Business and Society

Strategy, Ethics, and the Global Economy

SECOND EDITION

Business and Society

Strategy, Ethics, and the Global Economy

Alfred A. Marcus
University of Minnesota
Carlson School of Management

IRWIN

Chicago • Bogatá • Boston • Buenos Aires • Caracas
London • Madrid • Mexico City • Sydney • Toronto

Irwin Book Team

Executive editor:	Kurt L. Strand
Editorial assistant:	Kimberly Kanakes
Marketing manager:	Michael Campbell
Production supervisor:	Pat Frederickson
Project editor:	Karen M. Smith
Senior designer:	Heidi J. Baughman
Compositor:	Graphic Composition, Inc.
Typeface:	10/12 Goudy Old Style
Printer:	Quebecor/Fairfield

Times Mirror
Higher Education Group

Library of Congress Cataloging-in-Publication Data

Marcus, Alfred Allen, 1950–
Business and society : strategy, ethics, and the global economy / Alfred A. Marcus.—2nd ed.
p. cm.
Earlier ed. published under title: Business & society.
Includes bibliographical references and index.
ISBN 0-256-16202-6
1. Business ethics. 2. Social responsibility of business.
3. Business and politics. I. Marcus, Alfred Allen, 1950–
Business & society. II. Title.
HF5387.M3454 1996
658.4'08—dc20 95-40751

Printed in the United States of America
2 3 4 5 6 7 8 9 0 QF 2 1 0 9 8 7 6

To my family—

My wife, Judy; my sons, David and Ariel; my mother, Alice;
and to the memory of my father, James (1912-1992)

May each generation learn:

"What is the right path that a person should choose?
That which honors the person and brings honor from humankind."

PREFACE

The challenges that businesses face are strategic in nature. They require leadership, the capacity to align the firm with the social forces that affect it, and vision, the ability to provide a sense of purpose for the firm and its stakeholders. The challenges pertain to values and the relationship of the corporation to society, government and global competition, energy and the physical environment, and the social and legal effects of technology. This book examines the strategic decisions managers have to make and illustrates them with numerous cases and real-world examples. Among the cases designed to provoke thoughtful discussion about dilemmas that managers confront are the following:

- A unique series evaluating companies such as Wal-Mart, Phillip Morris, ADM, and 3M as investment risks.
- A special series on the Republican Party's Contract with America.
- A case on a self-proclaimed socially responsible firm similar to Anita Roddick's Body Shop (see "Transforming the Soul of Business").
- A new case on the electric vehicle (EV) industry as a response to California's air quality standards.
- The book has numerous ethical vignettes that relate to the experiences of managers, plus several revised and updated cases on companies such as Dayton Hudson and Ceridian.

The chapters provide key conceptual tools and background information that readers need to analyze the cases. Each chapter has at least one case that follows it, and some have mini-cases and real-world examples in the text. The academic tone in this edition has been modified for better acceptance.

The second edition has benefited from the feedback of readers and reviewers. It has:

- 31 full-length cases, as opposed to 15 in the original volume.
- New chapters and revisions of old chapters with an increased focus on tools managers can use and situations and problems that businesses have encountered.
- Increased coverage of Japan's troubled economy.
- An update on the economy of a unified Germany, and how it is affecting the rest of Europe.
- A discussion of the rebound of the U.S. economy and whether it can be sustained.
- A new chapter on the need for ethics, with developments in the U.S. Sentencing Code and a description of one company's ethics program.

- Expanded coverage of corporate politics and U.S. trade policy.
- Increased emphasis on corporate downsizing and change.

This book is especially strong with respect to cases dealing with the automotive, computer and electronic, and retailing industries. Enviromental management (eco-management) continues to get in-depth coverage, while the energy chapter concentrates on the period of the Gulf War and its aftermath. Technological changes, new product introductions, and the social and legal factors affecting them remain key themes.

The Book's Focus

Even with these changes, important continuities exist between the first and second editions of this book. The main emphases continue to be:

1. *Ethics and Public Policy.* The standard ethics and public policy topics treated in business and society courses are found in this book: the debate about social responsibility, corporate governance, business and politics, the historic relationship between business and government, mergers and acquisitions, women, minorities, consumerism, and poverty.

2. *The World Economy.* This book addresses business practice throughout the globe—a requisite for any modern business and society text. It has comparative material on Japan; the European nations, including the former Soviet bloc countries that are trying to introduce free market economies; the oil-producing countries of the Middle East; the dynamic nations of the Pacific Rim; and developing states such as India.

3. *Natural Resource and Environmental Issues.* The treatment of natural resource and environmental issues is comprehensive and up-to-date. The book views these issues in an international context and in light of global competitiveness. Principles related to ethics and the proper sphere of markets and government are applied in chapters on energy and environmental issues.

4. *The Impact of Technology.* This book gives extensive treatment to technology, from which managers should be able to derive many practical ideas. The impacts of technology on society are considered, and the tort system, which has had such a profound impact on business practice in recent years, is explained in a way that is meaningful to managers.

Additional Features

Additional features that make this book distinctive are the following:

Social Responsibility and World Economic Changes. The discussion of world economy extends to sections on ethics and social responsibility and law and public policy. From the outset, the connection is made between social responsibility, individual values, and economic growth. The international dimension is included with a discussion of the Lockheed bribery scandal and corporate governance in the Japanese firm.

Normative and Social Psychological Approaches to Ethics and Social Responsibility. The approach to ethics and social responsibility is not just normative; it is social-psychological. Some of the improtant literature in this area (e.g., Milgram and Kohlberg) is summarized. An individual and organizational context is provided for ethical dilemas in the corporation.

Historical Dimensions of Normative Ethics. A clear historical discussion of normative ethics is given with extensive development from the classical writings; the deotological (rights-based) tradition of Kant is contrasted with teleological concepts from modern utilitarianism; political philosophy is covered in the works of the founders of the American republic and contemporaries such as Rawls and Nozick; a critique of both deontological and teleological traditions is made from the perspective of modern analysts such as Freud who stressed the role of passions and instincts in governing human behavior.

The Rationale for Government. In this era of diminished expectations about the capabilities and reduced means for government worldwide to accomplish worthy objectives, students are given a perspective on the role that economists believe governments should play and the actual roles governments have played in economic development; the theme of contrasting normative economic theory with actual behavior is taken up repeatedly throughout the book. For example, the theory of the firm proposed by economists (agency theory) is contrasted with actual firm behavior observed by management scholars (behavioral theory).

Different Views on the Appropriate Government Role. Three different views on the appropriate role of government—the traditional liberal, the contemporary liberal, and the neoconservative—are contrasted with updates on the developments in contemporary ideologies; insights are provided about the conservative views of recent American administrations and about the controversy surrounding industrial policies that are supposed to make the U.S. economy more competitive internationally.

The Performance of the U.S. Economy in International Competition. How well the U.S. economy is doing in international competition is considered; its strengths and weaknesses in comparison with Japan and other nations are discussed in light of recent debates about free trade.

Comparative Performance of Nations. Several of the world's economies are discussed in light of values, government policies, and the international market orientation that is necessary for growth.

Reasons for the Rise of Economies. While many of the economies in the world have declined since 1973, some countries, (e.g., South Korea and Taiwan) have seen exceptional growth; reasons for this growth and whether it can be sustained are examined.

The Importance of the Natural World and the Environment. This book explicitly recognizes the importance of the natural world in providing businesses with essential raw materials (from nature) and in being a receptacle for the waste generated during production and consumption (to nature); the role governments and markets play in energy and environmental policy is emphasized in relation to the application of earlier concepts about the appropriate role for governments, markets, and individual values.

International and Comparative Aspects of Energy and Environmental Problems—Ethical and Managerial Dimensions. The international and comparative aspects of energy and environmental issues are stressed with sections on developments in Europe, Japan, and the United States; the ethical issue is considered in relation to the environmental movement and the challenges it poses to business; the discussion of these environmental issues ends with a list of actions managers can take.

The Role of Technology in Creating the Conditions for Economic Growth. The important role of technology in creating the conditions for economic growth and prosperity is taken up with emphasis on international competition (e.g., competition with Japanese technology) and the obstacles to bringing any new idea to fruition; few other texts explicitly consider the important role of technology and technological innovations that are transforming the U.S. and world economy.

The Problem of Managing Technological Risks. The impacts on people of new technologies are considered; how society and the corporation manage the potential danger of technological risks is dealt with in sections on controversial topics such as the risks of everyday life and the value of a human life.

Legal and Liability Aspects of New Product Development—The United States and Other Countries Compared. The legal and liability aspects of product development and technological innovation in the United States and Japan are discussed, and students are asked to consider different proposals that have been made for reforming the tort liability system in the United States.

Alfred A. Marcus

Acknowledgments

The Strategic Management and Organization Department at the Carlson School at the University of Minnesota has been very supportive to me in the writing of this new edition of *Business and Society.* I want to again pay tribute to my colleagues Norman Bowie, Bruce Erickson, Andy Van de Ven, Ian Maitland, Stefanie Lenway, Stuart Albert, and Phil Bromiley. Norm and Stefanie wrote cases for the second edition. Many of those who assisted me with the first edition, completed while I was on sabbatical at the Sloan School of Management at MIT, are again owed my thanks: John Carrol, Michael Cusumano, John Ehrenfeld, Rebecca Henderson, and James Maxwell at MIT; Barry Mitnick, University of Pittsburgh; James Post, Boston University; Ed Epstein, University of California, Berkeley; Rogene Buchholz, Loyola University, New Orleans; Allen Kaufman, University of New Hampshire; Rich Wokutch, Virginia Polytechnical Institute; and Robert Goodman, University of Wisconsin–Madison. I am also indebted to my former Ph.D. students Gordon Rands, Isaac Fox, and Mark Weber. Mark Weber wrote the teacher's manual for this second edition. The special contributions of other students is cited in the individual chapters. Senior sponsoring editor Kurt Strand of Richard D. Irwin creatively managed this project and kept me on a reasonable schedule. He took the place of the very able Libby Rubenstein, who was developmental editor for the first edition. John Pipkin of the University of Minnesota was a loyal and devoted word-processor for the first edition; he solved the many problems I created. Sharon Hansen of the Strategic Management Research Center at the University of Minnesota helped me through the difficult task of making revisions for the second edition. Mark Jankus wrote or helped write many case studies and the teacher's manual for the first edition. His fresh attitude toward the material and ability to think in an organized fashion was greatly appreciated. Don Geffen, with whom I worked on many environment, energy, and safety projects when I became the director of the Strategic Management Research Center, helped write new cases for this edition. I am grateful for the rigorous and systematic way this former physics professor and securities analyst approaches problems. William McEvily, Susan Feinberg, and Annette Berger, Ph.D. candidates at the Carlson School, also authored new cases that appear in the second edition. They are smart and well-trained and on their way to successful academic careers. Others to whom I owe a debt of gratitude are the reviewers of this manuscript for Irwin; they are listed below. I hope I have done justice to their many valuable suggestions in this second edition.

Reviewers for this edition: Joseph A. Petrick, Wright State University; Barry M. Mitnick, University of Pittsburgh; Robert Wright, University of Phoenix; and Kenneth E. Hoffman, Emporia State University.

Reviewers for the First Edition: Robert Chatov, SUNY-Buffalo; Philip Cochran, Pennsylvania State University; Edwin Epstein, University of California, Berkeley; Nancy Hanawa, University of California, Berkeley; Mayra Leatherwood, University of Illinois at Springfield; Lee Preston, University of Maryland; Kathleen Rehbein, Marquette University; and David Vogel, University of California, Berkeley.

A. A. M.

Contents in Brief

PART I

Introduction: The Strategic Business Environment

PART II

Values and the Corporation's Relationship to Society

PART III

Government and Global Competition

PART IV

Energy and the Environment

PART V

The Social and Legal Effects of Technology

Contents

PART I

Introduction: The Strategic Business Environment

PART V

THE SOCIAL AND LEGAL EFFECTS OF TECHNOLOGY

PART

I

INTRODUCTION

The Strategic Business Environment

CHAPTER

1

Managing in Turbulent Times

The environment of an organization in business, like that of any other organized entity, is the pattern of all the external conditions and influences that affects its life and development. The environmental influences . . . are technological, economic, physical, social, and political . . . in all these categories change is taking place at varying rates. Change . . . necessitates continuous monitoring . . . Executives . . . must be aware of those aspects of their company's environment . . . that will affect their company's future.

Kenneth Andrews, *The Concept of Corporate Strategy*

Introduction and Chapter Objectives

To sustain and renew themselves, corporations must be in harmony with society's needs and values. Leadership is the capacity to deal with the broad social forces that affect a corporation's viability and success. In this chapter, examples from the experiences of a number of companies are provided, including Ameritech, General Motors (GM), IBM, Coca Cola, and Motorola. The book's key themes are introduced: the changes that affect a corporation—changes in values that affect its relationship with society; changes in government policies that influence its global competitiveness; changes in the availability of energy and in the environment that impact its operations; and social and legal developments that affect its capacity to innovate. The chapter concludes with a discussion of corporate vision.

The Capacity to Deal with Broad Social Forces

leadership
The capacity to deal with the broad social forces that affect an organization's viability and success.

Broad social forces drive corporate success and failure. This book has been written to help you understand these forces. The capacity to deal effectively with them is the essence of **leadership.** Corporations are not only looking for functional experts but leaders. (The results of a typical survey are shown in Exhibit 1–1.) They also are searching for the people

EXHIBIT 1–1 The Need for Management Talent

In seeking management talent for your company today, how urgently needed is:	*Percent Responding As Very Urgently Needed*
Leadership	53%
Operations management	28
Marketing	27
Finance	13
Organizational behavior	11
Accounting	3

NOTE: Numbers do not add up to 100 percent because of multiple responses.

who can create a vision of the future, energize and motivate people to achieve that vision, overcome the barriers to change, and adapt the organization to changing circumstances.

Confronting Massive Change

One corporation that confronts broad social forces is Ameritech, a large telecommunications company that provides local service throughout the Midwest.[1] Once part of AT&T, it came into being after the 1984 federal court ruling that broke up the Bell system into a long-distance company, which still goes by the name of AT&T, and several local carriers (the "Baby Bells") such as Ameritech.[2]

The other local carriers are USWest, Bell Atlantic, Southwestern Bell, Bell South, Pacific Telesis, and NYNEX. Still regulated monopolies, with total revenues of $84 billion in 1993 and operating profits of $17 billion, they earned about a quarter of their sales and a third of their profits from access charges that the long-distance companies paid them for relaying calls to local customers. Another $10 billion in sales came from high-margin toll calls between cities and suburbs. Though the toll calls cost no more than local ones, regulators allowed local carriers to charge up to five times as much for them.

Ameritech devotes considerable attention to public policy, which is critical to the company's success. The telecommunications company contributes to many public policy organizations, such as the Brookings Institution, the Cato Institute, the Hudson Institute, and the Manhattan Institute.[3] It tries to influence the intellectual debate, because the way this debate is framed and carried out has an important effect on Ameritech's bottom line.

Many of the public policy organizations that Ameritech backs are staunch supporters of free-market principles. Their approach fits well with the company's political agenda, which seeks to remove restraints on its ability to compete in markets in the United States and abroad. While competitors have gradually gained access to markets previously reserved for local carriers, the latter have not had the same freedom to enter markets of their choosing. Not only are U.S. local carriers still subject to numerous regulatory restrictions at home and abroad, but also they have had to sue for the right to enter the long-distance telecommunications business.

Long-distance companies have avoided paying access charges by running direct-access lines to office buildings, thus bypassing the local carriers, but the local carriers are forbidden to compete in this rapidly growing and lucrative business. Between 1990 and 1994, their compound annual growth rate was 2.3 percent and their compound annual increase in operating profits was 0.9 percent. In contrast, the long-distance carriers grew at a rate of 4.3 percent, and their profits expanded at a rate of 10.0 percent. The local carriers have actively pursued legal and legislative remedies, but the process is tedious and they have suffered many setbacks.

Meanwhile, they made efforts to expand abroad. Ameritech had operated solely in the United States, but it now tried to establish a global presence. In France it created a partnership with the state-owned telecommunications company, French Telecom; in Poland it set up a state-of-the-art wireless network cellular system.

Technology was very important to Ameritech. It became involved in many high-tech applications: Compuserve, NEXIS, automatic teller machines (ATMs), and the fiber optic network. The evolution toward digital technology has had a major impact on how local carriers like Ameritech would compete. It was predicted that cellular service in the early 21st century would cost no more than local phone service and that hand-held communicators would allow people to scribble notes with an electronic stylus and send them wirelessly anywhere on earth. The U.S. government was auctioning off huge blocks of airwaves, and companies would bid more than $15 billion for the right to build a new generation of cellular systems.

In Harmony with Society's Needs and Values

A second example of the need for a corporation to be in harmony with society's needs and values is General Motors (GM). In 1946, Peter Drucker published a book about GM called *The Concept of the Corporation*.[4] GM was a pioneer, one of the first companies to have specialized functions (accounting, marketing, finance, and production), and to have divisional management with separate profit centers. It introduced horizontal and vertical integration, developed niche marketing (separate models for people in different socioeconomic classes), and created a worldwide presence. Drucker believed that the leaders of nearly all corporations copied GM's methods. In 1972, he still saw General Motors as a leader, but the company was "in deep trouble . . . because it is . . . at odds with basic needs and values of society and community."[5]

In 1980, U.S. automobile manufacturers controlled more than 80 percent of the domestic market. By 1990, this control had slipped to less than 70 percent. Imports remained steady with about 20 percent of the market, but transplants—foreign cars built in the United States—made major gains.[6] The ease by which the Japanese introduced lean production methods into the United States surprised many observers.

GM and the other U.S. car makers had many challenges to confront as the 1990s began (see Case 2–A, "General Motors: Turning Around a Corporate Giant," at the end of Chapter 2). GM suffered a precipitous decline in earnings, enduring record losses of $4.5 billion in 1991 and $23.5 billion in 1992. The 1992 loss was the largest ever for a U.S. corporation. With market share down, the company was forced to continue making cuts in the workforce. After closing 10 assembly plants, 4 engine factories, and 11 parts plants in the 1980s, it still needed to lay off 54,000 production workers and 26,000 white collar workers.[7]

For every car it sold, GM lost on average $1,500 more than Chrysler and $1,650 more than Ford.[8] With an aging workforce, GM had high health care costs, ranging from $600 to $900 per vehicle sold, and health care was not an issue that was likely to go away soon.[9] The cost of health care in the United States was expected to grow to some $1 trillion, nearly 15 percent of the gross national product (GNP) by the year 2000.

GM had been cutting costs and reducing the size of its workforce for nearly a decade, but industry analysts believed that the company had not done enough. They claimed that the nearly 100,000 white collar workers it employed were a huge burden on its productivity. GM had more capacity and people relative to sales than either Ford or Chrysler.[10]

GM also faced large regulatory challenges. In a typical year, GM had to spend 5 to 7 percent of its capital budget on government regulations.[11] The 1990 Clean Air Act was likely to greatly add to this bill. The company's credit rating had been downgraded, adding $200 to $300 mill to its borrowing costs. Cash for new product development was hard to find.

The board of directors took a more active role in seeking a solution to what ailed the company. It could no longer resist shareholder pressure, especially from large institutional shareholders, to change the company's leadership. The board replaced the company's president and relieved the beleaguered chairman of his duties as chair of the board's executive committee.

Despite its problems, GM still had a success to tout—the development of the Saturn, an entirely new car.[12] Saturn was a very special accomplishment. No other U.S. automaker had been able to profitably make a small car that rivaled in quality one made by the Japanese. The Saturn was so successful that GM was unable to keep up with demand. When it tried to boost production, employees resisted increasing output in favor of maintaining quality.[13] They felt that their jobs depended in the long run more on quality than on sales.

Saturn's approach to labor relations was to give workers the right to participate in all decisions from the plant floor to the boardroom. In contrast with GM's other divisions, workers were treated as co-owners with as much a stake in the company as executives or shareholders. This treatment was unique in a company known for its top-down, bureaucratic decision making and antagonistic labor-management relations.

The Need to Innovate

GM was undergoing fundamental change. Its static way of doing business was no longer adequate. The company was not atypical. Many U.S. corporations were in the throes of restructuring. Two large department store chains, Allied Stores and Federated Department Stores, were driven into bankruptcy. Major television networks were taken over—CBS by the Tisch family, NBC by General Electric, and ABC by Capital Cities Entertainment.[14] Fox started a major new network, and additional competition came from cable and videos.

No corporation was immune, but IBM's decline was one of the most surprising.[15] IBM's fall from greatness was analogous to the disintegration of the Soviet Union and the demise of communism. The parallels about the curse of bigness and the ineptitude of bureaucracy provide a cautionary lesson for all managers.

IBM had been the strongest, proudest, and most powerful of U.S. corporations. It was considered to be a near-perfect embodiment of what was best in U.S. management. However, in 1991 and 1992, the company's losses averaged more than $4 billion, and its 1993 losses topped $8 billion.[16] The problems of IBM were heralded as the surest sign of a U.S. lapse from greatness. John Akers, the CEO, who watched his company's profits plummet, admitted to taking his "eye off the ball."[17]

In a company where lifetime employment was virtually guaranteed, 170,000 people were laid off. IBM cut employment from a peak of over 400,000 employees in 1984 to about 200,000 employees in 1992.[18] Putting an end to lifetime employment broke a near-sacred trust the company had with the workforce. Not only were jobs cut but many employees were reassigned. To put its workers in closer touch with customers, 20,000 staff and laboratory workers were moved to the sales force.[19] To keep pace with a market teeming with small and agile competitors, IBM empowered the remaining workforce, decentralized authority and decision making, and motivated its managers to take risks. The old management structure had prevented change. Divisional politics and top-down decision making had foiled talent and creativity and blocked employee innovation.

Despite great technical prowess, including two Nobel Prizes for its researchers in the late 1980s, IBM rarely was first on the market with new products (see Exhibit 1–2), and these products inspired little user passion or excitement.

Like GM's directors, those of IBM had to act. They ousted Akers as CEO and in an unprecedented move brought in an outsider, Lou Gerstner, Jr., a former American Express and RJR-Nabisco executive.[20] While workforce reductions and an unexpected increase in demand for mainframes, occasioned by the positive business cycle, allowed IBM to regain profitability, Gerstner had trouble changing the IBM culture.[21] Infighting, feuding divisions, and paralysis threatened an ambitious plan to develop a whole new series of products around more advanced power chips that were a generation beyond Intel's Pentium.

If you had invested $1,000 in IBM stock on July 31, 1982, it would be worth $857 in

Exhibit 1–2 IBM's Troubles

- 1993 loss of $8 billion
  "We took our eye off the ball." (ex-CEO John Akers)
- Follows the leader
- Product appearance time lag:

Mincomputer	11 years
Personal computer	4 years
Workstation	5 years
Laptop	5 years

Can't keep pace with small, nimble competitors

1992. GM did better: $1,000 worth of its stock in 1982 was worth $1,520 in 1992. However, compared with other blue-chip companies, both giants were near the bottom in terms of value returned to investors (see Exhibit 1–3).

Critical Alignments Between Corporations and Society

GM and IBM are examples of what can happen to a corporation that does not stay in touch with society's needs. The requirement that a company understand social needs and values and adjust to them has never been greater. This book is dedicated to helping you deal with this issue. It addresses the following questions:

- To what extent do changes in values affect the corporation's relations with society?
- To what extent do changes in governments affect its global competitiveness?
- To what extent do energy and environmental issues affect its operations?
- To what extent do social and legal developments affect its capacity to innovate?

The organization of the book is designed to help you analyze, manage, and cope with the critical alignments managers must make between their corporations and society.

Changes in Values

The business system has experienced scandals that have resulted in questions about its integrity and legal and ethical standing. The roles of greed and self-interest versus altruism and other-regarding behavior in the economy and the business system need to be examined. What is the purpose of the firm? Whose interests does it serve?

The insider trading schemes of Dennis Levine, Ivan Boesky, Michael Milken and others during the 1980s have been characterized as the greatest criminal conspiracy the

Exhibit 1–3 The Market Value of a $1000 Investment As of July 31, 1982, and 10 Years Later

	1982	*1992*
Coca Cola	$1,000	$13,392
Phillip Morris	$1,000	$12,909
Merck	$1,000	$12,011
Boeing	$1,000	$7,330
General Electric	$1,000	$5,118
Procter & Gamble	$1,000	$4,899
Sears	$1,000	$2,261
General Motors	$1,000	$1,520
Caterpillar	$1,000	$1,454
IBM	$1,000	$857

financial world has ever known. The former *Wall Street Journal* correspondent James Stewart wrote about these scandals in *Den of Thieves*.[22] The scandals led to the demise of Drexel Burnham Lambert, a respected investment house.

The important ethical issues that managers should consider, however, go beyond these well-publicized scandals. Reasons why ethics matter will be provided in this book, focusing on classical ethical dilemmas between organizations and the individual, and between means and ends. This book contains numerous examples in which you can practice ethical reasoning. In addition to examining personal ethics, it will focus on such controversial topics as executive pay and managing diversity.

Changes in Government Policies and Global Competitiveness

Government is important both because of the constraints it imposes on business and the opportunities it generates. Trends in government budgets and taxes, trade and antitrust legislation, deregulation, and defense spending have important effects on U.S. companies. Also important have been trends in the international economy: the opening up of the former Communist countries and their attempts to convert to market economies, the relationships between prosperous and poor nations, the redefinition of capitalism and socialism, changes in the military balance and in the regimes of some nations, and other worldwide developments. The rationale for government, the prospects for sustaining worldwide economic development and growth, and the comparative advantage of nations are important topics that managers must consider.

The present era is one of massive political change. The Berlin Wall is down. Eastern and Central Europe are no longer Communist. The German state has been unified, while the Soviet Union and Yugoslavia have been shattered. Francis Fukuyama, author of the best-selling *The End of History and the Last Man* and former state department employee, sees inexorable progress toward democracy and free markets.[23] The striving to satisfy material needs and provide individuals with dignity and freedom are worldwide phenomena of immense importance. However, Fukuyama notes that people are driven by motives more deep-seated than the desire for physical comfort alone. They want identity—recognition, glory, and prestige. These wants, Fukuyama believes, are at the root of another major trend in the world: an upsurge in ethnic tensions and fundamentalism.

Fukuyama argues that the clash is between two opposing world forces. The motivation behind the one is mostly economic: the creation of a commercially homogenous global culture based on similar tastes in music, computers, food, and other consumer goods. The motivation behind the other is primitive and leads to retribalization, war, and bloodshed: nation pitted against nation, culture against culture, and people against people.[24] Parochial hatreds have resurfaced at the same time that markets, technology, and a single-world culture have progressed. In the early 1990s, more than 30 wars were raging in the world.

Popular culture tends to create a single, universal society. *The Cosby Show* was the most popular television program in South Africa. Free markets stimulate scientific and technical progress. New communication technologies are developed (e.g., the Internet) that lead to novel behaviors that breed interdependence and increased world stability. Freedom and markets are a universalizing force. They provide for common experiences and the sharing of languages and even currencies. The U.S. dollar, for instance, is the most accepted currency in the states of the former Soviet Union. Despite these positive trends, bloodshed and ethnic warfare grow.

Where will it lead? T. H. Marshall, the English sociologist, divides the modern period into three eras. The 18th century was one of human rights: freedom of speech and religion, and equal justice before the law. The 19th century brought the right to vote. The 20th century created the welfare state with various kinds of entitlements: health care, social security, and protection from unscrupulous business practices. Progress was never smooth. Ideological counterthrusts, profound conflict, and bloodshed often preceded major advances. Yet progress occurred. Now, as a new millennium approaches, it is unclear where the world is headed. Will future generations face a world of chaos, anarchy, and violence, or is the world moving toward an open and growing economy where each person will enjoy greater prosperity and freedom?[25]

These trends create dilemmas for business. For example, emerging markets are risky in the states of the former Soviet Union and China. Corrupt old bureaucrats worked in predictable ways according to unspoken rules. New entrepreneurs do not yet recognize that to stay in business they have to honor contractual obligations.

Competing in Global Markets

The stakes for companies are very high. An example, is Coca Cola. Its growth and profitability in North America have been very limited. Recent sales increases on this continent averaged about 1 percent annually. Cola product sales were down from 75 to 70 percent in the U.S. market. To maintain market share in the intense competitive battles with rival PepsiCo required very costly advertising, flashy commercials, and the hiring of hot celebrities from the worlds of music, fashion, and sport. Europe, on the other hand, offered great potential for growth. Consumption of soft drinks was only a third that of the United States, and it was increasing at a rate of 8 percent per year. Profit margins, moreover, were 50 percent higher than they were in North America. Of its worldwide profits of $2 billion, Coke earned 80 percent abroad.[26]

FedEx, on the other hand, mistakenly assumed that it could re-create its U.S. successes in Europe. In the United States, revenues for rapid package delivery were $20 billion and 3 million packages were sent every day. FEDEX wanted to duplicate this triumph in Europe. It spent vast sums on expansion, but never realized a return. Daily intra-European shipping did not grow to more than 150,000 packages. Overcapacity and high fixed costs led to huge losses for FEDEX. It had to sell off its European holdings and abandon the market.[27]

Another company affected by global developments was Cargill. This immensely profitable privately owned corporation was the world's largest trader in grain. However, it experienced a slowdown in its international grain business as once-hungry customers like China produced more grain and imported less, and the states of the former Soviet Union could not afford the grain. A full 40 percent of Cargill's assets were invested in foreign operations. Doing business globally proved very unpredictable, and Cargill's sales in the early 1990s fell nearly 20 percent.[28]

Cargill tried to reduce its dependence on grain by expanding into food processing and developing businesses in diverse areas such as meats, steel, and financial services, but it did not have experience in consumer markets. Control of the company had been in the hands of 40 family members who owned 100 percent of the stock. Some of them were seeking to turn the stock into cash. For the first time, the company was headed by a nonfamily member. If Cargill went public, security analysts and pension fund managers were likely to demand that it divest businesses in depressed industries like steel and move out of unstable countries like Brazil, Russia, and China.[29]

Changes in Energy and in the Environment

The relationship between humans and the physical environment also underwent fundamental change. All corporations relied on the critical resource of oil. It signified not only physical power, but political and economic power. The world's known reserves of this resource were eight times greater in the 1990s than they were in 1950. In both 1973 and 1979, Persian Gulf rulers unexpectedly interrupted supplies. Prices rose dramatically and the world economy suffered. Alternative energy sources, which would make the world less dependent on oil, were still in the development stage. The problems of using nonrenewable energy were apparent, including depletion of the ozone layer, global warming, and disposing of hazardous and nonhazardous wastes.[30]

Economic growth was needed to provide for the world's population, yet achieving that growth in the face of environmental problems was very difficult. Africa already suffered from drought, famine, civil wars, mass misery, and political social instability. Environmentalists believed in limits to growth. Growth did not make us happy, they said. They pointed out that about a third of the U.S. population in the 1990s described itself as being happy, about the same number as in 1957, though growth in national product (GNP) had more than doubled.[31]

Virtually no business in the world was immune from paying attention to environmental issues whether they involved resource extraction and use, processing, manufacturing, packaging, sale, or disposal of products. The natural world was both the source of the critical resources that corporations needed and the receptacle for their waste by-products. A better understanding of energy and environmental issues was incumbent upon managers. The consequences of not understanding them were gains not realized and losses which could be avoided.

Social and Legal Effects of Technology

Technology was important because scientific discoveries led to new products as in genetic engineering, new production techniques such as robotics, and forms of corporate management brought about by the spread of computers. Changes in transportation, solutions to product safety and reliability problems, and developments in pollution control were important to how companies did business. The promise of technology, however, often came into conflict with people's fears about its unforeseen dangers. Technological innovation was affected by the legal climate in the United States and other countries, which helped to determine how to manage technological risks. Managers must understand the innovation process and the liability rules that accompany new product introductions.

Economist Lester Thurow wrote that leadership in high technology involved not only the invention of new products but also the development of new process technologies that allowed people to produce goods and services, cheaper, better, faster. The United States spent only one-third of its money on new processes and two-thirds on new products while Japan expended the opposite. The VCR, fax, and CD were not invented in Japan, but they became Japanese products because of Japanese manufacturing capabilities. Japan was noted for enhancing the status and pay of production people and appointing chief executive officers (CEOs) with technical backgrounds who understood process technologies. In Japan and Europe, 70 percent of CEOs typically were engineers; in the United States only 30 percent were.[32]

To improve its position in process technologies, the United States had to upgrade its labor force. GM's experience with a robotized Cadillac factory was that it could not obtain sufficient numbers of technically sophisticated workers to run the factory. Sustainable competitive advantage meant more skilled workers, flatter organization charts, and the use of process teams in close contact with customers.

Progress was possible. Take Xerox as an example. Under attack from Canon, Minolta, Ricoh, and Sharp, which cut Xerox's U.S. market share from 80 to 13 percent between 1976 and 1982, Xerox introduced a quality program. Employees resisted; many felt that the money should be spent on equipment, and they compared the company's new empowerment program to communism. However, Xerox stuck with this program. A "gang of eleven"—a group of young mavericks who roamed around plants—benchmarked Xerox's performance against the best of its competitors and tried to make customer satisfaction number one. Without these efforts, Xerox could not have survived.[33]

Motorola was another example. In five years it cut defects from 40 per 6,000 components to 3.4 per 1 million components. It did so in very simple ways; for example, by reducing the number of parts and having them snap together rather than be joined by screws or fasteners. By pushing responsibility down the ranks and demanding perfection, Motorola saved more than $700 million in manufacturing costs.[34]

Vision

vision
A sense of purpose, reason for being, and guiding philosophy that motivate and unify a company's workforce.

Managing in a time of turbulence requires **vision**—a sense of purpose, a reason for existence, and a guiding philosophy that will motivate and unify a scattered workforce and make it more competitive.[35] People who have that vision are like Steven Jobs, the cofounder of Apple, who defined his company's purpose as making "a contribution to the world by making tools for the mind that advance human kind." A company with vision was Merck, which frequently led the list of most admired U.S. corporations. Its mission statement read: "We are in the business of preserving and improving human life. All of our actions must be measured by our success in achieving this." Disney's vision was "to make people happy."

Sam Walton, the founder of Wal-Mart (see the case study at the end of this chapter) formulated the following **abiding principles** for his company.[36]

1. Commit to your business.
2. Share your profits with all your associates (employees) and treat them as partners.
3. Motivate your partners.

4. Communicate everything you can to your partners.
5. Appreciate everything your associates do for the business.
6. Celebrate your successes.
7. Listen to everyone in your company.
8. Exceed your customer's expectations.
9. Control your expenses better than the competition.
10. Swim upstream.

Two Stanford University Business School professors, James Collins and Jerry Porras, listed 179 corporate CEOs identified by their peers as the most visionary. From 1920 to 1990, the companies of these CEOs outperformed the stock market by a factor of 50.[37] Vision was a synonym for success, if not its cause.

Conclusions

To manage a modern corporation is not easy. Companies are in jeopardy. Managers must become adept at dealing with a rapidly changing world. They must have a vision that motivates the workforce and makes a company successful in the long run. They must align their corporations with society, which means bringing them in closer accord with social values and ethics, governments and global competition, energy and environmental issues, and the social and legal forces affecting technology.

Making these adjustments is not easy. Many corporations have tried to make these adjustments. Some have not been successful. The cases that follow this chapter will give you practice in dealing with the problem.

Discussion Questions

1. What are the key attributes of leaders? How do leaders differ from functional experts?
2. Describe the broad social forces that faced Ameritech? How did Ameritech respond to public policy? What is your evaluation of its response? How is Ameritech's response likely to help the corporation?
3. What are the main challenges facing GM? Do you agree with Peter Drucker's view that GM is in deep trouble because it is at odds with the basic needs and values of society?
4. What were the causes of IBM's decline? How are IBM's problems similar to those of GM and Ameritech? In what ways are they different?
5. Imagine that you were on the board of directors of one of IBM, GM, or Ameritech. What advice would you give to management?
6. What are some of the important ethical issues that managers should consider?
7. What arguments does Francis Fukuyama make about the post-Communist world?

What kind of divisions will plague the world? What impact will these divisions have on business?

8. Describe the global issues affecting Coca Cola, FedEx, and Cargill. How can these companies best handle these issues?
9. To what extent do energy and environmental issues pose a threat to business? To what extent do they provide opportunities?
10. What is Thurow's argument about the difference between U.S. and Japanese capabilities in technology?
11. How have companies like Xerox and Motorola responded to the challenges of technology? Are their responses appropriate for all companies?
12. Do you know corporations that have a vision statement? What are these vision statements? Why do they matter?

Endnotes

1. Ameritech, *Annual Report 1991*.
2. Andrew Kupfer, "The Future of the Phone Companies," *Fortune*, Oct. 3, 1994, pp. 94–106.
3. "The Good Think-Tank Guide," *Economics*, Dec. 21–Jan. 3, 1992, pp. 49–53.
4. Peter Drucker, *The Concept of the Corporation* (New York: Mentor, 1946).
5. Ibid, p. 248.
6. General Motors, *Public Interest Report*, 1992.
7. "GM Can't Downshift Fast Enough," *Business Week*, Dec. 30, 1991, p. 37.
8. "Getting General Motors Going Again," *Economist*, May 2, 1992, pp. 77–78.
9. Alex Taylor, "The Road Ahead at General Motors," *Fortune*, May 4, 1992, pp. 92–97.
10. "GM Slices and GM Slashes But the Flab Survives," *Business Week*, Dec. 23, 1991, p. 27.
11. "GM Leaders Go on the Record," *Fortune*, March 9, 1992, pp. 49–57.
12. "Richard Lefauve and Arnoldo Hax, "Managerial and Technological Innovations at Saturn Corporation," *MIT Management*, Spring 1992, pp. 8–20.
13. "At Saturn, What Workers Want . . ." *Business Week*, Dec. 2, 1991, pp. 117–18.
14. Ken Auletta, *Three Blind Mice* (New York: Random House, 1991).
15. Joel Dreyfuss, "Reinventing IBM," *Fortune*, Aug. 14, 1989, pp. 30–39.
16. David Kirkpatrick, "Breaking Up IBM," *Fortune*, July 17, 1992, pp. 44–58.
17. Carol Loomis, "King John Wears an Uneasy Crown," *Fortune*, Jan. 11, 1993, pp. 44–48.
18. Allen Myerson, "IBM to Eliminate 25,000 Jobs in 1993 . . ." *New York Times*, Dec. 16, 1992.
19. "The New IBM," *Business Week*, Dec. 16, 1991, pp. 112–18.
20. David Kirkpatrick, "The Hunt for Mr. X: Who Can Run IBM," *Fortune*, Feb. 22, 1993, pp. 68–72.
21. Stratford Sherman, "Is Gerstner Too Cautious to Save IBM?" *Fortune*, Oct. 3, 1994, pp. 78–90.
22. James Stewart, *Den of Thieves* (New York: Simon and Schuster, 1991).
23. Francis Fukuyama, *The End of History* (New York: Free Press, 1991).
24. Ibid. Also see Benjamin Barber, "Jihad Vs. Mcworld," *Atlantic Monthly*, March 1992, pp. 53–66.
25. David Warsh, "A Liberal Story for . . ." *Boston Sunday Globe*, Sept. 15, 1991, p. A37, A43.
26. "Soda Pop Celebrity," *Economist*, June 6, 1992, p. 83; and "The Thirst of Champions," *Economist*, June 6, 1992, p. 83.
27. "Federal Express," *Economist*, June 6, 1992, p. 83.

28. "At Cargill, the Ties that Bind . . ." *Business Week*, Nov. 18, 1991, pp. 91–96.
29. Ronald Henkoff, "Inside America's Biggest Private Company," *Fortune*, July 13, 1992, pp. 83–89.
30. Daniel Yergin, *The Prize* (New York: Simon and Schuster, 1991).
31. "Africa—Two Droughts," *Economist*, May 23, 1992, pp. 46–49; and "Dark Greens," *Economist*, September 12, 1992, p. 99.
32. Lester Thurow, "The New Economics of High Technology," *Harpers Magazine*, March 1992, pp. 15–17.
33. Brian Dumaine, "How to Win a Quality War with Japan," *Fortune*, July 27, 1992, p. 162.
34. Barnaby Feder, "At Motorola Quality Is a Team Sport," *New York Times*, Jan. 21, 1993, p. C2; and "Future Perfect," *Economist*, Jan. 4, 1992, p. 61.
35. "The Vision Thing," *Economist*, Nov. 9, 1991, p. 81.
36. "Sam Walton in His Own Words," *Fortune*, June 29, 1992, pp. 98–106.
37. James Collins and Jerry Porras, "Organizational Vision and Visionary Organizations," Unpublished Research Paper no. 1159 (Stanford, Calif.: Stanford Graduate School of Business, 1991).

Case 1-A
Wal-Mart

Meeting the Challenges to Its Way of Doing Business[1]

Wal-Mart Stores, Inc., headquartered in Bentonville, Arkansas, had total sales in 1993 of $67.35 billion and total profits of $2.33 billion. It employed 375,000 people. Its main competitors (and their annual sales) were Dayton Hudson Corp. ($19.23 billion), Federated Department Stores ($7.23 billion), May Department Stores ($11.53 billion), Melville Corporation ($10.44 billion), Nordstrom, Inc. ($3.59 billion), and J. C. Penney Company ($18.98 billion). In 1993, Wal-Mart's revenues were up 21 percent and profits advanced 17 percent.[2]

Despite these impressive gains, Wal-Mart was attacked by social activists for many of its activities, ranging from purchasing cheap items that relied on labor in Third World countries to the company's prohibition of employee romances.[3] It was engaged in an increasingly demanding price war with other discounters. Its margins were the lowest in the company's history.[4] The National Advertising Review Board forced Wal-Mart to retract from an advertising campaign in which it had proclaimed: "Always the Lowest Prices, Always." Company expansion into Canada and Mexico was greeted with citizen opposition. Wal-Mart was even sued by a small town pharmacist in Arkansas for predatory pricing.

An institutional investor had held more than $500,000 worth of stock in Wal-Mart for the past 10 years and had earned substantial profits. It was now considering whether to increase its stake in Wal-Mart, reduce it, or keep it steady, but it was concerned with the social, political, and legal climate in which Wal-Mart was operating. Was this climate still conducive to Wal-Mart's growth and profitability?

The investor asked Joanne Magnuson, an analyst with Alliance Capital, to give her opinion of Wal-Mart as an investment risk. This case first provides a detailed analysis of Wal-Mart's financial position and then an analysis of the broad issues. The question for Joanne Magnuson was the bearing that the issues would have on Wal-Mart's future performance.

Company Description

Wal-Mart, by expanding sales at a compound annual rate of 33 percent or more for over 15 years, had become the world's largest retailer. It owned and operated 2,082 discount stores, 77 Supercenters, and 427 Sam's Clubs in 49 states, Puerto Rico, Mexico, and Canada, plus an array of other businesses including TCBY, Builder's Warehouse, and Advanced Environ Recycling. Wal-Mart's discount stores appeared in three formats: the original chain of average-sized discount stores, now in 43 states and located primarily in smaller communities with an average population of 15,000; a chain of larger Supercenter stores located in metropolitan areas; and a chain of Sam's Wholesale Clubs, also located in metropolitan areas.

The Supercenters were a combination of discount store and supermarket on 15 acres of land. The added sales usually more than covered the higher operating costs. Return on investment (ROI) at the Supercenters averaged 36 percent compared with 30 percent at Wal-Mart stores. Sam's Wholesale Clubs had the lowest ROI of the three, 20 percent.

At the end of 1993, the company purchased 100 PACE Wholesale Clubs from Kmart to convert into Sam's Stores. It was converting 112 Canadian stores bought from Woolworth into discount stores and was building another 110 discount outlets around the country. It also was expanding or relocating 70 other stores. Its plans included the construction of five new Supercenters and the conversion of 65 discount stores into Supercenter stores. Twenty new Sam's Wholesale Clubs were scheduled to open in 1994. With a few exceptions, including California, Wal-Mart expanded from its home base of Arkansas by creating efficient distribution centers. Most stores were within a 450-mile radius of a distribution center. Four new distribution centers were opened in 1994. In that year capital expenditures approached $3 billion.

As of 1994, total store space in operation was 158 million square feet. The ratio of sales per square foot was $426. Dayton Hudson had a ratio of $204 and Federated Department Stores about $170. Hardgoods accounted for 65 percent of Wal-Mart's total sales. Wage costs were an estimated 16 percent of sales. Management and the Walton family owned 42 percent of the outstanding stock with a market value as of August 1994 of over $23 billion.

Gross Margins

Wal-Mart's gross margins were 21.9 percent, not an indication of profitability or good management but of the sector of the retail industry in which Wal-Mart operated and the strategy it employed in a very competitive market. Discount stores have lower gross margins than department stores. Wal-Mart, the epitome of cost-conscious management, steadily reduced its gross margins from 27.3 percent in 1984 to less than 22 percent in 1993. An important factor in the decline in Wal-Mart's gross margins was the company's expansion into the "wholesale club" format, which operates on low margins and high volumes. The addition of low-margin grocery products in the Supercenters also contributed to this decline.

Nevertheless, Wal-Mart's central philosophy was to continually drive down costs and lower its prices, even if it meant reducing its gross margin. Kmart, with 1993 gross margins at 27 percent, down only slightly from 1984's margin of 29.1 percent, steadily lost market share to Wal-Mart even while it maintained higher gross margins. In other words, Wal-Mart's declining gross margins were not a sign of weakness but of its competitive strength and aggressiveness.

Net Margins

Wal-Mart's net margins declined from 4.2 percent in 1984 to 3.5 percent in 1994. This decline came about largely because of the increased importance of Sam's Wholesale Club. Sam's operated with very high volumes and low margins as did the grocery operations in the Supercenters. During this time, Wal-Mart's earnings grew at a compound annual rate of 27 percent although, given the company's greatly increased size, this growth rate slowed to about 20 percent in more recent years.

Wal-Mart continued to take market share from its competitors through its strategy of driving down prices and increasing sales per square foot. The company posed a severe competitive threat to all other retailers.

Return on Total Capital

Among its competitors, Wal-Mart consistently maintained the highest returns on capital, although there was a substantial decline in the magnitude of these returns. During 1984–1988, return on capital for Wal-Mart averaged 19.4 percent and was increasing; in 1988 it reached 21.2 percent. However, the five-year period from 1989 to 1993 saw a downward return on capital, averaging only 17.3 percent and hitting a low of 13.3 percent in 1993. Other discount chains also experienced substantial declines. Wal-Mart's decline, however, was due not only to the overall decline in the retail sector but also to the company's increasing activity in metropolitan areas where costs were higher than in the rural areas where it first dominated.

Market Valuation

Investors recognized Wal-Mart's sterling long-term earnings growth rate, and the company's price earnings (P/E) ratio continued to be very high compared with the market average. Long-term stockholders of the stock, including many Wal-Mart employees, benefited greatly from the stock's legendary price rise. Adjusting for five 2-for-1 stock splits, Wal-Mart stock sold between $1.37 and $2.87 only 10 years ago. With its October 1994 price of $25 per share, an investor holding the stock since the end of 1983 enjoyed a compound annual return of about 25 percent.

The stock price peaked in early 1993 at $34, however, causing investors and employees to be less pleased with the company's market performance during 1993–1994. As Wal-Mart grew in size its earnings growth rate started to decline and the company's P/E ratio compared with all listed stocks also declined.

The Special Culture

Heavy competition forced Wal-Mart to be constantly vigilant to keep its costs down and stay competitive. It achieved this goal by means of a hyperproductive culture in which its employees, called "associates," were expected to work very hard for low wages. The payoff for their relentless work ethic was that they would become rich if the stock price went up, because they were guaranteed a certain part of their compensation in company stock. Employee morale was hurt when the stock price failed to advance as expected. Since the death of founder Sam Walton in 1992, Wal-Mart's stock performance had not been as strong as it once was.

Other parts of company culture were also unique. Wal-Mart relied on what it called a "servant leadership;" it provided employees with what they needed—merchandise, capital, information, and inspiration—to serve customers, and it developed in its managers and employees a perverse pride in acknowledging mistakes and correcting them.

Costs were kept down through a well-developed information infrastructure designed to customize merchandise at individual outlets with a detailed point-of-sale replenishment system. This system was based on keeping track of more than 6,000 customer purchasing variables, including the time of day customers made their purchases. The goal was to customize each linear foot of shelf space at each department at each store so that the right quantity of goods was always available at the right time.

A Pattern of Diminished Performance

Whatever the explanations might be, Wal-Mart showed a clear pattern of diminished performance: lower gross and net margins, lower returns on capital, and a slowing growth rate. Competitors who studied the Wal-Mart model were compelled to cut their own prices to stay in business. Even merchants in some of the smaller communities where Wal-Mart had established its presence learned how to find market niches and provide services that their giant competitor did not address. While these actions did not necessarily take market share from Wal-Mart, they did close some potential areas of growth. These reactions by competitors put additional pressure on Wal-Mart to continue to intensify its cost-cutting efforts.

As the dominant retailer in the United States, Wal-Mart found that maintaining an expansion rate of 15 percent per year was increasingly difficult. With more of its expansion activity directed toward the suburbs of major metropolitan areas, Wal-Mart had to confront its competitors head-on. It also was difficult to generate continued sales growth of nearly 10 percent at the same stores when a high $400 sales per square foot was being extracted. Indeed, same-store sales growth had been dropping along with the new store expansion rate, accounting for Wal-Mart's diminished earnings growth rate.

Global Expansion

A second wind for growth became possible through Wal-Mart's large-scale campaign of expansion throughout North America. It had joint ventures with Cifra S.A. in Mexico and with Lojas Americanas in Argentina and Brazil. In Canada, Wal-Mart purchased 122 Woolco discount stores to revamp and upgrade to make them comparable to its U.S. Wal-Mart stores. Despite these new avenues for growth, management had clear incentives to intensify its cost cutting in its domestic stores and, therefore, to stabilize its profit margins.

Wal-Mart met some problems as well as successes. Its Mexico City store was ordered closed for 72 hours in 1993 for violating import and consumer information regulations. Wal-Mart characterized the incident as a "misunderstanding." Canadians referred to the Woolco purchase as an invasion of hard-driving U.S.-style retailing, which was likely to cannibalize small communities by means of cutthroat business practices from a juggernaut out to crush the competition.[5]

Public Relations Difficulties

Wal-Mart's halo was beginning to fade. Many detractors attacked the company but perhaps the most serious challenge came from the National Advertising Review Board, a watchdog panel of 70 advertising professionals and public interest members who spearheaded the industry's self-regulatory efforts. While the board did not have the power to enforce its regulations, it could refer cases to the Federal Trade Commission. In a case brought before it by the Better Business Bureau and Target department stores, the board decided against Wal-Mart, saying that it could not continue to use its slogan "Always the Lowest Prices, Always." The board determined that this slogan could mislead some shoppers, because it was impossible for a merchant to know that all of its prices were always the lowest.

Wal-Mart modified its slogan to "Always Low Prices, Always." It also agreed to discontinue store displays that listed its price and the price a purported competitor charged for the same item. Target had attacked Wal-Mart with newspaper ads claiming that Wal-Mart misled its customers about Target's prices.[6]

Accusations of "Predatory Pricing"

An equally difficult challenge for Wal-Mart came from Dwayne Goode, the owner of American Drugs, Inc., a small Arkansas drug chain. Goode accused Wal-Mart of selling prescription drugs and 20 health and beauty items below cost in order to drive out the competition. Ultimately, this tactic would lead to the demise of nearly all the long-established merchants in small U.S. cities.

Wal-Mart did not dispute the facts. It admitted that in each market it prepared a list of products and then called its competitors to see what they were charging. Wal-Mart then made sure that it charged less so it could retain its title of being the low-cost leader.

The basic concept was an old one in retailing: that an individual store should be willing to take losses on a few items to assure its overall profits. A store engaged in the common practice of "loss-leader" pricing to draw customers into the store. Management expected that customers would buy high-profit items as well as the loss-leaders, making the overall customer relationship profitable.

Goode, however, argued that this practice represented predatory pricing and was illegal because the intent was to drive out the competition. Once the competition was gone, Wal-Mart would be in a position to hike prices and charge what it pleased.[7]

This suit was very closely watched as it was upheld in a lower court in 1992. On appeal it could go all the way to the Supreme Court. Friends-of-the-court briefs were filed on behalf of Wal-Mart by Citizens for a Sound Economy, the National Taxpayers Union, and other groups, who contended that the very future of American capitalism was at stake.

Predatory Pricing and Antitrust Law

Since the enactment of the Sherman Antitrust Act in 1890, regulation of monopoly and restraint of trade has been a part of the U.S. legal system. The act outlawed conspiracies in the restraint of trade. Price-fixing clearly constituted a conspiracy. Subsequent legislation (e.g., the 1914 Clayton Act) expanded on the meaning of restraint of trade to include tied contracts, exclusive dealerships, and predatory pricing. The Celler-Kefauver Anti-Merger Act of 1950 prohibited the acquisition of the assets of another firm in order to lessen competition.

Predatory pricing was defined as selling below costs. Because measurement problems were associated with calculations of the costs, **intent** to exclude a competitor was a very important criterion. Average balance-sheet costs were used as a proxy for long-term marginal costs. Proof of sales below average balance-sheet costs with intent to exclude establishes a prima facie case of predatory pricing. How Wal-Mart would fare in the case brought against it by pharmacist Goode could have an important bearing on its future profitability.

Joanne Magnuson had to decide whether, with all this change, Wal-Mart remained a good investment. Should the institutional investor up its stake in the company, reduce it, or keep it steady? What strategy should the investor adopt vís-a-vís the company?

Discussion Questions

1. What factors accounted for Wal-Mart's success?
2. What challenges was it now facing?
3. To what extent could its special culture survive Sam Walton's death?
4. Would Wal-Mart succeed with its global expansion? Could it reproduce its business success abroad?
5. Would Wal-Mart's retreat with respect to its slogan of "always the lowest prices" hurt it?
6. Would the charges of predatory prices damage Wal-Mart?
7. What advice should Joanne give to the institutional investor?

Endnotes

1. This case was written by Donald Geffen and Alfred Marcus.
2. "Wal-Mart Stores," *Value Line*, May 27, 1994, p. 1653; *Wal-Mart: Annual Report 1994*.
3. "And the Winner is Still . . . Wal-Mart," *Fortune*, May 2, 1994, p. 62.
4. "Company Reports: Wal-Mart Earnings Climb, But Kmart Shows a Decline," *The New York Times*, May 17, 1994, p. 5D; "Wal-Mart: CEO Calms the Masses," *Arkansas Business*, June 13, 1994, Sec. 1, p. 1; "Wal-Mart Stores, Inc. Earns $500 Million," *Arkansas Business*, June 13, 1994, Sec. 1, p. 24.
5. "Wal-Mart: The Canadian Invasion/How May I Help You?" *Minneapolis Star Tribune*, April 11, 1994, p. 10A; "Wal-Mart Renovation Tab Tops $275 Million," *Calgary Herald*, May 28, 1994, p. 3E; "Wal-Mart Signs on Big Macs as New Woolco Snack," *Toronto Star*, May 31, 1994, p. 6B; "Company News: Wal-Mart to Continue International Expansion," *The New York Times*, June 4, 1994, Sec. 1, p. 37. "Company News: Giant Wal-Mart Store Ordered Shut, Temporarily," *The New York Times*, June 24, 1994, p. 5D.
6. "New Dayton Hudson CEO Seen as Aggressive, Creative," *Minneapolis Star Tribune*, April 15, 1994, p. 1D; "The Media Business: Advertising—Appenda: Wal-Mart to Change Its 'Always' Slogan," *The New York Times*, May 26, 1994, p. 18D; "Wal-Mart Dumps 'Low-Price' Slogan," *Newsday*, May 26, 1994, p. 65A; "Wal-Mart to Alter 'Always' Slogan after Panel Deems It Misleading," *Minneapolis Star Tribune*, May 26, 1994, p. 1D.
7. "Small Fry Takes on Wal-Mart," *Newsday*, June 10, 1994, Sec. 1, p. 65.

CHAPTER

2

Adjusting to Changes in the Strategic Business Environment

Innovative companies are especially adroit at responding to change in their environment . . . when the environment changes, these companies change too. As the needs of their customers shift, the skills of their competitors improve, the mood of the public perturbates, the forces of international trade realign, and government regulations shift, these companies tack, revamp, adjust, transform, and adapt.

Thomas J. Peters and Robert H. Waterman, *In Search of Excellence*

Introduction and Chapter Objectives

The purpose of this chapter is to provide frameworks and concepts to help adjust a corporation to changes in the strategic business environment. The discussion centers on the effects of the strategic business environment on the firm and strategies you can use to align companies with these environmental forces. The managerial role in strategic change is considered. Can managers make a difference? How effective can they be in aligning their organizations with changing external conditions?

External Conditions Affecting a Corporation's Performance

The external conditions and influences that affect a corporation's performance have many dimensions:

- The values, ideologies, and culture of a particular period of time.
- The structure of an industry.
- The factors that managers view as relevant and that they know with certainty.
- Their relationships with other organizations that affect their success.

Analyses of these conditions differ in important ways, as will be shown in this chapter.

The Broad Approach

broad approach to strategic business analysis Examines values, ideologies, structural aspects of society, government policies, and technological changes.

The **broad approach to strategic business analysis** covers the entire gamut of values and ideologies characteristic of an era. These values and ideologies are linked to the structural aspects of a society, government policies, and technological changes.[1] This approach categorizes the culture within which the organization operates, the ideology and dominant values of society; the government agencies which are involved in setting policies in areas such as antitrust, environmental protection, safety, and antidiscrimination; the state of knowledge; and the progress and state of technology.[2]

Practitioners of the broad approach include popular writers like John Naisbitt who helps corporations cope with uncertainty by spotting trends. Among the broad trends that Naisbitt follows are decentralization, networking, and the transformation from an industrial to an information society. Weiner Edrich Brown, a pioneer in social forecasting, monitors change in pollution, personal injury, technology's opportunities and impact on people, and prospects for the Third World. Yankelovich Skelly & White, a social research firm owned by Saatchi & Saatchi, the English advertising agency, has identified 35 widespread social trends such as rejection of authority and female careerism.

Other practitioners are Perception International, Inferential Focus, Williams Inference Service of Massachusetts, and the Business Intelligence Program of SRI International. They try to counter the business training many managers obtain in undergraduate and master's programs in business administration that teaches them to think in rational, linear terms and to value only what they can quantify. The problem with this type of thinking is that it leads us to assume that the future will look like the present.

Some of the trends that the practitioners have spotted have proven to be very useful. For instance, Perception International predicted an increased demand for television programs based on the proliferation of television stations throughout the world. The increase in the value of MCA's film libraries enabled investors in that company to make substantial profits. Southwestern Bell decided to create a Silver Pages Directory for the elderly based largely on the Naisbitt Group's prediction of the growing influence of this age group. Sometimes the trend spotters were wrong; in 1983 Inferential Focus predicted that Japanese companies would dominate the personal computer market.[3]

Probably a business person who avidly read, saved, and categorized articles in specialty trade magazines and general publications such as *The New York Times*, *The Wall Street Journal*, *Business Week*, *The Economist*, and *Fortune* could do as well as the practitioners of this type of broad analysis. However, most business people do not have the time to systematically read and analyze this information.

Scenario Planning

The worldwide Royal Dutch Shell Group long ago developed an approach to **scenario planning,** that would allow it to respond well to information from broad analysis. Shell found that planning in an increasingly turbulent and fluid business environment was proving exceedingly difficult. Forecasting errors were frequent in the face of dramatic and unprecedented changes. The best known econometric forecasts, for example, almost always failed to anticipate major shifts in the economy such as the price shocks caused by the

1973–1974 OPEC oil embargo, the 1978–1979 acceleration in inflation, and the 1980–1982 recession.

Instead of a single, best forecast, Shell developed scenarios for a variety of different possibilities. Shell needed a better understanding of the long-term oil market and if there would be major changes in price and in the competition among fuels (for example, coal versus oil). Since long lead times were necessary for projects in the petroleum business, it developed implications from the consideration of four possible futures:

1. Surprise free.
2. A tripling of oil prices by petroleum exporting nations, which would lower economic growth and depress demand.
3. A growing emphasis on "me-first" values and leisure, which would also depress growth.
4. Increased demand for oil alternatives such as coal and nuclear power.

Shell then examined the major actors—producers, consumers, companies, and governments—and how they would respond to these scenarios.

Company executives had trouble thinking in terms of strategic responses to alternatives that they did not consider possible at the time. They were being asked to have a deeper insight into the system and how it worked, both the predetermined and uncertain elements. Ultimately, they were much better prepared than their competitors to handle the havoc that ensued in the energy industry as the 1970s progressed (see Chapter 13 on energy policies).[4]

The Industry Structure Model

Unfortunately "a definitive conceptual framework" capable of "guiding and interpreting the full range of economic, technological, social, and political forces" that affect an organization's performance does not exist.[5] As a consequence, the ability to forecast, let alone cope with, large-scale, unpredictable change in the environment is not perfect.

industry analysis Examines competitive forces in an industry: buyers, suppliers, substitutes, potential entrants, and direct competitors.

A broad approach needs to be linked to industry conditions and managerial tasks. Scenarios should be joined with **industry analysis.** The competitive forces that govern an industry are buyers, suppliers, substitute products and services, potential entrants, and strategic groups of directly competing firms (see Exhibit 2–1).[6] These elements establish immediate opportunities and threats. They are influenced in turn by social values, government policies, energy and environmental issues, and technology. Technological innovations, for instance, make production scale economies possible, which in turn make it difficult for competitors to enter an industry, thereby protecting an organization from competitive change.

Industrial structure is not static; industries evolve and change. Their emergence typically follows a pattern of fragmentation, consolidation, maturity, and decline which is accompanied by fierce global competition. As industries mature, the challenges managers face change.

EXHIBIT 2–1 Industry Structure Model

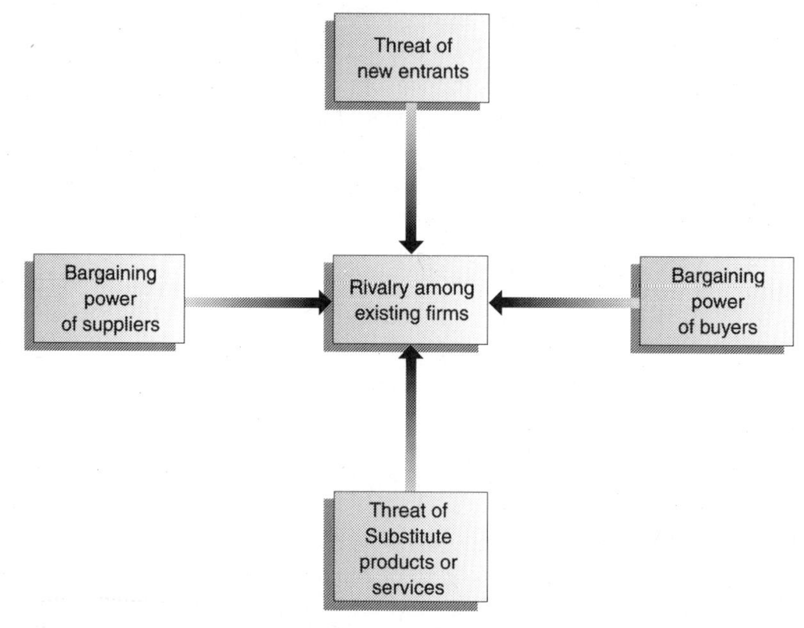

The Cognitive Model

The extent to which managers correctly perceive external conditions is unclear. Managers' cognitive abilities are limited and perceptions do not match objective reality. Managers scan external conditions that affect their organizations selectively. Elements that influence and distort how they perceive threats and opportunities include their age and the historic events they have experienced, the information that is available to them, the indicators used by the organization to judge its performance (see Chapter 4), and relationships that have been forged with other organizations.[7] The **cognitive model** analyzes how organizations gather and filter information and how managers interpret events.

cognitive model Analyzes organization's information gathering and filtering systems and managers' interpretation of events.

Cognitive schemes and biases lead managers at different levels in the organization to perceive events differently. Managers categorize events, assess the consequences, and consider appropriate actions based on these schemes and biases. External conditions are perceptual in nature and depend on the information gathering and filtering systems of the organizations and the managers' interpretations of events.[8]

Enactment, Selection, and Retention

External conditions become meaningful to managers through a process of enactment, selection, and retention (See Exhibit 2–2).[9] Enactment refers to the activities that isolate these conditions for closer scrutiny. Events that differ from expectations, such as indications of poor employee morale, complaints about product quality, or near-accidents bring

EXHIBIT 2–2 How External Conditions Becomes Meaningful to Managers

Enactment	Conditions are isolated for further scrutiny
Selection	Use of prior understandings to make sense of the irregularities
Retention	Storage of the information gained after irregularities have been confronted

conditions to the attention of managers. The process of selection refers to the effort to use prior understandings to make sense of these irregularities. Retention is the storage of the information. The reformulated knowledge gained after the irregularities have been analyzed is retained in the organization's files and in individuals' memories, and it is used when the organization confronts similar situations later.

A Critique of the Cognitive Model

While the role of perception, psychological states, and cognitive processes is important, objective environmental conditions should not be disregarded. Environmental understanding cannot be reduced to "perceptions alone," for it then becomes nothing more than the "psychoanalysis of managers." A social reality exists outside managerial cognition, which is not merely a reflection of managers' subjective and intersubjective experience.[10]

Managers try "to understand, make sense out of, and respond to" an objective world, but they are uncertain in their knowledge of this world. This uncertainty reflects itself in different ways. Managers are unsure of how cause-and-effect relationships work in the world; they have trouble assigning probabilities to future events; and they cannot know for sure what the outcomes of their decisions will be.[11]

Environmental Uncertainty

Uncertainty affects nearly everything that managers do. The sources of this uncertainty are insufficient information and an inability to effectively combine and use the information that exists. Managers may have too much information and are unable to discriminate between the relevant and irrelevant[12] or how the parts relate to the whole. Some parts of the milieu (e.g., relations with suppliers, competitors, government, or financial institutions) may generate more uncertainty than others.

Three types of uncertainty can be distinguished: state, effect, and response (See Exhibit 2–3).[13] **State uncertainty** refers to incomplete knowledge about external influences and their relations; sociocultural trends, demographic shifts, government policies in the United States and elsewhere in the world, technological developments, industry shifts (suppliers, competitors, and consumers), and so on.

Effect uncertainty refers to the impact of external forces on the organization. Information about external conditions may be adequate, but managers may not understand how these conditions combine to affect their organization.

EXHIBIT 2–3 Three Types of Uncertainty About External Conditions

State	Incomplete knowledge about external influences and their relations
Effect	Uncertainty about the impact of external forces on the organization
Response	Lack of knowledge of response options and/or inability to predict consequences of response choice

Response uncertainty refers to a "lack of knowledge of response options" and/or an "inability to predict the likely consequences of a response choice."[14] External forces and their impact on the organization may be known, but managers may not know how to respond with uncertainty.[15]

Uncertainty generally is assumed to be negative. Managers take steps to overcome it or to reduce or absorb its impacts on the organization. However, some managers may actually try to increase uncertainty since it opens the possibility for change.[16]

The Organizational Field Model

So far conditions external to the corporation have been defined as broad social forces and narrow competitive conditions. They have been viewed in objective and subjective terms and presented as a major source of managerial uncertainty. Often the actions of other organizations with whom the managers relate bring the uncertainty to the attention of managers. Thus, external conditions also should be viewed in terms of these organizations.

organizational field model
Emphasizes the relationships between the corporation and other organizations.

The **organizational field** model emphasizes organizations' dependence on one another. Managers contend with external circumstances by making exchanges or having transactions with managers of other organizations. They relate to organizations in the industrial structure model such as buyers, suppliers, and competitors but are not restricted to them. Managers also relate to trade associations and government regulatory agencies.[17]

The organization is part of an open organizational system, depending on resources generated by other organizations to survive. It has to "negotiate" or "navigate" between the opposing demands and expectations of these organizations. Supporting organizations may include customers, suppliers, government agencies, and financial institutions. If supporters are unsatisfied in either an economic or normative (value) sense, they can switch allegiance to competitors. The relative power of the organization depends on its ability to forge close ties with supporters so that they do not switch allegiance. To keep these close ties, it must supply the supporters with what they need, and in turn it acquires the resources it needs to survive.[18]

Turbulence

Some environments are more interconnected and heterogenous than others; that is, managers have to relate to more organizations, and the pattern of linkages between them is denser and more difficult to understand. The discussions of General Motors and IBM (see Chapter 1) made it clear that few organizations operate in munificent environments with an ample and assured supply of resources. Most find that external conditions are rapidly changing and so is the ability to acquire the resources they need.

Fluctuations in the ability to acquire resources may be experienced as a wave function (see Exhibit 2–4).[19] A wave has a velocity of change (its frequency), degree of change over time (the amplitude of this change), and the predictability of change (the extent of directional deviation). Frequency is the number of peaks or valleys experienced, amplitude the height and depth of these peaks and valleys, and directional deviation the sameness in the pattern of the peaks and valleys over time.[20] For most organizations the flow of resources is neither steady nor predictable.

Nonmunificent, complex environments have been described as disturbed, unstable, volatile, and unpredictable. Environmental turbulence is central to models of strategic choice, organizational failure, and executive turnover. Extreme turbulence puts the organization in jeopardy, threatens its survival, and takes away the opportunities managers have to freely determine the organization's fate. Turbulent environments severely test managers' adjustment capabilities.[21]

Matching Internal Strengths and Weaknesses with External Opportunities and Threats

SWOT
Identifies the match between the organization's strengths and weaknesses and external opportunities and threats.

Managers cope with rapid change in external conditions. Strategies, the patterns of resource allocations they make over time, reflect their responses to volatile environments. Successful strategies should match the organization's internal strengths and weaknesses with the external opportunities and threats it faces.[22] The acronym for this type of analysis is **SWOT:** *S* stands for strengths, *W* for weaknesses, *O* for opportunities, and *T* for threats. Strength and weakness analysis identifies distinctive competencies, the characteristics of

EXHIBIT 2–4 Flow of Resources over Time

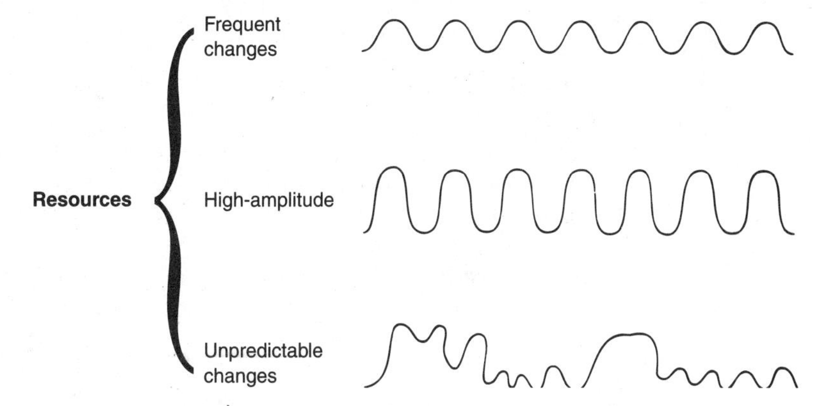

an organization that allow it to successfully compete with other organizations. By matching internal strengths with external challenges, managers can enhance the effectiveness of an organization.

Strategy *content* refers to the specifics of what is decided about the corporation's goals, scope, and competitive approaches. Strategic *process* refers to how these decisions are made. Content results in a *position* with respect to the firm's product and markets and how it is trying to achieve competitive advantage in relation to firms offering similar goods and services. Process is a *perspective* "through which problems are spotted and interpreted and from which streams of decisions flow."[23]

Strategic Content

corporate-level strategy Selecting a corporation's products and markets.

Both corporate and business levels make content decisions. Managers use **corporate-level strategy** when selecting the firm's products and markets. They define the businesses in which the firm will operate and the companies against whom it will compete.

An important content issue is the degree of business diversification and the relatedness of the business that a firm operates. On the one hand, managers have to decide whether there is less risk in being in an unrelated business. They must consider the appeal of the conglomerate structure. On the other hand, they must decide whether specialization offers economies of scale, scope, or learning. They must weigh the advantages of horizontal versus vertical integration, the gain that can be won from mergers or acquisitions.

business-level strategy Deciding how the corporation will compete in product/market domains.

Business-level strategy answers different questions. Once managers decide which environments the firm will call its own, the issues are how to compete in them. Managers must first make decisions about price and quality. Then they have to deploy resources in marketing and sales, manufacturing, R&D, accounting, and control to reflect these choices.

Strategic Topologies

Strategic topologies are common business strategies across organization types, technologies, and industries. A number of different topologies exist: uniqueness, life cycle, and adaptation.[24]

Uniqueness. Michael Porter argues that performance depends on a firm's ability to influence the forces that determine its profitability.[25] These forces are the threat of new competitors, rivalry among existing competitors, threat of substitute products, and the bargaining power of buyers and suppliers. A firm influences these forces by generating strategic advantage through uniqueness. Uniqueness derives from overall cost leadership, differentiation, or focus (see Exhibit 2–5).

Cost leadership signifies high market share and/or favorable access to raw materials. A firm typically adopts an aggressive strategy of construction of efficient scale facilities, tight cost and overhead control, avoidance of marginal customer accounts, and cost minimization in areas such as R&D, service, sales force, and advertising.[26]

Differentiation means that a firm offers unique products or services along several di-

EXHIBIT 2–5 Uniqueness

Focus	Degree of specialization, width of product lines, target customer segments, geographic markets
Low cost	Price, high volume, homogenous product, experience curve effects, investment in cost minimizing facilities and equipment, economies of scale and scope in production, advertising, distribution, and procurement
Differentiation:	
Customer	Advertising and sales force, brand identification with customer, distribution channel, company-owned outlets, specialty outlets, broad line outlets, extent of company-owned forward integration, extent of company-owned service network, engineering, credit
Supplier	Product quality, raw materials, specifications of product, tolerances, special features, captive supplier (extent of backward integration)

mensions such as brand image, technology, features, customer service, or dealer network. These unique features attract a premium price. The attributes can be varied in quantity or combined in different ways to differentiate the product. In consumer goods industries, advertising is the most obvious method of achieving differentiation.

Focus signifies that the firm has a narrow strategic target. It emphasizes a particular consumer group or segment of a product line. Cost leadership and differentiation can be combined with focus.

The low profitability strategy is being "stuck in the middle." Organizations tend to move toward the middle; therefore strong leadership is needed to prevent this drift. The generic strategies imply different organizational arrangements, control procedures, and incentive systems. Implementing them successfully means using a different set of resources and skills. A firm therefore cannot be successful applying two strategies at once. The resources and skills that work for one strategy are not interchangeable with those that succeed with another.

Life Cycle. The first stage is to develop a new product or service (see Exhibit 2–6).[27] The interest of the organization is in long-term growth through the exploitation of new market opportunities. The organic structure (i.e., loose, innovative, unbureaucratic) prevails. Marketing, technology, and R&D are stressed. The organization seeks out and appraises opportunities. It invests large sums in launching and developing new products and processes, and it engages in extensive market development and the pursuit of market share. Flexibility of operations and technological risk taking are the hallmarks of this strategy. The aim is to generate long-term earnings, not short-term profits.

The second stage is to stabilize the market. If the organization operates in a homogenous market, it competes through price/cost margins. It pursues a cost-leadership approach using tight mechanistic structures (i.e., rigid, control-oriented, bureaucratic) and efficient manufacturing processes and procedures to produce a limited set of products. Another

EXHIBIT 2–6 The Life-Cycle Topology

Develop	New markets, technological risk taking
Stabilize	Cost leadership or differentiation
Turnaround	Survival, reverse cash flow problems
Harvest	Wind down, sell, or liquidate

stabilization strategy is differentiation. The organization creates a niche that makes it difficult for competitors to penetrate. It defends its brand name or other product characteristics. It emphasizes specialization, high quality and distinctive service, convenient distribution, or close customer contact. By focusing on the customer's specific needs regarding the product, profitability is maintained in a mature market.

A third stage may be to achieve a turnaround with survival as the goal. The company has an urgent need to reverse cash flow problems, stop the hemorrhaging, and rebuild. After a tightening of operations, there can be a redirection of the units worth saving. Thus, cost-efficiency and controls are introduced and product lines are rationalized by phasing out unprofitable assets, units, and products. Reorganization through diversification, expansion, acquisition, merger, or integration may follow.

A final stage may be to harvest the business. The company decides to wind down, sell, or liquidate assets that do not meet performance criteria, such as return on assets (ROA). It eliminates assets that are incompatible with the core business, culture, or perceived expertise of the company, or that do not fit with the strategic direction. Harvesting can be imposed by the situation, it can be planned, or it can be emergent—that is, a decision made after trial-and-error efforts to change the situation. There may be significant exit barriers that affect the ability to carry out this strategy, including legislative, social, and moral issues as well as management pride and competitiveness.

Adaptation. When the environment of an organization is stable (see Exhibit 2–7), the appropriate strategy is to be a *defender*. The organization adopts a highly cost-effective single core technology. It engages in intensive planning and centralized control to maintain stability. A mechanistic structure is necessary.[28]

When the environment of the organization is broad and continuously expanding, the appropriate strategy is to be a *prospector*. The organization monitors a wide range of environmental conditions in search of new product and market opportunities. It relies on flexible technologies with a relatively low degree of routinization. Under these conditions an organic structure is necessary.[29]

In a mixed domain, the appropriate strategy is to be an *analyzer*. The organization attempts to locate and exploit new product and market opportunities, while clinging to its base of traditional products and customers. It develops a dual technical core representing stable and flexible components and a dual structure reflecting mechanistic and organic elements.

The *reactor* fails to appropriately take into account either stable or changing environmental conditions. It does not align itself with its environment, stressing neither cost-

EXHIBIT 2–7 Adaptation

	Defender	*Prospector*	*Analyzer*
Environment	Stable	Expanding	Stable/expanding
Technology	Cost-effective	Flexible	Cost-effective/flexible
Planning	Centralized	Opportunistic search	Centralized/opportunistic search
Organization	Mechanistic	Organic	Mechanistic/organic
Reactor	Fails to align technology, planning, and organization with the environment.		

effectiveness nor new products and markets, or some combination of the two. Alignment between strategy, environment, technology, and structure is not made; therefore performance deteriorates.

process-level strategy Choosing the formal and informal management systems and structures to carry out a strategy.

Process. Firms make **process-level strategy** decisions about the types of formal and informal management control systems and structures they will have. Within this realm, the systems for data collection, event reporting, tracking, monitoring, guiding, and controling are important.[30]

The organization records past events and compares them with what it plans to accomplish. These efforts produce "alert" messages. When something goes wrong, the organization acts to correct deficiencies, and it exercises control when no actions have been taken. Documents and reports produced as events occur show how the firm corrects errors and aligns its expectations with reality.

Through organizational processes, managers steer the firm through troubled environments. They test environments for obstacles not originally anticipated. The ways that managers handle discrepancies show something about the long-standing norms that govern the organization's relationships with its employees and the outside world. They are an indication of the organization's culture, ideology, and basic paradigm of interpreting and interacting with the world.

Strategic Change

This book is dedicated toward making better choices in turbulent environments. The premise is that organizational effectiveness depends on the ability to adapt. The strategies chosen are the means by which management aligns the corporation with society.

Managers are challenged by rampant social changes. Globalization causes intense competitive pressures. Government policies, such as deregulation, shift conditions under which firms operate. The government provides and then takes away incentives for investment. It introduces and removes trade barriers, duties and quotas, health and safety standards, and antitrust regulations. Its macroeconomic policies affect economic growth, employment, and the inflation rate. Technological discontinuities also have major effects. Changes in strategy should influence organizational performance by restoring or improving the organization's alignment with these conditions.

Can Managers Make a Difference?

Executives in high performing companies are supposed to scan the environment "more frequently and more broadly than their counterparts in low-performing companies."[31] Can managers make a difference with better information? The organizational ecology school of thought views external conditions as determining organizational success and survival.[32] Managers have little influence. The availability of capital and financial resources, technological innovation, the expansion of market opportunities, and the political stability needed to engage in future-oriented behavior originate in factors that are external to the corporation and which determine its success.

Biological analogies are applied—variation, selection, and retention and survival are determined as corporations pass through inevitable cycles of creation, growth, and decline. There is little managers can do. In contrast, institutional theorists believe that managers can influence organizational performance. They do so by achieving a degree of harmony with social forces.[33] Certainly, these conditions limit managerial freedom, but managers still have an element of choice in how to respond. They learn by copying what other organizations do; they use constraints to their advantage. External forces offer encouragement to undertake certain activities, and managers decide to follow up on these opportunities, some with more vigor and imagination than others. Managers are not at the mercy of external forces; they interact with and change them.

One way to understand the dilemma of determinism versus choice is to see that some situations involve more freedom than others (see Exhibit 2–8).[34] These situations require different strategies. When choice is restricted, managers may feel constrained to be "defenders" of an existing niche or position. When choice is open, they can be "prospectors" continually searching for new profit-making opportunities. When some choices are limited and others open, they can be "analyzers" who defend existing strengths and look selectively for new opportunities. The weakest position occurs when choice is open but managers fail to choose.

Aligning the Organization with Multiple Contingencies

Strategy, then, is aligning a corporation's external conditions with its internal strengths and weaknesses. This alignment must be matched by linking managerial values and ideals with society's values and expectations. There is no best way to accomplish such an alignment: Judgment and values play an important role.[35]

EXHIBIT 2–8 Choice and Determinism

		Choice	
		High	*Low*
Determinism	*High*	Analyze: some options open	Defend: few options available
	Low	Prospect: many options open	React: failure to grasp available options

macrocongruence The match between external conditions and the corporation's internal structures.

microcongruence The match between the internal structures and individual behavior.

Organizational performance is the result of a fit between context, structure, systems, style, culture, technology, reward systems, tasks, and personnel. If the fit is good, the organization will prosper. If it is poor, then it probably will not. **Macrocongruence** should exist between external conditions and internal structures, and **microcongruence** should exist between internal structures and individual behavior.

For example, it is not enough for a CEO to declare that the goals of the organization are ethical behavior, international expansion, environmental responsibility, and technological innovation. The organization must be aligned internally and externally to accomplish these goals. Otherwise it cannot accomplish its goals.

Since organizations operate in contexts of multiple and conflicting contingencies, it is necessary to recognize multiple and equally effective organizational strategies and designs for coping with these contingencies.[36] Multiple possibilities create the conditions for choice: The greater the number of equally effective options, the more managers can choose. Performance then may be subject to **equifinality:** "that is, the same outcomes can be achieved in multiple ways."[37]

Continuous and Discontinuous Change

Strategic change is not a simple function of choice in a placid environment. It depends on realigning the organization with many rapidly changing external conditions. In every organization, small adjustments in magnitude "tend to be interspersed with periods of discontinuous shifts in pattern."[38] In some circumstances, the fundamental shifts are smooth; they occur incrementally, the result of accumulated, common everyday experience. Their significance is not appreciated until after the fact. What seems trivial at the moment and only tactical in nature, proves in the end to be strategic in nature and of the utmost importance.

While major shifts are hardly noticed in some situations, in others they are disruptive interruptions that cannot be ignored. Discontinuous change occurs infrequently, but when it does it has great impact. It creates havoc: People are laid off, divisions are sold, established patterns of doing business are swept away, and nearly everything comfortable and familiar is turned topsy-turvy. The memory of the cataclysmic event lies embedded in the collective memories of members of the organization. As a point of comparison, it helps define what the organization becomes.[39]

Pressures for Change

External conditions create the pressures for strategic change. A corporation not aligned with its environment will be ineffective. Forces for change must overcome forces of inertia. A good example is General Motors, a company that had trouble effectively adjusting to change because the forces of inertia were so strong (see Case 2–A).

The costs of being mismatched with the environment have to be greater than the costs of change. The awareness that a misalignment or gap needs to be redressed is not sufficient. Strategic change will not take place unless there is both the capacity and desire for change. Resources have to be available for change, and stakeholder groups must believe that the change is fair and just to overcome possible opposition.

Conclusions

This chapter defines the strategic environment of the corporation. Strategies are the process by which corporations adjust to changing external conditions. Shell's approach to scanning the environment and developing scenarios are discussed. Distinctions are drawn between strategy content and process. Three topologies are presented: uniqueness, life cycle, and adaptation. The views of organizational ecologists and institutional theorists about managerial freedom are examined. Microcongruence, it is argued, has to match macrocongruence if managers are to make a difference: The internal incentives have to match the external strategy if a strategy is to be effectively implemented.

Discussion Questions

1. Compare and contrast the notion of the broad environment with the industry structure model. Give some examples of broad analysis and why it might be useful to a firm. What are the relationships between these two notions of the organization's environment?
2. What point is made by those who consider the cognitive environment to be important? What is meant by enactment, selection, and retention? Is there an objective environment? What is your opinion?
3. Some managers complain that they don't understand what is happening in the environment. Others say they understand what is happening but they don't know how it will affect their organization. Still others say that they understand how it affects their organization but they do not know what to do with the information. What do these three statements illustrate? Which type of uncertainty is the most important?
4. What is the organizational field model?
5. Environmental turbulence may be viewed in terms of the velocity, amplitude, and predictability of change in resources. How useful is this depiction?
6. What does SWOT stand for? What kind of analysis does it call for? To what extent is this type of analysis useful? Is it easy to carry out?
7. What is the difference between strategy content and strategy process?
8. What is the difference between corporate and business strategy?
9. Explain the differences between defenders, prospectors, analyzers, and reactors.
10. Explain the differences between cost leadership, differentiation, and focus. Do you agree that the low-profit strategy should be in the middle?
11. What is the product life-cycle approach to strategy? How does it differ from other approaches?
12. How do organizational ecologists answer the question: Can managers make a difference? How do institutional theorists answer this question? Which view, in your opinion, is correct?

13. What is the difference between macrocongruence and microcongruence? Why are both needed?
14. What does equifinality mean? What does it imply for organizational behavior?

Endnotes

1. D. Bell, *The Coming of Post-Industrial Society: A Venture in Social Forecasting* (New York: Basic Books, 1973); G. Lodge, *The New American Ideology* (New York: Alfred A. Knopf, 1975).
2. R. Butler and M. Carney, "Strategy and Strategic Choice: The Case of Telecommunications," *Strategic Management Journal*, 1986, pp. 161–77.
3. Myron Magnet, "Who Needs a Trend-Spotter?" *Fortune*, Deccember 9, 1985, pp. 51–56.
4. Pierre Wack, "Scenarios: Uncharted Waters Ahead," *Harvard Business Review*, September–October 1985, pp. 73–89; and "Scenarios: Shooting the Rapids," *Harvard Business Review*, November–December 1985, pp. 139–50.
5. R. Lenz and I. Engledow, "Environmental Analysis: The Applicability of Current Theory," *Strategic Management Journal* 7 (1986), p. 340.
6. M. Porter, *Competitive Strategy* (New York: Free Press, 1980).
7. R. B. Duncan, "Characteristics of Organizational Environments and Perceived Environmental Uncertainty," *Administrative Quarterly* 17 (1972), pp. 313–27; J. M. Pennings, "Strategically Interdependent Organizations," in P. C. Nystrom and W. H. Starbuck, eds., *Handbook of Organizational Design* 1 (New York: Oxford University Press, 1981), pp. 433–55; J. G. March and H. A. Simon, *Organizations* (New York: John Wiley, 1958); A. Tversky and D. Kahneman, "Judgment under Uncertainty: Heuristics and Biases," *Sciences* 185 (1974), pp. 1124–31; S. Keisler and L. Sproul, "Managerial Response to Changing Environments: Perspectives and Problem Sensing from Social Cognition," *Administrative Science Quarterly* 37 (1982), pp. 548–70.
8. D. C. Hambrick, "Environmental Scanning and Organizational Strategy," *Strategic Management Journal* 3 (1982), pp. 159–74; R. Ireland, M. Hitt, R. Bettis, and D. De Porras, "Strategy Formulation Processes: Differences in Perceptions of Strength and Weaknesses Indicators and Environmental Uncertainty by Managerial Level," *Strategic Management Journal*, 1987, pp. 469–85; W. H. Starbuck, "Organizations and Their Environments," in M. Dunnette, ed., *Handbook of Industrial and Organizational Psychology* (Chicago: Rand-McNally, 1976), pp. 1069–124.
9. K. Weick, "Enactment Processes in Organizations," in B. Staw and G. Salancik, eds., *New Directions in Organizational Behavior* (Chicago: St. Clair Press, 1977).
10. H. K. Downey, D. Hellreigel, and J. W. Slocum, "Individual Characteristics as Sources of Perceived Uncertainty Variability," *Human Relations* 30 (1977), pp. 161–74; A. H. Van de Ven., A. L. Delbecq, and R. Koenig, "Determinants of Coordination Modes within Organizations," *American Sociological Review* 41 (1976), pp. 322–38; H. K. Downey, D. Hellreigel, and J. W. Slocum, "Environmental Uncertainty: The Construct and Its Operationalization, *Administrative Science Quarterly* 2 (1958), pp. 409–43; F. Milliken, "Three Types of Perceived Uncertainty about the Environment: State, Effect, and Response Uncertainty," *Academy of Management Journal*, 1987, p. 134; L. Jauch and K. Kraft, "Strategic Management of Uncertainty," *Academy of Management Review*, 1986, pp. 777–90; G. Morgan, "Paradigms, Metaphors, and Puzzle Solving in Organization Theory," *Administrative Science Quarterly* 25 (1980), p. 608.
11. Milliken, "Perceived Uncertainty," p. 133; Duncan, "Characteristics of Organizational Environments," p. 313.
12. W. E. Gifford, H. R. Bobbitt, and J. W. Slocum, "Message Characteristics and Perceptions of

Uncertainty by Organizational Decision Makers," *Academy of Management Journal* 22 (1979), pp. 458–81.

13. Milliken, "Perceived Uncertainty." p. 135.
14. Ibid., p. 137.
15. P. R. Lawrence, and J. W. Lorsch, "A Reply to Tosi, Aldag and Storey," *Administrative Science Quarterly* 18 (1973), pp. 397–98.
16. March and Simon, *Organizations;* R. M. Cyert, and James G. March, *A Behavioral Theory of the Firm* (Englewood Cliffs, N.J.: Prentice Hall, 1963); Jauch and Kraft, "Strategic Management"; R. E. Miles, and C. C. Snow, *Organizational Strategy, Structure, and Process* (New York: McGraw-Hill, 1978); Ian I. Mitroff and Ralph H. Kilmann, "Teaching Managers to Do Policy Analysis: The Case of Corporate Bribery," *California Management Review* 20 (1977), pp. 47–54.
17. J. Pfeffer and G. R. Salancik, *The External Control of Organizations: A Resource Dependence Perspective* (New York: Harper and Row, 1978); O. E. Williamson, *Markets and Hierarchies: Analysis and Antitrust Implications* (New York: Free Press, 1975).
18. Pfeffer and Salancik, *External Control;* L. J. Bourgeois and W. G. Astley, "A Strategic Model of Organizational Conduct and Performance," *International Studies of Management and Organization* 9 (1979), pp. 40–46.
19. Wholey and Brittain, "Characterizing Environmental Variation," *Academy of Management Review,* 1989, pp. 867–82.
20. Ibid.
21. F. E. Emery, and E. L. Trist, "The Causal Texture of Organizational Environments," *Human Relations* 18 (1965), pp. 21–32; H. E. Aldrich, *Organizations and Environments* (Englewood Cliffs, N.J.: Prentice Hall, 1979).
22. Aldrich, *Organizations and Environments;* H. Mintzberg and J. A. Waters, "The Mind of the Strategist(s)," in S. Srivastava, ed., *The Executive Mind* (San Francisco, Jossey-Bass, 1983); K. Andrews, *The Concept of Corporate Strategy* (Homewood, Ill.: Richard D. Irwin, 1987).
23. Ari Ginsberg. "Measuring and Modeling Changes in Strategy: Theoretical Foundations and Empirical Directions," *Strategic Management Journal,* 1988, pp. 559–75.
24. T. Herbert and H. Deresky, "Generic Strategies: An Empirical Investigation of Topology Validity and Strategy Content," *Strategic Management Journal,* 1987, pp. 135–47; N. Venkatraman and J. Grant, "Construct Measurement in Organizational Strategy Research," *Academy of Management Review,* 1986, pp. 71–87.
25. M. Porter, *Competitive Strategy* (New York: Free Press, 1980); J. Woodward, *Industrial Organizations* (Oxford: Oxford University Press, 1965).
26. E. Segev, "A Systematic Comparative Analysis and Synthesis of Two Business Level Strategic Topologies," *Strategic Management Journal,* 1989, pp. 487–505; Porter, *Competitive Strategy;* C. Hill, "Differentiation versus Low Cost or Differentiation and Low Cost: A Contingency Framework," *Academy of Management Review,* 1988, pp. 401–12; A. Murray, "A Contingency View of Porter's 'Generic Strategies,'" *Academy of Management Review,* 1988, pp. 390–400; R. Wright, "A Refinement of Porter's Strategies," *Strategic Management Journal,* 1987, pp. 93–101.
27. Most of this section was adapted from Herbert and Deresky, "Generic Strategies," pp. 135–47.
28. Woodward, *Industrial Organizations;* J. Woodward, *Management and Technology: Problems of Progress in Industry,* Series No. 3 (London, HMSO, 1958); R. E. Miles, and C. C. Snow, *Organizational Strategy, Structure, and Process* (New York: McGraw-Hill, 1978).
29. Woodward, *Industrial Organizations.*
30. S. Kotha and D. Orne, "Generic Manufacturing Strategies: A Conceptual Synthesis," *Strategic Management Journal,* 1989, pp. 211–31.
31. R. Daft, J. Sormunen, and D. Parks, "Chief Executive Scanning, Environmental Characteristics, and Company Performance," *Strategic Management Journal,* 1988, pp. 123–39.

32. D. Wholey and J. Brittain, "Organizational Ecology: Findings and Implications," *Academy of Management Review*, 1986, pp. 513–33.
33. W. Scott, "The Adolescence of Institutional Theory," *Administrative Science Quarterly*, 1987, pp. 493–511.
34. M. Lawless and L. Finch, "Choice and Determinism: A Test of Hrebiniak and Joyce's Framework on Strategy-Environment Fit," *Strategic Management Journal*, 1989, pp. 351–65; L. G. Hrebiniak and W. F. Joyce, "Organizational Adaptation: Strategic Choice and Environmental Determinism," *Administrative Science Quarterly*, September 1985, pp. 336–49.
35. Andrew Van de Ven and R. Drazin, "The Concept of Fit in Contingency Theory," *Research in Organizational Behavior*, 1985, pp. 333–65.
36. N. Venkatraman, "The Concept of Fit in Strategy Research: Toward Verbal and Statistical Correspondence," *Academy of Management Review*, 1989, pp. 423–44; L. Fry and D. Smith, "Congruence, Contingency, and Theory Building," *Academy of Management Review*, 1987, pp. 117–32; D. Hambrick and D. Lei, "Toward an Empirical Prioritization of Contingency Variables for Business Strategy," *Academy of Management Journal*, 1985, pp. 763–88; A. Ginsberg, and N. Venkatraman, "Contingency Perspectives of Organizational Strategy: A Critical Review of the Empirical Research," *Academy of Management Review*, 1985, pp. 421–34.
37. Hrebiniak and Joyce, "Organizational Adaptation," p. 338.
38. A. Ginsberg, "Measuring and Modeling Changes in Strategy: Theoretical Foundations and Empirical Directions," *Strategic Management Journal*, 1988, pp. 559–75.
39. M. L. Tushman and E. Romanelli, "Organizational Evolution: Interactions between External and Emergent Processes and Strategic Choice," in B. M. Staw and L. L. Cummings, eds., *Research in Organizational Behavior* 8 (Greenwich, Conn.: JAI Press, 1985).

Case 2–A
General Motors

Turning around a Corporate Giant[1]

How should General Motors (GM) manage in turbulent times? A-LINE-MENT, a major international consulting group, is brought in to advise the company's 14-member strategy board, the most important decision-making body at GM, with representatives from GM's manufacturing, engineering, marketing, finance, personnel, logistics, purchasing, and communications divisions.

In 1993, the board met more than 600 hours, or more than one-third of the work year. Richard Wagoner, head of the North American car division, described what the board does:

> You figure out where the big holes are—where your costs are out of line or where you are weak in the marketplace. That suggests where you ought to dig. So you get some data together, present them . . . kick them around. Some . . . issues have been identified by people down in the organization who want to get input . . . Sometimes there is an issue that affects one area, but you bring it to the board to get it exposed to the other guys. We recently put together a team on health care. They come in every quarter and say, "Here's what we have been doing, here's our new initiative, here are the early results, here's where we are having trouble, and here's where you didn't support us." It is . . . logical . . . not rocket science.[2]

The board wants three major recommendations about the initiatives it should take to assure the company's continued growth and profitability. These initiatives should be aligned with society's values, changes in government and global competition, trends in environmental and energy policies, and currents in technology and the laws affecting technological development. They should be based on a sound analysis of possible developments in the strategic business environment and GM's options for dealing with that environment.

You are not the first group of consultants from whom the strategy board has sought advice. Your specialty is to bring companies into closer harmony with society's needs and values, but you will have to be very persuasive to have the board listen to your recommendations. As you read about GM's recent troubled history, you realize how difficult your assignment will be.

The Competitive Situation in the Early 1990s

The competitive situation at General Motors at the beginning of the 1990s was still uncertain despite a decade of the most far-reaching strategic changes the company had ever made. The world's largest industrial company sold more cars than any other automaker in the world, but its market share was about a quarter lower than it had been in 1980. It was not clear that the changes initiated by GM Chairman Roger Smith in his decade-long tenure had positioned the company to regain its position as the industry's leader.

In the summer of 1990, Smith retired from the chairmanship. His successor, Robert Stempel, assumed control. After a decade of substantial growth in car sales, the economies of the United States and other major industrial nations entered a sluggish, recessionary phase. Smith's changes at GM were put to the test by the economic downturn.

Stempel had worked at GM for 32 years and was the first engineer to run the company, which had traditionally been led by people with finance backgrounds. GM's workers and dealers were enthusiastic about the prospect of a "car guy" leading the company, but it wasn't clear that Stempel's approach would be much different than Smith's. "We made our decision to go with the long-term view, and it's paying off overseas, in trucks, and in our acquisitions," he told an interviewer. "We just have to stay the course in North America."[3]

Stempel's tenure as the head of GM was very short. After losses of $4.5 billion in 1991 and $23.5 billion in 1992, he was replaced by Jack Smith, an accountant with an MBA who had worked for GM for more than 30 years, most recently at the healm of its successful European auto division.

Roger Smith's Initiatives

Under Roger Smith, the company had taken four major initiatives: a joint venture with Toyota, the development of a completely new car (the Saturn), a restructuring of GM's five divisions, and the acquisition of two high-tech subsidiaries, Electronic Data Systems (EDS) and Hughes Aircraft. However, continued innovation by GM's domestic and foreign competitors gave the company little breathing room as it strove to work out the knots in its ambitious restructuring efforts.

1. NUMMI — The Joint Venture with Toyota. In 1983 GM announced that it would participate in a 50–50 joint venture with Toyota to build 200,000 small cars per year at a plant in Fremont, California. GM hoped to learn the secrets of Japanese automaking methods, while Toyota would gain experience in operating facilities in the United States. The joint venture surprised and worried other automakers, who anticipated that cooperation between the number one and number three automakers would reduce competition in the small car market. Antitrust concerns also prompted the Federal Trade Commission to undertake an exhaustive study of the proposed deal, and only after the two partners agreed to terminate the venture no later than 1996 did the FTC give permission to proceed.

The new company was called New United Motor Manufacturing, Inc. (NUMMI). The 1983–1996 time frame would give the company time to move through three complete car development cycles at the plant. The first car made would be a version of a car Toyota already produced and sold in Japan, but it would be marketed in the United States under the Chevrolet Nova brand name. Toyota would produce the drive train and several other components in Japan and would ship them to the NUMMI plant for stamping and assembling operations.

Under the terms of the agreement, GM would contribute the Fremont plant (which had been closed the year before) and cash, for a total investment of $100 million. Toyota would contribute $100 million in cash and would manage the plant, choosing the venture's CEO and top management and implementing Japanese production and management techniques.

These techniques would be a major departure from previous practice for a GM operation. NUMMI would use a "just-in-time" inventory system to minimize inventory expense, save space, and increase quality by providing no stockpiles of parts to cushion the effects of defective components. In another production innovation, production teams would be responsible for developing their own schemes for coordinating body movement, parts location, and the time required to do the job.[4]

These changes aside, GM executives were surprised at how little new technology was used at the plant. One noted, "I was amazed that they basically used 1950s technology, and they did a heck of a job with it. All the press lines were the same as the older types, except, of course, they were new presses. But it wasn't anything fancy."[5]

The real innovations at the NUMMI plant were in the selection and management of the workforce. The number of job classifications was reduced to four from nearly 200. Prospective employees underwent an intensive 35-hour screening process and, when hired, were guaranteed they wouldn't be laid off. New employees were extensively trained in the production philosophies of Toyota. Toyota based its workforce management philosophy on the assumption that employees wanted to do a good job and would do so if treated respectfully and given the responsibility to improve the quality and efficiency of their output. Workers were rewarded for learning how to do other jobs in the plant. A work team even had permission to stop the entire production line if a problem was spotted. Quality control would be ensured by attention to detail at each step of the production process rather than by an inspection when the car was completely assembled, the standard practice at other GM plants.

The idea of giving employees so much control was foreign to GM's traditional management philosophy, which assumed an adversarial relationship between management and labor and that intimidation was required to make an employee work. GM workers often had little or no idea of how much their particular production job contributed to the assembly of a car. One GM manager recalled how, at another GM plant, he brought two production workers to the defect repair area to show them how the repair personnel had to disassemble a significant portion of a car to weld in a part that the two workers had consistently failed to install. Their response: "'You mean to tell me that bracket holds the sunshade?' [The worker] had been doing this job for two years and nobody had ever told her what part she was welding."[6]

By 1986 NUMMI was in operation and a year later it seemed to be a success. Worker productivity had increased to the point where one study estimated it would cost $750 more and require 50 percent more employees using the same technology at the old Fremont plant to assemble the same car. GM ranked the Nova as one of its best-built vehicles. Toyota was impressed enough to decide to begin assembling 15,000 Corolla FX16s at the plant.[7]

Employee morale was also high. Absenteeism had dropped from 22 percent (at the old Fremont plant) to 2.5 percent. Workers had positive things to say about the new management philosophy: "I learned a different meaning for the word respect—one that doesn't include fear," said one. "My responsibility now is to the team, which works together like a family to solve problems and do the job. And no one places blame when something goes wrong."[8]

Unfortunately, it seemed as though GM was ill-prepared or unwilling to seriously apply the lessons learned at NUMMI to its other operations. Industry analyst Maryann Keller wrote that GM's top management had expected to learn primarily technological lessons from NUMMI and was unprepared to change the GM culture to adopt the management philosophy that was at the heart of NUMMI's success.[9] GM rotated teams of managers through NUMMI, prepared training tapes and other instructional materials on the NUMMI concepts, and took thousands of managers on plant tours, but it had no established plan for incorporating the new concepts at its other facilities. NUMMI-trained managers who moved to other GM divisions generally found that their new ideas received an unfriendly reception. Some left for jobs elsewhere.

Though NUMMI was profitable in its first two years of operation, it lost approximately $100 million in 1988. Sales of the Nova were weaker than expected and were expected to fall by 50,000 units to about 150,000 cars in 1988. Analysts attributed the disappointing sales figures to a weak marketing effort by Chevrolet, competition with other subcompacts, and a brand name (Nova) that buyers associated with a less-respected car in the past.[10] The 1996 cutoff date was rapidly approaching and GM had not decided what to do with the NUMMI workforce when the operation was disbanded.

Nonetheless, GM had learned some lessons from NUMMI. The 1987 contract with the United Auto Workers (UAW) inaugurated a new kind of management-labor relationship codified in an agreement known as The Quality Network. Committees composed of management and labor representatives would work together cooperatively to improve efficiency based heavily on the teamwork and continuous improvement concepts of the NUMMI operation. The UAW was guaranteed that no plants would be closed, and the plan made no distinction between hourly and salaried employees—all were expected to contribute.[11] Whether the inertia of GM's corporate culture could be overcome remained to be seen.

2. **Starting Saturn.** The same year that the NUMMI venture was announced, 1983, GM signaled another innovative project: the Saturn car, named after the rockets that propelled man to the moon. The Saturn would be the first new GM brand name since 1918. The new company's mission would be to "market vehicles developed and manufactured in the United States that are world leaders in quality, cost and customer satisfaction through the integration of people, technology and business systems and to transfer knowledge, technology and experience throughout General Motors."[12]

The concept of designing a car company from the ground up sprang from Smith's belief that GM needed to develop a leading-edge product if it was to have a chance of remaining number one in the future. Keller said the old approach wasn't working anymore.

> Every competitive effort turned into a frightful reduction of the global reality. If customers wanted small cars, the company would chop a foot off big cars; if customers wanted economy, it would eliminate luxury features such as air conditioning; if customers loved the Honda, it would build a model that was its interpretation of what a Honda was.[13]

As it was originally envisioned, the Saturn plant would be fully automated. The most advanced robotics and automation technologies would assemble more of the car than ever before. A highly computerized accounting and management system would make the whole operation paperless. An innovative labor-management agreement unlike anything seen before in the U.S. auto industry would be developed, as well as a separate franchise and dealer system.

As the planning phase progressed, the degree of automation and computerization was scaled back, but much remained that was new, especially in the way the workforce was managed. Japanese management techniques like those used at NUMMI would be utilized. Eighty percent of the workforce would be guaranteed lifetime employment. There would be no hourly workers; instead, workers would be paid a salary based on 80 percent of the national average autoworker's wage, with additional pay based on an incentive plan which rewarded good worker performance. There would be no more than five job classifications (one for production workers) and all employees would share one cafeteria.[14]

The Saturn production workers would enjoy more autonomy than workers at any other automaker's plants, including the Japanese. They would participate in the hiring process and would approve new additions to their work team (the workers were organized into 165 teams of 10 employees each). They would make most of the decisions concerning how to organize their work flow and would have authority to stop the entire line if a problem developed. They were responsible for the financial performance of their part of the operation, and had the power to veto or modify decisions concerning the purchase and installation of the equipment they used.[15]

The original plans called for a $5 billion investment in the project, which would begin producing 500,000 import-fighting cars at the new plant in Spring Hill, Tennessee, in 1990. As the years passed, however, the plans were scaled back. Only 3,000 new workers would be employed instead of 6,000. The project's budget was cut to $1.7 billion and output halved to 250,000 cars. The cars would be more expensive and larger than originally envisioned, yet company analysts still expected the project to run in the red for 15 years because of the huge fixed start-up costs.[16]

GM had announced new products before (e.g., the X-cars and J-cars), which were supposed to beat the Japanese at their own game, and had fallen short. After the fanfare with which Saturn was announced and covered by the media, GM's credibility was at stake. It couldn't afford another well-publicized failure.

Some analysts wondered what Saturn really had to offer the corporation. If the car was a money-loser before it ever hit the showroom floor, then its value had to be in the lessons the corporation would learn by producing the car. Unfortunately, by 1989 it seemed that the personnel management lessons learned through the NUMMI experience were making the most innovative aspect of the Saturn project seem redundant.[17]

Some industry observers questioned the wisdom of Saturn's marketing plan (which, among other things, called for the car's advertising to make no mention of the company's relationship to GM). The editor of a trade newsletter was skeptical: "They're not going to steal market share from the Japanese. It's more likely that they'll cannibalize other GM products, so for the company it will be a net wash in market share."[18]

The initial reviews of Saturn in 1990 were generally lukewarm. *Autoweek*'s comments were typical: "We are neither over- nor under-whelmed. We are merely whelmed, at least by import standards."[19] Ultimately, the car took off. *Consumer Reports* and other rating bodies gave it very high marks, an unusual outcome for a GM vehicle. Demand was high, but the initial investment also had been high and it took GM more than three years after the first Saturns rolled off the production line for it to come near to breaking even. Other GM divisions continued to resent the high subsidies paid for the Saturn experiment.

3. **Major Restructuring.** By the early 1980s, GM's top management realized that the corporation's organization was an impediment to the adaptability required to respond to the rapid changes in the global auto industry. Since 1916 GM had been composed of five separate divisions—Chevrolet, Pontiac, Buick, Oldsmobile, and Cadillac—that operated independently of one another. Two other major divisions, Fisher Body and General Motors Assembly Division (GMAD), were responsible for the engineering and tooling/assembly operations. Until 1984, a car division could develop the design for a car completely independent of the engineering and assembly divisions. It would then pass the design on to Fisher Body, which would engineer the body to comply with design, and then pass that on to GMAD, again without consulting the other divisions. GMAD would then prepare the dies and stamping operations and assemble the car. All divisions reported in a strictly vertical fashion, with the top management resolving all problems. There was no interaction between lower-level people.[20]

As competition in the industry heated up, and costs and quick responses to market changes became more important, the flaws of the ossified management structure became impossible to ignore. It was not enough for a designer to find a solution to a technical flaw in some car part—implementing the solution could take years. "You have to produce fifty thousand studies to show that it's a better solution," complained one employee. "Then you have to go through ten different committees to get it approved."[21]

A consulting firm, McKinsey and Company, was brought in to assess the situation. It concluded that Fisher Body and GMAD had become bureaucratic empires unto themselves and that a complete reorganization was in order.[22] In January 1984, the reorganization was implemented in one quick organizational convulsion. The five car divisions were divided into two supergroups: BOC—Buick, Oldsmobile, and Cadillac; and CPC—Chevrolet, Pontiac, GM of Canada, NUMMI, and Saturn. The Fisher Body and GMAD divisions were split in two and absorbed into both super groups. Henceforth, each supergroup would be responsible for all aspects of development for its own products, including design, engineering, manufacturing, assembly, and marketing. The old divisions would continue to serve as marketing arms.[23] Within each supergroup, Product Development Teams composed of representatives from the design, engineering, and marketing functions, as well as representatives of suppliers, would take responsibility for one of the 50–60 major components of a new vehicle design. In this way, Smith hoped to facilitate the kind of rapid response to market demands that the company had lacked.

That the reorganization did not proceed smoothly was not surprising, considering the extent to which old loyalties and old ways of doing business were ingrained in the company's culture. Many of the 10,000 employees of Fisher Body viewed the change as akin to a hostile takeover.[24] Further compounding the problem were subdivisions within Fisher Body which considered themselves to be largely independent of Fisher Body.

Still, Smith expected that the company might require years to fully adjust to the changes. "We changed the structure in six months; moved all the boxes around. The systems will take three to five years. The style might take ten to fifteen years," he noted.[25]

By the late 1980s, the reorganization seemed to have been at least partially successful. The quality of GM's cars was higher than it had been at the beginning of the decade, and the organization was more flexible. Still, corporate headquarters had not been subject to reorganization and the company's culture had hardly changed. The two supergroups could possibly develop into smaller versions of the old GM, complete with bureaucratic logjams. The head of the CPC supergroup had already organized his group along functional lines with a strictly vertical chain of command, which meant that disputes had to be resolved at the highest levels of management, just as in the old structure.[26]

4. **High-Tech Diversification.** In 1984, while GM was adapting to the changes wrought by the reorganization, the company made its biggest acquisition to date: a \$2.55 billion buyout of Electronic Data Systems (EDS), a firm that designed and operated data processing systems. Founded by billionaire entrepreneur H. Ross Perot, the company was the third largest in its field and was flourishing; its earnings per share quadrupled between 1980 and 1983.[27]

Roger Smith thought EDS would be good for GM in a number of ways. The automaker had 200 IBM mainframe computers and a 200,000 terminals, but no centralized data processing system to coordinate interdepartmental operations. At the time, the company's different departments frequently used different computer systems, making electronic communication between departments impossible. The system's inefficiency was estimated to cost GM \$600 million per year.[28] Smith envisioned EDS developing a new data processing systems for GM that would coordinate the collection of financial and operations data throughout the company, process health care claims (the company used 187 different health care carriers and its health care costs came to \$450 per car in 1983), and link dealers to the company's financial subsidiary and car divisions, among other things.

Smith also felt that exposure to EDS' highly competitive corporate culture would be good for GM. The company was known for its rigorous training and testing program, strict code of ethics, and emphasis on results. As an observer put it,

> Candidates for employment were rigorously screened, and would be rejected if even the smallest detail didn't line up correctly . . . EDS could sometimes feel like a boot camp, with Perot playing the role of unbudgeable drill sergeant . . . He pushed employees to their limits, expecting them to do the impossible. The important thing was the goal—to get the job done, no matter what.[29]

Where compensation at EDS was based largely on performance incentives, at GM it was based on seniority. Poor performance by a GM employee often went unaddressed for years. One former employee remembered a co-worker whose performance was rated as unsatisfactory or poor from the day he was hired until the day he was fired—16 years later. Only about 100 salaried employees were fired each year of a white-collar workforce of nearly 150,000.[30]

The merger of the 8,000 GM computer employees with the 6,000 EDS employees did not go smoothly. There was no clear strategy for integrating the two companies. The news that they would be absorbed into the EDS organization hit GM employees hard. Already distressed that they would lose their generous GM pensions and benefits (they would receive shares of a new class of GM stock instead), they were further alienated by the approach taken by EDS staffers assigned to the GM plants. Over the New Year holiday the EDS staff inventoried the GM computer equipment and left bright orange EDS stickers on it all. Some GM employees began to wear the stickers on their foreheads. Hundreds of GM data processing employees quit and others were fired by the EDS management, which was still independent of GM under the terms of the buyout agreement.[31]

Despite the difficulties, by 1986 EDS had modernized GM's health care claim processing system, saving the company $200 million annually. By 1987 it had nearly completed a private international satellite communications network that would allow GM to communicate among its branches and save hundreds of millions in telecommunications costs. By 1989 EDS was one of the corporation's most profitable businesses, contributing $423 million in earnings, contrasting sharply with the loss of nearly $1 billion by the company's North American car operations.[32]

A year after buying EDS, GM outbid Ford and Boeing to acquire the Hughes Aircraft Company, a major defense contractor and think tank. The $5 billion price tag was almost double the cost of EDS and made the purchase the largest non-oil acquisition in history.[33]

Hughes developed a wide range of electronic defense systems that were used in everything from aircraft and weapons guidance systems to surveillance satellites. The company employed 26,000 engineers and more than 1,450 PhDs who were developing more than 100 different technologies for use in 12,000 products and services. Among other things, the company developed computer systems and software, a capacity Smith hoped to utilize by having Hughes help automate GM's computer-integrated manufacturing systems. Hughes was grouped with GM's Delco Electronics and Delco Systems Operations subsidiaries and the instrument and systems display subgroup of the AC Spark plug division to form GM Hughes Electronics Corporation (GMHE).

Smith believed that high-tech acquisitions like Hughes and EDS would make GM the world leader in automotive technologies well into the 21st century. Hughes would provide GM with a pool of elite technical experts to develop futuristic automotive technologies like night vision systems, a satellite-based vehicle identification and location system, automotive collision-avoidance and near obstacle detection systems, and others. The acquisition would also further diversify GM into the defense, electronics, and aerospace industry, providing a hedge against declines in the automobile business.

Others thought less of the deal. Hughes had recently been penalized by the military for missing deadlines, inflating costs, and poor workmanship. "We've poured billions and billions into Hughes for the past forty years and they've never built a successful missile," said a Pentagon official at the time.[34] Recurring problems with the company's Maverick missile program had led Congress to attempt to find a more reliable supplier.

Critics also doubted whether a developer of one-of-a-kind big-ticket defense systems would have much to offer the auto industry, which relies on mass-produced components with low-unit costs.

Perot, a member of GM's board of directors, argued strongly against the purchase: "We can become so preoccupied with using capital to solve our problems that the front-end investment will be so large that it alone will make it difficult for GM to be competitive."[35] In a letter to Smith he noted: "The Japanese are not beating us with technology or money. They use old equipment, and build better, less expensive cars by better management, both in Japan and with UAW workers in the U.S."[36] (Perot's share in GM was later bought back by the company for $700 million.)

The Challenge Ahead

By 1990, GM had spent $77 billion in its decade-long effort to modernize its plants, automate its equipment, and develop new car models. Its truck and foreign car operations were doing well, earning more than $3.5 billion in 1989, but the North American car business continued to lose money. Despite the huge investment, car and truck assembly efficiency had only improved 5 percent since 1980, compared with a 31 percent improvement at Ford. The company operated the 11 least-efficient plants in the country. GM's cars cost an average of $250 more to build than Ford's, and $750 more than Japanese models made in the United States, making it the industry's high-cost producer. Profitability per vehicle fell from $588 per vehicle in 1984 to $12 per vehicle in 1989. All told, the company sold a third less cars than it had a decade before and its market share had fallen almost 12 points to 34.7 percent. During the same period the Japanese manufacturers' combined market share had increased 10.4 percent. Further clouding the future of GM's domestic sales was the fact that, according to a survey of 35,000 U.S. car owners, customers under age 45 preferred Japanese cars by a two-to-one margin over GM's.[37]

Compounding GM's problems was the fact that growth in the domestic motor vehicle market had leveled off during the 1980s, and showed little promise of improving in the 1990s. Total U.S. auto and truck sales grew at a 4.6 percent annual average rate during the 1950s and 1960s, but had only grown at a rate of 0.5 percent since 1973. Because of a deceleration in the growth of the driving-age population and number of households in the 1980s, the market wasn't growing as fast as it had in the past. Further, owners were holding on to their old vehicles longer—an average of 7.6 years in 1985, compared to 6.4 years in 1979—because of a decline in household savings and because the vehicles were better made than in the past and didn't wear out as fast.[38]

Much of the increased market share of the foreign manufacturers was due to the success of their "**transplants**"—manufacturing facilities built in the United States. The voluntary import quotas that had restricted the number of cars Japan could export to the United States had prompted the Japanese manufacturers to look for new ways to penetrate the U.S. market. Establishing production facilities in the United States became economically attractive to Japanese manufacturers in the 1980s as the value of the dollar fell relative to the yen (more than 40 percent between 1985 and 1989), and Japanese cars produced in the United States were unlikely to be affected by any protectionist legislation that Congress might pass.

Honda opened the first transplant operation in 1982. By 1990 seven more Japanese-owned plants had been built in the United States with a combined production capacity of 1.6 million vehicles annually, about 12 percent of the total U.S. new car/light truck capacity. The transplants helped Japanese manufacturers continue to expand their share of the market: for every percentage point increase in the market share of transplant vehicles, the market share of U.S. producers dropped 2/3 of a point, and the market share of imports dropped 1/3 of a point. GM was the domestic producer whose market share was suffering the most at the hands of the transplants.[39]

Not all of the news was bad. GM had made dramatic progress in its effort to improve the quality of its cars. The number of defects per 100 vehicles had dropped 77 percent to 168, nearly as good as the Japanese average of 121.

Jack Smith's Tenure

Jack Smith took over at General Motors in April 1992 when the U.S. car market was turning up after a four-year decline and the accelerating value of yen made Japanese imports less competitive. The company earned $2.5 billion in 1993. By 1994 it sold more than 15 million cars, up from 12.5 million in 1991. Employment in its U.S. car and truck divisions, however, was down to 361,000 people. It had laid off 74,000 workers in the United States since 1991, but it still employed over 700,000 people worldwide. At corporate headquarters more than 20,000 white-collar workers had lost their jobs, but analysts believed that 25 percent of the 70,000 remaining white-collar employees were more than the company needed.

GM still was losing market share in the U.S. market. In 1994 its share of the U.S. auto market dipped from 35.5 percent a year earlier to 33.4 percent, and its share of the truck market was at 28.4 percent from 31.5 percent the previous year. GM's cars cost more to build than those of Chrysler or Ford and they took longer to develop. Average labor costs per vehicle at GM were nearly $2,500, while at Chrysler they were about $1,800 and at Ford about $1,600. It took Chrysler just 32 weeks to bring the Neon to market and 35 weeks for Ford to bring the Mustang to market, while it took GM 38 weeks to bring the Chevy Lumina to market.

While the quality of GM's high-priced brands—Cadillac, Buick, and Oldsmobile—were above average, the quality of its low-priced Chevrolets and Pontiacs, which account for more than 50 percent of its sales, were well below that of Toyota, the industry leader. Indeed, according to J. D. Power and Associates, Chevrolets had twice as many quality defects as Toyota.

Still, it was too early to tell if the changes Smith was making were having an effect. GM's culture was known for its complacency, myopia, and preservation of the status quo. Accountants dominated the giant headquarters bureaucracy. The company was also out of touch with customers. Jack Smith's time at the healm was characterized more by incremental tinkering than radical reform.

Cutting Fleet Sales. The first action Smith took was to cut fleet sales to rental car companies from 800,000 units to 400,000. GM sold the cars at a discount to the rental car companies in order to keep up its market share and have its factories stay busy. However, the rental car companies then sold the cars after only a few months, which undercut GM's ability to sell its new models.

Centralizing Purchasing. The second step Smith took was to centralize purchasing in the hands of the controversial José Ignacio Lopez de Arriortua, a Spaniard who had worked for Smith in Europe. Lopez was a firebrand who tore up contracts and demanded double-digit price cuts from suppliers. He treated suppliers ruthlessly rather than develop long-term partnerships based on trust. To obtain lower bids, he even shared proprietary product blueprints with competitors.

Though he saved $4 billion in purchasing costs, Lopez generated immense antagonism. The low-cost parts he received were not always the best. They might cost less but added time to production. For example, an ill-fitting ashtray from a low-cost supplier caused a six-week shutdown of a Buick factory in Texas.

Suppliers threatened to withhold investment in technical research for GM because they feared they might not recover their costs. They claimed that they would take their new technology to Ford or Chrysler. Lopez, meanwhile, defected to Volkswagen, taking with him many company secrets, for which GM sued him. GM had to send its new purchasing head to visit all the suppliers to regain their confidence.

Reducing the Number of Platforms. The third action that Smith took was to reduce the number of basic car platforms from 12 to 6. GM's model in this action was Chrysler. Chrysler's revitalization was attributed to the use of interdisciplinary project teams (members came from engineering, design, purchasing, and marketing) for its very successful LH (facetiously called "last hope") model. GM, however, had been using project teams for nearly a decade. They simply had not worked. The engineering person was more beholden to the engineering department than to the team, and the purchasing person's loyalties were to purchasing, and so on. At GM, unlike Chrysler, the team concept never was fully implemented. The teams became an arena for endless bickering between departments.

The problem at GM remained execution. Conflicting agendas, divisions, and egos made it hard to get anything done. The question was whether Smith's revamped company could meet the ambitious goals he had set for the new models of Chevrolet, Pontiac, Oldsmobile, and Buick mid-size cars due in dealers' showrooms in 1997–1998. Investment costs for the 600,000 vehicles made in 1988 were $5.9 billion per year; Smith was planning on investing only $1.6 billion to make more than 700,000 vehicles per year. Development time in 1988 had been 72 months; Smith planned to cut this to 37 months. Assembly hours per vehicle would be reduced from 39 to under 19 hours. The number of parts would be slashed from 3,200 to 2,300, the number of plants from five to three, and the number of combinations needed to make these vehicles from nearly 2 million to under 1,000. Whether these goals could be met would be the true tests of Jack Smith's leadership. GM's future still was in doubt.

Discussion Questions

1. Evaluate the actions taken by GM Chairman Roger Smith during the 1980s. To what extent were his initiatives aligned with society's values, with changes in government and global competition, with energy and environmental policies, and with developments in technology and the laws affecting technological development? Were they the right actions to take? Was General Motors in a better position at the end of the decade than it was at the beginning?
2. What should Roger Smith's successors do? Was Jack Smith on the right track? To what extent were his initiatives aligned with society's values, with changes in government and global competition, with energy and environmental policies, and with developments in technology and the laws affecting technological development? Which of his actions were positive? Which were negative? What advice would you give Smith about what he should do?
3. How would General Motors best be able to survive in the world auto industry? What three steps should it take to turn itself around? What would you propose to GM's strategy board? How would you justify your recommendations?

Endnotes

1. This case was written by Mark C. Jankus and Alfred Marcus.
2. Alex Taylor, "GM's Turnaround," *Fortune*, October 17, 1994, p. 66.
3. Ibid., p. 55.
4. M. Keller, *Rude Awakening: The Rise, Fall, and Struggle for Recovery of General Motors* (New York: William Morrow, 1989), p. 132.
5. Ibid., p. 137.
6. Ibid., pp. 127, 129.
7. Ibid., p. 131; J. L. Badaracco, Jr., "The 'New' General Motors," Harvard Business School Case No. 9–387–171, rev. February 1988, p. 5.
8. Keller, *Rude Awakening*, p. 142.
9. Ibid., pp. 135–42.
10. J. L. Badaracco, Jr., "General Motors in 1988," Harvard Business School Case No. 9–388–118, rev. April

1988, p. 6; "General Motors' Asian Alliances," Harvard Business School Case No. 9–388–094, rev. May 1988, p. 5.

11. Keller, *Rude Awakening*, pp. 242, 249–50.
12. Ibid., p. 248.
13. Ibid., p. 93.
14. Badaracco, "The 'New' General Motors," p. 7.
15. J. Szczesny, "The Right Stuff," *Time*, October 29, 1990, p. 76.
16. Keller, *Rude Awakening*, p. 163.
17. Ibid., p. 249.
18. Szczesny, "The Right Stuff," p. 78.
19. "To Saturn and Beyond," *Fortune*, November 5, 1990, p. 12.
20. Keller, *Rude Awakening*, p. 100.
21. Ibid., p. 106.
22. Ibid., p. 109.
23. Badaracco, "The 'New' General Motors," p. 8.
24. Keller, *Rude Awakening*, p. 114.
25. Badaracco, "The 'New' General Motors," p. 15.
26. Keller, *Rude Awakening*, p. 120.
27. Badaracco, "General Motors in 1988," p. 7.
28. Keller, *Rude Awakening*, p. 147.
29. Ibid., p. 149.
30. Ibid., p. 31.
31. Badaracco, "General Motors in 1988," p. 8.
32. A. Taylor, "The New Drive to Revive GM," *Fortune*, April 9, 1990, p. 53.
33. Badaracco, "The 'New' General Motors," p. 13.
34. Keller, *Rude Awakening*, p. 168.
35. Ibid., p. 173.
36. Ibid., p. 172.
37. Taylor, "The New Drive," pp. 53, 57, 60; C. P. Work, "Detroit's Drive for the Fast Lane," *U.S. News and World Report*, January 22, 1990, p. 41.
38. M. F. Bryan and J. B. Martin, *Realignment in the U.S. Motor Vehicle Industry*, Federal Reserve Bank of Cleveland, June 1, 1991.
39. Ibid.

CHAPTER

3

The Contest for Corporate Control

Shareholders, Stakeholders, and Public Policies[1]

In a free-enterprise, private property system, a corporate executive is an employee of the owners of the business. He (or she) has direct responsibility to his (or her) employers. That responsibility is to conduct the business in accord with their desires, which generally will be to make as much money as possible while conforming to the basic rules of society, both embodied in law and those embodied in ethical custom.

Milton Friedman, "The Social Responsibility of Business Is to Increase Its Profits"

More than ever, managers of corporations are expected to serve the public interest as well as private profit . . . Management must be measured for performance in noneconomic and economic areas alike . . . Corporations operate within a web of complex, often competing relationships which demand the attention of corporate managers. The decision-making process requires an understanding of the corporations' many constituencies and their various expectations.

The Business Roundtable, 1981

Introduction and Chapter Objectives

The contestants for corporate control are, on the one hand, broad social forces: **economics,** the foundation of the business system, dictates that the firm maximize returns to investors; **laws,** a prerequisite for operating, require the firm to play by the rules of the game; and **ethics** dictate that the firm do what is right and good. On the other hand, stakeholders—owners, customers, employees, suppliers, communities, and competitors—have expectations and try to control the corporation. In addition, the public policy process has a claim, as the corporation is expected to operate within the spirit and letter of this process. These opposing views of corporate control are reviewed in this chapter.

The Hidden Hand

hidden hand
In increasing a person's wealth, the individual engages in deals with other people that unintentionally benefit society by increasing its wealth.

The founders of the American republic assumed people were driven by self-interest.[2] The Constitution established a system of checks and balances to protect against its excessive pursuit. Adam Smith, author of *The Wealth of Nations* (1776), considered that the more a person pursued self-interest, the more the person would unwittingly—by means of the **"hidden hand"**—enrich society:

> Every individual . . . neither intends to promote the public interest, nor knows how much he is promoting it . . . By directing his industry in such a manner as its produce may be of the greatest value, he intends only his own gain, and he is in this . . . lead by an invisible hand to promote the end which was not part of his intention.[3]

Smith argued that a person promotes society's interests (does good) by doing well (promoting his or her own interest).

People do not think about what is right or wrong or about what is good and bad in business. They think about the bottom line. Profit drives progress. It stimulates people to offer a valuable good or service to others. It leads them to innovate and specialize. It increases the economic productivity and efficiency of society, adds to its wealth, and makes all people better off. Profit elevates people above the miserable conditions to which they otherwise would be subject. Without free markets, Smith believed, people would live primitively and without hope.

Adam Smith was a moral philosopher. In the 18th century, economics as an organized discipline did not exist. Smith believed that the pursuit of gain must be tempered by moral virtue.[4] It cannot be accomplished without self-restraint and delayed gratification. "Parsimony" is necessary for a person to advance and the economy to grow. People must keep themselves from "prodigality." They must save, invest, and postpone gratification. If they become too wealthy, they lose these traits.

Smith sympathized with the workers. He was aware of the dangers of specialization. To increase society's wealth, workers had to concentrate on narrow tasks, which they performed very proficiently. This concentration on simple, repetitive tasks dulled their intelligence.

In the *Theory of Moral Sentiments* (1759), Smith discussed how people acquire sympathy for others by imagining how it would feel to be in the other's position. As revealed in this oft-quoted passage from *The Wealth of Nations*, to succeed in a capitalist system, a person must think of someone else's needs and desires:

> . . . man has almost constant occasion for the help of his brethren, and it is in vain for him to expect it from their benevolence only. He will be more likely to prevail if he can interest their self-love in his favour and show them that it is for their advantage to do for him what he requires of them. Whoever offers to another a bargain of any kind, proposes to do this. Give me that which I want, and you shall have this which you want, is the meaning of every such offer . . .[5]

Smith also believed in the need for powerful laws and ethics. No society can exist unless the laws of justice are tolerably observed and humans abstain from injuring each other.

Managers as Agents of Shareholders

Following the lead of Smith, Frederick Hayek and Milton Friedman developed a management approach which holds that the primary responsibility is to maximize returns to shareholders within the confines of laws and ethical principles. The objective of the firm is to reward owners subject to the constraints that managers obey the laws of society and follow ethical norms.

The Duties of an Agent to a Principal

Agency
Acting in behalf of another person's interests, as managers act in the interests of shareholders, doctors in the interests of patients, or pilots in the interests of passengers.

Hayek and Friedman see managers as the "trustees" or "agents" of shareholders. Shareholders are the "principals" whose interests the managers must serve. **Agency** means that managers consent to act in behalf of, or in the interests of, shareholders. Ideally, the principal would carry out the actions, but because of time, expertise, or distance an agent is appointed to act to carry out the principal's wishes as precisely as possible. The agent usually receives monetary renumeration. Agent-principal relations are common and are critical to all kinds of economic activity—employers and employees, doctors and patients, and aircraft pilots and passengers. Whenever someone is hired to fulfill a function that the other person cannot carry out, the person who has been hired is the other person's agent.

The main concern with agency-principal relations is that the agent may have other interests that take precedence over the interests of the principal. How is the principal to monitor the agent's behavior to assure that the agent carries out the will of the principal? How is the principal to determine whether the agent acted in good faith in pursuing the principal's interests? The principal can make sure that the agent's actions coincide with the principal's interests by establishing appropriate incentives and by incurring monitoring costs designed to limit any discrepant behavior by the agent. Still, it is virtually impossible for the principal to guarantee that the agent will always make optimal decisions from the principal's viewpoint. Incentive and monitoring instruments are limited by time and the principal's money resources.

When disputes occur between principal and agent over contractual agreements, the principal has the right to take away his or her consent and end the agreement. The agent must obey the principal's instructions, but obedience is not the only basis for the fiduciary relation. Trust, faith, care, and loyalty also are important. The agent has a duty to not knowingly violate the reasonable directions of the principal. The penalty for violations is to lose the job as agent and incur liability. However, if the principal's instructions are unreasonable, the agent has no duty to obey. Unreasonable instructions are those that:

- Are illegal, unethical, and contrary to public policy.
- Threaten the physical well-being of the agent.
- Violate ordinary business custom.
- Are impossible or impractical to carry out.
- Conflict with other contractual duties or duties of the agent.

Hayek's View

Hayek argues that the main responsibility of managers is to the principals. That duty is to increase shareholder wealth.[6] Other corporate constituencies and stakeholders such as employees, customers, and residents of the communities where a corporation is located are important only insofar as they affect the relationship between owners and managers. The rights of other claimants to the corporation's resources are limited because in the event of bankruptcy the shareholders are the last to be paid back. They are the **residual claimants** who are most at risk. Managers are trustees for stockholders who bear the ultimate risk for the decisions managers make.

residual claimants Shareholders have the highest claim on the corporation's profits because, in the event of bankruptcy, they are last to be paid back.

limited liability Under the law, only that portion of the owner's property that is tied up in the owner's corporation is at risk.

Hayek begins with the legal definition of the corporation. As it is chartered under the various laws of the different American states, the corporation pursues economic activities meant to benefit shareholders *and* society. The corporation is a legal person capable of entering contracts. Its owners have **limited liability,** which means that not all of the owners' property is at risk, only that portion tied up in the corporation. This arrangement is very effective for raising the large sums of capital needed by modern industry. It means that shareholders readily move their capital toward attractive, wealth-creating opportunities. The result is the efficient use of capital.

However, limited liability also is a privilege in return for which the corporation is expected to serve the public. The corporation's social role is to use the resources it has to increase social output. Managers are obligated to put the corporation's resources to their most productive uses.

Managers serve the shareholders in putting the corporation's resources to work. Even though profit is the goal, generally accepted rules of decency and even charitableness are binding on the corporation as are strict rules of law. The corporation's purpose is to secure the highest long-term return on capital given the legal and moral rules that prevail in society.

According to Hayek's view, however, to compel corporations to use resources for specific ends other than long-term maximum return on capital is likely to produce "undesirable results." The doctrine that corporate policy should be guided by "social considerations" is mistaken.[7] For one thing, the range of such considerations is very wide. Many different political, charitable, educational, and other ends can be brought under its heading. To allow managers to use corporate funds in ways that managers believe are socially appropriate would "create centers of uncontrollable power never intended by those who provided the capital."[8] It would vest decision-making powers in managers selected for their capacities in an entirely different field—that is, for their abilities to use resources efficiently in production.

Hayek admits that the actual influence of shareholders is often slight. The separation of ownership and control places shareholders in a subordinate position with managers often dictating to shareholders rather than acting on the basis of their recommendations.[9]

Friedman's Position

Milton Friedman's view is that only people, not businesses, have responsibilities. These people are the individual proprietors and managers. The proprietors have the right to do with their money as they please. If they wish to spend it on socially beneficial projects, that is their prerogative. However, managers are employees of owners and are responsible to them. They have to make as much money as possible for shareholders while conforming to the rules of society embodied in law and ethical custom.[10]

In a hospital or school, the managers' goal may be other than profit, but in the corporation managers are responsible to the owners. They serve as "agents" of the owners of the corporation and their primary responsibility is to them. While the Constitution vests the tax function in public authorities elected by the people, managers have no right to "tax" shareholders for social purposes.

Shareholders choose managers solely for their ability to run the company effectively, to produce a product, finance it, and sell it. Outside the corporation, managers may take on other responsibilities (to church, family, or conscience), but as employees of the owners of a corporation, they have no right to exercise these responsibilities, which would be spending someone else's money and reducing the profits due others. If corporate profits are to be spent on charity, the underprivileged, the environment, or other worthy causes, the money should be spent freely and separately by owners, not by managers acting for them.

In any event, how are the managers to decide how this money is to be spent? What specific expertise do they have in the area? Moreover, if the managers decide to spend the shareholders' money on unauthorized purposes, won't the shareholders abandon the company? Won't the price of the company's stock decline precipitously? Won't managers be fired for dereliction of their duties? The system, according to Friedman, prevents managers from "exploiting" shareholders even for "unselfish" social purposes. It requires that if managers wish to do good, they do so "at their own expense."[11]

Friedman nonetheless admits that if managers spend the shareholders' money for social purposes and can at the same time increase the profits of the firm, then doing so is legitimate. For example, the firm provides amenities to a community, and this in turn attracts better quality employees who are more loyal to the corporation and willing to work harder, then this activity is appropriate. Similarly, if by making charitable donations, the managers reduce the corporation's tax burden, then this activity too is appropriate. Friedman accepts "enlightened self-interest" as a legitimate activity of managers, but he expresses his disgust for managers who cloak their profit-making motivations under the guise of social responsibility.[12]

Ultimately, Friedman opposes "social responsibilities in any sense other than the shared values of individuals." His ideal is the market where "no individual can coerce any other, all cooperation is voluntary, [and] all parties to such cooperation benefit or they need not participate." Friedman prefers markets to democratic decision making because even in a democracy, after people have voted, they must conform.[13]

Managerial Control

The Hayek and Friedman view is a normative one. Analysts and commentators such as A. Berle and G. Means have tried to change the focus of the debate from what ought to be to what is.[14] They argue that in reality managers dominate shareholders. Even Hayek

Real-World Example

Creating Shareholder Value

Alfred Rappaport, professor of finance at Northwestern University, argues management focus on accounting numbers such as growth in earnings per share will not necessarily lead to maximum returns for shareholders (see Chapter 4). Returns to shareholders should be defined as dividends plus the increase in the company's share price.[15]

Managers should use discounted cash flow techniques, which are the essential means for analyzing shareholder value creation, not only for buying and selling businesses but for ongoing planning and performance monitoring of all business strategies. The essence of this approach is to estimate the economic value of an investment by discounting forecasted cash flow by the cost of capital.

Rappaport shows how "basic value drivers"—sales growth rate, operating profit margin, and working and fixed capital investment—are incorporated into shareholder value calculations. There are difficulties and uncertainties in making estimates (e.g., future sales growth rates, income tax rates, and equity risk premiums), but only the market impounds information from the company and other sources into its valuation of the company's future prospects. Market prices are "a signal to the company about the level of expected accomplishments needed if shareholders are to earn the required rate of return on the company's shares."[16]

Rappaport argues that "one of the most destructive canards in business is the notion that the stock market has a short time horizon," which has led many companies and the financial community to a preoccupation with short-term performance. However, it is essential to distinguish between the scurrying of investors and the fundamental forces that determine market prices. Investors often see long-term implications in current information and the market is often willing to pay a premium for companies providing evidence of sustainable competitive advantage.[17]

admits that what should be is not what is—while shareholders should be dominant, they often are not, and it is the managers who frequently control the corporation.[18]

These concerns go back at least as far as Adam Smith, who had identified the potential problems that could arise with the separation of ownership from control:

> The directors of such (joint-stock) companies, however, being the managers rather of other people's money than of their own, it cannot well be expected, that they should watch over it with the same anxious vigilance with which the partners in a private copartnery frequently watch over their own. Like the stewards of a rich man, they are apt to consider attention to small matters as not for their master's honour, and very easily give themselves a dispensation from having it. Negligence and profusion, therefore, must always prevail, more or less, in the management of the affairs of such a company.[19]

Berle and Means's thesis is that the modern corporation draws its capital from an increasingly dispersed group of investors, while at the same time it concentrates greater economic power in the hands of a relatively few managers:[20]

> Those who control the destinies of the typical corporation own so insignificant a fraction of the company's stock that the returns from the running of the corporation profitably accrue to them in only a very minor degree. The stockholders, on the other hand, to whom these profits of the corporation go, cannot be motivated by those profits to a more efficient

> use of the property, since they have surrendered all disposition of it to those who control the enterprise.[21]

If the managers act in a rational, self-interested fashion, they will use the corporate property under their control to benefit themselves rather than the shareholders.

Variations on the Managerialist Premise

managerialist premise The corporation is dominated by self-interested managers who take actions contrary to shareholder interests (e.g., they maximize aggregate profits or growth, instead of return to equity).

There are many variations on the **managerialist premise**—the argument that managers maximize their own wealth at the expense of shareholders. Since their salaries are at least partially based on the firm's growth, they may be motivated to expand firm size beyond the level that maximizes shareholder wealth. Once the constraints of the shareholder are satisfied, managers can use retained earnings to maximize growth, trying to achieve a growth rate greater than the one that would maximize shareholder value.[22]

Another view is that managers use discretionary profit, (i.e., profit above the necessary minimum required by stockholders) to increase staff and administrative expenses and to raise the level of perks and emoluments; these expenses provide managers with the salary, status, prestige, and security they seek.[23] Still another view is that managers maximize their lifetime income by avoiding risk and making decisions that produce stable financial results.[24] The managers attempt to achieve steady growth in sales and earnings even though better investment opportunities might, with added risk, provide a higher return to the owners.

A very strong theme in the managerialist argument is that managers are likely to be more risk-averse than shareholders. John Kenneth Galbraith maintains that managers are conservative and risk-averse in their efforts to earn returns. They "put prevention of loss ahead of maximum return."[25] It is desirable to achieve planned results but even more important to avoid unplanned disasters.

Managers seek to avoid unnecessary risks that might diminish their direct control. Interested chiefly in their own survival, they seek to retain power and status. To ensure demand for the corporation's products, they engage in extensive advertising and support government policies that maintain full employment. To ensure stable prices for labor and raw materials, they seek long-term contracts with suppliers. They prefer to finance the firm's investments through retained earnings rather than debt, and they try to generate adequate cash flow for reinvestment while avoiding the constraints connected with borrowed funds.[26]

According to the managerialist view, managers are less interested in maximizing shareholder returns than in maximizing their survival and security at shareholder expense. They seek the highest growth in sales but only if the risk level is acceptable, and if growth is achieved, they should have job security, frequent promotion, and adequate pay.

Why are managers likely to be risk-averse? Both individual and institutional investors are more diversified than managers. Individual investors may not hold diversified portfolios, but institutional investors who dominate the marketplace do. The most important possession of managers, on the other hand, is their job, from which they expect a discounted earnings stream until retirement. With the job comes fringe benefits, plus stock options that are not easily transferable and make lateral mobility costly and difficult.

Managers may see conglomerate growth as a means to protect their own interests through diversification, but such growth is not in the interests of shareholders who can diversify on their own. Since managers cannot spread their risks or escape them as easily as investors, they are likely to be more firmly tied to the company's fortunes. As a consequence they are more risk-averse than shareholders.

Critics have attacked the managerialist premise, and empirical support for it does not appear to be especially strong.[27] After examining the power exercised by family owners, institutional investors, lenders, and government regulators, E. S. Herman concluded that active power and control does in fact lie with managers. However, he acknowledged that other parties as well as the board of directors had latent power that could serve to constrain managerial discretion. Latent power was "exercisable within limits, under constraints, and on a contingent basis."[28] J. E. Heard noted that institutional investors were sometimes able to defeat antitakeover proposals made by management or secure the removal of such proposals before a vote following discussions with management.[29] Mizruchi suggested that such instances were clear examples of control by shareholders and further argued that the ability of the board to use unobtrusive control to set the boundaries within which management makes decisions was an example of true control.[30]

The Board of Directors

These studies bring up an important point. The board of directors is supposed to control managers in the name of the shareholders. It has six primary functions:[31]

1. Select, regularly evaluate, and, if necessary, replace the chief executive officer.
2. Determine management compensation and review succession planning.
3. Review and where appropriate approve the financial objectives, major strategies, and plans of the corporation.
4. Provide advice and counsel to top management.
5. Select and recommend to shareholders an appropriate slate of candidates for election to the board of directors; evaluate board processes and performance.
6. Review the adequacy of systems to comply with all applicable laws and regulations.

Supported by data on the ouster of CEOs by boards of directors, Mizurchi argued that boards did exercise a great deal of real control, even if it was through the holding of latent power.[32]

Boards of directors have become more active in ousting CEOs in recent years. Under pressure from shareholders, GM removed Robert Stempel as CEO and chairman and installed John Smale, the retired CEO of Procter & Gamble. Outside directors played a key role in overthrowing Stempel. Outside directors also forced a change in CEOs at Ford (Petersen) and Chrysler (Iacocca).[33]

Whether directors are becoming more involved is a complicated question. GM directors waited until the company's market share declined by 8 percent before they did anything. Nonetheless, all boards of directors have been under increasing pressure from shareholder activists and large institutional investors like the California Public Employees Retirement System (CALP), which have been focusing on underperforming companies, evaluating CEO performance, and taking initiatives to limit CEO compensation (see Chapter 8). It is hard to overcome board inertia; directors generally do not want to be perceived as troublemakers. It is hard for them to define what would constitute justifiable grounds for intervention. They are reluctant to discipline people who often are good friends. Their responsibilities are very broad but they work for only 12 to 14 days a year and for what they consider to be meager pay.

Another argument is that managers are controlled by the job market. The outside labor market prevents potential agency problems because managers are evaluated on the basis of the firm's performance, and managers acting in self-interest want to maximize their future compensation and job flexibility. In addition to competitive labor markets for executive talent, other factors that can induce managers to adopt a shareholder orientation are a relatively large managerial ownership position (see Chapter 8), compensation tied to shareholder returns, and the threat of takeovers.[34]

The Stakeholder Approach

stakeholder approach Rather than serving shareholders first, managers choose which stakeholders or group of stakeholders (e.g., customers, employees, communities) to favor.

The **stakeholder approach** examines the relationships that the corporation has with various groups that surround it such as shareholders, suppliers, customers, and employees. This approach suggests that managers should decide "what they stand for," and then formulate and carry out a strategy based on the interests they favor. It provides generic strategies meant to be "broad descriptions" of what the corporation "stands for" and how it should make trade-offs about stakeholder concerns (see Exhibit 3–1).[35]

Company Statements of Stakeholder Interests

Many firms have stakeholder strategy statements. Hewlett-Packard is dedicated to the dignity and worth of its individual employees; Aetna Life and Casualty believes that tending

EXHIBIT 3–1 Generic Stakeholder Strategies

Narrow stakeholder strategy:
Maximize benefits to one or a small set of stakeholders (management, labor, suppliers, shareholders, governments, customers, affected communities, and others).

Financial strategy:
Maximize benefits to stockholders.
Maximize benefits to all financial stakeholders, including banks and analysts.

Utilitarian strategy:
Maximize benefits to all stakeholders (greatest good for the greatest number).
Maximize average welfare level of all stakeholders.
Maximize benefits to society.

Social justice strategy
Raise the level of the worst-off stakeholders.

Social harmony strategy
Maintain or create social harmony.
Gain consensus from society.

Real-World Example

Japanese and American Managers

Aligning stakeholder expectations with economic, legal, and ethical obligations is one of management's major challenges (see Exhibit 3–2).[36]

Japanese and U.S. managers have different views concerning how to meet this challenge. When Japanese managers are asked to whom *should* the firm belong and to whom *does* the firm belong, and what *should* be and what *is* the corporation's most important goal (see Exhibit 3–3), they give different answers than U.S. managers.[37] It is much clearer who is in charge of the American firm: shareholders, not employees. Japanese managers are dedicated to making a contribution to society through achieving profit for expansion. U.S. managers are dedicated to making a contribution to society through shareholder returns. U.S. managers emphasize shareholder returns much more than their Japanese counterparts.

EXHIBIT 3–2 A Framework for Aligning Stakeholder Expectations with the Corporations' Economic, Legal, and Ethical Obligations

	Obligations		
Stakeholders	*Economic*	*Legal*	*Ethical*
Owners	______	______	______
Customers	______	______	______
Employees	______	______	______
Community	______	______	______
Competitors	______	______	______
Suppliers	______	______	______
Social activists	______	______	______
Public at large	______	______	______
Etc.	______	______	______

to the broader needs of society is essential to fulfilling its economic role; and J. C. Penney Company tests every policy, method, and act so that it is right and just.[38]

Perhaps Johnson & Johnson's stakeholder strategy is the most famous example (see Exhibit 3–4):[39] Johnson and Johnson consistently receives high rankings for community and social responsibility in *Fortune*'s annual surveys of top business officials.

The Business Roundtable Statement on Stakeholders

The Business Roundtable was a group made up of CEOs from the largest companies in the United States. It claimed to speak for the entire business community. In 1981, the Business Roundtable issued a statement on stakeholder strategy. Some excerpts are given below.

EXHIBIT 3–3 Japanese versus U.S. Managers

	Percent of Responses	
	Japanese Managers	*U.S. Managers*
To whom should the firm belong?		
Employees	30%	25%
Society	25	7
Shareholders	24	54
Customers	10	8
Senior managers	7	1
Community	3	5
State	1	0
To whom does the firm belong?		
Employees	31%	1%
Society	5	2
Shareholders	23	64
Customers	11	2
Senior managers	26	30
Community	1	0
State	3	1
What should be the most important goal?		
Contribution to society	68%	45%
Profit for expansion	16	14
Employee welfare	9	5
Shareholder returns	6	34
Environment	1	2
What is the most important goal?		
Contribution to society	12%	7%
Profit for expansion	86	31
Employee welfare	1	1
Shareholder returns	0	61
Environment	1	0

Customers have a primary claim for corporate attention. Without them, the enterprise will fail . . .

Employees expect not only fair pay but also such conditions as equal opportunity, workplaces that protect health and safety, financial security, personal privacy, freedom of expression, and concern for the quality of life. Experience has shown that employees will perform well for corporations that have earned their loyalty, rewarded their performance, and involved them in the decision making process . . .

Corporations most closely touch people's lives in the individual communities where they operate. Here they are expected to be concerned with local needs and problems—schools, traffic, pollution, health, recreation . . .

The corporation's first responsibility to society is to maintain its economic viability as a producer of goods and services, as an employer, and as a creator of jobs . . .

Shareholders have a special relationship to the corporation . . . The corporation must be profitable enough to provide shareholders a return that will encourage continuation of investment. . . . The expectation of near-term gain can exert pressure to subordinate long-term

Exhibit 3–4 Johnson & Johnson's Stakeholder Strategy

We believe our first responsibility is to the doctors, nurses and patients, to mothers and all others who use our products and services. In meeting their needs everything we do must be of high quality. We must constantly strive to reduce our costs in order to maintain reasonable prices. Customers' orders must be serviced promptly and accurately. Our suppliers and distributors must have an opportunity to make a fair profit.

We are responsible to our employees: the men and women who work with us throughout the world. Everyone must be considered as an individual. We must respect their dignity and recognize their merit. They must have a sense of security in their jobs. Compensation must be fair and adequate, and working conditions clean, orderly and safe. Employees must feel free to make suggestions and complaints. There must be equal opportunity for employment, development, and advancement for those qualified. We must provide competent management and their actions must be just and ethical.

We are responsible to the communities in which we live and work and to the world community as well.

We must be good citizens—support good works and charities and bear our fair share of taxes. We must encourage civic improvements and better health and education.

We must maintain in good order the property we are privileged to use, protecting the environment and natural resources.

Our final respnosibility is to our stockholders. Business must make a sound profit. We must experiment with new ideas. Research must be carried on, innovative programs developed, and mistakes paid for. New equipment must be purchased, new facilities provided, and new products launched. Reserves must be created to provide for adverse times.

When we operate according to these principles, the stockholders should realize a fair return.

> objectives to more immediate profit considerations. Despite such expectations, management needs to maintain a long-term perspective.
>
> Balancing the shareholder's expectations of maximum return against other priorities is one of the fundamental problems confronting corporate management. The shareholder must receive a good return but the legitimate concerns of other constituencies also must have the appropriate attention.[40]

The Business Roundtable's statement was attacked by the economist Paul MacAvoy. In a *New York Times* article, MacAvoy maintained that a concern with constituencies "implies that the large corporation is a political entity subject to the votes of interest groups, rather than an economic organization subject to the market test for efficient use of resources." He argued that "the corporation should be using its resources to maximize investment returns, so as to stimulate the investment required to produce the largest amount of goods and services for which consumers are willing to pay . . . unless social and charitable activities reduce long-run marginal costs or increase consumer demand than they divert resources from the social goals inherent in maximum production."[41]

The Business Roundtable replied that it recognized that a corporation's first responsibility was "to make available to the public quality goods and services at fair prices, thereby earning a profit that attracts investment to continue and enhance the enterprise, provide jobs, and build the economy." However, "chief executive officers who have been out there facing reality know that they are surrounded by a complicated pattern of . . . expectations

[and] they have to be concerned not only about shareholders but about . . . constituent groups."[42]

Revision of the Business Roundtable Position

In 1990, the Business Roundtable issued a statement, *Corporate Governance and the American Economy,* which revised its original position on stakeholders in light of the competitive challenges U.S. companies faced abroad.[43]

> As an economic entity chartered by the state, each corporation finds itself in heavy competition not only with other U.S. corporations but also with the products and services of foreign corporations, and with business organizations that are as diverse as individual entrepreneurs to nations or consortiums of nations . . .
>
> Corporate governance is sometimes erroneously compared to political governance. Although surface similarities exist between the election of boards of directors and the election of legislative bodies, the fundamental purposes of the corporation as an economic entity are quite different from those of a political body . . . A corporation has as its prime purpose the long-term optimization of economic outcomes . . .
>
> It is important that all stakeholder interests be considered, but impossible to assure that all will be satisfied.

The new Roundtable position was more in accord with the classic views of Hayek and Friedman. It had evolved now that conditions governing business were different in the 1990s.[44]

Plural Interests

behavioral theory
A theory that holds that the corporation is a coalition of different interests each of which may be benefited to different degrees at different points in time.

The **behavioral theory** developed at Carnegie-Mellon University in the late 1950s and early 1960s was in many ways supportive of the stakeholder approach. This theory is empirical rather than normative; that is, it studies how decisions are made as opposed to prescribing how they should be made. It holds that the corporation is a coalition of groups with varying goals and interests. The corporation makes decisions at different points in time that favors these different groups.[45]

The origins of behavioral theory can be found in the following arguments. The depiction of decision making as the rational pursuit of predetermined objectives, whether they be profit, growth, or competitive advantage, is not accurate. The view which assumes that "corporate management has considerable discretion, is analytical and rational, and can plan comprehensively" is too narrow.[46] The behavioral theory assumes that firms have multiple centers of power. Groups from within the firm and without—managers, workers, stockholders, suppliers, bankers, customers, lawyers, accountants, and regulatory officials—have different subgoals that they pursue simultaneously. At least five internal subgoals (production, inventory, sales, market share, and profit) are involved. The actual goals of the organization as a whole are ambiguous. They reflect the bargaining among various internal units as well as pressures from society.[47]

Pressure is exerted by customers, suppliers, and regulatory agencies. For the firm's survival, the search for customers is critical. A major reason for business failure is a company's inattention to markets. From suppliers the firm must obtain labor, materials, and equipment, which are important because they influence costs and prices. Regulatory agencies impose constraints by legal action or by the implied threat of legal action. As E. A. Grefe comments:

> If the chief executive officer's attention is focused solely on share of the market, the market itself could vanish or be severely restricted by regulation. Witness the experience of any number of industries: nuclear power, tobacco, candy, cereal, bottling, chemical, paper, oil, to name but a few.[48]

However, regulatory agencies can also provide opportunities for competitive advantage and improving public image.

A large corporate organization has numerous groups of participants. Inside the corporation, these participants have different status, job assignment, geographic location, educational background, career aspiration, attitude toward the firm, and expectations. Their inherently different interests lead to a diversity of forces, sometimes in opposition, which affect managerial decisions. Boards of directors, though they have direct authority, have limited power. Exxon's large board meets infrequently, and it is a forum for the exchange of information, not an arena for challenging the decisions of internal management.[49]

Behavioral theorists believe that in the short run firm behavior is a complex amalgam of many forces—stockholders, employees, and the community, internal and external coalitions with different interests and goals, and leadership—all of which may make a difference, like a political entity, in influencing outcomes.[50] Decision making involves groping gradually for solutions over time, usually without radical policy changes. Herbert Simon argues that the search for "satisfactory" financial success takes precedence over simple profit maximization. Though targets exist for financial well-being, managers are not strict profit maximizers.[51]

Public Responsibility

public responsibility The corporation is responsible to citizens through the public policy process and, as well as shaping the process, is shaped by it.

A final approach to corporate control is that of **public responsibility.** The growth of government involvement in the economy after World War II led to the development of this approach. The public responsibility approach holds that corporations are shaped by public policy processes that affect primary and secondary areas. The primary area consists of the organization's "functional role": its "exchange relationships with the market." The secondary area covers the effects of production, sales, procurement, and employment, and other business activities, including the "neighborhood effects," and the "use by others of the merchandise and services sold."[52]

Managerial responsibility is not supposed to extend beyond the secondary involvements. It is not the task of managers to better social conditions or resolve social problems. Unlike the stakeholder approach, this approach does not require the corporation to be sensitive to the "complaints" of all social groups. Instead, public policy should be regarded as an objective guide to what managers should do; individual moral and ethical insights are less important.

Laws and the public policy process are the ultimate arbiters of the communities' expectations about corporate behavior. Public policy includes the spirit as well as the letter of the law, and it reflects the changing environment that extends from "accepted standards" to "specific laws and requirements" and "newly emerging viewpoints and issues."

The corporation and government form an "interpenetrating" system; neither is completely controlled by the process nor does it completely control it.[53]

An important objective of management is to overcome constraints on its ability to respond to public policy developments. These constraints include the organization's structure and leadership, its ability to motivate and reward managers, and the financial formulas used in making decisions. Responses to public policies involve a number of stages from awareness to commitment to implementation. (see Exhibit 3–5).[54]

Regulatory Growth

Regulatory growth in the late 1960s and early 1970s came to embody the focus on laws and public policies. It signified a so-called second managerial revolution. The first revolution was the shift from owners managing their enterprises to the joint-stock company where ownership and management were separated. The second revolution gave government decision makers vast powers and increasing control over key areas of managerial decision making, including manufacturing and the introduction of new products and services. The critical challenge for management was how to respond to the public control that emanated from government and the shifting public policy process.[55]

Special Public Affairs Units

In the 1970s and 1980s, many firms developed and enhanced their capabilities for responding to the public policy process by creating special public affairs departments or units (see Chapter 9). Varying with the needs of an industry and individual companies, these units brought many important activities together (see Exhibit 3–6).[56]

A successful public affairs program should enhance a firm's credibility, facilitate a timely and appropriate response to issues, and have a positive financial impact.[57] From 1982 to 1985, the average number of employees in public affairs grew from 8.7 to about 15 persons per firm despite declining government regulation and a sympathetic administration in Washington.[58]

EXHIBIT 3–5 Response Stages

1. *Awareness:*
   Managers recognize the existence of a problem. They can be early or late in their ability to detect an emerging public policy issue and can lead or lag in their response to an issue.
2. *Commitment:*
   Managers decide on a course of action. They can choose actions such as buffering the corporation's internal operations from emerging public policy issues to altering both a company's internal operations and the external environment.
3. *Implementation:*
   Managers organize to carry out the course of action they have chosen. They attempt to achieve goals that they have set for their organizations.

Exhibit 3–6 Activities of Public Affairs Units

1. *Issues management.* Public affairs departments help to identify important social, political, economic, and technological developments and to integrate this information into strategic planning.

2. *Government relations* (federal, state, and local). Public affairs departments monitor legislative and regulatory developments, assess their implications, and try to affect the course of public policiy.

3. *Public relations.* Public affairs departments communicate information about the firm to the media.

4. *International relations.* Public affairs departments promote company interests in foreign capitals and in international forums.

5. *Investor and stockholder relations.* Public affairs departments often take charge of company communications with investors, brokerage houses, and other financial institutions.

6. *Corporate contributions.* Frequently, public affairs departments coordinate company contributions to the community.

7. *Institutional advertising.* To heighten public awareness, public affairs departments often engage in image building through such means as nonproduct, corporate advertising.

8. *Employee communications.* Public affairs departments also may produce newsletters and other communications that help gain the support of employees, stockholders, customers, and local citizens for the corporation.

Additional Steps to Enhance Public Affairs Management

In recent years, corporations have taken additional steps to enhance public affairs management. In the 1970s and 1980s, they created corporate political action committees or PACs.[59] The purpose of PACs is to make donations to political candidates for federal office. Under electoral reform laws passed after the Watergate scandal, companies are allowed to solicit funds for candidates subject to certain limitations, such as the amount that an individual employee can give to a particular candidate.

Firms made "grass roots" efforts to motivate employees, stockholders, customers, suppliers, and local citizens to become politically active.[60] This might include writing a letter to a congressperson or local politician, signing a petition, marching in a demonstration, or expressing an opinion on a television or radio talk show.

Another change that took place in the way corporations managed the political and social environment was the involvement of chief executive officers in national political organizations. You will recall the Business Roundtable statement on stakeholder strategy. The chief executive officers who made up the Roundtable headed the largest corporations in America.[61] In the 1970s, CEOs became directly involved in establishing a political agenda for the American business community, taking positions on issues of vital concern, and personally lobbying Congress and government officials.

Public Policy Advocacy Advertising

Another notable development in corporate public affairs was the use of advertising to do public policy advocacy. Companies promoted their particular positions on public policy matters in advertising space on the editorial pages of major newspapers and magazines.

Real-World Example

William G. McGowan—Effective Corporate Public Affairs Leader[62]

In the 1960s, technological changes began to radically transform the telecommunications industry. Companies wanted to connect their telephone lines to computers in order to transmit and process information from different plant locations. They wanted to share leased lines. But AT&T was not being responsive to their requests. Microwave Communications Incorporated (MCI), a new company, proposed to take advantage of microwave technology to set up a private line between Chicago and St. Louis. This line would be more flexible than the ones provided by AT&T, but AT&T resisted and in a long drawn out regulatory proceeding that lasted from 1963 to 1969 it blocked MCI from proceeding.

In 1968, the late William G. McGowan joined MCI. A hard-driving executive from Scranton, Pennsylvania, McGowan had received his M.B.A. from Harvard and had a successful career working as a consultant and executive for many firms. McGowan's first move as chief executive officer was to relocate corporate headquarters to Washington, D.C. In Washington, he looked for political allies to fight AT&T but could find none. No trade association in the telecommunications industry was willing to take on the industry behemoth. Telephone users, even large ones, were afraid to offend AT&T. The financial backers of MCI were small entrepreneurs who had little political clout or sophistication. In developing an opposition to AT&T, McGowan had to act alone. His aim was no less than to divest AT&T of its local subsidiaries, and he marketed his ideas to policy makers in much the same way a company would market its product to consumers. McGowan found that a group of officials in the Federal Communications Commission, the White House, and the Justice Department were willing to listen. They too felt that competition in the telecommunications industry would have benefits—additional innovation would result from an effective check on AT&T's monopoly power and consumers would have lower telephone rates. McGowan articulated his objectives in terms of broad social goals. He established with a number of other small companies the Ad Hoc Coalition for Competitive Telecommunications (ACCT) in 1976 to pursue these goals.

McGowan's efforts in building MCI involved (1) maintaining venture capital, (2) lobbying, (3) exploiting loopholes in the laws that would allow MCI to expand its services, and (4) providing telecommunications services to existing customers. He did not regard the initial FCC decisions that opened the door for MCI, especially the Specialized Carrier Decision of 1971, as being sufficient. He constantly pushed at the FCC to broaden the frontiers of competition. Finally, in 1974 MCI started an antitrust suit against AT&T. This suit lasted for nearly 10 years, during which time McGowan heightened visibility for his firm by portraying AT&T in a negative manner.

McGowan's political strategy was essential to his company's business success. He needed access to government officials and he obtained it. By the middle of the 1970s it was impossible to resolve a telecommunications issue without first hearing from McGowan. McGowan's persistence paid off because one of the important outcomes was permission for MCI and others to compete in offering long-distance telephone service. When deregulation took place, McGowan used his visibility as spokesperson for the procompetition forces to enhance the image of MCI and make it a leader in the long-distance telephone market. He was a master at combining the individual interest of his firm with the broader public interest in telecommunication's deregulation.

The idea was not new because corporate views on public policy issues have been presented throughout this century. However, in 1969 Rawleigh Warner, Jr., newly elected chairman and CEO of Mobil, and Bill Tavoulareas, the company's president, inaugurated a new program to reach the public directly through a newspaper campaign. A young labor lawyer,

Herbert Schmertz, was appointed head of public affairs with the responsibility to make this campaign successful.

Mobil's intention was not only to inform the public about Mobil's particular needs but also to deal with matters of public interest. For example, when the *New York Times* opened its editorial pages to advertising copy, Mobil bought the space and used it to argue for a better transportation system and for improved health care, policies that appealed to liberal opinion. In March 1975, when television station WNBC in New York produced a miniseries on the oil industry that Mobil thought was biased against the oil companies, Mobil responded with full-page advertisements titled "Whatever Happened to Fair Play?" in the *New York Times* and *The Wall Street Journal*, complaining that the series was inaccurate and unfair.[63]

Surveys by Lou Harris and other pollsters showed that Mobil's advocacy advertising caused the public to regard Mobil more favorably than other oil companies. Although the ads were noticed by public policy makers, they had little or no affect on formulating policy on issues concerning the oil industry.

Other significant developments in corporate public affairs were the proliferation of ad hoc coalitions and the increased involvement of specialized consulting firms and lobbying groups.[64]

Maximizing Ethical Behavior

In short, we have argued that the corporation has economic, legal, and ethical obligations that it owes its stakeholders. It cannot afford to shirk its responsibilities to any of them (see Exhibit 3–7). Management response is filtered through organizational processes and individual psychology. Friedman and Hayek suggest that these obligations are separate and that economics is dominant. Norman Bowie has proposed a revised framework suggesting that ethics underlies both the economic and legal obligations.[65] In accord with his argument, Milton Friedman's maxim should be modified: Rather than maximize returns to investors subject to legal and ethical constraints, managers should maximize ethical behavior. As a by-product, they will enhance profits and minimize legal liabilities.

The revised framework (see Exhibit 3–8) is based on the following two arguments.

EXHIBIT 3–7 Avoid Ethical Shirking to Stakeholders

To owners	Managerial salaries, benefits, perks at owner expense
To employees	Factor of production manipulated for gain No respect for privacy, freedom of speech, safety
To customers	Intent to cheat, deceive, mislead; no fair value, full information
To community suppliers	Plant closings, pollution violations, no charity, delaying payments, failure to honor debts

1. There is much overlap between individual interest and ethics. Of course, the overlap is not perfect. Cases of spontaneous altruism (see Chapter 6) occur where people sacrifice their lives for others without any obvious benefit to themselves; for example, soldiers jump on grenades to save their buddies, or passengers in downed airplanes enter a burning plane to save someone else's life at the expense of their own.

People may carry out these acts purely for the pleasure they get in fulfilling a duty. A clear conscience is preferable to guilt and regret. However, a reputation for being trustworthy has some concrete benefits. It can be valuable because others treat us as we have treated them. In addition, if you are regarded as trustworthy, you are more likely to be given positions of authority and responsibility that require trust. Altruism is reciprocal: We act benevolently in the hope of being rewarded with similar kindness.

EXHIBIT 3–8 Initial and Revised Frameworks

A. Initial framework

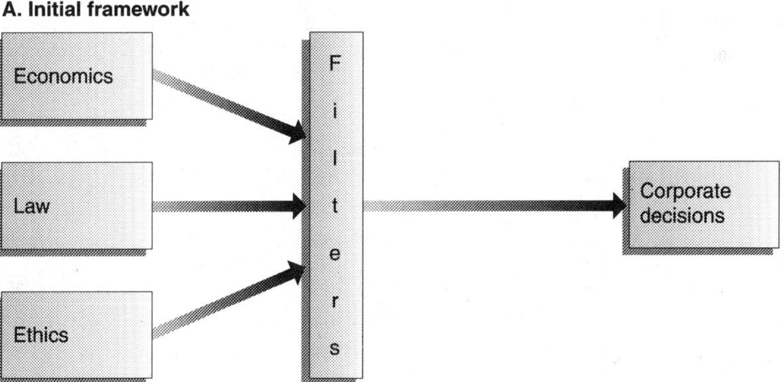

"Maximize returns to shareholders subject to legal and ethical constraints"

B. Revised framework

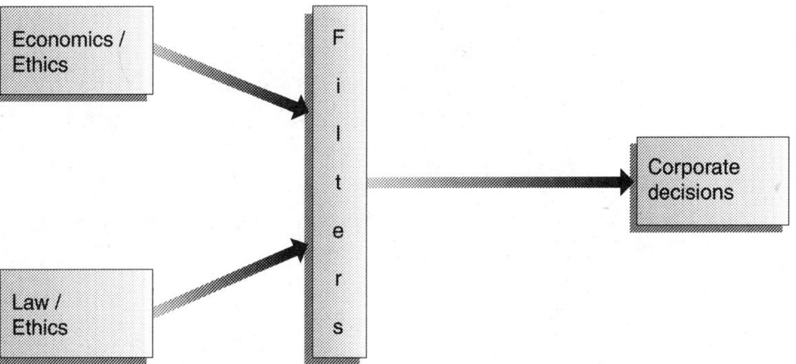

"Maximize ethical behavior and as a byproduct enhance profits and minimize legal liabilities"

2. The legal and ethical obligations of corporations also may be more connected than is commonly thought, but situations exist where these obligations conflict. For example, it is legal but not ethical to fire a person for no reason. On the other hand, certain moral acts—for example, protesting against human rights violations in China—are ethical but not legal. Nonetheless, the law frequently embodies fundamental ethical notions. The *Uniform Commercial Code*, for instance, requires that one bargain in good faith. Labor law forbids gross inequality in bargaining position or coercion. Consumer law prohibits deceit. The legal philosopher Ronald Dworkin argues that where statutes are vague or in conflict, the judges will decide difficult issues on ethical grounds.

The "hedonic paradox" means that the more a person seeks happiness the less likely the person will find it. In the same way, the more managers seek profits the less likely they will achieve them.

The main obligation that corporations have—to make money in a legal and in an ethical fashion—may be the cause of fewer conflicts than one would think. Kenneth Dayton, former chair of the Dayton Hudson Corporation said, "We are not in business to make maximum profits . . . We are in business . . . to serve society. Profit is our reward for doing it well" (see Case 3-A in this chapter).

Conclusions

Starting with Adam Smith, different theories of corporate control have been articulated. The approaches reviewed are the classic (or agency) approach that emphasizes shareholders; the managerialist critique of that approach, which suggests that managers, not shareholders, dominate; the stakeholder approach, which suggests that managers can choose which of many stakeholders to favor; and the public policy approach.

Hayek and Friedman's positions are that managers should increase shareholder profits within legal and ethical constraints. When managers act as executives, they are the agents of shareholders who own the corporation. The relationship of managers to owners is a contractual one based on norms implicit in agency relationships.

The agency approach is contradicted by the managerialist argument, which maintains that managers run corporations in their own interests. The managers take actions that are less risky than owners would take on their own, because their assets are specialized and more closely tied to the corporation than those of the owners who usually have diversified portfolios. The managers also focus on growth rather than profitability and provide themselves with perks. Managerialist premises, however, have been challenged by the role that boards of directors play. Takeovers and the market for managerial talent also limit managerial discretion.

The stakeholder approach finds support in the idea that in real-world situations managers face conflicting demands. Their behavior is a function of different sets of responsibilities influencing their actions. These responsibilities work through organizational and psychological influences best described by the behavioral theory, which holds that neither shareholders nor managers control the corporation. Instead, a shifting coalition of interests is in charge that biases decisions in unique ways.

The public responsibility approach comes from the growing regulation of the corporation and the corporation's response to this regulation. Corporations have become more involved in the public policy process through a number of mechanisms. Finally, we have made the point that often it is in the corporation's interest to maximize ethical behavior and, as a by-product, to achieve financial success. Some of the implications of this argument will be taken up in the next chapter.

Discussion Questions

1. Elaborate on agency relationships. What problems does the principal face in controlling the agent's behavior? When is the agent justified in not obeying the principal?
2. Compare and contrast Frederick Hayek's view of the corporation with that of Milton Friedman.
3. What is meant by "separation of ownership from control?" What is the practical difference of separation of ownership from control?
4. Can boards of directors exert effective control over the corporation? What other means do shareholders have for controlling the corporation?
5. Which stakeholder groups have the chief influence on decision making in a firm? How do they exert this influence? What effect does it have?
6. Compare and contrast the five generic strategies. Why would a company choose a social justice strategy?
7. What would Milton Friedman say about Johnson & Johnson's stakeholder strategy? Would you agree with him?
8. Who won the debate between the Business Roundtable and Paul MacAvoy? What are your reasons for thinking so?
9. Why did the Business Roundtable modify its statement?
10. What is the principle of public responsibility? Why did it come to prominence? How does it differ from the principle of social responsibility?
11. In what ways did corporations enhance their capabilities for public affairs management in the 1970s and early 1980s?
12. What is your opinion of the way William McGowan founded MCI? What other opportunities might exist for using the public policy process to create new businesses?
13. Is business involvement in the political process fair? Are important nonbusiness interests unrepresented or underrepresented in the public policy process because they lack the resources that businesses can command? Should the laws be reformed to reduce business involvement in politics?
14. What is the hedonic paradox? What is its implication for managing a corporation?
15. In what ways are laws consistent with ethics? In what ways are they not consistent?
16. What is your view of the maxim: "Maximize ethical behavior and as by-product

enhance profits and minimize legal liabilities." Is this maxim realistic? Does it make any sense?

Endnotes

1. I would like to acknowledge the assistance of the following doctoral candidates at the University of Minnesota who contributed to parts of this chapter and the next: Linnea Van Dyne, Isaac Fox, Kent Miller, Gordon Rands, and Doug Schuller; M. Friedman, "The Social Responsibility of Business Is to Increase Its Profits," reprinted in Charles S. McCoy, *The Management of Values* (Boston: Pitman, 1985), pp. 253–60.
2. The Federalist Papers (New York: New American Library, 1961).
3. Adam Smith, *The Wealth of Nations* (New York: Modern Library, 1965).
4. J. Q. Wilson, "Adam Smith on Business Ethics," *California Management Review* 1 (1989), pp. 59–72.
5. Smith, *The Wealth of Nations*.
6. Milton Friedman, "Social Responsibility of Business," pp. 253–60; Frederick Hayek, "The Corporation in a Democratic Society: In Whose Interests Ought It and Will It Be Run?" from H. I. Ansoff, ed., *Business Strategy*, 1977, pp. 225–39.
7. Hayek, "Corporation in a Democratic Society,"
8. Ibid.
9. Ibid.
10. Friedman, "Social Responsibility of Business."
11. Ibid.
12. Ibid.
13. Ibid.
14. A. Berle and G. Means, *The Modern Corporation and Private Property* (New York: Harcourt, Brace and World, 1967).
15. Alfred Rappaport, "Selecting Strategies that Create Shareholder Value," *Harvard Business Review* 3(1981), pp. 139–49; "Corporate Performance Standards and Shareholder Value," *The Journal of Business Strategy* 4 (1983), pp. 28–38.
16. Ibid.
17. Ibid.
18. Hayek, "Corporation in a Democratic Society."
19. Smith, The *Wealth of Nations*, p. 700.
20. A. Berle and G. Means, *The Modern Corporation and Private Property* (New York: Harcourt, Brace and World, 1967); M. Weidenbaum and M. Jensen, *Introduction to the Modern Corporation and Private Property*, Working Paper 134 (St. Louis: Center for the Study of American Business, September 1990); L. S. Zacharias and A. Kaufman, *The Problem of the Corporation and the Evolution of Social Values*, Working paper MG 87/88 #2, Management Research Center, School of Management (Amherst: University of Massachusetts, 1987).
21. Berle and Means, *The Modern Corporation*, pp. 8–9.
22. R. Marris, *The Economic Theory of "Managerial" Capitalism* (London: Macmillan, 1964).
23. O. Williamson, *The Economics of Discretionary Behavior* (Chicago: Markham, 1967); Marris, *"Managerial" Capitalism*.
24. W. Baumol, *Business Behavior, Value and Growth* (New York, Harcourt, Brace and World, 1959).
25. John K. Galbraith, *The New Industrial State* (Boston: Houghton Mifflin, 1967), p. 215.
26. G. Donaldson and J. Lorsch, *Decision Making at the Top* (New York: Basic Books, 1983).

27. E. S. Herman, *Corporate Control, Corporate Power* (Cambridge: Cambridge University Press, 1981); G. Bentsen, "The Self-Serving Management Hypothesis: Some Evidence," *Journal of Accounting and Economics* 7 (1985), pp. 67–84; R. D. Kosnik, "Greenmail: A Study of Board Performance in Corporate Governance," *Administrative Science Quarterly* 32(1987), pp. 163–85.
28. Herman, *Corporate Control*, p. 23.
29. J. E. Heard, "Pension Funds and Contests for Corporate Control," *California Management Review* 29, no. 2 (1987), pp. 89–100.
30. M. S. Mizurchi, "Who Controls Whom? An Examination of the Relation between Management and Boards of Directors in Large American Corporations," *Academy of Management Review* 8, no. 2 (1983), pp. 426–35.
31. Business Roundtable, *Corporate Governance and American Competitiveness* (New York: Business Roundtable, March 1990), p. 7; I. Kesner, "Directors' Characteristics and Committee Membership: An Investigation of Type, Occupation, Tenure and Gender," *Academy of Management Journal* 31, no. 2 (1988), pp. 66–84; A. Stalnaker, *The Board of Directors and the Chief Executive Officer*, Formal Publication, No. 74 (St. Louis: Center for the Study of American Business, June 1986).
32. Mizurchi, "Who Controls Whom?" pp. 426–35.
33. Myron Magnet, "Directors, Wake Up!" *Fortune*, June 15, 1992, pp. 85–92.
34. E. Fama, "Agency Problems and the Theory of the Firm," *Journal of Political Economy* 88 (1980), pp. 288–307.
35. R. E. Freeman, *Strategic Management: A Stakeholder Approach* (Marshfield, Mass.: Pitman, 1984).
36. Archie Carroll, "The Pyramid of Corporate Social Responsibility," *Business Horizons*, July–August 1991, pp. 39–48.
37. Hajime Miyazaki, "Employeeism and the Spirit of Japanese Capitalism," Ohio State University, summary tables from *Nakkei Surveys*, pp. 42–3. The U.S. comparison is based on surveys with over 250 U.S. managers that I have carried out.
38. Business Roundtable, *Corporate Ethics: A Prime Business Asset* (New York: Business Roundtable, 1988); J. Dresang, "Companies Get Serious about Ethics," *USA Today*, Dec. 9, 1986, p. B1; W. Hewlett, "Hewlett-Packard: What Is the HP Way?" in *The HP Way*; S. B. Middlebrook, "Aetna Life & Casualty: Philosophy and Direction," in *Taking Part*, Aetna company report, 1982; J. C. Penney, "The Penney Idea," *Business Ethics at J.C. Penney*, 1913.
39. Business Roundtable, *Corporate Ethics*; R. W. Johnson, "Johnson & Johnson: Our Credo," 1979.
40. Business Roundtable, "Statement on Corporate Responsibility" (New York: Business Roundtable, October 1981).
41. P. W. MacAvoy, "The Business Lobby's Wrong Business," *The New York Times*, Dec. 20, 1981, quoted in T. G. Marx, ed., *Business and Society* (New York: Prentice Hall, 1981), pp. 158–64.
42. A. C. Sigler, "Roundtable Reply," *The New York Times*, Dec. 27, 1981, quoted in T. Marx, ed., *Business and Society: Economic, Moral, and Political Foundations* (Englewood Cliffs, N.J.: Prentice Hall, 1985).
43. Business Roundtable, *Corporate Governance and American Competitiveness.*
44. Norman Bowie, "New Directions in Corporate Social Responsibility," *Business Horizons*, July–August 1991, pp. 56–65; Norman Bowie, "The Firm as a Moral Community," Discussion Paper No. 141, Strategic Management Research Center, University of Minnesota, July 1990; Norman Bowie, "Fair Markets," *Journal of Business Ethics*, 1988, pp. 89–98.
45. R. M. Cyert and James G. March, *A Behavioral Theory of the Firm* (Englewood Cliffs, N.J.: Prentice Hall, 1963); L. Gomez-Mejia, H. Tosi, and T. Hinkin, "Managerial Control, Performance, and Executive Compensation," *Academy of Management Journal* 30, no. 1 (1987), pp. 51–71.

46. E. A. Murray, "Strategic Choice as a Negotiated Outcome," *Management Science* 24 (May 1978), pp. 960–72.
47. Cyert and March, *A Behavioral Theory of the Firm*.
48. E. A. Grefe, *Fighting to Win: Business Political Power* (New York: Harcourt Brace Jovanovich, 1981), p. 13.
49. A. J. Parisi, "The Men Who Rule Exxon," *The New York Times Magazine*, August 3, 1980, pp. 19–25.
50. H. Mintzberg, D. Raisinghani, and A. Theoret, "The Structure of Unstructured Decision Processes," *Administrative Science Quarterly* 21 (June 1976), pp. 246–75.
51. H. Simon, "On the Concept of Organizational Goal," *Administrative Science Quarterly*, June 1964, pp. 1–22, quoted in H. I. Ansoff, ed., *Business Strategy*, pp. 240–263.
52. L. Preston, and J. Post, *Private Management and Public Policy*, 1975, pp. 14–43, 94–106.
53. Ibid.
54. R. W. Ackerman, *The Social Challenge to Business* (Cambridge, Mass.: Harvard University Press, 1975); R. W. Ackerman, "How Companies Respond to Social Demands," *Harvard Business Review* 51, no. 4 (July–August 1973), pp. 88–98.
55. W. Lilley and J. C. Miller, "The New Social Regulation," *The Public Interest*, Spring 1977, pp. 49–62; R. J. Penoyer, *Directory of Federal Regulatory Agencies — 1982 Update* (St. Louis: Center for the Study of American Business, 1982), p. 1; P. Weaver, "Regulation, Social Policy, and Class Conflict," *The Public Interest*, Winter 1978, pp. 45–64; M. L. Weidenbaum, "The Future of Business-Government Relations in the United States," in M. Ways, ed., *The Future of Business* (New York: Pergamon, 1979), p. 49.
56. S. Lusterman, *The Organization and Staffing of Corporate Public Affairs* (New York: The Conference Board, 1987); J. A. Sonnenfeld, *Corporate Views of the Public Interest: Perceptions of the Forest Products Industry* (Boston: Auburn House, 1981); G. Starling and O. Baskin, "Pfizer Corporation: Strategy, Organization, and Implementation in the Public Affairs Function," *Issues in Business and Society: Capitalism and Public Purpose* (Boston: Kent Publishing, 1985), pp. 29–51; A. Kaufman, E. Englander, and A. Marcus, "Structural Aspects of Issues Management: Transaction Costs and Agency Theory," paper presented at the Eastern Academy of Management Meeting, 1987.
57 P. Andrews, "The Sticky Wicket of Evaluating Public Affairs: Thoughts About a Framework," *Public Affairs Review* 6 (1986), pp. 94–105; A. M. Kaufman, E. J. Englander, and A. A. Marcus, "Structure and Implementation in Issues Management: Transaction Costs and Agency Theory," *Research in Corporate Social Performance and Policy* 11 (1989), pp. 257–71; A. Marcus and A. Kaufman, "The Continued Expansion of the Corporate Public Affairs Function," *Business Horizons* 31 (1988), pp. 58–62; "Managing the Headquarters—Overseas Relationship in Public Affairs," *Perspectives: International Public Affairs*, January 1985; "Government Relations: Prerequisite for Doing Business in Asia," *Perspectives: International Public Affairs*, Fall 1985.
58. A. Marcus and M. Irion, "The Continued Growth of the Corporate Public Affairs Function," *The Academy of Management Executive*, August 1987, pp. 249–52.
59. R. E. Cohen, "Congressional Democrats Beware—Here Come the Corporate PACs," *National Journal*, August 9, 1980, p. 1305; M. Glen, "The PACs are Back Richer and Wiser to Finance the 1980 Elections," *National Journal*, December 24, 1979, pp. 1982–4; A. Matasar, "Corporate Responsibility Gone Awry?: The Corporate Political Action Committee," Paper prepared for the 1981 Annual Meeting of the American Political Science Association, New York, September 3–6, 1981; J. S. Shockley, "Corporate Spending in the Wake of the Bellotti Decision: National Implications," Paper prepared for the American Political Science Association convention, New York, 1978.
60. G. Keim and C. Zeithaml, "Corporate Political Strategy and Legislative Decision Making,"

Academy of Management Review 11, no. 4 (1986), pp. 828–43; A. A. Marcus, *The Adversary Economy: Business Responses to Changing Government Requirements* (Westport, Conn.: Quorum Books).

61. K. McQuaid, "The Roundtable: Getting Results in Washington 81," *Harvard Business Review* 59 (May–June 1981), pp. 114–23.
62. D. Yoffie, "Corporate Strategies for Political Action: A Rational Model," from Marcus, Kaufman, and Beam, *Business Strategy and Public Policy*, pp. 43–60.
63. R. Buchholz, W. Evans, and R. Wagley, *Management Response to Public Issues* (Englewood Cliffs, N.J.: Prentice Hall) pp. 186–200.
64. G. Keim and Zeithaml, "Corporate Political Strategy and Legislative Decision Making, pp. 828–43; R. E. Cohen, "The Business Lobby Discovers That in Unity There Is Strength," *National Journal*, June 28, 1980, pp. 1050–55; R. Reich, "Regulation by Negotiation or Confrontation?" *Harvard Business Review* 59 (May–June 1981), pp. 82–92.
65. Ibid.

Case 3–A
Dayton Hudson

New Strategies[1]

Originally a family-owned retailer established in 1902 in Minneapolis, Minnesota, Dayton Hudson went public in 1967 and in 1969 merged with Hudson, a department store chain based in Detroit. By 1993, Dayton Hudson (DH) had 174,000 employees and nearly 900 stores in 33 states, in three major businesses: Target, Mervyn's, and the department store chain, which includes Dayton, Hudson, and Marshall Fields. Target's more than 500 stores are located primarily in the Midwest, Southeast, and Southwest. Mervyn's over 200 stores are primarily in the West (California), and the 60-odd department stores are found mostly in the Midwest. In 1967, when DH went public, 46 percent of its business came from its department stores, 30 percent from specialty retailers, and 23 percent from Target. Today, the Target stores account for more than 60 percent of DH's revenues.[2]

Divisional Performance

Target started operations the same year as its main competitors, Wal-Mart and Kmart, but it is substantially smaller. While Wal-Mart has sales of more than $55 billion and Kmart has sales of more than $39 billion, Target's sales are about $10 billion. Target is able to compete with these retailing giants because of the unique niche it has carved. It not only offers general merchandise (e.g., toothpaste) at a discount, but provides inexpensive, fashionable items (apparel and home fashions) in stores that it tries to make consistently good looking.

In contrast, Mervyn's has been in constant trouble. In 1993, DH's revenues increased to $19.2 billion from $17.9 billion, and its operating profits grew to $1.11 billion from $1.09 billion. Net income of $375 million was 2.1 percent higher than the prior year. Target's operating profit grew by $80 million and operating profit by $40 million. But Mervyn's sales declined from $4.5 billion to $4.4 billion and its profits fell by more than 37 percent. Sales were up by 7 percent at Target and up by 6 percent at the department stores while at Mervyn's they declined by 1 percent.[3]

While some of Mervyn's problems can be attributed to the weak California economy, Mervyn's straddles the line between department store and discounter, and has no stable niche. Mostly, it competes with Sears and Penneys, but it must also fend off challenges from both the lower-priced discount chains (e.g., Wal-Mart, Kmart) and the more "trendy" department stores (e.g., Nordstrom's, Bloomingdales, Macy's, Saks Fifth Avenue, and Neiman-Marcus). For years, Mervyn's has been a deadweight on DH's earnings, and the company has been seeking a way to turn it around.

Executive Turnover

In the summer of 1994, Kenneth Macke, DH's CEO, was forced to retire after 10 years.[4] Macke had many accomplishments to his credit. He divested the firm's specialty retailers (including the bookseller, B. Dalton) and concentrated the company's capital in Target. Thanks in large part to the stock market crash of October 1987, he repelled a $6 billion hostile takeover attempt by the Haft family, owners of Crown Books and a drugstore chain. The State of Minnesota passed anti-takeover legislation, making it the responsibility of managers not only to offer the highest return to shareholders but to serve all of a corporation's stakeholders including customers, suppliers, and communities (see Exhibit 1).

Macke, however, was unable to achieve the consistent 15 percent per year earnings growth that shareholders expected. Since 1987, DH's earnings had been very inconsistent, with 1992 profits below levels posted in 1989 and 1990.

Macke's successor was Robert Ulrich. Like Macke, Ulrich was formerly head of the Target division. He had advanced upward in the company by means of marketing and merchandising skills. Described as intensely competitive, aggressive, and creative, he was an analytical and aloof person who presumably would be able to make the tough decisions DH needed to become more profitable.[5]

Media and community groups asked Ulrich about his vision for Dayton Hudson. Community groups were especially anxious that his drive to strengthen the company economically might lead to a reversal in the pattern of the company's historic giving.

Exhibit 1 Minnesota Anti-Takeover Legislation

- The board of directors of a target company are supposed to take into account the interests of a wide variety of groups in exercising business judgment.
- The board is authorized to consider the "interests of employees, customers, suppliers, creditors, the economy of the state and nation, community and societal considerations, long-term and short-term interests of shareholders, including the possibility that these interests may be best served by the continued independence of corporations."
- The law prohibits the sale of the target company's assets to pay debts incurred in financing a hostile takeover for five years.
- Golden parachutes and the payment of greenmail are virtually prohibited.
- Approval of a majority of disinterested shareholders is required before a bidder can gain voting rights for a controlling share of the stock.
- Approval of a majority of the disinterested members of the board of directors (those who are neither managers nor representatives of the bidders) is required before the bidder can enter any business combination with the target company.

Strategy for the Divisions

For DH's divisions, Ulrich had specific economic goals. He wanted to enhance Target's reputation for value pricing. The advertising campaign was "Expect More, Pay Less." Like Wal-Mart, DH granted store managers the autonomy to learn the competitors' lowest prices. Managers could then reduce prices in response. This strategy cut into margins, but it was meant to achieve higher comparable store sales.

Ulrich's aim was to transfer the value pricing scheme to Mervyn's. Already, he had sent a SWOT team from Target to Mervyn's to slash prices to boost sales. To keep inventories at a minimum and sales high, he also had Mervyn's switch from private label goods to brand names.

His strategy for the department stores also involved lower prices. His aim was to lower the gap between the department stores and the more moderately priced retailers like Penney. He wanted to broaden the department store base and attract more price-conscious shoppers.

Cost-Cutting. In many ways DH was far behind Wal-Mart and even Kmart in crucial areas such as opening new superstores, which combine food and general merchandise, and entering global markets. To get prices down in all three divisions and to revive Mervyn's would be a large challenge. Carrying through would require major cost-cutting.

Cost-cutting always had been a way of life at DH. The company pushed suppliers very hard so that the savings could be passed on to customers. It had never hesitated to lay off workers when necessary. After buying Marshall Fields for $1.1 billion in 1990 and integrating it with its own computer system, DH layed off more than 1,000 Field employees in buying, marketing, information systems, and finance. Soon after DH consolidated its warehouse and distribution centers (from six to four) and eliminated more than 600 jobs. In 1992, it cut more than 600 jobs from its Minnesota department stores. DH also proved a very tough bargainer with Hudson employees, who voted in 1990 to join the UAW.

Unique MCI Contract. Perhaps, the most unique relation with a supplier was the contract DH established with MCI. This deal originated in DH procuring the services of EPIC USA, a telecommunications and information systems consulting group. It asked EPIC to help set up a long-distance network with a single vendor. The purpose was to take advantage of economies of scale through bulk purchases, something that had not been previously tried.

MCI was hired as the sole vendor for all of DH's stores, which were placed under a single telecommunications umbrella that would handle long-distance and video transmission, critical store inventories, and credit card information. The new pooling of services was expected to reduce telecommunications costs by 10 percent.[6]

Streamlining the Organization. Ulrich also cut unnecessary management levels in an effort to streamline the organization and speed up decision making. In his view, speed was a way of life. Unnecessary barriers between divisions had to be broken down and decision making had to become more rapid. Ulrich cleaned house and eliminated many top level positions (e.g., the vice chair and chief administrative officer at the department store division).

Micromarketing. Another Ulrich initiative was to enhance DH's capacity for micromarketing. Micromarketing was the effort to customize a local trend at a particular store or a particular group of stores based on the climatic, ethnic, legal, geographic, and social differences of markets (e.g., selling unique logo-bearing apparel in different markets). Ulrich was prepared to spend one-third of DH's capital budget on technology to improve its operations and distribution capabilities by means of sophisticated inventory management methods that could predict consumer demand for colors, sizes, and styles on a store-by-store basis.

Community Contributions

DH had a reputation for community giving. It made grants to the Minnesota Orchestra and to public television. It gave money to hurricane victims, to Habitat for Humanity to build homes, and it helped start, with prominent child care organizations, a nationwide public service campaign to educate parents about quality day care and how to find it. Yet, its community involvement sometimes got the company into trouble. It got caught between pro-life and pro-choice forces on the abortion issue. It gave money to Planned Parenthood, and it faced a temporary boycott of its stores. Also, gay and lesbian groups accused it of being one of 11 U.S. companies that had regressive workplace policies. DH's response was to deny having these policies and to announce that it would be selling a new line of gay and lesbian greeting cards.[7] How DH would handle such social issues also would have a bearing on its future.

Former chairman Macke had written about the company:

> Our . . . philosophy has always been that we exist to serve society—not just to make money . . . The Dayton Family built this company on a broad definition of success: we succeed when we are good stewards for all stakeholders. Since 1946 we have invested considerable leadership—and 5 percent of our federally taxable income—in social action and arts programs in the communities where we operate . . . I believe the communities we are in are stronger for the effort. Healthy communities are more livable and productive for everyone including retailers. Over time our philosophy has also given us a competitive advantage. It affects everything from sales to purchasing and recruiting—even takeover defense. It's part of our identity, and it works for us and the communities we serve.[8]

The Dayton Foundation was set up by the Dayton family in 1917 to promote "the welfare of mankind everywhere in the world." In 1976, when the family still owned about 40 percent of the common stock, Kenneth Dayton commented: "Our current practices grew out of a private sense of social obligation that my grandfather had when he started this company. He was a very charitable man who made substantial contributions to the community." Bruce Dayton, another member of the founding family, said: "Business can take the initiative in addressing the priority needs of our society."[9]

Like other companies, DH's stated goal was growth and return on equity: "to grow and earn at a rate commensurate with the best in the industry." However, it also had a policy of using 5 percent of its federal taxable income (the maximum allowed under the tax code) "to improve the quality of life" in the communities in which the corporation and its operating companies are located.[10]

Conservative shareholders mocked such practices. In 1973, DH was virtually alone among U.S. companies giving 5 percent to social programs. It took a leadership role in encouraging other Twin Cities companies to set up such programs; in 1976, the Chamber of Commerce formally set up a "Five Percent" club for Twin City firms. DH's contribution policies were somewhat different from other companies in that they emphasized social action and the arts, not health, welfare, and education. Some of the funds were given by operating companies directly to their local communities, and most were spent in Minnesota. In 1974, when profits fell and the company's stock reached an all time low, the contribution program was reviewed, but the company decided to maintain its "unique leadership posture."[11] DH also had formal programs in equal employment and advancement opportunity, consumerism, energy conservation, environmental impact, and community development. Each year the heads of the operating companies had to report on their social responsibility programs, and about 5 percent of their incentive compensation was based on their social performance.[12]

First among Retailers for Social Responsibility

In 1993, a *Fortune* magazine survey ranked DH first among retailers for social responsibility. Its community contributions cost it $24 million that year, the largest sum for a U.S. retailer. It was included in *The 100 Best Companies to Work for in America* and *The Best Companies for Minorities*.

Its community involvement gave it a distinctive position in the marketplace (see Exhibit 2). New CEO Ulrich was asked about his views by anxious community groups concerned that his drive to cut costs and strengthen the company financially would leave DH less committed to its historic social policies.

What should Ulrich do? What is the best way for him to align the company's community involvement with its need to become more profitable?

Discussion Questions

1. What were the reasons for Macke's retirement?
2. What is Ulrich supposed to be doing as his replacement?
3. What effect will Ulrich's plans have on Dayton Hudson's history of community giving?
4. Should Dayton Hudson revise its past approaches to community involvement?

EXHIBIT 2 Dayton Hudson: 1993 Community Involvement

- Dayton Hudson's $10 million, seven-year Child Care Aware initiative has trained more than 9,000 child care providers in 32 communities located in 18 states.
- Dayton Hudson made a $140,000 grant to KLRN-TV in San Antonio, Texas, to support production of "Heritage," a 13-week series on a range of contemporary issues produced from a Latino perspective.
- Dayton Hudson awarded $50,000 to Christians United in Business Endeavors for the Genesis Project in Detroit, an employment program for economically disadvantaged youth.
- Our social action giving helps people, including young people, to prepare themselves and their families for fully independent economic and social participation in society. Our employment strategies help women to leave or avoid welfare and assist others to succeed at work and in careers.
- Our arts giving promotes excellence and innovation in artistic expression. The Comprehensive Arts Support Program (CASP) encourages selected arts organizations to set goals and objectives and to measure results. CASP now supports the efforts of the largest budgeted arts organizations in Chicago and the Twin Cities.
- Dayton Hudson donated $50,000 to Loring Nicollet Bethlehem Community Center in Minneapolis for a variety of inner city education and employment programs, including a "reverse commute" program, placing adults in suburban workplaces.
- Dayton Hudson divisions embarked on several new partnerships, including the participation of Marshall Field's in the Chicago Arts Partnership and Target's commitment to Habitat for Humanity, through which 50 new homes for low-income families will be built by the end of 1994.
- Our employees are active in countless local civic and volunteer projects. This dedication is exemplified by our combined employee and corporate support of the United Way, which totaled more than $13 million in 1993.
- Dayton Hudson donated more than $230,000 through the American Red Cross to assist victims of flooding along the Mississippi basin and of fire and earthquake in Southern California. Additional merchandise donations of blankets, hygiene products, bottled water, diapers, and formula were also made.
- Dayton Huson continued to receive numerous awards for community giving activities. Awards included the Silver Anvil Award from the Public Relations Society of America, the Sidney R. Yates Arts Advocacy Award in Illinois, the United Way of America Summit Award for Volunteerism, as well as citations from various governors, state legislators, and state education and child care associations.

EXHIBIT 2 *(concluded)*

Dayton Hudson Foundation/Corporation

Dayton Hudson Foundation manages contributions to Minneapolis/St. Paul metropolitan area programs for the Corporation and Twin Cities-based operations, Target and Dayton's. The Foundation also manages a small national giving program and provides major funding for special initiatives of all operating divisions. The Foundation's giving priorities are to assist economically dependent adults to achieve long-term work in the mainstream economy, and to develop and sustain professional arts programs and the work of living artists.

1993 Grants	*Number*	*$*
Twin Cities		
Social Action	108	$2,862,100
Arts	71	2,969,528
Miscellaneous	19	500,560
Other	2	128,350
National	48	539,800
Corporate	58	275,998
Total	306	$7,276,336

1993 Grants by Focus	*$*
Social Action	$10,600,380
Arts	9,870,024
Miscellaneous	3,505,727
Total	$23,976,131

1993 Key State Grants	*$*
California	$ 4,838,257
Florida	874,917
Illinois	1,711,504
Michigan	2,053,397
Minnesota	7,072,316
Texas	1,509,261
Other States	5,916,479
Total	$23,976,131

Mervyn's

1993 Grants	*Number*	*$*
Social Action	360	$1,681,755
Arts	177	2,140,370
Miscellaneous	140	683,902
Total	677	$4,506,027

Target

1993 Grants	*Number*	*$*
Social Action	813	$4,581,048
Arts	690	3,098,225
Miscellaneous	220	1,609,860
Total	1723	$9,289,133

The Department Store Division

1993 Grants	*Number*	*$*
Social Action	168	$1,152,200
Arts	212	1,408,401
Miscellaneous	142	344,034
Total	522	$2,904,635

Endnotes

1. This case was written by Alfred Marcus.
2. Dayton Hudson Corporation, *Annual Report* 1993.
3. "Dayton Hudson President Predicts Turnaround for Troubled Mervyn's Chain Within the Next Year," *Star Tribune*, June 25, 1994, p. 1D.
4. "Top Dayton Hudson Officer Retiring," *The New York Times*, April 15, 1994, p. 4D; "Ken Macke Exits Top Job at Dayton Hudson," Minneapolis-St. Paul *Star Tribune*, April 15, 1994, p. 1A.
5. "Company News; Dayton Hudson Plant to Test Supercenter Format," *The New York Times*, March 12, 1994, p. 37, Section 1; "New Dayton Hudson CEO Seen as Aggressive, Creative; Ulrich got Target Center Name; Launched Attack on Wal-Mart Ads," *Minneapolis Star Tribune*, April 15, 1994, p. 1D; "New Dayton Hudson CEO Starts Cleaning House, Arranging Team; Vice Chairman's Job Eliminated; Target Chief Named," *Minneapolis Star Tribune*, April 30, 1994, p. 1D; "Grabbing Dayton Hudson by the Throat," *Business Week*, May 2, 1994, p. 38; Sally Apgar, "Dayton's Due for a Makeover," *Minneapolis Star Tribune*, June 21, 1994; Sally Apgar, "Is Target the Aim of Dayton Hudson?" *Minneapolis Star Tribune*, Jan. 16, 1995, pp. 1–5D.
6. "Dayton Hudson Chooses MCI for Communications; Single System for all Stores Is Expected to Reduce Retailer's Costs by 10 Percent," *Minneapolis Star Tribune*, March 25, 1994, p. 3D.
7. "Gay and Lesbian Theme Greeting Cards are in the Cards at Dayton Hudson; Dayton's Store in Minneapolis, Two Field's in Chicago Will Test Cardthartic Line," *Minneapolis Star Tribune*, February 17, 1994, p. 1D.
8. Doug Tompkins, Ralph Nader, et al., "The Meaning Limits, and Promise of Socially Responsible Business," *Utne Reader*, September–October 1993, pp. 67–74.
9. Canthorn, Dayton Hudson Corporation.
10. Ibid.
11. Dayton Hudson Corporation, *Annual Report*, 1986; Dayton Hudson Corporation, *Community Involvement Report*, 1989; Dayton Hudson Corporation grants list, 1989; Canthorn, Dayton Hudson Corporation.
12. Ibid.

Case 3–B
Ceridian
On the Right Track?[1]

In 1993, Larry Perlman was the 13th highest paid CEO in the Twin Cities. His base salary was $600,000 and his total compensation with bonuses earned him more than $1 million that year.[2] After spinning off Control Data Systems (CDS) to shareholders in 1992, for the first time in 10 years Ceridian had two straight years of profitability (see Exhibit 1). Perlman had to decide if Ceridian finally was on the right track. Had he moved it beyond the visionary ideas of its founder and dominant figure, William Norris, into a niche where it could effectively compete in the long run?

Synopsis of Ceridian

The newly reconstituted Ceridian employed 7,600 people and provided businesses with payroll processing, employer, and human resource services. It supplied technology-based services and products to defense and governments worldwide and did media and marketing research. It had a growing presence in the tax-filing market. In 1993 it purchased Systems Tax Services, an electronic tax-filing company. It also acquired Tesseract, a key purchase because it brought in new customers and saved Ceridian $15 million in software development costs. Ceridian was well-positioned to benefit from a

EXHIBIT 1 Ceridian's Financial History
(in millions of dollars)

	Revenues	*Net Profits*	*Net Worth*
1984	$5,027	$ 90	$1,776
1985	3,680	(256)	1,203
1986	3,347	(37)	991
1987	3,367	(111)	1,048
1988	3,628	2	1,054
1989	2,935	(13)	412
1990	1,691	31	457
1991	1,525	(7)	446
1992	830	39	101
1993	886	50	111

pattern of increased outsourcing of such data processing functions. More and more companies were subcontracting their information technology needs and focusing on their core activities, which would work to Ceridian's advantage.[3]

Control Data Systems (CDS)

Now independent of Ceridian, Control Data Systems (CDS) was doing better, but was still having troubles. In 1993, it had a profitable year. It earned about $8 million on revenues of more than $400 million,[4] but was still not close its goal of increasing earnings to 10 percent of revenues. CDS was shifting from its proprietary Cyber mainframe toward reselling computers from a variety of vendors. Its goal was to be a systems integrator that would mix and match different suppliers' machines. It continued to employ about 3,000 people worldwide, but in 1993 had to announce cutbacks of 6 percent of its workforce because of the European recession and delays in obtaining export licenses for computers ordered by China. The cutbacks were financed out of a $60 million reserve fund set up for downsizing.

Perlman's Speech to Employees. In October 1993, Perlman addressed Ceridian employees:

> Today, few companies can realistically offer stable, lifelong employment. Ever-changing technologies create volatile markets. The rapid growth of markets outside the United States makes the global competitiveness of American goods and services more critical than ever. Taken together, these factors means that companies often have to move very quickly, creating abrupt and painful transitions for people caught in their midst.
>
> This is a fundamental national problem. Since 1989, the United States has lost 1.6 million manufacturing jobs. And it isn't just a manufacturing sector issue. Between 1979 and 1992, the Fortune 500 companies terminated an average 340,000 people a year. Unemployment for managers in the United States has increased three and a half times faster than the overall unemployment rate. When you bring these macroeconomic forces down to the individual company level, it means decisions that affect individuals, not statistics. That is where pain occurs. Ceridian is not immune to these forces. To grow and be profitable, we are constantly reviewing—and changing if necessary—the mix of businesses and the products that each one offers. As part of the strategic planning process, we ask of each business: Is this the best investment to build value for shareholders? . . . We can't afford to ignore these questions . . . We have to make decisions and act every day for the ultimate good of shareholders . . . These decisions often affect people's jobs . . . For all the above reasons, the ideas about work life that most of us grew up with—job security, comprehensive benefits, a one-career work life—have changed dramatically. This leads people to feel disconnected and, frankly, a little bit

lost. It's hard to ask people for loyalty when we can't guarantee jobs. What we can do is redesign work so that individual experiences are positive. By empowering employees to operate as freely and flexibly as possible, we can compensate for some of the insecurity we feel and at the same time create a strong company that can provide a more valuable employment experience.

We can also focus on developing a sense of community within Ceridian so that people feel some responsibility for each other and for the organization. I am convinced that having a sense that we belong to a community and that we care about the people around us is worth working for.[5]

Repositioning the Company

Ceridian thought that people saw the company as a quality provider of payroll and human resource services but did not believe that the image accurately portrayed all that it did. Therefore, it interviewed industry consultants, over 100 customers, and account and sales representatives. Not surprisingly, Ceridian learned that it presented many different faces: a supplier of payroll and other services, an information management company, an employer services company, and as a competitor of ADP.

The message to the marketplace was confusing. So, the company tried to reformulate its mission statement: "We create tools that help employers manage the employment relationship."[6]

The company's vision was "to become the premier partner in providing exciting, quality solutions that enable our customers to optimize their most important asset—their people."[7] Ceridian was trying to help companies maintain and manage a quality, diverse workforce. It met employer needs for payroll processing, human resources management, tax filing, employee assistance, and benefits administration. The benefits of outsourcing for a customer were lower operating costs and less burden on in-house staff. The new positioning statement was going to be built into training and sales material and would be the driving force for decisions about product enhancements and development.

The Employee Assistance Program: EAR. An important part of the strategy was to better leverage its employee assistance program, called EAR (Employee Advisory Resource). Statistics showed that at any given time, 15 to 20 percent of the U.S. population need help with a problem: alcohol or chemical abuse; emotional, financial, or legal problems; family problems; and problems in the workplace. Employees had to struggle with problems that distracted them from their jobs, lowered their productivity, and possibly affected their long-term health and well-being.

EAR provided employees with immediate telephone access to professional counselors 24 hours a day, seven days a week. The calls were confidential and anonymous when desired. EAR was composed of professional trained staff in mental health, substance abuse, work-related problems, and law. It had a network of resources around the country to help with long-term problems requiring in-person contact.

Ceridian's Origins

From its roots in the Control Data Corporation, Ceridian had come a long way. Control Data Corporation was started in July 1957, when William Norris and 11 other engineers defected from Univac (Sperry-Rand). By 1986 Control Data had $2.6 billion in assets and $3.3 billion in sales, making it one of the major players in the computer business. CDC was recognized as a BUNCH member (Burroughs, Univac, NCR, CDC, Honeywell) chasing industry leader IBM.

The primary business of CDC was computing hardware, peripheral equipment, and computer services. CDC's initial expertise evolved around developing computing power for the scientific, engineering, aerospace, and defense markets. It pioneered a program in which it built the world's first supercomputer under the guidance of Seymour Cray. (Cray later left CDC and started his own company.)

Industry pressures forced CDC to diversify from hardware to computer services in the early 1960s. It first moved into markets for general peripheral products (for the original-equipment manufacturer market) and data services. The peripheral products division grew rapidly, fueled by the growth of minicomputers and to some extent microcomputers in the 1960s–1970s. By 1982 peripherals were a billion-dollar business, and with nearly half of the disk drive market, CDC dominated the peripherals industry.[8]

CDC used its mainframe capabilities to establish time-sharing and data processing services. Engineering and professional services also became important revenue sources. CDC also provided support services for these programs. Perhaps CDC's most ambitious endeavor in the nonhardware area was the development of the PLATO system. PLATO utilized minicomputers to run software for training and educational programs for businesses and government agencies and secondary school students. By late 1987, the company's investment in PLATO was nearing $1 billion, yet the operation had never covered its costs.[9]

Commercial Credit Corporation (CCC) was a large independent financing company, which CDC purchased in 1968 to provide leasing arrangements for purchasers of its large mainframe systems. While providing the needed cash infusion and leasing services that CDC required in the late 1960s and early 1970s, CCC was never successfully assimilated. In 1987, the company gave up its final 18.3 percent stake in CCC.[10]

Problems at CDC. The year leading up to these sales was not a happy one for CDC. In 1985, CDC posted record losses during a general slump in the computer industry.[11] The peripheral products group, once CDC's "cash cow," was hit hard by competition from Japan and lower margins per unit. Gross margins on sales and rentals of computer equipment dropped 12 percent from the year before. Lenders refused to advance more money, and the company had to sell some assets to raise money.[12]

Declining product quality was another contributor to CDC's troubles. The company did not spend enough money to stay on the leading edge of computer technology. CDC also did not anticipate the proliferation of personal computers, which proved detrimental to its computer service business. Demand for mainframes was flat and the development of a new supercomputer drained the company's resources.[13]

Despite these difficulties, many critics focused on the controversial views of its founder William Norris. They criticized his autocratic management style, citing it as a contributing factor in CDC's downturn. He was said to "manage by intuition," refusing to allow market research on the need for PLATO before it began operations.[14] He refused to allow marketing research before launching PLATO because it would "uncover all the problems" and "we'd never go into it."[15]

Business Week said CDC had to dispose of some assets and William Norris was one of them.[16] In the early days, decisions had been made at the lowest possible level with the support of upper-level management. This created an entrepreneurial environment, but when Norris moved away from involvement in day-to-day operations and into social responsibility programs, the company's financial performance began to deteriorate.

William Norris's Vision

> One of the great delusions of our time is that government alone is primarily responsible for meeting the major needs of society. Unfortunately, that has proven to be neither achievable nor realistic because our society has been going downhill . . . Deterioration in our society will continue unless and until substantial corporate resources are invested to help meet major needs as profit-making opportunities in cooperation with government and other sectors.[17]—William Norris (1986)

CDC possessed unique resources, notably technology, to meet these unmet social needs. The challenge was to find ways to convert society's unmet needs into profitable business opportunities.[18]

Norris was confident that his strategic direction would strongly position Control Data for the next quarter century. Norris believed government and charities were limited in the amount of social amelioration they could accomplish. Business should take the lead. Government was relegated to a support role for CDC. Government should provide incentives (e.g., enterprise zones, tax breaks) to encourage the private sector to partake in social programs.[19] However, Norris also believed that business social programs should not be handouts. He said that such programs must "be a business success before [they] can be a social success."[20] By 1979, CDC had a 15-member committee with an annual budget of $3 million to develop programs that would address social problems.

Cooperation between business, government, and social groups was part of the business strategy of CDC, and CDC joined the government in a number of social ventures.[21] Some of CDC's ventures with the government can be traced to the military background of its founders, but others resulted from rising technology transfer and diffusion in the world. The EAR program was a successful surviving program that CDC initiated under Norris's direction.

Larry Perlman's Vision

> There is no measurement of earnestness per share or trying per share or good intentions per share. Only earnings per share count.—Larry Perlman (1987)

Larry Perlman, who came after Norris in 1987, was known as a "troubleshooter" who had the ability to turn companies around. An intensely competitive person, he was aware that he was operating in a very difficult situation. His appointment as CDC's president was the toughest assignment he had to face.[22]

A St. Paul native, Perlman earned a law degree from Harvard after doing his undergraduate work at Carleton College. For 14 years he had practiced law before becoming general counsel at Medtronic, a medical device manufacturer in the Twin Cities. When Medtronic's U.S. pacemaker division was suffering from product quality problems, declining credibility, and dwindling market share, Perlman was asked to head the division. He did so successfully for three years before returning to private law practice.

Perlman was a "small" and "compact" person who looked like the skier, runner, fly fisherman, and squash and tennis player that he was. There was "something efficient about him." He seemed "to contain no unnecessary material, nothing lanky or bulky." In a 1985 speech, however, Perlman condemned the "lone ranger style of management—the classic male tough guy, solitary and imperturbable," and he blamed the problems women were having in reaching upper management positions on men's inability "to accept the female characteristics they themselves have—sensitivity, intuition, and eagerness to cooperate as well as compete."[23]

Perlman joined CDC in 1980 first as general counsel and then as head of Commercial Credit Corporation (CCC) which had got into trouble when it ventured into too many businesses and its expenses were higher than those of its competitors. First, Perlman cut back CCC to the businesses where it did well. Then he recommended that CDC sell the division, arguing that as a computer manufacturing and service company it could not successfully compete in the financial industry. The decision to sell Commercial Credit was controversial because CCC had been an important contributor to CDC's earnings.[24] As executive vice president of the company and president of its Data Storage Products Group (DSP), his next assignment, Perlman learned what it meant to battle for survival. In 1985 DSP had $800 million in assets and 20,000 employees. He cut both in half, firing three quarters of DSP's upper-level executives. Perlman, however, did not view himself as a hatchet man. He believed that the work force reductions were "necessary to get expenses down."[25] DSP was basically a manufacturing operation in a company that was becoming increasingly committed to providing computer services.

Now, Larry Perlman had to make sure that he was on the right track in steering Ceridian into the future. Did it have the right business strategy? Did it have the right social philosophy? How should it forge an appropriate connection between its business and social philosophies?

Discussion Questions

1. What do you think of William Norris' social vision? To what extent does his social vision relate to Control Data's declining financial performance?
2. How does Larry Perlman differ from William Norris? What situation does he confront? What changes has he made? Have these changes been for the better?
3. Has Ceridian totally abandoned the legacy of William Norris because of its financial troubles? Should Norris's vision of social responsibility play any role in the company?
4. Is Ceridian on the right track? What should Perlman do now?

Endnotes

1. This case was prepared by Alfred Marcus and Douglas Schuller with assistance from Mark Jankus.
2. "Executive Compensation: What Twin Cities Executives Are Making," *Minneapolis Star Tribune*, Oct. 18, 1993, p. 4D.
3. Ceridian, "Repositioning for the 1990s and Beyond," *Inside Focus*, special edition 8, no. 7.
4. Steve Alexander, "Control Data Systems Earns $982,000," *Minneapolis Star Tribune*, Oct. 22, 1993, p. 4D.
5. "Interview with Larry Perlman," *Current* (company publication), October 1993, pp. 1–2.
6. Ibid.
7. Ibid.
8. F. S. Worthy, *William C. Norris: Portrait of a Maverick*.
9. *Value Line Investment Survey*, November 6, 1987, p. 1089.
10. Standard & Poor Corporation, "Company Profile Report, Control Data Corporation," October 22, 1987, pp. 1–4.
11. R. Broderick, "Corporate Culture: Norris at Colonnus," *Corporate Report Minnesota*, February 1986, p. 126.
12. D. Hertzberg, "As GAF Pursues, Will Carbide Adopt Pac Man Defense?" *The Wall Street Journal*, December 10, 1985, p. 3; P. Houston and G. Bock, "Control Data's Struggle to Come Back from the Brink," *Business Week* 14 (1985), pp. 62–63.
13. Broderick, "Corporate Culture"; Worthy, *William C. Norris*.
14. F. S. Worthy, "Does Control Data Have a Future?" *Fortune*, December 23, 1985, pp. 24–26.
15. Eric J. Savitz, "The Vision Thing," *Barron's*, May 7, 1990, p. 10; Worthy, "Does Control Data Have a Future?" pp. 24–26.
16. G. Bock, "Has the Street Given Up on Control Data?" *Business Week* 30 (1985), pp. 48–49.
17. W. C. Norris, "Applying Technology: The Key to the Future," *Journal of Business Strategy* 6 (1986), pp. 38–46.
18. D. Kelly, "Doing Well Doing Good," *Corporate Report Minnesota*, December 1981, pp. 106–8.
19. Norris, "Applying Technology."
20. Worthy, *William C. Norris*, p. 114.
21. J. P. Shannon, "Choose Partners and Dance," *Corporate Report Minnesota*, June 1983, p. 158.
22. D. J. Tice, "Troubleshooter," *Corporate Report Minnesota*, September 1987, pp. 72–77.
23. Ibid.
24. J. Dubashi, "The Do-Gooder," *Financial World*, June 27, 1989, pp. 70–74; Tice, "Troubleshooter."
25. Tice, "Troubleshooter."

CHAPTER

4

Financial and Social Performance

It is a stunning if disturbing fact of corporate life in the 1990s. A lot of senior people at very large companies have no idea what made their organizations successful.

Stephen Fraidin, Fried, Frank Harris Shriver & Jacobson, 1994

If you don't demand something out of the ordinary, you won't get anything but ordinary results.

Charles Jones, EDS, 1994

There is no evidence anywhere that ramming something down people's throats is an effective management tool.

Peter Scott-Morgan, Arthur D. Little, 1994

Introduction and Chapter Objectives

How do we know a firm is doing well? How should we evaluate its performance? Some of the financial and nonfinancial aspects of firm performance are discussed in this chapter. The organization's social performance—its ability to satisfy external constituencies—is considered, and the relationships between social and financial performance are discussed.

Judging Success

The ability to cope with external change is critical to an organization's success, but by what measure do you judge this success? Useful performance measures help assess the quality of a firm's adaptation to changing external conditions, but performance must be defined. The concept may seem simple, but it has been the subject of great debate.[1]

Basic Terminology and Definitions

Although performance is at the core of management and is the test of any strategy, there is less than complete agreement about basic terminology and definitions. A number of issues have impeded efforts to achieve a consensus.

1. What is the appropriate *level of analysis*—the individual, the work unit, or the organization as a whole? Should concern center on the business unit or the corporate entity?

2. How should the concept of performance be differentiated from *organizational effectiveness*, which includes nonfinancial aspects of success and includes the human and ethical aspects of the organization? The organization has to be judged for meeting broader societal expectations as well as for meeting the financial goals of investors.[2]

Measurement

accounting measures Record a firm's past performance.

financial measures Capture investors' anticipation of a firm's future performance.

Evaluation of measurement approaches should lead to improved understanding of the underlying concept of performance, but difficulties remain. Two types of basic economic indicators exist: (1) **Accounting measures** include sales growth, profitability (return on investment, return on sales, return on equity), and earnings per share. (2) **Financial measures** (the stock market valuation of the company) include stock returns, market to book value, and Tobin's Q (ratio of market value to replacement cost of assets). Accounting measures record past performance; financial measures capture the investors' sense of a company's future potential. For example, biotech firms often make no profits (accounting), but they have high stock market values because of their performance potential.

Limited reliance should be placed on investor impressions because it is difficult for investors to accurately assess a company's future potential. Accounting data also may be limited; there is ample scope for manipulation through different depreciation policies and the varied treatment of certain revenue and expenditure items.[3]

In assessing a firm's performance, one needs some relevant basis for comparison. Firms differ depending on the markets in which they compete. Typically, in benchmarking a company's performance, you compare it with that of its competitors or you compare it to the performance of a large sample of all other companies, such as the Fortune 500 listing of major manufacturers. Also, it is necessary to have a historical perspective, to examine trends over time (see the Real-World Example on the next page).

Complications

Assessing a firm's performance obviously is complicated. Performance is largely a result of *operational success* in key areas such as market share, new product introduction, product quality, marketing effectiveness, manufacturing, and technological efficiency. However, operational success is hard to measure.

In their best-selling book on "excellent companies," T. J. Peters and R. H. Waterman used a simple financial screen to distinguish "excellent" from the "nonexcellent" companies. A firm had to be in the top half of its industry in four of the six measures Peters and Waterman used: compound asset growth, compound equity growth, ratio of market to book value, average return on total capital, average return on equity, and average return on sales.[4] These measures, however, do not capture such important dimensions as the quality of internal processes or the ability to manage external stakeholders, such groups as shareholders, suppliers, customers, employees, communities, and government.[5]

Real-World Example

SciMed Life

SciMed Life Systems is a manufacturer of disposable devices used in the treatment of coronary heart disease, primarily catheters for use in angioplasty procedures. It employs 1,300 people. Total 1993 sales and those of its competitors are listed below:

Eli Lilly & Co.	$6.50 billion
Medtronic, Inc.	$1.40 billion
SciMed Life	$ .26 billion
Cordis Corp.	$ .26 billion
St. Jude Medical	$ .25 billion
Datascope Corp.	$ .17 billion

In 1993, SciMed Life earned $50 million in profits, and its operating margins were 34 percent, the second highest among its competitors, a place SciMed Life has occupied since 1989. Operating margins in this high-risk sector generally were well above the industry average of 13.5 percent. Though still very strong, SciMed Life's margins had been declining since 1991. Lilly, Medtronic, St. Jude, and Cordis had more stable margins than SciMed Life and their margins had been growing.

SciMed Life's net profit margins or return on sales in 1993 were 18.8 percent. The company only became profitable in 1988 and its net margins, then at 14.3 percent, had expanded rapidly to peak at 28.7 percent in 1991, which put it second among its competitors. However, SciMed Life had been unable to sustain that position, and by 1993 it had dropped to third place. Net margins for its competitors were more stable and had been growing. SciMed Life's 1993 return on equity was 25 percent, but, with the exception of Datascope, all its competitors had done better.

SciMed Life's market performance in 1993, as measured by its price/earnings ratio of .88, compared to a large sample of companies (followed by the Value Line investment service was the lowest among its competitors). The company's P/E ratio had been going down for several years; in June 1994, Medtronic's P/E ratio was 1.24 while that of Cordis was 1.34.[6]

SciMed Life was profitable with high margins, high returns on capital and equity, and high employee productivity, but investors were not rewarding it chiefly because its economic performance compared with its competitors had been eroding. However, other factors were involved. The external environment provides some indication of what was happening. The maturing of the medical products business and the possibility that major health care legislation might be passed were taking their toll. Investors were uncertain about SciMed Life's expansion into Japan and Europe and the results of continued high spending on R&D. Moreover, SciMed Life had lost an important patent dispute with Pfizer and by 1995 would not be able to produce a profitable product (rapid-exchange catheters). Thus, its alignment with social forces made investors apprehensive.

Peters and Waterman also relied on a measure of innovativeness. Industry experts were asked to rate companies on their innovation record and their ability to adapt to changing circumstances. However, the ratings by industry experts capture only a single dimension of performance, and the judgment of experts may be a poor basis for evaluation.[7]

Different performance measures can be combined and analyzed together. A factor analysis of 14 indicators reveals four dimensions. Profitability/cash flow and relative market position capture the *static* elements of performance; change in profitability and cash flow and growth in sales and market share capture the *dynamic* elements. However, combining different dimensions of performance into a unified concept may be misleading since it masks conflicts and trade-offs, such as the conflict between long-term growth and short-term profitability.[8]

Bala Chakravarthy has distinguished excellent from nonexcellent companies in the computer industry by using measures based on nearness to bankruptcy, slack, and company reputation.[9] Nearness to bankruptcy is assessed using *Z scores*, which measure survivability by showing the limits below which a firm cannot slip. They are a function of working capital/total assets, retained earnings/total assets, earnings before interest and taxes/total assets, market value of equity/book value of total debt, and sales/total assets.[10]

slack
The resources remaining after a company has met its obligations to its primary stakeholders.

To examine company ability to adapt to future environments, the generation and investment of slack may be relevant. **Slack** is a measure of the cash remaining after the company has met its obligations to its primary stakeholders (i.e., customers, suppliers, shareholders, employees). Indicators of the capacity to generate slack are profitability (cash flow by investment, return on sales, and return on total capital), employee and capital productivity, and the ability to raise long-term resources (market-to-book and debt-to-equity ratios). Excellent firms are likely to generate and invest more slack than nonexcellent firms. Higher investments in research and development and in new product development will be particularly significant.[11]

Corporate reputation may be assessed using *Fortune* surveys of knowledgeable industry experts who have ranked firms based on their ability to satisfy stakeholders. The stakeholders are stockholders (quality of management, value as a long-term investment, financial soundness, use of assets), customers (quality of products, innovativeness), employees (ability to attract and keep), and community (social responsibility). However, their subjective quality places limits on the extent that reputational rankings can be used to distinguish excellent from nonexcellent companies.[12]

"Fit"

Based on the idea that performance reflects a match between key organizational characteristics and external conditions, the concept of "fit" can be used to differentiate companies. There is a need to establish fit between: (1) industry structure and competitive context; (2) organizational structure and external conditions; (3) management systems and organizational structure; and (4) management style and strategic context.[13] It may even be necessary to synchronize all the so-called "7–Ss"—strategy, structure, systems, style, shared values, staff, and skill. The concept of achieving a fit between the organization's strengths with environmental opportunities, however, is very complicated. Defining these concepts and assessing the fits an organization has with external conditions is difficult and time-consuming.

Effects That Cannot Be Captured by Economic Performance

These concepts are useful, but they only go so far because businesses affect society in ways that cannot always be captured. A full understanding of these effects and their relationships to a firm's economic performance is needed. Measuring a firm's social performance, however, is very tricky.[14] The social accounting movement in the United States quickly lost momentum not only because of measurement difficulties but also because firms did not want to set up additional accounting systems that had no generally accepted standards.

Social Performance

social performance An organization's capacity to meet demands and expectations of constituencies beyond those linked directly to its products and markets.

Social performance has been defined as the organization's ability to meet the demands and expectations of *external constituencies* beyond those linked directly to its products and markets. A better definition requires listing all the external constituents and measuring their satisfaction, obviously a very complicated task, which becomes more complicated because companies are selective concerning the stakeholders they take into consideration and the actions they take to develop relationships with them.[15]

A number of methods can be employed to assess social performance. First, you can do a content analysis of annual reports, but you must pay attention to the use of annual reports for purposes of impression management. The reports may systematically underrepresent the company's social performance because management does not want investors to know the costs; or the reports may systematically overrepresent the company's social involvement to create the impression of sensitivity to nonmarket factors and ward off attacks by social activists. Another reason for overrepresenting social performance in annual reports is to rationalize poor economic performance by claiming that it is a consequence of events beyond the company's control.[16]

You also can rely on the rankings of the Council of Economic Priorities (CEP). The CEP pollution performance index, for example, is based on an investigation of company pollution control records. However, it refers to only one aspect of social performance, and companies are selective in the types of social performance they choose to emphasize.[17] Moreover, the CEP rankings are the judgments of a particular organization with a point of view (pro-environmental) that may not be generally shared.

Social performance is also measured by reputational indexes that rely on the perceptions of individuals who are not direct constituents of the organization. Ratings of this type have been performed by an editor of *Business and Society Review*, business persons, and MBA students. *Fortune* magazine also provides a rating of corporate reputation to measure social performance. Still another method is to find out whether companies have social responsibility programs.[18] All of these methods are imperfect. At the end of this chapter is the MIT Sloan School of Management's questionnaire used to assess corporate social performance. MBA students devised this questionnaire to evaluate the social performance of the companies that recruit at the school (see Case 4–B).

Social Investment Funds

Socially responsible rating services and investment funds also evaluate company performance. Their aim is to help people invest with a "clean conscience."[19] They believe that socially responsible investments are likely to be profitable because companies that can deal creatively with pollution, safety, and employment problems will be innovative in other areas as well. Socially responsible investment in the United States grew from $4 billion in assets in 1984 to $62.5 billion in 1991.[20]

Kinder, Lydenberg, Domini & Company, an investment service specializing in "social choice" investing, has evaluated more than 800 companies in nine areas: community relations, employee relations, environment, military contracting, nuclear power, product liability, South African involvement, women and minority issues, and "other." Franklin Research and Development of Boston evaluates corporate environmental activities. The Dreyfus Third Century Fund ranks companies according to social criteria and then selects the most profitable ones for its investments. The Calvert Managed Growth Portfolio first assesses the financial performance of companies and then compares the companies with others in the industry on social issues. The New Alternatives Fund focuses on natural resource investments in solar and alternative energy companies.

The problem of course is that no consensus exists for what constitutes socially responsible investing. Definitions may be either more or less restrictive. Comparisons may be made within an industry or between industries. The socially responsible funds rely on government enforcement data and interviews with corporate officials. They may have trouble reconciling inconsistent company behavior; for example, Fort Howard Paper Company has played a leading role in recycling paper but it also has played "hardball politics," using "job blackmail," the threat that it may lay off workers, to get its way with the Wisconsin Clean Air Act. It is also the largest paper mill source of PBC, a chemical compound used in manufacturing that has harmful effects on humans.[21] Some of the funds emphasize "positives"—demonstrated commitment to the environment or efforts that go beyond legal requirements. They also tend to include corporations that sell systems to analyze, clean up, or protect the environment. Other funds emphasize "negatives," identifying companies whose records should keep investors away.

Connecting Economic and Social Performance

Though no single best way to assess social performance exists, it is useful to consider different relationships that can prevail between economic and social performance.

1. Profitability and social performance are *positively* related: Profitable firms are better social performers.
2. Profitability and social performance are *negatively* related: Profitable firms are poorer social performers.
3. The relationship between economic and social performance is *not linear:* Highly profitable and unprofitable firms, for example, are poor social performers.
4. There is *no relationship* between economic and social performance.[22]

1. A Positive Relationship. Why would a positive relationship exist between economic and social performance; that is, firms that have a good effect on society are also highly profitable? The direction of causation plays a very important role. Perhaps companies can afford to be "good." If economic performance influences social performance then well-to-do companies *can afford* good social performance. Their economic performance affects their capability to undertake programs to meet social demands. Firms need excess resources to be good social performers because social performance involves substantial costs and only firms with these resources are capable of absorbing these costs.[23]

If the direction of causation is reversed, a different interpretation is in order. Good social performance contributes to economic performance. It pays to be good. In what sense can this be true?

1. The *quality and skills* of good social management may also apply to the economic sphere; management excellence in one area has some bearing on excellence in the other. Socially aware and concerned management may possess the skills needed to run a superior company in the traditional financial sense. These skills may be sensitivity to outside forces and creative adjustment to external pressures.[24]
2. Social performance may benefit the corporation by creating *goodwill*, a very important asset because it exerts positive pressure on employees, customers, government officials, bankers, investors, and other important constituencies to be favorably disposed to the corporation.[25]
3. If a company is perceived as a good social performer, it may cause *employee morale* to rise and result in increased productivity. Fewer strikes and work stoppages can more than offset the costs of social responsibility.
4. A reputation for social performance may enhance *customer loyalty*. Satisfying customers' claims for perceived quality may be easier than satisfying their claims for better products.
5. Goodwill may ease tensions with *government officials*, making it less likely that the corporation will pay large fines or become involved in lengthy suits.

Good economic performance may be a precondition for good social performance, and it may be a consequence of good social performance. *Beneficent cycles* exist when strong economic performance contributes to strong social performance, which in turn contributes to strong economic performance. *Vicious cycles* exist when poor economic performance contributes to poor social performance, which in turn contributes to poor economic performance.[26]

The lives of two 19th-century American businessmen, Andrew Carnegie (founder of U.S. Steel) and Julius Rosenwald (founder of Sears), illustrate these approaches. Carnegie's approach was to be profitable in order to be philanthropic. By contrast, Rosenwald's philosophy was to identify social needs as the basis for profitable business opportunities. Both approaches represent enlightened self-interest. Peter Drucker writes that "in the years to come, the most needed and the most effective—indeed perhaps the only truly effective—approach . . . will be identifying social needs as the basis for profitable activities."[27]

Thus, the corporation can benefit from socially responsible behavior. By providing consumers with safe products, it assures their loyalty. By granting employees pleasant and safe working conditions, it reduces absenteeism and turnover and leads to increased productivity. By being a good corporate citizen and supporting the arts and charitable organizations, it enhances the quality of life and attracts a better quality workforce. Sensitivity to changing societal expectations makes the corporation a better financial performer; this in turn increases the chances for the corporation to be a better social performer.

2. "Bad" Firms That Prosper. Firms that have both a bad effect on society and are also highly profitable indicate a simple trade-off between social performance and economic performance. Firms cannot afford both. The bad firms prosper at the expense of society, while the good firms suffer on account of their social performance. Social performance is detrimental to economic performance because it imposes costs. Paying these costs puts the firm at disadvantage compared with competitors who have weak social performance. Milton Friedman argues that firms should not volunteer social performance activities because their primary obligation is to shareholders.[28]

3. A Nonlinear Relationship. The relationship between social and economic performance may not be linear. If not, it implies that too much social performance or too little is detrimental to the firm's economic performance. Thus, an inverted U-shaped curve shows that a firm's economic performance is likely to be enhanced only if its social performance is somewhere *in the middle*. Firms in deep economic trouble are most likely to cut back on their social spending while firms with an extremely positive economic performance may have achieved their success at the expense of society.

4. No Relationship. Finally, it is possible that no relationship exists between social and financial performance. When this happens, other factors dominate. The relationship between a company's social and economic performance has to take into account the industry, size of company, availability of slack resources, age of assets, age of the firm, and other factors. The specific risk and performance patterns in an industry are likely to be important. Stakeholders focus their demands on the most conspicuous industries and firms, often the largest in an industry. However, large companies usually have financial, managerial, and technical know-how and are able to achieve economies of scale or scope in social performance. They also are likely to have more bargaining power with government officials, which allows them to obtain concessions or delays in implementing social demands. It will probably cost older firms more to upgrade old facilities for purposes such as pollution control. These firms also may have more rigid organizational structures that permit less managerial flexibility in responding to social demands.[29]

Does It Pay to Be Good?

Many empirical studies have considered the relationship between social and financial performance. A review of them indicates the following:

- Seven showed a positive relationship between social and financial performance.
- Three showed a negative relationship between corporate social performance and corporate financial performance.
- One showed a positive relationship between the promotion of women and financial performance and a negative relationship between charitable contributions and financial performance.
- One showed a U-shaped relation, meaning that *extreme* social performance (good or bad) was negatively related to financial performance.
- Two found no effect.[30]

Few of the studies found that it paid to be "bad." However, it has been previously indicated that it is difficult to measure social performance, and the studies used different means for assessing financial performance. One study used corporate crime (Federal Trade Commission violations) and philanthropy as measures of corporate social responsibility and correlated them with return on assets (ROA) and return on sales (ROS) for the 500 largest corporations in the United States between 1979 and 1982. Five-year ROA and ROS measures were significantly lower for companies with a high crime rate and a low rate of philanthropy. It was unclear, however, whether firms with more crimes and less philanthropy suffered financially, or whether firms that committed more crimes and made smaller contributions did so because of poor financial performance.[31]

Another study tried to clarify whether financial performance follows or precedes social performance. It showed that a company's previous financial record, measured by stock market and accounting figures, influences its subsequent social performance ratings, relying on *Fortune*'s survey of corporate executives and analysts as the measure of social performance. The relationship between prior social responsibility ratings and subsequent financial performance is positive but not statistically significant. The authors conclude that good financial performance is a precondition for good social performance, but good social performance is not necessarily a precondition for good financial performance.[32] Not all socially responsible actions contribute to corporate profitability. The moral responsibilities individuals have cannot be contingent upon the expected gain. Some activities have to be pursued even at financial cost simply because they are right.[33]

The Stock Market as a Deterrent to Dubious Behavior

The classic theory of the firm rests on the idea that managers are the agents for the owners, so increasing shareholder wealth is the appropriate way to judge managerial behavior. Negative stock market returns, therefore, should discourage managers from engaging in dubious behavior. Concern for company shareholders should prevent prudent managers from engaging in ethically dubious behavior.[34]

Indeed, the stock market often reacts negatively to ethically dubious behavior. There have been abnormal reductions in stock market returns following accusations of bribery, fraud, and illegal political contributions. There also have been abnormal reductions in the aftermath of automobile recalls, the Three Mile Island (1979) and Bhopal (1984) tragedies, and major airline accidents. Managers who acted as the true agents of their shareholders would not allow their companies to fall into these predicaments.[35]

However, negative stock market returns raise some interesting questions. First, how *effective* are they as a deterrent to dubious behavior? If negative returns are effective, then managers have to be aware of them, but how strong is the signal that shareholders send to managers, and how capable are managers of perceiving that signal? If market returns slip for a short period and then rebound, how much attention will managers pay to them? Shareholder signals have to be very clear.

A more fundamental question is how *appropriate* are shareholder returns as a deterrent to dubious behavior? The classic theory of the firm emphasizes the stock market valuation of the company. Nonetheless, the investor's model is qualified to read that the responsibility to earn profits for shareholders is bound by the claims of laws and ethics.[36] Other claims have to be consistent with shareholder interests.

If other interests violate those of shareholders, then the classic theory provides no guidance. A different ethical standard (see Chapter 7), derived from religious sources such as the Sermon on the Mount or from philosophical sources such as Immanual Kant's formulation of the categorical imperative, demands an unconditional devotion to what is "right." If shareholder interests conflict with what is "right," then the needs of shareholders have to be sacrificed.

Indeed, managers may face situations where shareholder returns conflict with ethical standards. Under these circumstances the shareholder reaction is an inducement, not a deterrent, to dubious activities. Shareholder returns tell managers to do one thing. Ethical behavior tells them to do another. It is up to the managers to decide. They have to make a choice. This time the classic theory provides no guidance; qualified to read that managers should maximize shareholder returns within the bounds of laws and ethics, it does not say how to reconcile conflicts between ethics and profits.

Thus, it may be incumbent upon managers to lay prudence aside and adopt a more rigorous ethical standard, one that may be at odds with shareholder interests. They cannot simply rely on shareholder returns as a guide to ethical behavior. If the rational pursuit of self-interest always comes before moral duty, then humanity is the loser. The most dependable deterrent to dubious activity is moral duty and awareness of the consequences of one's actions: treating people with respect, as ends not means, and as autonomous creatures not subject to managerial coercion. These standards have relevance regardless of the short-term effect on shareholders.[37]

The Performance of Socially Responsible Investment Funds

Prudential Securities has assembled and assessed the performance of nine *model* portfolios, each put together around a single social theme (see Exhibit 4–1).[38] The overall performance of these portfolios was quite strong compared with Standard and Poor's (S&P) 500, but actual social investment funds did not perform nearly as well. None of them did better than the S&P 500 during 1988–1993. Investing in socially responsible stocks, then, is not a guarantee of success. Although there may be some connection between social and financial performance, the motive for social performance cannot be solely financial gain.

What Is Social Responsibility?

The question of what a corporation's social responsibilities are is tricky. Corporations indeed have obligations to society, but these obligations raise the following questions.[39]

1. *Are the obligations voluntary?* Do managers volunteer to assume obligations because they are devoted to various principles (e.g., religious, democratic, or humanistic), or do they undertake them because of laws and the threat of punishment?

2. *What do these obligations consist of?* Do they involve philanthropy or consist of an obligation to use the corporation's technical skills and resources to solve social problems? Did the following represent corporate responsibility?—Westinghouse's efforts to enter the field of public transportation, Control Data's attempts to develop software packages to

EXHIBIT 4–1 Model Investment Portfolios

A. Model Socially Responsible Investment Portfolios
(compared with the S&P 500, 1990–93)

Average of Nine Model Portfolios:	*Average Annual Return (percent)*
No EPA violators or nuclear utilities	17.3%
No top 100 weapons contractors	15.9
No toxic polluters	15.8
Pro-labor	15.3
S&P 500	**15.3**
No cigarettes, liquor, and gambling	15.0

B. Actual Socially Responsible Investment Portfolios
(compared with the S&P 500, 1988–93)

S&P 500	**14.2%**
Parnassus	13.0
Dreyfus Third Century	12.6
PAX World	10.8
Calvert Social Investment	10.0
New Alternatives	9.8
Amana Income	9.5
Calvert Ariel Growth	9.1

Real-World Example

Social Responsibility and the Emergence of a New Type of Corporate Leader

Social responsibility remains an illusive concept. Some U.S. corporations have seen the emergence of a new style leader, Ed Arzt, for example, the CEO of Proctor and Gamble (P&G), who is described as tough, demanding, and wanting results. Arzt has shifted the focus of P&G's management training from teamwork and trust to individual accountability. To beat the competition, he wants quantum leaps in quality and speed of execution. He pushes so hard that some employees feel abused and leave; 13,000 were laid off in July 1993. With the emphasis on short-term financial results, employees feel like replaceable cogs in a machine.[40]

To what extent is Ed Arzt a socially responsible leader? His response might be: "I'm taking frustrated, unproductive workers and challenging them to work as a happy, efficient unit. My responsibility to the shareholders is to make a profit and survive well into the future. If some employees think that I have created a white-collar sweatshop, that is their problem."

help underprivileged youth, and DuPont's programs to recycle waste and sell its pollution control expertise. Or were these opportunities for financial gain?

3. *Why should managers be socially responsible?* Do they try to achieve broad public acceptance out of concern over government encroachment on private decision making? the desire to be good citizens in their communities? or a fear of violence and social disruption?

These issues are not easy to resolve.

Social Responsibility Statements

Statements on social responsibility abound. This chapter will conclude with a selection of them:[41]

> Many define "socially responsible businesses" as the activities a company engages in outside its normal line of business: community involvement and direct philanthropy . . . Even more important than these efforts are the contributions a company makes in business activities. Business starts with providing superior products and services. If we meet our customers' needs successfully we will grow, and as we grow, we will make another significant contribution to our community—we'll provide meaningful jobs for growing numbers of people.
>
> H. B. Atwater, Jr., former chairman and CEO of General Mills

> An important hallmark of a socially responsible company is participation in public/private collaborations to address major social needs as business opportunities. Most critical is the need for more good jobs. The source of most good jobs is innovation, which is the process of creating new products.
>
> William Norris, founder of Control Data Corporation

> . . . first to obey the law . . . Second to invest their funds and train their workers for future prosperity . . . Third to go beyond the law and exercise exemplary achievements in consumer, worker, environmental, and community progress.
>
> Ralph Nader, consumer advocate

> . . . socially responsible business is an oxymoron. Businesses . . . will continue in the name of "increasing stockholder value" to be destructive and pollute, either by toxics or by polluting the environment of the mind, promoting banal products, monocultures, and increased consumer insecurities about status, age, speed, individualism, and so on.
>
> Doug Tompkins, cofounder of a clothing and lifestyle design company and founder of the Foundation for Deep Ecology

> A socially responsible business is not only one that provides a return to owners . . . but also creates high-quality products and/or services, provides rewarding jobs to employees, and does all this within the laws and mores of the countries in which it operates. Achieving any one of these ends is challenging. Accomplishing them all is very complex.
>
> Jay Lorsch, Harvard Business School

> A socially responsible businessperson would be: someone who treats employees, customers, vendors, shareholders, and the general community in the same way he or she would like to be treated; in other words, someone who applies the Golden Rule to all stakeholders; someone who could live with his or her actions, decisions, and policies being disclosed regularly on the

front page of the newspaper; someone who is able to consider and understand the broader implications of his or her actions.

Roger Hale, president and CEO of Tennant Corporation

The debate over corporate social responsibility took on a new significance for companies in the 1970s as society turned its attention to equal opportunity, pollution control, energy and natural resources, and consumer and worker protection. Advocates of corporate social responsibility maintained that corporations had a broader array of responsibilities that went beyond the mere production of goods and services for profit. They argued for a long-term or enlightened view of self-interest. On the other hand, critics of the social responsibility doctrine argued that in a capitalist society economic performance was a corporation's primary social responsibility. If the corporation did not serve shareholders first, it would be unable to serve society.

Conclusions

Organizational performance has financial and nonfinancial dimensions. The relationships between financial and social performance have been explored. We have tried to understand four possible relationships between financial and social performance: positive, negative, nonlinear, or no relationship. The chapter gives reasons why these relationships might exist and summarizes the evidence concerning whether it "pays to be good." It concludes with a discussion of the argument that the organization should strive to do what is right and be good whether or not it pays. The next chapter delves more deeply into these questions.

Discussion Questions

1. What level of analysis is most appropriate in performance assessment?
2. To what extent is organizational effectiveness synonymous with the financial performance of the organization?
3. What is the difference between accounting and financial measures of success?
4. What does "fit" imply?
5. How do you determine whether a company is innovative?
6. How useful is company reputation as a measure of success?
7. What is meant by *slack?* Why is it important?
8. What is social performance? How can it be measured?
9. Why might there be a positive relationship between corporate social and financial performance?
10. Why might there be a negative relationship between corporate social and financial performance?
11. Why might there be an inverted U-shaped relationship between corporate social and financial performance?

12. Why might there be no relationship?
13. What is the practical difference if these relationships prevailed? Should people do what is right regardless of the consequences?
14. To what extent is socially responsible behavior in the corporation's self-interest?
15. To what extent can one rely on the stock market as a deterrent to dubious behavior?

Endnotes

1. B. Chakravarthy, "Measuring Strategic Performance," *Strategic Management Journal*, 1986, pp. 437–58; R. T. Lenz, "Determinants of Organizational Performance: An Interdisciplinary Review," *Strategic Management Journal* 2 (1981), pp. 131–54; J. Child, "Management and Organizational Factors Associated with Company Performance—Parts I & II," *Journal of Management Studies* 2 (1974), pp. 175–89, and 12 (1974), pp. 12–27.
2. D. E. Schendel and C. W. Hofer, eds., *Strategic Management: A New View of Business Policy and Planning* (Boston: Little, Brown, 1979); P. S. Goodman and J. M. Pennings, eds., *New Perspectives on Organizational Effectiveness* (San Francisco: Jossey-Bass, 1977); R. Steers, *Organizational Effectiveness: A Behavioral View*, The Goodyear Series in Management and Organizations (Santa Monica, Calif.: Goodyear, 1977); M. T. Hannan, J. Freeman, and J. W. Meyer, "Specification of Models for Organizational Effectiveness," *American Sociological Review* 41 (1976), pp. 136–43.
3. J. McGuire and T. Schneeweis, "An Analysis of Alternate Measures of Strategic Performance," paper presented at the Third Annual Conference of the Strategic Management Society, Paris, 1983.
4. T. J. Peters and R. H. Waterman, *In Search of Excellence: Lessons from America's Best Run Companies* (New York: Harper & Row, 1982).
5. R. E. Freeman, "A Typology of Enterprise Strategy," *Strategic Management: A Stakeholder Approach* (Boston: Pitman), pp. 101–107.
6. "Despite Posting Record Revenues, SciMed Has Flat 2nd-Quarter Earnings," *Minneapolis Star Tribune*, Sept. 22, 1992; "SciMed Life Systems Inc. Reports Earnings for Quarter to August 31," *The New York Times*, Sept. 22, 1992, p. 23D; "Complaint Against SciMed Amended," *Minneapolis Star Tribune*, Oct. 8, 1992, p. 3D; "Short-Sellers Cozy Up to SciMed's Volatile Stock," *Minneapolis-St. Paul City Business* 10 (Oct. 30, 1992), p. 7.
7. Peters and Waterman, *In Search of Excellence*.
8. C. Y. Woo and G. Willard, "Performance Representation in Business Policy Research: Discussion and Recommendation," paper presented at the 23rd Annual National Meetings of the Academy of Management, Dallas, 1983. The 14 indicators are return on investment, return on sales, growth in revenues, cash flow/investment, market share, market share gain, product quality relative to competitors, new product activities relative to competitors, direct cost relative to competitors, product R&D, variations in ROI, percentage point change in ROI, and percentage point change in cash flow.
9. Chakravarthy, "Measuring Strategic Performance."
10. E. I. Altman, *Corporate Bankruptcy in America* (Lexington, Mass.: Heath Lexington Books, 1971); J. Argenti, *Corporate Collapse: The Causes and Symptoms* (New York: John Wiley, 1976).
11. Chakravarthy, "Measuring Strategic Performance."
12. Ibid.
13. Chakravarthy, "Measuring Strategic Performance"; M. Porter, *Competitive Strategy* (New York: Free Press, 1980); B. D. Henderson, *Henderson on Corporate Strategy* (Cambridge, Mass.: Abt

Books, 1979); P. Lawrence and J. Lorsch, *Organization and Its Environment* (Boston: Harvard University Press, 1967); R. E. Miles and C. C. Snow, *Organizational Strategy, Structure, and Process* (New York: McGraw-Hill, 1978); H. Mintzberg and J. A. Waters, "The Mind of the Strategist(s)"; in S. Srivastava, ed. *The Executive Mind* (San Francisco: Jossey-Bass, 1983).

14. Mintzberg and Waters, "The Mind of the Strategist(s)"; K. W. Kapp, *The Social Costs of Private Enterprise* (Cambridge, Mass.: Harvard University Press, 1950); A. C. Pigou, *Economics of Welfare*, 4th ed. (London: Macmillan, 1960); A. Ullman, "Data in Search of a Theory: A Critical Examination of the Relationships among Social Performance, Social Disclosure, and Economic Performance of U.S. Firms," *Academy of Management Review*, July 1985, pp. 545–57.
15. M. A. Keeley, "Social Justice Approach to Organizational Evaluation," *Administrative Science Quarterly* 23 (1978), pp. 272–92; R. H. Kilmann and R. P. Herden, "Towards a Systematic Methodology for Evaluating the Impact of Interventions on Organizational Effectiveness," *Academy of Management Review* 3 (1976), pp. 87–98; Pfeffer and Salancik, The External Control of Organizations.
16. R. W. Ingram and K. B. Frazier, "Environmental Performance and Corporate Disclosure," *Journal of Accounting Research* 18 (1980), pp. 614–22.
17. B. L. Kedia and E. C. Kuntz, "The Context of Social Performance: An Empirical Study of Texas Banks, in L. E. Preston, ed., *Research in Corporate Social Performance and Policy*, vol. 3 (Greenwich, Conn.: JAI Press, 1981), pp. 133–54.
18. J. McGuire, A. Sundgren, and T. Schneeweis, "Corporate Social Responsibility and Firm Financial Performance," *Academy of Management Journal*, 1988, pp. 854–72; Kedia and Kuntz, "The Context of Social Performance."
19. Irwin, "Clean and Green."
20. Social Investment Forum, May 1991.
21. Ibid.
22. Ullman, "Data in Search of a Theory," pp. 545–57.
23. Cyert and March, *A Behavioral Theory of the Firm* (Englewood Cliffs, N.J.: Prentice Hall, 1963).
24. G. J. Alexander and R. A. Buchholz, "Corporate Social Responsibility and Stock Market Performance," *Academy of Management Journal* 21 (1978), pp. 479–86.
25. B. Cornell and A. Shapiro, "Corporate Social Responsibility and Financial Performance," *Academy of Management Journal* 27 (1984), pp. 42–56.
26. A. Marcus, "Responses to Externally Induced Innovation: Their Effects on Organizational Performance," *Strategic Management Journal*, 1988, pp. 387–402.
27. P. Drucker, "The New Meaning of Social Responsibility," *California Management Review*, Winter 1984, pp. 53–63.
28. M. Friedman, "The Social Responsibility of Business Is to Increase Its Profits," reprinted in Charles S. McCoy, *The Management of Values* (Boston: Pitman, 1985), pp. 253–60.
29. P. L. Cochran and R. A. Wood, "Corporate Social Responsibility and Financial Performance," *Academy of Management Journal* 27 (1974), pp. 42–56.
30. Ullman, "Data in Search of a Theory," pp. 545–57.
31. R. Wokutch and B. Spencer, "Corporate Saints and Sinners: The Effects of Philanthropic and Illegal Activity on Organizational Performance," *California Management Review*, Winter 1987, pp. 62–78.
32. McGuire and Schneeweis, "Analysis of Alternate Measures of Strategic Performance."
33. C. G. Luckhardt, "Duties of Agent to Principal," in M. Snoeyenbox, R. Almeder, and J. Humber, eds., *Business Ethics: Corporate Values and Society* (New York: Prometheus Books, 1983), pp. 115–21.
34. Friedman, "The Social Responsibility of Business," pp. 253–60; A. A. Marcus, "Deterring Dubious Business Behavior," *Executive Excellence*, September 1990, pp. 11–12.

35. G. Jarrel and S. Peltzman, "The Impact of Product Recalls on the Wealth of Sellers," *Journal of Political Economy* 83 (1985), pp. 512–36; A. A. Marcus and R. S. Goodman, "Corporate Adjustments to Catastrophe: A Study of Investor Reaction to Bhopal," *Industrial Crisis Quarterly* 3 (1989), 213–34; P. Bromiley and A. Marcus, "The Deterrent to Dubious Corporate Behavior: Profitability, Probability and Safety Recalls," *Strategic Management Journal* 10, pp. 233–50; W. N. Davidson, P. R. Changey, and M. Cross, "Large Losses, Risk Management and Stock Returns in the Airline Industry," *Journal of Risk and Insurance* 57 (1987), pp. 162–72; W. N. Davidson and D. L. Worrell, "The Impact of Announcements of Corporate Illegalities on Shareholder Returns," *Academy of Management Journal* 31 (1988), pp. 195–200; A. A. Marcus and R. S. Goodman, "Compliance and Performance: Toward a Contingency Theory," *Research in Corporate Social Performance and Policy* 8 (1986), pp. 193–221; A. A. Marcus and R. S. Goodman, "Victims and Shareholders: The Dilemmas of Presenting Corporate Policy During a Crisis," *Academy of Management Journal* 2 (1991), pp. 281–305.
36. Friedman, "The Social Responsibility of Business,"
37. Immanuel Kant, *Foundations of the Metaphysics of Morals;* D. Vogel, "Ethics and Profits Don't Always Go Hand in Hand. *Ethics: Easier Said Than Done* 1 (1989), p. 60.
38. Kristin Davis, "Clean Money," *Kiplingers*, October 1993, pp. 37–42.
39. W. C. Frederick, "From CSR_1 to CSR_2: The Maturing of Business-and-Society Thought," Working Paper No. 279, Graduate School of Business, University of Pittsburgh, 1978.
40. "No More Mr. Nice Guy at P&G," *Business Week*, February 3, 1992, pp. 54–56; Walter Kiechel, "When Management Regresses," *Fortune*, March 9, 1992, pp. 157–58.
41. Doug Tompkins, Ralph Nader, et al., "The Meaning Limits, and Promise of Socially Responsible Business," *Utne Reader*, September–October 1993, pp. 67–74.

Case 4–A
Transforming the Soul of Business[1]

Darlington Foods is an integrated wholesaler and retailer of high-quality food products. It provides gourmet foods to supermarket chains and specialty stores in the United States and Europe under the well-known brand names of "Full Flavor," "Good-For-You," and "Healthy Delite." Partly through acquisition, its sales have more than doubled in the past 10 years, but profits have been disappointing.

	Sales (000s)	*Operating Income (000s)*	*Net Loss (000s)*
1991	$28,380	$1,554	$ (1,043)
1992	35,595	(6,351)	(10,353)
1993	49,020	(4,155)	(6,975)

The top management team consists of company president and CEO Robert Dennis, 39, an undergraduate engineering graduate with a Ph.D. in educational administration from the University of Kansas; executive vice president Carl Martin, 49, who attended the University of Utah and worked for the Albertson and Super Value grocery chains; retail sales vice president Kevin J. O'Brien, 31, a graduate of the Harvard Business School; marketing vice president Jane Wyman, 40, who attended the University of Houston and worked for Dayton Hudson; and chief financial officer (CFO) Benson Siegel, 59, a CPA from the University of California, Berkeley, who used to run his own business.

The founder of the company, Maxine Chu, and the former CFO, Brian Kensington-Fuller, were forced to resign because of the company's poor performance.

Before the monthly executive team meeting in November 1994, O'Brien proposed to send five senior employees to a conference on "Transforming the Soul of Business: Profit, Competition, and Conscience on the New Frontier," which would be held in Hilton Head Island, South Carolina, February 8–12, 1995.[2] This proposal was part of O'Brien's ongoing effort to make the company a more socially responsible entity, along the lines of Ben and Jerry's and the Body Shop.

O'Brien believed that the key to restoring Darlington's profitability was to align it with upscale consumers who would appreciate a socially conscious profile. Doing so was not only a way to restore profitability, but the right thing to do. "This company should be governed by conscience," O'Brien was fond of saying. "It should not be a slave to short-term profits. If we do the right thing, everything will work out for the better."

The cost of sending the five employees to Hilton Head would be about $6,000. However, Darlington had not provided conference trips to employees in the past, so this marked a break with precedent.

Benson Siegel, the newest member of the executive team, had about a week until the next meeting to look over the conference brochure. On the title page, it advertised "Innovative Techniques for Making a Profit While Making a Difference," "How to Make Your Business a Positive Agent for Social Change," and "Step-by-Step Strategies to Build Your Company and Make it Thrive."

The mission of the conference sponsor, the National Institute for a New Corporate Vision, was "to foster an evolution that encourages balance: a thriving corporate life, self-fulfillment, and meaningful personal relationships." Other companies that would be represented at the conference were Stonyfield Farm, Seventh Generation, Crip Publications, Reebock, Deja Foods (a maker of footwear from recycled soda bottles, tires, and latex), After the Fall Products, Odwalla (all-natural fruit juices), Motherwear, and Republic of Tea. The conference promised sessions that would address topics such as extraordinary customer service, incentives that work, employee empowerment, thinking globally, fostering creativity, employee ownership, collaborative communication styles, entrepreneurial spirit, reengineering, systems thinking, teamwork, and giving back to the community.

Siegel did not know what to think. A liberal Democrat, a successful entrepreneur, and philanthropist, he also had been known as a hard-driving person when he owned his own business. He felt that he had kept his priorities straight: "When in the office, use your head—keep your heart at home" was his motto.

Siegel was not inclined to support O'Brien's initiative and considered it his duty to bring some common sense to the executive team. He had been brought in to tame the youthful, disorganized exuberance of Maxine Chu, the company's talented but flawed founder, and Kensington-Fuller, the prior CFO. O'Brien had been Chu's favorite and Siegel felt that the initiative was a leftover that should no longer be a part of Darlington's way of doing business.

Siegel was unsure how other members of the executive team stood on the conference. Though all of them had been hired by Chu, none completely shared her point of view. They were competent professionals who had done what Chu asked, but had not displayed much leadership. Darlington never had gone far in implementing the "creative capitalism" ideas O'Brien promoted. Chu believed these ideas were a matter of personal conviction and had been careful not to let them intrude deeply into the business. One reason she did not push hard was her fear of antagonizing customers, especially the large supermarket chains.

Siegel thought the culture at Darlington was a bit flaky and rather disorganized. He joked that it gave him a mild sensation of being captured by a cult. Chu was not dogmatic; O'Brien was another matter. No doubt about it, Siegel thought, O'Brien was extremely bright, but he was also arrogant and self-righteous, qualities that Siegel detested. Siegel feared O'Brien. He considered him single-minded, intolerant, excruciatingly pure, a fanatic; there was no telling how far he might go.

Siegel then read an article about how several socially conscious businesses had been unable to live up to their ideals. Ben and Jerry's deserted its much vaunted pay scale, which had meant that the CEO could earn only seven times the salary of a person who scooped ice cream. Stride Rite took its factories out of inner city locations and shipped jobs to low-wage countries in Asia, like Nike, its rival. The most interesting part of the article concerned a glaring expose about the Body Shop that had appeared in *Business Ethics: The Magazine of Socially Responsible Business*.[3]

Titled "Shattered Image," it told the tale of a disgruntled former Body Shop franchisee, who ended up losing over $10,000 a month because of alleged discrepancies between what the Body Shop owners promised and what they delivered. The Body Shop was being investigated by the Federal Trade Commission for its treatment of franchisees. The article also claimed that the Body Shop used outmoded product formulas that relied on nonrenewable petrochemicals, and that it had a history of quality control problems, which had led to the selling of contaminated products.

Though a multimillionaire with an estimated net worth of over $200 million and a yearly income of $1.3 million, Anita Roddick (CEO of Body Shop) had proclaimed that she saw herself not only as a creator of profits for her shareholders but as "a force for good, working for the future of the planet." She had sought "enlightened capitalism" as "the best way of changing society for the better:"

> I think you can trade ethically, be committed to social responsibility and global responsibility and empower your employees without being afraid of them. I think you can rewrite the book on business.

But the article claimed that Roddick was a master of hype and image building and not much substance. Siegel sent copies of this article to all the members of the executive committee. He could not wait for the executive meeting.

O'Brien was not going to be done in by Siegel. He decided to invite a guest to the meeting, Laura Scher, a former MBA classmate of his, a person he believed was above reproach and represented the best of the new capitalism. Scher had graduated from Harvard in 1985 near the top of her class, but like O'Brien had not chosen the path to easy and quick riches. She refused a lucrative Wall Street offer and created her own company, Working Assets Funding Service, whose purpose was to do well by doing good.

The company started by offering a donation-linked credit card. Then it came up with a charity-connected long-distance phone service. Both businesses allowed people to donate to various left-wing, feminist, and environmental causes while carrying out their everyday transactions. *Inc.* magazine named Working Assets one of the 500 fastest growing privately held companies in the United States in 1993. Its revenues had increased from $2 million in 1991 to nearly $35 million in 1993. It had more than 130,000 long-distance subscribers.[4]

O'Brien wanted Scher to convince the members of the executive committee that Darlington Foods could succeed by doing good. The soul of the company, however, first had to be transformed. The company needed an entirely new business ethic. The way to start was to allow the five employees to go to Hilton Head.

Foreseeing the coming battle, the other members of the executive committee were not sure how to react. What should Darlington Foods do? How should it steer between the powerful points of views of its talented executive committee members? Who was right about this issue—Benson Siegel or Kevin O'Brien?

Discussion Questions

1. If you were Benson Siegel, how would you prepare yourself for the next meeting of the top management team? What would be your goals? What would you hope to accomplish?

2. If you were Kevin O'Brien, how would you prepare yourself for this meeting? What would be your goals? What would you hope to accomplish?
3. As a member of the management team, what are your views about the future of Darlington Foods and the differences between key members of the management team? Should employees be sent to the conference in Hilton Head?

Endnotes

1. This case was written by Alfred Marcus.
2. National Institute for a New Corporate Vision, First International Conference, 1995.
3. "Being Cruel to Be Kind," *Business Week*, October 17, 1994, pp. 51–53; Jon Entine, "Shattered Image," *Business Ethics*, September/October 1994, pp. 23–30.
4. Jane Gross, "She Took One Look at the Age of Greed and Made a Quick Left," *New York Times*, November 7, 1993, p. 8F.

Case 4–B
The Sloan School Ethics Questionnaire

Scott Seidewitz, a second year student in the MBA program at the Sloan School of Management, is the co-director of the students' ethics group. This group has decided that the Sloan School should mail a questionnaire on corporate ethics to all recruiters at the school. Linda Stantial, Director of the Career Development, is willing to go along with the request, but it has met some unexpected opposition from other students and from some of the people in the administration. The cover letter is shown in Exhibit 1, and Exhibit 2 contains the complete questionnaire.

Discussion Questions

1. What do you think of this questionnaire?
2. Should business schools survey prospective employers in this manner?
3. What are the risks?
4. What are the benefits?
5. Would you be interested in the results?
6. Would you use the results to make employment decisions?
7. What items do you find objectionable? What items would you leave out of this questionnaire?
8. What would you add to the questionnaire? Why?

Exhibit 1 Cover Letter

January 31, 19xx

Dear ______________________________,

In recent years, the students of the Sloan School of Business at MIT have placed an increasing emphasis on personal values when making career decisions. As a result, students have become interested in learning more about prospective employers' organizational policies and sense of social responsibility. To provide students with information along these lines, the Sloan Business Ethics Group has prepared the enclosed Questionnaire on Corporate Policies and Ethics. We invite you to help us in this effort by completing the questionnaire and returning it to Sloan School of Management's Career Development Office by March of this year.

With the support of the Career Development Office, the Sloan Business Ethics Group is sending the Questionnaire on Corporate Policies and Ethics to all companies that recruit at Sloan. The questionnaire covers a variety of topics in which students expressed interest in a schoolwide survey. In order to make the questionnaire manageable to recruiting firms, we have limited it to four pages and worded questions as neutrally as possible. Questions generally require either yes or no answers or simple numerical information. In a few instances, we also request brief descriptions of corporate policies or historical experiences.

The Sloan Business Ethics Group will summarize and publish the results of the questionnaire in a booklet to be available to students in the Sloan Career Development Office. We will publish responses as provided by recruiting firms, without ratings or comment. For comparison, we will accompany responses with the percentage of companies responding yes or no to each question or, for numerical responses, the mean and range of responses by industry, company size, and entire population. Copies of the actual surveys and additional information returned by companies will also be available to students in a separate binder.

The Questionnaire on Corporate Policies and Ethics is an opportunity both to help students make informed career decisions and to help companies attract M.B.A.'s with similar values and goals. We understand that some of the information requested may be sensitive in nature, and that different companies will be willing to provide different levels of information. Any questions left blank will simply be marked "no response." We encourage you to answer as many questions as possible and provide any additional information or comments which you think will be useful to prospective recruits.

If you have any questions about the questionnaire or the Sloan Business Ethics Group, please feel free to call me at ____________ or Linda Stantial, Director of the Career Development Office, at ____________. We hope you will join us by returning your completed questionnaire by March 3.

Sincerely,

Scott V. Seidewitz
Co-Director, Sloan Business Ethics Group

EXHIBIT 2 Sloan Recruiter Questionnaire

Sloan Business Ethics Group
Questionnaire on Corporate Policies and Ethics

Please feel free to provide additional information about any question.

I. Company Information

1. General information:
   Company name: ____________________
   Address: ____________________
   ____
   Contact person (name): ____________________
   (title) ____________________
   Phone: ____________________

2. Company size:
   What were your company's sales in the most recent fiscal year? $ ____________________
   What were your company's assets at the end of most recent fiscal year? $ ____________________
   How many people does your company currently employ? ____________________

3. Ownership:
   Your company is: Publicly owned ______ Privately owned ______
   Wholly owned subsidiary of ____________________
   In what country is your company headquartered? ____________________

4. Does your company have a mission statement, credo, or other statement of purpose?
   Yes ___ No ___ If yes, please attach a copy.

II. Charitable Contributions and Community Service

1. Does your company make direct charitable contributions? Yes ___ No ___
   Does your company have a charitable foundation? Yes ___ No ___
   If yes to either, what amount of cash contributions did your company and/or charitable foundation donate in the latest fiscal year? $ __________
   What percentage of worldwide corporate pretax profits is this? ________
   (Optional) Attach a description of your charitable contributions program, including names of recipients and amounts received.

2. Does your company make in-kind contributions (product donations)?
   Yes ___ No ___
   If yes, what was the value of in-kind contributions in the most recent fiscal year? ___
   Does your company perform pro bono work for nonprofit organizations?
   Yes ___ No ___
   If yes, what percentage of client-hours is spent on pro bono work? ___

3. Does your company match employee contributions to charitable organizations? Yes ___ No ___
   If yes, at what ratio are they matched? ________ Up to what contribution amount?
   ____

4. Does your company have an employee volunteer or executive loan program?
   Yes ___ No ___
   (Optional) Attach a description of your employee volunteer/executive loan programs.

EXHIBIT 2 *(continued)*

III. Environment

1. To what extent does your company have formal programs promoting:

	Company-wide	*Only in Specific Locations*	*None*
Recycling	____	____	____
Use of recycled office materials	____	____	____
Energy conservation	____	____	____
Car or van pooling and/or public transportation use	____	____	____
Reuse or recycle of manufacturing inputs (N/A_)	____	____	____
Reduction of wastes, emissions, and effluents from manufacturing processes (N/A ____________)	____	____	____
Design and production of ecologically sound products (N/A ____________________)	____	____	____

(Questions 2 and 3 apply only to manufacturing firms. Nonmanufacturing firms may leave blank.)

2. Does your company have a designated corporate environmental official?
   Yes ___ No ___
   If yes, what percentage of her/his time is spent on environmental matters? _____
3. Has your company been cited by the EPA or other federal or state agencies for violations of environmental laws or regulations in the past five years? Yes ___ No ___
   If yes, how many times have you been cited in:

	Number of Violations	*Amount of Fines*
Past year	____	____
Past 5 years	____	____

(Optional) Attach a description of the nature of violations and penalties.

IV. WORK FORCE BENEFITS AND POLICIES

(Please limit responses in this section to *U.S. operations only.*)

1. To what extent does your company offer maternity leave benefits?
   Companywide ___ Only at some locations ___ Not offered ___
   If offered, how many weeks of leave do you provide:

	Paid Leave	*Unpaid Leave*
With current position guaranteed	____	____
With comparable position guaranteed	____	____
With comparable or lesser position guaranteed	____	____

To what extent does your company offer paternity leave benefits?
Companywide ___ Only at some locations ___ Not offered ___
If offered, how many weeks of leave do you provide:

EXHIBIT 2 *(continued)*

	Paid Leave	*Unpaid Leave*
With current position guaranteed	____	____
With comparable position guaranteed	____	____
With comparable or lesser position guaranteed	____	____

2. What type of assistance does your company offer for child and/or elder care?

	Child care	*Elder care*
Subsidized on-site care, all locations	____	____
Subsidized on-site care, some locations	____	____
Reimbursement	____	____
Referral	____	____
No assistance	____	____

3. To what extent does your company offer the following types of flexibility in hours and work place?

	All Locations	*Some Locations*	*No Locations*
Flextime	____	____	____
Reduction of hours following parental leave	____	____	____
Work-at-home arrangements	____	____	____

4. Do you extend the same benefits provided to married employees to unmarried employees who meet defined domestic partner criteria for:
   Unmarried homosexual couples? Yes ___ No ___
   Unmarried heterosexual couples? Yes ___ No ___
5. Does your company have a policy on sexual harassment? Yes ___ No ___
   (Optional) If yes, please provide a copy.
   Does your company have a designated person outside of the supervisory hierarchy with whom employees can confidentially discuss concerns about sexual harassment?
   Yes ___ No ___
   Do you offer awareness training to discourage sexual harassment? Yes ___ No ___
   If yes, what percentage of employees have participated in it? __________

V. ADVANCEMENT OF MINORITIES AND WOMEN

1. Please indicate the percentage representation of minorities in your company:

	African-American	*Hispanic*	*Asian*	*Native American*
U.S. work force	____	____	____	____
U.S. management staff (exempt employees)	____	____	____	____
Senior management team (executive or partner level)	____	____	____	____
Board of directors	____	____	____	____

EXHIBIT 2 (concluded)

2. Please indicate the percentage representation of women in your company:
   U.S. work force ______
   U.S. management staff (exempt employees) ______
   Senior management team (executive or partner level) ______
   Board of directors ______
3. Does your company have officially sanctioned support groups for:
   Women? Yes ___ No ___ Lesbians and gays? Yes ___ No ___
   Minorities? Yes ___ No ___

VI. LEGAL/POLITICAL RECORD

1. Have any state or federal government agencies cited your company for major violations of labor, occupational safety, product safety, advertising, securities, or equal opportunity laws or regulations in:
   Past year? Yes ___ No ___
   Past 5 years? Yes ___ No ___
   If yes, please describe (attach additional sheets, if necessary):
   ____
   ____
2. Does your company sponsor a political action committee (PAC)? Yes ___ No ___
   If yes, how much did it contribute to political campaigns in:
   the 1987–88 election cycle? __________
   the 1989–90 election cycle? __________
   (Optional) Attach a listing of your PAC's contributions for the above election cycles.

VII. INTERNATIONAL OPERATIONS AND INVESTMENTS

1. Does your company have operations outside the U.S.? Yes ___ No ___
   If yes, do the policies described in your answers to this questionnaire apply to (check one):
   All international operations ______
   Some international operations ______
   U.S. operations only ______
2. Does your company have operations in non-OECD (less industrialized) countries?
   Yes ___ No ___
   If yes, does your company require that these operations abide by the health and safety regulations of:
   The United States? Yes ___ No ___
   Each individual country? Yes ___ No ___
3. Does your company offer the same level of benefits to employees in non-OECD countries as given to employees in the U.S.? Yes ___ No ___

Please return to Sloan Career Development Office, 50 Memorial Drive, Cambridge, MA 02139

PART

II

Values and the Corporation's Relationship to Society

CHAPTER

5

WHY ETHICS MATTER

It is not a matter of being a Goody Two Shoes. It is a matter of being practical. The notion that nice guys finish last is not only poisonous, but wrong.
Martin Josephson, ethics consultant

Introduction and Chapter Objectives

This chapter provides four reasons why ethics should matter to corporations: (1) to enhance their competitiveness, (2) to preserve their legitimacy, (3) to deter white-collar crime, and (4) to promote trust and prevent debilitating conflict. It discusses why people often are not ethical and concludes with advice on how to enhance ethical behavior.

Why Do Ethics Matter?

Companies spend large sums of money on ethics programs. A 1991 survey of Fortune 500 companies by the Ethics Resource Center at Bentley College showed that over 40 percent of the companies held regularly scheduled ethics workshops and seminars. More than 20 percent had board ethics committees and ethics programs of various kinds. Many companies had ombudsmen for ethics and encouraged employee whistle-blowing (see Exhibit 5–1).[1]

Peers and subordinates use anonymous questionnaires to rate Northrup Corporation managers on their ethical behavior. After attending a required ethics seminar, new 3M employees are asked to carry a pocket card that helps them work through ethical problems (see Exhibit 5–2). Martin Marietta's ethics program cost the company more than $2 million a year, including lost production time and organizational costs. The salaries and travel expenses of ethics office personnel amount to almost $400,000 a year. What do these companies expect to gain from their ethics programs?

EXHIBIT 5–1 Ethics Activity in Large U.S. Corporations
(50,000 or more employees)

Written ethics guidelines	95%
Ethics training	47%
Hotline/reporting channel	28%
Board ethics committee	23%
Corporate ethics office	15%

EXHIBIT 5–2 3M's Pocket Guide to Corporate Ethics

A Seven-Step Guide
For Working Through Ethical Problems

Step 1 Identify all critical facts.
Step 2 Identify key values of all players.
Step 3 Identify the driving forces in the situation.
Step 4 Work through a worst-case scenario and its effects on the players.
Step 5 Identify key values and ethical principles that you would uphold.
Step 6 Write down an outline of your action plan.
Step 7 Identify organizational changes that could prevent this situation in the future.

Statement of 3M Corporate Values

We are committed to:

- Satisfying our *customers* with superior quality and value.
- Providing *investors* with an attractive return through sustained, high quality growth.
- Respecting our *social and physical environment.*
- Being a company that *employees* are proud to be a part of.

The Ethics Check Questions

1. Is it legal?
2. Is my action the right thing to do?
3. Can my action stand public scrutiny?
4. Will my action protect 3M's reputation as an ethical company?

Reason 1: To Enhance Competitiveness

Declining U.S. economic competitiveness is often attributed to moral faults—greed, selfishness, and arrogance. In 1992, *Boston Globe* columnist Mike Barnicle wrote:

> We're on the ropes for a lot of reasons. Our schools have broken down. We turn out lawyers and accountants while Japan graduates engineers and scientists. Our concept of family and neighborhood has disappeared. Our idea of morality and honor is covered with dust. We cut corners, use drugs by the bundle, and operate under tax codes that force everyone to become crooks . . . we have . . . been badly wounded by greed, selfishness, and the arrogant shortsighted policies of American management . . . They are only in it for the money. They couldn't care

> less about inferior products, consumer satisfaction, contaminated work space, or labor unrest . . . We are rushing toward permanent mediocrity because of a pack of . . . assorted greedheads . . . It's an old story. Those at the top specialize in packaging, manipulation, self promotion, and lining their own pockets.[2]

Cohesive, cooperative societies like Japan and South Korea, where the moral fabric is apparently less frayed by myopic policies and the avarice and acquisitiveness of haughty managers, are supposed to be gaining on the United States.

The former premier of Japan, Kichi Miyazawa, was a persistent critic of U.S. society. He pointed to a decline in the work ethic and said that Americans were hooked on the easy "paper wealth" of Wall Street—junk bonds and leveraged buyouts—and to financial wheeling and dealing. Overpaid managers were responsible for low-quality U.S. products that could not compete with products from Japan. Miyazawa claimed that "Americans don't throw themselves wholly into work on Monday because they play too hard on Saturday and Sunday." He was alluding to the typical Japanese workweek, which is six days, not five.

Richard Gephardt, now Democratic minority leader in the House of Representatives, said that Miyazawa's statements were "ignorant expressions of Japanese racism," that Americans worked hard every day, and that U.S. productivity was higher than that of Japan.[3]

Juliet Schor, a Harvard University economist, wrote that Americans do work hard. The U.S. workweek, after declining to 39 hours in 1970, has increased ever since. Each year, the typical U.S. worker puts in more hours than a worker in 1970. U.S. workers also are subject to greater time pressures at home. Leisure has shrunk. Diverse unpaid charitable activities, formerly carried out by voluntary associations, are no longer done. Civic participation in noble causes has declined.[4]

Employers, on the other hand, like the long workweek, since they can thereby avoid the expense of hiring and training new workers and paying them fringe benefits, including very expensive health insurance. U.S. labor unions are weak and employees lack bargaining power. In Germany, where unions are strong, the typical work week is 35 hours and the average worker gets six weeks of paid vacation. Some U.S. corporations have problems with overworked employees. Their productivity is declining. Medtronics had to limit the amount of employee overtime work because it could not afford a drop in the quality of its sensitive medical products.

Moreover, the ethical problems to which Miyazawa refers are not restricted to the United States alone. Japan was scandalized when respected financial institutions such as the Sumitomo and Sanwa Banks diverted large sums of money to trucking companies controlled by the Japanese mob. Members of the Japanese parliament, the Diet, illegally obtained more than $80 million in return for granting new routes and service areas to the trucking companies. The mob arbitrated disputes from auto accidents to business deals, and it persuaded reluctant owners to abandon their property when new economic development was pending. The web of corruption that engulfed Japanese society played a part in weakening this powerful nation.[5]

Ethics and economic competitiveness are related. The turnaround of an underdeveloped society is connected to ridding itself of corruption. When the Mexican economy showed improvement, this performance was ascribed to less rampant corruption. Similarly, when companies like Goodyear turn around, we often see it in ethical terms: the restoration of trust is regarded as an important reason for the company's improved economic performance. The 19th-century French observer of American society, Alexis de Tocqueville, remarked that the United States became "great because it was good."[6] Virtuous behavior often is a necessary condition for economic achievement because it entails saving, thrift, hard work, honesty, and conscientiousness.

Ethical Values and Economic Growth. The sociologist Daniel Bell relates the ethical values of a society to the competitiveness of its economic institutions. He discerns a movement in American values "from the Protestant ethic to the psychedelic bazaar." The **Protestant ethic** and Puritan temper were based on "work, sobriety, frugality, sexual restraint, and a forbidding attitude toward life." They were the result of an agrarian, small-town way of life where the clergy held sway and a person was expected to be accountable.[7]

Protestant ethic Values associated with the rise of Protestantism, emphasizing hard work, thrift, frugality, and self-improvement.

In 20th-century America, a consumption ethic of hedonism, pleasure, and play eroded this ethic. The automobile, movies, and radio eliminated rural isolation and created a common culture devoted to spending and material possessions. Items once considered luxuries spread to the middle and lower classes. People manifested success not by saving and abstinence but by lavishly displaying the "lifestyles" they could afford to acquire. Gratification of the impulses rather than their suppression became the norm.

There is a conflict between American business and these values. Effective business practice requires a reliance on the principles of economy, efficiency, optimization, and functional rationality that may conflict with current cultural traditions in the United States and other advanced industrial nations. In newly industrializing nations, on the other hand, one often finds greater adherence to the traditional tenets of the Protestant ethic. People in these nations value hard work, thrift, frugality, honesty, and self-sacrifice for the purpose of economic success. Thus, the question of ethical values is a broader one than the personal salvation of individual managers. It concerns economic growth and the competitiveness of American business in the world economy.

Reason 2: To Preserve Legitimacy

A second reason why ethics matters is to preserve legitimacy. If a company's products are considered illegitimate, it will have to struggle to keep them on the market. For instance, when Dow Corning was accused of putting a breast implant on the market that adversely affected the health of millions of women, the effects on Dow Corning's bottom line were negative. The company's stock fell by 15 percent despite the fact that implants represented only 1 percent of its revenues and the company seemed to have adequate insurance to cover potential litigation. Though Dow Corning had an ethics program in place for 18 years, no questions had been raised. Dow Corning now has been forced to declare bankruptcy.

Sears is another example. In 1992, consumer affairs representatives from the states of California and New Jersey alleged that the company's auto centers had misled customers and charged them for unnecessary repairs. The California Department of Consumer Affairs threatened to revoke the licenses of 72 Sears auto centers in California. Sears had been in financial trouble since 1990 when it fell to third place in retail sales behind Wal-

Mart and Kmart. It had introduced many cost-cutting measures and eliminated as many as 50,000 jobs.

Management put pressure on all employees to increase sales. Clerks in Sears stores began to earn more of their wages from commissions. Auto mechanics had a new wage structure with a large piecework component. The incentive was to lure people into the store with low posted prices and then to exaggerate the amount of work that had to be done so that the mechanics could earn a decent income. Many Sears mechanics cooperated with government investigators. Sears auto centers constituted 9 percent of the company's total retail revenues and 5 percent of total profits. During the height of the controversy from June 1 to June 19, the company's stock declined from $48.25 per share to $38.12 per share.[8]

Cigarettes are another example. The investor Warren Buffett said that what he likes about the cigarette business is that "it costs about a penny to make a pack, you sell it for a dollar, it's addictive, and there's fantastic brand loyalty."[9] U.S. cigarette consumption, however, declined at a rate of more than 2 percent per year during the late 1980s and early 1990s. Consumption fell off in Europe, too. Since more than one million Americans and Europeans supposedly die each year from cigarette-related causes, the $40 billion U.S. market and $50 billion European market would appear to be in jeopardy. Demands have been made to completely outlaw cigarette advertising. The successful Joe Camel advertising campaign was particularly controversial. While critics challenged it as unethical marketing, Camel increased its market share among 18–24 year olds from 4 to 7 percent.

Cigarette manufacturers feel that they are being forced to move to other parts of the world—Africa, Asia, and the states of the former Soviet bloc—where opposition to smoking is not as widespread. Worldwide consumption of cigarettes is growing at a rate of more than 2 percent per year. The question is whether this growth can continue when the legitimacy of the product is so vigorously contested (see Case 5–A on Philip Morris).[10]

A fourth example is Fuller Chemical. It has an outstanding reputation for social responsibility in areas such as pollution control, community giving, recycling, and feeding the poor.[11] Nonetheless, *The Progressive* magazine cited Fuller for selling glue to children in Central and Latin America. The children inhaled the glue because getting high allowed them to forget their hunger and loneliness, but the glue destroyed their brains and kidneys. The article suggested that Fuller use mustard oil or noxious chemicals to deter the children from inhaling the glue. Fuller considered the suggestion ridiculous, but it was under intense pressure to do something because the challenge to the legitimacy of its products damaged its reputation for social responsibility (see Case 5–B).

A final example comes from Prudential Securities, which was accused of selling risky real estate and energy partnerships to retirees and others and calling them safe investments. It was claimed that Prudential dealers misrepresented the safety of some $8 billion worth of risky limited partnerships and lied in promotional materials about the return that investors could expect. Customers throughout the country deluged the company with nervous phone calls. How could a company that had so aggressively pursued their trust and business have committed such acts? Prudential took out full-page newspaper advertisements to reassure the public that the fraudulent acts had been eliminated and that people could again put their trust in the company.

The government showed that branch office employees who engaged in the fraudulent practices had been inadequately supervised. To increase their commissions, these employees churned clients' accounts without authorization and got unwitting clients to sign agreements to allow the risky trading. When a loss showed up on an account statement, they deceived clients by calling it a "back-office error." For defrauding thousands of investors, Prudential Securities agreed to an immediate payment of $371 million in restitution and fines. The settlement was likely to be the largest in history for a security firm.[12]

These cases suggest that corporate ethics do matter. A company cannot afford to let the legitimacy of its products come into question.

Reason 3: To Deter White-Collar Crime

Ethics also matters because of the role it plays in deterring white-collar crime.[13] This type of crime costs the United States an estimated $14 to $40 billion a year compared with $4 billion a year from street crime. One could cite many incidents of high-level white-collar crime; two examples will be noted briefly: Defense Department procurement frauds perpetrated by Melvyn Paisley, assistant secretary of the Navy under Ronald Reagan; and phony profits generated by Joseph Jett, Kidder, Peabody & Company's former chief government bond trader.

Paisley distorted the bidding process by deflecting contracts for hundreds of millions of dollars of weapons systems to those who paid secretly for his assistance. Implicated in the scandal were United Technologies, Unisys, Loral Corporation, Teledyne, Martin Marietta, and Grumman. Former Grumman chairman John O'Brien pleaded guilty to two counts of fraud. Paisley was sentenced to serve time at a minimum-security prison near Las Vegas for leaking confidential information, rearranging the playing field, and persuading his Pentagon colleagues to favor companies that gave him money. As a result, all Pentagon contractors have had to tighten their ethical compliance codes. Unisys paid the largest penalty—$163 million in fines. Like other companies, it established new channels, such as 24-hour telephone hotlines, to encourage whistle-blowing. (See the Real-World Example on Martin Marietta's ethics program.)[14]

At Kidder, Peabody, Jett generated a phony $350 million in profits by stripping and reconstituting Treasury bonds, turning the bonds into separate components of interest and principal and vice versa, and manipulating the firm's trading and accounting systems. Sham trading in 1993 amounted to $1.7 trillion, which permitted Jett's zero-coupon trading desk to achieve mammoth profits. Jett claimed that his supervisors knew about his activities. Internal auditors never caught the ruse though the false profits constituted 27 percent of the fixed-income unit's profits. No one ever noticed the disparity between the volume of profits and the absence of cash. Michael Carpenter, the 47-year-old head of Kidder, and a personal friend of Jack Welch, the CEO of General Electric (GE), which owned Kidder, operated the business from 1989 to 1994 without a broker's license, a violation of Securities and Exchange Commission rules. Carpenter and Edward Cerullo, Jett's supervisor, were forced to resign, and GE felt it had to sell the troubled investment unit.[15]

The big headline-grabbing stories of white-collar crime capture our attention, but small violations also add up. The long list of minor offenses includes petty theft, taking sick time when a person is not sick, getting paid for overtime not worked, taking long lunch and coffee breaks, purposely performing slow or sloppy work, faking injury to receive

Real-World Example

Martin Marietta's Ethics Program[16]

The defense industry came under great scrutiny in the early 1980s with the great jump in defense spending in response to Reagan administration initiatives. Many companies were suspected of winning contracts by fraud and making defective products. A blue ribbon commission, headed by David Packard of Hewlett-Packard, recommended that the industry govern itself to prevent increased government regulation.

Eighteen defense contractors, including Martin Marietta, created the Defense Industry Initiative on Business Ethics and Conduct in 1986. They promised a written code of conduct, employee training, and the encouragement of employees to report violations without fear of retribution. Rather than be subject to increased regulation, the defense contractors would voluntarily disclose to the government their legal violations and take other actions.

Standard Martin Marietta training in the early 1980s had included a "Hellfire and Brimstone" speech from the associate general counsel, who said: "We'll stand behind you if you make an innocent mistake. But if you deliberately violate the law, you won't get support." But now Martin Marietta realized it would have to do more. It set up its ethics program in September 1985. The program was governed by a steering committee of senior managers including the corporate president, CFO, and general counsel. The board of directors authorized a 12-page Code of Ethics. This document was mailed to all 60,000 employees at their homes. All of them had to send back a card acknowledging that they had received the code.

Martin Marietta's Code of Ethics emphasized the company's unifying principles: integrity, people, teamwork, and excellence. It reaffirmed the company's commitment to its employees, customers, communities, shareholders, and suppliers; announced the establishment of an ethics office; and encouraged employees to anonymously report violations of the code to the ethics office. (Employees were given a toll-free number they could call.) The company also connected incentive compensation to the code and provided employees with an additional publication to clarify what the code meant. Between 1986 and 1988, all employees received training in how to interpret and use the Code of Ethics.

By 1991, the ethics office was receiving up to 10,000 calls annually. Some merely involved clarifications of the code: Employees wanted advice about what to do in a particular situation. Other calls—nearly 600 in 1991—disclosed incidents of dubious behavior. These cases had to be closely examined and resolved. Of the 40 percent of cases that were corroborated, discipline had to be taken, corrective actions made, or changes in corporate policy carried out. For employees, discipline might mean counseling, oral and written reprimand, transfer, suspension without pay, or termination.

Many cases had to do with personnel issues: salaries, promotions, assignments, and supervision. Others involved inaccurate or false records, waste, conflicts of interest, drug use, theft, discrimination, harassment, safety problems, defective quality, procurement violations, and even sabotage. If a case could not be resolved within 90 days, it was brought to the attention of a local company executive. A case not resolved within 120 days was brought to the central steering committee.

Many employees resented the program because it put them under suspicion. Some managers thought that the process undermined their authority. Others felt that personnel issues were inappropriate for an ethics committee and should be handled by the human resources staff. Confidentiality was a serious concern. The most difficult problems often were raised anonymously. The complainant needed to be protected from retaliation. Another issue was fairness. Every year, about three complaints of unfair actions taken by the ethics committee were brought before a state labor board.

Real-Life Ethical Vignettes

1. John was a bookkeeper at a small business. The owner's son occasionally took money from the cash drawer for entertainment. Because John kept the books, the son asked him to conceal the cash withdrawals. What should John do?

2. You are asked to go to a midwinter conference in San Juan, Puerto Rico. During the three-day schedule, only two workshops pertain to your job. Should you go? If you go, should you attend the workshops or play in the 80° weather?

workers' compensation, working under the influence of drugs and alcohol, taking care of personal business on company time, removing company property or merchandise, using company long-distance telephones or copy equipment for personal use, and taking kickbacks from a supplier.[17] (See the real-life ethical vignettes above.)

Few people can say that they never have engaged in any of these petty offenses. However, the accumulation of these offenses contaminates the work environment and reduces organizational effectiveness. In addition, an estimated 1 percent of corporate revenues are lost to dishonest activities, which force corporations to put in place elaborate and expensive controls that often demean employees.

Employee dishonesty is a result of motivation, opportunity, and rationalization. By means of tests, interviews, and background checks, employers can try to screen out employees with dishonest intentions (see Case 5–C). Employers then must be careful to limit the opportunities for newly hired employees to commit a dishonest act. Finally, employers have to limit the rationalizations an employee may use to do something wrong. Most people need to rationalize acting contrary to ethical principle. For example, they need to feel that they are underpaid, that the company owes them, or that they are simply borrowing stolen property and will pay it back later. They want to think that the company has cheated them and that their revenge is justified. They also want to feel that all employees are acting this way and therefore it must be right (see the real-life ethical vignette on the next page).

Rising incidents of white-collar crime are leading employers to run more detailed reference checks on new hires, to review and improve internal controls, and to establish and upgrade corporate codes of conduct. Most frauds are discovered by means of internal controls, notification by an employee, internal audits, or special investigations. Poor internal controls or management override of internal controls that should be in place often explain why fraud takes place. Obviously, there is a difference between employees who steal for their own gain, like Melvyn Paisley, and employees who pad their own pockets but also make the company look good financially, such as Joseph Jett. In the latter case, the incentive to catch the offending party is not very high.

Sentencing Guidelines
U.S. government rules by which a company can be prosecuted if an employee violates a law, even without company knowledge.

Under the U.S. **Sentencing Guidelines** of 1991, a company can be prosecuted if an employee violates a law, even without company knowledge. The fines for owners, managers, and employees of companies who violate any of the more than 800 different federal statutes are 10 to 20 times higher than they were in the past. Government attorneys gener-

Real-Life Ethical Vignette

After a leveraged buyout, Browning Machinery had a huge debt. People believed that they were constantly "under the gun." They justified using copiers, faxes, envelopes, and postage for personal use by saying that the "discipline of debt" forced them to work harder. They had been forced to make concessions in pay and benefits while shareholders, raiders, and top management reaped undeserved rewards. As a supervisor at Browning Machinery, what should you do to combat this attitude?

ally go after the people at the top. If an indictment occurs, there is a 90 percent chance of conviction or a guilty plea. Fines can be 95 percent lower for businesses that have implemented codes of conduct and effective compliance programs prior to a violation, but *having* programs and *using* them are often very different. Many ethics plans gather dust on corporate shelves. Employees have to feel comfortable with a plan before they will use it.

Studies of White-Collar Corporate Crime

Studies of white-collar crime can provide insights and raise interesting questions.

1. *Are managers rational about corporate crime?* Do they calculate the benefits of illegal activities to themselves or to their company and compare them to the probability of detection multiplied by the costs of getting caught. If so, the way to reduce corporate crime is by changing the cost-benefit calculus, imposing more onerous consequences on the offenders (e.g., larger fines, more public shame and humiliation), and increasing the likelihood of catching offenders (e.g., larger enforcement budgets).[18]

2. *Do declining economic conditions affect the performance of illegal acts?* When there is a downturn in organizational performance, depression within an industry, or a general recession, organizational crime may go up. Criminal acts can appear more attractive as the environment becomes constrained. As economic pressure on the firm increases, managers also may get desperate and feel justified in committing illegal acts. Illegal behavior has been found to increase in a scarce (i.e., nonmunificent) environment characterized by prior poor performance (measured by return on equity and return on sales) in the industry. Firms that violate the law are less profitable than firms in general but are no less profitable than other firms in their industry.[19]

3. *What is the role of ethical climate in illegal behavior?* It is not surprising that financial strain is often viewed as a reason for dubious behavior. Violations can increase sales and profits, improve market share, and help cut costs. However, aren't all firms motivated by the desire to improve their economic performance? Does it really make a difference if a firm is under the additional stress of economic decline? The relationship between economic performance and corporate illegality has been found to be weak; other factors operate to separate violating from nonviolating firms including "different ethical climates."[20]

Environmental stress provides a motive for dubious activities, but it is not its cause. For that one must turn to the climate of the organization and the control mechanisms that permit illegal activity, and the personality and character of the individuals involved. In the final analysis, illegal behavior is a matter of free choice.

Criminal behavior has to be "learned" in isolation from the rest of society and in close association with those who define such behavior favorably. This theory of criminal behavior is called **referent group theory.** In some companies, employees identify so completely with the company's production, profit, growth, and other goals that they subordinate their individual values to those of the company (see Chapter 6) and lose a sense of their own identity. Their values and personality structure are fragile and are broken by strong company and other pressures.[21]

referent group theory Criminal behavior is learned in isolation from society and from associates who regard such behavior favorably.

Case studies suggest that corporate illegalities become a way of life in some organizations. When asked to give their own reasons why corporate crime takes place, organization members rarely mention economic pressures but point instead to the ethical climate and the influence of leadership. Highly mobile leaders more interested in financial results and career advancement than in the firm's reputation create a weak climate for employee resistance to corporate illegality.[22]

Size can make a difference. Dominant companies in uncompetitive industries may be able to pass costs on to consumers and therefore be more compliant. However, in large organizations with strong hierarchical relations, lower-level employees may feel that they are supposed to achieve profit and growth targets without regard to ethical and legal considerations. In large, complex organizations, illegalities occur because the division of labor protects upper-level persons with a "veil of ignorance." Superiors do not want to know how results have been obtained so long as the results are achieved.[23]

Reason 4: To Promote Trust

A final reason that ethics matters is to promote trust and prevent debilitating conflict. Successful companies are built on a network of trust that binds management, employees, and shareholders. Troubled companies cannot sustain this trust.

Organizational Citizenship. In *Organizational Citizenship Behavior: The Good Soldier Syndrome*, Dennis Organ attributes much of corporate success to discretionary activities that are not directly recognized in the formal reward system but which in aggregate promote effective functioning.[24] This is called **organizational citizenship.** In other contexts, these attributes would be called altruism, neighborliness, sportsmanship, and courtesy. They imply avoiding petty grievances and excessive complaining about real or imagined slights. One should help others who have tasks or problems regardless of any direct personal reward or recognition. These prosocial behaviors are the essence of civic virtue—responsible participation in life of the organization.

organization citizenship Discretionary activities, not formally rewarded by the incentive system, that promote organizational effectiveness.

John Kotter and James Hesketh of the Harvard Business School find that long-term corporate success is more common in companies where trust and organizational citizenship are in place. A company has to show that it cares equally about all its stakeholders and has to pay special attention to customers and employees. Investment analysts chose 12 companies that were governed according to these values and 20 companies that were not. Since 1950, the companies that adhered to the values increased their revenues by 12 times, expanded their workforces by 8 times, and increased their share prices by 12 times. Net profits grew by 756 percent as opposed to 1 percent in the companies that lacked these corporate values.[25]

Debilitating Conflict. In the absence of trust, debilitating conflict can arise in an organization. Issues of fairness and the division of spoils divide a company and make it difficult to function. Time-consuming and complex arguments over the division of revenues and profits hurt the Arthur Andersen accounting firm in the early 1990s. The partners in the company's two major divisions—accounting and computers—fought one another bitterly over the issue of compensation.

The accounting partners generated less revenue per person but were better paid. The computer partners produced higher growth rates and profit margins but had no influence in decision making. The accountants adhered to the rule that 70 percent of the allocation of shares had to be linked to seniority. They argued that their investment had built up the computer business; now that it was flourishing they had every right to the profits. Their concern was that the computer partners might defect.

To prevent computer partners from joining Andersen's rivals, the accountants introduced "noncompeting" clauses into the contracts of the computer partners. This clause did not apply to the accountants. The accountants fired the head of the computer division, claiming that he was plotting to leave and to take other partners with him.

The conflict went on for years. Eventually Arthur Andersen split into two separate businesses. It changed its allocation formula from seniority to performance.[26]

Prosocial Behavior. Prosocial behavior is supposed to be at the core of Herman Miller's success. Herman Miller is a manufacturer of office and health care furniture in Zeeland, Michigan. The company appears frequently on lists of the best managed and most admired corporations in the United States. It has been cited for the superior quality and design of its products. The company has a good record on women—it is regarded as one of the best companies in which a woman can work—and the environment. A leader in cutting costs by cutting waste, Herman Miller has reduced product packaging, created its own waste-to-energy plant, and sells or swaps many recyclable materials. Since 1950 sales have increased from $2 million to $865 million. Limits are placed on how much more the CEO can earn than the average worker.[27]

Max Depree, the founding chairman of the company, made a covenant with his workers. He claims to owe them a rational environment that values their trust and in turn provides them with human dignity. He gives them the opportunity for personal development and self-fulfillment. In his book, *Leadership Is an Art*, Depree maintains that strong values and open communication are needed for successful management. People identify with an organization's spirit, sense of joy, beauty, and excellence. They need a setting of equality, which values their contributions and does not crush their initiative.

Obstacles to Being Ethical

If being ethical is in the corporation's interest, why is so difficult for employees to live up to ethical expectations?—because there are many temptations: greed, pressures to perform, fear of failure, a sense that no one is ethical, lack of character, self-absorption, and an inability to respect the law.[28] An investment banker, whose yearly income exceeds $1 million, sells insider tips for which he collects a briefcase stuffed with $700,000. Savings and loan officers in Texas with six-figure incomes steal from their institutions to buy Rolls-Royces and take personal trips to Paris. A defense contractor, whose firm has $11 billion in annual sales, charges the government $100,000 for a plastic cap on a stool leg.

The average employee, affected chiefly by the expectation to perform, may be less greedy than fearful. He or she may believe that achieving corporate objectives is what matters, but how these objectives are achieved is not particularly relevant.[29]

In an economic slowdown, managers subject their employees to increasing pressure. Employees learn that it is acceptable to misstate an occasional sales figure, manipulate a customer, exploit a competitor, prevaricate to the boss, or overlook corporate wrongdoing because the company needs to survive.

Fear of failure drives many employees to wrongdoing. People want to keep their jobs, but their companies face rising competition on a global scale. More overseas companies have entered U.S. markets. More domestic industries have been deregulated. To keep up with one's rivals, it may be necessary to cut corners.

Baby-boomers who reach the top fear being crowded out, and they develop anxiety about falling behind economically. Insecurity increases in households headed by 25- to 34-year-olds when median real family income declines 6.4 percent, as happened from 1979 to 1987.

Lack of character is at the root of many of our moral difficulties. Surveys show that among 18–30-year-olds, 70–80 percent admitted cheating in high school, 40–50 percent admitted cheating in college, and 24 percent confessed to placing false information on their résumés. **Character** has been defined as a combination of empathy and self-control.[30] Empathy is the willingness to take into account the rights, needs, and feelings of others. Self-control is the willingness to take into account the more distant consequences of present actions—to be future oriented rather than wholly present oriented.

character
A combination of empathy, the capacity to consider the feelings of others seriously, and self-control, the ability to take into account long-term consequences.

An increasingly level of self-absorption can be traced to the "me" generation and "do your own thing" of the 1960s. These narcissistic tendencies were exacerbated by growing mobility and isolation as people moved from job to job and community to community, weakening the ties to their own communities and families. The 1980s were a period of conspicuous consumption, careerism, and self-centeredness. It was permissible to enrich oneself without bounds, and spend and flaunt a lot of money. At the same time, respect for the law diminished, replaced by a cowboy-like attitude that institutions and the rules that govern them were not worthy of honor.

Ways to Enhance Ethical Behavior

The 1990s may yet prove to be different. Seven ways to enhance ethical behavior are outlined below.

Know and Use Ethical Principles. These principles will be developed in more detail in subsequent chapters. For now, it is sufficient to be aware of four.

1. The Golden Rule: Act in way that you want others to act toward you.
2. The categorical imperative: Respect all people; treat them as ends not simply means; act in a manner that could be considered a universal rule of behavior (i.e., don't make exceptions for yourself).
3. The utilitarian principle: Try to achieve the greatest good for the greatest number.
4. The TV test: Be certain that you could explain your actions comfortably to a national television audience.

However valid in the abstract, these principles may be in conflict with each other, as we shall see.

Act in a Way That Prevents Harm to People and Companies. Know the consequences of failure to act according to this precept. Alamo Rent-a-Car had to refund $3 million to customers it overcharged for repairs. The practice of bribery and sloppy accounting to get business abroad may affect one's domestic business. Cargill refuses to engage in bribery and will not operate in certain countries because bribery is rampant.

Act in a Way That Keeps You from Going to Jail. Fines under federal racketeering laws (RICO) reach into the hundreds of millions of dollars for many offenses—antitrust, securities, contracts, fraud, bribery, kickbacks, and money laundering. Ivan Boesky, of "greed is good" fame, spent time in a Lompoc federal prison camp. Michael Milken was sentenced to 10 years in prison and had to pay $600 million in fines and restitution. Leona Helmsley was convicted of tax fraud and served time in prison.

Act in a Way That Avoids Public Humiliation. Do not do anything on the job that you would not want your mother to watch on the morning news. However, many Watergate figures and others implicated in scandals have profited. They have received large amounts of money for book contracts, speaking tours, or TV docudramas.

Act in a Way That Preserves Your Job. Citicorp fired its president and senior executive of its credit card processing division for overstating revenues. AMEX (American Express) fired executives who failed to follow company policy and write off accounts of customers who went bankrupt. NYNEX fired marketing people who wrote improper reports that resulted in unjustified commissions.

Set Realistic Goals for Subordinates, So They Won't Cheat. Reward admirable behavior, but do not reward employees whose numbers look good without checking whether corners were cut to achieve the good results.

Act in a Way That Promotes Peace of Mind. Ultimately, you must see that consuming things is unlikely to satisfy your longing for meaning. You will get no satisfaction from working for an employer whose main values are dishonesty, infighting, and self-aggrandizement. Christopher Noon, a successful Chicago area developer, said, "The reason we're here on earth is not just to earn money and drive a BMW."[31] "What do we care about? What do we stand for? We are not the sum of our possessions," George Bush said at his 1988 inauguration, "We all want to save, nurture, and share."

A recent headline proclaimed: "Money Is No Longer Top Concern For MBAs." The article that followed reported a Duke University survey of 650 MBA students at 11 leading schools. The survey found that 70 percent of the students would not work in certain industries because of ethical and political concerns. About 82 percent of the students would not work for tobacco companies—the financial mainstay of Duke University; 36 percent would avoid firms with environmental problems; 26 percent would avoid liquor marketers; and 20 percent would avoid defense contractors.[32] How do you feel about these matters? Are there companies for whom you would not work?

Conclusions

This chapter has provided four reasons why ethics matter. It has discussed obstacles to ethical behavior and ways to remove those obstacles. Stephen Covey, head of a firm that does leadership development around the world, starts his seminars on principle-centered leadership with a quotation from the French Jesuit philosopher Pierre Teilhard de Chardin: "We are not human beings having a spiritual experience. We are spiritual beings having a human experience." Covey has formulated seven habits belonging to highly effective people.[33]

1. Be proactive—take the initiative and be responsible.
2. Begin with the end in mind—start with an image of outcomes conforming to values you cherish.
3. Put first things first—discipline yourself to subordinate your feelings, impulses, and moods to your values.
4. Think win-win.
5. Seek first to understand, then to be understood—listen to others to empathize with them and then reply.
6. Synergize—create wholes greater than the sum of the parts.
7. Sharpen the saw—cultivate the essential dimensions of your character: physical, mental, emotional/social, and spiritual.

Covey maintains that these maxims help breed the behaviors—fairness, integrity, honesty, dignity, service, quality, and excellence—that have been part of every major enduring ethical system, social philosophy, and religion.

Discussion Questions

1. Why do companies have ethics problems?
2. How useful is 3M's Pocket Guide to corporate ethics? What are the guide's strong and weak points?

3. As the top officer of a corporation, how would you respond to Mike Barnicle's column about corporate greed?
4. Do you think Japanese Premier Miyazawa is right about American work ethics? Explain your answer.
5. What does Daniel Bell mean by the "Protestant ethic"? Why is it important?
6. Why did the Sears auto mechanics cheat? Who is to blame?
7. What is your view of the Joe Camel marketing campaign? Was it unethical?
8. To what extent were *The Progressive*'s charges against H. B. Fuller Company unfair?
9. Compare the wrongdoing at Prudential, the Defense Department, and Kidder, Peabody. Who is to blame for what went wrong?
10. Assess Martin Marietta's ethics program. Is it a good one? Why or why not?
11. What do the studies of white-collar crime suggest about its prevention?
12. Why does organizational citizenship thrive in some organizations and not in others?
13. Compare and contrast the cultures at Arthur Andersen and Herman Miller. How do you explain the difference?
14. Why aren't some people ethical?
15. What can be done to enhance ethical behavior?

Endnotes

1. Institute of Management Accountants, "More Companies Adopt Ethics Policies,"; "Standards of Ethical Conduct for Management Accountants," *Management Accounting,* Feb. 1994, p. 22; Kenneth Labich, "The New Crisis in Business Ethics," *Fortune,* April 20, 1992, pp. 167–76.
2. Mike Barnicle, "Why Our Society Is Falling Apart," *Boston Globe,* Jan. 13, 1992, p. 18.
3. Colin Nickerson, "Japan's Premier Hits U.S. on Work Ethic," *Boston Globe,* Sept. 25, 1994, p. 1/7.
4. Juliet Schor, *The Overworked American* (New York: Basic Books, 1991).
5. James Sterngold, "Another Scandal in Japan," *Sunday New York Times News of the Week in Review,* Jan. 13, 1992, p. 3.
6. Nancy Perry, "What's Powering Mexico's Success," *Fortune,* Feb. 10, 1992, pp. 109–15; Peter Nulty, "The Bounce is Back at Goodyear," *Fortune,* Sept. 7, 1992, pp. 70–72; quoted in Brenton Schlender, "The Values We Will Need," *Fortune,* Jan. 27, 1992, pp. 75–77.
7. Daniel Bell, *The Cultural Contradictions of Capitalism* (New York: Basic Books, 1976), pp. 54–57; D. Vogel, "Business Ethics Past and Present," *The Public Interest* 102 (1991), pp. 49–64.
8. Michael Santoro, "Sears Auto Centers (A)," Harvard Business Case, Dec. 13, 1993.
9. Quoted in *The Economist,* May 16, 1992.
10. "The Tobacco Trade," *Economics,* May 16, 1992, pp. 21–24.
11. H. B. Fuller Company, 1993 *Community Affairs Report;* H. B. Fuller Company, 1993 *Annual Report.*
12. "Not So Prudent," *Economics,* Aug. 31, 1991, pp. 59–60; Hubert Herring, "Ever Get Burned by a Fast-Talking Broker?" *The New York Times,* Oct. 24, 1993, p. 2F; Kurt Eichenwald, "Fraud Accord Has Prudential Phones Ringing," *The New York Times,* Oct. 23, 1993, pp. 15, 23; Barnaby Feder, "Limiting the Statute of Limitations," *The New York Times,* Oct. 23, 1993, pp. 15, 23.

13. Ann Merrills, "Stealing from the Hand That Feeds You," *Minneapolis Star Tribune*, Oct. 3, 1994, pp. 1D, 7D.
14. Irwin Ross, "Inside the Biggest Pentagon Scam," *Fortune*, Jan. 11, 1993, pp. 88–92.
15. Terrence Pare, "Jack Welch's Nightmare on Wall Street," *Fortune*, Sept. 5, 1994, pp. 41–48; "Questions About Kidder," *Business Week*, Aug. 22, 1994, pp. 60–63.
16. Lynn Sharp Paine, "Martin Marietta: Managing Corporate Ethics (A)," Harvard Business Case, Sept. 14, 1992.
17. Banning Lary, "Why Corporations Can't Lock the Rascals Out," *Management Review*, Oct. 1989, pp. 51–54.
18. P. Bromiley and A. Marcus, "The Deterrent to Dubious Corporate Behavior," *Strategic Management Journal* 10 (1989), pp. 233–50; G. Geis and R. F. Meier, *White-Collar Crime: Offenses in Business, Politics and the Professions* (New York: Free Press, 1977).
19. Szwajkowski, "Organizational Illegality: Theoretical Integration and Illustrative Application," *Academy of Management Review*, 1985, pp. 558–67.
20. P. C. Yeager, "Analyzing Corporate Offenses: Progress and Prospects," *Corporate Social Performance and Policy*, 1986, pp. 93–120; P. Asch and J. J. Seneca, "Is Collusion Profitable?" *Review of Economics and Statistics* 58 (1976), pp. 1–12.
21. E. H. Sutherland, *White Collar Crime* (New York: Holt, 1949), p. 234.
22. Geis and Meier, *White-Collar Crime*; M. B. Clinard, *Corporate Ethics and Crime: The Role of Middle Management* (Beverly Hills, Calif.: Sage, 1983).
23. P. C. Yeager, "The Politics of Corporate Social Control: The Federal Response to Industrial Water Pollution," unpublished Ph.D. dissertation, University of Wisconsin, Madison, 1981; Peter C. Yeager, "Structural Biases in Regulatory Law Enforcement," paper presented at the Annual Meetings of the Society for the Study of Social Problems, Washington, D.C., 1985.
24. Dennis Organ, *Organizational Citizenship Behavior: The Good Soldier Syndrome* (Lexington, Mass.: Lexington Books, 1990).
25. John Kotter and James Heskett, *Corporate Culture and Performance* (New York: Free Press, 1992).
26. "Civil War at Arthur Andersen," *Economics*, Aug. 17, 1991, pp. 66–67.
27. "The Magic of Herman Miller," *Industry Week*, Feb. 18, 1991, pp. 11–17; "Herman Miller," *Business Week*, Sept. 16, 1991, pp. 51–56.
28. Ronald Henkoff, "Is Greed Dead?" *Fortune*, Aug. 14, 1989, pp. 40–49.
29. Gene Laczniak, "Business Ethics: A Manager's Primer," *Business*, Janurary–March 1993, pp. 23–29.
30. James Q. Wilson, *On Character* (Lanham, Md.: AEI Press, 1991).
31. *Fortune*, August 14, 1989, p. 46.
32. Eric Randall, "Money Is No Longer Top Concern for MBAs," *USA Today*, June 11, 1994, p. 1.
33. "Corporate America, Dr. Feelgood Will See You Now," *Business Week*, Dec. 6, 1993, p. 52; Ani Hadjian, "What's So Effective About Stephen Covey?" *Fortune*, Dec. 12, 1994, pp. 116–26.

Case 5–A
Philip Morris Companies, Inc., and the Cigarette Controversy[1]

In her second assignment (her first was Wal-Mart, discussed in Case 1–A), Joanne Magnuson, new analyst for Alliance Capital, was asked to give her opinion of Philip Morris as an investment risk.

EXHIBIT 1 Sales and Profits, 1993–1994 ($ billions)

	Sales		Profits	
	1993	*1994*	*1993*	*1994*
Domestic tobacco	$7.9	$8.0	$2.8	$3.3
International tobacco	8.5	9.5	2.4	2.8
North American food	20.9	21.3	2.4	2.5
International food	9.4	9.3	1.1	1.2
Miller beer	3.4	3.7	.4	.4
Totals	$50.1	$51.8	$9.1	$10.2

An institutional investor had held more than $500,000 worth of stock in Philip Morris for the past 10 years and had made substantial capital gains. This investor was now considering whether to increase its stake in Philip Morris, reduce it, or keep it steady. Its concerns had much to do with the social, political, and legal climate in which Philip Morris was operating. This case first provides a detailed analysis of Philip Morris's financial position and then an analysis of these issues. The question for Joanne Magnuson was the bearing that the cigarette controversy would have on Philip Morris's future performance.

Description

Philip Morris is the largest consumer products company in the world with revenues twice that of Procter and Gamble. Its brands include Marlboro, Benson and Hedges, Chesterfield, Miracle Whip, Jell-O, Oscar Mayer, Entenmann, Toblerone, Maxwell House, Post Cereals, Sealtest, and Kool-Aid (see Exhibit 1). The company is headquartered in New York City and has 161,000 employees. Its main competitors, with their total sales for 1993 are American Brands ($13.7 billion) and RJR Nabisco Holdings ($15.1 billion). Philip Morris possesses a 45 percent share of the U.S. cigarette market.[2]

The company entered the food business through acquisitions of General Foods in November 1985, Kraft Foods in December 1988, and two European companies, Jacobs Suchard AG in August 1990 and Freia Marabou in April 1993. Philip Morris also owns the Miller Beer Company. Philip Morris's sales productivity ratio is a very high $378,000 per employee. It is the largest advertiser in the world, spending over $2 billion a year on media advertising. It is a large and frequent contributor to many causes, including the NAACP, the United Negro College Fund, the Boy Scouts, the Girl Scouts, the United Way, the National Multiple Sclerosis Society, and the National Association on Drug Abuse. It supports the Joffrey Ballet, the Morgan Library, the Guggenheim Museum, the American Museum of Natural History, and the National Gallery of Art. A company document explains its philosophy on corporate giving: "We believe that business activities must make social sense and that social activities must make business sense."

Operating Margins

Philip Morris's 1993 operating margins were 16.1 percent—a blend of high margins in tobacco and lower margins in food and beer. Overall operating margins for Philip Morris have been fairly stable for the past 10 years. The surge to 20.5 percent in 1992 was probably a one-time blip and the sharp decline in 1993, coupled with the first earnings decline in 15 years, resulted from the turmoil of consumer price resistance and a voluntary cut in the price of Marlboro by 40 cents a pack. On April 2, 1993, now referred to as Marlboro Friday, Philip Morris reduced the retail price of its famous brand to compete with cheaper generic brands that had cut its market share to 22 percent. The immediate result was a huge decline in revenues, but after a year the market share, at 27 percent, was the highest ever. Operating margins recovered in 1994, running over 17 percent.

Of its two major tobacco competitors, RJR enjoyed the highest margins and American Brands the lowest. The differences are predominantly due to the different business mix in each firm. RJR has proportionately more tobacco and its food subsidiary, Nabisco, has higher margins than Philip Morris's food operations. American Brands has only a small market share of U.S. cigarette sales and a high proportion of tobacco sales abroad where margins are lower.

The 1993 operating margin of Philip Morris's food business compared with that of other food companies shows how weak the company's food business is.

Company	Margin
Kellogg	21.2%
Campbell Soup	18.5%
Heinz	17.0%
Hershey	16.3%
General Mills	15.3%
Sara Lee	11.6%
Philip Morris Food	11.0%

A comparison of Miller's 1993 operating margins with those of competing brewers shows that the beer business also is very weak. It is puzzling why the company has not sold or spun off the Miller Brewing Company after all these years.

Market Valuation

Tobacco stocks no longer sell at market multiples. Philip Morris has not had an annual average P/E multiple higher than the market since 1981. Prior to 1982, the stock often sold at a premium to the market. The reasons for the change are obvious: fears of litigation (so far the industry has won every case based on the cigarette warning label), declining consumption in the United States, expectations of declining consumption abroad, the threat of higher taxes on cigarettes, and the realization that much of the company's rapid earnings growth (earnings per share have averaged 19.5 percent growth for the past 10 years!) is due to unsustainable price increases. The lackluster performance of the food group and Miller has not helped the company's multiple either.

Until 1992, however, Philip Morris's relative P/E had been steadily climbing toward 1.0, reaching 0.95 in 1991. Consumer resistance to higher cigarette prices, higher taxes, and restrictions on smokers have probably ended that climb. In 1992, the stock price peaked at $86.63. In the fall of 1994, Philip Morris was selling under $60 per share after hitting a low of $45 in 1993. The stock rebounded in part because the board voted to increase the dividend by almost 20 percent and gave its approval to a three-year $6 billion stock buyback program. However, investors who bought the stock in 1980 at $4.50 were lucky enough to sell at $80 in 1992; and with nerves strong enough to hold on through every litigation scare, they received an average annual compound return of over 30 percent.[3]

Discussion

Despite welcome figures in parts of its business, Philip Morris has a series of problems that cloud its future. Cigarette use in the United States is continuing to decline, especially among the more affluent sectors of the society. Price increases of 10 to 15 percent per year can no longer be sustained because consumers will give up brand loyalty if the price difference is right. Attempts to discourage smoking have intensified, and sharp tax increases, the best way to stop young teenagers from taking up the habit, appear inevitable. New litigation dangers have appeared because government warning labels fail to alert consumers to the possibilities of addiction. New judges appointed by President Clinton may make the federal courts more hostile to tobacco and more likely to remove the judicial protection granted the companies by the warning label.

The growth for Philip Morris is now coming from foreign sales of cigarettes as management aggressively promotes overseas sales.[4] The U.S. federal government has forced many countries to open up their markets to American cigarettes and even to permit the advertising of U.S. brands in countries where cigarette ads are banned.

It is only a matter of time, however, before foreign governments realize the burden that cigarettes are going to place on their publicly funded health care systems and try to reduce consumption. Hence, Philip Morris does not have a clear path to continued growth in its tobacco business. For this reason, powerful shareholders such as pension funds have started to demand that management spin off the company's tobacco holdings from its other businesses.[5] So far the new management that took over after the resignation of CEO Michael Miles in June 1994 has resisted this demand.

The food operations are a disappointment, though neither General Foods nor Kraft Foods were outstanding companies before Philip Morris acquired them. Operating margins for this sector are lower than those of other large food companies. Health-conscious consumers are eating fewer dairy products and avoiding many of Philip Morris's packaged products that are heavily laden with sugar while soft drinks are replacing coffee among the younger generation. The breakfast cereal business is a great business, but Post does not have the market share and supermarket shelf space of Kellogg and General Mills. Miller Beer remains a problem. It is woefully lacking in margins at all comparable to those of the competition.

Philip Morris management is clearly under pressure to produce. It must get margins up in the food operation and do something about Miller Beer. It must find investment opportunities for the $2 billion in cash generated by the tobacco business each year. A lot of management's attention will be focused on the overseas cigarette business and on domestic political and judicial issues affecting cigarettes. Shareholder pressure may grow to spin off less profitable divisions and leave only a food and beverage company.

The top management of the food divisions have to actively focus on improving their margins and sales. Cost-cutting is an important ongoing issue.

Management Succession at Philip Morris

On June 17, 1994, Michael Miles unexpectedly resigned as chairman of the board and CEO. Miles was known for the dramatic move he took when he lowered the price of Marlboro cigarettes. This move raised the brand's share from under 20 percent to over 28 percent and dealt a decisive blow to the low-price brands, which had been gaining on Marlboro.[6]

Advances in earnings were slow to follow, as 1993, the year of the price cut, proved disastrous for the cigarette manufacturer. However, sharp earning gains in 1994 demonstrated how shrewd the price cut had been.

A Reluctance to Aggressively Argue the Case for Smoking. Miles' departure may have occurred because of his reluctance to aggressively argue the case for cigarette smoking. Many in the company believed that Philip Morris was losing the public relations battle. It had to undertake a public relations campaign to defend the legitimacy of its product.

The perception created by the media, one which was gaining ground among analysts and investors, was that the tobacco industry was in the midst of a slow but inevitable decline because it would not be able to withstand the onslaught from antismoking forces.

These perceptions were linked to pressures applied by pension funds (like TIAA-CREF) and mutual funds (like Fidelity) to get the company to split the food from the tobacco business. Institutional investors argued that the food division should be split from the tobacco division to save Philip Morris from tobacco's ultimate demise.[7]

In 1988, the Surgeon General of the United States found that smoking was not only dangerous but addictive; more than 420,000 Americans die each year from cigarette smoking, more than die from homicide, suicide, AIDs, automobile accidents, alcohol, and drug abuse. The antismoking Clinton administration threatened to impose additional taxes on tobacco manufacturers to finance health care reform. It banned smoking in government agencies, including the Pentagon, and was considering legislation that would extend the ban to all public places.

The Food and Drug Administration (FDA) made an aggressive and well-publicized bid to regulate tobacco as a dangerous drug. The evidence seemed to be mounting that people in the industry knew of the health risks of smoking and that it was addictive, even when they publicly denied such knowledge. Internal documents at Brown and Williamson (maker of Kool and Viceroy brands) indicate that company executives grappled with the idea of revealing to the Surgeon General what they knew about cigarette hazards as far back as 1963. One of the documents concludes: "We are . . . in the business of selling nicotine, an addictive drug." The executives decided to keep silent, not disclose their research results, stop work on a safe cigarette, and carry out a campaign of obfuscation.[8]

The Tobacco Product Liability Project, a 10-year-old program to support lawsuits against the cigarette manufacturers, was making inroads. Health care agencies around the country initiated lawsuits to seek refunds for treating smoking-related illnesses. A coalition of attorneys filed what was likely to be the biggest class action suit of all time on behalf of every American who had ever smoked. Melvin Belli, one of the leading attorneys said: "We will prove that the tobacco industry has conspired to catch you, hold you, and kill you."

An attorney also brought a $5 billion suit on behalf of flight attendants who claimed to have been harmed by secondary smoke. R. J. Reynolds planned to introduce a safer, low-smoke cigarette called Eclipse, which would emit very little second-hand smoke and have less tar and nicotine than other cigarettes, but attorneys bringing liability suits against Reynolds argued that the company was, in effect, admitting that its current cigarettes were not safe.

In June 1994, executives of the major tobacco companies faced six hours of grilling before the Health and Environment Subcommittee of the U.S. House of Representatives. The confrontation took place following the publication of a 1993 Environmental Protection Agency (EPA) report that classified, for the first time, second-hand smoke as a carcinogen. The EPA estimated that more than 3,000 nonsmoking Americans die annually from lung cancer simply because they have been too close to other people's smoke. These findings were confirmed by a Louisiana State University Medical Center study showing that women exposed to their husband's tobacco smoke had a 30 percent greater chance of getting lung cancer than women in smoke-free environments.

Ultimately, such attacks would add up. The lawsuits, legislation, and regulatory proposals battered the cigarette maker. Miles was an aloof, uncommunicative nonsmoker, who came from the food side of Philip Morris, and he was replaced by the company's hardened tobacco men and smokers, who had always run the company.

Miles favored splitting the company in two, but he was opposed by Hamish Maxwell (of Maxwell House Coffee), the company's former board chairman and still a powerful member of the executive committee. Maxwell had been the architect of the diversification that combined the food companies (General Foods and Kraft) with Philip Morris, and he did not want his efforts undone.[9]

A Media Campaign to Blitz the Opposition. The new management team of William Murray (chairman) and Geoffrey Bible (CEO) had spent their entire professional lives in the tobacco industry.[10] They were determined to defend the cigarette business at any cost. They were armed with facts and figures about the contribution of the tobacco industry to the economies of the United States and the world, its role in paying taxes and reducing budget deficits (the industry was the largest taxpayer in the country), and its positive contribution, as a strong export industry, to reducing the trade deficit.

Emphasizing smokers' rights, which were being curtailed in prohibitions against smoking throughout the country, the new management team stressed the importance of individual liberty and choice in the decision to enjoy the pleasures of smoking. They contested the scientific findings that linked smoking and the passive absorption of smoke to disease. They announced that they would go on the offensive to remove smoking bans in restaurants and public places in California.

In an early press conference, Geoffrey Bible declared the new management team's intention of defending the industry and the rights of consumers. He demonstrably and incessantly chain-smoked Marlboro menthols to the point where some members of the media in the small and unventilated room protested that they were ill. The combative Bible was a proud smoker and drinker who had built international tobacco into an $8.5 billion business. Described as a "fanatic" who was "on the edge all the time," he inspired fear among the people who worked for him. Bible was driven by a "strong work ethic," and he promised to barnstorm the country with a media campaign to blitz the opposition.

Bible claimed that the company's advertising campaign would authoritatively rebut the critics. Its advertising campaign was directed by the well-known Young and Rubicom agency, which had effectively altered public perceptions of controversial issues in the past. In June 1993, the company sued the EPA for alleging that secondary smoke was a carcinogen. In March 1994, it organized a demonstration by tobacco workers against the proposal to raise the cigarette tax.

Philip Morris had many reasons to be optimistic. The new Republican majority in both Houses of Congress surely meant less government pressure. The company pointed to polls showing that more people, especially the young, women, and minorities, were smoking. There was a revival in the thinking that smoking was pleasurable, that it eased tension, aided concentration, and made a person happier. Faith Popcorn, an observer of popular trends, talked about the "pleasure revenge"—a revolt against the puritanism of an overly health-conscious nation.

Reasons for Accepting Smoking. The top executives of Philip Morris had various reasons for accepting smoking. A revealing article in the *Sunday New York Times* (March 20, 1994), quoted many of them.[11] Stephen Parrish, senior vice president for external affairs, was quoted as saying:

> . . . my daughter came home from school, and said: ". . . tomorrow we're going to talk about drugs . . . We're also going to talk about cigarettes and whether they're addictive." . . . I told her that a lot of people believe that cigarette smoking is addictive but I don't believe it . . . the Surgeon General says some 40 million people have quit smoking on their own . . . But if she asked me about the health consequences, I would tell her that I certainly don't think it's safe to smoke . . . But it's a choice. We're confronted with choices all the time . . .

David Dangoor, executive vice president for international operations, said:

> Everybody knows that smoking must be a terrible idea . . . Yet they do it. Why? . . . People do all sorts of things to express their individuality and to protest against society. And smoking is one of them, and not the worst . . . In a lot of countries, its incredibly important to the whole welfare state that we sell our products to collect taxes.

Craig Fuller, senior vice president for corporate affairs, said:

> We think smokers and nonsmokers alike have rights. And they ought to be accommodated . . . Among our strongest brands is Marlboro . . . It gives us cash flow, a financial base . . .

William Campbell, president and chief executive officer of Philip Morris USA, said:

> My girls ask why I smoke. And I can only answer that I enjoy it, and I think I'm informed about it. And I tell them, "You'll be facing decisions like this one when you're an adult . . ."

Victor Crawford, a lobbyist for the Tobacco Institute, said:

> And January 3 of '92 I got the diagnosis of throat cancer . . . I have no animosity. I've got nobody to blame but myself . . . I'm not proud of having lobbied for them . . . Do I feel guilty about what I did? Yeah.

Discussion Questions

1. Would you invest in Philip Morris?
2. Would you advise your clients to invest in this company?
3. What reasons would you give for investing or not investing in Philip Morris? Would they be only financial reasons?
4. To what extent do financial considerations alone mean a client should not invest in Philip Morris?
5. To what extent are the reasons for not investing ethical in nature? Should these ethical reasons affect your decision making?

Endnotes

1. This case was written by Donald Geffen and Alfred Marcus.
2. "Philip Morris," *Value Line*, June 23, 1994, p. 1876; "Philip Morris Posts Income Gain in Quarter," *The New York Times*, July 13, 1994, p. 4D.
3. "For Philip Morris, Another Adversary: Stockholders," *Business Week*, July 4, 1994, p. 26; "Market Place: Who Wants Philip Morris with Its Problems? Many Investors Do," *The New York Times*, July 24, 1994, p. 8D; "Big Investors Pressing Philip Morris," *The New York Times*, June 21, 1994, p. 4D.
4. "Philip Morris in Ukraine," *The New York Times*, June 1, 1994, p. 5D.
5. "Philip Morris Decides Not to Split Its Units," *The New York Times*, May 26, 1994, p. 1D; "A Rumor of War in the Philip Morris Boardroom," *Business Week*, June 13, 1994; "Philip Morris Chairman Unexpectedly Resigns," *The New York Times*, June 20, 1994, p. 1D; "Philip Morris Chief Leaves Name-Brand Legacy," *The New York Times*, June 21, 1994, p. 1D.
6. "Philip Morris: Man Friday," *The Economist*, June 25, 1994, p. 65.
7. Jonathan Freeland, "Showdown at the Last Gasp," *The Guardian*, June 9, 1994, pp. 2–3.
8. Phillip Hilts, "Tobacco Company Was Silent on Hazards," *The New York Times*, May 7, 1994, p. 1/9.
9. "Philip Morris Will Stay in One Piece," *Business Week*, June 6, 1994, p. 42.
10. "A 'Smokin' Marlboro Man," *Business Week*, Sept. 19, 1994, pp. 59–62; "Philip Morris Plans Smoking Campaign," *The New York Times*, June 27, 1994, p. 7D; "Philip Morris Goes on the Offensive," *The New York Times*, June 22, 1994, p. 3D; "Philip Morris on Offensive in California," *The New York Times*, May 16, 1994, p. 1A.
11. Roger Rosenblatt, "How Do Tobacco Executives Live with Themselves," *New York Times Magazine*, March 20, 1994, pp. 34, 51, 74.

CASE 5–B
H. B. FULLER IN HONDURAS[1]

In the summer of 1985, H. B. Fuller's Resistol product was implicated in glue sniffing among Honduran street children. A wire service quoted a newspaper article:

> They lie senseless on doorsteps and pavements, grimy and loose limbed, like discarded rag dolls. Some are just five or six years old. Others are young adults, all are addicted to sniffing a commonly sold glue that is doing them irreversible brain damage . . . Resistol is a contact cement glue, widely used by shoe repairers, and available at household goods stores everywhere . . . In some states of the United States, glue containing addictive narcotics . . . must also contain oil of mustard—the poisonous chemical used to produce mustard gas—which makes sniffing glue so painful it is impossible to tolerate.[2]

Though other drugs are abused by children in Central America, the term *Resistolero* became synonymous with street children, whether or not they used inhalants. The question for H. B. Fuller was how to respond to this situation.

The H. B. Fuller Company

A St. Paul, Minnesota, manufacturer of glue, mucilage, inks, bluing, and blacking, H. B. Fuller had sold its products worldwide for a long time. In 1941, the company was purchased by Elmer Andersen. During World War II, the company thrived, but Andersen was not satisfied with business success alone; he wanted the company to be socially responsible. Andersen took an active role in Minnesota politics, first serving in the state senate from 1949 to 1959; he was elected governor in 1960. In 1971, he was succeeded as president of the company by his son Tony, who continued seeking international growth and corporate responsibility. Andersen remained as chairman of the board of directors.

Like other Minnesota firms (see Case 3–A on Dayton Hudson), H. B. Fuller contributed 5 percent of its earnings to charity. It also had a showcase, energy-efficient, environmentally sensitive research center, and it had been listed by *Fortune* as one of the best U.S. companies for which an employee could work. In late 1986, Elmer Andersen received this letter:

> I heard part of your talk on public radio recently, and was favorably impressed with your philosophy that business should not be primarily for profit . . . However, on a recent trip to Honduras, I spent some time at a new home for chemically dependent "street boys" who are addicted to glue sniffing. It was estimated that there are 600 of these children on the streets in San Pedro Sula [a city of 300,000] alone. The glue is sold for repairing tennis shoes and I am told that it is made by H. B. Fuller in Costa Rica. These children also suffer toxic effects of liver and brain damage from the glue . . . Hearing you on the radio today, I immediately wondered how this condemnation of H. B. Fuller could be consistent with the company as I knew it . . . and with your business philosophy. Are you aware of this problem in Honduras, and, if so, how are you dealing with it?

Three years later, Dick Johnson, vice president for corporate relations, received a call from a stockholder whose daughter was serving with the Peace Corps in Honduras. The daughter questioned how H. B. Fuller could claim to have a social conscience and continue to sell Resistol, which was "literally burning out the brains" of the children in Latin America?

Honduras

The country at the center of the controversy, Honduras, was extraordinarily poor. In 1989, the population was slightly less than five million; 65 percent of all households lived in poverty. Infant and child mortality rates were high, life expectancy low, and adult literacy was estimated at less than 60 percent.

A mountainous nation with few natural resources, Honduras relied mainly on banana and coffee exports for income. A vast migration to urban centers was taking place. The capital, Tegucigalpa, had one of the fastest urban growth rates in Central America. It was common for more than seven persons to live in a single windowless room with dirt floors. Unemployment was high and wages low. Children often left school at an early age and took to the streets, either shining shoes and selling newspapers or roaming around with nothing to do.

Resistol, the product abused by the children, was used in homes, schools, and industry. It was indispensable in shoe manufacturing and repair, leatherwork, and carpentry. Unlike water-based cements, it set rapidly, had strong adhesion, and was water resistant.

Resistol was sold by Katvio Chemical Industries SA, a wholly owned subsidiary of H. B. Fuller. Katvio was one of the 500 largest private corporations in Latin America. Fuller gave its country managers in Latin America a high degree of autonomy because of rapid currency fluctuations and unstable political conditions. Like its parent, however, Katvio also stressed the ethical obligations of its managers.

When reports first surfaced in 1983 of substance abuse by children, Katvio hired an advertising agent. It informed the newspapers that Resistol was not the only product used by street children; moreover, glue sniffing was not caused by the company but was a social problem. Katvio asked the newspapers to stop using the term *Resistolero* as a synonym for "drug addict."

By 1985, social activists who worked with the children asked that mustard oil be added to the product to prevent its abuse. Fuller's corporate hygiene staff, however, found toxicology reports that mustard oil causes cancer. It was extremely destructive to the mucous membranes, upper respiratory tract, eyes, and skin, and resulted in nausea, dizziness, headaches, severe irritation, burns, edema, and asthma. In addition, its shelf life was less than six months. Instead of reformulating Resistol, the president of the Solvent Abuse Foundation for Education called for education as the only viable approach.

In 1987, Katvio set up community affairs councils to respond to community needs. The councils made several contributions to organizations working with street children. In March 1989, however, the Honduran congress passed legislation prohibiting the introduction into the country of contact adhesive products that did not include oil of mustard.

The Fact-Finding Mission

A fact-finding mission led by Dick Johnson visited Honduras shortly after the law was passed. Among the things it considered was that Resistol not be sold in small packages, which would make it less affordable. The economic circumstances of Honduras, however, made larger packages economically unfeasible. Another issue was that the law requiring mustard oil had not been implemented. An election was three months away, and officials had decided to delay implementation until a new government was in place.

The Honduran government received more than $2.3 million in U.S. aid, but in 1989 it was more than $248 million in arrears on foreign debt payments. Negotiations over $300 million in aid from the International Monetary Fund, the World Bank, and the United States had been suspended.

H. B. Fuller had a number of options. It could pursue a government relations strategy, hoping that the law might be repealed or abolished. Or it could pursue a community relations strategy and establish ties with private agencies that were trying to help the children. One such organization was

CONATSI, a private agency started in 1989, which had a program to improve the quality of services to children, promote interchange of experiences, coordinate human and material resources, offer technical support, and promote research. CONATSI, unfortunately, was underfunded and understaffed.

What does corporate citizenship require in a situation like this? H. B. Fuller had to make its decision in accord with its long-standing policies of corporate responsibility.

Discussion Questions

1. Was education a viable approach to ending glue sniffing? If so, would it work?
2. What was wrong with the mustard oil solution? How should H. B. Fuller respond to its critics who advocated the use of mustard oil?
3. How should H. B. Fuller handle this incident?
4. How would H. B. Fuller's tradition of social responsibility affect its response?

Endnotes

1. This case was originally written by Norman Bowie and Stephanie Ann Lenway. It was adapted for this book by Alfred Marcus.
2. Peter Ford, "Glue Sniffing Among Honduran Street Children," an InterPress Service feature.

Case 5–C
Recruiting Ethical Employees

Shearson-Lehman and Dennis Levine[1]

Jane Martin sat down at her desk and opened the file of background materials her consulting firm's client, Shearson-Lehman, had provided. The personnel department of Shearson-Lehman had a problem (see Exhibit 1). In the wake of the insider-trading scandals that had swept Wall Street beginning in 1986 with the arrest of former Shearson-Lehman employee Dennis Levine, the reputation of the financial services conglomerate, like the rest of the major investment banking houses, was suffering. This was a matter of concern because a reputation for integrity, trustworthiness, and confidentiality, which can inspire confidence in potential clients, was an essential asset for a bank.

Further, tradition was at stake. Bankers like to believe that theirs is a gentlemanly profession, a profession with an ethical code that demands honesty and strict observance of banking rules and regulations by those fortunate enough to find a place in the field. The widely publicized account of how a network of important figures in the financial community, including Levine, noted arbitrageur Ivan Boesky, investment banker Martin Siegel, financier Michael Milken, and others, had used highly confidential information about upcoming mergers and acquisitions to amass personal fortunes had shredded the reputation of the investment banking community as a whole.[2] Shearson-Lehman also was concerned because a 1988 law makes brokerage houses potentially liable for their employees' insider trading.

The question facing Shearson-Lehman was what, if anything, could or should be done to modify the company's recruitment process. Part of the problem, however, was that the ambition that had driven people like Levine to illegal acts to enrich themselves was also a part of the psychological makeup of the most successful employees. To prosper in the highly competitive mergers and

EXHIBIT 1 Wall Street Fines, 1987–1992

	1991 Capital ($ millions)	*1987–92 Fines ($ thousands)*
Merrill Lynch	$11,783	$107.2
Salomon Brothers	11,097	2,583.5
Shearson Lehman	8,079	1,310.5
Goldman Sachs	6,390	11.8
Morgan Stanley	5,820	51.5
Drexel Burnham	2,143	2,507.0
Paine Webber	1,866	951.0
Bear Stearns	1,836	63.2
First Boston	1,700	61.0
Dean Witter	1,424	84.0
Prudential	1,420	801.5
Smith Barney	1,040	37.5
Donaldson, Lufkin	900	5.0
Kidder-Peabody	674	351.6
Nomura	669	182.0
Morgan Securities	646	1.0
A.G. Edwards	417	2.5
Kemper	294	2.0
Oppenheimer	249	26.0
Paine		

acquisitions (M&A) field, a person had to be aggressive, driven, and ambitious enough to put in long hours and thrive under the mental pressure generated by billion-dollar deals, where clients might earn hundreds of millions of dollars and the investment banks might earn millions in fees. Zeal and ambition were welcome commodities in a new employee, but the Levine episode seemed to demonstrate that an employee's ambition had to be tempered with a respect for the rules and with at least a minimum measure of honesty.

Shearson-Lehman was considering whether to require all prospective employees to take a pencil-and-paper honesty test.[3] A variety of such tests were available, but their use was controversial. Questions about an applicant's attitudes toward theft, for example, could be considered as an invasion of privacy and offensive by potential employees. The validity of the tests was also in question. Perhaps there were other, better methods for ensuring that only reasonably honest people were hired. Somehow the firm had to find a way to balance the need for aggressive, ambitious employees with the equally important need to maintain a good reputation.

The Rise and Fall of Dennis Levine

The history of the Levine episode was as follows.[4] At the time of his arrest in May 1986, Dennis Levine was well on his way to achieving his lifetime goal of wealth and power. At 33 he was a managing director in the M&A department of Drexel Burnham Lambert, at that time the hottest investment banking house on Wall Street. Levine's $1 million annual salary and $11.5 million in insider trading profits had given him a solid start toward achieving his goal of *real* wealth, which he personally pegged at $100 million. In early 1986, everything seemed to be going his way. A year later, he was trading cigarettes for contraband plates of linguini with claim sauce behind bars at a federal prison.

Levine described the personality trait that got him into trouble as an "inability to set limits."[5] Born to a solidly middle class family and raised in Queens, Levine was an unremarkable high school student academically, but he had a knack for making people believe in him. He learned salesmanship by making cold calls for his father's home renovation business, but it wasn't until his junior year at City University of New York's Baruch College that he found a field that excited him enough to really apply himself: the high-stakes, get-rich-quick world of investment banking.

His idols were the dealmakers, the people who worked behind the scenes putting together mergers and acquisitions and who made millions in the process.[6] An investment banker could earn $500,000 a year before he was 30, drive Porsches and live at the best addresses in Manhattan, dine every night at the most fashionable restaurants, and ride to work in a limousine. Levine was captivated by the promise of this lifestyle and energetically pursued a job in the field.

After receiving an MBA at Baruch in 1976, Levine hit Wall Street in his banker's pinstripes and began putting his charm to work. He came up empty-handed in his search for an entry-level position in the investment banking field. He had no useful social connections, no Ivy League degree, and not even a track record that might persuade someone he was worth a try.

Levine was able to get a job in the corporate counseling department of Citibank, where he gained the real-world experience that was the only shortcoming on his résumé about which he could do anything. After a year of developing hedging strategies for clients with foreign currency exposures, he was hired by Smith Barney Harris Upham & Company, an investment banking and stock brokerage firm, in 1978. He worked a year in corporate finance at the firm's branch in Paris before returning to New York where he was made an associate in the firm's M&A department.

At Smith Barney, Levine began to capitalize on the inside information he was privy to as a member of an investment banking team that companies first approach when they consider an acquisition. An acquiring firm generally offers a premium or greater than market price for a target's shares. If one can buy shares in a target firm, or better still play the futures market in anticipation of an acquisition, immense profits can be made in a short period of time with little risk. Doing so, however, is illegal. The Securities and Exchange Act of 1934 bans "any manipulative or deceptive device" which the courts have interpreted as meaning that corporate insiders cannot trade on information important enough to affect investor's decisions before this information is publicly disclosed. In 1980, Levine flew to the Bahamas and opened a secret brokerage account in the name of "Mr. Diamond" with a branch of Bank Leu, a Swiss bank. Under cover of the Bahamas' privacy laws, Levine felt sure that his clandestine trading activity would be undiscovered, and he began placing regular buy and sell orders for the stocks of companies that he learned were takeover targets.

By this time, Levine had already established a network of contacts with whom he traded information on upcoming mergers and acquisitions. He was particularly eager to develop relationships with the lawyers on the Street, since they, like the investment banks, were usually among the first parties approached by CEOs interested in a takeover. These lawyers had two commodities prized by Levine: potential clients to be won for his employer, and information to be used for his personal profit.

It was partly to improve the quality of information available to him that Levine began looking for another position in 1981. Smith Barney was not a major M&A firm and it appeared doubtful he would be promoted to a partnership there in any case. He didn't have to search long; Lehman Brothers Kuhn Loeb, then the major M&A house and desperate for people with experience, snapped him up within a few weeks after he made his interest in moving known.

Shearson-Lehman's Statement

All new Lehman employees, including Dennis Levine, had to sign the following statement:[7]

> **Confidential Nature of Information.** It is essential that all information concerning any business carried on in this office, whether security transactions or otherwise, should be kept completely confidential. The stock-in-trade of a banker is his integrity and his respect for the confidence that others place in him. There can be no excuse for failure to observe this fundamental principle.

Despite signing this statement, Levine began to cash in on his inside information in earnest while at Lehman Brothers. Between 1982 and 1984 he made 22 illegal trades, the most profitable of which involved a tender offer made by Lehman client American Stores for the Jewel Companies. After learning in early 1984 that American Stores intended to make an offer, Levine began buying Jewel stock through his Bank Leu account, gradually accumulating 75,000 shares at $49.25 apiece. When American Stores went public with a tender offer of $70 per share, Levine racked up $1,206,275 in profits. During his tenure at Lehman Brothers, he took in about $5 million through illegal trades.

In early 1984 Shearson American Express bought Lehman Brothers and Levine began to look for another job. With Lehman no longer a privately held company, no partnerships were available.

In February 1985 he was hired by Drexel Burnham Lambert, the acknowledged up-and-coming M&A firm in New York. The Drexel partners knew of Levine's reputation as someone who had reliable and profitable ties to Wall Street's information network, and they agreed to his terms of employment: $1 million a year to start and the managing directorship of the Drexel M&A department.

The Drexel culture suited Levine well. Drexel employees were expected to produce results; how they managed to do so was not a matter of great interest. Levine continued to develop his network of contacts and bring in business for the firm.

May 1985 was an important month in Levine's life. First, he scored his biggest insider profit, taking in $2.7 million on 150,000 shares of Nabisco that he bought when he learned Nabisco and R. J. Reynolds were planning a merger. Second, the Securities and Exchange Commission (SEC) began a series of investigations that ultimately led to his downfall.

The banker at Bank Leu was making personal trades based on Levine's information. The Bank Leu official wasn't the only person "piggybacking" on Levine's trades. A Merrill Lynch broker in Caracas, Venezuela, through whom Bank Leu executed many of Levine's trades, also took advantage of the apparently faultless timing demonstrated by the Bahamian bank as it executed Levine's trades.

In May 1985, the SEC received an anonymous letter tipping them off to the Caracas broker's trading activities. The broker led the SEC to Bank Leu, and after 10 months of investigations and negotiations, Bank Leu was given special permission by the Bahamian government to violate its privacy laws and expose Levine. In return, Bank Leu was granted immunity from prosecution.

In New York, Levine pleaded guilty to two counts of tax evasion, one count of securities fraud, and one count of perjury. To reduce his sentence, he agreed to expose his accomplices. To help trap Ivan Boesky, Levine made tape-recorded calls to the arbitrageur to get Boesky to implicate himself. It worked. Boesky in turn exposed others, including Michael Milken, who had single-handedly popularized corporate takeovers funded by junk bonds.

Levine spent 15 months in the Lewisburg federal prison in Pennsylvania. After his release, he developed a business advising companies about raising money or executing deals. Levine has also lectured at several top business schools on the subject of ethics, and professes remorse for his trespasses:

> I will regret my mistakes forever . . . I've gained an abiding respect for the fairness of our system of justice: For the hard work and creativity I brought to my investment banking career, I was well rewarded. When I broke the law, I was punished. The system works.[8]

Drexel Burnham Lambert was itself made the subject of SEC investigations and eventually pleaded guilty to six felony counts related to securities fraud. The firm paid a record $650 million fine, and eventually filed for bankruptcy protection in February 1990.[9]

Illegal Information in the 1990s

The illegal use of insider information remains a very important issue in the investment banking community in the 1990s.[10] Unexplained increases in stock prices and trading volume continued to accompany a high percentage of the large deals made, for example the 1994 purchases of American Cynamid by American Home Products, Gerber by Sandoz, Grumman by Northrup, and Intuit by Microsoft. The perception that the market was rigged against small investors remained an issue, since use of insider information makes the market appear unfair.

In 1994, the SEC brought a record of 45 insider trading cases, exceeding the previous high of 43 it brought in 1989. The SEC was more sophisticated in its capacity to find inside traders. For instance, it can do an electronic search to determine everyone from a certain zip code who trades in a stock. It has records of anyone who has been involved in suspicious trading in the past.

The Securities and Exchange Act, passed in 1934 in response to trading practices that contributed to the 1929 stock market crash, regulates securities sales and purchases.[11] It is set up to prevent stock market manipulation and deception. The landmark 1968 *SEC* v. *Texas Gulf Sulphur Co*. established the main precedent for insider trading. In that case, Texas Gulf made a significant find of minerals in the province of Ontario. It stopped drilling for a few months while it acquired land around the site. Meanwhile, company employees and those they tipped made stock purchases without letting the investing public know about the discovery. They went so far as to deny press rumors about the find. SEC rule 10b-5 promulgated in 1942 states that no person can make "affirmative misrepresentations, half-truths, or omissions in connection with the purchase or sale of securities." The courts ruled in the case that a person having material insider information has to disclose it or not trade in the securities, because all investors trading in public security markets should have an equal right to relevant information.

The 1980 *Chiarella* v. *United States* ruling is somewhat different. Chiarella worked for a financial printer. Though the names of acquired companies involved in takeovers and acquisitions are kept from documents until a final printing, Chiarella was able to deduce these names and trade on the information. The Supreme Court reversed a prior court's conviction of Chiarella on the grounds that the sellers in these transactions had not directly placed their trust and confidence in Chiarella. Therefore, he was under no obligation not to use the information.

Another important case is 1983 *Dirks* v. *SEC*. Dirks was an investment analyst who specialized in the insurance industry. A former officer in an insurance company told him that the assets of the company were vastly overstated because of massive fraud in the company. Dirks analyzed the company and was able to obtain confirmation from other former company officials that the insurance company's records had been doctored. Dirks did not personally trade on the information, but he told others. They benefitted by unloading their stock before it was publicly known that there was fraud involved and by purchasing "put" options on the futures market. The SEC censured Dirks for not making the information public, but the Supreme Court overturned the censure on the grounds that such a ruling would exert an inhibiting role on market analysts. It would make them less likely to conduct future fraud investigations. By allowing them to reap benefit from their activities, they would be more likely to vigorously investigate.

A final case involved former University of Oklahoma and current Dallas Cowboy football coach Barry Switzer. In the 1984 case of *SEC* v. *Switzer*, the courts decided that Switzer could use information he overheard, while sunbathing at a secondary school track meet, to trade in shares, and that he could tip off his friends to this information, since those who disclosed the information did not intend Switzer to hear what they were saying, nor did Switzer intend to acquire information from them.

How to interpret these cases appears to be the following. If a friend says to you that his company is performing well, you can buy stock in that company because the friend has not told you anything material enough to affect investors' decisions. However, if, as a psychiatrist, your patient says something about the possibility of his company dealing with a hostile takeover, you cannot trade in that information because it has not been acquired for that purpose. It breaks the confidential nature of your relationship with client. However, if you just overhear two people talking about a takeover deal, it is legal to invest. You have no assurance that these people are insiders and neither you nor they intended that you should have the information. On the other hand, if a high ranking person in your organization tells you about a likely takeover, neither you nor anyone you might inform is allowed to trade on this information. If you use material, non-public information from a well-recognized, reliable source, you will be prosecuted.

Other Major Players in the Insider Trader Scandals of the 1980s

More than 60 insider-trading cases have been prosecuted since the mid-1980s, involving people linked to the financial services industry, from investment bankers to lawyers to reporters. The most publicized cases are summarized below.

Paul Thayer. Thayer was a successful World War II fighter pilot, commercial aircraft pilot for TWA, chairman and CEO of the aerospace conglomerate Ling-Temco, chairman of the U.S. Chamber of Commerce, and deputy Secretary of Defense under Ronald Reagan. While serving on the board of Anheuser Busch, he leaked confidential information to friends about a possible Campbell Taggart acquisition. Thayer's friends purchased shares of Campbell Taggart in the open market.

Ivan Boesky. Ivan Boesky made his living as an arbitrageur, one of the breed of financiers that step in when deals are announced or rumored to be in the works and buy the stock in question at a lower price than the raider has offered. Stockholders who would rather not wait until the tender offer is actually made sell to the arbitrageur, who then racks up hefty profits if and when the deal actually goes through. Boesky commanded more than $3 billion in buying power and legitimately earned more than $100 million for himself this way.[12]

For some reason, his legitimate earnings weren't enough. Boesky developed a network of contacts throughout the financial community, including Levine and Martin Siegel with whom he traded inside information on upcoming deals. When Levine turned him in to the federal investigators, Boesky pleaded guilty to one count of conspiring to file false statements with the SEC and paid a $100 million fine. In December 1987, he was sentenced to three years in prison.

Martin Siegel. Dennis Levine wasn't the only Drexel Burnham Lambert investment banker who had a history of illicit financial arrangements with Ivan Boesky. Martin Siegel, co-head of Drexel's M&A department and an expert in defense-oriented takeover maneuvers, had taken a total of $575,000 in payments from Boesky in return for inside information on several deals Siegel worked on while employed by Kidder, Peabody, & Co. in the mid-1980s. When Boesky began cooperating with SEC investigators in order to lighten his sentence, he turned in Siegel.[13]

Siegel came from a modest background marked by financial problems. His father had filed for bankruptcy protection when Siegel was a young man, and the experience had made an impression on him. He lived modestly for years after he began earning large salaries, saving most of his money. When Siegel remarried in 1981 and soon afterwards had a child and built a new home, his personal expenditures began to outdistance his income. During that vulnerable period, he began trading information for payoffs from Boesky.

Terrified of being caught, Siegel insisted that Boesky pay him in cash. Boesky couriers would meet Siegel in a public place and hand over a suitcase full of greenbacks, which Siegel would use for household expenses and pocket money.

During 1983 and 1984, Siegel supplied Boesky information on upcoming M&A deals including

Diamond Shamrock and Natomas, Getty Oil and Texaco, and Carnation and Nestle. Eventually, Siegel ceased giving Boesky leads. After moving to Drexel in early 1986, Siegel gave up his illegal activities altogether, but his past caught up with him when Boesky turned him in. Siegel pleaded guilty to two felony counts and agreed to pay a $9 million fine. He was permanently barred from working in the securities industry.

Michael Milken. The "Mozart of the money markets" was, like the musical genius, interested in his field from an early age. Michael Milken was helping his accountant father prepare clients' tax returns at age 10. By the time he graduated from the Wharton business school, he had already developed expertise in the area of finance he almost single-handedly made a household word: junk bonds.

Milken was the founder and head of the High Yield and Convertible Securities Department at Drexel. He specialized in helping Drexel clients (both companies and corporate raiders like T. Boone Pickens) who were unable or unwilling to raise capital by borrowing from banks or insurance companies to do so with junk bonds. Milken and his subordinates earned handsome fees by finding a pool of investors willing to buy the less-than-investment-grade debt issued by these companies.

Milken made himself a billionaire and Drexel one of the richest and most powerful investment firms on Wall Street, but along the way he engaged in several violations of the federal securities, tax, and mail fraud laws, among others. Working with Boesky, Milken arranged to have the Boesky organization buy stock that a Drexel client wanted to sell. By quietly selling the stock to Boesky, who subsequently sold it at a loss (made up by Drexel), the client was able to make more on the sale than it would have if the public had learned the sale was occurring. On other occasions, Boesky asked Drexel to buy stock Boesky wanted to sell for the same purpose. A Drexel employee kept track of the profits and losses on these transactions; if Drexel owed Boesky some money, Milken would engineer some bond trades that would benefit Boesky.

Milken also was involved in defrauding the investors of the Finsbury Fund, an investment fund for foreign investors managed by a Drexel client. In order to reimburse Drexel for the commissions paid to salesmen of the fund, Milken arranged with the client to overcharge Finsbury Fund shareholders on their transactions. In another violation, Milken engaged in securities transactions designed to allow a client to generate short-term losses for the reduction of personal income tax liability.

In April 1990, Milken plead guilty to six charges and agreed to pay a $200 million fine and $400 million in restitution to defrauded investors and clients. He was permanently barred from the securities industry and faced up to 28 years in prison. Even with the $600 million fine, Milken's personal fortune was still estimated at more than $1 billion.

Upon being released in 1993 after spending 22 months in prison, Milken, among other things, taught a weekly course at the UCLA School of Business. Apparently unrepentant, he presented himself as a visionary like Galileo who also had been imprisoned for his actions. Milken cited the 1980s not as a time of rampant greed, but a period of enormous charitable giving. Some students viewed him as a "great man, a martyr, and not a crook." Others resented his presence in an institution of higher learning.[14]

Honesty Tests: Are They Useful?

Pencil-and-paper honesty tests are designed primarily to help employers identify job applicants that may be a bad risk for theft of company property. Employee theft costs business around $10 billion per year. At least 5,000 companies use honesty tests, and there are dozens of different honesty tests on the market.

The following types of questions are common to most honesty tests:

- Questions inquiring into the applicant's attitude towards theft and other illegal activity;
- Questions probing beliefs about the frequency and extent of theft in our society;
- Questions examining the applicant's punitive attitudes towards theft;
- Questions dealing with whether the applicant has considered theft, how easy they believe it would be to accomplish, and how likely they think it is that they would be caught;
- Questions that ask the applicant to assess their own honesty;
- Questions that ask outright whether the applicant has engaged in employer theft previously; and
- Questions designed to detect whether the applicant's answers are lies.

Studies of the validity of honesty tests have been inconclusive. Depending on the cutoff used by the firm, anywhere from 25 to 75 percent of applicants will fail an honesty test.[15]

Critics of the tests point out that there is no irrefutable link between a person's performance on a test and his or her actual behavior on the job. Still, experts note that the tests incorporate the best strategies that psychologists have come up with for assessing honesty, and contend that "while it is acknowledged that each of the validity strategies used to date has flaws, what stands out is the consistency of positive findings across tests and across validity strategies."[16]

These experts also note that not everyone agrees that the best way to curb employee theft is improved screening procedures. Some argue that the problem lies in the culture and norms of the organization and that the solution is to be found in developing a more positive and honest climate.

Minicases for Assessing Prospective Employees

An alternative to using honesty tests to screen new employees is to present them with minicases and see how they will respond. A recruiter then assesses an applicant's judgment to see whether the person will fit into the highly competitive yet morally demanding securities industry. Here are some examples of minicases that Shearson-Lehman could use:[17]

- You take a break from work and go to lunch with a friend. Your mention of what you have been working on leads to a discussion about ethics in the financial services industry. Your friend cannot understand why insider trading is illegal. Your friend reasons that even though a person trading on inside information is enjoying an advantage unavailable to the investing public, no one is forced to sell them any shares. Whoever decides to sell the shares has done so freely and presumably has received about what they expected to get for them. Who is really hurt? How should you answer?
- You are a security analyst, responsible for advising a pool of investors who put their trust in your advice. You get a call from an acquaintance who works for a company whose stock some of your clients hold. He tells you that the company has just filed a certain type of report, and tells you that "there's some information on page 76 you might be interested in." You know from experience that this type of report is filled with technical detail that few analysts bother to fully examine. If the information indicates that it would be prudent for your clients to sell their holdings in the company, should you act on the tip?
- You are at a party, trying to relax and put the ethical questions of the day behind you. You talk with a reporter from a major financial publication who tells you that he has written a story detailing the self-serving behavior of the top management of a company whose stock you've been recommending to clients. The reporter says he expects the story to be published within a week. This is the first you've heard of any alleged improper dealings by that management team. You're not sure the allegations are true, but you do know the

company's stock price is likely to be affected. By extension, so will your clients who own the stock. Is it be ethical to use this information? Are there circumstances where it clearly would or would not be ethical to use it?

- You are a vice president of a brokerage house that provides both investment banking services to corporate clients and brokerage services for retail customers. You learn that one of your corporate clients has suffered a large, unreported loss. Unfortunately, the client corporation is on your "recommended buy list" and your brokers have been advising your retail customers to purchase the stock. If you do nothing, the brokers will continue advising clients to buy stock in a company that is in trouble. If you act to protect the retail customers, you may be using confidential information improperly. What are the ethical steps, if any, that you could take to protect your retail customers?

Discussion Questions

1. What should Jane Martin recommend to Shearson Lehman?
2. How would you answer the dilemmas posed by the minicases?
3. Why did the financial scandals in which Dennis Levine and others were involved take place?
4. Should Shearson Lehman adopt a form of honesty testing to weed out dishonest job applicants? What was the extent of the company's responsibility in this respect?
5. What other steps could the company take to ensure ethical behavior by its employees without stifling the ambition and initiative necessary in an investment banker?

Endnotes

1. This case was prepared by Mark Jankus and Alfred Marcus.
2. L. P. Cohen, "Milken Pleads Guilty to Six Felony Counts and Issues an Apology," *The Wall Street Journal*, April 25, 1990, p. A1; L. P. Cohen, "How Michael Milken Was Forced to Accept the Prospect of Guilt," *The Wall Street Journal*, April 23, 1990, p. A1; G. Crovitz, "Milken's Tragedy: Oh How the Mighty Fall before RICO," *The Wall Street Journal*, May 2, 1990, p. A15; M. Milken, "Text of Michael Milken's Statement in Court," *The Wall Street Journal*, April 25, 1990, p. A12.
3. P. R. Sackett and M. M. Harris, "Honesty Testing for Personnel Selection: A Review and Critique," in H. J. Bernardin and D. A. Bownas, eds., *Personality Assessment in Organizations* (New York: Praeger, 1985), pp. 236–76.
4. "The Inside Story of an Inside Trader," *Fortune*, May 21, 1990, pp. 80–89; M. Stevens, *The Insiders: The Truth behind the Scandal Rocking Wall Street* (New York: G. P. Putnam's Sons, 1987).
5. Stevens, *The Insiders*.
6. Ibid.
7. Stevens, *The Insiders*.
8. "The Inside Story of an Inside Trader," pp. 80–89.
9. B. D. Fromson, "The Last Days of Drexel Burnham," *Fortune*, May 21, 1990, pp. 90–96; J. B. Stewart and D. Hertzberg, "SEC Accuses Drexel of a Sweeping Array of Securities Violations," *The Wall Street Journal*, September 8, 1988, p. A1.
10. "Insider Trading," *Business Week*, Dec. 12, 1994, pp. 78–82.
11. Aaron Levine, *Economic Public Policy and Jewish Law* (Hoboken N.J.: Ktav Publishing, 1993), pp. 115–59.
12. J. Fierman, "The Paranoid Life of Arbitragers," *Fortune*, November 9, 1987, pp. 97–109.
13. Fromson, "The Last Days of Drexel Burnham," pp. 90–96; Stewart and Hertzberg, "SEC Accuses Drexel . . . ," p. A1.

14. Cohen, "Milken Pleads Guilty . . . ", p. A1; Cohen, "How Michael Milken Was Forced to Accept the Prospect of Guilt," p. A1; Crovitz, "Milken's Tragedy," p. A15; Francis Clines, "An Unfettered Milken Has Lessons to Teach," *The New York Times*, Oct. 16, 1993, pp. 1, 9.
15. Sackett and Harris, "Honesty Testing for Personnel Selection," pp. 236–76.
16. John L. Casey, Ethics in the Financial Marketplace.
17. Scudder (New York, 1988).

CHAPTER

6

REASONING ABOUT ETHICS

Group Norms and the Individual

The human brain is, in large part, a machine for winning arguments, a machine for convincing others that its owner is in the right—and thus a machine for convincing its owner of the same thing. The brain is like a good lawyer: given any set of interests to defend, it sets about convincing the world of their moral and logical worth, regardless of whether in fact they have either.

Robin Wright, *The Moral Animal*, 1994

If . . . ethical conflict still exists after exhausting all levels of internal review, a management accountant may have no other recourse on significant matters than to resign . . .

The Institute of Management Accountants, "Standards of Ethical Conduct"

Introduction and Chapter Objectives

This chapter starts with a discussion of changing ethical values and why people reason ethically. It shows the limitations of moral common sense and provides a framework for handling ethical dilemmas. The chapter then moves to group norms versus the individual. There are five vignettes that illustrate this dilemma. Psychological experiments that show people compromising their personal values for collective goals are discussed. The problem of being ethical in the context of an organization is presented, as are the sources of an ethical personality and the reasons for altruism. This chapter concludes with a discussion of self-interest and altruism as determinants of human actions.

Changing Ethical Values

Businesses operate in a context of changing ethical values. Polls show declining public confidence in business. The United States is a scandal-plagued society. In recent years,

Ethical Vignettes

Personnel Issues

1. My company is experiencing rough times. Management wants to lay off half the production workers, then immediately hire back most of them as temporary workers. This will cut costs by reducing the costs of permanent workers. What should I say?

2. My group works together well. We are self-motivated and highly conscientious. We consistently receive high ratings. This year we took on additional work and responsibilities and performed better than last year according to all the objective ratings used by the company. Still, we are told that our raises and bonuses will be lower to give other people in the company the chance to be rewarded for their good work. What should we do?

3. A woman who works for me took disability leave two months before her baby was born. She was supposed to write a procedures manual but didn't get the job done because she needed bed rest. What should I write in her annual performance review?

4. You are in a position to promote a person to the vice presidency of your company. You consider her a star employee. However, the personnel manager does a routine background check and finds that the employee has not, as claimed on her résumé, received her MBA. What should you do?

Americans have witnessed many scandals, including influence peddling by top political appointees, cheating of their congregations by television evangelists, collusion among military contractors, and bribery at the Pentagon. Managers, however, usually face less dramatic ethical situations. A high percentage of managers' problems have to do with personnel issues such as firing employees, promoting them, or taking them on and off projects.[1]

Though commonplace, the ethical dilemmas found in business are nonetheless extremely troubling. They consist of relationships between people that might cause harm. **Ethical predicaments** may be defined as situations that involve actual or potential harm. They involve actions that affect the freedom and well-being of others, and arise when one wants to do "the right thing," but does not know what it is. Ethical predicaments exist when conflict occurs between values, between groups and individuals to whom one is obligated, which is discussed in this chapter, and between means and ends (see Chapter 7).[2]

ethical predicaments Situations of actual or potential harm, involving conflicts between values, opposition between individuals and groups, and controversy about means and ends.

Why People Do Not Reason Ethically

People have many reasons for not wanting to reason ethically. They argue from the standpoint of relativism: Since there are many equivalent paths to follow, it does not matter which one is chosen. People also add cynicism to relativism. Ethical arguments cannot be won or lost. They are not scientific, factual, or subject to proof and counterproof, but are based on feeling and illogical convention. In the end, people believe that egoism and selfishness always dominate. Humans pursue their own interests without regard for others. They give only to get what they want. They love because they want to be loved, and love only those that love them, hating or being indifferent to the rest of humanity. According to such views, people are driven by instinct; they do what feels good. People are not free, and ethics cannot be taught; it is an afterthought, an ideology created by the powerful to suppress the powerless.[3]

Socrates's Reply to Cynicism. In Plato's *Republic*, Thrasymachus of Chalcedon, a sophist and teacher of rhetoric in Athens, raises a remarkably similar question, to which Socrates replies.

> *Thrasymachus:* Is not injustice more profitable than justice? Innocent as you are yourself, Socrates, you must see that a just man always has the worst of it. Take a private business: when a partnership is wound up, you will never find that the more honest of the two partners comes off with the larger share; and in their relation to the state, when there are taxes to be paid, the honest man will pay more than the other on the same amount of property; or if there is money to be distributed the dishonest will get it all . . . So true is it Socrates, that injustice, on a grand scale is superior to justice . . . and "right" . . . means simply what serves the interest of the stronger party; "wrong" simply means what is for the interest and profit of oneself . . .
> *Socrates:* I am delighted with your answer, Thrasymachus; . . . Please add to your kindness by telling me whether any set of men—a state or an army or a band of robbers or thieves—who were acting together for some unjust purpose would be likely to succeed, if they were always trying to injure one another. Wouldn't they do better if they did not?
> *Thrasymachus:* Yes, they would.
> *Socrates:* Because, of course, such injuries must set them quarreling and hating each other. Only fair treatment can make men friendly and of one mind.[4]

Socrates tries to win the argument by shifting the focus from the individual to the group. Collective success, he argues, is based on fair treatment. Even a band of thieves has to treat its members fairly. Injustice undermines the cooperation necessary for the group to be effective.

The answer is ingenious, but is it right? Do you agree that fairness is needed for even thieves to function well? Think of the power of a dictatorial leader who can intimidate an entire organization. Couldn't this kind of leader be successful? If you were Thrasymachus, how would you respond to Socrates?

Why People Reason Ethically

In ethical dialogue people marshal facts and construct theories to justify what they do. Observe children, who test their actions against each others' ethical principles with cries of "That's not right!" and "It isn't fair!" From childhood on, a person's actions are subject to challenge and justification.[5]

We dismiss people who cannot provide an explanation for what they do. Take a tree. Its appearance gives pleasure, but it cannot explain or defend itself unless humans are prepared to make arguments in its behalf (e.g., environmentalists). The tree cannot help but grow in a certain beautiful way. We admire the beauty of a tree but not its character since the tree lacks freedom of choice. Praiseworthy actions require freedom and justification. To maintain integrity and self-worth, humans deliberate, ponder, and reflect. In *The Ethics of the Fathers*, a collection of rabbinic sayings, Hillel maintains: "If I am not for myself, who will be for me?"; but, he quickly adds: "If I am only for myself, what am I?" Another rabbinic sage contends that "the right path that a person should choose" is one which "honors the person who does it, but which also brings honor from humankind."

People give meaning and consequences to their actions by deliberation. Managers especially are in positions where conflicting rights are at stake and different parties are affected by the decisions they make. Their judgments have to be defended and explained. Managers must think about who will be hurt and how to avoid harm. Their ability to handle their jobs is affected by their capacity to reason ethically.[6]

Moral Muteness

Unfortunately, many managers are reluctant to ask ethical questions. They tend to discuss issues as if their motivations are solely practical; their concerns are with organizational interests and economic good sense. The situations are labeled as judgment calls, professional matters, or strategic concerns rather than ethical ones. The managers try be prudent and are "mute" about ethical discussion. They avoid the use of ethical language and define conflicts in nonethical terms. Serious consequences—undue managerial stress and decreased influence for ethics—may arise from their failure to directly confront ethical issues.[7]

In day-to-day behavior, individuals use different and often conflicting principles to justify their behavior. Some argue that conventions should govern: In business, do as others do or risk financial loss. Others hold that "might equals right": Seize what advantage is possible without regard to social laws and customs. Still others have an intuitionist ethic and do what "feels right."[8]

Some companies have ethical codes that employees may invoke to justify what they do. A common business practice requires employees to ask of themselves whether under the "full glare of examination by associates, friends, and family they would remain comfortable with their decisions."

Moral Common Sense

A good starting point in reasoning about ethical issues is moral common sense.[9] Certainly, a person should try to adhere to the following principles:

- Avoid giving harm to others.
- Respect the rights of others.
- Do not lie or cheat.
- Keep one's promises and contracts.
- Obey the law.
- Prevent harm.
- Help those in need.
- Be fair.

However, how does a person reconcile conflicts between these principles? What do the principles mean when applied to specific situations? For instance, what if avoiding harm to others requires lying and cheating? To save lives threatened by terrorists, isn't it acceptable to lie and even to strike back violently against the terrorists? On the other hand, is it right to kill a healthy individual and distribute the person's body parts to save the lives of a dozen people needing transplants? How should values be weighed against values in a particular case?

These problems cannot be easily solved. They make ethical discourse necessary. Philosophers believe that people should reason about ethical issues and that with practice they can improve their judgment.

A *Framework for Ethical Dilemmas*

Business ethicists provide the following questions to help deal with ethical dilemmas:

- What principles are involved?
- What groups or individuals have a stake in the outcome?
- Whom are you as a manager serving?
- Whom might you as a manager injure? How badly?
- What principles should guide you in making a decision?
- Are these principles clear? Are they in conflict?
- Could you describe these principles to the company's board of directors? To your family?
- Could you explain these principles in court? To the media? To your fellow workers?
- Would the decision you make seem right a year from now?
- Would the decision seem right 20 years from now when someone writes a history of the company?

Group Norms versus the Individual

Let us apply these questions to moral dilemmas that pit group values against the individual. In the remainder of this chapter, the focus is on these conflicts between the individual and the organization. What are the rights of individuals in relation to those of the organization? What obligations do individuals have? What obligations does the organization have to them? What obligations do individuals have to fellow employees? Vignettes on the next page illustrate this type of dilemma.

Ethical dilemmas, however, take place at a variety of levels:

1. The individual: Concern is with personal and professional behavior and the meaning of terms such as trust, honesty, and integrity.
2. The organization: The survival of the organization may come into conflict with individual standards of ethical conduct.

Ethical Vignettes

Group Values and the Individual

1. The Eccentric MBA. After looking for a job for six months, a new college graduate obtains the kind of work she has been seeking. It seems to her that this is a once-in-a-lifetime opportunity. She can get in on the ground floor in a new and expanding business that promises all the challenges, excitement, and monetary renumeration she wants. The job pays extremely well for an entry-level position, so she will be able to get an apartment for herself and live without the restrictions imposed by parents and roommates. The catch is that the job is in a very sensitive industry that requires very high standards of personal conduct. The job demands conformity and integrity. The company recently was hurt and embarrassed by a scandal caused by an irresponsible employee. Image is critical to the industry. As a result of this experience, the company now requires that new employees take a personality test. The results are carefully scrutinized to determine whether the employee will fit in and be a good team player. The company cannot afford to hire people who will rock the boat; many controls are in place to ensure that employees play by the rules. For example, employees must adhere to a dress code and fill out a detailed form daily accounting for their activities.

The new graduate admittedly is an eccentric who has carefully cultivated a lifestyle that makes her stand out from others. She is not used to being hemmed in by an organization. She does what she wants when she wants. Independent-minded, she resents being told how to behave. She is contemptuous of the personality test and does not see what relation it could possibly have to her job performance. Nevertheless, she knows that if she guesses correctly at the expected responses on the personality test, she will be less likely to be questioned by the company's psychologist and more likely to be hired immediately. She also needs the job even if it means curbing her independent ways and pretending to be like everyone else. Her failure to find work in the past six months is beginning to be stressful. At the same time, she wonders how well she will perform in a company that expects everyone to behave the same. What should she do?

2. The Avid Environmentalist. You are the owner of a bank and your best employee is president of a local environmental group. Recently, the group has protested vigorously against a hazardous waste dump owned by a company that is a subsidiary of your most important client. You believe that the environmental group's sensationalized campaign against your client is grossly unfair and is based on blatant lies and distortions, not on a true estimate of the risks involved in the situation. You are inclined to tell your employee that she will be fired if she does not cease her irresponsible actions as head of the environmental group. Only last year you were embarrassed by the media when they barged into your bank to interview an employee who was heavily involved in the pro-life movement. At that time, you explicitly told all employees to keep their private causes to themselves and away from the workplace. What should you do?

3. A Tight-Knit Group of Brokers. You have worked together with three other brokers in the same company for the past 12 years. The four of you are the best of friends, with strong personal ties going back 30 years; you grew up with these people, knew their families, and went to the same elementary school and the same church. Nevertheless, it is a surprise when one of the four reveals that he has been successfully trading on "tips" from an unmentioned source. You know that your friend has been having personal financial difficulties, but things seemed to be improving. Now you think you know why.

Your friend invites you and the other members of the group to join in the trades based on the tips. You, too, face financial challenges as your children approach college age and apply to private schools with high price tags. Your parents are aging and face a deteriorating financial situation. You have recently become concerned about dipping into your savings merely to meet monthly living expenses.

One of your friends eagerly accepts the offer to trade based on the tips, but another argues that doing so may be against the law. She says that the trades are not worth the risk of getting caught, that she is in no way interested in hurting her family or career, and that she might not participate in a cover-up if an investigation occurs.

Your trader friend explains his scheme. It seems foolproof, though perhaps of doubtful legality. The risks of getting caught appear minimal. What should you do?

4. Polishing an Image. You have just received your MBA and for the past year and a half have worked as a financial accountant for a company that is having talks about a proposed merger with another firm. A director of the company approaches you to enlist your support in "polishing the company's image" for the upcoming merger talks. She asks for "some terrific forecasts of industry growth and market share" to give her "some leverage" in the talks. She says, "Be a good team player and do what I say, and it will all work out for the best."

You are not naive. You know that the figures you choose as the basis for the forecasts and the approach and techniques you employ can influence the results. On the one hand, you could massage the data to paint a fairly rosy picture of the company's future. On the other hand, you could analyze the data to show pitfalls ahead and the prospects of rough going. Standards among accountants vary. The rules applying to the numbers a person brings to the table in merger talks seem to give you substantial leeway. You like the job and the company. You have formed many close ties to the people involved, including the director, who is a role model for you. What should you do?

5. Down the Drain. After a yearlong search, you finally have a job in the industry of your choice. The industry is high status and dynamic, and has excellent growth potential. Landing a job in this industry makes you the envy of your fellow graduates in the MBA program. However, you discover that the company is using a recently banned chemical as a cleansing agent, which is then flushed down the drain. When you ask why the company is acting in this fashion, you are told that it has a large supply of the chemical in storage and that it is only using up the remaining amount—to waste what is left would be silly. To safely dispose of the cleansing agent is a bother, and the alternative compound proposed by the government is very expensive. Moreover, you are told that company officials believe the government has been overly cautious in banning the chemical because the company has had no past reported health problems related to it. Your supervisor tells you, "Don't be naive. Real companies operate differently than you expect. If you want to succeed in this company, you'll have to go along." What should you do?

3. Society: The justness and appropriateness of specific policies are debated in areas such as child care, defense procurement, and national security.
4. The economic system: The dilemma is whether capitalism as it is practiced in the United States and other countries in the world is just and appropriate or whether alternative forms of capitalism are more just and better able to meet people's needs.

Obeying Orders

Employees in modern organizations can be put in compromising situations where their personal values conflict with organizational practices. They have to decide what to do. In a series of experiments conducted in the late 1950s, the social psychologist Stanley Milgram considered the tension between organizational requirements and individual conscience.[10] Over 1,000 subjects were involved in these experiments, which were repeated in numerous universities. The basic situation involved telling an individual to inflict punishment upon another person whenever the other person made apparent learning errors. As the other person gave what seemed to be an incorrect answer, the subject in the experiment was instructed to increase the level of electric shock the person was to receive.

The purpose was to determine how far people would go in inflicting increasing pain on a protesting victim. The victim was a professional actor and the subject was a randomly chosen individual who had volunteered for the experiment. Would people stop inflicting pain after hearing grunts, verbal complaints, demands to be released, vehement and emotional protests, or agonizing screams from the victim?

As it turned out, a substantial portion of the subjects, although they might display obvious distress and express outrage to the person in authority who was conducting the experiment, continued to inflict pain on the victims. They continued to increase the level of electric shocks no matter how much pleading they heard from the victim to be released.

Milgram infers from these experiments that people are unlikely to defy authority even in the face of an obvious moral imperative. Normal and otherwise reasonable people have a capacity for abhorrent, immoral acts committed simply because they are obeying leaders.

What explains the apparent willingness of one person to inflict pain upon another? First, people appear to be committed to doing their jobs and to doing them well (in this case, the job is to inflict pain when the victim makes an incorrect answer) even when the destructive consequences of what they are doing is clear to them. People want to be viewed as competent performers. They understand that society consists of persons who are carrying out narrow and specialized jobs. They believe that the broader tasks of setting goals and assessing the morality of situations are entrusted to others—someone else oversees what is taking place and assumes responsibility.

binding factor
A desire to uphold a promise or complete a task without regard for the ethical consequences.

Second, while people may recognize that they are doing wrong, they have trouble carrying out the values they hold. "**Binding factors,**" such as a desire to uphold the promise to conduct the experiment and the awkwardness of a withdrawal, lock people into the situation. They then become consumed by the narrow technical details of their job and lose sight of the broader implications.

Third, as they become involved in the task, people lose a sense of responsibility. They see themselves simply as the agents of an external authority; they feel like they are just carrying out their duty. This point of view is adopted by people operating in large organizations where they are locked into a subordinate status in the authority structure. Such people tend to believe that the activities of the organization are benevolent and useful to society and justify the inconvenience that any particular person suffers. Quite simply, the ends of the organization, defined for them by others, justify the organization's means.

Finally, once having caused suffering to the victim, the people start to see the victim as unworthy. The victim deserves punishment because the victim is unable to answer the question that has been given. The subject gradually perceives the victim as having some basic defect in intellect or character. This stereotyping of the victim has very broad implications for how disadvantaged minorities are treated in our society.

Employees in the modern corporation often are asked to carry out orders that they cannot accept. The separation between order givers and those who carry out the order creates problems. Since order givers cannot fully observe whether the order has been faithfully carried out, they tend to be indifferent to the methods used to get the job done, so long as the job is successfully accomplished. Employees, who cannot fully comprehend what they have been asked to do, tend to maintain that they are "just following orders" whether the action is right or wrong. These views blunt moral responsibility and invite people to blame others should moral standards be violated.[11]

Being Ethical in the Context of an Organization

People sometimes have to rebel against outrageous orders. Such behavior in an organizational context, however, poses difficult dilemmas. Should a person contribute to unethical behavior or resist and try to end it? By opposing unethical behavior, the person is likely to suffer unpleasant consequences—punishment, dismissal, shunning by colleagues, and banishment to distant locales or uninteresting and unchallenging assignments.[12]

There are many ways to follow one's conscience and defy unethical or unreasonable authority (see Exhibit 6–1). Before publicly exposing unethical practices, a person can inform or threaten a higher-level manager. If this does not work, the person can conscientiously object to, quietly refrain from, or sabotage the implementation of unethical behavior.

While actions taken against the organization can be effective, they have important limitations. First, the person might be wrong about whether the organization's actions are indeed unethical. Second, the person is likely to damage organizational relationships by coercing people into doing things they otherwise would not do. Even if the person is right, the organization can be hurt unnecessarily. The person's actions can create a climate in the organization in which others feel that "might makes right." By using coercion to compel people to end the unethical practice, the person may contribute to a climate in the organization in which people believe that the only way to get things done is to use force.

Thus, a person might want to consider changing the organization by being a part of it rather than against it. "The self," according to the Protestant theologian Paul Tillich, "affirms itself as participant in the power of a group."[13] This model is more like the one found in Japan, where a person brings about change by being part of the group. In the United Sates, the individual takes on the lonely but romantic fight against the organization.

Working with people in the organization, however, has its limitations. First, it requires achieving compromises that are satisfactory to the contending parties. Of course, doing so may not always be possible. Second, it requires a strong capacity for leadership, but not all people have this capacity. Moreover, no matter how hard one tries to make changes from within, to do so is impossible because some organizations have very strong cultures (e.g., consensus or authoritarian) that resist change. Thus, a person is left with

EXHIBIT 6–1 Confronting Unethical Behavior

		Voice	
		Yes	*No*
Loyalty	*Yes*	Work with others to change behavior	Accept behavior
	No	Blow the whistle	Exit the organization

the dilemma of deciding whether to compel change as an individual separate from the organization or to lead change as part of the organization.

The Sources of Ethical Behavior

Why would a person be willing to challenge the organization? The sources of this type of altruistic behavior (bad for the person but good for society) have been investigated by many scholars; however, their explanations provide no simple answers about why a person would be willing to make the sacrifices to challenge unjust authority (see Exhibit 6–2).

whistle-blower
A person who challenges the actions taken by the organization to which they belong by publicly exposing them.

Whistle-blowers, people who challenge their organizations for the sake of some higher value, tend to be conservative. They are highly devoted to their work and to their organization. However, they have been asked to violate what they consider to be the standards of appropriate workplace behavior. They then feel that they are defending the true mission of the organization, that by engaging in some form of courageous dissent or protest they are the true organizational loyalists. Whistle-blowers engage in protest against the

EXHIBIT 6–2 Reasons to Challenge Authority on Ethical Grounds

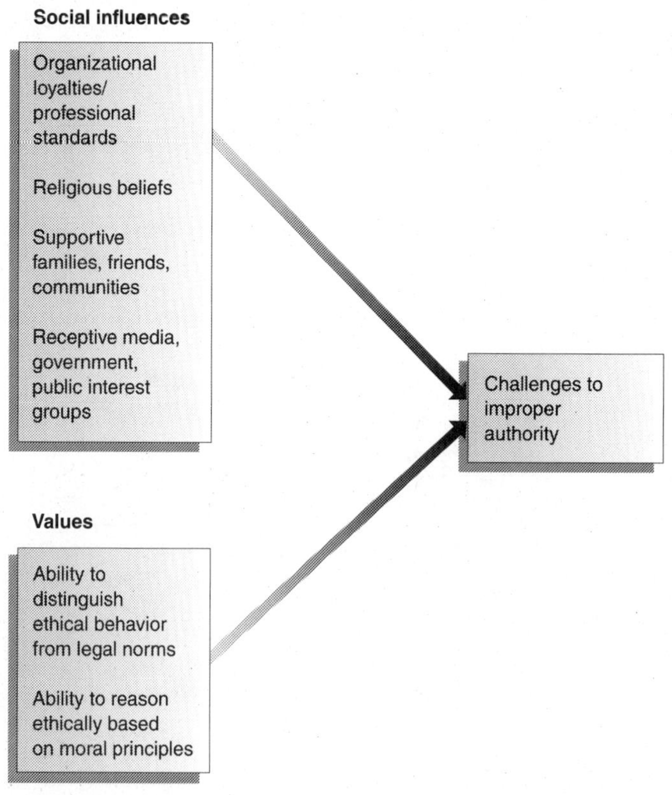

organization at great personal cost. They face harsh reprisals, blacklistings, dismissals, transfers, and personal harassment. What sustains them is their professional ethics, religious beliefs, supportive friends, families, and communities, a receptive media and government, and public interest groups that are willing to take them seriously.[14]

Since ethical behavior requires self-sacrifice, a person's behavior when tested by moral challenges cannot be easily predicted. Ethical behavior may require breaking the rules of society that are otherwise functional in that they permit people to live with each other. Ethical behavior and legal norms are not necessarily equivalent. Ethical behavior requires more than the determination of whether a particular action is legal.

It might not be possible to teach this type of behavior. Theory and practice do not always coincide. Simple people sometimes meet ethical challenges better than people with immense learning (consider the German philosopher Martin Heidegger, who was an early supporter of Hitler). One may be an ethical person and never have studied ethics. On the other hand, a person who has devoted a lifetime to ethical study may not act always ethically.

Developing an Ethical Personality

How do people develop ethical personalities? They obtain their values from family, school, and neighborhood. They acquire ethical grounding from religious institutions. They learn their behavior from peers and popular culture—music, the movies, and television. According to psychologist Lawrence Kohlberg, ethical sensitivity requires an appreciation for collective interests, rules, and laws that promote long-run community interests.[15] This type of appreciation develops as the person matures. A child has no sense of communal interests. Influenced by praise and displeasure, the child is affected mainly by reward and punishment. Concerned with personal gratification and affected by authority, the child has no sense that it is obeying rules because they promote the common good.

An adolescent, however, has a changed perspective. The adolescent focuses on the group and group norms. In trying to conform to the expectations of parents and peers, of home, school, and church, adolescents learn proper behavior from the surrounding groups. But adolescents, like children, conform without knowing why. They obey rules because rules are there to be obeyed, not because they have an intrinsic understanding of their purpose.

According to Kohlberg, only adults with a universal orientation and the need for justification based on moral principles reach the pinnacle of moral sensitivity. These adults are at the **"postconventional autonomous stage"** because they are willing to accept rules, not merely because society says so, but because they understand their function and purpose. They understand what the rules mean and what they are trying to accomplish. They can give a rational defense of their actions and are not likely to obey authority simply because obedience is expected.

postconventional autonomous stage The peak of moral sensitivity when a person can give a rational explanation of his or her actions and is not simply bound by conformity or the fear of punishment.

Reasons for Optimism: People Are (at Least Sometimes) Altruistic

As mobility increases and the community's influence declines, self-fulfillment and self-gratification can take the place of the common good.[16] Feeling good may take precedence over doing or being good. People are driven to pursue the good things in life (e.g., money,

EXHIBIT 6–3 Reasons for Saving

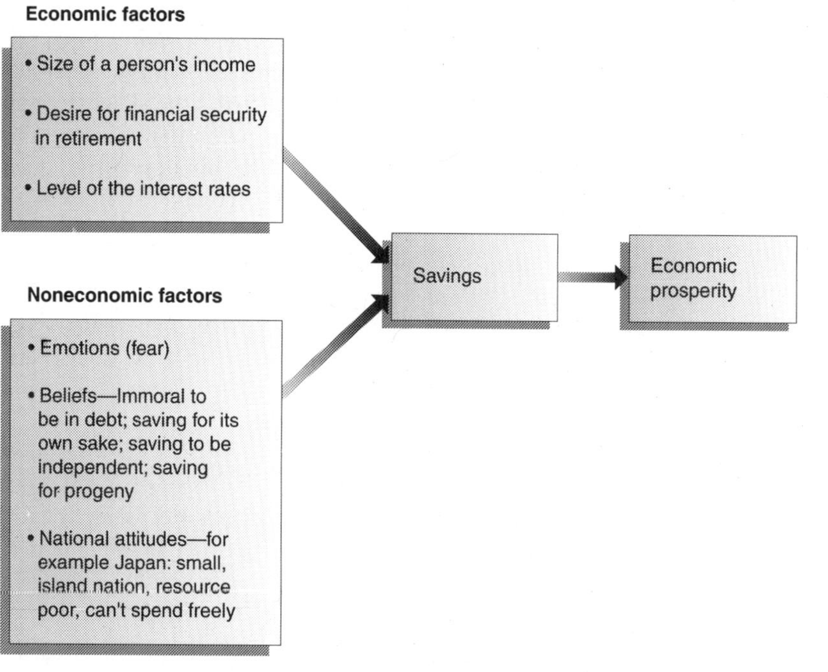

power, and sex), rather than to pursue a life that is good. However, studies have found that in many surprising and unanticipated ways people remain ethical. They take into account interests broader than their own selfish ends.

Experiments have shown that people mail back "lost" wallets to strangers with the cash intact. A high proportion of people asked to aid a person in distress on the streets of New York did so.[17] People tend to support public television. They do not always cheat when there is little chance of getting caught. They vote when they know that their vote will make no difference. Throughout history people have risked their lives for others and for causes, from non-Jews who saved Jews in Nazi Germany to Freedom Riders who marched against segregation in the American South. The main reward to these people was "the inner sense of having done what is right."[18]

Even purely economic behavior cannot be completely understood if the propensity for self-sacrifice is not considered. Saving, for instance, is of prime importance to economics (see Exhibit 6–3). Savings and investment are key attributes of social development. Long-run prosperity is impossible without them. Nonetheless, such behavior cannot be explained only in terms of self-interest. The economic explanation is that it is a consequence of the size of a person's income (the more income, the more saving), the desire for financial security in retirement, and the level of the interest rate (the higher the interest rate, the more the saving). Economists are the first to admit that these factors do not explain all the variance observed. Emotional factors such as fear and moral and societal values lead a person to save. People may believe that it is immoral to be in debt, that one should save for its own sake, that one should save to be independent of the welfare system and of one's children, and that one should save because of the obligation to one's progeny (i.e., they deserve an easier start in life).

In addition, certain national attitudes lead to the propensity to save. The Japanese, for instance, perceive themselves to be the crowded inhabitants of a resource-poor island that has few economic endowments. If they do not judiciously save and invest, they, their children, and their children's children will be doomed to a terrible poverty. A concern for unborn future generations is not necessarily an expression of a rational self-interest, which says it is better to consume now than to worry about what is to happen long after one is dead. Without moral commitments, there are insufficient incentives and penalties to save, and without savings a market economy would not prosper.

Many of the relationships needed to develop an economy depend on noneconomic feelings and ethical norms. People may not be able to articulate why they follow these norms, which become a matter of habit. However, if people failed to obey the contracts and implicit promises that are upheld by moral commitments, the system could collapse. If everybody acted as though promises and contracts had no meaning, prolonged economic activity could not take place.

Distinguishing between Psychological Egoism and Prudential Altruism

Certainly the desire to gain at someone else's expense is a powerful motive. Egoism cannot be denied, but distinctions have to be made about what it means. Some people argue in favor of strict **psychological egoism** in which all motivation is reduced to self-interest. Even recognized heroes are denounced for promoting their selfish and parochial ends. If people mistakenly overlook what is in their best interests and behave altruistically, the strict egoist view insists that the main motivation is still selfishness. People who love others, for example, do so only because they expect to be loved themselves.

psychological egoism The reduction of *all* motivation to self-interest.

This viewpoint is not inconsistent with a **prudential altruism.** The desire for distinction and recognition, if not monetary and other rewards, can lead a person to do good. If, in treating others well, people are acting only to make their own lives more agreeable, who is to fault them if they achieve positive results. If kindness results merely from the fear of anarchy (what the English philosopher Thomas Hobbes called "a solitary, poor, nasty, brutish state of nature"), then this fear is beneficial.[19] Everyone is better off when people are allowed to pursue their self-interests within limits and without threatening the social order. Society becomes more secure and stable.

prudential altruism Treating other people well because of a desire to make one's own life more safe, secure, and agreeable.

Self-interest surely is relevant, but may not be the sole factor that explains people's behavior. People are under the influence of pleasure and moral duty simultaneously; "there are important differences in the extent each of these sets of factors is operative under different historical and societal conditions, and within different personalities under the same conditions."[20] Self-interest dominates some of the time, but there are instances when people act on principles.

If people do everything for purely selfish reasons, they will stop the action when the selfish reasons disappear. However, if they act because what they are doing is inherently right, they will continue with that behavior regardless of how their interests are affected. They will continue "in the face of opposition" because they will have "internalized the values" that justify the actions.[21]

Conclusions

This chapter has tried to show the following:

- People constantly engage in ethical debate. They have a need to justify what they do.
- By asking a number of relevant questions, they should be able to reason better about the ethical dilemmas they face.
- Individuals working in an organization may face conflicts between adhering to their personal ethical values and carrying out the policies of the organization. What is common practice in the organization may conflict with the individual's ethical point of view. The individual then may have to choose between being loyal to the organization and struggling for change from within it or leaving the organization and fighting for change from without.
- Self-interest is a powerful motivating force. When totally unrestrained, however, it can lead to social anarchy. Thus, most people realize that they should control their self-interest; that is, they believe that it needs to be controlled as well as unleashed. Prosperity for people requires a modicum of social harmony, built upon commonly shared values of respect for each person.
- At times, each person must put aside self-interest for the sake of some higher principle.

Discussion Questions

1. Reasons people give for not thinking ethically are relativism, cynicism, egoism, and that behavior is instinctual. Do you agree with these reasons? How would you refute them?
2. Is Socrates' response to Thrasymachus convincing? Why or why not?
3. Can ethics be taught? Can it be learned?
4. In the experiments that Milgram conducted, why did people obey authority? What do you think of these reasons? Are they good ones?
5. Even in the face of an obvious organizational wrong, what are some reasons for not being a whistle-blower? What are some alternatives to blowing the whistle?
6. What effect has the decline of schools, families, neighborhoods, and religious institutions had on individual values? To what extent do you think people adhere to a "feel good" ethic as opposed to a "do good" or "be good" ethic?

7. Is voting a good example of altruistic behavior? If individual votes are unlikely to make a difference in the outcome, why do people vote?
8. Distinguish between psychological egoism and prudential altruism?

Endnotes

1. H. C. Bunke, "Should We Teach Business Ethics?" *Business Horizons* 4 (1988), pp. 2–8; W. Shapiro, "What's Wrong: Hypocrisy, Betrayal and Greed Unsettle the Nation's Soul," *Time*, May 25, 1987, pp. 14–17; Kathy E. Kram, Peter C. Yeager, and Gary E. Reed. "Decisions and Dilemmas: The Ethical Dimension in the Corporate Context," in *Research in Corporate Social Performance and Policy* (Greenwich, Conn.: JAI Press, 1989), pp. 21–54.
2. Barbara Ley Toffler, *Tough Choices* (New York: John Wiley, 1986); R. A. Cooke, *Ethics in Business: A Perspective*, Arthur Andersen & Co., 1988; Declaration of the Rights of Man and Citizen; K. Goodpaster, *Ethics in Management* (Boston: Harvard University Graduate School of Business Administration, 1984).
3. R. Edward Freeman and Daniel R. Gilbert, Jr., *Corporate Strategy and the Search for Ethics* (Englewood Cliffs, N.J.: Prentice Hall, 1988); George A. Steiner and John F. Steiner, *Business, Government, and Society: A Managerial Perspective* (New York: McGraw-Hill, 1991); Norman E. Bowie, *Challenging the Egoistic Paradigm*, Discussion Paper No. 142, Strategic Management Research Center, University of Minnesota, 1990; Robert H. Frank, *Passions with Reason: The Strategic Role of the Emotions* (New York: W.W. Norton, 1988); Sigmund Freud, "From Civilization, War and Death," in *The University of Chicago History of Western Civilization, Topic X: Problems of the Twentieth Century* (Chicago: The University of Chicago Press, 1964).
4. Plato, *The Republic*, trans. by M. Cornford (New York: Oxford University Press, 1967).
5. Bruce A. Ackerman, *Social Justice in the Liberal State* (New Haven: Yale University Press, 1980); Tom L. Beauchamp and Norman E. Bowie, *Ethical Theory and Business*, 2nd ed. (Englewood Cliffs, N.J.: Prentice Hall, 1983); Freeman and Gilbert, *Corporate Strategy and the Search for Ethics*.
6. Toffler, *Tough Choices*.
7. F. B. Bird and J. A. Waters, "The Moral Muteness of Managers," *California Management Review* 1 (1989), p. 73; Kram, Yeager, and Reed, "Decisions and Dilemmas."
8. Stiener and Stiener, *Business, Government, and Society*; George A. Steiner and John F. Steiner, *The Union Carbide Corporation and Bhopal*, 1988.
9. K. Goodpaster, *Ethics in Management* (Boston: Harvard University Graduate School of Business Administration, 1984).
10. Stanley Milgram, *Obedience to Authority* (New York: Harper & Row, 1975).
11. J. Q. Wilson, "Adam Smith on Business Ethics," *California Management Review* 1 (1989), pp. 59–72; K. M. Eisenhardt, *Agency Theory: An Assessment and Review* (Stanford, Calif.: Department of Industrial Engineering and Engineering Management, Stanford University, 1988); C. G. Luckhardt, "Duties of Agent to Principal," in M. Snoeyenbos, R. Almeder, and J. Humber, eds., *Business Ethics: Corporate Values and Society* (New York: Prometheus Books, 1983, pp. 115–21; W. W. Manley and W. A. Shrode, *Critical Issues in Business Conduct: Legal, Ethical, and Social Challenges for the 1990s* (New York: Quorum, 1990); B. M. Mitnick, *The Concept of Constituency*, Working Paper No. 376 (Pittsburgh, Pa.: Graduate School of Business, University of Pittsburgh, n.d.); J. W. Pratt and R. J. Zeckhauser, eds., *Principals and Agents: The Structure of Business* (Boston: Harvard Business School Press, 1985).

12. Richard P. Nielsen, "Changing Unethical Organizational Behavior," *The Academy of Management Executive*, 3 (2), p. 123; M. Velasquez, D. J. Moberg, and G. F. Cavanagh, "Organizational Statesmanship and Dirty Politics: Ethical Guidelines for the Organizational Politician," *Organizational Dynamics*, Autumn 1983, pp. 65–80.
13. Nielsen, "Changing Unethical Organizational Behavior."
14. Myron Peretz Glazer and Penina Migdal Glazer, *The Whistleblowers: Exposing Corruption in Government and Industry* (New York: Basic Books, 1989); J. P. Near, "Whistle-Blowing: Encourage It!" *Business Horizons* 1 (1989), pp. 2–6.
15. L. Kohlberg, "Moral Development," in *International Encyclopedia of the Social Sciences*, vol. 10, D. L. Sills, ed. (New York: Macmillan & Free Press, 1968); L. Kohlberg, *Moral Stages: A Current Formulation and Response to Critics* (New York: Karger, 1983).
16. R. N. Bellah, *Habits of the Heart: Individualism and Commitment in American Life* (Berkeley: University of California Press, 1985).
17. A. Etzioni, *The Moral Dimension: Toward a New Economics* (New York: Free Press, 1988); H. A. Hornstein, E. Fisch, and M. Holmes, "Influence of a Model's Feelings about His Behavior and His Relevance as a Comparison to Other Observers' Helping Behavior," *Journal of Personal and Social Psychology* 10 (1968), pp. 222–26; Latane and Darley, 1970; H. A. Hornstein, H. N. Masor, and K. Sole, "Effects of Sentiment and Completion of a Helping Act on Observer Helping: A Case for Socially Mediated Zeigarnik Effects," *Journal of Personality and Social Psychology* 17 (1971), pp. 107–12.
18. Etzioni, *The Moral Dimension*.
19. Richard T. DeGeorge, *Business Ethics*, 2nd ed. (New York: Macmillan, 1986).
20. Etzioni, *The Moral Dimension*, p. 63.
21. Ibid.

Case 6–A
High Value Discount Appliances[1]

The High Value (HV) chain of discount appliance stores, started in 1978 with the merger of three smaller chains, had achieved sales in excess of $2 billion in a mere 12 years under the respected leadership of its CEO, George Sutherland.[2] Investors included major banks, insurance companies, real estate developers, Fortune 500 companies, and investment banking houses. High Value was touted by the business press as one of the most outstanding new companies in the United States during the last 20 years. It was especially praised for its internal culture. *BizEd Magazine* chose it as one of the 10 best companies for which to work. The culture of the organization was described as "fresh, dynamic, exciting." High Value had managed to create a "protected, family feeling, without the stifling atmosphere that sometimes prevails inside families."

Business and Sports

Sutherland came from old New England stock, was a pillar of the community, was active in his church, and had an impeccable reputation for business integrity. He was a major patron of the arts, an important contributor to the Republican party, and a part-owner of two major league sport franchises, one in Cleveland and the other in Oakland. A soccer player during college at Dartmouth, Sutherland had devoted much of his life to making soccer a national sport comparable to baseball or football. In 1983, he founded the USA Soccer League, which now has teams operating in eight cities. High Value and the USA Soccer League were indistinguishable to many people; as the league's main corporate sponsor, High Value attached its name to nearly all of the league's activities.

You are a former college soccer star from the University of Illinois and a continuing soccer enthusiast who is introduced to Sutherland after a 1986 match in New York City. Although nearly 20 years his junior, you immediately develop a rapport. It so happens that your wife's first cousin is a close associate of Sutherland's and an investor in a number of the same businesses. Sutherland invites you to a weekend aboard his yacht. You also play tennis and golf with him and are amazed at his skill in both these games.

Not only do you like Sutherland, but also the group of young, athletic, and talented men and women whom he has gathered around him—up-and-coming lawyers, accountants, marketing and advertising people, and journalists. You fit right in with this hard-working, hard-playing crowd. You are surprised that, contrary to expectations, none are callous or self-centered. They are a warm, caring group, extremely supportive of one another, devoted to Sutherland, and accepting of you.

You grew up in the Midwest and have no extended family or friends in New York City, where you now work. For six years, you were employed by a major accounting firm, but you did not become a partner and were let go. Now you have an unchallenging job in a large bank, but you see no future for yourself in banking.

Promoting Sport to Benefit Business

On August 3, 1990, after a fairly brutal tennis game, Sutherland asks whether you would like to become his personal assistant. The work sounds a little nebulous, but the salary doesn't. You must support two young children and a wife, and though you lack experience in retailing, you could leave the bank with no regrets. It never felt like home. It was a place to punch a clock. Everything was bound by dry and impenetrable rules. The people barely said hello. You were bored stiff and you had only started there. You accept Sutherland's offer.

Your new job is a whirlwind of excitement. What you do has scarcely any connection with High Value. You are the liaison to the world of professional soccer. You are in contact with major celebrities and become a central figure in promoting the success of the new soccer league. You even come up with the idea of changing High Value's logo to a soccer ball, to make the connection between the company and the soccer league even clearer in people's minds.

On July 4, 1992, after a tennis game at his estate, Sutherland asks you to go into his private office and bring him some files to look at by the pool. You trip on a chair in his office and the contents of the files scatter across the floor. Upon picking them up, you inadvertently see a memo from Sutherland to the CFO. The memo reads as follows:

> There are no irregularities in the statements of inventory or accounts receivable, as alleged by Garcia. These are judgments calls, as we all know. There is no reason to be conservative in making these calls and to make it appear as if our profits are any less than they are. You realize as well as I do that every year we are subject to an independent audit by the respected firm of DuPers and LienBold. How can we fool such experienced auditors into believing that our inventory and accounts receivable are less than reported? Explain the situation to Garcia, thank him for his diligence, transfer him to a part of the company where he no longer can be concerned with these matters, and provide him with appropriate renumeration for his efforts. The so-called issue of irregularities is not an issue, as we both know.

Pessimism and Decline in the Sport League

Despite the U.S. recession, High Value's reported profits the prior year had suffered little. Sutherland earned a substantial bonus and was able to cash in on stock options worth more than $8 million.

The soccer league, on the other hand, was having difficulties. It had always been hard for professional soccer to take off in the United States. Sutherland again dipped into his personal fortune to provide it with an infusion of cash.

The next year is not especially good for High Value. Maybe the company has overextended itself by opening too many new stores. Sales continue to climb, but the competition has intensified, and margins and profits are down. Still, most investors continue to have faith in the company and there is no dearth of funds for additional expansion. However, investors are asking more questions. Why has High Value been so successful? Analysts are beginning to carefully scrutinize the company's records.

The situation for the USA Soccer League deteriorates further. American fans are losing interest. Attendance is down and a number of franchises are near bankruptcy. Without a major infusion of new money, the league is in jeopardy of folding. Sutherland has been on the telephone for days trying to persuade his wealthy friends to commit more dollars, but they see the league as a losing proposition and refuse to cooperate.

After your tennis match with Sutherland on July 4, 1993, you find him in an uncharacteristically pessimistic mood. He says: "There is not much more I can do. My bonus and stock options this year will be nowhere near what they were last year. From now on, we are going to have to play things a lot closer to the vest at High Value. The league could fold. I have sunk as much cash as I can into this endeavor. We both know that High Value has plenty of cash. We could borrow $10 to $15 million temporarily to keep the league going. What do you think? No one would have to know."

How do you react?

Discussion Questions

1. How do you respond to Sutherland? What do you do?
2. If a friend presented this dilemma to you, what would you tell him to do? What are the issues? What is at stake? What is the appropriate way to behave?

Endnotes

1. This case was written by Alfred Marcus.
2. Laurence Barton, *Ethics: The Enemy in the Workplace* (Cincinnati: South-Western College Publishing, 1995), pp. 131–42.

CHAPTER

7

Reasoning about Ethics

Means versus Ends

Every rational being exists as an end in himself and not merely as a means to be arbitrarily used by this or that will. In all his actions, whether they are directed to himself or to other rational beings, a human being must always be regarded at the same time as an end . . . i.e. . . . an object of respect.

Immanuel Kant

If the hypothesis were offered us of a world in which . . . millions kept permanently happy on the one simple condition that a certain lost soul on the far-off edge of things should lead a life of lonely torture, . . . even though an impulse arose within us to clutch at the happiness so offered, how hideous a thing would be its enjoyment when deliberately accepted as the fruit of such a bargain.

William James, "The Moral Philosopher and the Moral Life"

Introduction and Chapter Objectives

Managers face difficult ethical choices that involve basic questions about what is right and wrong and what is good and bad. In this chapter, conflicts between two moral traditions are introduced. According to one of these traditions, treating *each person* with dignity and respect is the most important consideration. The other regards the greatest good for *the greatest number* as the most important consideration. This chapter provides vignettes to help you reason about these ethical dilemmas.

Conflicts between Means and Ends

A brief analysis of the opening quotations is an appropriate place to start. Surely, as William James, the American philosopher and psychologist, notes, it is not right to allow a person to suffer. And Immanuel Kant, the 18th-century German philosopher, says that every person has the right not to be used by others arbitrarily. However, can individual suffering be justified by the *good* achieved for the group who are made happy? To achieve noble *ends*—"millions kept permanently happy"—can one rely on nasty *means*—that a single person "should lead a life of lonely torture"?

Kant's answer seems direct: One must *always* regard the individual with respect. However, he qualifies this in saying we are to regard people "not merely as means"; that is, he suggests that "at the same time" we *should* view people as ends, we inevitably see them as means.

In his rendering, William James points to the tragic character of the dilemma. Even if the group decides that its happiness justifies an individual's suffering, can the group easily live with its decision? Its happiness is muted by the consciousness of the unhappy bargain it has had to strike.

This situation illustrates one of the fundamental concerns of ethics. Do the ends justify the means? Does the happiness of many override a single person's distress and sorrow? Ethical choices in business often are as tragic. They involve bitter trade-offs between apparently irreconcilable values. Right and wrong has to be balanced against good and bad.

Balancing Right and Wrong Against Good and Bad

The following examples illustrate these trade-offs. Agents of the Central Intelligence Agency (CIA) serve righteous *ends* in protecting American foreign policy interests; nonetheless, in the pursuit of these noble ends the CIA routinely relies on *means* (e.g., lying, deception, and violence) that violate accepted canons of right and wrong. On the other hand, the ends of Nazi soldiers certainly were vile—to conquer other nations and impose upon them a system that systematically brutalized and subordinated the conquered population. However, in pursuing these ends, the Nazi soldiers *may have* adhered to some principles of common morality (fidelity, love, and sympathy) in their dealings with each other.

The Italian political philosopher Niccolò Machiavelli argued in *The Prince* (1513) that worthwhile ends often justify efficient means; that is, to achieve ends of overriding importance may require unscrupulous means. Almost everyone would agree with Machiavelli that under some circumstances the ends do justify the means. For example, when a terrorist asks where a child is hiding, one is permitted to lie. However, Stalin was not right to murder more than 20 million Russians and imprison many more to impose his brand of communism.

The conflict between means and ends is at the root of philosophical discussion about ethics. Thus, it is worth reviewing the concepts, theories, and arguments of that debate.

Ethics Defined

Ethics is systematic inquiry into human conduct to discover both the rules that ought to govern human action and the goods that are worth seeking.[1] Two different, but related, questions are central to this pursuit: what is right or wrong, and what is good or bad? The questions led to the development of two major traditions of ethical reasoning. One tradi-

deontology Ethical reasoning concerned with the proper means—what is right and wrong.

tion is called **deontology** after the idea of duties or rights. It teaches that people have a responsibility to do what is right and to avoid doing what is wrong. For instance, people should love their neighbors and treat others with respect. The reason people do this is that they are rational, autonomous, and free. Kant said that people should apply universal rules to their conduct, acting only in ways that they would want *everyone* else to act under the circumstances. According to Kant, you cannot make an exception for yourself.[2]

teleology Ethical reasoning concerned with the proper ends, what is good and bad in life.

The second tradition is called **teleology** because it is concerned with the ends of action, or what is good or bad in life. No fine line, however, can be drawn between these two traditions. An interest in ethics requires reflection on both of them. Modern ethical thinkers ask what do the main ethical concepts mean? Can these concepts be defined? Is it possible to reach ethical conclusions that are universally accepted?

Doing What Is Right

Golden Rule The universal maxim with Judeo-Christian roots that would have you do unto others as you would have them do unto you.

On the surface, ethical standards differ, yet there is a core of similarity that runs through ethical systems that negates claims of total relativism. The **Golden Rule**—do unto others as you would have them do unto you—is a universal idea with origins in both Judaism and Christianity as well as in non-Western religions such as Buddhism and Confucianism. In Buddhism, it is expressed as, "Hurt not others with that which pains yourself." The excellent companies in Peters and Waterman's best-selling book often displayed this type of behavior, as the managers tried to treat their employees, customers, suppliers, shareholders, and other stakeholders with the same respect that they would have liked to have received.[3]

All but the most extreme cynics believe that humans should do what is right by treating others with dignity. People have a duty, a moral obligation, to do so. In everyday discussion, this duty is signified by the word *ought*. In the Judeo-Christian tradition this ought is positively expressed as the Golden Rule: people are obligated to love their neighbors as themselves.

Going beyond the Golden Rule

The Golden Rule may not be a sufficient guide to action. In fact, starting with the New Testament, it has been criticized (see Exhibit 7–1). In the Sermon on the Mount, Jesus was more demanding of people. He said that they should not simply love their neighbor as themselves:

> I say unto you love your *enemies*, bless them that curse you, do good to them that hate you, and pray for them that despitefully use you and persecute you . . . For if you love those who love you, what reward have you? Do not even the common people do the same? . . . Be you therefore perfect.

Immanuel Kant was also a critic, however friendly, of the Golden Rule.[4] For example, he was concerned that it might be applied perversely by wicked people. A sadomasochist, for instance, believes that it is right to harm others and to be harmed by them because hurting

EXHIBIT 7–1 The Golden Rule and Its Critics

The Golden Rule	*Critiques of the Golden Rule*
"Love your neighbor as yourself."	What about your enemies? Are they not deserving of love?
	If a person loves being harmed, can the person harm others?

and being hurt are how such a person wants to be treated. A business person too might believe that inflicting harm and being the recipient of such harm was acceptable; it was part of the natural order of the dog-eat-dog business world. "Do unto others before they do it unto you" might be this person's motto. Kant formulated the famous categorical imperative in his treatise on *The Metaphysics of Morals* (1785) at least partially to combat the possibility that people would use the Golden Rule in such a perverse way.

Treating Others with Respect

Kant went beyond the Golden Rule by positing that the moral ought is unconditional—it is binding regardless of a person's wishes, desires, or interests. Some of the connotations of the word *ought* do not concern morals. There is a logical ought used in mathematical statements to indicate necessity, and a prudential ought usually used in statements about money and riches, for example, "Hard work and thrift ought to make a person wealthy."[5]

categorical imperative To treat others with respect, as ends and not merely as means, regardless of the circumstances and consequences for oneself.

As Kant expressed it, the **categorical imperative** is the duty to regard other human beings with unconditional respect. Be just in your dealings with your fellow human beings, he argued, treat them as ends and not merely as means. This principle cannot be abrogated. It exists regardless of whether we want to treat others with respect or not, whether it helps or harms us, whether it is prudential to do so and we receive financial gain or suffer financial loss. The categorical imperative permits no exceptions.[6]

Kant's idealism does not rule out the possibility that people will to a degree treat others as objects of manipulation; he admits that they will do so, but argues that they should not be treated merely as means.

Universalism

Kant's categorical imperative also requires that a person ask if a proposed action is consistent with universal standards of conduct. Would a person be willing to live in a world where *everyone* behaved in the manner contemplated? For example, would a person be willing to live in a world where everyone inflicted harm and was a victim of the harm inflicted by others? Would a person be willing to live in a world where everyone's ends are achieved by violent means, where everyone lied, cheated, bribed, or discriminated against persons of a different race or religion? If you lie, Kant would ask, are you willing to let everyone lie? If everyone lied, of course, it would be impossible to tell whether anyone was telling the truth, and it would be impossible for society to function. Similarly, if everyone cheated, bribed, or discriminated, social order would disintegrate. Transactions among people would be impossible.

Autonomy

Kant also believed in people's autonomy; they should knowingly submit themselves to universally valid moral principles. People are not subject to blind instincts and sensations. They are rational and can control their passions. The distinctive human quality is the ability to formulate universal laws and to abide by them.[7]

Inalienable Rights

Kant lived at the time of the great revolutions in America and France, and his ideas are largely in accord with those expressed by the leaders of those revolutions. People were deserving of respect, Thomas Jefferson held, because certain "truths" are "self-evident, . . . [that] all men are created equal." People "are endowed by their Creator with certain inalienable rights; that among these are life, liberty, and the pursuit of happiness." The leaders of the French Revolution, similarly, proclaimed that human beings have natural rights to "liberty, property, security, and resistance to oppression." Liberty is defined as "the power to do anything that does not injure others." People also should have the right to freedom of religion and of opinion "provided that their manifestation does not disturb the public order established by law." They should be guaranteed the right to "freely speak, write, and print subject to responsibility for the abuse of this freedom." For the makers of the French Revolution, property also was "an inviolable and sacred right." No one can be deprived of property "unless legally established public necessity obviously demands it and upon condition of a just and prior indemnity."[8]

The rights, or entitlement, model of ethics, represented by Kant and the leaders of the American and French revolutions, holds that individuals have a right to be treated in ways that ensure their dignity, autonomy, and respect.

Kant's Rationality and Human Instinct: Are They Compatible?

Although a critic of the Golden Rule, Kant supports the universal aspect of the biblical injunction to love your neighbor as yourself. The self in the Bible is based on a belief that people are created in the divine image. For Kant, the unique aspect of people that gives them their potential for morality is their rationality, their ability to articulate reasons for their actions, and their freedom, their ability to engage in autonomous action based on the reasons they give.

In contrast, 20th-century thinkers commonly view people as driven by impulses beyond their control (see Exhibit 7–2). Compare Kant's notion of humanity with that of Sigmund Freud, the founder of psychoanalysis, who wrote that "the inmost essence of human nature consists of elemental instincts, which are common to all men and aim at

EXHIBIT 7–2 The Categorical Imperative and Its Critics

Kant's Categorical Imperative	*Critiques of the Imperative*
Treat others with respect: An unconditional principle.	Are people rational?
Universalism: Everyone should behave in this manner.	Are they free to do what they want?
Human autonomy: People knowingly submit themselves to universal laws.	Is an ethics based on intentions, not consequences, adequate?
Inalienable rights: Everyone has the right to such things as life, liberty, and the pursuit of happiness.	Haven't these rights been systematically violated in the totalitarian dictatorships of the 20th century?

the satisfaction of certain primal needs." Humans, according to this view, are driven by impulses, not reflection: "We assume that human instincts are of two kinds: those that conserve and unify which we call erotic or else 'sexual' and secondly the instincts to destroy and kill which we associate as the aggressive or destructive instincts." These impulses represent the desire to love and hate. They are too complex to be called either good or bad.

Freud believed that each of the instincts is "every whit as indispensable as its opposite" and that "an instinct of either category can operate but rarely in isolation . . . Only exceptionally does an action follow on the stimulus of a single instinct . . . As a rule several motives . . . concur to bring about an act." Even ideal motives, according to Freud, are made up of contradictory elements that are camouflages for destructive urges.[9]

The Betrayal of the Intellectuals

The tendency to denigrate rationality and to view humans as bundles of elementary drives and instincts has been criticized by post–World War II European intellectuals. The Dutch thinker Julien Benda wrote about "the teaching of modern metaphysics which exhorts man to feel comparatively little esteem for the truly thinking portion of himself and to honor the active and willing part of himself;" he complains that modern thinkers tend to assign "a secondary rank to the mind." He condemned "a whole literature [that] has assiduously proclaimed the superiority of instinct, the unconscious, intuition, the will as opposed to intelligence."[10]

In *The Road to Serfdom*, the Nobel Prize–winning economist Friedrich Hayek wrote that the instinctual element in behavior was harnessed by totalitarian dictatorships to impose their will. Since a person in a totalitarian society does not choose to do good or evil, but is forced to do so, Nazi and Communist totalitarianism deprived people of their autonomy and took away their ability to exercise moral judgment. In these societies Hayek believed that people "have no title to praise," because they are "outside the sphere of individual responsibility [where] there is neither goodness nor badness nor opportunity for moral merit . . ."[11]

Intentions and Consequences

Another criticism of Kant is his stress of motives and neglect of consequences. Kant taught that other people should be treated with respect, that one should have goodwill toward them. However, does appropriateness of *motives* (as Kant believed and as the Christian tradition taught) make an action right, or is it the goodness of *consequences* (as utilitarians propose)?

John Dewey, the 20th-century American philosopher, argued that motives—the intention to treat people with respect—are less important than deliberation on consequences: "We are reasonable when we estimate the import or significance of any present desire or impulse by forecasting what it would come or amount to if carried out." Dewey advises people to deliberate about the proposed action by means of an "**imaginative rehearsal.**" They should consider the consequences of their actions in terms of good or evil. People should imagine the consequences and plan their actions according to their dislike or approval of these consequences.[12]

imaginative rehearsal To consider the consequences of one's actions by contemplating the likely goodness or badness of what will happen.

Kant's views are deontological; they focus on the rightness or wrongness of actions in themselves. Dewey's views are teleological; they focus on the purpose of actions; moral worth is determined by a consideration of the action's consequences, not the actor's intentions.

Considering an action's consequences puts a great burden on our time and analytical capabilities. We must develop many options, consider who might be affected, and weigh the results. We have to dwell on whether the action is good or bad in light of its manifold consequences, a difficult task.

Good and Bad

Questions of right and wrong force people to examine their *intentions*, but in so doing they may miss the *consequences* of their actions. Instead of right and wrong, what ends are we trying to achieve? We are not thinking in terms of immediate ends, such as tomorrow I have to finish the budget report, or personal ends, such as I would like to increase my net worth by 75 percent in the next five years. We are thinking about the ultimate ends worth pursuing in life.

For classical philosophers in the tradition of Plato and Aristotle, the ultimate end is wisdom. Wisdom yields virtuous character and behavior: the capacity to combine means and ends—to have sympathy for others and take into account the long-term consequences of our decisions.[13] For modern thinkers, the ultimate end is a calculus of pleasure and pain best summarized by Jeremy Bentham's reference to "the greatest good for the greatest number."[14] This utilitarian precept (discussed later in this chapter) has a serious limitation, which is alluded to by William James: The concern for the *greatest* good can prevent us from taking the rights of an individual seriously. To what extent must the "greatest good for the greatest number" be built upon the pain and suffering of particular individuals?

EXHIBIT 7–3 Means versus Ends: A Classic Ethical Dilemma

		Means	
		Right	*Wrong*
Ends	*Good*	Acceptable actions	Unclear?
	Bad	Unclear?	Unacceptable actions

Many business situations involve questions of ends versus means (see Exhibit 7–3). Managers try to do something good, but feel they have no choice but to use vile means; or the methods they employ are totally acceptable, but they are used to accomplish some nefarious end.[15]

Resolving these difficulties is no simple task, but by reasoning about them you can improve your judgment. The five ethical dilemmas on the next page illustrate the conflict between means and ends.

Intrinsic and Extrinsic Good

intrinsic good
An ultimate good that is valued as an end in itself, as opposed to an extrinsic good that has only instrumental value.

What is meant by a good or bad consequence? The word good is used in so many different contexts—a good job, a good movie, a good apple, a good feeling, and so on.[16] No one would maintain that any of these uses is the highest good. One must distinguish between things valued for what they are good for and final goods valued for themselves. The former are *extrinsic* because they are instrumental in character and valued only for what they provide. Final goods are **intrinsic goods** because they have inherent value. They are the ultimate goods, the reason that all other goods are worthwhile. Aristotle says, ". . . there is some end of the thing which we desire for its own sake (everything else being desired for the sake of this) . . ."[17]

Extrinsic goods are means to an end, rather than ends in themselves. Thus, we go to the dentist not because doing so is a final good but because it allows us to achieve some more important aim. We may go to college because we want a higher paying job, not because we value a college education in itself. We earn money because we seek to provide for our children and improve the quality of our lives, not because we value the money in itself and seek to accumulate it simply for the sake of accumulating.

Wisdom and Virtue versus Pleasure and Pain

Aristotle felt that virtue is "concerned with passions and actions and in these there is excess, defect, and the intermediate." He believed that "excess and defect are characteristic of vice, and the mean of virtue." He said that a person can "fail in many ways . . . while

Ethical Vignettes

The Conflict between Means and Ends

1. A Fundamental Breakthrough. You are the research director for a pharmaceutical company. You believe that the company's claims about a product you helped develop, if not outright mendacious, are exaggerated. The product could endanger the lives of the people it is supposed to help. You are also aware that the pharmaceutical company is no longer growing as rapidly as it once was, that it has had few major new products reach the market in recent years, and, as an insider in the industry, that its exaggerations are typical.

Moreover, it takes millions of dollars in profits from successful products to recoup the losses from unsuccessful ones. Product development is a very expensive proposition and "misses" outnumber "hits" by a wide margin. Only by making substantial profits from its few successful products can the company afford the research needed to keep your research team adequately funded. But that is not the only issue. You believe that only through an adequately funded research team can your company benefit society, and your research team may be close to a fundamental breakthrough in the fight against AIDs. What should you do?

2. Managing New Ventures. You work for Brighten Enterprises, a Fortune 500 company with annual sales of more than $23 billion. Your company has been on the cutting edge in new product innovation. It has grown rapidly and has produced many good jobs that help stimulate the local economy. Recently, you persuaded a small company with about $1 million in sales, to purchase, finance, install, and maintain new equipment that would be used almost exclusively for deals with Brighten. You promised Sunshine Electronic Devices and Precision Equipment that it could possibly earn $70 million in sales over 10 years. The total cost of the equipment was about $15 million.

It was a big step for Sunshine, but one which it was eager to take. You got along well with Sunshine managers and looked forward to working with them. The negotiations lasted more than 18 months and you were pleased with the capability of Sunshine's people. The equipment was now more than 65 percent installed.

Brighten Enterprises, however, was hit with some bad news in the second quarter of 1992. Marketing forecasts were not met and revenues were 10.5 percent lower than anticipated. Your unit was hardest hit; sales were down by 31 percent. Although your business is cyclical, these numbers surprised you.

Top management at Brighten decided that your unit could not afford any new investments at this point. All new projects were terminated immediately until a fuller evaluation could be carried out and decisions made about restructuring. Though your job was secure because of your strong track record in product development, Sunshine was sure to suffer. Without the Brighten contracts, Sunshine could not service its debt. It faced bankruptcy. More than 300 Sunshine workers might lose their jobs.

You thought that this scenario probably had been played out before. Sunshine had taken a chance while Brighten, cautious as usual, had cut its losses. It was a brilliant way to manage the risk of new ventures. Brighten is the local powerhouse, the engine that gives dynamism to the economy and provides many people with jobs. Its impact is also large at the national and international level, and its health is more important than that of Sunshine. Sunshine can be sacrificed, or so you think. What should you do?

3. A Tight Schedule. The Gulf War is raging and your job is meeting specifications for a large-scale military contract on a very tight schedule. A second manufacturer waits for components produced by your company to assemble the final product. The government had been extremely dissatisfied with late delivery by prior component suppliers. Your company was chosen chiefly because of its ability to deliver goods on time.

The specifications for the component require work from a certified welder. Unfortunately, the two welders with whom you usually work are unavailable; one is on vacation and the other, who has a long history of unexplained absences, called in sick. You are in luck, however, because the apprentice welder is available. He has worked with you for more than two years and does excellent work.

In fact, you believe that his work is better than that of the certified welders. You trust him completely.

You allow the apprentice to weld the component, but check that the job is done correctly. X-ray inspection shows that the job appears perfect. As closing time approaches, more than 99 hours of the 100 inspection hours specified in the contract have been completed. The component has to be shipped by the end of the day or there will be production bottlenecks. The 100-hour inspection requirement, you believe, is arbitrary: 99 plus hours are just as good.

The driver in your carpool is ready to leave. You start to sign the certification papers, to apply the inspection sticker, and to call shipping to pick up the welded component. You will be awarded a bonus for meeting the deadline. Should you get in the van and congratulate yourself on a job well done?

4. Where Highways Dare Not Go. You are a marketing professional who is offered a promotion that places you as the leader of a team developing a new recreational vehicle. This vehicle has a rough ride and few amenities but can travel at high speeds and take people to places "where highways dare not go." The vehicle will be marketed to young people interested in thrills and adventure. The product will have to sell at a low price, so there will be severe limits on engineering and material costs. The vehicle might have safety problems. Foreign competition has created financial difficulties, but your company is betting on this product becoming very profitable. Accepting the promotion would put you in line for a top management spot. Should you take the job?

5. Risk Perception. You work for a small but prestigious and respected marketing research firm. An attorney from a legal firm representing the cigarette manufacturers' association asks your supervisor to have your firm do a study of the scientific literature on risk perception. This request seems odd because it is not the kind of work your company usually does. Moreover, your supervisor is reluctant to do work for a firm that represents the cigarette manufacturers. He tells the attorney to look elsewhere.

The attorney persists, saying that he wants your firm to do the study. Your supervisor then demands a huge fee, expecting that the attorney will back off. Surprisingly, the attorney accepts the demand.

Your firm certainly could use the business because of the current down cycle in the economy. Your supervisor confides to you that if his wife knew that he was accepting this job she would be extremely upset. Her father smoked two packs of cigarettes a day and died of lung cancer at the age of 50. However, your supervisor rationalizes that it is "only an academic survey" and that he won't get further involved even if it means testifying in court.

You know from your brother, who is an attorney, that risk perception is a hot topic in the courts and that your supervisor could easily become embroiled in a trial. The cigarette manufacturers have escaped paying damages to people who have contracted diseases from smoking because of the warning label on the package. This label shifts the burden of proof to the smoker, who is assumed to know the risks and to have voluntarily assumed them. If an attorney for a person harmed by smoking could prove that the warning label was not adequate in communicating the risk of smoking, cigarette manufacturers could face huge liabilities.

Your supervisor asks you to do the literature review and suggests that you take the lead in client contact. This may be an opportunity for you to develop some business on your own and to create an independent reputation. However, you also understand that the evidence you unearth could be very helpful to the law firm, which will use it only to advance the interests of the cigarette manufacturers.

You are uncertain about your feelings. If someone wants to smoke and risk getting cancer, isn't that the person's business? Why is it the fault of the cigarette manufacturers? What should you do?

to succeed is possible only in one way" and "to miss the mark easy, to hit it difficult." Accordingly, a person must act as if he or she were an archer trying to hit a target. "Shall we not, like archers who have a mark to aim at, be more likely to hit upon what is right?"[18]

Unlike the ancients who sought to understand virtue, many modern thinkers consid-

EXHIBIT 7–4 Utilitarianism and Its Critics

Utilitarianism	*Critiques of Utilitarianism*
Consider consequences.	Are people capable of forecasting the consequences of their actions?
Aim for happiness.	What is happiness?
Seek pleasure, avoid pain.	Is there a better way to establish what happiness is than in monetary terms?
Try to achieve the greatest good for the greatest number.	What about wisdom, virtue, courage, friendship, and beauty—do they get counted?
	What happens to the rights of individuals and groups?

ered pleasure as the highest good and pain as the greatest evil, a belief associated with the Utilitarians, whose founder was the 19th-century English philosopher Jeremy Bentham. Community interests were an aggregate of individual pleasures and pains, which add up to "the greatest good for the greatest number."[19]

Utilitarians suggest that people add units of happiness and unhappiness together to arrive at a measure of happiness or total pain and pleasure (the so-called hedonic calculus). Then society can make more rational decisions about what to do. In doing these calculations, economists are at an advantage because they can work with a quantitative unit: money. Thus, economists have produced indicators of national economic performance like the gross national product (GNP). They have advocated the use of cost-benefit analysis before proceeding with individual policies and programs. These quantitative techniques are systems of national accounts that aggregate at the national level information that business people gather about their firms.

While these indicators are useful, they nevertheless have a concreteness that prevents people from grappling with more fundamental questions; for instance, what is happiness? Does it consist of friendship, knowledge, courage, and beauty in addition to material things upon which a money value can be placed?

Is happiness the same as quantified units of pleasure? What about a dissatisfied Socrates, according to a famous question asked by John Stuart Mill; is he not better off than a satisfied hog? Should the preferences reflected in the price system be the sole criteria for assessing moral value? (See Exhibit 7–4.)

The Tyranny of the Majority

Utilitarianism aims to maximize happiness, but in paying attention to happiness in general, it can ignore individual happiness. What happens to the rights of minorities when the majority (or some benevolent utilitarian dictator claiming to represent the majority)

Real-World Example

The Destructive Potential of Factions

The founders of the American republic were aware that democratic government could be hurt by competing factions:

> A factious spirit has tainted our public administration . . . By a faction I mean a number of citizens whether amounting to a majority of minority of the whole who are united and actuated by some common impulse of passion, or of interest, adverse to the rights of other citizens, or to the permanent and aggregate interests of the community . . . [20]

The roots of faction are in the different capabilities of human beings. Differing capabilities yield different economic circumstances. From the different capabilities result "unequal distribution of property." Unequal distribution yields different "sentiments," and different sentiments produce the division of society into different groups and interests:

> Those who hold and those who are without property have ever formed distinct interests in society. Those who are creditors and those who are debtors . . . a landed interest, a manufacturing interest, a mercantile interest, a moneyed interest, with many lesser interests grow up of necessity in civilized nations and divide them into different classes actuated by different sentiments and views.[21]

The division of society into classes with different interests is dangerous but it cannot be avoided. The rights of contending factions have to be protected, according to the founders.

> There are . . . two methods of removing the causes of faction: the one by destroying the liberty which is essential to its existence, the other by giving to every citizen the same opinions, the same passions, and the same interests . . . the first remedy . . . [is] . . . worse than the disease . . . The second expedient is as impracticable as the first would be unwise. As long as the reason of man continues fallible, and he is at liberty to exercise it, different opinions will be formed.[22]

Since the causes of faction cannot be removed, relief can be sought only "in the means of controlling its effects."

decides what the greatest good for the greatest number is? Would the rights of individuals and groups be suppressed?

American democracy was designed to deal with this issue. Sensitive to abuses of the majority, the founders established a complex system of governance to assure that individual and group rights are not violated. They created a republic that would protect citizens from the tyranny of the majority. The cure for the brute force of the majority is representative government, not direct democracy, and a country large and diverse enough to prevent any single faction from imposing its view on the rest.[23]

Similar principles can be applied in an organization to promote plural views and protect minority interests. When diverse interests are represented, minority rights are more secure. However, with diversity of interests comes the problem of disruptive, cantankerous, and potentially destructive factions, about which the founders of the American republic also had much to say (see the Real-World Example above).

Reviewing the Deontological and Teleological Traditions

So far, different principles for addressing ethical dilemmas have been discussed. The deontological tradition maintains that a person's intent should be to treat others with *respect*.

An act has moral value only if all people have been treated as possessing dignity and worth, and people have the right to be treated with dignity because they are human beings with inalienable rights to life, liberty, and the pursuit of happiness. *Universalism* also belongs to the deontological tradition. An act can be justified only if it can be applied universally. A person has to be consistent with regard to moral choices and not hypocritical. A person's motives, not the consequences of the person's actions, are important from the deontological perspective. The teleological tradition, on the other hand, stresses outcomes, not motives. From it derives the *utilitarian* principle that actions should result in the greatest good for the greatest number.

Means and Ends: A Basic Moral Dilemma

The two major ethical traditions pose a dilemma when juxtaposed against each other. Right and wrong questions, on the one hand, are those of means,—proper conduct. Good and bad questions are those of ends—the purposes such conduct serves. The conflict between means and ends constitutes the core of many ethical dilemmas.

Consider individual goals, such as becoming successful in life and not being humiliated by failure. They are not universal principles to be equated with the greatest good, justice, and liberty. Yet they are the types of goals that motivate people.[24]

People may engage in ethically dubious behavior because they want to achieve these goals. They rationalize their actions by claiming that the ends justify the means; in other words, success justifies the dubious behavior that may be necessary to achieve that success. Equally as important as success is the fear of humiliation that comes with failure. Sometimes this fear is based on very realistic concerns, such as a concern about economic security. At other times, the fear is simply one of not wanting to look bad or to be wrong. These fears may drive people to ethically dubious acts.

People often define themselves in terms of achievement in their jobs and careers. If they do not attain the success they seek, they open themselves up to ethical compromise and may commit dubious acts. The end—to maintain their self-esteem—justifies the means.

Another manifestation of ends conflicting with means is how people at different levels in an organization view the issues the organization faces (see Exhibit 7–5).[25] Typically, people lower in the hierarchy stand for a deontological ethics that calls for treating people with respect. People higher in the organization stand for a teleological ethics that emphasizes the "greatest good" for the organization as a whole.[26]

People lower in the hierarchy frame ethical questions as helpful or hurtful to the welfare of individuals. They care about their friends and colleagues in the organization who may be hurt by decisions made at the top. They are reluctant to lay off people they know and respect. People higher in the organization do not have the same reluctance about these cuts and justify layoffs in terms of the organization's survival. They frame ethical questions as broad policy issues that involve the organization's welfare, not the welfare of the individuals who have been harmed. The ends justify the means the organization uses to accomplish its objectives.

In 1993, Pope John Paul II issued an encyclical, *Veritatis Splendor* (The Splendor of Truth), which provides his perspective on these issues.[27] He states that some actions are

EXHIBIT 7–5 Ethical Principles at Different Levels in the Organization

		Typical ethical principle
Organization level	High	Greatest good for the greatest number
	Low	Welfare of individual employees

universally wrong, regardless of the consequences. Rape, for instance, is categorically unacceptable regardless of circumstance and consequence. Even if a spy or drug agent had to commit a rape to gain access to destroy a tyrant or drug kingpin, it would be forbidden. The evil of rape cannot counterbalance any good that may come from it. Our own moral reasoning must contain absolutes that do not justify the ends.

Final Considerations

Ethical dilemmas are difficult. They involve conflicts between deeply held and often opposing principles. There is no easy way out and yet one must still give account and justify what one has done.

With respect to the resolution of difficult choices, a few pieces of advice may be useful.

1. If two apparently irreconcilable principles are in conflict, one should make sure that there really is an ethical dilemma. Is there some ingenious way out that will allow one to proceed without violating any moral rule? Consider all the facts, then rethink the problem. Try to redefine the situation before caving in on moral principles. Establish firm limits and do not go beyond them in making ethical compromises.

2. Philosophers distinguish between act utilitarianism and rule utilitarianism.[28] The former calls for actions that are always in accord with the greatest good for the greatest number. Breaking the rules, lying, and even killing are justified if the greater good is served. **Rule utilitarianism** means that certain rules cannot be violated under any circumstances because they guarantee the existence of society. The ultimate justification for these rules is an appeal to social utility. Without such rules (e.g., the prohibition against murder), society could not maintain itself.

rule utilitarianism Certain rules that guarantee the existence of society that cannot be violated under any circumstances.

3. Be aware that some situations are tragic and cannot be resolved either through redefinition or the use of sophisticated distinctions. A person can do only one thing: carefully give reasons why some principles take precedence over others. Provide justifications for the actions you take.[29] Understand that moral rules still have meaning under these circumstances, that their violation is an unfortunate exception. Do not give in to absolute relativism which leads to pure anarchy, or the inability to make any moral distinction or judgments.

It is not easy for humans to be just and to preserve a sense of integrity in an imperfect world. The 20th century, for all its material progress, has been a brutal period with wars, genocide, and the degradation of the human spirit. The question posed by the Christian theologian Reinhold Neibuhr is relevant: In situations where a person's survival is at stake and people are acting unjustly, can a person maintain a sense of integrity? Can a person be moral in an immoral society?

Conclusions

This chapter has presented eight moral principles from the writings of various ethical philosophers. Some of these are deontological principles relating to right and wrong and some are teleological principles relating to good and bad. The principles are:

1. Treat others with respect (Kant).
2. Investigate the consequences of one's actions (Dewey).
3. Evaluate one's actions in terms of a higher good (Aristotle).
4. Behave in a virtuous manner, balanced with precision between extreme states of passion (Aristotle).
5. Strive to maximize pleasure and minimize pain (Bentham, Mill).
6. Assess actions in terms of the greatest good for the greatest number (Bentham, Mill).
7. Avoid causing unnecessary suffering to individuals and groups (James).
8. Take into account a broad range of interests when making decisions (the founders of the American republic).

These principles, as suggested by the vignettes in this chapter, can be applied to many business decisions.

Discussion Questions

1. Define ethics. What does it mean? What is an ethical dilemma?
2. Why are managers reluctant to discuss ethical issues? Why do they insist on referring to them as organizational or economic matters?
3. Are all ethical principles relative? Explain your answer.
4. What is the difference between the deontological and the teleological tradition in ethics?
5. Explain Immanuel Kant's critique of the Golden Rule.
6. To what extent did Kant envision any exceptions to his rule of treating others with respect? Can this rule really be unconditional and absolute?
7. To what extent are people rational? To what extent are they controlled by passion and instinct? What do you think (or feel)? What difference does your answer make?
8. In your view, which is more important—motives or consequences? Why?

9. What is the difference between an intrinsic good and an extrinsic good?
10. How would you answer the criticisms raised against utilitarianism?
11. Can a person be happy in an unjust society? What do you think (or feel)?
12. If faced with William James's hypothesis of keeping millions permanently happy on condition that one person lead "a life of lonely torture," what would you do? If the one person were a statistic, for example, one chance of cancer in 10,000, what would you do? How would you justify your decision?

Endnotes

1. O. A. Johnson, ed., *Ethics: Selections from Classical and Contemporary Writers*, 3rd ed. (New York: Holt, Rinehart and Winston, 1974).
2. Immanuel Kant, "Foundations of the Metaphysics of Morals," in O. A. Johnson, ed., *Ethics: Selections from Classical and Contemporary Writers*, p. 205.
3. T. J. Peters and R. H. Waterman, *In Search of Excellence: Lessons from America's Best Run Companies* (New York: Harper & Row, 1982).
4. T. L. Beauchamp and N. E. Bowie, *Ethical Theory and Business*, 2nd ed. (Englewood Cliffs, N.J.: Prentice Hall, 1983).
5. Johnson, *Ethics: Selections from Classical and Contemporary Writers*.
6. Kant, "Foundations of the Metaphysics of Morals," p. 205.
7. R. T. DeGeorge, *Business Ethics*, 2nd ed. (New York: Macmillan, 1986).
8. "Declaration of the Rights of Man and Citizen," in *The University of Chicago History of Western Civilization, Topic VIII: The French Revolution, Liberalism, Nationalism* (Chicago: University of Chicago Press, 1964).
9. Sigmund Freud, "Civilization, War and Death," in *The University of Chicago History of Western Civilization*, Topic X: *Problems of the Twentieth Century* (Chicago: University of Chicago Press, 1964).
10. Julien Benda, "The Betrayal of the Intellectuals," in *The University of Chicago History of Western Civilization*, Topic X.
11. F. Hayek, "Excerpts from the Road to Serfdom," in *The University of Chicago History of Western Civilization*, Topic X.
12. John Dewey, *Ethics* (1908, reprint Carbondale, Ill.: Southern Illinois University Press, 1978).
13. R. McKeon, *Introduction to Aristotle* (New York: Random House, 1947); Plato, *The Republic*, trans. M. Cornford (New York: Oxford University Press, 1967); L. Strauss, *Natural Right and History* (Chicago: University of Chicago Press, 1953).
14. Jeremy Bentham, "An Introduction to the Principles of Morals and Legislation," in Johnson, ed., *Ethics: Selections from Classical and Contemporary Writers*, pp. 228–39.
15. Beauchamp and Bowie, *Ethical Theory and Business;* DeGeorge, *Business Ethics;* Kenneth E. Goodpaster, *Some Avenues for Ethical Analysis in General Management*, Harvard Business School Paper No. 383-007 (Cambridge: Harvard University Business School, 1982); L. G. Hrebiniak and W. F. Joyce, "Organizational Adaptation: Strategic Choice and Environmental Determinism," *Administrative Science Quarterly*, September 1985, pp. 336–49; Johnson, *Ethics: Selections from Classical and Contemporary Writers;* C. Mills, *How Good a Person Do I Have to Be?* Report from the Institute for Philosophy and Public Policy, 198?, pp. 12–15.

16. Johnson, *Ethics: Selections from Classical and Contemporary Writers*.
17. Aristotle, "The Nicomachean Ethics," in Johnson, *Ethics: Selections from Classical and Contemporary Writers*, pp. 47–76.
18. Ibid.
19. John Stuart Mill, *Utilitarianism* (Oxford: Blackwell, 1986).
20. *The Federalist Papers* (Garden City, N.Y.: Anchor Books, 1966).
21. Ibid.
22. Ibid.
23. Ibid.
24. Michael Josephson, "Ethic in Business: An Overview," *Ethics: Easier Said Than Done* 1, no. 2 (1989), pp. 40–43; J. Sigler and J. Murphy, "Business Ethics: Action Needed," *Ethics: Easier Said Than Done* 1, no. 2 (1989), p. 60; W. Smithburg, "Corporate Ethics," *Ethics: Easier Said Than Done* 1, no. 2 (1989), p. 60.
25. LaRue Tone Hosmer, *The Ethics of Management* (Homewood, Ill.: Richard D. Irwin, 1987).
26. K. E. Kram, P. C. Yeager, and G. E. Reed, "Decisions and Dilemmas: The Ethical Dimension in the Corporate Context, in *Research in Corporate Social Performance and Policy* (Greenwich, Conn.: JAI Press, 1989), pp. 21–54.
27. Peter Steinfels, "The Encyclical," *The New York Times*, Oct. 16, 1993, p. 9.
28. DeGeorge, *Business Ethics*.
29. Bruce A. Ackerman, *Social Justice in the Liberal State* (New Haven: Yale University Press, 1980).

Case 7–A
Reengineering Phantom[1]

CEO Marina Delatorre was in trouble with the board for her reluctance to move quickly in reengineering Phantom Savings and Loan.[2] The stock was selling far below its true value, according to board members, because Delatorre had not demonstrated her willingness to implement a reengineering effort that would recalibrate all the bank's processes for enhanced productivity. The board suspected that Delatorre was dragging her feet because of an aversion to laying off employees.

The company's president, Eugene Trascher, had no such wariness. He had brought in a team of consultants from the well-regarded TACK firm to help him achieve his goal of a 30 to 40 percent reduction in operating expenses. TACK had already completed much of the study. Rather than examining the company by division, department, or function, it had divided the company into core processes such as customer operations, customer support, and customer contact. Then it made direct process observations. TACK also sent consultants and company personnel to visit companies like GTE and Avis for inspiration and ideas about the best practices. Lessons from these visits were molded into the final recommendations. Some of the findings appalled Trascher; for example, Phantom bought 83 different brands of personal computers each year.

The consultants now wanted to proceed beyond the first-phase diagnostics to broad-scale implementation. They had written the script for the reengineering exercise and wanted to continue guiding the effort. They talked of finding the optimum solutions for crafting the new process platforms and engaging in the phase-out diagnostics. TACK produced a thick book of 350 changes it wanted to make from consolidating work centers to simplifying procedures for approving customer service.

In making their presentation to the board, the team asked for a large-scale, one-time charge against earnings (65 percent for expenses and 35 percent for capital).

TACK said that if its fixes were implemented they would generate an internal rate of return (IRR) of 987 percent and a payback on investment in two years. If the consulting team could achieve only one-quarter of its goals, the company still would see a 211 percent IRR and a three-year payback. While these numbers were enthusiastically received by board members, one director questioned the costs of the layoffs, claiming that they were low and that actual costs would be two to three times as much.

When questioned about the human side of the layoffs, one of the TACK consultants replied: "Hey, we're taking a bunch of frustrated, unproductive people and transforming them so that they can do their work better. We're involved in saving their jobs, not destroying them." He said that employees would be retrained at a leadership session called "New and Better Ways to Win at Work." They would learn about initiative, teamwork, accountability, open communications, respect for diversity, and coaching, rather than managing. These were the "survival skills they would need whether they stayed at Phantom or ended up somewhere else."

In 1992, Phantom had $151 million in losses compared with a profit of $356 million the previous year. The future would be a difficult one with deregulation continuing, consolidation in the industry, and the engagement of all the players in serious cost-cutting. To compete, Phantom would have to purge itself of all marks of inefficiency.

Phantom had a large multistate branch network active in the western United States and Texas. It employed 26,432 people; TACK sought to cut up to 7,000 from the payroll. Phantom said that the details of the buyout packages would be announced in two weeks. If enough people did not voluntarily accept the packages, the company would push them out.

Delatorre thought that Trascher's plan, though ruthless, was brilliant. She and other top managers were immune from the pain, but for many employees the pain was real. To lose a job is traumatic. It destroys the person's esteem and hurts his or her family. After previous cutbacks, 160 employees had banded together to bring a class-action suit against Phantom for age discrimination. Delatorre then had asked the Human Resources Department to do a follow-up study to determine how many of the laid-off employees now had jobs. After three years, more than half were still unemployed.

Delatorre wondered about the commitment and loyalty of the remaining employees if the company again laid off employees in response to complex issues that perhaps could be better addressed in another manner. Would further turmoil in the company completely shatter morale? She believed that when these additional factors were weighed, the costs of reengineering would prove greater than the benefits. When she addressed her concerns to Trascher, he replied flatly: "If we refuse to lay off these people, our losses will only mount, and the longer we delay the worse it will be." What should Delatorre do?

Discussion Questions

1. What do you think of Trascher's position? Is it justified?
2. What is your view of the role that TACK consultants played in this case?
3. What dilemma does the CEO confront? If you were Marina Delatorre, what would you do? Why?

Endnotes

1. This case has been written by Alfred Marcus.
2. Phantom is a fictional company. The problems of *actual* companies are explored in these two articles: "The Pain of Downsizing," *Business Week*, May 9, 1994, pp. 60–69; Louis Richman, "When Will the Layoffs End?" *Fortune*, Sept. 20, 1993, pp. 54–56.

Case 7–B
The Lockheed Bribery Case

Do the Ends Justify the Means?

Steel and Concrete Structures Engineering, Inc. (SCSE), is an international firm employing 690 people in 11 countries. It does work all over the globe. One of its most important functions is to sell its services in this marketplace. Every year, it offers all employees a three-day training session that focuses on corporate ethics and customer relations.

As part of this year's training, SCSE has invited two business school professors to discuss the Lockheed bribery case. As an experienced marketing person who has sold many SCSE projects throughout the world, your job is to comment on what the professors have to say.

First, you read some of the material prepared by the Training Department on corporate ethics.

> Ethics deal with standards of conduct and morals. An ethical person is one who does what his or her conscience says is right. Since standards differ from person to person, what is ethical in a business relationship is what is commonly considered just and moral. Good ethics result in good business and bad ethics in bad business. If we treat a customer, supplier, or employee dishonestly, word will get out and others will retaliate or avoid future dealings with the company. Our view is that the drive to be profitable and meet payrolls forces some businesses to use shady practices, but in the long run such businesses will not come out ahead. Our advice to you is to always do what is right. In the long run, companies whose employees do what is right will come out ahead. In dealings with customers, we want you to think of the customer's best interest. Represent factual material honestly. Complete your contractual obligations on time and within budget. Internally, we want you to uphold the highest level of professional conduct. We encourage your participation in civic affairs, and we will not tolerate sexual harassment or discrimination in employment practices.

Next, you listen as the session on the Lockheed bribery case begins.

Moderator: One of the most difficult dilemmas faced by U.S. businesses operating abroad is the question of illegal payments. Should American companies engage in this activity when it is accepted business practice, albeit illegal? Should they engage in it when it seems necessary to obtain contacts and to open up new business? The Lockheed bribery scandal of the mid-1970s is an interesting example of this dilemma.

Because of Lockheed's desperate straits as a company—it had just been bailed-out by a federal government loan guarantee—the company's existence was at stake.[1] Many jobs would be lost if the company did not obtain a sufficient number of orders for its L-1011 Tristar commercial aircraft. Was it right for Lockheed to have bribed foreign officials in an effort to get them to buy its aircraft?

Here are some of the details related to the decision by Carl Kotchian, Lockheed's president, to pay $3.8 million in bribes to Japanese officials. Kotchian did not go to Japan intending to bribe Japanese officials. Although directly responsible for the negotiations for the sale of the planes, he spoke no Japanese and had to rely on advice and representation from executives of a Japanese trading company retained as an agent. The trading company represented Lockheed in all deliberations with the prime minister and the prime minister's office, and Kotchian did not have direct contact with the government officials who would make the actual decision. His contact was limited to the technical and functional representatives of Japan's airlines.

The negotiations extended over a period of 70 days, during which Kotchian stayed in a hotel room in downtown Tokyo. He was subject to hurried meetings and continued suggestions that the decision would be made soon except that something, an unnamed something, was not in place.

Kotchian had no firm knowledge of whether his competitors had supplied that unnamed something, but he suspected that they had or would be willing to do so.

Lockheed had failed to obtain contracts for the L-1011 from Italy, Germany, and Sweden, and a large order was essential to bring unit sales close to the break-even point and to repay at least partially the expense of designing and building the aircraft. If the Nippon order, which meant more than $430 million in revenues, was not forthcoming, it would be another blow to sales momentum. This in turn would mean a slowdown in new design projects and the layoff of engineers and production workers. Kotchian felt it was his duty to protect a large workforce in Burbank, California. If Lockheed lost its fourth foreign order in a row, not only would the jobs of these workers in Burbank be jeopardized but so would Kotchian's own job. Kotchian felt that a bribe of 0.8 percent of the face value of the order was a small price to pay when so much else was at stake.

Our first speaker to comment on this case will be James Utility. Our second speaker will be Jerry Dialectic. Both are business school professors. To conclude our debate on this dilemma, an experienced marketing person from our company will offer his opinion.

James Utility: You may be surprised at the position I am taking, but I would like to justify Mr. Kotchian's decision. Most ethical rules are not categorical. Even rules that people should keep their promises (or not lie, cheat, bribe, and violate the law) have clear exceptions. I would argue that "a sound ethics requires that rules sometimes be broken." Almost everyone would agree that a person could break a promise to sell a friend a patent, which that friend would in turn sell to Iraq to make advanced guided missiles.

I would make the following distinction. Categorical rules cannot be violated under any circumstances. Prima facie rules, however, may be violated in favor of more pressing obligations. Prima facie rules should not be violated if other things are equal: however, in the complex circumstances of international business, situations do not conform to simple maxims. Under these circumstances, violating an ethical rule may be ethical or ethically required.

My argument is that the Lockheed situation should be assessed from a utilitarian perspective, in which it is clear that the positive ends outweigh the negative means. The decision to bribe Japanese officials was ethical. A corporation engaged in lying, covering up, and cheating to get what it wanted. It took unfair advantage of its competitors. However, there are other considerations: the health of American businesses that engage in international trade, the overall health of the U.S. economy, and the benefits of the sale to management, stockholders, and employees. The $400 million that Lockheed would receive for the planes would go a long way toward restoring Lockheed's fiscal health. It also would provide savings to taxpayers in the form of revenues generated and unemployment benefits avoided. Management has an obligation to stockholders to earn reasonable return, to employees to try to assure job security, and to society at large to promote U.S. economic well-being through the success of the company.

Certainly, the company would be doing harm by helping corrupt officials stay in power. The costs of the bribe would be passed along to consumers, and it might result in inferior and possibly dangerous products being put on the market. Another aircraft manufacturer probably would have paid the bribes if Lockheed didn't, and Lockheed believed that the Tristar was an acceptable, if not a technically superior, plane. From the standpoint of endpoint ethics, I argue that such payments are ethical if the product is good and someone else would have made the bribe anyhow. The rules against bribery are only prima facie rules. Bribery cannot be condemned in all situations.

I remind you that the Foreign Corrupt Practices Act of 1977 makes it a crime to offer payments to foreign officials to obtain or retain business. A company can be fined up to $1 million. Officers of the company who participate in or have reason to know of violations can be fined up to $10,000 and receive up to five years in prison. However, I believe that it is an unjust law that is hurting American business in international competition.[2] Under certain conditions, I see no reason why a company should not try to evade it.

Jerry Dialectic: My argument is that the only way to defend Lockheed is to cite necessity, that the company had no other choice because of the economic factor. The company cannot be defended based on the moral factor of the rightness or wrongness of its decision. To prevent bribery from taking place, certain questions should be posed. You should consider:

1. What is the worst thing that can happen if you engage in bribery?
2. What will be the effect on future business?
3. What will be the effect on the company's image?
4. How will it affect the corporation's philosophy of management?
5. How will it affect the control managers have over the corporation?
6. How will it affect the kind of employees the company attracts?
7. How will it affect the company's customers?
8. How will it affect the company's relationships with competitors?
9. What will it do to the managers as human beings? Will it erode their moral fiber?
10. How will it affect the status and quality of products, R&D, and innovation in the company?
11. Is bribery the kind of practice with which the company wants to be identified?

If these questions are asked, and the probing with respect to them is profound, I am convinced that you will not engage in bribery.[3]

Discussion Questions

1. As an experienced marketing person listening to the two business school professors, what is your response?
2. How should SCSE approach this issue?
3. Do the ends justify the means in this case?
4. How should employees be advised to handle cases such as the Lockheed bribery?

Endnotes

1. B. Pendergast, *Note on Lockheed Aircraft Corporation*, Case 9–372–013 rev. (Boston: Harvard Business School, November 1976).
2. James Utility's views are based on M. Pastin, "Case: International Bribery," in *The Hard Problems of Management: Gaining the Ethics Edge* (San Francisco: Jossey-Bass, 1986), pp. 117–23.
3. Jerry Dialectic's views are based on Ian I. Mitroff and Ralph H. Kilmann, "Teaching Managers to Do Policy Analysis: The Case of Corporate Bribery," *California Management Review* 20, no. 1 (1977), pp. 47–54.

CHAPTER

8

Reasoning about Ethics

Inequality and Diversity

Imagine a hundred yard dash in which one of the two runners has his legs shackled together. He has progressed 10 yards, while the unshackled runner has gone 50 yards. How do they rectify the situation? Do they merely remove the shackles and allow the race to proceed? Then they could say that "equal opportunity" now prevailed. But one of the runners would still be forty yards ahead of the other. Would it not be the better part of justice to allow the previously shackled runner to make up the forty-yard gap; or start the race all over again.

Lyndon Johnson, 1963[1]

For the first time, we realized that diversity is a strength as it relates to problem solving. Before we just thought of diversity as the total number of minorities and women in the company like affirmative action.

Ernest Drew, CEO of Hoechst Celanese, 1994[2]

Introduction and Chapter Objectives

This chapter begins with the philosophical debate about justice and liberty. It then covers the issues of unequal pay in the corporation and discrimination against women and minorities. Important laws and court cases about discrimination are summarized. The chapter also provides ethical vignettes about sexual harassment and affirmative action and draws implications for corporate policies and programs.

Justice and Liberty: The Philosophical Debate

The relationship between individual well-being and the collective good is taken up by the modern political philosophers John Rawls and Robert Nozick. Rawls justifies inequality only if it is "reasonably expected to be in everyone's advantage and attached to positions and offices open to all." His principles of justice are:

> First: each person is to have an equal right to the most extensive basic liberty compatible with a similar liberty for others. Second: social and economic inequalities are to be arranged so that they are both (*a*) reasonably expected to be to everyone's advantage, and (*b*) attached to positions and offices open to all.[3]

These principles, he maintains,

> are a special case of a more general conception of justice that can be expressed as follows. All social values—liberty and opportunity, income and wealth, and the bases of self-respect—are to be distributed equally unless an unequal distribution of any, or all, of these values is to everyone's advantage.[4]

Rawls combines Kant's respect for each individual with the utilitarians' preference for the greatest good for the greatest number. Each person deserves the same basic right to equality unless it is in the collective interest that there be some inequality (e.g., to motivate people to make greater effort and contribute more to the common good).

Rawls argues from the perspective of a "veil of ignorance." He maintains that we would freely accept these conditions if we did not know our own race, sex, degree of wealth, or natural abilities. He holds that the advantage of acceptance is a sense of fairness and the willing cooperation of everyone in society, even the less well situated.

Robert Nozick takes a different view. He stresses liberty and the rights of people to acquire property.

> If the world were wholly just, the following inductive definition would exhaustively cover the subject of justice . . .
>
> 1. A person who acquires a holding in accordance with the principle of justice in acquisition is entitled to that holding.
> 2. A person who acquires a holding in accordance with the principle of justice in transfer, from someone else entitled to the holding, is entitled to the holding.
> 3. No one is entitled to a holding except by repeated applications of 1 and 2.[5]

While the highest good for Rawls is some form of justice, for Nozick it is liberty, the ability of people to forge their own destinies without communal interference. Nozick writes:

> We might say: From each according to what he chooses to do, to each according to what he makes for himself (perhaps with the contracted aid of others) and what others choose to do for him and choose to give him of what they've been given previously . . . So as a summary and great simplification . . . we have: From each as they choose, to each as they are chosen.[6]

Nozick maintains that a person who legitimately obtains wealth is entitled to it regardless of how it affects equality or inequality. Starting with pay inequality, a number of examples of inequality as they relate to the corporation will be examined in this chapter.

Pay Inequality

In 1930 when Babe Ruth was asked why he earned more than President Herbert Hoover, he replied, "Because I had a better year." Can the same be said of CEOs of major U.S. corporations? In 1993, the median chief executive salary and bonus in the 350 largest U.S.

companies was $1,174,398, up from $1,095,000 in 1992. In a book titled *In Search of Excess: The Overcompensation of American Executives*, Graef Crystal found a negative relationship between top management compensation and corporate performance.[7] CEO pay kept rising in the 1980s even after the 1989 recession. In 1990, the median pay increase in the 350 largest U.S. companies was 6.7 percent, while shareholder value (i.e., share price plus dividends) fell by 9 percent. Rand Araskog of ITT earned $3.9 million in 1990, up 63 percent from the previous year, not including free shares and other payouts valued at $7.5 million. ITT's earnings per share, however, increased by only 12 percent. The California Public Employees Retirement System and United Shareholders Association sued the company, and ITT's board of directors voted to change the reward system.

The salaries paid to corporate executives have not been closely tied to performance. Giant companies announced vast layoffs, at the same time that top executive pay increased substantially. Since 1972, the salaries of executive officers of major corporations have doubled in terms of real money. Government pay was down 25 percent in the same period.[8] The average 1993 salary of CEOs in the United States was 157 times greater than the average wage of workers. In 1980, the difference had been 42 times greater. In Japan, the average salary of CEOs in 1993 was 32 times greater than the average wage of workers.[9]

CEOs in the United States earned nearly double the figure earned by CEOs in other countries (see Exhibit 8–1). No less a pundit than former Vice President Dan Quayle quipped: "Unconnected to performance, the pay of CEOs is galloping forward faster than [that of] production workers, corporate profits, industrial production, the national debt, the population of India, the number of channels on cable TV, and just about everything including newly created independent republics in formerly East bloc nations."[10]

Pay of nonunion salaried workers increased 4.9 percent in 1992 and 4.5 percent in 1993, while CEO pay jumped 8.1 percent in 1992 and 8.1 percent.[11] These trends do not reflect supply and demand according to Derek Bok, former president of Harvard University.[12] Bargaining over compensation is a highly subjective process that is easily manipulated by the incumbents. A CEO who also is chair of the board represents a direct conflict of interest, because the chair decides who sits on the board and the board decides how much compensation the CEO gets. Outside directors on the board at most companies are

EXHIBIT 8–1 Highest Paid Executives: 1993 ($ millions)

	S. Weill (Travelers Inc.)	*G. Fischer (Eastman Kodak)*	*G. Levin (Time Warner)*	*J. Meillor (General Dynamics)*
Salary	$ 1.0	$ .33	$ 1.1	$ .67
Bonus	3.0	.15	4.0	1.4
Perks	.25	5.0	.24	12.9
Long-term incentives, stock grants	41.4	19.9	15.9	5.4
Total	$45.7	$25.4	$21.2	$20.3
5-year return to shareholders (annual rate)	30.8%	9.2%	11.7%	27.3%

frequently CEOs themselves, and thus they are part of the same job market and have no reason not to increase the CEO's pay.

Prodded by activist shareholders and threats of increased intervention from the government, company boards have had to devote more time to the issue of compensation.[13] In 1993 the Securities and Exchange Commission (SEC) imposed new disclosure rules for corporate pay. Proxy statements have to reveal the CEO's pay in addition to the pay of the four other highest paid executives. The earnings of CEOs and top management are enhanced by **stock options,** the option to buy future shares at a fixed price. When share prices fall below a fixed price some companies had routinely cancelled old stock options and substituted new ones at lower prices. Under new SEC rules, companies are required to reveal all repricing of stock options for the past 10 years.

stock options
A form of payment to executives which provides them the opportunity to buy shares of a company's stock in the future at a price fixed earlier.

Heeding shareholder criticism to align corporate pay with performance, boards have been placing greater emphasis on stock options.[14] Even outside directors are being paid more in stock than in retainers. Nearly 20 percent of all major corporations have guidelines that require, or at least strongly urge, top management to invest between 1 and 10 percent of their annual salaries in company stock. The CEO and chairman of Cabletron Systems made only $52,000 in 1993, but 504 of the company's 3,300 worldwide employees earned more. Most of the compensation of the CEO and chairman came from selling the stock he owned in Cabletron. In 1993, the fear that the stock market boom would not continue and that Democrats would exact high taxes from high-paid executives led many of them to exercise their stock options. Michael Eisner of Walt Disney had compensation of $203 million, $202.3 million of which were redeemed stock options.[15]

The important question is whether such large compensation to CEOs really makes their companies better. Harvard University Business School professor John Kotter argued that U.S. companies need leadership, which cannot be motivated by mere money. Edward Deming, the quality guru, opposed large compensation packages on the grounds that they destroyed teamwork. Harvard finance professor Michael Jensen defended the large pay; he expressed the view that while Japanese and German managers can be motivated by loyalty and peer pressure, U.S. managers, because of the individualism of our society, respond only to money. However, Jensen strongly advocated aligning executive pay with performance. The best way to accomplish that was to make executives the owners through **leveraged management buyouts.**[16]

leveraged management buyout
A group of managers, with the assistance of people in the financial community, buys a publicly traded company and make it a private company.

A growing proportion of takeover activity in the United States in the 1980s occurred as leveraged management buyouts. After a buyout, the firm no longer is traded on public stock markets. The aligning of the interests of management and shareholder interests is accomplished through debt expansion that subjects managers to new levels of discipline and control and reduces their discretionary use of funds.

Inequality among Functional Areas

Another example of corporate pay inequality is in the functional areas. For a list of average salaries for various corporate jobs in 1992 (see Exhibit 8–2).[17]

Production personnel and engineers were relatively underpaid compared with people in finance. Does it seem fair that people who actually make goods are paid less than those who finance these activities?

EXHIBIT 8–2 Average Annual Corporate Salaries for Various Jobs in 1992

	Junior Professional (3–5 years' experience)	*Senior Professional (10 or more years' experience)*
Human resources	$42,700	$109,100
Marketing and sales	$55,500	$122,600
Engineering	$61,000	$118,300
Production and operations	$64,600	$ 93,000
Information systems	$66,300	$101,200
Finance (analyst, bond trader, merger and acquisition specialist)	$75,000	$175,000+

Inequality in Society

Corporate inequality reflects inequality in U.S. society. Since 1977, the pretax incomes of the top 1 percent of households has increased by 70 percent, while the pretax income of the average household has grown by only 9 percent. Though the middle class is weaker, mobility in U.S. society remains high: 80 percent of high-income Americans are first-generation, self-made successes. However, children of very poor parents still find it difficult to rise to the top.[18]

Fewer of the very rich are CEOs; 31 percent were CEOs in 1992, down from 44 percent a decade earlier. Big gains were made by sports stars, entertainers, and professionals such as accountants and consultants. About 20 percent of America's richest people were entrepreneurs who created entirely new enterprises and markets, while Fortune 500 companies were laying off millions of workers. These entrepreneurs often were iconoclasts and mavericks who worked to develop an idea they truly loved although it seemed impractical. Money was a by-product of their dreams, not the end in itself. Many promoted health fads or saving people through nutrition, exercise, and other means.

Immigrants were another group that made sharp advances in the 1980s.[19] In the past, restrictive immigration laws had severely curtailed immigration into the United States, but in 1965 the administration of Lyndon Johnson put an end to the notorious national origin quotas that had been in place. Since then the United States has witnessed a vast influx of people with ambition and drive who are often willing to work long hours at difficult jobs and whose children are overachievers in subjects like science and mathematics.

Discrimination

discrimination
The act of judging people not on their abilities but on their membership in groups that are subject to negative stereotyping.

Inequality extends to the inability of the corporation to fully incorporate women and minorities. **Discrimination** means that individuals are not free to compete on the basis of their abilities, and are judged instead on membership in a particular group, and subject to negative stereotypes built up around that group.

In business relationships, people should be judged on their merits as individuals.

When a mutually advantageous deal is not consummated because one of parties belongs to a group that is discriminated against, then the deal makers are not the only losers. The interests of society as a whole are not served. The group to which a person belongs—gender, race, national origin—has no bearing on a business relationship. The basis of that relationship is the special blend of skills, products, and services the parties to a business relationship have to offer. A society that consistently violates this principle is likely to remain backward.

Equal Employment Opportunity and Affirmative Action

The laws against discrimination subject companies to two sets of requirements. First, they must conform to equal employment opportunity requirements and not discriminate on the basis of sex, race, ethnic background, religion, handicap, age, or veteran status. Second, companies are expected to carry out affirmative action programs. The demand to treat people alike—as individuals regardless of their sex, race, ethnic background, religion, or any other characteristic—comes from the Civil Rights Act of 1964, which states that job discrimination is illegal. **Affirmative action** is the requirement to accord special treatment to groups that have suffered discrimination in the past. It has its origins in a 1961 executive order issued by President Kennedy. Court cases support both doctrines.[20]

affirmative action The requirement to accord special status to groups that have suffered discrimination in the past.

Equality of opportunity by itself does not produce equality of results. Disadvantaged groups suffer not only from prejudice, which has kept them from fully participating in the economy, but also from the results of this prejudice, which is a lower socioeconomic status than that of the population as a whole (see the Lyndon Johnson quotation at the beginning of this chapter). They do not begin at the same level. A special status is necessary to raise their social and economic condition so that they can compete on an equal footing, but affirmative action has brought on a backlash and has subjected minorities to resentment.

Women

After World War I, women made up about 20 percent of the U.S. workforce. After World War II, the figure was close to 25 percent. Today, it is more than 45 percent (see Exhibit 8–3).[21]

Despite great progress, women still have barriers ("the glass ceiling") to reaching the top of corporations because CEOs want to pass the job on to someone in their own image and likeness.[22] In 1993, more than 40 percent of all managers (up from 32 percent in 1983), and 40 percent of all law graduates (up from 30 percent in 1983) were women, but only 4.8 percent of senior managers were women (up from 2.9 percent in 1986). Thirty-five percent of all MBA students were women, but only 5 percent of executives were women. Women earned just 75 cents for each dollar that a man earned (up from 65 cents in 1982). Women out of college in the 25–34-year-old age group increased their earnings from 85 percent to 90 percent of that of their male counterparts between 1981 and 1991. However, the pay gap widened for women 45–54 years old, whose income was only 62 percent that of similarly educated men in that age group. Women-owned business firms,

EXHIBIT 8–3 Women in the Workforce

	1990	*1985*	*1980*
Workers who are women	45.4%	44.4%	42.4%
Number of corporate CEOs	3	3	2
Corporate boards with women directors	56	45	36
Women-owned sole proprietorships	30.4	28.1	26.1
Self-employed women	35.9	33.3	30.0
Women's Median Weekly Earnings as a Percentage of Men's Earnings			
	1990	*1985*	*1983*
Engineers, architects, surveyors	89%	79%	82%
Mathematical and computer scientists	79	80	75
Executives, administrative, managerial jobs	65	66	64
Percentage of Professionals Who Are Women			
	1990	*1985*	*1983*
Executive, administrative, managerial jobs	40%	36%	32%
Engineers	8	9	6
Mathematical and computer scientists	36	31	30
Physicians	19	17	16
Lawyers and judges	21	18	16

on the other hand, were the fastest growing segment of the economy, employing more than 6.5 million people. These businesses were strongest in retail trade and services. Like men, women established their own businesses to gain autonomy and control over their careers, but another reason was the desire for work flexibility because of family considerations.[23]

Sexual Harassment

During the controversy about Clarence Thomas's nomination to the Supreme Court, the Harvard sociologist Orlando Patterson wrote:

> We must face certain stark sociological realities: in our increasingly female, work-centered world, most of our relationships, including intimate ones, are initiated in the workplace; gender relations . . . are complex and invariably ambiguous.[24]

Surveys suggest that 80 percent of the people in companies are aware of romantic affairs that have developed in the workplace, and 90 percent see the affairs as negative.[25] Employee romances start, lead to gossip, create hostilities, and strain relationships. Couples in high-level management positions create special complications. They may not be able to confront each other or they may form powerful alliances against others. When the couples break up, it puts a strain on the entire organization.[26]

sexual harassment Unwelcome sexual advances, requests for sexual favors, and other verbal or physical conduct of a sexual nature that are a condition of employment or create an intimidating, offensive, or hostile work environment.

According to the Equal Employment Opportunity Commission (EEOC), **sexual harassment** consists of unwelcome sexual advances, requests for sexual favors, and other verbal or physical conduct of a sexual nature that are a condition of employment or create an intimidating, offensive, or hostile work environment.[27]

Most men (66 percent) think sexual harassment in the workplace is greatly exaggerated, but most women (32 percent) do not. A relatively high percentage of women say that they feel they have been harassed; that is, unwanted advances were made in which the woman's refusal would have lead to loss of promotion, raise, or job. Many more women resent the subtle forms of harassment such as off-color jokes, unnecessary touching, and being called "sweetie" or "honey." Unwanted propositions, lewd remarks, and even physical assault are a problem in any office.[28]

The two classes of harassment defined under the EEOC guidelines are (1) requests by a supervisor for sexual favors in return for job benefits and (2) a hostile work environment. In *Meritor Savings Bank* v. *Vinson* in the mid-1980s, the court accepted an atmosphere of sexual aggression, even without economic injury, as constituting harassment.

Judicial decisions in the 1980s made a company financially responsible for harassment by its employees unless the company had taken action to prevent the offenses and had responded vigorously when they occurred. Many companies set up policies (see Exhibit 8–4) and started training and other programs to combat harassment.

General Motors has a one-day workshop that all supervisors must attend. DuPont has a four-hour workshop called "A Matter of Respect"; 65,000 workers have attended. Honeywell, Corning, and DuPont have 24-hour hotlines. At DuPont, workers who call the hotline do not have to identify themselves, confidentiality is assured, and calling does

Exhibit 8–4 AT&T's Policy toward Sexual Harassment

AT&T's sexual harassment policy prohibits sexual harassment in the workplace, whether committed by supervisory or nonsupervisory personnel. Specifically, no supervisor shall threaten to insinuate, either explicitly or implicitly, that an employee's submission to or rejection of sexual advances will in any way influence any personnel decision regarding that employee's employment, wages, advancement, assigned duties, shifts, or any other condition of employment or career development.

Other sexually harassing conduct in the workplace that may create an offensive work environment, whether it be in the form of physical or verbal harassment, and regardless of whether committed by supervisory or nonsupervisory personnel, is also prohibited. This includes, but is not limited to, repeated offensive or unwelcome sexual flirtations, advances, propositions, continual or repeated verbal abuse of a sexual nature, graphic verbal commentaries about an individual's body, sexually degrading words being used to describe an individual, and the display in the workplace of sexually suggestive objects or pictures.

Sexual harassment in the workplace by any employee will result in disciplinary action up to and including dismissal and may lead to personal, legal, and financial liability.

Employees are encouraged to avail themselves of AT&T's internal equal opportunity complaint procedure if they are confronted with sexual harassment. Such internal complaints will be investigated promptly, and corrective action will be taken where allegations are verified. No employee will suffer retaliation or intimidation as a result of using the internal complaint procedure.

Source: AT&T Policy Statement, 1992.

not mean bringing charges. Every complaint filed must have an immediate response from the employee's supervisor or someone in the personnel office.

If an investigation is warranted, the company undergoes the difficult task of fact-finding. Since there are usually neither witnesses nor physical evidence, and it is difficult to show that the advances were not wanted, fact-finding is complicated. It is important to know whether the victim repeatedly told the accused person that the advances were not welcome. Resolution of these cases has to be quick. DuPont's policy is to resolve most cases in 3 to 20 days. When allegations prove to be true, the company will either transfer

Decision Dilemmas

Sexual Harassment[29]

1. The Business Trip Three people from Fairfax Professional Services go on a business trip. The male partner is in his mid-40s and is married. The third-year female analyst is in her early 30s, and the newly hired MBA is in her mid-20s. The business trip is a success; the employees secure a new project that will bring $1 million worth of business to the company. That evening they celebrate. The male partner has too much to drink and asks questions about the female analyst's sex life. He moves closer to her and puts his arms around her. She is visibly shaken and begins to cry. She moves away from the male partner, reminding him that she has just become engaged, and tries to change the subject. The MBA is upset about what she has witnessed. The next day she urges the analyst to file a sexual harassment complaint, but the analyst refuses. She says that the male partner is simply having a midlife crisis: "That's the way it is around here. I don't want to jeopardize my chance to work on important accounts or obtain a promotion, and I don't want to be branded a troublemaker." On her own, the MBA brings the incident to the attention of the Human Resources Department. It makes some discreet inquiries and learns that the partner has a reputation for occasional heavy drinking and, apparently, has had consensual affairs with other junior employees. However, no one has ever brought a formal complaint against him. The human resources staff tell the MBA that she cannot file a formal complaint herself, but must convince the analyst to do so. What should she do?

2. No Touching Felton Consumer Products Company has an explicit policy of "*no* sexual touching" between employees. Helen, a member of John's staff, has received poor performance reviews, but nonetheless believes that she should be promoted. She files a letter of complaint with the Human Resources Department, alleging that John embraced his secretary Emily on company property. The department begins an investigation by interviewing people in the company. It asks them for complete confidentiality, but leaks occur, and word of the inquiry spreads, hurting the reputations of both John and Emily and making it difficult for them to carry out their jobs. Their department is at a standstill with bitterness and acrimony on all sides. Helen complains that other employees are siding with John and Emily, and that she is being ostracized. Emily's story is that she received a phone call about her niece's death in an automobile accident and that John was only comforting her. What should the Human Resources Department do?

3. "Boys Will Be Boys" After having lunch with a customer, a salesperson alleges sexual harassment. She claims that the customer made unwelcome offensive comments followed by physical contact to which she objected. She expects her company to take immediate legal action. If it fails to protect her, she will sue. When confronted, the customer claims that "boys will be boys," and that what happened was "nothing more than a joke," an "innocent flirtation," and perhaps a "chance for a relationship." This customer represents an organization that constitutes one-quarter of the company's business. The company discovers that this salesperson also complained of sexual harassment in her previous employment. What should it do?

or terminate the offender. A number of decision dilemmas are provided to afford a sense for how complicated the issue of sexual harassment is.

Minorities

The issue for minorities is not advancement but entry into the corporate world. Of the minority groups that have experienced discrimination in the United States, African Americans have been the most economically disadvantaged.[30] Their average family income is about half the average income of white families, and the gap has grown in recent years.[31] A disproportionate number of the black population is young and still lives in the South where incomes are lower. Blacks are 12 percent of U.S. households, but own only about 4 percent of the country's wealth. The unemployment rate among blacks is about twice that of whites. Studies have shown that whites also advance more quickly in the hiring process than blacks.

Educated African Americans usually get off to a good start, but their careers lag behind those of their white counterparts. Although many African Americans with MBAs received higher starting salaries than whites with that degree, they did not advance as quickly in the organization. Most black MBAs were still in entry-level positions after five years, while most white MBAs had advanced to middle management positions or better.[32]

During the 1990–1991 recession, African Americans were more often laid off than whites. At Dial Corporation, blacks represented 26.3 percent of the workforce, but they lost 43.6 percent of the jobs. At W. R. Grace, they were 13.1 percent of the workforce, but lost 32.2 percent of the jobs. Black losses were highest in blue-collar jobs. Blacks showed some gains in obtaining managerial, professional, and technical positions, but in these areas they continued to represent only 5.2 percent of the workforce. In addition, fewer blacks are considered for such jobs because only 13 percent of them have a college education compared with nearly 25 percent of the whites and 39 percent of Asian Americans. The main reason for disproportionate job loss among African Americans during the recession was low seniority and heavy concentration in jobs that were eliminated. Continued deindustrialization, abandonment by companies of inner-city facilities, and movement to parts of the country with small black populations also played a role.[33]

Many companies increased overall minority hiring during the recession, so that their record for all minorities, including women, looked very good. The Office of Federal Contract Compliance (OFCC), which investigates discrimination, only audits records of overall minority employment. Indeed, Hispanics and Asian Americans gained many jobs, and OFCC had no grounds for making complaints.

The equal employment and affirmative action programs that exist have tended to help better educated, more upwardly mobile African Americans but these programs have done little for the hard-core underclass of unskilled, unemployed African Americans who are often unprepared to hold a job. Forty-three percent of black children are born poor. Two-thirds are born to unwed mothers. Despite gains in wealth, the poverty rate (income below $14,000 for a family of four) has failed to budge in the last 20 years. About 33.3 percent of African Americans live below the poverty level, as opposed to 11.6 percent of whites. Among Hispanics, 29.3 percent live below the poverty level (see Exhibit 8–5). The black poor are hurt the most by structural changes in the economy because these have not created many new unskilled manufacturing jobs.

EXHIBIT 8–5 People below Poverty Level, 1992

	Number (millions)	Percentage
White	24.5	11.6%
Black	10.6	33.3
Hispanic	6.7	29.3
All races	36.9	14.5

Source: *World Almanac 1995,* p. 383.

Public Policies and Court Cases

The public policies and court cases that cover the problems of women and minorities are numerous. The following section reviews major civil rights legislation, affirmative action programs, and antidiscrimination court cases.

Civil Rights Legislation

The 1964 Civil Rights Act was a landmark act that forbade discrimination in employment based on race, color, religion, sex, or national origin. As amended it requires all companies with 15 or more employees to report each year the number of women and minorities on each step of the employment ladder in the company. It also stipulates that no employer is required "to grant preferential treatment to any individual or to any group because of the race, color, religion, sex, or national origin of such individual," or because of any imbalance in the total number or percentage of people belonging to these groups. The Civil Rights Act upholds an employer's right to "apply different . . . conditions . . . of employment pursuant to a bona fide seniority or merit system . . . provided that such differences are not the result of an intention to discriminate."[34] The EEOC, which administers the Civil Rights Act, issues guidelines on employment discrimination, investigates charges of discrimination and makes public its decisions, and litigates noncompliance cases.

Affirmative Action. As noted earlier, the Kennedy and Johnson administrations issued executive orders in the early 1960s to bring about affirmative action. In 1971, the Labor Department, which administered the executive orders, required federal contractors to determine if they were utilizing minorities in the same proportion as they were found in the area labor force.[35] If not, the contractors would have to establish government-approved goals concerning hiring, retention, and promotion, and they would have to set up timetables for achieving these goals. The standard for minority employment used by the Labor Department is the proportion of minorities living in an area or in the Standard Metropolitan Statistical Area (SMSA) surrounding a business. The concentration of minority employees at lower echelons in a company also can be evidence of discrimination.

The Reagan administration came out very strongly against affirmative action maintaining that it believed in the concept but not in the "police approach" developed by Carter administration officials.[36] W. Bradford Smith, head of the Justice Department's

Civil Rights Division, said that "racial and sexual preferences are at war with the American ideal of equal opportunity for each person to achieve whatever his or her industry and talents warrant."[37]

Shelby Steele, an African American writer, admits that "affirmative action robs us of our dignity. It says that color, not our hard work, can bring us advancements." Nevertheless, affirmative action has opened many doors to people of color; in this way, it has forced many companies to take action. It has decreased racism by prodding integration, but it also has forced minorities to deal with the skepticism of white workers who often assume that minority employees have been hired only because of antidiscrimination legislation. Minorities often feel that they have to work twice as hard to prove themselves, which can shatter their self-esteem.

Other Laws against Discrimination

Laws were passed in 1967 against age discrimination (i.e., discrimination against people between the ages of 40 and 70); in 1973 providing for affirmative action in the hiring of the handicapped; in 1974 providing for affirmative action in the hiring of Vietnam veterans; and in 1978 against discrimination toward pregnant women. This legislation covered a large proportion of the American population.

Court Cases

Landmark court cases have affected the way antidiscrimination and affirmative action laws have been implemented. Companies first learned to take these laws seriously in 1971 when in the case of *EEOC* v. *AT&T*, AT&T was found guilty of discrimination and made a $45 million settlement to cover back wages. Also, 1971 was the year of *Griggs* v. *Duke Power*, in which the Supreme Court found that a high school education and the passing of tests not related to a job were not relevant employment characteristics. "The Civil Rights Act," the Court said, "proscribes not only overt discrimination but also practices that are fair in form, but discriminatory in operation. The touchstone is business necessity. If an employment practice which excludes Negroes cannot be shown to be related to job performance, the practice is prohibited."[38]

In 1981, the Ninth Circuit Court of Appeals reaffirmed the basic thinking in *Griggs*. In *Fernandez* v. *Wynn Oil Co.* a woman did not get the job as director of international relations because the company believed that men in South America would not feel comfortable dealing with a woman in a position of responsibility. The court did not accept that there was any relationship between job performance and gender in this case.

Connecticut v. *Teal*, decided by the Supreme Court in 1982, had a similar outcome. In this case, 23 percent of black employees had been promoted to be supervisors of a welfare department, while only 14 percent of white employees had been promoted. To be promoted, all employees had to take a test, which 46 percent of the blacks failed and only 20 percent of the whites failed. Supervisors then picked who was to be promoted on the basis of seniority, letters of recommendations, and past performance reviews. Winnie Teal failed the test, but claimed that it was not job related. The Supreme Court supported her contention.

There have been four major affirmative action cases. Undoubtedly the most famous is the 1976 *Bakke* v. *University of California* decision. A white male applicant to medical school at the University of California Davis charged reverse discrimination against the university because it reserved 16 out of 100 places in its medical school class for minorities. Bakke claimed that his qualifications were superior to those of many of the minority applicants admitted, and the Supreme Court agreed that he had been a victim of reverse discrimination. It ordered Bakke admitted and prohibited quota admissions of minorities and separate evaluations of minorities without comparison to other applicants. However, in a very important qualification, it did allow race to be considered as a factor in admission. The court said that a "properly devised admissions program" can involve "the competitive consideration of race and ethnic origins."[39]

A second important affirmative action case was decided in 1979 in *Weber* v. *Kaiser Aluminum*. Brian Weber was a white male worker in a Kaiser Aluminum plant in Louisiana. Like Bakke, he charged the company with reverse discrimination. He said that he had applied for entrance into a training program sponsored by the company and the United Steel Workers that would have doubled his pay and given him a better job. The program called for selection of 50 percent blacks. At Kaiser prior to 1974 less than 2 percent of the craft workers were black even though blacks constituted 39 percent of the area's labor force. Weber was not chosen despite the fact that he had more seniority than the blacks who had been selected. Even so, the Supreme Court decided against Weber, holding that Kaiser's affirmative action program was not court-ordered. It was voluntary and private and within the "spirit of the law." The program did not discharge any white workers and did not create a total obstacle to their promotion. The program was simply a temporary measure to eliminate a serious racial imbalance and therefore was acceptable.[40]

A third important case was decided in 1983 in *Firefighters* v. *Stolts* when the Supreme Court decided that 15 African Americans hired by the Memphis Fire Department could be laid off during a budget crisis using a seniority rule that laid off the last hired first, even though this rule meant that disproportionately more blacks than whites would be laid off. After arguments were heard from attorneys appointed by the Reagan administration, the Court held that the Civil Rights Act did not require seniority systems to be changed to remedy past discrimination.

The final case, *Crosson* v. *Richmond*, was decided in 1989. The Richmond City Council, five of whose nine members were black, took actions that the Supreme Court ruled were unacceptable. Half of the city of Richmond is African American, but less than 1 percent of the city's prime construction contracts had been granted to black businesses. The city council set aside 30 percent of prime contracts to be subcontracted to minority businesses. Crosson Company, a white-owned mechanical plumbing and heating company, lost a bid to supply toilets to the city jail because it was not willing to use a minority-owned subcontractor. It then challenged the city council's requirement, and the Supreme Court sustained the challenge. The Court accepted that the ordinance violated the white contractor's right to equal protection under the law. The court said that laws favoring blacks over whites had to be judged by the same constitutional test as laws favoring whites over blacks. Justice Sandra Day O'Connor wrote that racial discrimination even for "laudable purpose" is not "benign," and that "racial classifications" even with "assurances of good intention" are "suspect."[41]

Decision Dilemma

Affirmative Action

A large, privately owned manufacturer and distributor of snack foods is hiring to fill an entry-level position in its accounting department. The personnel coordinator informs the Accounting Department manager that he has concerns about the company's lack of diversity and that the job opening is an excellent opportunity to make progress. The newspaper ad yields 10 applicants, two of whom are minorities. Six candidates are judged worthy of interviews, including both minority candidates even though one lacks the necessary background experience to qualify for the job. After the interviews, the Accounting Department manager determines that a white male is best qualified for the job. What should the personnel coordinator do—hire the most qualified candidate? hire the most qualified minority candidate? reopen the job search?

Implications of Affirmative Action for Corporate Policies

With respect to hiring, companies should try to work within the following framework:[42]

1. Standards should not be lowered.
2. Unqualified people should not be hired.
3. Standards used to evaluate people clearly should be job-related.
4. If a woman or minority person is better qualified, then clearly pick the woman or minority person; to not do so is discriminatory.
5. If a woman or minority person is equally qualified—and if the woman or minority person is underrepresented in comparison to the working population in the area—pick the minority person; doing so is in the spirit of affirmative action requirements.
6. What should a company do if a woman or a minority person is clearly qualified, but a majority person is more qualified? Are minimum or above standards of qualification sufficient when another candidate is more qualified? Under these circumstances, it is important for the company to consider:
   a. The degree to which the woman or minority person is underrepresented in the job in question.
   b. The extent of the gap in the qualifications level between the woman or minority person and the majority person.
   c. The degree to which the woman or minority person could rapidly grow in the job to the point where such a person would quickly catch up with and perhaps surpass the currently more qualified majority person.
   d. The degree to which the company can devote the time, energy, and attention to the woman or minority person to assure that such rapid progress was possible.
   e. The job's immediate importance for the safe and efficient operation of the business.

f. The side-benefits to the company of having a woman or minority person in terms of employee understanding and acceptance of diversity, community relations, and/or fulfilling legal mandates and requirements without compromising product quality or integrity.

Corporate Programs

Many companies have hired full-time diversity managers and have tried to make their organizations more hospitable to people of both sexes and many national origins.[43] Companies explain why they have these programs. First, they have to have such programs. They are not just a legal requirement. Dramatic demographic shifts are occurring in the workforce; by the year 2000, 85 percent of the people entering the labor pool will be women, minorities, or immigrants. Second, companies say that some of their best employees are women and members of minority groups. Third, the marketplace is made up of people of different sexes and races. Therefore, their companies should reflect the marketplace. Finally, diversity brings a broader perspective to problem solving. They cite a study showing that ethnically diverse teams of business students outperformed all-white teams. The all-white teams got off to a faster start but the ethnically diverse teams quickly surpassed the white teams, especially in producing more innovative solutions to problems.

The diversity program at Hoechst Celanese, a large chemical company, rests on the following principles:

1. CEO involvement.
2. Diversity as a criterion in evaluating employee performance.
3. Making sure that the concerns of white males are addressed.
4. Scrutinizing compensation for fairness.
5. Using diversity training that avoids combativeness, an emphasis on guilt, and contempt.
6. Celebrating differences.
7. Improving the supply of diverse workers by active recruitment at colleges and universities.
8. Maintaining commitment during downsizing.

Diversity Training

Diversity training is a very common practice among large U.S. corporations. In any given year, more than 50 percent of U.S. companies will hold some kind of diversity training. Monsanto has workshops to dismantle prejudices. More than 5,000 employees have been through the six-day sessions, which are run by a consultant.

Horror stories have been told about some of these training sessions, however. Those who oppose the training claim that the trainers are unqualified, that the training leaves employees angry and confused, and that the session fees are too high. Proponents of the training admit that company support is often thin, that CEOs are aloof and do not encourage employee participation, and that companies make no effort to follow up on the training.

By its very nature, diversity training is uncomfortable. People have to discuss beliefs and feelings in front of fellow workers, and have their values and assumptions challenged. Training sometimes crosses the line from discomfort to abuse when a group such as white males is singled out as the only one that must change.

Work-Family Programs

Many companies also have initiated work-family programs of various kinds including day care centers and counseling on how to deal with aging parents. From 1971, the number of companies providing day care has grown from 11 to more than 4,000 (see Case 8–A). Companies are trying to bolster productivity by eliminating the unnecessary distractions of family life.

Managerial Questions

Managers might ask a number of questions about discrimination, including the following:

- Society needs to invest in education to produce better elementary schools and more qualified and able people. Are discrimination and affirmative action simply legal and economic matters, or do they entail broader voluntary activities on the part of the corporation?
- Public policy issues concerning discrimination and affirmative action are extremely contentious. The corporation can play a very influential role. How should the corporation contribute to the public policy-making debate? A need exists to reexamine welfare and health policies, and to strengthen drug prevention. Can the corporation play a role in these areas?
- The United States is a heterogenous society with strict legal guidelines against discrimination. This is not true of many of the nations with whom the United States competes. How can the United States harness its heterogeneity for the country's benefit? What are the implications of women and minority issues for global competitiveness and for the vitality of American business in the international marketplace? Appreciation for other peoples and cultures is a competitive strength when it is fostered appropriately.

Conclusions

Societies cannot function without a sense of fairness. Societies whose sense of fairness is consistently violated perform less well because significant groups are excluded and their contributions are not elicited. Economists once expected a widening gap between rich and poor in the developing countries.[44] Today the standard wisdom is that economic equality is not only compatible with economic growth but that it can contribute to it. In rapidly growing Asian countries such as South Korea, income disparities have declined while they have increased in South American and African countries with slower economic growth. Income disparities have been going up in the United States for the last 20 years, and the rate of economic growth is not as high as it once was.

This chapter has discussed inequality in the corporation, beginning with corporate pay and continuing with discrimination against women and minorities. The chapter distinguished between equal employment opportunity programs, which require that companies treat all people as individuals, and affirmative action programs, which require companies to treat people as members of groups. Some of the important issues linked to the rapid entry of women and minorities into the workplace, including sexual harassment, have been raised. This chapter has presented the main provisions of civil rights legislation and executive orders that guide public policies, and it has reviewed major court cases involving this public policy. Guidelines for corporate hiring policies and some examples of corporate diversity programs conclude the chapter.

Discussion Questions

1. Define discrimination. Why is it wrong? Is inequality of pay justified?
2. Distinguish between equal opportunity and affirmative action. Why have both of these principles guided federal policies?
3. What is white backlash? Why has it come into existence?
4. Discuss equal employment opportunity and affirmative action from the perspective of either the deontological or teleological standards.
5. How can managers eliminate subtle workplace biases?
6. You are the public affairs office for a major corporation. Write a memo about the role of the corporation in affecting public policies about women and minorities.
7. How should women and minorities be treated in corporate mission statements?
8. What is your feeling about office romance? Are you for or against it? Why?
9. Why do you think women receive lower pay for the same work? What should be done about it?
10. How large is the economic gap between black and white Americans? What responsibilities do corporations have to narrow this gap?
11. What does the 1964 Civil Rights Act say about preferential treatment?
12. What is sexual harassment?
13. Why was the Reagan administration opposed to affirmative action? Was this opposition justified?
14. What principles were established in the *Griggs*, *Bakke*, *Weber*, and *Richmond* cases? As a corporate personnel officer, what should you learn from them?
15. What kind of hiring policies should companies have concerning women and minorities?
16. What kind of policies should companies have concerning sexual harassment?

Endnotes

1. Robert K. Fulwinder, *The Reverse Discrimination Controversy* (Totowa, N.J.: Rowman and Littlefield, 1980), p. 95, cited by George A. Steiner and John F. Steiner, *Business, Government, and Society*, 4th ed. (New York: Random House, 1985), p. 545.
2. Faye Rice, "How to Make Diversity Work," *Fortune*, August 8, 1994, pp. 79–89.
3. J. Rawls, *A Theory of Justice* (Cambridge: Harvard University Press, 1971).
4. Ibid.
5. R. Nozick, *Anarchy, State and Utopia* (New York: Basic Books, 1975).
6. Ibid.
7. Geoffrey Colvin, "How to Pay the CEO Right," *Fortune*, April 6, 1992, pp. 61–69.
8. Brian Dumaine, "A Knockout Year for CEO Pay," *Fortune*, July 25, 1994, pp. 94–103.
9. Shawn Tully, "What CEOs Really Make," *Fortune*, June 15, 1992, pp. 94–99; "Bosses Pay," *The Economist*, Feb. 1, 1992, pp. 19–22; "Why Down Means Up," *The Economist*, Oct. 19, 1991, p. 86.
10. "Executive Pay: The Party Ain't Over Yet," *Business Week*, April 26, 1993, pp. 56–64.
11. Joan Lublin, "Looking Good," *The Wall Street Journal*, April 13, 1994, pp. R1–2; Joan Lublin, "Work Now Get Paid Later," *The Wall Street Journal*, April 13, 1994, p. R2; Joan Lublin, "What You Don't Know," *The Wall Street Journal*, April 13, 1994, p. R2.
12. Derek Bok, *The Cost of Talent* (New York: Free Press, 1993).
13. Timothy Schellhardt, "Passing of Perks," *The Wall Street Journal*, April 13, 1994, p. R2; Joan Lublin, "Director's Cut," *The Wall Street Journal*, April 13, 1994, p. R5; Julie A. Lopez, "A Better Way?" *The Wall Street Journal*, April 13, 1994, p. R6.
14. Joan Lublin, "Study Finds Pay of More CEOs is Stock-Based," *The Wall Street Journal*, Nov. 12, 1993, pp. B1, B12.
15. Dumaine, "A Knockout Year for CEO Pay" pp. 94–103.
16. Colvin, "How to Pay the CEO Right," pp. 61–69.
17. Nancy Perry, "If You Can't Join 'Em, Beat 'Em," *Fortune*, Sept. 21, 1992, pp. 58–59.
18. Louis Richman, "The Truth about Rich and Poor," *Fortune*, Sept. 21, 1992, pp. 134–46; Anne Fisher, "The Debate over the Very Rich," *Fortune*, June 29, 1992, pp. 42–54.
19. "The New Americans," *Economics*, May 11, 1991, pp. 17–20.
20. Philip Mason, *Race Relations* (London: Oxford University Press, 1970).
21. Steiner and Steiner, *Business, Government, and Society*, p. 540.
22. "Women in the Workplace," *The Wall Street Journal*, October 18, 1991, p. B3.
23. Valerie Reitman, "It's All Relative," *The Wall Street Journal*, April 13, 1994, p. R7; "Women at the Top," *John Naisbitt's Trend Setter*, Nov. 11, 1993; Ann Fisher, "When Will Women Get to the Top?" *Fortune*, Sept. 21, 1992, pp. 44–56.
24. Orlando Patterson, "Race, Gender, and Liberal Fallacies," *New York Times*, Op-Ed, Oct. 20, 1991, p. 15.
25. Robert E. Quinn, "Coping with Cupid," *Administrative Sciences Quarterly*, March 1977.
26. Eliza Collins, "Managers and Lovers," *Harvard Business Review*, Sept.–Oct. 1983.
27. 29 C.F.R. 1604. 11 (a) 1987.
28. Eliza Collins and Timothy B. Blodgett, "Sexual Harassment . . . Some See It . . . Some Won't," *Harvard Business Review*, March–April 1981.
29. Margot Slade, "Sexual Harassment," *New York Times*, March 27, 1994, Sec. 4, pp. 1, 6.
30. Rochelle Sharpe, "In Last Recession Only Blacks Suffered Net Employment Loss," *The Wall Street Journal*, Sept. 14, 1993, pp. 1, A14.
31. Timothy Schellhardt, "Data on Average Wealth of Blacks Suggests Economic Gap with Whites is Widening," *The Wall Street Journal*, June 20, 1983, p. 11.

32. David Ford, "Blacks in Management," *UTD Advance*, March 1984, p. 3.
33. Sharpe, "In Last Recession," pp. 1, A14.
34. Committee on Labor and Public Welfare, U.S. Congress, Senate Subcommittee on Labor, *Compilation of Selected Labor Laws Pertaining to Labor Relations*, part III, (Washington, D.C.: U.S. Government Printing Office, 1974), pp. 591, 610, 612.
35. U.S. Equal Employment Opportunity Commission, *Affirmative Action and Equal Employment: A Guidebook for Employers*, vol. 1 (Washington, D.C.: U.S. Government Printing Office, 1974).
36. "The New Bias on Hiring Rules," *Business Week*, May 25, 1981, p. 123.
37. Stuart Taylor, "Breaking New Ground on Affirmative Action," *New York Times*, May 21, 1986, p. A28.
38. *Griggs* v. *Duke Power*, 401 U.S. 424, 1971.
39. *Allan Bakke* v. *The Regents of the University of California*, 553, p. 2d 1152, 1976.
40. *Weber* v. *Kaiser Aluminum*, 99 S.Ct. 2721, 1979.
41. Cited in L. Greenhouse, "Court Bars a Plan Set up to Provide Jobs to Minorities," *New York Times*, January 24, 1989, p. A1, 16, 19; see also E. A. Bronner, "Plan to Help Minority Firms Is Struck Down," *Boston Globe*, January 24, 1989, pp. 1, 7.
42. Steiner and Steiner, *Business, Government, and Society*, p. 546.
43. Mary Kane, "Serious About Sensitivity," *Star Tribune*, Dec. 1, 1994, p. 1D/2D; see also Rice, "How to Make Diversity Work," 1994.
44. Sylvia Nasar, "Economics of Equality," *New York Times*, January 8, 1994, p. 17/26.

Case 8–A
Child Care at Atlantic Information Systems[1]

Only 10 percent of U.S. households fit the mold in which the husband is the sole supporter of both the wife and children. In 40 percent of households, both spouses work, and another 6 percent of all households is composed of single parents. Sixty-six percent of the women who work have children under the age of 18; 59 percent have children under the age of 6.[2]

About 2,599 U.S. companies now are helping employees with their child care needs.[3] The help ranges from being direct providers of day care, to arrangements with independent agencies for modified work schedules. The reasons companies give are that doing so aids in recruiting, morale, productivity, and quality. It is also supposed to lower accident rates, absenteeism, worker stress, tardiness, and turnover.

For instance, Control Data Corporation compared its employees who took advantage of in-house child care with those who did not and found a lower rate of absenteeism (4.4 percent as opposed to 6.0 percent) and turnover (1.8 percent as opposed to 6.3 percent). The effects are greater in companies with large numbers of women employees.

Often companies become involved because of employee initiative. Employees ask or tell the company through various mechanisms (e.g., confidential letter writing, requests to employee assistance programs, or special advisory committees) that they seek child care assistance. Companies respond because of their sense of obligation to employees. They want to help employees with their problems. It is a way to create a family environment and sustain close personal ties between employer and employee.

A large group of companies, though, have not become involved. They are skeptical about the gains and worry about the costs, the insurance arrangements, parents' complaints, quality control problems, and the issue of equity.

This case is about the dilemma faced by Atlantic Information Systems when a group of its employees requested that the company provide child care.

The Company

Atlantic Information Systems Inc. is a medium-size firm with two complementary lines of business. Its 700 professionals advise other organizations about data storage and processing systems. They also produce and market customized software systems for a variety of business functions. In addition to its professional staff, the firm includes 100 employees whose work is administrative, clerical, or janitorial.

When Lester Barks, the founder and CEO of Atlantic, started his business, he recognized that he would require employees with both high-level technical skills and sophisticated communication skills. Thus, he chose to locate his firm in southern New Hampshire. By locating there, he knew that he would be able to recruit his staff from the high-quality labor pool made up of the many distinguished graduates from business schools in the New England area. Barks' analysis proved to be correct. He recruited well and was able to infuse the staff with his own energy and appetite for work. As a result, the firm grew rapidly, developing a strong reputation for innovative designs and good customer service.

From the beginning, Barks had believed in rewarding people for their work, but had also tried to keep fixed costs to a minimum. Thus, although he had established a generous profit-sharing plan, he tried to hold the line against the expansion of employee benefits programs. This policy had been working reasonably well. As long as the company's young, well-educated employees kept getting their substantial paychecks, they seemed content to solve their own personal and career problems.

As the firm and its employees matured, however, sentiment toward the firm's personnel policies seemed to shift. The people who had the skills and experience Barks needed to run his business also had young families to care for. The conflicting demands of jobs and families were proving to be problematic for many people. In particular, the firm's location outside the urban mainstream made it difficult for employees to find high-quality care for their preschool children.

The Request that Atlantic Provide Child Care

Recently, several employees had approached Barteau Weber, the vice president for personnel, with a strongly worded request that Atlantic examine its personnel policies with a view toward adopting practices that were more in keeping with the needs of the work force. In particular, they asked that Atlantic consider opening a company-sponsored child care center. They argued that the company should establish and support a high-quality child care center as a way of reducing demands on their time and concentration that detracted from their ability to focus on their jobs. In addition, they pointed out that predicted changes in the structure of the work force were likely to make such a center a prerequisite for recruiting and retaining qualified employees in the future.

Weber knew that this request was not the product of a few overly demanding whiners. Indeed, the request had been put together by a self-appointed committee consisting of half a dozen of the firm's most respected employees and had been signed by more than 50 people. Furthermore, Weber knew that, within just the past three months, two highly valued senior systems designers had resigned. Rather than returning to work after the six-week parental leave the company allowed, they quit because they were unable to arrange for suitable child care. Weber had overheard many informal conversations focusing on these concerns, and, of course, there was always a certain amount of absenteeism that could be attributed to people staying home to take care of sick children.

Weber was aware that many companies around the nation were establishing child care centers, but he had little technical knowledge of how they were structured or how much they cost. Moreover, he felt certain that Barks would resist the idea of getting involved in such a venture. Nevertheless, he felt that it was his responsibility to bring the matter to Barks' attention.

Barks' Opposition

As he expected, Barks said he was not in favor of having the company get involved in providing solutions to employees' personal problems. As they discussed the matter further, Barks said, "It's not the start-up costs I'm concerned about. We've got space here, and we can afford the initial investment. But this is not a one-time thing. The operating costs are likely to be high, and they'll go on and on. What will we do if times get hard? If we start this, it's going to be difficult to shut it down if we decide we can no longer afford it." Weber acknowledged that there would be some expense involved, but observed that maintaining the firm's competitive position depended on retaining its highly qualified employees, an observation that could hardly be contested in a knowledge-intensive firm such as Atlantic. He said the problem was too important to ignore, and was likely to become even more important in the years ahead.

Barks said: "That may be true, but this problem only affects a part of our work force. Some people don't have children at all, and others have children that they managed to raise without any help from us. How are they going to feel if they see the company spending its money on an expensive program that benefits only a few employees?" Weber said it would probably be a good idea to survey the company to see how people felt about the issue, but pointed out that he'd never heard anyone say anything negative about it.

After some further grumbling, Barks eventually acknowledged that it might be worthwhile to "do something," and asked Weber what he would recommend. Weber hesitated, saying that he'd need some time to gather information about costs. He also pointed out that since other companies already had programs in place, it might be useful to find out about their experiences. Barks agreed to the delay, but said: "I want to see a full analysis of the problem and your recommendations within two weeks. If this is as important as you say it is, we might as well get moving on it. We should find out what everybody thinks about this idea. We can't act without finding out how serious this problem is, and how people who don't have kids feel about it. So do some investigating, and get back to me with your ideas about what you think we should do and why. Even if we start now, it's going to be some time before we can make a decision on this because I'll want to talk it over with the executive committee. You'd better draft a statement on this that we can distribute to everyone. Tell them we're working on it and will get back to them."

Weber's Assignment

Weber accepted the assignment, went back to his office, and sighed. He was enthusiastic about day care, but already overburdened, and did not see how he could gather all the information he needed and come up with a recommendation in two weeks. The only way to meet Barks' deadline was to hand off the task to an assistant.

He made a few quick phone calls to find out how to approach the problem. Then he called Eliot Beckman into his office and said: "I have a great assignment for you. Mr. Barks wants us to figure out whether we should set up a company day-care center. We'll need to look into the pros and cons and figure out how much it will cost. I've done a little bit of background work, but I need you to do some further analysis and put together a set of recommendations. He's looking for us to help him figure out what the company's policy should be. Of course, you know he didn't get where he is today by just waving his hands at problems. He's going to want all the details laid out so that he can judge the situation for himself."

Continuing his instructions, Weber said: "The first thing you'll need to do is get some sense of how big this issue is. You can use electronic mail to ask people whether they have preschool kids, and, if so, whether they would be interested in having a day-care center at work. And ask them for any other questions, concerns or ideas they have about the topic."

Eliot turned to leave, but Weber called him back saying: "We'll need to let people know what we're up to. Give them a few days to respond to your E-mail message, and then draft a memo to go to everybody under my signature. We want to let them know we're studying this issue. Some people are getting pretty hot about this, so we need to cool down the fires a little while we figure this out. Be careful how you say it, though. We want to let the people who are concerned about this know that we're taking them seriously, but we don't want to give the impression that we're caving in to the demands of a few complainers. If we decide to go ahead with this, we want people to think it's a good idea for the company as a whole."

Eliot's Task

Eliot began his work by sending off an E-mail message to everyone on the staff. In the message, he asked people to tell him whether they had preschool kids and whether they would be interested in a company-sponsored child care center. He also invited them to send any comments or questions they had about the idea. After some research, he learned that there were a variety of issues to consider besides cost.

After reviewing the research, he was ready to draft his memos. The memo to the staff had to:

- Announce that the company was studying the problem and explain the rationale for the investigation.
- Describe the investigation itself.
- Acknowledge the viewpoints of all employees with regard to the child care issue.
- Invite comment.

The memo to Mr. Barks had to:

- Acknowledge that some employees opposed employer-sponsored child care.
- Present the expense analysis for both high-and medium-quality centers.
- Make an argument about what the company should do.

Eliot's research suggested the following about (*a*) the costs of day care and (*b*) the personnel of Atlantic. He also had (*c*) the results of the employee survey with which to work and (*d*) estimates of child care fees and estimated usage levels.

(*a*) Annual Costs for Day-Care Centers Designed to Accommodate up to 96 Children

Estimates are based on current costs in the mid-Atlantic region, and include all operating expenses but exclude the capital costs of construction/renovation and equipment. The medium-quality center meets state licensing standards. The high-quality center meets standards established by the National Association for the Education of Young Children. The data were from Resources for Child Care Management of Morristown, New Jersey, a national organization.

Food includes food, supplies, and staff necessary to serve breakfast, lunch, and an afternoon snack.

Medium- and high-quality centers: $46,000.

Supplies includes diapers, medical supplies, and other disposable, nonclassroom items.

Medium-quality center: $10,000.
High-quality center: $12,000.

Transport includes the annual cost of a 17-passenger school bus.

High-quality center only: $8,000.

Classroom supplies includes consumables (paper, paint, etc.), replacement toys, games, books, and so on.

High-quality center: $9,200.
Medium-quality center: $7,500.

Insurance provides $5 million comprehensive liability and student accident insurance.

Medium- and high-quality centers: $11,040.

Enrichment covers specialists (dance, music, etc.) and field trips.

High-quality center only: $5,000.

Management includes an annual management fee (based on an average of $50,000 annually).

Space includes opportunity cost, maintenance, and utilities at $20 per square foot.

Medium-quality center: 5,000 sq. ft.
High-quality center: 10,000 sq. ft.

Fringe includes taxes and a cafeteria benefits plan for day-care staff.

Medium-quality center: $54,341.
High-quality center: $83,204.

Staff Development includes outside workshops, tuition reimbursements, conferences, and materials.

High-quality center: $4,000.
Medium-quality center: $2,000.

Staff Salaries for High-Quality Center. Assumes four lead teachers at $23,000, three teachers at $21,000, seven assistant teachers at $16,000, 31 hours/week of part-time help at $6.50/hour, one director at $35,000, one assistant director at $30,000, one secretary at $20,000, one nurse at $30,000, and one nurse's aide at $14,000 (for sick-child care staff).

Staff Salaries for Medium-Quality Center. Assumes four lead teachers at $19,000, two teachers at $17,000, five assistant teachers at $14,000, 31 hours/week of part-time help at $5.00/hour, one director at $25,000, one assistant director at $20,000, and one secretary at $15,000.

(*b*) Personnel Data—Atlantic Information Systems

Average cost to recruit a professional employee: $15,000.

Average cost to recruit a nonprofessional employee: $1,000.

Average salary for professional staff, one to five years of service: $75,000.

Average salary for professional staff, 6–10 years of service: $87,000.

Average salary for administrative staff: $44,000.

Average salary for clerical and janitorial staff: $28,000.

The average parent misses five days of work per year per child due to a child's illness or the breakdown of childcare arrangements.

Turnover attributable to childcare problems is eight professionals/year; child care-related turnover of nonprofessionals was not measured.

(*c*) Results of Employee Survey

Number of parents of preschool children in the current work force: 215.

Number of children/parents who will be using center: 1.

Percentage of parents interested in employer-sponsored child care program: 45 percent.

Percentage of parents interested in employer-sponsored child care of professional rank: 65 percent; percentage nonprofessional: 35 percent.

Number of employees who oppose employer-sponsored child care: 15.

(*d*) Child Care Fees and Anticipated Usage Level

Anticipated fees employees would pay for childcare: $75/week for professional employees; $50/week for nonprofessional employees.

Anticipated level of use of childcare center: 49 weeks/year/child.

Discussion Questions

1. What should Eliot Beckman say in his memo to Atlantic Information System's employees?
2. What should Eliot Beckman say in his memo to Mr. Barks?
3. Should corporations provide day care for their employees? Why or why not?

Endnotes

1. This case was written by Jolene Galegher.
2. D. Friedman, "Child Care for Employees' Kids," *Harvard Business Review* 86 (1986), pp. 28–34.
3. J. D. Auerbach, *In the Business of Child Care* (New York: Praeger, 1988).

Part III Government and Global Competition

CHAPTER

9

Benefiting from Public Policies

International Trade

We simply knew we could not leave Japanese competitors the isolation in Japan, while they prospected in our home market. We set about using very commercial and political means to influence change . . .

Robert Galvin, former CEO of Motorola[1]

Introduction and Chapter Objectives

This chapter introduces you to the importance of government in affecting the fortunes of companies, and it provides examples showing how this is done. It explores the differences between responding to market demands and responding to public policies. It presents a strategic approach to managing the corporation's relations with government.

This chapter also introduces the topic of global competition, focusing on trade policy, explaining David Ricardo's principle of comparative advantage, tracing the evolution of U.S. trade policy, and describing how the General Agreement for Trade and Tariffs (GATT) works. The chapter concludes with a discussion of the comparative strengths and weaknesses of four major world economic powers: Germany, Japan, the United Kingdom (U.K.), and the United States.

The Impact of Public Policy

In theory, businesses compete in unfettered free markets as privately owned, profit-maximizing entities. In reality, they are affected by public policies forged by government at home and countries throughout the globe where they operate. An example is Levi Strauss & Company, the privately owned apparel company, which expanded internationally in the 1980s to serve new markets and buy products from additional suppliers.[2] Buying certain foreign-made products subjected Levi Strauss to criticism from activist groups, which claimed that working conditions in factories outside the United States depended on child labor and a prison workforce, and that poor plant safety and environmental conditions were common. The activists uncovered human rights violations in many of the foreign plants.

The values and image of Levi Strauss were at stake. It sent audit teams to make a detailed assessment of its suppliers. After being visited by auditors, 30 percent of the suppliers agreed to improvements, but 5 percent refused to make changes and no longer work for Levi Strauss. On its own, the company decided to end all arrangements with Burmese suppliers, and it chose to exit China by 1995.

The decision to leave China was a painful one. Levi Strauss could no longer rely on a cheap, highly skilled work force. It would be precluded from selling to an immense market in the world's most rapidly growing economy. But Levi Strauss did not feel comfortable with Chinese policies, and it believed it had no choice but to pull out.

Government Effects on Business

Governments set the tone for business operations throughout the world. They provide a fundamental framework that determines what businesses can and cannot do. Firms strive for sustainable competitive advantage based on superior products, constant innovation, and the creation of assets that cannot be imitated by their competitors. Their success depends on national endowments—capital, labor, and natural resources.[3] It also depends on intense domestic rivalry, sophisticated buyers, and the clustering of firms. Universities, financial institutions, and suppliers concentrate in areas of economic excellence such as the Silicon Valley. A number of factors that make for a company's success are influenced by government.[4]

Government plays an enormous role in determining how well a company does. Among the influences government has are:

1. Research and development (R&D) programs, which help make innovation possible. The aerospace and semiconductor industries in the United States owe a heavy debt to the U.S. government for the research it financed.
2. **Infant industry protection,** which includes special subsidies to industries in their early stages, allowing them to achieve the economies of scale they need to become world-class competitors.
3. Help in reviving declining industries.
4. Aiding labor market mobility by retraining workers.
5. Supporting the start-up of small businesses that cannot obtain backing from private capital markets because of the risk involved.
6. Vigorous enforcement of antitrust and consumer protection laws to ensure that competitive market conditions exist for business development.
7. Tough laws that challenge businesses to come up with creative ways to solve environmental and occupational safety and health problems.
8. Competition among local governments for businesses to locate in their region to stimulate job creation and expand the tax base.
9. Providing subsidies ranging from loan guarantees to tax breaks (see Case 9–A on Northwest Airlines).

infant industry protection
Protective tariffs to keep out foreign competitors so that new industries can get started.

Managers have to know how to maneuver through a host of government-related issues. The effects of government on business strategy and performance range from tax policies and subsidies to regulations on prices, products, and profits. Government can control entry into the market through licenses, permits, charters, concessions, patents, and franchises. It can structure markets through trade and antitrust policies, and it may directly compete with firms through public enterprise.

Federal, state, and local governments also aid businesses by providing the necessary infrastructure. They build roads, bridges, dams, airports, and railways. They finance police protection, public education, public parks, libraries, and the justice system. They purchase goods and services from business, including weapons, office furniture, computer software, and economic and policy analyses. Government policies influence business conditions from interest rates to growth rates, unemployment, and prices.

Rapid changes in government policies at home and abroad in recent years have made businesses increasingly subject to a climate of uncertainty. This integration of public policy and business strategy around issues such as global competitiveness corresponds to a growing merger between government and the economy through many types of policies—macroeconomic, national security, trade, and regulation—that meaningfully affect a firm's performance and operations.[5]

Reconciling Business and Political Interests

For any business to succeed, it is critical that management have the capacity to understand the origins and impacts of public policies. Business actions must be consistent with the institutional rules and arrangements that governments establish as well as the competitive conditions in the marketplace. Managers must be able to integrate and reconcile their business and political interests.

United Airlines quickly learned this lesson. In the debates leading up to the deregulation of the airline industry, United vigorously supported lifting market controls. However, it was less prepared than its competitor American in dealing with the challenges of an open market. American Airlines, whose CEO Robert Crandall led the charge against deregulation, was more successful in making innovations in the immediate postderegulation period with its frequent flier mileage program and a renegotiated contract with the airline pilots' union. Its responses to deregulation enabled American to take market share from United.[6]

Responses to government, unlike the market where the price system dominates, require a different set of skills. Managers have to take into account voting, majority rule, and due process in democratic societies. They need strategies to influence public opinion, interest groups, administrative bodies, legislatures, the courts, and the media as much as strategies to guide their interactions with customers, suppliers, and competitors. For company strategies to be effective, they must be consonant not only with the firm's internal competencies and competitive strengths, but they also must conform to public policies.

Issues, Interests, Information, and Institutions

To manage corporate public affairs (see Chapter 3), managers must pay attention to issues, interests, information, and institutions.[7] Issues are disputes moving toward resolution.

How they are settled has the potential to benefit or hurt a firm. The firm's actions will influence how the dispute is decided. An example of an important issue was the court's decision to break up AT&T following an antitrust suit against this corporate giant.

Many interest groups have a stake in an issue, and they mobilize to affect the decision-making process. Businesses themselves lobby, make political contributions, and present their cases before the courts and administrative agencies. Trade associations conduct some of this activity. Today many companies have set up their own political offices in Washington, D.C., and in state capitals. They also have established full-time staffs at corporate headquarters to analyze emerging issues and manage their political activities. In addition, firms rely on law firms, lobbyists, and other specialized intermediaries to speak for them.

Sometimes, issues lead to conflicts between different businesses. At other times, the conflicts involve corporations and environmentalists, labor unions, women, ethnic and racial minorities, and consumers. The media plays a key role in defining the issues and presenting different points of view.

All interests bring the information they know to bear. Companies, for instance, run full-page ads in major newspapers, testify in Congress, sponsor specialized studies and reports, and try to influence public opinion. Their capacity to articulate and advance positions using available information is a critical resource in their ability to achieve their goals.

Institutions are the bodies that make public policy and have the right to take binding action. In the United States, they are the executive, legislative, and judicial branches of government, which exist at all levels of government from the states to the national government. The complex sharing of power among different branches of government is illustrated by the Federal Communications Commission (FCC). Congress has given it broad authority over the telecommunications industry, but it is the president who selects the commissioners who serve on the FCC. The commissioners are appointed to staggered terms, so that no president has complete control over them. FCC decisions have local impact; for example, the right to operate a television station. Its decisions also are subject to judicial appeal. The courts, which interpret statutes passed by Congress, can overturn and modify commission rulings. Congress itself continually revises these statutes with new amendments.

The diversity of institutions means that affected businesses have access to different layers of government. Losers might hope to win the battle the next time the issue is brought up in a different context. Also, though an issue is on the agenda, public policy making bodies can refuse to act. Without consensus, stalemate can prevail for substantial periods of time. The best recent example is U.S. health care reform, where no action was taken despite long debate.

Coping with Public Policies

issues management The process by which corporations identify, evaluate, and respond to emerging issues.

Issues management is the process by which corporations identify, evaluate, and respond to emerging issues. In engaging in this activity, managers should ask the following questions:

- How will an issue influence the profitability and productivity of the company?
- How will an issue affect competitive conditions in the industry?

- What is likely to determine the outcome?
- How can the company exert its influence?
- How must the company adapt to changes that the issue is likely to bring into being?
- In what ways will the company have to modify its business practices and structure?

The growing connection between public and private policies has led many firms to reexamine how they manage issues. Companies increasingly are trying to transform public policy constraints into opportunities for gain. The firm's ability to manage its relationships with public policy making bodies can be an important strategic advantage.[8]

A Strategic Orientation

Businesses have many choices in their response to public policies. They can fight all the way and do only what is required, or they can be progressive and take a leadership role. Their responses can be reactive and defensive or accommodative and proactive.

A company with a proactive orientation will try to identify the competitive impacts of alternative public policies. Public policies can have different effects on firms within an industry. Larger and more efficient firms may have low costs because of economies of scale. Smaller, recent entrants to a market may have low costs because of their flexibility and ability to make rapid progress on the learning curve. In either situation, the low cost position provides opportunities for gain. Competitors might have to cope with changes in public policies at a later time and with more bother, greater expense, and a tarnished image.

opportunism
The effort to transform public policy constraints into opportunities for gain.

Opportunism is the effort to transform public policy constraints into opportunities for gain. For instance, 3M has created a highly successful Pollution Prevention Pays (3P) program in response to growing environmental regulations (see Chapter 15). Honda developed the revolutionary CVCC engine in response to air pollution requirements (see Case 12–B on Chrysler and Honda).

Opportunism usually is a thought-out, long-term strategy that is part of overall business practice. An opportunistic firm follows up its awareness of the competitive implications of policy changes by anticipating how the issue is likely to develop. The firm plans its responses to expected events, but it must also consider unlikely contingencies.

The Stages of Issues Management

The stages in managing an issue are (1) formation—issue identification, analysis, development of a range of responses, and selection of a specific response; (2) development of an implementation plan; and (3) assessment of the results. Relevant questions at different stages in issues development are:

Formation

1. How do coalitions and movements for political change come into existence? How do they get issues on the public agenda?

2. How do businesses, public interest associations, and others influence government decision making?
3. How is legislation transformed into government programs?

Implementation

1. How do government officials interpret and administer government programs?
2. How do they respond to the pressures from external parties?
3. What effect do government programs have on external groups and interests?

Evaluation

1. What coalitions have formed in favor of or in opposition to policy innovation?
2. What obstacles hinder the institutionalization of policy changes?
3. What actions can be taken to overcome these obstacles?

Collective action is only one choice open to companies pursuing their interests. The decision to work together with other firms, like other business decisions, is subject to the test of profit potential. Because participation in a group imposes costs on the members, the firm will weigh these costs against the benefits of participation.

anticipatory strategy A company's effort to improve its competitive position and increase public support by responding early to public issues.

As a general rule, an **anticipatory strategy** is preferable to a reactive one. An organization that anticipates public expectations will have more options. It can improve its competitive position and increase public support while still meeting profit and performance goals expeditiously. However, foot-dragging or stonewalling is reasonable in some cases. Therefore, strategic analysis is needed.

Legitimacy and Advantage

legitimacy The extent to which a corporation's goals, purposes, and methods mesh with those of society.

Though corporate advantage is a prime objective of public affairs participation, legitimacy is also important. **Legitimacy** is the extent to which a corporation's goals, purposes, and methods mesh with those of society. Managers find that legitimacy is a difficult problem because of its intangible and subjective qualities. The values held by society are fluid and diverse; at any point in time, managers might be able to find some subgroup that espouses values consistent with corporate activities. Therefore, managers have the option to conform to society's values, to change these values, or to align themselves with a subgroup that holds a minority viewpoint.

Business success in influencing politicians depends on building coalitions within the context of emerging and ongoing social and political movements. The influence a business exerts is a result of its ability to fuse its demands with a program that has wider appeal. In politics, beliefs are as important as interests, and positions must be justified in terms other than mere self-interest. The pursuit of advantage has to be tempered by a concern for legitimacy.

Trade Policy

The issue of trade policy has become a top priority at many companies. Let us look at two examples.

Real-World Example

Monsanto: Competitive Cooperation

Monsanto has tried to develop a strategic approach to public policy. The company calls the approach *competitive cooperation*, competitive because issues management has a material impact on the company's competitiveness measured by the achievementof corporate goals; and cooperative because diverse issue agendas require issue-by-issue coalition building, even with traditional adversaries (e.g., environmentalists).[9]

Monsanto has changed from a capital-intensive, largely chemical commodity company into a firm that concentrates on proprietary, patented products. In doing so, the company has tried to harness issues management to assist it directly in the pursuit of its strategic goals. To reduce the likelihood of surprise, elaborate scanning systems have been installed to identify and list emerging issues that might affect the firm. Monsanto also has established an Issue Identification Committee, made up of 13 key and senior managers, which has identified 10 broad areas of concern, including global competitive challenges, the management of technology, and the management of multinational business. Hundreds of publications are read and thousands of clippings assembled to make managers aware of external social and political trends in a new and more comprehensive way.

A high-level Emerging Issues Committee has been formed to focus attention on these issues. Richard Mahoney, Monsanto's CEO, wanted to be sure that senior executives were making the best use of their time with public issues. Mahoney set up a process that determined the priority of issues of greatest concern to the company and about which it could have greatest influence. To narrow the list of issues, he advised that the effects of a particular issue on the company's assets and business direction should determine its place on the list.

Cataloging the universe of issues facing Monsanto led to the creation of a regularly updated Public Issues Book with summaries of 170 different issues. The company evaluated and sorted these issues on a division-by-division basis to provide managers with issues that were key to their operations. The Executive Management Committee reviewed the list. Its highest priorities were fair trade, biotechnology regulation, intellectual property rights, agricultural policy, and hazardous waste policy. Fair trade was in the foremost position because Monsanto does business in more than 100 countries. A high-level executive was assigned to each issue and a detailed action plan drawn up. For each issue, the company outlined specific objectives and action steps. It routinely checks performance against the plans and has responsible executives provide the Executive Management Committee with periodic reports.

Toys 'R' Us versus LSRSL.[10] To gain entry to the Japanese market, Toys 'R' Us, the U.S. toy discount retailer, had to fight Japan's Large-Scale Retail Store Law (LSRSL), which gives local (i.e., Japanese) retailers the right to review, comment on, and oppose the building of any new large store. The stated purpose of the LSRSL is to control the retail activities of large stores, secure business opportunities for local retailers, and provide sound development of the retail trade without hampering the benefits to consumers. The law applies to establishing and extending buildings for a retail business whose size exceeds 500 square meters. In principle, it allows large stores to open a business only upon giving notification to the Ministry of International Trade and Industry (MITI), which must then review each application. If MITI believes that the activity of the large store may damage local small retailers, it can advise the applicant to postpone opening the store and to reduce its business space.

The LSRSL was a formidable barrier to the entry of Toys 'R' Us into the Japanese market. To overcome this barrier, the company first formed a joint venture with McDonald's to obtain that company's expertise about the Japanese regulatory system and store location policies. Next, Toys 'R' Us petitioned the U.S. government for assistance. It wanted the government to make the toy firm's difficulties an international trade issue and to pressure the Japanese to loosen up their administration of the LSRSL. The Japanese promised to revise the law to make it easier for U.S. discounters to establish themselves in Japan. In 1991, Toys 'R' Us finally opened its first Japanese outlet. Without U.S. government assistance, however, it is unlikely that the company would have successfully resolved the matter as soon as it did.

CEMEX.[11] Another example is Cementos Mexicanos (CEMEX), the largest North American cement producer. In the 1980s, the Mexican company tried to enter the U.S. market. Almost immediately, U.S. producers and labor unions filed an antidumping petition with the U.S. International Trade Commission (ITC), claiming that they had been injured by imports. The ITC decided in favor of the U.S. manufacturers and imposed a 58 percent duty on the Mexican imports.

CEMEX appealed to the U.S. Court of International Trade (CIT) and the U.S. Court of Appeals, but it lost in both instances. It then petitioned through the General Agreement on Trade and Tariffs (GATT), which decided in favor of CEMEX, but the U.S. government, which has the right to withhold its approval of a GATT ruling, refused to go along. CEMEX was forced to restrict its entry into the U.S. market to states like Arizona and California, where cement prices are high, and to keep out of Florida where prices are low because of the way the ITA computes dumping margins.

International trade issues have come to dominate corporate politics to a far greater extent than in the past. It is worth delving deeper into this matter because corporate public affairs managers have to increasingly grapple with this type of complicated issue.

Free Trade

If the United States is falling behind in international commerce, to what extent should it move away from its traditional commitment to free trade? To what extent should it remain committed to these policies? Adam Smith argued that free trade stimulated competition and provided opportunities for countries to specialize and to achieve economies of scale. Countries would produce what they were best at making and trade for the rest. However, what if a country's economy was weak? What if it was not good at making anything and had no absolute advantage in any area? To understand this situation David Ricardo, the early 19th-century British economist, formulated the principle of **comparative advantage,** perhaps one of the most powerful in economics.[12] Comparative advantage says that countries should specialize in producing the goods they make best and import other goods.

comparative advantage David Ricardo's principle of international trade, which states that countries should specialize in producing goods it makes best and import other goods.

If it takes 10 hours of labor to make a gallon of wine and 20 hours to make a pound of cheese in Greece and it takes 60 hours of labor to make a gallon of wine and 30 hours to make a pound of cheese in Turkey, Greece is more productive than Turkey in both commodities. It has the *absolute* advantage in wine and cheese, but its *comparative* advantage is in wine while Turkey's *comparative* advantage is in cheese. It makes sense for Greece to specialize in wine production and for Turkey to specialize in cheese production. The two countries should trade with each other because both will be better off; however, since Greek workers in this instance are more efficient than Turkish workers, they will earn more income.

Trade does not make earnings across countries equal when productivity differs, it simply makes both countries better off than they otherwise would be. Tariffs and quotas, on the other hand, reward inefficient domestic producers and make goods more expensive (and less plentiful) for domestic consumers. The economy has less reason to be innovative. Consumers in economies insulated from international competition have to pay higher prices for lower-quality goods and services.

Smoot-Harley and Its Aftermath

In 1930, the U.S. Congress passed the Smoot-Harley Tariff Act, which established the highest general tariff rate structure in U.S. history. Country after country retaliated, world trade stagnated, and the Great Depression, already underway, deepened and became global.[13] Why did the U.S. Congress ignore the warnings of experts? Why did it raise tariffs to unprecedented levels? The power of special interests seeking import protection dominated the legislative process. Though most people benefit from international trade, the firms and industries whose home markets will be diminished suffer. They are concentrated, organized, and capable of pressing their interests in the political arena. In contrast, the broad mass of consumers who benefit from foreign trade is diffuse and its interest in any particular trade issue is usually slight. For free trade to have a chance, antiprotectionist counterweights must be in place.

The process of creating these counterweights started in 1934 when Congress passed the Reciprocal Trade Agreements Act. This act authorized the president to negotiate and implement tariff-cutting pacts with other countries. The law had an effect. By 1942, U.S. exports returned to their predepression levels. After a long history of passing comprehensive tariff bills, Congress, with some exceptions, stopped making product-specific trade law. It relinquished that task to the executive branch.[14]

GATT

Since 1947, the world has benefitted from the General Agreement on Tariffs and Trade (GATT), which has promoted free trade. Its secretariat monitors the trade policies of 117 member nations. Originally composed of 23 countries, the GATT's purpose was to fight against the legacy of protectionism, which had severely hurt the world economy in the period between the two world wars and had made the Great Depression worse.[15]

The GATT works on the basis of three principles. The first is *reciprocity;* if a country lowers its tariffs against another country's exports, the other country is expected in turn to lower its tariffs. The second principle is *nondiscrimination*, by which no country should grant favorable trade treatment to another country or groups of countries. The third principle is *transparency:* Countries replace nontariff barriers such as import quotas with tariffs, and then make these tariffs binding by promising not to raise them.[16]

Between 1948 and 1973, the GATT was very successful. The growth rate in international commerce went up 7 percent each year after 1948 after having grown at a rate of only .5 percent per year between 1913 and 1948. From 1950 to 1980, the sum of imports and exports rose from 8.4 percent of the U.S. GNP to 21.1 percent. The increase for West Germany (Germany was not united until 1990) went from 25.4 percent to 57.3 percent and for Japan from 20.1 percent to 31.2 percent.[17]

Today, more than 70 percent of U.S. products and services are in markets where they face foreign completion. The largest increases in world trade followed the so-called Kennedy Round of negotiations that lasted from 1963 to 1967. Cuts of 50 percent and more were made on more than two-thirds of the products of industrial countries. Between 1969 and 1973, world exports more than doubled.[18]

Unfortunately, the result of this burgeoning trade was a call for protectionism. Specific sectors of the economy had trouble adjusting to the new competition. Under the GATT, however, countries were restricted in what they could do. Only developing countries and advanced nations with severe balance-of-trade problems could use quotas. A country had to consult with other GATT nations before raising a tariff and it had to provide affected nations with compensation. Countervailing duties were allowed only if imported goods had been subsidized. Special duties were sanctioned only if charges of dumping could be proved; that is, an importer had to sell goods at below cost.

Because of these restrictions, countries resorted to more subtle forms of trade protection: voluntary export restraints (bilateral quotas), public subsidies, and nationalistic procurement policies. The Tokyo Round of GATT talks, which lasted from 1973 to 1979, was successful in lowering tariffs (the weighted average tariff rate went down from 7 percent to 4.67 percent), but it was unsuccessful in eliminating ambiguities in the treatment of nontariff barriers.[19] The 1990 round of GATT negotiations—the Uruguay Round—was extremely complicated and very hotly contested. However, new agreements were reached to lower agricultural trade barriers and to deal with questions of intellectual property and services.

Against Free Trade

Throughout the world, a new nationalism has surfaced and, with it, arguments against free trade and for protectionism have gained momentum. Briefly, these arguments consist of the following:

1. National security reasons justify the violation of free trade principles. A country needs certain vital industries in case of war.
2. Violating free trade principles for the sake of job protection is justified. Low wages provide the developing countries with an unfair trade advantage that robs the developed countries of jobs. Much of international trade is in the form of intrafirm transactions wherein a company exports manufacturing to low-wage countries.
3. Some countries create unfair trade advantages. They do so by means of tax incentives and selected subsidies to companies, such as government-sponsored R&D, preferential loans, and giving companies the freedom to collude. Foreign companies that cannot compete with the subsidized companies should be allowed to violate free trade principles to put themselves in a better position to compete.
4. During the infant industry stage, special subsidies and protection in various forms

from import restrictions to reduced tax are appropriate, provided they are removed when the industry gains strength and matures. Infant industry protection has long been accepted in international trade theory: To build comparative advantage in particular industries, a country may have to protect them when they are young.

5. It might be justifiable to violate free trade principles to obtain more favorable terms of trade. Threatening a country with a tariff can help open the country's markets to foreign goods.[20]

Trade wars, whereby countries retaliate against the protectionism of other countries, are extremely damaging to the world economy, however. A severe decline in world trade would hurt everyone except special interests.

Remedies for Firms Harmed by Foreign Competition

The U.S. government has established a number of remedies for firms and industries that allege they have been harmed by imports.[21] The main components of U.S. trade law can be found in the 1974 Trade Act. The remedies available to businesses are:

- Offsetting duties in special cases
- Antidumping measures
- Temporary relief (the escape clause)
- Trade adjustment assistance
- Deals in special cases (voluntary export restrictions and orderly marketing arrangements).

In 1897, Congress allowed the imposition of special offsetting duties if it found that foreign governments were unduly subsidizing exports. The 1921 Anti-Dumping Act permitted similar measures if foreign sellers were unloading goods in the U.S. market at prices below those in their home market. In a 1943 agreement with Mexico, the U.S. government drew on precedents to establish an "escape clause," which allowed an affected industry to appeal for temporary relief if it could prove injury from the results of U.S. trade policies.

The 1962 Trade Expansion Act brought major revision and codification of the escape clause. It also introduced the idea of trade adjustment assistance as an alternative or supplement to tariff relief. Workers and companies adversely affected by imports could seek government financial, technical, and retraining assistance.

Under a special section of the 1956 Agricultural Act, the president had the authority to negotiate bilateral export limitation agreements with foreign governments on textiles or textile products. Presidents Eisenhower, Kennedy, and Nixon used this authority to get deals for voluntary export restraints (VERs) on textiles. The idea of establishing VERs and orderly marketing arrangements (OMAs) was extended to automobiles and steel.

Between 1979 and 1980, the foreign share of the new-car market in the United States increased from 17 percent to over 25 percent; the 1982 agreement limited the Japanese to no more than 25 percent of the U.S. market. To get around the limitation, the Japanese automakers increased their export of luxury models to the U.S. market and raised prices. They also made investments in U.S. car manufacturing facilities not covered by the agreement. Though it increased employment in the U.S. automobile industry by 55,000 in the early 1980s, the auto agreement with Japan raised the prices paid by consumers an estimated 4.4 percent. U.S. automakers benefited by $2.6 billion and those in Japan benefited by $2.2 billion.

A similar agreement was negotiated between the U.S. government and each country supplying steel to the United States. In 1984, the U.S. government set the limit on steel imports to the U.S. at about 20 percent through the use of VERs. Again, the costs to consumers has been very high. Industrial users of steel have had to pay higher costs, which they have passed on to consumers. To get around the quotas, foreign steel manufacturers have entered specialty steel markets not covered by the agreement. This prompted U.S. specialty steel makers to petition the U.S. government for relief.

These special deals were used because they circumvented national and international rules. They got around national rules because the U.S. government did not have to prove injury or limit the duration of protection. They avoided GATT requirements that permit other nations to impose equivalent trade restrictions unless the United States offers compensation in the form of offsetting tariff reductions.

The Omnibus Trade Act of 1988

Under the Omnibus Trade and Competitiveness Act of 1988, the U.S. government became even more vigilant in trying to remove nontariff barriers.[22] The act strengthened U.S. trade negotiators' leverage and gave the government negotiating authority for the Uruguay Round of trade talks. The act also required notification of plant closings and expanded assistance to workers who lose their jobs.

Super 301 provision Gives the U.S. government the right to name priority unfair trading practices and countries.

Under the **Super 301 provision** of the act, the U.S. government had the right to name "priority" unfair trading practices and "priority" unfair trading countries. When this is done, a 12-to-18-month period of negotiations takes place to remove the cited nation's trade barriers. In 1989, Japan was cited for exclusionary government procurement practices for supercomputers and satellites and for technical barriers preventing forest product imports. Brazil was cited for quantitative import restrictions and India for trade-related investment barriers and for closure of its insurance market to foreign firms.

The Super 301 provision opened the door for U.S. businesses to present cases against Japan. In 1990, Allied-Signal maintained that Japan put together a business combination to develop and market a product to compete with Allied-Signal's amorphous metal alloys. It also claimed that the Japanese government tried to keep Japanese firms from purchasing its alloys and that Japan held up an Allied-Signal patent application for 11 years before approving it. To relieve the tension in U.S.-Japan relations, the chief U.S. trade representative reached an agreement with Japan in which Allied-Signal withdrew its complaint and Japan agreed that its utilities could buy transformers that use Allied-Signal's metals.[23]

Exporting Mechanics

In addition to negotiating trade agreements for U.S. companies, the American government provides numerous other types of trade assistance. The export market is far more complicated than producing and selling for the domestic market.[24] The Department of Commerce has 47 local U.S. offices that provide information about trade and investment opportunities abroad, foreign markets, and financing and insurance, tax advantages, trade exhibitions, documentation, and licensing and import requirements. Most its offices have a business library and lists of people who are experienced in exporting. Many state governments have similar offices.

The Business Counseling Section of the International Trade Administration also provides advice to exporters. Programs in the Export-Import Bank and Overseas Private Investment Corporation offer information about political conditions in various countries. The State Department, an additional source of information, works with large commercial banks and industry trade associations.

In selecting a foreign market, a prospective exporter can study the *Foreign Trade Report* published by the Bureau of the Census. It includes statistical records of the merchandise shipped from the United States to foreign countries. *Overseas Business Reports* provides details on marketing strategies for individual countries. U.S. embassies and consulates prepare *Foreign Economic Trends* with country-by-country data on business conditions. International economic indicators, demographic data, and market share reports can be obtained from other government reports. For a nominal annual subscription fee, TOPS (the Trade Opportunities Program) will make matches between individual firms and particular business opportunities.

Developing an export marketing strategy involves deciding what is unique about the product and how it will stand up to the foreign competition. The product may have to be modified for the foreign market. The quality image is important because American products have slipped in recent years. Questions about production capacity, promotion and advertising, training and translation, distribution, and customer service should be considered. For instance, to what extent will the product have to be disassembled for shipping? All of these questions bear on the final price of the product.

The U.S. producer can sell the good directly overseas or rely on an intermediary for both sales and shipping. There are many types of intermediaries. Foreign firms often use commission agents to find foreign products they need. Country-controlled buying agents fulfill the same function. Export management companies, on the other hand, purchase U.S. goods for sale abroad, and the manufacturer usually bears the risk. To enhance the practicality of exports by small- and medium-sized companies, joint trading companies may be established. It is also possible to rely upon conventional sales representatives, wholesale outlets, and government purchasing agents. In making all of these decisions, business people will find government agencies useful.

Though one hears a great deal about U.S. trade deficits, much less is heard about exports. The United States is the world's largest exporter. Its exports valued at more than $500 billion per year outdistance both Germany and Japan, the world's number two and number three exporters. Boeing is the largest exporting company, but most of the increase in U.S. exports in recent years has come from small- and medium-size businesses.

Comparing National Strengths and Weaknesses

Trade theory holds that each economy in the world builds up unique advantages and disadvantages and that by means of mutually beneficial transactions everyone benefits. For the world to prosper, there should be a division of labor among the world's major trading partners. In what follows, some of the advantages and disadvantages of four major indus-

Exhibit 9–1 Strengths of National Economies

Germany	Japan	United Kingdom	United States	
chemicals	electronics	services	computers	defense
plastics	equipment	consumer goods	software	aerospace
machinery	steel	publishing	biotech	health care
printing	transportation	advertising	consumer goods	entertainment
optical	office computing	luxury items	forest products	leisure
	cameras	leisure	agriculture	
		consulting		

trial nations—Germany, Japan, the United Kingdom, and the United States—are compared (see Exhibit 9–1).[25]

Germany. The particular strengths of the German economy are in chemicals, plastics, machinery, printing, and optical products. The economy is adept at complex production processes that require a high degree of precision. There is strong domestic rivalry for prestige in science and technology. A pragmatic, technical management aims to master and dominate sophisticated market segments. It puts a stress on quality, premium high performance products that command high prices. The Germans try to compete based on quality and differentiation, not on cost.

Germany has a large domestic market, sophisticated buyers, and an international orientation among its companies. Banks hold shares in companies and bank executives serve on company boards. To a greater extent than in the United States or the United Kingdom, ownership is in private hands. The firms tend to be small, hierarchical, well disciplined, and owner-managed. For all these reasons, German firms have a long-term perspective; they are not as preoccupied with quarterly profits.

These advantages have not prevented major declines in the steel, coal, shipbuilding, and apparel industries. Germany has relatively few natural resources, with the exception of coal and coke, and domestic markets are saturated in many areas. The government imposes tough product standards and has demanding environmental laws. Consumers are sophisticated, but also cautious and conservative and not easily swayed by image marketing. In any event, television and radio advertising on the public media in Germany is limited. A product does not make rapid headway if intangible brand name and mass communication is critical to its success.

German businesses have not been strong in consumer products. In business services, they have been held back by high wages. Public ownership and regulation have inhibited innovation in telecommunications, transportation, and electric power. Management education is weak, electronics and computer industries have failed to flourish, and the pace of small business formation has been slow. Finally, group decision making has retarded innovation, and a creeping financial orientation in addition to poorly developed risk capital markets have prevented further progress.

Germany has faced a huge burden in integrating the formerly Communist East. Employment and environmental difficulties could hold the unified Germany back (see Chapter 11).

Japan. Japanese strengths are in electronic products, heavy equipment, steel- and transportation-related industries, autos, office machines, computing equipment, and cameras. Although Japanese companies have R&D programs, they do much of their technology sourcing abroad. Project teams are able to bring new products into production very quickly. The emphasis on product quality remains great even though Japan has long ago overcome the image of producing cheap goods.

The dynamism of the Japanese economy has been promoted by intense domestic rivalry, demanding buyers, cooperative suppliers, rapid upgrading of technology, and an international orientation. Savings and investment are high and capital investment strong. Investment has been aimed at creating large, efficient facilities with the latest technology. Since World War II, the Japanese approach has been to scrap old production facilities and build new ones rather than make incremental adjustments.

Sophisticated domestic buyers insist on the latest model of car, electronic product, or camera with the most up-to-date features. Japanese companies have been aware that presentation and packaging is an important part of sales, and the mass media and advertising business are well developed.

Japanese companies expect a great deal from their suppliers. World-class suppliers have developed cooperative long-term relationships with Japanese companies. The flow of information is very important. Trading companies help exporters penetrate foreign markets. Distribution channels, however, are dominated by diverse and highly fragmented outlets, not the uniform mass-marketing channels such as supermarkets and discount chains that dominate in the United States.

The goals of Japanese business usually are defined in term of market share. Companies try to maintain employment, achieve economies of scale, and outdo rivals. A considerable amount of public information is available on the economy, as is production and market share information.

Still, the Japanese economy has weaknesses in some areas. It lags behind foreign competition in chemicals, plastics, food and beverages, and personal consumer products. Japan has a paucity of raw materials, and labor is in short supply and very expensive.

United Kingdom (U.K.). The strengths of British industry are in services, consumer goods, and trading. The country has a large capital pool and a favorable geographic location; its economy has a cost advantage in advanced human resources, which provide it with an important edge in consulting, publishing, and advertising. Certainly it has not hurt the U.K. to have English as the international language of business. Great Britain is a leading maker of luxury and leisure goods and entertainment.

British industries are recognized internationally by their brand names (e.g., Schweppes "bitter lemon"), and they have competed well in many areas, including consumer packaged goods, alcoholic beverages, food, confectionery products, personal products, household furniture, insurance, auctioneering, money management, pharmaceuticals, and entertainment and leisure. Gains in petroleum and petroleum-related products were made with the discovery of North Sea oil.

British disadvantages are a lack of domestic rivalry and a downward slide in living standards that have eroded domestic demand. Many exports are to Commonwealth members, which are chiefly underdeveloped countries with low-income buyers. While many parts of the economy have been successful, the core manufacturing areas in the north and Midlands have been declining for a long period of time and show few signs of revival. The U.K. has had to rely heavily on foreign inputs and machinery for its industry. Losses have been greater than gains and few positions exist where industry is unusually strong.

Investors often are short-term institutional buyers whose major concern is share price appreciation and dividends. There has been an explosion of acquisitions and takeovers. British companies appear to be merging rather than competing. Managers frequently lack the strong profit motivation or market share orientation found in the United States.

The U.K. seemed to have fallen into a comfortable pattern of slow decay. Widespread state ownership and regulation following World War II retarded dynamism and innovation and contributed to the stodgy attitude and dependency on protocol, form, and bureaucracy in companies. Government-directed intervention in the form of subsidies, consolidation, and protection did not work. And labor unions were no help to Britain moving ahead. Notable failures occurred after the government encouraged mergers to create world-class companies in steel, autos, machine tools, and computers. The government's choices of promising technologies led to few commercial successes. The alteration of power between Conservative and Labour parties brought on sharp policy reversals on matters such as government ownership. The United Kingdom was in a downward cycle, so that it became very hard to turn the economy around, but trends in the 1990s have been better.

The United States. The U.S. economy is strong in computers, packaged software, biotechnology, consumer goods, and services; however, 15 of the top 25 U.S. industries are natural resource–based, which reflects their relative abundance in the country. Despite increasing cutbacks, the United States has a commanding position in defense, aerospace, and related fields that are affected by government spending, and it remains strong in health care, entertainment and leisure, and consumer and business services.

The United States has many remaining advantages: scientific research, especially in the fundamental disciplines; the media, chain stores, and modern marketing; and financial services and money management capabilities. The country remains a good place to start new businesses. The average productivity of the workforce is as high as any other nation, but real wages are declining.

Broad segments of U.S. industry (e.g., autos, machine tools, semiconductors, consumer electronics), however, have been losing competitive advantage. The United States has very large trade deficits, weak and uneven productivity growth, and low rates of business investment. It has been slow to adopt new process technologies, upgrade its facilities, and introduce new products and features. Its science and technology are superb, but these have lagged in converting into competitive industries. Relatively low wages and high employee availability have lowered the pressure to automate. Manufacturers have been making mass-produced standardized disposable goods for a large domestic market where consumers have had an insatiable demand for credit. Goods are often made with compromises in product design, quality, and service. The relationship between producers and suppliers has been competitive and at arms' length.

Companies have become easy targets for takeovers, so management has tried to head them off by boosting short-term earnings and restructuring in a way that has not always been in the long-term interests of the company. Mergers and alliances have been carried out to create stock market excitement, but relatively little capital has gone into new plants, products, and technology. Unrelated diversification and downsizing undermine competitiveness. Companies seek government protection to deal with the competition, claiming that foreign competitors are engaged in uncompetitive acts such as dumping.

Conclusions

In a global competitive environment, close ties between business and government mean that the issues management function takes on increasing importance. The process by which a corporation identifies, evaluates, and responds to emerging political, social, and economic trends that affect it significantly is critical for its long-term success. Issues management has special importance for firms involved in global commerce, as the examples show.

The viability of the firm is supposed to depend on its ability to produce at low cost and meet market demand. However, firms often seek relief from the pressures of a competitive market. They act opportunistically toward public policy, trying to obtain government subsidies, entry restrictions, protection from new products and technologies, and prices that guarantee profits. Government policies protect many firms from the market's judgment. Whatever the merits or demerits of a public policy from a broad social perspective, it is likely to create individual competitive winners and losers. Armed with competitive analysis, firms are able to participate more effectively in the public policy process.

Discussion Questions

1. Provide some example of government effects on business.
2. What are some of the differences between responding to market demands and responding to public policies?
3. Define what is meant by issues, interests, information, and institutions. Why are they important?
4. What is issues management? What is a strategic approach to issues management?
5. What are the different stages in issues management? What kinds of questions are relevant at the different stages?
6. What is meant by corporate legitimacy? Why is it important?
7. Describe and assess Monsanto's issues management program.
8. Why has trade policy become a top priority at many companies? Give some examples.
9. Explain David Ricardo's principle of comparative advantage.
10. Provide a description of how U.S. trade policy has evolved since the Smoot-Hawley Act.

11. What is the GATT? How does it work?
12. What are some of the arguments against free trade? Assess these arguments.
13. What remedies do U.S. firms have against alleged harm by unfair foreign competition?
14. Describe the purpose and major provisions of the 1988 Omnibus Trade Act.
15. Describe some of the assistance the federal government provides for exports.
16. Compare the economic strengths and weaknesses of Germany, Japan, the United Kingdom, and the United States.

Endnotes

1. John Coleman, "Motorola's Japan Strategy," Harvard Business School Case, April 1987.
2. David Baron, "Integrated Strategy: Market and Non-Market Components," Stanford Graduate School of Business paper, May 11, 1994.
3. M. Porter, "The Competitive Advantage of Nations," *Harvard Business Review,* 1990, pp. 73–93.
4. Willis Emmons, "Public Policy and the Manager," Harvard Business School Case, Sept. 2, 1993.
5. Alfred Marcus, Allen Kaufman, and David Beam, eds., *Business Strategy and Public Policy* (Westport, Conn.: Greenwood Press, 1987).
6. Alfred Marcus, "Airline Deregulation, Business Strategy, and Regulatory Theory," in *Public Policy and Economic Institutions* (Greenwich, Conn.: JAI Press, 1991), pp. 325–350.
7. Baron, "Integrated Strategy."
8. Alfred Marcus, *The Adversary Economy* (Westport, Conn.: Greenwood Press, 1984).
9. Steve Littlejohn, "Competition and Cooperation," in Marcus, Kaufman, and Beam, eds., *Business Strategy and Public Policy,* pp. 19–31.
10. "Guess Who's Selling Barbies in Japan Now?" *Business Week,* Dec. 9, 1991, pp. 72–73; see also Baron, "Integrated Strategy."
11. Baron, "Integrated Strategy."
12. J. D. Gwartney and R. L. Stroup, *Economics: Private and Public Choice* (San Diego: Harcourt Brace Jovanovich, 1987); D. B. Yoffie, *Note on Free Trade and Protectionism*, Working Paper 383-174, Harvard Business School, 1983; D. B. Yoffie and J. W. Rosenblum, "Zenith and the Color Television Fight," Case No. 383-070, Harvard Business School, 1982; D. B. Yoffie and J. K. Austin, "Textiles and the Multi-Fiber Arrangement," Case No. 383-164, Harvard Business School, 1983.
13. Stephanie Lenway, *The Politics of U.S. International Trade* (Marshfield, Mass.: Pitman, 1985).
14. David Baron, *Business and Its Environment* (Englewood Cliffs, N.J.: Prentice Hall, 1993); see also Destler, 1986; and Lenway, *The Politics of U.S. International Trade*.
15. "Jousting for Advantage," *The Economist,* September 22, 1990; N. Vousden, *The Economics of Trade Protection* (New York: Cambridge University Press, 1990).
16. Ibid.
17. Yoffie, *Note on Free Trade and Protectionism*.
18. Ibid.
19. Ibid.
20. Ibid.
21. Destler, 1986.
22. J. S. Lublin, "U.S. Food Firms Find Europe's Huge Market Hardly a Piece of Cake," *The Wall Street Journal,* May 15, 1990, p. A1; B. Stokes, "Off and Running," *National Journal,* June 17, 1989, pp. 1562–66.

23. Baron, *Business and Its Environment.*
24. M. L. Whicker and R. A. Morre, "Policies to Build a More Competitive America," Paper presented at the American Political Science Association Annual Meetings, 1987.
25. M. Porter, *The Competitive Advantage of Nations* (New York: Free Press, 1990); J. Chipman, "On the Concept of International Competitiveness," Discussion Paper 118, Strategic Management Research Center, University of Minnesota, 1989; R. T. Kudrle, "Business-Government Relations Abroad: What's Important for the U.S.?" Discussion Paper 81, Strategic Management Research Center, University of Minnesota, 1987; S. A. Lenway, "Between War and Commerce: Economic Sanctions as a Tool of Statecraft," *International Organization* 42 (1988), pp. 397–426; J. A. Limprecht and R. H. Hayes, "Germany's World-Class Manufacturers," *Harvard Business Review,* Nov.–Dec. 1982, pp. 106–114; P. S. Nivola, "More Like Them? The Political Feasibility of Strategic Trade Policy," Paper prepared for the Annual Meeting of the American Political Science Association, San Francisco, Aug. 30–Sept. 2, 1990; M. Porter, "The Competitive Advantage of Nations," *Harvard Business Review,* March–April 1990, pp. 73–93; "The New Germany: The Spontaneous Union," *The Economist,* June 30, 1990; "Two Germanys United Would Pose Challenge to Other Economies," *The Wall Street Journal,* Nov. 13, 1989, p. A1; "West Germany: Heading for Unity," *The Economist,* Oct. 28–Nov. 3, 1989.

Case 9–A
Northwest Airlines Financial Package[1]

In May 1991, the Minnesota state legislature hastily passed enabling legislation that allowed state and municipal governments to offer Northwest Airlines (NWA), a Minnesota-based airline carrier, a financial package of low-interest loans, tax credits, and grants that would allow it to restructure its debt and locate its new airplane maintenance facilities within the state.[2] Provisos made sure that a complete review of the airline's finances would be conducted prior to final approval. On December 17, 1991, the legislature approved the $838 million partnership between Northwest Airlines, the State of Minnesota, and other parties which included the Minneapolis/St. Paul Metropolitan Airports Commission (MAC), the Cities of Duluth and Hibbing (where the maintenance facilities were to be located), St. Louis County, the Iron Range Resource Rehabilitation Board (IRRRB), and the privately owned Northern States Power, the local gas and electric utility. The legislation was celebrated and denounced in the local and national media and hotly debated in the state where the size of the package and its attendant risk was perceived to be excessive. *U.S. News & World Report* and *Barron's* voiced criticism of the package, and a group of local business people who objected to the use of taxpayers' money to support a private corporation formed the Citizens' Committee to Stop the NWA Loan. As the financial condition of the airline continued to slip during the two years that followed, Northwest was considering a proposal to change the conditions of the original deal. Should it go ahead with this proposal? If it did, how should it present it to the public and the other parties involved?

Background on Northwest Airlines

Northwest Airlines is the fourth largest U.S. airline carrier. Maintaining its corporate headquarters in Eagan, Minnesota, it employs an estimated 18,000 state residents. It is part of an industry that has undergone profound changes since it was deregulated in 1978. Excess capacity, price wars, and poor earnings for all carriers have lead to numerous bankruptcies and consolidations.

After a brief period of profitability in the mid-1980s, the industry was battered by record losses during 1990–1993. Since then, it has returned to profitability. The wave of losses were attributed to the Gulf War, escalating fuel costs, continuing price wars, and a major recession that led to a decline in passenger traffic.

Industry consultants maintain that if an airline is to survive in the 1990s, it must be large and develop a global presence. American, Delta, and United have been very aggressive in expanding their routes and acquiring assets from failing carriers. NWA, which merged with Republic Airlines in 1986, has been engaged in similar strategies. In the late 1980s, extensive orders for new aircraft were placed by all carriers in response to the need to retire aging aircraft, meet noise reduction regulations, increase fuel efficiency, and boost capacity to capture larger market shares. In October 1986, Northwest Airlines agreed to buy up to 100 Airbus A320 jetliners from Airbus Industrie, the European aircraft manufacturing consortium.

In March 1989, NWA disclosed that an unnamed investment group headed by former director and Disney executive Gary Wilson and financier Al Checchi had proposed to acquire the company. A takeover battle soon ensued as the group of potential owners expanded and the bidding war raised the price of a Northwest share from $60 to $121. On June 19, Northwest agreed to accept the offer of the Checchi-Wilson group for $3.65 billion. The group included KLM (Royal Dutch Airlines), and San Francisco investors Blum & Associates, and Elders, Inc., of Australia. Checchi and Wilson invested $40 million of their own money and borrowed $3 billion more.

The new management team acted to improve performance while increasing capacity and global market share. To address its competitive and regulatory pressures, Northwest had to expand its Airbus purchases and step up its acquisition of the assets of failing airlines. Additionally, buying a new fleet required that the airline build new maintenance bases. All these plans required a fresh influx of capital at a time when the airline's own recent leveraged buyout had left the company saddled with debt and enormous interest payments.

Searching for a Site for New Maintenance Bases. The company's previous management had been seeking a location outside Minnesota at which to build the new maintenance bases, but by early 1990 it was common knowledge that the new owners wanted a Minnesota site. Officials at NWA said that although other states had made similar financial offers, the carrier preferred to locate the maintenance bases in Minnesota because of the company's historically good relationship with the state.

At the same time, public officials from Duluth and Hibbing were trying to entice the airline into building the bases in their cities. These two cities are located in the heart of the Iron Range, an economically depressed region of northeastern Minnesota. The maintenance bases were expected to generate over 1,500 high-paying airplane mechanic jobs and 1,000 construction jobs, creating an important ripple effect in the local economies. Each of these cities as well as the Metropolitan Airports Commission presented NWA with separate financing offers in the first quarter of 1990. These initial offers were deemed insufficient by NWA officials who terminated talks in October 1990.

The Metropolitan Airports Commission (MAC) can be considered an arm of the state although it has its own taxing district. Approximately 75 percent of MAC's revenues come from Northwest, making the airline's survival important for MAC's financial health. Officials from Duluth approached MAC and suggested that they join forces in order to structure a more extensive financial package. At this time Jim Oberstar, the congressman who represented Duluth and Hibbing, became involved and took the lead negotiating role. By early 1991, he had formed a coalition of groups with interests in the bases: MAC, the Cities of Duluth and Hibbing, St. Louis County (within which Duluth and Hibbing are located), the Iron Range Resources and Rehabilitation Board (IRRRB), and Northern States Power. IRRRB was formed to administer a grants program to spur economic growth in the deeply depressed Iron Range, which had not experienced the benefits of the state's growth-oriented policies. It was the first member of the group to approve its part of the package—$35 million in bonds and $10 million in grants.

In February 1991, the state's governor instructed the Commissioner of Trade and Economic Development to begin working with the congressman and other public officials to draft legislation that would give the partnership authority to negotiate with Northwest. Two months later a bill was put before the state legislature requesting authorization to provide Northwest with an $838 million financial package of low-interest loans, tax incentives, and two Airbus maintenance bases which the airline would lease from the state. In total, the project promised to create 1,500 new jobs for the employment-starved Iron Range.

Legislative Passage. After three intense weeks of lobbying, the legislation was passed with a proviso that final approval was made contingent upon an assessment of the airline's financial condition and its ability to meet the obligations of the loan agreement. The governor and the legislature's leadership warned that if the legislation was not passed, Northwest might move its 18,000-employee headquarters from Minnesota. The presence of the NWA corporate headquarters in the Twin Cities metropolitan area makes it one of four or five metropolitan areas in the United States that are a major airline hub. As a hub, the Minneapolis/St. Paul International Airport had more passengers flowing through it (and therefore revenue) than would have been generated otherwise by the surrounding community. In 1991, 38 percent of the 19 million passengers that went through the airport were making connections.

The Twin Cities' status as a hub for Northwest Airlines had significant impact on the state's economic health. In addition to the direct jobs provided by the airline, a MAC study concluded that 35,575 jobs in the state were heavily dependent on available air services. Northwest and its employees generated $216 million in state and local taxes. The expected economic benefits of the maintenance bases included an annual direct payroll of $1 million as well as considerable ripple effects.

The reality was that if the airline failed, the Twin Cities would have to face losing many of its direct flights and becoming a spoke to another hub instead of a critical intersection on global air routes. It was difficult to imagine the effect this could have on its business community which, for the most part, supported the financing package.

The airline spent $700,000 for lobbying the legislature. On December 17, 1991, despite organized vocal opposition and many reservations about the airline and the industry, the legislative commission responsible for final approval gave the partnership its blessing.

Tough Financial Going after the Deal

In January 1992, state officials met near the Hibbing airport for the groundbreaking ceremony for the maintenance center that would provide 500 high-paying jobs.[3] Another maintenance center would be built near Duluth, providing additional jobs. Six months later, Northwest collected the first $270 million of its aid package in the form of an operating loan from MAC backed by the taxpayers of the seven-county Twin Cities metropolitan area. Although the airline's financial position was somewhat precarious, it was anticipated that the expected economic upturn and assistance provided by the coalition would improve its overall health. In 1992, however, a reintroduction of price wars instigated by American Airlines plunged Northwest Airlines into a deeper financial crisis. It posted losses of up to $2 million per day in May of that year alone.

On May 26, 1992, company CEO John Dasburg sent a letter to all employees saying that the airline would need concessions in order to survive. NWA's employees are represented by three unions: (1) the Airline Pilots Association, (2) the Teamsters Union, and (3) the International Association of Machinists and Aerospace Workers (IAM). NWA enjoys generally good relations with its unions and employees. Improved employee morale—part of the corporate strategy to build the airline—had been observed since the buyout in 1989. Employees and unions were visible in their support of the original financial partnership with the state; the pilots union had even offered to contribute a portion of the financing—an offer turned down by the company. However, the road to major concessions by labor that would allow the airline to survive was not smooth. The airline had to lay off more than 2,000 workers. After a year of negotiations, nearly $900 million in concessions that gave employees a 30 percent stake in the company were approved by the executive council of the Airline Pilots Association, averting Chapter 11 bankruptcy filing by hours.

During the year of negotiations with its unions, the airline was forced to take other drastic measures to avert bankruptcy. On December 7, 1992, Northwest's executives announced the completion of a $2.2 billion financing package that included loans, debt deferral, and the cancellation of 74 of the new Airbus orders. Additionally Airbus Industrie and Boeing agreed to provide aircraft financing despite the cancellation or deferral of NWA orders. KLM, which owns an equity position and whose future as a global carrier depends on the success of Northwest, and Bankers Trust, which also holds an equity position, participated in the deal.

Turnaround and Questions about Fulfilling Obligations. In the two years after the legislature approved the financial partnership with Northwest Airlines, a lawsuit filed by members of the opposition, the worsening financial condition of the airline, and the cancellation and delay of aircraft orders prevented the state from issuing the bonds needed to finance the bases. The airline then reported a near record profit of $112 million in the third quarter of 1993 compared with a $20 million loss for the same quarter in 1992. Checchi and Wilson's share of the airline, for which they had paid $40 million, was now worth $250 million. The question remained, however, whether the bases would be built according to the original plan. Though the airline put itself in a position of potential default on its contract with the state and MAC, it announced that it no longer needed the bases. The commissioner of the Minnesota Department of Trade and Economic Development, Peter Gillette, said that renegotiating the deal with the airline was out of the question. IAM workers threatened to file a lawsuit against the state, MAC, and the airline, claiming that Northwest had no power or authority to renegotiate its agreement without legislative authorization.

Northwest was considering making a proposal to build only a smaller base at Duluth, which would employ 350 people, and to create another 500 lower-paying reservation jobs at Chisholm, another Iron Range city. It would build no base at Hibbing and would put up only one-sixth of the $60 million needed for the proposed projects. The rest would be provided by the state, the City of Duluth, and the IRRRB. In exchange, Northwest would incur no penalty for changing the terms of its agreement with the state. Senator Doug Johnson, a Democratic legislator from the Iron Range, suggested that the state was lucky to have Northwest around. If it cost a lot of money for a broken promise, so be it.

Discussion Questions

1. What should Northwest do? Should it follow through on its original plan? Should it try to gain acceptance for the new proposal? Should it scale back even further?
2. Whatever it does, how should it present itself to the public, to powerful state legislators, and to the various groups that had supported it in the past?

Endnotes

1. This case was written by Annette Berger with the assistance of Alfred Marcus.
2. *Minneapolis Star Tribune*, Jan. 5, 1993; *Minneapolis Star Tribune*, June 21, 1992.
3. Monika Bauerlein, "Northwest's New Deal," *City Pages*, July 20, 1994, pp. 6–18.

Case 9–B
Motorola and Japan[1]

Motorola is involved in nearly all aspects of communications technology from semiconductors to cellular phones, transceivers, and base stations that link the cellular phones to land-based telephone networks. It vigorously exports these products throughout the world, and has enlisted the aid of the U.S. government to help it open markets in Japan and elsewhere. Among U.S. companies, it is known for its aggressive stance. The question it faces is how much further to push this policy. To what extent can it strongly protest Japanese imports when it tries to enter Japanese markets? Will the aggressive trade policies it has pursued hinder its efforts to sell cellular phones and pagers? The Japanese might decide against buying the products of such a relentless critic. To push its policy further would be counterproductive if the Japanese retaliated. An additional consideration is that its vigorous pursuit of protectionism has started to hurt other U.S. companies. Loyal customers like Apple, that make PCs with Motorola's chips, are paying more for the chips and are starting to lose market share. PC costs for consumers are up because of the trade restrictions for which Motorola has fought. Should it modify its aggressive stance?

Background on Motorola. Motorola's roots are in the consumer products business.[2] In 1928, it developed the first car radio. By the 1970s, however, it had almost completely abandoned consumer products, concentrating instead on high-tech industrial goods—cellular phones, radios, pagers, and semiconductors for civilian, defense, and aerospace applications. With $5.4 billion in sales, Motorola was one of the world's largest electronics and communications companies. As a Baldridge Award winner, its reputation for quality and scientific excellence was outstanding. From the beginning, Motorola met Japanese inroads with an uncompromising stand to run its business better than the Japanese. It also made a series of aggressive counterthrusts into the Japanese markets. It soon discovered, however, that the Japanese did not play by the same rules as everyone else.

After the U.S. government gained a commitment in 1980 from the Japanese telecommunications company NTT to seek procurement contracts from foreign as well as domestic suppliers, Motorola was frustrated by the unwillingness of NTT officials to see Motorola representatives and to tell them what product specifications were and how to submit a proposal. Motorola was told that mid-level Japanese managers wanted to retire with jobs at Japanese firms like NEC, Fujitsu, and Hitachi; if they cooperated with Motorola, they would jeopardize their chances of doing so. Motorola had also brought successful patent infringement cases in telecommunications against the Japanese in the early 1980s.

To advance its position in semiconductors, Motorola bought a Japanese company. Nonetheless, the Japanese share of the world market continued to grow, reaching 44 percent by 1986 compared with the U.S. share of 43 percent. In D-RAMs, Japan controlled more than 75 percent of the market. Motorola and Intel decided to exit this market and concentrate instead on microprocessors. Motorola was a strong supporter of U.S. government efforts to reach an agreement with the Japanese to increase their purchase of foreign-made chips to more than 20 percent of the Japanese market over five years.

Motorola also was known for its aggressive efforts to alert government officials and business executives to the dire consequences of not paying attention to the Japanese challenge. Not all U.S. firms, however, felt as strongly as Motorola. In trade disputes with the Japanese, IBM and AT&T generally kept a lower profile. McDonnell Douglas, Hughes Communication, and other firms that were winning Japanese contracts expressed satisfaction. Only GTE and Rockwell seemed as dissatisfied with the Japanese as Motorola was.

Japanese Industry Promotion Policies

Motorola was particularly concerned about the industry promotion policies of the Japanese government.[3] From 1945 to 1960, when Japan tried to reconstruct its economy after its devastating defeat in World War II, it operated under near wartime conditions of regulation and control. The Japanese Parliament passed a law in 1946 that gave the government enormous power to intervene in economic activities. The government could ration all commodities for consumption and production and prohibit or restrict their usage and shipment. Many of these regulatory powers remained in effect until the early 1960s.

Starting in the 1960s, Japan entered its famous rapid period of growth. Through trade protection, tax advantages, and subsidies, the Ministry for Trade and Industry (MITI) promoted what it considered to be key industrial sectors. It selected these industries on the basis of their potential for productivity expansion and market growth. The economy moved from a reliance on agriculture and light industry (e.g., textiles) to dependence on heavy industry (e.g., steel and autos). Exports exploded. The GNP expanded at an average annual rate of more than 10 percent from 1960 to 1970.

In 1962, MITI's proposed Law for Extraordinary Measures for the Promotion of Specific Industries encountered opposition from business and was defeated. The defeat of this law signified a turn in government policy. The government then announced plans for trade liberalization. Dismantling the system of restricting imports by means of licenses and foreign exchange quotas was a major spur to productivity growth because Japanese manufacturers feared foreign penetration of domestic markets and in anticipation made efforts to improve productivity and quality and upgrade facilities. By the end of the 1960s MITI's role was largely symbolic. It suggested directions toward which the Japanese economy should move. Its visions and plans were supported by coordinating private firms and providing them with incentives.

The Fall-Off in Growth in the 1970s. Since 1970, the Japanese economy did not have the same strength as it did in the 1960s. It was hurt by a number of factors beyond its control such as President Nixon's decision to end the postwar fixed exchange rate system and the OPEC oil embargo that resulted in huge oil price increases. In 1974, the unemployment rate doubled and for the first time in the postwar period, Japan's GNP declined. In 1977–1978, the value of the yen rose rapidly, and in 1979–1980, the second oil shock occurred.

Many Japanese industries were hurt badly and clamored for protection. Japan, however, continued to achieve stunning trade surpluses with almost all its trading partners. Thus, it continued to reduce tariff barriers, making Japanese tariff rates among the lowest in the world. In principle, Japan was committed to free trade. It had policies to help industries hurt by free trade's consequences. Through the Law to Aid Depressed Industries, it gave assistance to workers to relocate and train themselves for new jobs. It also allowed capacity reduction cartels to form in selected declining sectors. These cartels helped restructure these industries.

The government, too, took the initiative to support civilian R&D. In 1987, both the United States and Japan were spending about 2.5 percent of GNP on R&D. Japanese expenditures, though, were dominated by the private sector, with less than 20 percent of it government funded, while close to 50 percent was government funded in the United States. Copying a British idea, the Japanese formed technology research associations (TRAs) among private firms to conduct joint R&D with government assistance. The TRA for Very Large-Scale Integrated Circuits (VLSI) was composed of big computer manufacturers Fujitsu, Hitachi, Mitsubishi, NEC, and Toshiba. Its aim was to develop high-density high-speed semiconductors to be used in a Japanese-made computer that would challenge IBM's next generation mainframe. It produced more than 1,000 patent applications, many of which were thought to be the world's leading technology. However, the TRA for VLSI lost out when the momentum in the computer industry shifted from mainframes to PCs and networked systems.

Trade Disputes

Japanese-U.S. trade continued to be riddled with numerous disputes. If a U.S. company believes that Japanese products are being dumped on the U.S. market, it can file a petition to demonstrate that it has been injured. If the decision goes in its favor, a recommendation to the president can be made to impose a quota. The Japanese then can appeal to GATT, which can bring together a third-party panel to resolve the controversy if the disputants themselves cannot agree. The GATT Council, of which the U.S. is a member, must approve any ruling made by the third-party panel.

Between 1986 and 1989, the U.S. government gave final rulings on 23 injury cases, of which 13 were ruled as caused by dumping and other unfair Japanese trade practices. The Japanese did not appeal any of the cases to GATT. However, a number of disputes were not resolved in this manner. In notable steel, auto, and semiconductor cases, where the industry heavily pressured Congress and the White House to apply sanctions against the Japanese, the Japanese voluntarily agreed to restrain imports to the U.S. market. These settlements, while not explicitly against GATT clauses against protective duties, were in violation of the spirit of GATT.

Motorola's Stance. Motorola vigorously supported the semiconductor industry's actions against the Japanese. Along with the Semiconductor Industry Association, it alleged that Japanese firms were dumping on the U.S. market and denying market access to U.S. firms in Japan. It asked the Japanese to increase their purchase of foreign-made chips to more than 20 percent of the Japanese market.

Motorola supported the suits the industry association brought against the Japanese producers. When the U.S. government decided against the Japanese and started to impose duties, the Japanese promised: (*a*) not to export to the U.S. market at prices lower than fair market value; (*b*) to monitor third-country shipments of electronic products to the United States, so that they would not hurt U.S. competitors; and (*c*) to facilitate sales of U.S. products in Japan. The U.S. government, however, accused the Japanese of violating terms (*a*) and (*b*). It retaliated by raising duties on goods used in the United States. It brought additional action against the Japanese in front of GATT, which decided in favor of the United States. It was because of these pressures that the Japanese agreed to voluntarily restrict imports and promised foreigners to help them capture a 20 percent share of the Japanese market by 1993.

Trade Analyst Arguments. Trade analysts argued that a semiconductor agreement went against the interests of U.S. consumers. They cited research showing that voluntary export restraint arrangements in steel and autos had led to higher prices. Their argument went as follows:

1. The fair pricing rule under the U.S. antidumping law establishes a constructed value, which is the sum of direct and indirect costs and allows for a certain profit margin. However, it does not take into account the fact that Japanese producers can afford lower prices than their U.S. counterparts. Japanese semiconductor manufacturers, like NEC, spread their overhead over a much broader group of products than U.S. semiconductor manufacturers, since they produce not only semiconductors but PCs, telecommunications equipment, and other home appliances.

2. Fair pricing is built on a static notion of pricing. Costs diminish rapidly in the semiconductor industry as experience and production know-how accumulate. A more dynamic notion of pricing would take into account long-run marginal production costs after learning has taken place.

3. The only reason that the Japanese settle is fear of retaliatory tariffs on products completely different from those where alleged unfair practices occur (possible under the 301 provisions of the 1988 Omnibus Trade Act). The Japanese want to avoid an all-out trade war that will hurt producers and consumers throughout the world.

In short, the trade analysts argue that settlements benefit both Japanese and U.S. producers by creating what is in effect government-maintained producers' cartels. With competition restrained, producer earnings in both countries go up at the expense of consumers.

The Industry Association's Position. In 1993, Japan met its obligations under the import promotion agreement. Foreigners supplied 20 percent of the Japanese chip market in the fourth quarter of 1992, compared to only 16 percent the quarter before. In five years, the foreign chip makers' share of the Japanese market had more than doubled. The U.S. Semiconductor Industry Association was calling for further guaranteed targets in the face of stiff opposition from Japanese officials. It had an influential supporter in Laura Tyson, President Clinton's head of the Council of Economic Advisers, who favored forcing foreign countries to open their markets by threatening to raise new barriers against their exports.

American chip makers were doing extremely well, with Intel as the world's largest. It was argued that their success could have been achieved without government interference as standard Japanese memory chips were no rival for advanced U.S. chips and microprocessors. Decline in demand for the Japanese products and rise in demand for those made in the United States were the main reasons that outsiders captured 20 percent of the Japanese market. Trade fairs, seminars, and visits would have happened even without a trade agreement.

The agreement cost consumers up to $4 billion, according to calculations of Brookings Institution economist Kenneth Flamm. The cost was born mainly by U.S. computer companies like Apple. In 1989, the high costs of chips caused this company's profits to decline by a third. Apple, meanwhile, was a main customer of Motorola. Its weak economic performance dampened demand for Motorola's chips. In addition, new South Korean firms such as Hyundai and Samsung were emboldened to enter the U.S. market, and weak Japanese producers such as Oki, Sharp, and Sanyo were saved from potential bankruptcy.

Discussion Questions

1. In light of the charges against it and the changed industry conditions, what should Motorola do?
2. Should it support the industry association's position?
3. Should it continue its aggressive stance of pressuring the U.S. government to take a tough stand against the Japanese?
4. Are numerical targets a good policy for opening foreign markets?
5. Are there no better alternatives?

Endnotes

1. This case was written by Alfred Marcus.
2. David Yoffie and John Coleman, "Motorola and Japan (A)," Harvard Business School Case, February 1992.
3. M. Okuno-Fujiwara, "Industrial Policy in Japan: A Political Economy View," Stanford Center for Economic Policy Research, 1990, pp. 1–33.

CHAPTER

10

Why Governments Are Needed

We hold these truths to be self-evident, that all men are created equal, that they are endowed by their Creator with certain unalienable Rights, that among these are Life, Liberty, and the pursuit of Happiness. That to secure these rights, Governments are instituted among men deriving their just powers from the consent of the Governed.

Declaration of Independence

We the people of the United States, in Order to form a more perfect Union, establish Justice, insure domestic Tranquility, provide for the common defence, promote the general Welfare, and secure the Blessings of Liberty to ourselves and our Posterity, do ordain and establish this Constitution for the United States of America.

Constitution of the United States

Introduction and Chapter Objectives

Public policies come from governments, but why are governments needed? This question acquires great significance as governments throughout the world grow increasingly. They have expanded what they do, taken on new tasks, and run up huge deficits. In 1995, it was estimated that in 10 years the U.S. government deficit would increase from 2.3 percent of the gross domestic product (GDP) to 3.6 percent. The main reason for this increase was growth in entitlement spending (e.g., Social Security, Medicare, and Medicaid). Discretionary spending was projected to grow by 2 percent per year, while spending on entitlements was forecast to increase by 7 percent (see Case 10–A on the Contract with America at the end of this chapter).

Government deficits have seriously affected many nations in the world. They hurt national economies. With governments competing with businesses and consumers for scarce investment capital, interest rates soar. Credit becomes less available. Without foreign investment, government borrowing crowds out private investment. The problem of spiralling deficits raises the question: What is the appropriate role of government?[1] What activities should government carry out? More important, perhaps, what activities can it cease carrying out? What activities can be cut?

The founding documents of the United States provide alternate perspectives. The Declaration of Independence stresses that the main goal of government is to protect liberty, while the Constitution proposes that the main goal is to promote the common welfare. Adam Smith, writing in the same period, held that people should have the liberty to pursue their economic interests so long as there was a corresponding improvement in the social good.[2] If this liberty did not improve society, then government intervention was justified.

Many economists after Smith have debated the question of why government is needed. They usually start with the premise that markets are a superior means to organize production; governments are needed only to correct defects in the functioning of markets. Most economists agree that governments perform critical functions that cannot be performed adequately by markets (e.g., providing police protection, administering justice, and preventing pollution), but they do not agree that governments should be involved in the redistribution of income or take actions to smooth the business cycle. Economists also acknowledge that government actions are not always called for in the face of market defects. The gains from correcting the defects have to be weighed against the costs of administering the government programs. In this chapter, the arguments about why government is needed made by classic liberal, contemporary liberal, and neoconservative economists are compared.

The Need for Government

For business managers, hounded by unnecessary regulation and red tape, the question of why governments are needed is of real concern. The founders of the American republic did not question the need for government, but they were divided about why. The Declaration of Independence starts with the individual's right to life, liberty, and the pursuit of happiness, which government must protect. If government does not live up to its obligations, the people have the right "to alter or to abolish it" and to institute a new government. In contrast, the framers of the Constitution start with collective interests ("We the people"), which state that government should promote justice, order, and the general welfare, and to provide for the common defense.

These great documents reveal an enduring tension among Americans about why governments exist. Some people start from the premise that individual rights are paramount and governments exist to protect liberty, while others start from the premise that collective welfare is paramount and governments exist to further justice. Almost all U.S. politicians are pragmatic; to reach solutions to problems they draw upon arguments from both schools of thought.

In Economic Theory

consumer sovereignty Rule by consumers, or decentralized decision making in the market, rather than centralized control by the government.

While politicians are pragmatic about the role of government, economists offer the strongest body of theory on that role. Economists generally prefer **consumer sovereignty,** or decentralized decision making by consumers in the marketplace, to the centralized control of the government. This preference is based on the efficiency advantages of markets, but it is broader than that and includes economic and technological progress, a rising standard of living, social mobility, and political freedom.[3]

Markets have a number of efficiency advantages. First, they tend to achieve particular purposes at lower costs than government, or they accomplish these purposes better for the same costs. In this way, markets outperform government in static efficiency terms. However, they also outperform it in terms of dynamic efficiency; that is, they are better than government at promoting new technologies, improving product quality, and creating new products.[4] Finally, markets outperform government by stimulating organizational improvements, increasing worker and management motivation, and enhancing business decision making.[5]

Market Defects

One of the main proofs of markets outperforming government is illustrated by the newly industrialized economies of Asia, which are in striking contrast to the state-centered economies of the old Communist bloc countries. Nonetheless, almost all economists admit that markets are not perfect and have certain defects or shortcomings that should be corrected by government action (see Exhibit 10–1). For instance, economic efficiency requires competitive factor and product markets; that is, there must be full market knowledge, full market power by existing producers and consumers, and no obstacles to the free entry of new market participants. These conditions are seldom completely met by markets.[6] Another market defect is the possible inadequate protection of future rights and interests. Government intervention may be justified because private and public perspectives on the valuation of the present and future differ.

Public Goods

Economists admit that even if markets are operating according to theory, they do not provide certain types of public goods that are needed collectively and not individually.

EXHIBIT 10–1 Why Governments Are Needed

The Declaration of Independence:	To preserve liberty.
The Constitution:	To promote the common welfare.
Economic Theory:	To provide for public goods.
	To handle market defects, for example:
	Entry barriers.
	Insufficient consumer knowledge.
	Insufficient consumer power.
	Insufficient protection of future interests.
	To deal with spillovers and externalities.

public goods Broadly shared commodities that people tend to demand in quantities that private markets cannot provide.

Public goods are broadly shared commodities that people tend to demand in quantities that private markets cannot provide. Such goods would not be provided in sufficient quantities were it not for government intervention. For instance, when a given air quality improvement is achieved, the resulting gain is available to everyone. Those who pay for the benefit cannot exclude others from enjoying it. This condition also applies to other public goods, such as national defense, police protection, national parks, and highways. The private market incentive to provide public goods is deficient, even if the preference for them is high.

Spillovers and Externalities

Private market activities also create so-called spillovers or externalities. A positive spillover or externality exists when a producer cannot appropriate all the benefits of the activities it has undertaken. An example would be research and development that yields benefits to society (e.g., employment in subsidiary industries) that the producer cannot capture. Thus, the producer's incentive is to underinvest in the activity unless government subsidizes it. With positive externalities, too little of the good in question is produced; with negative ones too much is made. Negative externalities such as air pollution occur when the producer cannot be charged all the costs. Since the external costs do not enter the calculations the producer makes, the producer manufactures more of the good than is socially beneficial. With both positive and negative externalities, market outcomes need correction to be efficient.

Other Market Defects

Many economists accept that two additional market defects exist. First, to correct for apparent instabilities in the business cycle, the government can implement a variety of fiscal and monetary policies. By themselves, markets may not guarantee a high level of employment, price stability, and a socially desired rate of growth. While Milton Friedman accepts the earlier justifications for government intervention, he contests these premises.[7]

Second, market outcomes may violate cherished values about equality and justice. In the market, a person's distribution of goods depends on factor endowments (e.g., skill and inherited wealth) and the relative prices they command. Society, however, may consider this distribution neither fair nor just. Thus, government may redistribute income through the tax code or the alteration of inheritance laws.

Libertarians reject this argument for two reasons. First, they claim on moral grounds that what someone earns belongs to the person and government has no right to take it away. Second, they argue on practical grounds that if government routinely redistributes income, then the incentive to earn will decline. If this acquisitive instinct diminishes, society is worse off because the economy will not grow as fast.[8]

Imperfect Governments

Where a rationale exists for government involvement, it does not necessarily follow that the government is capable of effectively addressing the problem. While markets are imperfect, governments too have shortcomings, and their ability to correct market imperfections is limited.[9]

In each instance of a market defect, it is necessary to weigh whether the proposed government action would make things better. A helter-skelter approach, where the government tries to correct all that is wrong with markets without first making a careful analysis, is as dangerous to the economy as the defects. The many unintended consequences of this approach tend to complicate matters and make the situation worse rather than better. In the next section, three views of the appropriate role for government—the classic liberal, contemporary liberal, and neoconservative—are summarized and contrasted.

The Classic Liberal View

The best representative of this school is Milton Friedman. His 1962 book, *Capitalism and Freedom*, considered extreme in the 1960s, nearly became the standard wisdom during the Reagan years. Friedman views himself as a classic liberal, not a conservative, because his starting point, like that of Adam Smith, is in opposition to traditional societies that restricted individual liberty.

In traditional societies, people's ability to influence their future is affected by the group to which they belong and the beneficence of the ruling authorities. The modern revolutions that ushered in capitalism stripped away the importance of inherited categories such as peasant and aristocrat, Christian and Jew, or Caucasian and Hispanic. Market economies gave people the right to make transactions without being limited by these restrictions. States became governed by the rule of law rather than the arbitrary whims of kings and nobles.

Friedman has written that "an impersonal market separates economic activities from political views and protects men from being discriminated against in their economic activities for reasons that are irrelevant to their productivity."[10] No government body, no matter what higher purpose it appeals to, should stand in the way of economic liberty. The emancipation of individual talent, energy, and initiative is critical to achieving the economic growth that is synonymous with modern societies.

Friedman believes that a market system provides this freedom for the individual. In a market, people do business with one another, not because of some group to which they belong, but because they offer each other a good or service that is of high quality, low price, or has some other desirable feature.

If forced to choose, Friedman's primary allegiance is to the individual freedom that the market provides, even above economic prosperity. Since individual freedom is his primary value, Friedman's position has been labeled libertarian to distinguish it from economists who defend markets on utilitarian grounds (i.e., they yield prosperity). Markets are a superior means of social organization because they allow for voluntary cooperation based on free discussion, which is the purpose of a liberal society (see Exhibit 10–2).

Democratically elected governments, according to Friedman, have deficiencies that markets do not have. For instance, when a democratically elected government makes a decision passed by a majority, all citizens have to obey, even those who oppose the measure. Once made, the decision is binding on everyone. In contrast, each person in the

Exhibit 10–2 The Classic Liberal View

Markets are superior because they promote liberty:
Grant right to make transactions as individuals.
Permit free discussion/voluntary cooperation.
Not binding on those not subject to transactions (unlike government).

Governments needed when markets are not practical:
To protect people and the nation from coercion: "civil order."
To resolve disputes between conflicting parties: "rule maker and umpire."
To protect consumers from excessive market power: "technical monopoly."
To protect individuals from the actions of others: "neighborhood effects."
To act for those incapable or incompetent to act for themselves: "paternalism."

Governments in pursuing above should not restrict freedom of entry:
Retards technological innovation.

Governments should limit themselves to areas of technical competence:
Even with obvious market defect like pollution.

market decides if and how much of a particular good or service to acquire. Each chooses whether to buy, sell, or stay out of the market altogether. The individual makes this choice without being bound by the community's interests as represented by the will of a political majority.[11]

A political decision about national defense spending compels all citizens to conform to its mandate. No longer is each citizen in a position to weigh the evidence and choose how much national defense the person might need or want. However, Friedman recognizes that in the case of indivisible matters such as "protection of the individual and the nation from coercion," reliance on the market is not practical.[12] If each person or group chose the type of protection it wanted (its own weapons and weapon systems, private armies, and security forces), anarchy would result similar to that in Beirut during the 1970s and 1980s or Somalia in the early 1990s.

No settled society is possible under such conditions, nor can the orderly selling and buying necessary for the exercise of free choice in a market exist. So classic liberals accept the cost of relying on government to preserve civil order even if it strains the social fabric. Since the cost exists, reliance on government should be limited to the issues where people have common views and no alternatives are feasible. For example, nearly all people agree about the need for police that guarantee civil order and armies for external defense.

Appropriate Areas for Government

Thus, classic liberals accept that government has an appropriate role to play in certain areas. Besides domestic order and defense, it has an appropriate role as *rule maker and umpire*.[13] The interactions that take place in a market are like a game where the players have to respect the rules. These rules have to be interpreted, enforced, and modified.

When individuals have disputes, someone has to resolve them. A judicial system is needed.

Rule Maker and Umpire. People's freedoms come into conflict. One person's right to live, for instance, comes into conflict with another's desire to kill. The government has to guarantee that the freedom to maintain life takes precedence. The government also must be the arbiter between the freedom to combine and the freedom to compete. The European tradition has favored the freedom to combine, while the United States has inclined toward the freedom to compete. In Europe, competitors have had the right to fix prices, divide up markets, and take other actions to keep out potential competitors. In the United States, they have been restricted from doing so and have had to compete by selling better products.

Another case where freedoms conflict concerns the definition of property rights. For instance, does title to a piece of property give owners the right to the minerals in the ground below it or control over what goes on in the air above it? Can owners charge a nuisance price for noise if someone flies an airplane above their property, or must the owners pay the airplane pilots to stop them from making the noise? These are the kinds of questions the judicial system attempts to resolve.

Friedman includes the government's constitutional responsibility "to coin money" and maintain a monetary system as part of the responsibility to be a rule maker and umpire.[14] Friedman does not favor using monetary policies to stabilize economic activity. According to Friedman, the government should increase the money supply in accord with the historic growth rate of the economy (about 3 percent per year), and should not have discretionary authority to adjust the money supply to stimulate or suppress economic activity. As rule-maker and umpire, the government should be neutral.

technical monopoly The capacity of a company, because of its proficiency, to drive all competitors from the market.

Correct Market Defects. Classic liberals also believe that it is appropriate for government to correct market defects.[15] One of these defects is **technical monopoly,** that is, a company can gain near complete dominance because it is technically more proficient than its competitors. It might legitimately acquire some advantage—economies of scale or scope—that drive virtually all its competitors from the market. The government faces a difficult dilemma because technical monopoly reduces the choices that consumers have in the market. The dominant firm, if no substitutes exist for what it sells, can use its monopoly power to withhold the products from the market and arbitrarily raise their prices.

In many industries, it is possible for firms to gain market dominance via some type of technical advantage. In such industries as electric utilities, the argument that technical monopolies exist has been used to justify regulating utility prices and entry to the industry. Prices are regulated to prevent the monopolist from gaining unfair advantage over consumers. In exchange for limitations on the monopolist's profits, it is guaranteed entry restrictions. No firm can challenge its position, as the government does not let potential challengers compete with the dominant firm.

The United States has favored regulation to deal with technical monopoly. Many European nations, on the other hand, consider public ownership as the answer to this problem. Friedman offers a third alternative: Allow the monopoly to exist without government controls.[16] As long as the government does not enforce entry restrictions, the monopolist must always be on guard against the threat of technological challenge from a latent rival. If regulation were in place, it would not have to face this challenge. Entry barriers make its markets uncontestable, but they also shield it from technological change that can benefit the public. Free markets work when a firm has gained uncontested dominance through technical means, so long as rivals are not excluded entry into the market through regulation. Friedman's point is that technological stagnation is likely with public regulation.

neighborhood effect Negative by-products for society created as a result of a transaction between two parties who themselves may be better off.

Another type of market defect that classic liberals recognize is a **neighborhood effect.** The premise of a free market is that when two people voluntarily make a deal, society as a whole will become richer from the aggregation of many such deals. However, what happens if the transactions cause a by-product (e.g., hazardous waste) that society has to clean up? The parties to the transaction may be better off, but society as a whole has to pay the costs.

Friedman's answer to the neighborhood effect is simple: Society must charge the parties to the deal the costs of the cleanup because they are responsible. Whatever damage they generate has to be internalized in the price. By doing so, the market defect (i.e., the price of pollution, which is not counted in the transaction) is corrected. The market price then reflects the true social costs of the deal and the parties have to adjust accordingly. Thus, only deals in the social interest, will be consummated.[17]

To solve this dilemma, however, the U.S. government does not generally supplement the price system, but it regulates the polluter. Friedman maintains that whenever government intervenes in business activity, there is a cost in reduced freedom. He also questions whether government, even by imposing a tax or charge on the polluting parties, is able to determine what damage has been caused or what the monetary value of the damage is. When pollution is involved, the damage is often long term (increased sickness and disease) and intangible (reduced visibility). To collect, the government would have to set up a burdensome administrative apparatus.

Paternalism. A final area where government intervention is appropriate, according to Friedman, is to act on *paternalistic* grounds for those who are incapable or incompetent to act for themselves.[18] The word *paternalism* is an anachronism: remember, Friedman wrote his book in 1962. However, his argument still has merit. Markets demand a high level of capability and competence. People have to be able to reason about their self-interest, absorb information pertaining to it, and then successfully make transactions that make them better off. Not everybody is up to this task. Thus, Friedman provides the rationale for welfare state activities that protect people who are otherwise unable to care for themselves (for example, children, handicapped, and the mentally ill).

The classic liberals' rationales for government activities, even with these qualifications, are extensive. The government has a role to play in defending the nation, providing for law and order, defining property rights, adjudicating disputes, enforcing contracts, preserving competition, establishing a monetary framework, countering technical monopolies and neighborhood effects, and supplementing private charity by helping people who cannot otherwise help themselves. The list of appropriate government functions is quite large, but not as large as the actual list of programs that the government of the United States carries out. (see Exhibit 10–3).[19]

EXHIBIT 10–3 Federal Government Actions that Classic Liberals Cannot Justify

Price supports for agriculture.
Tariffs on imports or restrictions on exports.
Rent controls.
Wage and price controls.
Minimum wages.
Maximum interest rates.
Detailed regulations of particular industries.
Mandatory social security, old-age, and retirement programs.
Occupational licensing.
Public housing.
Military conscription.
The creation and maintenance of national parks.
The public delivery of mail.
Publicly owned and operated toll roads.

The Contemporary Liberal View

A good representative of the contemporary liberal school is the Harvard economist Richard Musgrave who, with his wife Peggy Musgrave, has written extensively on public finance. Contemporary liberals like the Musgraves also have a preference for decentralized decision making and individual choice by consumers in the marketplace. Their justifications for government activity rest on a variety of market imperfections with which classic liberals would agree.[20]

1. *Uncompetitive factor and product markets*. Free entry, full market knowledge, and market power on the part of producers and consumers are needed. Government assures competition and expands producer and consumer knowledge. Thus, it endeavors to prevent monopoly and require that warning labels be attached to products such as cigarettes.
2. *Public goods*. Government should provide such public goods as national defense, education, roads, and canals. Such goods would not be provided in ample quantities were it not for government intervention. The providers could not appropriate sufficient benefits for themselves to justify creating the amount demanded by the public.

Contemporary liberals differ from classic liberals in adding the following justifications to their list (see Exhibit 10–4):

3. *Justice and equality*. These cherished values may be violated by the market. Thus, government has to make adjustments in the distribution of income by means of the tax systems and other means such as the laws of inheritance.
4. *Employment, price stability, and growth*. The market system may not guarantee a high level of employment, price stability, and a socially desired rate of growth without government intervention. To correct instability in the business cycle, the government can use fiscal (budgetary) and monetary policies.

Exhibit 10–4 The Contemporary Liberal View

Governments needed to deal with market defects:
Uncompetitive factor and product markets.
Public goods.
Justice and equality.
Employment, price stability, and growth.

Even contemporary liberals, despite their commitment to a larger role for government, admit that governments can err and be inefficient in attempting to remedy market defects.

Three Functions

Contemporary liberals divide the appropriate functions of government into three categories: allocation, distribution, and stabilization. Conflicts can exist among these functions and resolving them is a major challenge that governments face.

Allocation. Both classic and contemporary liberals accept nearly the same position regarding allocation of public goods. All members of society, not just those who purchase the good, enjoy the benefits. The private market incentive for providing such public goods as national defense or police protection is not great, even if the preference for them is high. Therefore, government intervenes; in this instance, voting by ballot replaces free market decision making.

A distinction, however, must be made between public provision of goods and public production. While the public provision of goods is relatively high (at least 20 percent) in all countries in the world—both those with large public and those with large private sectors—in only a few countries is there a large degree of public production. The United States is roughly equivalent to other countries in the world with regard to the provision of public goods, but ranks low in public production (only 12 percent). Most public goods (e.g., weapons and weapons systems) in the United States are purchased from the private sector (i.e., the defense industry).[21]

distribution Government alteration of society's income toward greater equality.

Distribution. Contemporary liberals accept but classic liberals reject **distribution** as a government function. Unlike classic liberals, contemporary liberals argue that some alteration in the pattern of inequality is necessary. Contemporary liberals are critical of the tenet of welfare economics, the Pareto rule, that holds that a change in economic conditions improves the welfare of society when it makes the situation of Person A better without Persons B or C becoming worse off. Someone gains, but no one loses. However, this may mean that excessive concentrations of wealth exist at the top of the scale and inadequate incomes exist at the lower end. The blight of poverty then affects nearly everyone as it spawns crime, drug addiction, and numerous other social problems. Thus, contemporary liberals call for tax transfers that tax the wealthiest to subsidize low-income people. The cost is in deadweight losses that arise from the inefficiencies of administering government programs. Another cost is reduced efficiency for the economy as a whole as the wealthy may choose leisure over work.

stabilization
Government control over budgets and monetary policy is used to maintain high levels of growth and employment and low levels of inflation.

Stabilization. Another government function over which contemporary and classic liberals disagree is **stabilization.** There are substantial fluctuations in the business cycle; contemporary liberals believe that it is the role of government to try to control these cycles.[22] Unemployment and inflation may plague society unless government acts to change the level of aggregate demand by means of taxation and consumption. Of course, government, by making mistakes, could cause destabilization. This is the essence of Friedman's main critique of macroeconomic policies.

Moreover, economies do not operate in isolation but are linked to other economies by means of trade and capital flows. These flows have been increasing rapidly in the post–World War II period. They make it difficult for any single national government to control its economy by means of macroeconomic stabilization. International cooperation is needed but difficult to achieve. Still, there is agreement in most countries in the world to stabilize the business cycle by means of monetary and fiscal policies.

The Neoconservative View

neoconservatives
Economic view that considers government shortcomings before advocating that government act to correct market defects.

Many people who formerly were contemporary liberals became neoconservatives after the failure of government programs such as the War on Poverty and the Vietnam War. The views of neoconservatives have been elegantly summarized by Rand Institute economist Charles Wolf, Jr.[23] Classic and contemporary liberals admit that government failure is possible. **Neoconservatives** emphasize this possibility. They ask that the shortcomings of the government be compared with the shortcomings of the market before proposals to remedy market defects are carried out (see Exhibit 10–5).

The analysis of government failures should be expanded to include the following:

1. Government is often the exclusive provider of public goods and has near monopoly status.
2. Uncertainty surrounds the means of providing public goods (e.g., on education, what constitutes good teaching; on defense, what is needed to guarantee national security).
3. The unanticipated results of government activities (e.g., good intentions to provide for the poor may result in welfare dependence).

EXHIBIT 10–5 The Neoconservative View

Compare government shortcomings with market shortcomings:
Government exclusive provider.
Uncertain technology for providing goods.
Unanticipated results.

Neoconservatives judge markets and governments on the basis of efficiency and equity. In their emphasis on equity they resemble contemporary liberals. They have looked very closely at the definitions of equity. Rawlsian notions of equity favor the lot of the least advantaged in society before the lot of the most advantaged. (Marx would distribute to each person according to the person's needs and demand from each according to the person's abilities.) Neoconservatives favor equality of opportunity over that of outcome.

Neoconservatives accept public goods arguments for government intervention. There may be positive externalities from government investment in research and development—benefits not appropriable by firms operating in the private market.[24] Another case of underinvestment, if only private market forces are operating, is philanthropy, where the benefits are available to society at large (less crime, drug addiction, and fewer social problems) but the costs are borne exclusively by the donor.

In some cases of traditionally labeled "market failure," neoconservatives are skeptical of why government should be involved. Their arguments about technical monopoly, for instance, are similar to those made by Milton Friedman. So-called technical monopoly situations may not require government intervention if there are contestable markets. If new entrants can challenge the monopoly, its status is temporary. If a firm has to be constantly on guard against this situation, it cannot exploit consumers.

Acceptable Government Involvement

Neoconservatives accept a broad range of government involvement. First, government action is justified in providing regulatory services in such areas as the environment (where there are externalities), food and drug controls (where consumers lack information), and radio and television licensing (where there otherwise would be a monopoly). Second, it is justified in producing pure public goods such as national defense, police protection, and the administration of justice. These goods cannot be provided by the private sector. Third, the government is justified in producing quasi-public goods such as education, postal services, and health research. These goods may also be provided by the private sector (so there is some competition), but not in the quantities required by the public. Finally, some transfer programs such as social security and welfare are justified.

Neoconservatives believe that in theory these activities are justified, but in practice these offerings have proliferated too greatly. Wolf, for instance, argues that demand for government intervention is inflated for a variety of reasons (see Exhibit 10–6).[25]

EXHIBIT 10–6 Reasons that Demand for Government Programs Is Inflated

- Increased public awareness of market shortcomings.
- Less tolerance for these shortcomings.
- Greater degree of political organization and enfranchisement.
- The rewards to legislators and government officials to publicize problems and find solutions.
- Legislators' need to show that they are taking dramatic actions so that they will be reelected.
- The decoupling of burdens and benefits.

Decoupling of Burdens and Benefits

To explain government growth, neoconservatives emphasize the decoupling of burdens and benefits. Decoupling explains why some programs like gun control are so difficult to pass. The public that would benefit is large and dispersed, while those that would bear the burden—the gun lobby—are concentrated and well organized. On the other hand, some programs help specific groups, while the burden is widely dispersed throughout the public. The specific groups have a large incentive to organize and to appropriate the benefit, while the broad public, where each person may lose only a few dollars, has little incentive to organize and to oppose the program. Thus, farmers and retirees are formidable political blocs capable of winning substantial gains through the political process because of the decoupling of burdens and benefits. These two types of decoupling the neoconservatives call **microdecoupling.**

microdecoupling The dominance of small, concentrated special interest groups in politics over the larger, dispersed and less well-organized majority.

Another type of decoupling occurs when the vast majority enjoys the benefits of government programs, such as progressive taxation (because the vast majority is relatively poor), while a small minority bear the burden (the small but wealthy minority that provides most of the tax base). As long as political power is based on majority rule, there is a danger of the majority exploiting a minority in a democracy. This type of decoupling the neoconservatives call *macrodecoupling*.[26]

Government Incapacity

Neoconservatives also stress the incapacity of government to effectively manage programs that have been created. Conditions such as the following lead to ineffective management:

1. Without competition, it is hard for the government to provide services at adequate levels of efficiency and quality.
2. It is difficult to define and measure the output of government programs.
3. There is no bottom-line termination mechanism.

In a market, costs are linked to prices by consumers who decide what to buy. In government, revenues come from taxes linked only indirectly to services. Tax payers do not directly obtain goods or services for tax dollars. They express their will by voting. Politicians support programs they oppose, but they also vote for programs that taxpayers favored. The taxpayers cannot unbundle their support for politicians in the same way they unbundle their decisions to buy goods and services in the market.

The result is that government agencies have less need than businesses to be precise about their actions. The standards they use can be vague. Private internal goals may dominate and take precedence over public goals.

Additional problems affect the supply of government services. First, the systems that government is attempting to influence are very complex. Efforts to correct market failures in one area may create unanticipated consequences in another. In addition, although inequality of income is less of a problem, inequality of power and privilege among government officials can be problematic. When one group has the right to command and coerce another, abuses are likely.[27]

Traditional Conservatives

Although not a major part of present-day economic thought, another increasingly important group is traditional conservatives. They do not share the individualistic premises of the economists, do not value individual freedom as the highest good, and do not see free markets, inviolable property rights, and limited governments as the means to assure that freedom. Rather, they follow in the footsteps of Edmund Burke, the 18th-century British philosopher, who was a critic of the French Revolution and individual rights. The traditional conservatives argue that institutions like the family, church, and state are important in stabilizing the social order. These collective institutions, which help protect the delicate fabric of society and promote law and order, come before individual rights and liberties.

The Fusionist Conservative Coalition

The fusionist conservative coalition of the modern Republican party, which elected Ronald Reagan and George Bush, appealed to both classic liberals and traditional conservatives. Reagan, as a representative of this coalition, showed his hostility to big government and favored market forces. At the same time, he supported large increases in defense expenditures and maintained that the family and church should be relied upon to mitigate social problems. The eclectic forces brought together in the Republican coalition helps explain its inconsistencies on an issue like abortion, which classic liberals permit and traditional conservatives prohibit.

If their viewpoints are so different, how could classic liberals and traditional conservatives find a common home in the Republican party? An important reason is that they both vigorously opposed communism, the classic liberals for communism's repressing individual rights and markets, and the traditional conservatives for communism's atheism and its opposition to organized religion.[28] The demise of worldwide communism may spell the end of the coalition as religious elements threaten to dominate it.

Government in Practice

Government policies are not crafted by economic theoreticians but by politicians, and fathoming what politicians do and why they do it is a complicated matter. The deliberations that determine political outcomes are influenced by the constitutional system of checks and balances instituted by the founders of the American republic. The founders imagined a large country with diverse interests. Fearful of a powerful majority, they tried to create a system where no faction could dominate. The participants in political controversies, therefore, are wide-ranging and diverse. They include citizens, interest groups, corporations, trade associations, environmental organizations, federal bureaucrats, and the media. Different professional groups—scientists, physicians, engineers, and lawyers—provide expert opinion. Sages, seers, and pundits testify in front of congressional committees, appear on talk shows, and write columns for newspapers. Policy is affected by factual information, theory, beliefs, values, attitudes, conjectures, statistics, and anecdotes. When economists are consulted, it is simply as part of this process.

Among economists there is a broad consensus that, all things being equal, markets are superior to government in achieving efficient outcomes. There is consensus about market defects that justify government intervention to guarantee market efficiency. However, when it comes to applying principles, economists disagree.

Why Governments Have Grown

Governments have grown for many reasons, most of them not because of matters of economic principle. To get a sense of the magnitude of this growth, it is useful to compare 1929 statistics with current ones. In 1929, there were 68,000 civilian federal employees in Washington, and 500,000 federal civil servants in the nation, of whom 300,000 worked for the Post Office.[29] Nonetheless, the federal government was smaller than companies such as United States Steel, General Motors, and Standard Oil. By 1940, however, there were a million federal employees, and by 1970 nearly three million. To this day, the government surpasses most corporations in the number of employees.

Theories on why government has grown are plentiful.[30]

Economic Development. In undeveloped nations, taxes and social security contributions typically account for a much lower percentage of gross national product (GNP) than in developed nations. The "law of increasing state activity" attributes growth in government to the complex social changes associated with industrialization.

Party Politics. Whether a nation's government is controlled by left-wing or right-wing political parties provides a strong key to the relative degree of change in government spending. There is a strong positive correlation between the size of increases in the public sector and the degree to which left-wing parties dominate.

Voting. Alexis de Tocqueville, in his classic formulation, attributes the expansion of government expenditures to the spread of the franchise and an increase in economic equality.[31] As the franchise is extended, the income of the median voter declines. The median voter is able to redistribute income.

The Supply of Revenues. Economic development, party politics, and voting are demand-side theories. Other theories focus on the supply side, explaining government growth in terms of the public revenues that can be sustained through taxation. The bracket creep explanation of government growth, for example, holds that a progressive income tax, with inflation and unindexed brackets, moves taxpayers into higher marginal brackets and leads to increased revenues and a real increase in public expenditures. Decreases in self-employment lead to increases in taxable earnings, as employees who work for others are less able to under-report their income than are the self-employed.

Legislative Decision Making. Other explanations for increased government expenditures focus on institutions. For example, in a simplified world, legislators are likely to favor all bills benefiting their own districts. When the costs of such bills are allocated across all districts, legislators will agree to pass all bills so long as the ones that benefit their own districts are supported.

Bureaucratic Process. Another theory is that the size and the structure of the budget are the inadvertent result of bureaucratic drift.[32] How bureaucrats solve year-to-year problems influences the problems and sets of solutions available in subsequent years. Short-sighted yearly decisions lead to cumulative long-term problems.

The size and scope of governments in countries with different systems vary a great deal. The United States is behind many other countries in total taxes as a percentage of GNP. The relative size of the government sector is lower in the United States than in any other major developed country except Japan. No theory provides definitive guidance about what the size and scope of government should take in countries with different social, political, and cultural systems.

Conclusions

Economic theory is one of the main foundations for contemporary ideology about the state. Economists believe that markets are the superior means for organizing a nation's economic life; their preference is for a minimal state. Most believe that the individual consumer should be sovereign. Economists contrast *consumer sovereignty* with rule by government. Consumers should govern because individuals are best able to judge their needs and preferences through the transactions they make in the marketplace. Through the invisible hand of the marketplace, society prospers. Reflective of those marketplace transactions are the laws of supply and demand, which move the goods of a society to their most productive uses. No central planning agency of government can achieve with the same wisdom and foresight what freely cooperating consumers accomplish on their own.

Economists, however, are not anarchists about government. Most economists accept that government should play an important role: provide for the common defense, establish domestic order, make laws and settle disputes, regulate unfair business practices, protect citizens from monopoly and the undesired side effects (externalities) of market activities, and provide them with some of the collective goods (e.g., highways) they seek but which their voluntary behavior does not provide. The question is not so much one of permitting or not permitting government activity, but of determining the proper mix of government and markets in a well-functioning system.

Even though economists share a preference for markets and recognize that government has a role to play in correcting market defects, they divide with regard to the following points:

1. Classic liberals emphasize individual liberty and believe that big government is the gravest threat. They prefer a minimal state in which the functions and size of government are severely limited. Every infringement by government on individual rights is to be avoided.

2. Contemporary liberals begin with community values, such as justice and the common welfare, instead of individual happiness. To promote community goals, they accept that the government should try to smooth the business cycle and that its programs should redistribute income from the wealthy to the less advantaged (see the special feature, "On Property and Poverty"). In this way, all people are on a more equal footing in the competition that goes on in the marketplace.

Special Feature

On Property and Poverty

It is interesting to note that classic liberals and contemporary liberals both can appeal to John Locke's views on property.* Locke believed that property was the result of people's hard work, applied skills, and unusual talent and that therefore they were entitled to the fruits of their labor. On the other hand, he felt that no person should own more property than that person could properly use. According to this "spoilage principle," the government had the right to redistribute any excess.

With regard to poverty, the classic liberal would like to see problems like poverty solved by the voluntary actions of private charities and social welfare agencies, but recognizes that government might have to play a role. The contemporary liberal stresses that in an increasingly interdependent society, it is impossible for people to participate in the economy in isolation from each other. Whenever voluntary deals are made, they are likely to affect others who are not immediate parties to the deals. The right to freedom, moreover, is not sufficient if one does not also possess the means, that is, the resources and educational attainments, to express that freedom. Thus, government must give the disadvantaged a place to start in life so that they can catch up with the more advantaged.

All three ideologies agree that unless the problems of the disadvantaged are addressed, society will face more crime, social conflict, and discord, which will hurt everyone. The neoconservatives simply emphasize that there may be little that government can effectively do in this area.

*P. Navarro, *The Policy Game* (New York: John Wiley, 1984).

3. Neoconservatives are skeptical of the government's abilities to achieve public goals. They emphasize that whenever the government acts, unanticipated side effects that run counter to what the government intends can occur. Thus, in trying to provide for aid to the disadvantaged, the government may stifle individual initiative. While its aims are noble, the government's capabilities to remake society are limited.

Discussion Questions

1. Compare the views expressed in the Declaration of Independence and the Constitution concerning why government is needed? Are these views really so different?
2. Why do economists prefer markets to governments?
3. What is a market defect? Give some examples.
4. What is a spillover? Give an example of a positive and a negative spillover.
5. Are governments perfect? If so, what difference does it make?
6. Friedman cites the benefits of an "impersonal market." What are they?
7. What is wrong with democracy, according to Friedman? Why are markets superior?
8. Why can't the armed forces be privatized? Why can't the police be privatized? Would the justice system work better if it were privatized? Would jails and schools be better run if they were privatized? Isn't Friedman really a big government liberal?

9. What do you think about Friedman's argument about contestable markets (freedom of entry) in the case of technical monopoly?
10. Do you think pollution taxes are a good idea? Why or why not?
11. Why doesn't Friedman's paternalism argument justify social security?
12. What is a public good? Why does the government have to intervene to provide it?
13. How do the views of contemporary liberals differ from the views of classic liberals like Friedman?
14. How do the views of neoconservatives differ from the views of classic liberals like Friedman?
15. How do the views of neoconservatives differ from the views of contemporary liberals?
16. What is microdecoupling? What is macrodecoupling?
17. Why is government not better at providing goods and services to the public? Why is it not more efficient?
18. What is the fusionist conservative coalition?
19. What are some reasons for the growth of government?

Endnotes

1. Jonathan Rauch, "The Long Good-Bye," *National Journal*, Feb. 22, 1992, pp. 438–41.
2. Dennis Collins, "Adam Smith's Social Contract," *Business and Professional Ethics* 7, pp. 119–46.
3. M. Friedman and R. Friedman, *Free to Choose: A Personal Statement* (New York: Avon Books, 1980).
4. "Dear Landlord," *The Economist*, February 9, 1991, pp. 75–76 (a review of "Directly Unproductive Profit-seeking Activities," by J. Bhagwati, in *Journal of Political Economy*, 1982, p. 90); C. Wolf, Jr., *Markets or Governments: Choosing between Imperfect Alternatives* (Cambridge, Mass.: MIT Press, 1988).
5. H. Leibenstein, "A Branch of Economics Is Missing: Micro-Micro Theory," *Journal of Economic Literature* 17 (1979), pp. 477–502.
6. R. Musgrave and P. Musgrave, "Fiscal Functions: An Overview," in *The Politics of American Economic Policy Making*, ed. P. Peretz (Armonk, N.Y.: M. E. Sharpe, 1987), pp. 3–22.
7. M. Friedman, *Capitalism and Freedom* (Chicago: University of Chicago Press, 1962).
8. G. Gilder, *Wealth and Poverty* (New York: Basic Books, 1981).
9. Wolf, *Markets or Governments*.
10. Cited by P. Navarro, *The Policy Game* (New York: John Wiley, 1984).
11. Friedman, *Capitalism and Freedom*.
12. Ibid., p. 23.
13. Ibid.
14. Ibid.
15. Ibid.
16. Ibid.
17. Ibid.
18. Ibid., pp. 31–32.
19. Ibid.

20. R. Musgrave and P. Musgrave, "Fiscal Functions: An Overview from Musgrave and Musgrave," *Public Finance in Theory and Practice*, 4th ed. (New York: New York University Press, 1984), pp. 3–22.
21. Ibid.
22. Ibid.
23. Wolf, *Markets or Governments*.
24. Ibid.
25. Ibid.
26. Ibid.
27. Wolf, *Markets or Governments;* Richard Rose, "What if Anything Is Wrong with Big Government?" *Journal of Public Policy*, 1981, pp. 5–37.
28. Wolf, *Markets or Governments*.
29. B. D. Porter, "Parkinson's Law Revisited: War and the Growth of American Government," *The Public Interest*, Summer 1980.
30. Patrick Larkey et al., "Theorizing about the Growth of Government: A Research Assessment," *Journal of Public Policy* 1, pt. 2 (May 1981), p. 167; D. R. Cameron, "The Expansion of the Public Economy: A Comparative Analysis," *American Political Science Review* 72 (1978), pp. 1243–61; J. B. Kau and P. H. Rubin, "The Size of Government," *Public Choice* 37, no. 2 (1981), pp. 261–74; A. Meltzer and S. Richard, "A Rational Theory of the Size of Government," *Journal of Political Economy* 89, no. 5 (Oct. 1981), pp. 914–27; A. T. Peacock and J. Wiseman, *The Growth of Public Expenditures in the United States*, (Princeton, N.J.: Princeton University Press, 1961), as cited by P. Larkey et al., "Theorizing about the Growth of Government," p. 167.
31. Alexis de Tocqueville, *Democracy in America* (Oxford: Oxford World Classics, 1835).
32. C. E. Lindblom, "The Science of 'Muddling Through,'" in H. I. Ansoff, ed., *Business Strategy* (New York: Penguin Books, 1977), pp. 41–60.

Case 10–A
Contract with America (A): How to Respond?[1]

The 104th Congress begins work on January 4, 1995. The new Republican majority has promised to make a quick impact. The Contract with America program, upon which many Republican legislators ran, has these provisions:[2]

> *The Fiscal Responsibility Act:* A balanced budget tax limitation amendment and a legislative line-item veto to restore fiscal responsibility to an out-of-control Congress, requiring it to live under the same fiscal constraints as families and businesses. To do so will mean $500 to $700 billion in spending reductions over five years. The Republicans have promised to cut a number of programs.
>
> *The American Dream Restoration Act:* A $500 per child tax credit, repeal of the marriage tax penalty, and creation of American Dream Savings Accounts to provide middle-class tax relief.
>
> *The National Security Restoration Act:* Restoration of national security funding to strengthen national defense and maintain U.S. credibility around the world.
>
> *The Senior Citizens Fairness Act:* A raise in the Social Security earnings limit, which currently

forces seniors out of the workforce. This bill would allow a retiree to earn up to $30,000 before Social Security benefits are curtailed.

The Job Creation and Wage Enhancement Act: Small business incentives and a capital gains tax cut. The plan is likely to cost $56 billion over five years.

The Committee for Economic Development (CED) has to decide how to respond to the newest Republican proposals.[3] The CED is a research and education organization that seeks solutions to pressing social and economic issues that affect the long-term health of the U.S. economy. Made up mostly of business executives from large companies, the CED has for 50 years developed public policy recommendations that contribute to preserving and strengthening a free society, achieving economic growth, increasing productivity, providing equal opportunity, and improving the quality of life. Many of its recent pamphlets consider budget deficits and tax cuts.

You have been sent by the CEO of your company to attend the January 4 CED meeting. The purpose of this meeting is to hammer out a CED position on the new Republican proposals. You hear the following talk by the economist Martin Alford.

Monstrous Deficits: The Most Critical Problem Facing America?

Are monstrous deficits the most critical problem facing America?[4] Is the federal debt going to lead to a terrible cataclysm, to the end of America as we know it? After all, as comedian Robin Williams says, "What are a bunch of zeroes among friends?"

Deficits and Debt. Let's start with a few definitions and facts. The debt consists of accumulated loans to the U.S. Treasury in the form of interest-bearing bonds sold to private investors, government agencies, and the Federal Reserve Bank. The federal government normally sells these bonds because it does not have enough receipts from taxes and user charges to pay for its expenditures. It has to borrow because taxes are not high enough to cover expenditures.

Debt is a stock figure, like the amount of water in a bathtub at one time, but deficits are a flow figure, the amount of water running into the tub (see Exhibits 1 and 2). For most of the period since World War II, deficits were not a factor. However, the situation changed in the 1970s (see Exhibit 3).

EXHIBIT 1 Rising Deficits . . .

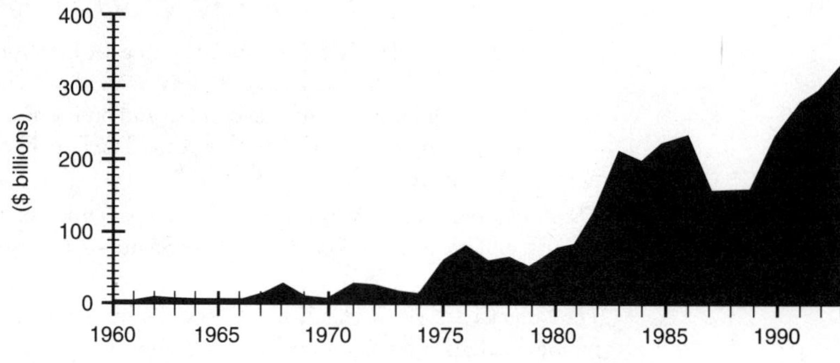

EXHIBIT 2 . . . and Rising Debt

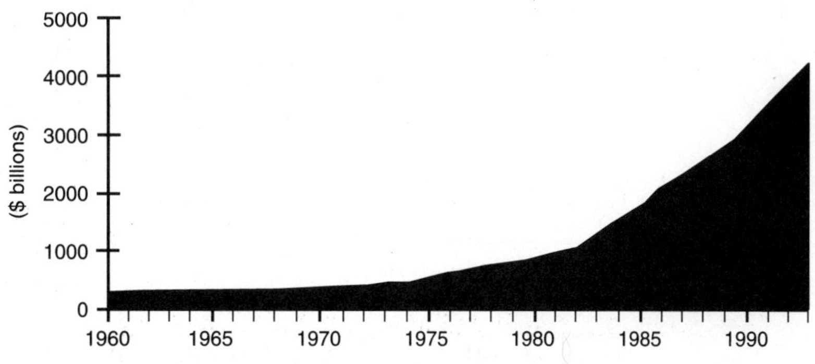

EXHIBIT 3 U.S. Federal Government Deficits and Debt, 1950–88 (in $ billions)

	Flow Deficits (% of GNP)			Stock Debt	
	Receipts	*Expenditures*	*Deficit*	*Amount*	*% of GNP*
1950–54	17.7%	18.0%	− .3%	$ 271	73%
1955–59	17.4	17.9	− .5	288	58
1960–64	18.1	18.8	− .7	317	49
1965–69	18.4	19.3	− .9	367	38
1970–74	18.4	19.6	−1.2	486	33
1975–79	18.3	21.3	−3.0	834	33
1980–84	19.1	23.2	−4.1	1,577	42
1985–88	18.9	23.2	−4.3	2,611	54

GNP = Gross national product.

Debt Run-Up during the 1960s and 1970s. President Lyndon Johnson thought he could conduct two wars at once (poverty and Vietnam) without raising taxes. After the Arab oil embargo and OPEC price increases for petroleum, the nation had to contend with stagflation—high inflation and low growth. Stop-and-go economic policies were the result. First, the U.S. government tried to curtail inflation by slowing the economy. When unemployment grew, it introduced a stimulus—a higher deficit. At more than 20 percent of national spending, the federal government has a large effect on aggregate demand. The English economist John Maynard Keynes prescribed a deficit as the cure for the Great Depression, but in an inflationary economy the deficit yielded higher prices. The spiral continued.

A Keynesian stimulus to spur demand when the economy is underperforming has to be matched by a contraction in government activity when the economy heats up; otherwise inflation is the inevitable result. Politicians, however, lacked the discipline to cut back government budgets.

EXHIBIT 4 All Government Tax Collections as Percentage of GDP, 1990

U.S.	30%
Japan	30
Canada	34
U.K.	35
Germany	37
Italy	40
France	43

GDP = Gross domestic product.

EXHIBIT 5 All Government Expenditures as a Percentage of the GDP, 1990

Japan	32%
U.S.	36
U.K.	41
Canada	44
Germany	45
France	50
Italy	52

GDP = Gross domestic product.

Reagan and Bush Tackle the Problem during the 1980s and Early 1990s. President Ronald Reagan promised but failed to reduce government expenditures. He cut tax rates and raised defense spending, hoping that with lower taxes people would have the incentive to earn more (the supply-side theory). As the economy picked up, Reagan believed that government revenues would grow and budgetary deficits decline. Unfortunately, his tax cuts were introduced during a terrible recession. The Federal Reserve Board was trying to put an end to the double-digit inflation that Reagan inherited from the Carter administration. It slowed the economy by cutting the money supply. A slower economy meant a rising deficit.

The debt swelled throughout the 1980s. To reduce it, either taxes had to be raised or expenditures cut. U.S. taxes were low compared with other countries (see Exhibit 4). However, President George Bush made a promise: "Read my lips; no new taxes." Though he broke the promise, the deficit kept growing.

U.S. expenditures compared to those of other industrialized nations also were low (see Exhibit 5), but the Democratic-controlled Congress would not let them go any lower. The result was a stalemate during Bush's presidency—neither higher taxes nor cuts in spending.

What Economists Thought. Most economists did not believe the debt was much of a problem.[5] Alan Blinder, Princeton University economist and now a member of the Federal Reserve Board, said: "A bloated deficit is more like having a few termites in the house: it's better to clean them out right away, but a little procrastination will do only a little damage, and an excessively toxic pesticide might do more harm than good."

Most economists argued:

1. The debt was not really harmful to future generations. Although debt financing implied higher future taxes, it also meant higher future incomes. Future generations, who would have

EXHIBIT 6 The Deficit and Saving as a Percentage of the GNP

Federal Deficit	*Deficit Net Private*	*Saving*
1961–70	−0.4%	8.3%
1971–80	−1.8	8.0
1981–90	−3.6	6.1

to pay back the deferred taxes, held interest-yielding bonds that would result in higher incomes.

2. The debt had not crowded out private investment as much as had been anticipated, based on the evidence from the 1980s. With the government deferring taxes into the future, people felt themselves to be richer. Between 1981 and 1990, they spent more and saved less (see Exhibit 6).

U.S. saving rates went down. With less savings available and government pressure on existing savings (to pay back the debt), real interest rates moved up. This deterred private investment. To a degree, private investment was crowded out, as economic theory holds; but the high-interest rates also attracted foreign capital, which made up much of the difference, so investment really didn't decline that much.

Indeed, when adjusted for inflation, investment did not appear to go down at all. But what did happen was that the dollar appreciated, and as it did so, the current account balance fell off dramatically. The budget deficit crowded out net exports rather than private investment. The budget deficit problem became a foreign trade deficit problem, a problem that the Federal Reserve addressed in the period leading up to the last presidential election, when to stimulate the economy out of the early 1990s recession, it deflated the U.S. dollar.

What Should Be Done?

Admitting that there are some costs to the federal deficits, what do most economists suggest should be done? There are two approaches, a more moderate and more radical one.

The Moderate Program. The moderates propose the following:

1. Since there is no time in the future when the federal debt must be paid off, our aim should be to stabilize interest costs as a share of GNP.
2. We should invest wisely, using federal expenditures for things, such as new highways and aircraft, that will last into the next generation. This will make it easier for our progeny to pay off the debt.
3. We should invest in education and R&D along with basic infrastructure, since only then will the next generation have the productive assets it needs to deal with the debt. These investments are to be preferred to transfer payments and expenditures for current services that will make no difference in the future.
4. We need some budgetary discipline. The Gramm-Rudman-Hollings Act has not worked. Congress delayed its implementation and the Supreme Court declared one of its provisions unconstitutional because it violated the separation of powers provisions. In its place, we might consider:

- A constitutional amendment mandating a balanced budget.
- A presidential line-item veto.
- A provision inversely linking congressional salaries to the size of the deficit.

Ultimately, moderates believe, as James Gwartney and Richard Stroup have written, that, "deficits are problematic, but not that troublesome."

The Radical Program. The radicals, including the Concord Coalition chaired by former senators Warren Rudman and Paul Tsongas, treat the deficit as a more serious problem. Among the proposals they advocate are:

1. Raise the marginal tax rate from 31 percent to 36 percent (it peaked at 92 percent in 1952, was cut to 50 percent in 1981 and 28 percent in 1986).
2. Reduce mortgage interest rate deductions (more than 80 percent goes to households with a greater than $50,000 a year income).
3. Cut the defense budget by at least $85 billion.
4. Require all other government agencies to eliminate 5 percent of their most outdated or unnecessary programs and reduce spending on what's left by 10 percent across the board.
5. Make Social Security benefits and federal pensions more fully taxable for the nonpoor elderly.[6]
6. Tax Medicare benefits received by the well-off elderly.[7]
7. End farm price support payments.
8. Gradually phase in a $2 per gallon increase in gasoline taxes over the next 10 years (making U.S. gasoline taxes more in line with those of other industrialized nations).
9. Tax employer-paid health care benefits.

The radicals argue that government benefits have to be proportional to need. In making cuts, government neutrality is needed, which means that intended or unintended subsidies to industries have to be eliminated. The radicals also argue that reform has to be comprehensive to overcome the opposition of special interests.

The New Republican Initiative. It is up to you how to respond to the new Republican initiative. The only warning I give is that the contract with America seems contradictory. On the one hand, it calls for a balanced budget; on the other, it calls for additional tax cuts, tax breaks, and increased defense spending. I am not sure we can have it both ways.

Discussion Questions

1. How do you respond to this speech?
2. What kind of memo do you write to your CEO explaining your view of the problem?
3. What position do you feel the CED should take?

Endnotes

1. This case has been written by Alfred Marcus.
2. Mike Meyers, "For the Middle Class: Many Happy Returns," *Minneapolis Star and Tribune*, Jan. 23, 1995, World & Nation section, pp. 6–19.
3. Richard Kirkland, "Today's GOP: The Party's Over for Big Business," *Fortune*, Feb. 6, 1995, pp. 50–62.
4. Rob Norton, "Taking on Public Enemy No. 1," *Fortune*, Oct. 19, 1992, pp. 84–87.
5. J. Yellen, "Symposium on the Budget Deficit," *Journal of Economic Perspectives*, 1989, pp. 17–21; E. Gramlich,

"Budget Deficits and National Saving," *Journal of Economic Perspectives*, 1989, pp. 37–54; B. D. Bernheim, "A Neoclassical Perspective on Budget Deficits," *Journal of Economic Perspectives*, 1989, pp. 55–72; R. Eisner, "Budget Deficits: Rhetoric and Reality," *Journal of Economic Perspectives*, 1989, pp. 73–93.

6. Neil Howe and Phillip Longman, "The Next New Deal," *Atlantic*, April 1992, pp. 88–99.
7. Ibid.

Appendix: Major Categories of Federal Income and Outlays for Fiscal Year 1993

On or before the first Monday in February of each year, the U.S. President is required by law to submit to the Congress a budget proposal for the fiscal year that begins the following October. The budget plan sets forth the President's proposed receipts, spending, and the deficit for the Federal Government. The plan includes recommendations for new legislation as well as recommendations to change, eliminate, and add programs. After receipt of the President's proposal, the Congress reviews the proposal and makes changes. It first passes a budget resolution setting its own targets for receipts, outlays, and the deficit. Individual spending and revenue bills are then enacted consistent with the goals of the budget resolution.

In fiscal year 1993 (which began on October 1, 1992, and ended on September 30, 1993), Federal income was $1,154 billion and outlays were $1,408 billion, leaving a deficit of $255 billion.

Federal Income

Income and social insurance taxes are, by far, the largest source of receipts. In 1993, individuals paid $510 billion in income taxes and corporations paid $118 billion. Social security and other insurance and retirement contributions were $428 billion. Excise taxes were $48 billion. The remaining $50 billion of receipts were from Federal Reserve deposits, customs duties, estate and gift taxes, and other miscellaneous receipts.

Federal Outlays

About 82% of total outlays were financed by tax receipts and the remaining 18% were financed by borrowing. Government receipts and borrowing finance a wide range of public services. Following is the breakdown of total outlays for fiscal year 1993.*

1. **Social security, Medicare, and other retirement:** $500 billion. These programs were 35% of total outlays. These programs provide income support for the retired and disabled and medical care for the elderly.

2. **National defense, veterans, and foreign affairs:** $344 billion. About 20% of total outlays were to equip, modernize, and pay our armed forces and to fund other national defense activities; nearly 3% went for veterans benefits and services; and about 1% went for international activities, including military and economic assistance to foreign countries and the maintenance of U.S. embassies abroad.

---

*These percentages exclude undistributed offsetting receipts, which were −$37 billion in fiscal year 1993. In the budget, these receipts are offset against spending in figuring the outlay totals shown above. These receipts are primarily for the U.S. Government's share of its employee retirement programs and rents and royalties on the Outer Continental Shelf. The outlay amounts do not total to $1,408 billion due to rounding.

Source of Appendix: U.S. Government Printing Office, #375-537, 1994.

3. **Net interest:** $199 billion. About 14% of total outlays were for net interest payments on the public debt.

4. **Physical, human, and community development:** $119 billion. About 8% of total outlays were for agriculture; natural resources and environmental programs; transportation programs; aid for elementary and secondary education and direct assistance to college students; job training programs; deposit insurance, commerce and housing credit, and community development; and space, energy, and general science programs.

5. **Social programs:** $254 billion. The Federal Government spent 11% of total outlays to fund Medicaid, food stamps, aid to families with dependent children, supplemental security income, and related programs. About 6% was spent for health research and public health programs, unemployment compensation, assisted housing, and social services.

6. **Law enforcement and general government:** $28 billion. About 2% of total outlays were for judicial activities. Federal law enforcement, and prisons; and to provide for the general costs of the Federal Government, including the collection of taxes and legislative activities.

The pie charts below show the relative sizes of the major categories of Federal income and outlays for fiscal year 1993.

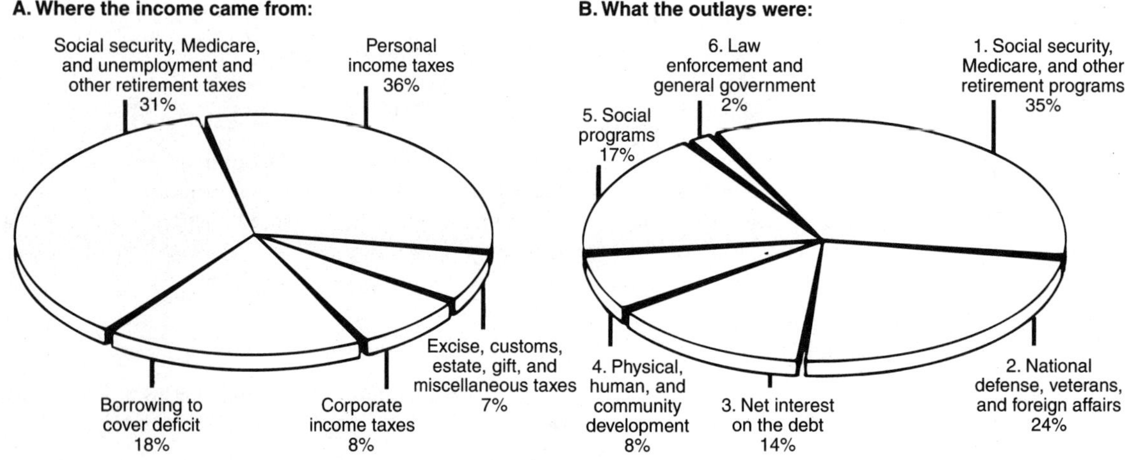

Case 10–B
Contract with America (B): Cutting Entitlements?

Only one-third of the federal budget has been in the president's control. Entitlement spending for such items as Medicare, Medicaid, and Social Security were outside his control, and very controversial politically. The Contract with America promised no cuts in these entitlement programs.

Medical spending, however, was very high. President Clinton's health care reform plan had been defeated. In any case, there had been serious debates about whether it would actually have lowered the deficit. Many studies actually showed that it would have raised the deficit.

Office of Management and Budget Director Alice Rivlin, in a memo to the president that was leaked to the press, maintained that the deficit would rise precipitously in the next century unless something was done to reign in spending on Medicare, Medicaid, and Social Security. The huge debt would cut into savings, raise real interest rates, and crowd out private investment.

A full 52 percent of the budget was in the form of mandatory spending, most of it for Social Security, Medicare, and Medicaid payments. The rest consisted of pensions for military retirees and government employees, benefits to veterans, farm price supports, student loans, child nutrition and food stamp programs, unemployment compensation, and other programs.

Of the 35 percent of the budget in the president's control, about one-half was committed to defense. Contract for America's promise under the National Security Restoration Act was to raise defense spending. The remainder of discretionary spending went to hundreds of programs from education to national parks to community development to the operations of such agencies as the Environmental Protection Agency and the National Science Foundation. The final 13 percent of the budget was in the form of interest on the debt.

In March 1994, Representative Gerald Solomon, a Republican from upstate New York, introduced a set of recommendations that would balance the budget early in the 21st century with only modest cuts in entitlements, no increases in taxes, and lower reductions in defense spending than the Clinton administration had proposed. It was the only program-by-program, line-by-line accounting of how the budget could be balanced within guidelines that were at all similar to those in Contract for America. Total reductions in federal spending would be 44 percent for the environment, 72 percent in agriculture, 32 percent in foreign aid, 29 percent in transportation, 40 percent in community and regional development, and 65 percent in energy.

Medicare and Medicaid spending would still have to be cut, according to this proposal, by 11 percent. Income security programs, welfare, and other programs for the poor would be reduced by 12 percent. Totally eliminated would be economic aid to Russia, almost all agricultural price supports, construction of the space station, grants for new sewer systems, subsidies for Amtrack and air service to remote places, economic development grants, the National Services Corps, and the legal services corporation. The FBI, the Center for Disease Control, and other federal programs would have less money to spend. A total of $700 million would be shaved off the national budget in five years. By the year 2000, more than $1 trillion would be saved. The Concord Coalition had a different plan. It was calling for higher taxes on wealthy Americans and taking away some Social Security benefits from more well-to-do elderly.

Discussion Question

What position should your company suggest that the CED take on the issue of reducing entitlements?

Case 10–C
Contract with America (C): Capital Gains Tax Cut?

President Bush signed a law that aimed to cut growth in the 1991–1995 debt by $482 billion through tax increases (he broke his promise of no new taxes), spending cuts, and savings, but the economy fell into recession and the savings and loan bailout occurred. Bush failed to cut growth in the debt.

In 1994, President Clinton reduced the deficit by $83–102 billion from the original estimates of $286–$305 billion. He was the first president in two decades to cut the deficit two years straight

(1993 and 1994). However, his accomplishment was only partially due to the changes he had made—the cuts in federal spending, changes in purchasing rules, and tax increases. The main reason for the lower debt was growth in the economy, though lower health care and Social Security costs (than had been estimated) and lower than expected costs for the savings and loan bailout also contributed.

A key to further reducing the deficit was for the United States to continue having a high level of economic growth, and the Republican Contract with America appeared to be the answer. Under the proposed Job Creation and Wage Enhancement Act, it was calling for cuts in capital gains taxes as well as other business incentives.

Profits on the sale of stocks, bonds, real estate, and other assets were taxed at 28 percent. The Republican argument was that a reduction in this tax would increase federal revenue, raise savings, and make capital less expensive for U.S. businesses. The reduction could be achieved by either lowering the maximum rate or by allowing taxpayers to exclude a portion of the gains from taxable income, which in effect lowers the rate. In the 1980s, taxpayers had a 60 percent exclusion right, which made the maximum tax 20 percent.

Another proposal was to adjust capital gains for inflation. Since a high percentage of the increased capital values is in the form of inflation, prominent economists like Martin Feldstein argued that they should not be taxed. The Republican proposal would exclude 50 percent of the gains from taxation and allow taxpayers to adjust gains for inflation. This plan would lower the top rate to 19.8 percent. Over time it would go down even further as it became adjusted for inflation.

Republicans also argued that a capital gains tax cut actually would stimulate tax collection. Taxpayers who had been reluctant to sell assets because of high capital gains taxes would feel free to do so. A Treasury Department study concluded that the 1990 Bush plan would have raised $12.5 billion over five years.

Some Democrats, however, countered that cutting the tax would boost the deficit. Congress' Joint Committee on Taxation concluded that the Bush plan would have cost the federal Treasury $11.4 billion over the same time period. In addition, it would benefit the rich, stimulate consumption, and rekindle a tax-shelter industry. The Joint Committee on Taxation concluded that about two-thirds of the tax savings under the Bush plan would go to people earning more than $200,000 a year.

In 1990 when President Bush proposed his capital gains tax cut, Democrats blocked it. Richard Gephardt, House Democratic Leader, called the proposal "nothing more than a giveaway for rich investors."

Discussion Question

What position should your company suggest that the CED take on the issue of adjusting capital gains?

Case 10–D
Walter Wriston and the Chrysler Bailout[1]

Walter Wriston was a firm believer in the benefits of a free market. As far as he was concerned, the market became less efficient whenever the government tried to influence it. In the long run, people were poorer on account of it. Wriston was fond of quoting Justice Hugo Black:

> The unrestrained interaction of competitive forces will yield the best allocation of our economic resources, the lowest prices, the highest quality, and the greatest material progress, while at the same time providing an environment conducive to the preservation of our democratic political and social institutions.[2]

Now Wriston had been asked to testify before the congressional banking committee that was holding hearings on the proposed bailout of the Chrysler Corporation. He had to decide what to say.

Citicorp's Stake in the Bailout

Walter Wriston was chairman of Citicorp, one of the largest banks in the world. Citicorp had the most capital funds of any privately owned bank holding company, with $5.9 billion, and had earned $541 million in 1979. The bank had both consumer loan services (serving 16 million individuals worldwide) and commercial loan services, and already held one of the largest shares of Chrysler's bank debt.

Under provisions of the proposed bailout, the banks, including Citicorp, would have to come up with an additional $680 million in new loans and debt forgiveness for Chrysler. Wriston didn't like the idea of loaning Chrysler more money. The automaker had lost more money in 1979 than any company in history. There was no doubt that better loans could be made to entrepreneurs with more promising business prospects.

Wriston had a fiduciary duty to invest funds wisely, and lending additional funds to Chrysler did not seem like a wise use of Citicorp's money. However, he was under intense pressure to make the loans to Chrysler. A great many jobs were at stake along with the economic health of the communities where Chrysler had plants—and perhaps the economic health of the whole nation. Congress would only authorize the $1.5 billion in loan guarantees it was considering if Chrysler's stakeholders would grant the company $2.6 billion in loans, wage and benefit sacrifices, and other financing.[3]

No stakeholder was exempt from being asked to make sacrifices. Banks, employees, suppliers, dealers, and shareholders were expected to contribute to the $2.6 billion total, even those who had loaned Chrysler less than $100,000. Legislators reasoned that if exceptions were allowed, each party would want to be excused from its obligations. Should Citicorp be part of this deal?

Government Bailouts

Wriston, who was philosophically opposed to government bailouts, did not know what to do. Federal efforts to save failing corporations were common. During the Great Depression the government's Reconstruction Finance Corporation (RFC) provided low-interest loans to failing businesses. The Small Business Administration continued the tradition of government assistance when the RFC ceased to exist. There had been several highly visible federal bailouts of large enterprises in recent years, including those of Penn Central and Lockheed.[4]

Penn Central. By the late 1960s, railroads were not a profitable business in the United States, particularly in the Northeast. Unfavorable federal tariff regulations, inadequate investment in maintenance of the railroads' assets, and the movement away from transportation by rail in favor of highways, waterways, and air all contributed to the industry's sorry financial situation. The 1968 merger of two of the largest railroads, the Pennsylvania Railroad and the New York Central, at first seemed like a step toward recuperation for the ailing Northeast lines. It was not to be. By mid-1970 the Penn Central railroad was bankrupt. Shaky from the start, the giant corporation lost more than $1 million per day in 1970 and by the summer its liabilities were almost three times the size of its assets.

A great many people had a lot to lose if the company was liquidated via bankruptcy proceedings. The company's creditors numbered 100,000. There were nearly as many employees with jobs on the line. About 200 Penn Central subsidiaries were served by a multitude of suppliers who would be hurt if the railroad failed. Communities throughout the Northeast could lose rail service. The financial markets, already shaken by recession and the war in Vietnam, could be upset. They might panic if what was the sixth-largest firm in the country when it was formed in 1968 collapsed.

The federal government therefore stepped in to rescue the company. In 1971 Congress created the National Railroad Passenger Corporation (Amtrak) and took over the nation's intercity rail passenger service. Congress created the Consolidated Rail Corporation (Conrail) in 1976 to take over the unprofitable freight operations of six bankrupt eastern railroads, including Penn Central. The government paid Penn Central a total of $2.1 billion for its railroad operations, and invested an additional several billion dollars in repairing its assets and making good on its debts.

The new Penn Central Corporation, no longer in the railroad business, was solidly profitable by 1980 as a diversified firm involved in a variety of energy, real estate, and entertainment businesses. The majority of railroad employees kept their jobs until retirement. Communities continued to be served by rail operations now under quasi-governmental control. The successor to Penn Central in running the railroads, Conrail, however, was still losing money in 1979.

Lockheed. Lockheed was one of the largest defense contractors during the 1960s, supplying the Pentagon with technologically sophisticated hardware like ballistic missiles for submarines. However, the company suffered a series of financially devastating setbacks late in the decade when it incurred large cost overruns on a number of defense contracts. It spent, for example, $3.7 billion to produce the C-5A military transport aircraft, which it had contracted to produce for $2.3 billion. Further, it only delivered 81 of the 115 planes called for in the contract.

Just as Lockheed's financial picture was worsening further due to cutbacks in the space program and defense contracts, serious problems with another contract developed. Rolls-Royce, the company that produced the engines for the L-1011 Tristar commercial aircraft Lockheed built, was in danger of imminent failure unless it received assistance from the British government. The British government agreed to rescue Rolls-Royce, but only if the U.S. government agreed to guarantee $250 million in loans that Lockheed needed to buy Rolls-Royce engines to complete the Tristar contract.

Debate on the Lockheed loan guarantee proceeded in the congressional banking committees through early 1971. Lockheed's supporters argued that over 50,000 jobs would be lost if the company folded. The already distressed aerospace industry would be threatened. All of the suppliers and subcontractors on the Tristar project, who had already advanced hundreds of millions of dollars, would be harmed, pushing many into bankruptcy. Moreover, national security would be hurt if a large defense contractor went out of business.

Over the objections of those who argued that such a bailout would set a bad precedent and was not really necessary (since Lockheed's missile and military aircraft divisions could have been reorganized and kept in business, or another defense contractor could buy the company), a loan guarantee bill was passed in August 1971. The bill contained provisions designed to ensure that the government had first claim on Lockheed's assets if the company went under, that no more than $250 million in guarantees would be outstanding at any time, and that the government would issue no loan guarantees if other sources of credit were available.

The guarantees reassured Lockheed's creditors, who restructured the company's debt and extended additional credit. Substantial foreign sales, a recovering economy, and more-lucrative government contracts all contributed to the company's improved financial condition, and Lockheed paid off the last of its government loans a few months before they were due in 1977.

Government Intervention in Germany and France

If the federal government were to help Chrysler, it wouldn't be the first time a nation had come to the aide of its auto manufacturers. The West German and French governments had both done so.

West Germany. By 1974, Volkswagen, the German automaker founded under the guidance of the Nazis in 1939, was in serious financial straits. The company's sales depended on a single model (the Beetle), which, though very popular up through the 1960s, was suffering from increasing competition from Japanese makes. In 1971 the company initiated a program to develop new models, but the program was expensive and fraught with difficulties. Rising competition offered the firm no breathing room. U.S. demand for Volkswagens was hurt by the 1974 recession and Japanese competition; sales fell 11 percent that year. Overseas production plants in Brazil and elsewhere required large capital expenditures and were not providing much of a return. The company needed help.

Since World War II, the West German government had adopted a largely noninterventionist policy with respect to rescues of firms in trouble. Bankers and businessmen in general opposed government intervention, fearing that government control might result. Instead, bailouts were usually financed by the banks whose investments in the troubled company were at stake. If there was any government intervention, it was usually at the state, rather than the federal, level.

When all else failed, though, the federal government was willing to step in. In Volkswagen's case, the federal and state governments agreed to finance an assistance program for the 40,000 workers that would be laid off as a result of a cost-reduction agreement between the labor unions and the company. The agreement gave Volkswagen enough time to develop a successful new model (the Rabbit), and by 1976 the company was profitable again.

France. The French government's attitude toward bailouts was significantly more interventionist than that of the German government. The French government played an active role in shaping French industrial policy, using taxes and loans to encourage business to operate in ways conducive to achievement of the government's social goals. The government had nationalized a number of important industries. Renault, the leading French automaker, had been nationalized in 1945, and though day-to-day operations were directed by business professionals, the government's public-policy goals still strongly influenced the firm's strategic decision making.

In the wake of the 1973 oil crisis, which threatened Renault's financial future, the company assimilated a number of companies in related tools and parts industries in accordance with a government-sponsored rescue plan. Renault formulated its expansion plans to take into account the government's interest in spreading manufacturing plants, and thus jobs, around the country rather than concentrating them in a few areas, even though concentrating the plants might be more profitable. In another case involving France's other automaker, the government's $310 million direct loan made possible Peugeot's takeover of Citroen in 1974–75. The Ministry of Industry also sent one of its top officials to join the company. Because Renault was owned by the French government and Peugeot-Citroen was a major employer, they could count on assistance from the French government if they got into trouble like Chrysler.

The History of the Chrysler Corporation

The problems that brought Chrysler to the brink of bankruptcy were, in some respects, the kinds of problems that Walter Chrysler had made a name for himself solving. An ambitious and confident man who had a talent for understanding engineering machinery, Chrysler enjoyed early success in the Buick division of General Motors by eliminating waste and inefficiency.

In the early 1920s, Chrysler was persuaded to come out of retirement to manage a series of failing auto makers: the Willys-Overland Company, and soon afterward, the Maxwell Motor company. Commanding a $1 million salary, he initiated the development of a completely new automobile featuring a high-compression engine. The new car, the Chrysler, was a smashing success, generating $4 million in profit for the firm in the first year on sales of 32,000 cars. In 1925 the name of the Maxwell Motor Company was changed, and the Chrysler Corporation was born.

Demand for the firm's cars developed quickly, and Chrysler acquired new manufacturing facilities by buying the Dodge Corporation in 1928 in what was at the time the biggest acquisition ever. Chrysler's strategy of "shallow" integration, in which it relied heavily on suppliers for parts rather than building its own, gave it great flexibility in an era of rapid automotive technological change. By the time Walter Chrysler retired in 1937, the company was completely free of debt, having paid off the last of the bonds it issued to finance the Dodge acquisition.

Walter Chrysler's successors did not oversee the same untarnished string of achievements as the company founder. As the automobile market evolved, innovative technologies became less important than automotive good looks. The company began losing market share in the early 1950s under top management that refused to follow the trend toward sharp-looking design. The company yielded second place (never to be regained) to Ford in 1953, and went from a 22 percent share of the market in 1951 to less than 10 percent in 1962. The company lost money during the 1958 recession and again the next year.

The Successful 1960s. In 1961, Chrysler hired a new president, Lynn Townsend, who quickly developed a strategy for recovery based on tightening up operations and expanding into the international auto market as well as nonautomotive domestic businesses. Townsend introduced the industry's first five-year, 50,000-mile warranty and oversaw the development of the best-designed automobiles Chrysler had offered for years. The company expanded into other businesses: real estate, chemicals, outboard marine engines, air conditioners, space technologies. It also expanded overseas; by the end of the decade, Chrysler had plants in 18 different countries.

The 1960s were a time of robust expansion in the American economy, and Townsend made sure Chrysler wasn't left behind. His 1963 $700 million, 10-year expansion plan expanded six-fold by 1965 as the company added large new manufacturing facilities and founded the Chrysler Financial Corporation to provide credit to dealers and customers. Townsend's plan seemed to work. The company's assets tripled between 1961 and 1968, while debt fell as a percentage of equity from 35 percent to less than 20 percent. Market share rose to 16 percent in 1968.

The Unfavorable 1970s. In 1970, however, a decade-long string of unfavorable economic developments and just plain bad luck began. The first of a series of oil price increases and a recession in 1970 hurt Chrysler's earnings. The company posted its first loss since 1961 in the last quarter of 1969. The expansion had depleted the firm's cash reserves and run up a long-term debt burden of $790 million, larger than that of General Motors. When profits softened, the company was forced to abandon plans to automate its operations and to develop a line of subcompacts to compete with Volkswagen. The new company president, John Riccardo, initiated a two-year austerity program that cut overhead by several million dollars.

By 1973, auto sales had recovered sharply and so had Chrysler's earnings. Riccardo attributed Chrysler's renewed success largely to its strategy of focusing on the company's profitable compact cars rather than pursuing the subcompact market. Chrysler's Dodge Dart and Plymouth Valiant were doing well in the compact market, and it made some profits in the big-car market. The company earned record profits on its highest ever sales in the second quarter of 1973 and was well into a $450 million program to restyle its large cars.

By early 1974, however, large cars were not what customers wanted. The Arab oil embargo in late 1973 put fuel economy at the top of car buyers' lists, and small cars accounted for half of all car sales. As the country suffered through several years of stagflation, Chrysler's situation grew more perilous. The company's inventories, already swollen by management policies that rewarded high production figures regardless of demand, expanded further. A *Business Week* cover photo featured some of the 360,000 new cars the company couldn't sell. A new austerity plan was implemented, and the jobs of four out of five of the company's engineers were eliminated. Research and development budgets were cut 19 percent. Investment in tools and facilities decreased 39 percent in two years. The company was fighting to stay solvent and in the process was sacrificing its ability to adapt to the future.

The years 1976 and 1977 offered a brief respite to the beleaguered company. Profits rose again as auto sales recovered and customers turned to the company's Aspen and Volare lines for the only luxury compacts on the market. Disaster struck, however, when numerous technical defects in the Aspen/Volare lines became evident. The cutbacks in engineering had taken their toll. By the end of 1977, Chrysler had spent more than a half million dollars just to mail the recall notices on the Aspens and Volares that had to be brought back for fixing. The Center for Auto Safety awarded the Aspen/Volare its "Lemon of the Year" award.

The Need to Increase Investment. It was clear to Riccardo that the company needed to dramatically increase its investment in the development of new vehicles. He proposed a $7.5 billion plan to provide all-new products and modernize the manufacturing facilities. To finance the restructuring, the company began selling off its foreign subsidiaries. Peugeot-Citroën bought an 85 percent interest in Chrysler's French, British, and Spanish plants for $530 million in cash and Peugeot stock. Peugeot also bought Chrysler's European financial subsidiary for $80 million. Volkswagen bought two-thirds of Chrysler's Brazilian operation for $50 million, and General Motors bought the company's Venezuelan and Colombian plants for $30 million. Chrysler stockholders reluctantly approved a new stock issue that raised $200 million.

These funds were not enough. The company lost more than $200 million in 1978 and more than $1 billion in 1979.

New Leadership: Lee Iacocca at the Helm. In late 1978, the company looked to new leadership to put the company back on its feet. It found it in Lee Iacocca, a 30-year veteran of Ford who had proven himself a tough, imaginative, and effective manager during his career there. His greatest success had been the Ford Mustang, introduced in 1964, and still a moneymaker for Ford. As he moved through the company's ranks to becoming president in 1970, he developed expertise in both product development and marketing, as well as a keen understanding of public relations: when the Mustang was introduced, he managed to get his and the car's picture on the front of both *Time* and *Newsweek*.

Fired in 1978 by Henry Ford II (who explained that he "just didn't like" him), Iacocca was quickly hired as the new president of Chrysler, with the understanding that he would become CEO when Riccardo retired. The move was applauded by most industry observers.

Revamping the Product Line. Most observers believed that the company needed to substantially revamp its product line. Chrysler wasn't producing and selling enough of the kind of cars people wanted to generate any earnings. To make a comeback required a substantial investment. There weren't many suitable assets left to sell. The commercial paper market was largely closed to the company since ratings on its bonds had plummeted due to its recent financial trouble. It could not expect much further help from its lenders. Chrysler had largely exhausted a last-ditch $567 million line of credit. Most of the lenders already had lent the maximum that regulations or bank policy would allow on a single firm. Desperate to keep the company running until the development programs could bring the promising new line of fuel-efficient, luxury compacts (code named K-cars) to market, Iacocca went to the government to ask for help.

The Development of the Bailout Deal

Chrysler needed at least $1.2 billion to make it through to 1982. It would need $334 million in 1979, $1.2 billion in 1980, and $600 million in 1981, of which $928 million could be covered by further asset sales, leaving a $1.2 billion gap. The company had discreetly tested the federal waters in late 1978 when Riccardo suggested to President Carter's chief domestic policy adviser, Stuart Eizenstat, that the company be exempted for two years from certain pending federal fuel economy and auto emission standards. Riccardo said that compliance would cost Chrysler many millions of dollars. The idea was scrapped later as it became clear that even drastic regulatory relief would not be enough to keep Chrysler solvent.

Another early proposal was that the government grant Chrysler a $1 billion advance on the tax credits it had accrued through the enormous losses of recent years. Corporations are allowed to deduct past business losses from current income in order to reduce tax liability. Chrysler had huge losses to write off against future earnings, but no prospect of any earnings in the near future. The idea was to write out a check to Chrysler for $1 billion in advance against the future tax benefits of the past losses. This proposal was also scrapped by Treasury Secretary William Miller, who disliked the precedent that this tax deal would set.

As late as 1978, Chrysler's management was against the idea of federally guaranteed loans, recognizing that such loans invariably shook public confidence in a business, something which would be disastrous for a car company's sales. Nonetheless, by late 1979 guaranteed loans were clearly the only viable option. Bills to provide loan guarantees to Chrysler had been introduced in the Senate and House Banking Committees, and the struggle over the final form of the guarantee began.

A number of legislators were skeptical of the plan to guarantee Chrysler loans and were determined to see that the federal government was not the only party with something at stake. William Proxmire, the Wisconsin senator who chaired the Senate Banking Committee, insisted that Chrysler stakeholders, who had much more to lose than the public at large, universally contribute to the bailout or there would be no legislation. Much of the discussion centered on just how much each of Chrysler's constituencies would be required to sacrifice and what form that sacrifice would take.

According to the proposed law, before the government issued any loan guarantees, Chrysler would have to get binding commitments from its constituents for financial aid totaling $2.6 billion. Each constituent's share was to be spelled out so that none of the parties could assume the government or another party would take up the slack. Chrysler union employees would give up wage increases, vacations, and other benefits worth $462.5 million, nonunion benefits would be reduced $125 million, and pension funds would be deferred to save $342 million. Another $628 million would be raised through additional asset sales. State governments would have to loan another $187 million. Canada would have to contribute $170 million in loan guarantees after 1982. Chrysler dealers and suppliers would purchase $63 million in convertible debentures. Finally, Chrysler's lenders, including Citicorp, would be expected to come up with $642 million by extending the maturity dates on existing loans, forgiving some interest, and deferring other interest payments.

Chrysler owed $4.8 billion to banks all over the world. About a quarter ($1.6 billion) was in loans to the car company, and the other three-quarters ($3.2 billion) was loaned to the Chrysler Financial Corporation, which was in relatively good shape. The $1.6 billion loaned to the car company broke down as follows:

Consortium led by Manufacturers Hanover	$567 million
Other U.S. lenders	$72 million
Japanese lenders	$400 million
Canadian lenders	$290 million
European lenders	$305 million
	$1.6 billion

Not a Good Risk. Chrysler was not a good risk for further loans, to say the least. By late 1979, the company was in blatant violation of many of the loans' covenants binding the company to minimum standards of fiscal soundness, and any one of the banks could have exercised its right to bring the automaker to court to demand payment, surely triggering a stampede of such requests.

If the Loan Guarantee Act was actually passed, and the banks were expected to make further loans to the company, bank officers would be presented with a tough decision. Every one of them, down to the smallest lender, would be required to ante up a share of the additional loans proportionate to their existing exposure.

There was some doubt over how the foreign lenders would respond. They were less vulnerable to patriotic appeals, and some of them, like many U.S. lenders, had no idea that their small involvement with Chrysler would put them on the spot.

Philosophically, Walter Wriston was against the bailout plan. If it was put in effect, he would have to be involved with it whether he liked it or not. He thus reviewed the arguments for and against Citicorp's participation.

The Case for the Bailout

The most frequently repeated reason for putting together a loan guarantee package was the number of jobs at stake. If Chrysler failed, according to Lee Iacocca, 140,000 Chrysler employees would be out of work, and as many as two million other people—families of workers, dealers, and suppliers—would be "severely impacted."[6] The economies of auto-producing states like Michigan would be seriously threatened, and even the national economy would feel the reverberations of a failure.

A Chrysler failure would cost the federal government anywhere from $3 to $15 billion in lost tax revenues and increased unemployment benefits, welfare payments, and food stamp programs. It would also put a strain on the Pension Benefit Guarantee Corporation, the federal guarantor of pension benefit plans like Chrysler's.

Proponents of a bailout pointed to precedents for government assistance: the Penn Central and Lockheed bailouts had been successes. Others argued that a Chrysler failure would imperil the national balance of trade as the Japanese rushed to fill in the gap left by Chrysler. The nation would lose the fuel-efficient luxury K-cars the company was working on, and there would be less competition in the U.S. auto industry.

Iacocca argued that there were no alternatives to the guaranteed loan program that would save Chrysler. Declaring bankruptcy and going through a Chapter 11 reorganization might work for some firms, but it wouldn't work for an automaker, he said. Customers would not know the difference between a reorganization and liquidation, and would cancel orders, cutting the company's cash flow. Suppliers would demand cash payment upon delivery. Dealers would lose their ability to finance purchases from the company. The company would go under. Bankruptcy simply wasn't a workable option.

The Case against the Bailout

Perhaps a bailout was the only way to save the company, but some, including Wriston, weren't convinced the company should be saved. Wriston felt that

> there [was] no avoiding the fact that a bailout was an attempt by the government to move economic resources to places where they would not otherwise go. Such distortions inevitably would lead to less, not more, productivity—and therefore to fewer jobs, less return of investment, and fewer bona fide lending opportunities for banks and everyone else.[7]

He sympathized with the view that the bailout would set a bad precedent, sending a message to large companies that they didn't need to be efficient because the government would be there to save them if they went bankrupt. It wasn't fair to small businesses that failed all the time. Those failures meant losses for investors, suppliers, employees, and banks, too. That was the price the market exacted for inefficiency. Why should big business be helped just because it could afford an army of lobbyists to capture Congress's attention?

Senator Adlai Stevenson III of Illinois argued that the real solution to the problem was to invest in a retraining and reallocation program for Chrysler workers who would lose jobs in a bankruptcy and not to prop up failing industries as did Great Britain, which had seen its economy gradually ruined as a result.

Wriston's Predicament

Wriston considered the arguments for and against the bailout. If a bailout plan was signed into law by the president, disbursements to Chrysler would be blocked if final commitments by every Chrysler constituent to contribute its share of additional funding were not forthcoming. If the bill were passed, and if Wriston decided not to join in, the whole deal would be scuttled, Chrysler would quickly fail, and fingers would be pointed at Citicorp and any other holdouts as the cause of failure.

In late 1979, Chrysler was nearly out of cash and had been ignoring its suppliers' bills. If a bailout wasn't worked out *soon*, there might as well be none, because the company would fold. On the other hand, Citicorp had a responsibility to its depositors to invest their money wisely.

Wriston had a difficult decision to make. What should he say to Congress? And if a bailout plan were enacted, should he participate or should he take the heat as the bank president who prevented the plan from proceeding?

Discussion Questions

1. When, if at all, is it justified for the federal government to help save a declining company?
2. What form should this help take?
3. What can be learned from precedents?
4. Describe the plan to bail out Chrysler? What exactly did it involve? What was the likelihood that it would be successful?
5. What should Walter Wriston say to Congress about the bailout? Should his bank participate, or should he try to stop the bailout?

Endnotes

1. This case was written by Mark Jankus with the editorial guidance of Alfred Marcus.
2. Statement of Walter Wriston, Chairman, Citibank, Hearings before the Senate Committee on Banking, Housing, and Urban Affairs, Part 2, November 16, 19, 20, and 21, 1979; 96th Cong., 1st sess., *Chrysler Corporation Loan Guarantee Act of 1979* (Washington, D.C.: U.S. Government Printing Office, 1979), p. 1284.
3. G. Starling and O. Baskin, in *Issues in Business and Society: Capitalism and Public Purpose* (Boston: Kent Publishing, 1985), pp. 29–51; R. B. Reich and J. D. Donahue, *New Deals: The Chrysler Revival and the American System* (New York: Times Books, 1985).
4. N. A. Bailey and C. Lord, "On Strategic Economics," *Comparative Strategy* 7 (1988), pp. 93–97.
5. Reich and Donahue, *New Deals*.
6. Ibid., p. 120.
7. Statement of Walter Wriston, p. 1284; M. B. Fuller, *Note on Auto Sector Policies*, Case 9–382–121, Harvard Business School, 1982.

CHAPTER 11

Government Support for Industry Competitiveness

Laissez-faire should be the general practice; every departure from it, unless required by some great good, is a certain evil.

John Stuart Mill

While America's commitments steadily increased after 1945, its share of world manufacturing and of world gross national product began to decline, at first rather slowly, and then with increasing speed . . . there is the country's industrial decline relative to overall world production, not only in older manufacturers, such as textiles, iron and steel, shipbuilding, and basic chemicals, but also . . . in robotics, aerospace technology, automobiles, machine tools, and computers . . . The uncompetitiveness of U.S. industrial products abroad . . . have . . . produced staggering deficits in visible trade . . .

Paul Kennedy, "The (Relative) Decline of America"[1]

Introduction and Chapter Objectives

This chapter examines the recent performance of the U.S. economy and the role of government in promoting competitiveness. It will show that by changing the size and structure of markets and the costs of doing business, government has affected businesses in many ways. Post-World War II policies were influenced by business cycle management and the growth of social regulation (e.g. occupational safety, pollution control, and affirmative action). These were followed by a wave of deregulation of controlled industries (e.g., airlines and banks). The current debate is whether the United States should have policies, like those in Japan and the European countries, that promote industry competitiveness. U.S. political traditions, however, differ from those in other countries. This chapter will look at the debate about government's role in promoting industry competitiveness.

The Performance of the U.S. Economy

The Japanese, along with other international rivals, are supposed to be eroding U.S. economic strength. Critiques of U.S. economic performance include the following:

- Having been hurt by declining mathematical scores among students, a glut of attorneys, and a shortage of machinists and skilled laborers, the productivity of U.S. manufacturing has fallen seriously behind that of other nations.[2]
- Too many American managers lack hands-on knowledge of technologies and production. They are experts in the arts of financial manipulation, mere **"paper entrepreneurs,"** who have no understanding of what happens on the factory floor.[3]
- American manufacturing is held back by a proliferation of rules and unnecessary control systems. It is well suited to making mass items in a predictable and routinized fashion, but it is not well suited to flexible manufacturing that involves skilled labor and rapidly changing technologies in knowledge intensive industries.[4]

"paper entrepreneurs" U.S. managers are charged with being experts in financial manipulation but lacking in knowledge and skills of basic technologies and production.

Some believe that "U.S. industry's loss of competitiveness . . . has been nothing short of an economic disaster."[5] It is no longer true that each generation of Americans can look forward to more comfortable conditions than its predecessors.

This dim view of U.S. economic prospects, however, is not shared by everyone.[6] Some feel that a relative decline of the United States was inevitable, natural, and indeed beneficial; certainly, it is not something about which to be alarmed. The easy superiority achieved by Americans after World War II was not sustainable. Indeed, U.S. intentions have been to help other nations achieve greater equality with the United States because it needed strong trading partners.[7] Through programs such as the Marshall Plan and the promotion of free trade, the United States contributed to the recovery of the Western European and Japanese economies.

How Well Has the U.S. Economy Been Doing?

A report issued in 1985 by President Reagan's Commission on Industrial Competitiveness claimed that the nation's ability to compete internationally was facing "unprecedented" challenges from abroad. U.S. world leadership and the ability to provide Americans with the standard of living and opportunities to which they aspired were at stake.[8] Contrary to these views, another report stated that with the exception of selected industries, the U.S. economy remained competitive with the economies of Japan and Western Europe.[9]

Signs of Decline

The signs of declining competitiveness were U.S. growth rates, which had fallen behind those of its international rivals (see Exhibit 11–1), and major trade deficits. By 1986, the current account (trade) deficit had reached $160 billion. In a host of critical industries from automobiles to textile machinery, imports increased as a percentage of the domestic market. New industries, moreover, were not springing up to replace the old and annual productivity increases had been falling, which did not portend well for the future.

EXHIBIT 11–1 Evidence of Declining U.S. Competitiveness[10]

Growth in GNP per Employed Person (%)

	1960–73	1974–78
U.S.	1.8%	.1%
Germany	4.7	3.0
France	4.5	3.0
U.K.	3.2	.8
Japan	8.9	3.2

U.S. Trade Gap

Exports as Percentage of GNP		Imports as Percentage of GNP		Trade Gap as Percentage of GNP	
1970	1980	1970	1980	1970	1980
9.3%	19%	9.3%	22.0%	0	3.0%

Weakened Industries:
Imports as a Percentage of the U.S. Domestic Market

	1960	1980
Automobiles	4.1%	27.0%
Consumer electronics	5.6	50.6
Cutlery	8.2	90.0
Steel	4.2	14.0
Machine tools	3.2	28.0
Textile machinery	6.6	45.5

Declines in U.S. Productivity Growth

	Average Annual Increase
1948–65	3.2%
1965–73	2.4
1973–78	1.1

Continued Strength in the Economy

In some areas, the U.S. economy showed surprising strength (see Exhibit 11–2).[11] Living standards remained equal to or above those in Western Europe and Japan. Social mobility was high. Almost half of the top 25 percent of earners in the United States fell from that position every seven years, and nearly half of the bottom 25 percent moved up. Compared with the economies of Europe and Japan, the U.S. economy was a powerful job creator. It absorbed the baby-boom generation and nearly 12 million legal and illegal immigrants, and created over 22 million jobs during the 1970s. The European economies, in contrast, had net job losses and high rates of unemployment. From 1960 to 1980, 30 million new jobs were created in the United States, but only 7.5 million in Japan and 2.5 million in

Exhibit 11–2 Evidence of U.S. Economic Strength

Per Capita Purchasing Power, 1992 (in U.S. $)

U.S.	$23,400
Japan	19,800
Canada	19,600
France	18,900
Germany	17,400
U.K.	15,900

Unemployment Rates in Major Industrialized Nations[12] (as a percent of total workforce)

	1995	1990	1985	1980	1970	1960
Japan	2.9%	2.1%	2.6%	2.0%	1.2%	1.7%
U.S.	5.4	5.5	7.2	7.1	4.9	5.5
U.K.	8.6	5.9	11.2	7.0	3.1	2.2
Germany	8.2	7.1	7.2	6.4	.5	1.1
Canada	9.6	8.1	10.5	7.5	5.7	6.5
France	12.6	10.2	10.4	6.4	2.5	1.5

Western Europe. U.S. unemployment rates fell behind those of most of its international competitors between 1985 and 1995. The exception was Japan, which had very low participation by women in the workforce.

Productivity Trends

According to the economist Paul Krugman, the most important indicator of competitive strength was productivity: "Productivity isn't everything, but in the long run it is almost everything."[13] In this area, the United States still held an absolute edge. In 1990, the average U.S. worker produced $45,000 in goods and services as opposed to $38,000 for the average German worker and $35,000 for the average Japanese worker. However, U.S. productivity growth averaged just 0.9 percent per year during 1973–1992, after averaging 3 percent per year from 1937 to 1972. Between 1972 and 1990, Japanese productivity grew at an annual rate of 3 percent and German productivity at an annual rate of 1.6 percent while U.S. productivity grew at only 0.5 percent per year. If these trends continued, Japan and Germany would overtake the United States in productivity.[14]

It is important to note that U.S. productivity gains often were achieved through curtailing wages and downsizing companies, while in Germany and Japan they were achieved by investment in new plant and equipment and in worker skills.[15] German and Japanese companies were constrained from pursuing low wages and layoffs by unions, social policies, and regulation. Managers in those countries could not hire, fire, and redeploy their workforces as readily as U.S. managers. They had to invest in new plant and equipment, education, training, and innovation. U.S. investment from 1987 to 1992 was the lowest among the Group of 7 nations.[16] At 10.7 percent of GDP in 1991, it represented only one-half the investment of Japan. Unsurprisingly, the typical machine tool in the United States was seven years older than that in Japan.

Service Sector Jobs

Millions of new jobs had been created in the U.S. service sector, which employed nearly 80 percent of U.S. workers. Labor-intensive jobs in this sector, such as health care and fast foods, were expanding. In contrast, manufacturing employment in the United States contracted from 26.4 percent of total employment in 1960 to under 20 percent in 1980.[17]

To thrive, many service industries such as finance, process engineering, and consulting, depended on a strong manufacturing base to create demand for what they had to offer. Historically, productivity growth had been most rapid in manufacturing. Technological progress was achieved through automation and economies of scale. On the other hand, the nation's largest sector, the service industries, depended on personal relations (e.g., medicine or hairstyling) where productivity growth remained sluggish because it was difficult to introduce gains. Though output in the service sector was hard to measure, the data suggested weak growth during the 1980s, only 0.7 percent annual increases in productivity compared with 3.8 percent in manufacturing.[18]

Service Sector Cutbacks During the Recession

The recession at the outset of the 1990s led to large layoffs in the service industries. Downsizing was common in banks, department stores, advertising agencies, and airlines, where cuts were made among middle managers, loan officers, and sales personnel. White-collar workers lost 41 percent of the jobs during the recession, the highest proportion on record. With growing global competition and the deregulation of telecommunications, transportation, banking, and insurance, these trends were likely to continue.[19]

core staffing
A company retains only a nucleus of permanent workers and contracts out the remaining jobs to temporary workers, part-time workers, and consultants.

Many service firms were moving toward a concept of **core staffing,** where the company retained only a shrinking nucleus of permanent workers and contracted out the remaining jobs to temporary workers, part-time workers, and consultants. Companies found it increasingly difficult to add full-time workers because of the cost of worker benefits (e.g., unemployment, health insurance, workers compensation and social security).

Many service companies also started to rethink the way they did their work. Work redesign, lean production, and total quality management were the rule. The Bank of Boston, for instance, changed the way it processed securities by consolidating the activity at a single location instead of 11 and reducing the number of computer systems from six to two.

Trade Imbalances

Service industries such as medical care, education, transportation, and government offered few opportunities for export. The country's merchandise trade balance, which in 1971 became negative for the first time in this century, continued along a negative path to reach record low levels (see Exhibit 11–3). The United States had a negative trade balance of $158.9 billion in 1990. Among its major rivals, only the United Kingdom had

EXHIBIT 11–3 Trade Balances and GNP Per Capita: 1990[20] (U.S. $ billions)

	United States	United Kingdom	France	Canada	Japan	Germany
Trade balance	$−122.3	$−37.6	$−17.8	$ 6.8	$ 52.2	$ 65.2
Imports	516.2	222.8	234.4	124.8	235.4	354.8
Exports	393.9	185.2	216.6	131.7	287.6	420.0
GNP per capita (U.S. $ thousands)	21.0	14.3	20.1	16.8	22.9	19.5

a similar negative balance. Other rivals had positive balances: Japan, $145.2 billion; Germany, $43.6 billion; France, $16.2 billion; and Canada, $9.2 billion.[21] The United States remained the world's leader in per capita purchasing power, but it trailed Japan in per capita GNP, largely because the GNP adjusts for the flow of money into a national economy from positive trade balances and resulting currency strength.

Manufacturing

U.S. decline was evident in capital-intensive manufacturing industries such as automobiles, steel, electronics, and home appliances. In these industries, improvement in productivity depends on capital investment; however, U.S. capital formation per employed person in the United States was down.[22]

Investment

Investment depends on savings, but U.S. savings rates also lagged behind other countries (see Exhibit 11–4). Capital costs in the United States, therefore, were higher. The weighted average of debt and equity costs after taxes during the 1980s was about 5.5 percent in the United States, 4 percent in West Germany, 3.5 percent in Great Britain, and 3 percent in Japan. Given Japan's advantage in capital costs, it was no surprise that its annual gross investment per factory worker was higher than that of the United States. This gap widened from a 40 percent lead during 1972–1982 to an 85 percent lead from 1982 to 1986.[23]

American businesses, like those in the United Kingdom, depended more heavily on equity financing than businesses in Japan or Germany. Equity holders assumed a part-ownership position—and the additional risks entailed—because they expected higher returns. This expectation put pressure on managers to produce short-term profits, and thus prevented as much investment in labor-saving equipment as the foreign rivals of the United States. Though productivity growth in the United States improved somewhat between 1986 and 1989, it still lagged behind that of other nations.

EXHIBIT 11–4 Personal Savings as Share of Disposable Personal Income

	United States	United Kingdom	France	Canada	Japan	Germany
1960	6.2	6.6	15.2	3.9	17.4	8.6
1970	8.3	9.2	18.7	5.6	18.2	13.8
1980	7.3	13.5	17.6	13.6	17.9	12.7
1985	4.5	9.7	14.0	13.3	16.0	11.4
1990	4.6	8.7	12.8	10.8	15.9	13.7

High Capital Costs

High capital costs meant that U.S. managers had to be extremely careful about the types of investments they made. They had to be able to demonstrate on a project-by-project basis that they could maximize returns or the projects would not be approved. The discount rate estimates used in cost projections made projects that promised big, immediate paybacks the favorites over long-term projects that promised gradual, less spectacular returns.

Dow Chemical estimated that its international competitors, which controlled 32 percent of the chemical market, paid three percentage points less for borrowed money and six points less for equity financing.[24] Dow's long-term spending had to be concentrated on a select group of technologies including engineering thermoplastics and pharmaceuticals, which were in related areas that complemented each other. Dow could wait only five years for these investments to start to pay off.

High-Tech Weakness

Weakness in manufacturing did not pose a serious threat if the United States continued to hold the lead in high technology, but the U.S. advantage in this area also deteriorated. The country lost market share in such high-tech industries as semiconductors, scientific and medical equipment, robotics, advanced fiber optics, and composite materials. The level of American inventions remained high, but the commercialization of new ideas into competitive products fell behind that of other nations.

High capital costs plagued computer giants like Control Data and Cray Research, which had to alter or abandon long-term plans to develop U.S. supercomputer technology. Although Control Data had invested $350 million in supercomputers, its bankers and shareholders were unwilling to spend at least $150 million more to wait for a possible payback. Cray Research also needed up to $200 million to complete its supercomputer projects; it even created a separate company for the venture called Cray Computer Corporation headed by Cray's founder, Seymour Cray, but Cray Computer did not last. In 1995, it filed for Chapter 11 protection under the Federal Bankruptcy Act.[25] This financial turbulence in the American computer industry put Japan's Hitachi, Fujitsu, and NEC, computer giants with no such problems, in a position to gain dominance in an important technology.

High capital costs have hurt technological development in particularly critical areas such as semiconductors, which are components to many other products. DRAMs are the semiconductor memory chip used in products from digital watches to supercomputers. The Japanese were able to gain control of a large percentage of this market, in part because they had lower capital costs that enabled them to continue to make high levels of investment even during downturns in the business cycle, something that no American manufacturer was able to do. While U.S. companies relied on the equity market to fund development and early manufacturing, the Japanese companies borrowed at one-quarter of the cost.[26]

U.S. companies hoped to overcome this disadvantage by forming a new joint venture. Called U.S. Memories, it included Intel, National Semiconductor, Advanced Micro Devices, LSI Logic, IBM, Digital Equipment Corporation (DEC), and Hewlett-Packard.[27] U.S. Memories tried to raise $1 billion in capital, half in equity from the member companies and the rest in debt. IBM, DEC, and Hewlett-Packard would be major consumers of the output of the new company, which would reduce much of the risk that chip makers standing alone previously faced (see Case 11–A on U.S. Memories at the end of this chapter).

Sometimes the rights to promising technologies were sold to overseas concerns because U.S. companies could not afford the development costs. In the late 1980s Allied-Signal Corporation's Bendix Electronics Groups became an innovator in the development of engine sensors and antilock brakes. However, to fully exploit these technologies the company would have to make a five-year investment of $1 billion. The German electronics giant Siemens was more willing and able to tolerate this expense. It purchased Bendix from Allied-Signal. Siemens' goals for the company were driven less by its monthly cash flow and more by what Bendix was doing to become a global leader in the technological areas in which it excels.[28]

The Call for Policies to Aid U.S. Industries

It could be argued that in a world of increasing international economic competition, the U.S. government had to take a more active role in enhancing the competitiveness of U.S. business. The best example was the Japanese government and its powerful Ministry of Trade and Industry (MITI), which played a role in that country's success.

Governments in other nations of the world routinely stimulated specific industries to promote exports (e.g., South Korea and textiles) and protect industries in decline (e.g., Germany and automobiles). They engaged in national planning or created complex systems of tariffs and subsidies that distorted free markets. They also tried to win an advantage in international trade by pegging their currencies to the dollar in a way that lowered export or import prices.

Another way government planners sought to gain a national advantage was by manipulating capital markets to encourage savings. If the flow of capital across international boundaries was restricted, the people in a country had to accept low rates of return, but industries benefited from low interest rates that stimulated investment and the modernization of industrial facilities. Governments then could use their influence on the financial system to direct investments toward industries they favored.

U.S. firms, it was argued, simply could not compete against subsidized and protected foreign firms unless the U.S. government had similar policies. Advocates of government

sunrise and sunset industries
The U.S. government should encourage the industries of tomorrow and phase out industries with no economic future.

assistance to industries argued that it was appropriate for the U.S. government to do the same as foreign governments. U.S. government officials should focus on the **sunrise industries** of tomorrow (e.g., biotechnology) and help ease the nation out of the **sunset industries** of yesterday (e.g., smokestack industries such as steel and coal).

Whereas, the opponents of these policies maintained that government officials were incapable of making these important decisions and that the market was better able to decide which industries had long-term potential, the advocates argued that the government had no choice but to become involved. They pointed to the many areas where the U.S. government already was involved in influencing the competitiveness of U.S. business (e.g., a host of federal rules and regulations that distort the operations of a free market). At a minimum, more coordinated government policy making was necessary.

The Government's Role in U.S. Economic Development

The United States started as a separate nation in 1776, the same year that *The Wealth of Nations* was published. Its author, Adam Smith, warned against a system of industrial policies that endeavors

> either by extraordinary encouragements to draw towards a particular species of industry a greater share of the capital of the society than what would naturally go to it; or, by extraordinary restraints to force from a particular species of industry some share of the capital that would otherwise be employed in it.[29]

Thomas Jefferson envisioned a nation of small proprietors and farmers, each with the liberty to conduct their own affairs as they saw fit.[30] The Federalists opposed Jefferson by promoting a vision of a strong central government that would play an active role in the nation's economic development. Alexander Hamilton, the Federalists' leader, believed that dispersed power would disrupt commerce and prevent the nation from making economic progress. Concentrating power in national institutions like a national bank would help further economic development. The easing of credit by the bank would stimulate commerce.

Since Hamilton's time, the federal government assisted in the building of railroads, canals, and harbors. It created roads and highways. It employed public funds to construct airports. It placed, at certain periods, high import taxes on products brought into the United States to protect American business. The 1896 Republican party platform advocated protectionism as the bulwark of American industrial independence and the foundation of U.S. development and prosperity.

Today, the federal government extends loans to the private sector with the Small Business Administration and the Federal Home Loan Bank system. In times of trouble, particular companies (e.g., Lockheed and Chrysler) have received government loans to bail them out (see Case 10–B on the Chrysler bailout). In addition, agriculture has been the recipient of a well-developed price support system. In addition, the U.S. government provides weather information and other navigational aids to the airline industry. Had it not been for the government, many businesses could not have started, would have failed, or would have been less profitable.

Assisting and Constraining Business

In the United States, a broad array of policies both assist and constrain business. They change the size of markets, the structure of markets, and the costs of doing business in an industry.[31] Government shifts the rules affecting commerce, but it also influences businesses more directly, simply by changing its purchases, since nearly a quarter of the nation's product is consumed by government (see Case 12–C on Alliant Techsystems).

The Size of Markets. Government's direct impacts come from the purchase of products or services (e.g., the defense industry). Indirect effects occur through policies that affect complements or substitutes for the products an industry sells. For the automobile industry, a critical complement is gasoline, whose price is affected by government policies. Highways are also affected by government policies. A substitute for auto travel is mass transit, which depends heavily on federal subsidies.

The Structure of Markets. The markets businesses serve are affected by the government. The patent system rewards innovation by granting a temporary monopoly, which is, in effect, a legal barrier to entry. Public regulation of gas and electric utilities has prevented competition and denied freedom of entry. Trade protection and antitrust actions have favored one industry over another. The extent of competition and the type of competition in an industry are influenced by government policies.

The Costs of Doing Business. Government policies also affect the costs of doing business. They vary the costs of inputs (e.g., raw materials, labor, and capital), thereby changing the overall cost structure. For instance, in addition to increasing the costs of all companies that rely on pollution-producing technologies, pollution requirements impact competitors—with different plant and equipment configurations—differently. In so doing, they create competitive advantage for some firms and competitive disadvantage for others. In contrast, government subsidies lower the cost structure in industries by reducing capital and other costs. Indirect subsidies, such as accelerated depreciation and tax credits, abound in the tax codes. Subsidies affect industries differently, favoring some industries over others. Likewise, government aid to education or sponsorship of R&D lowers the costs of firms and industries that require this aid.

Government policies have a large role to play in directing free-market forces. Michael Porter's model of business strategy identifies five forces that should be analyzed: rivalry among firms in an industry, the threat of new entrants, the threat of substitute products or services, the bargaining power of suppliers, and the bargaining power of buyers (see Chapter 2). The impact of these forces determines the ultimate profit potential of an industry. However, without a diagnosis of government policy, this analysis is incomplete.[32]

The Amount and Type of Involvement

Some commentators argue that from the American Revolution until about 1929, government involvement in the U.S. economy was minimal. U.S. businesses enjoyed relatively little interference and, as a consequence, flourished.[33] The reality, however, is that government involvement in the U.S. economy has always been significant.

EXHIBIT 11–5 A History of U.S. Government Involvement in Economic Activities

1887	Interstate Commerce Act
1890	Sherman Antitrust Act
1914	Clayton Act and Federal Trade Commission Act
1917	World War I: War Industries Board
1929–1933	Hoover presidency: Associationalist Policies
1933	National Industrial Recovery Act
1935	National Recovery Administration (found unconstitutional)
Late 1930s	New Deal: Selective regulation of key industries (e.g., airlines, communication, power)
1948	Employment Act
Early 1970s	Growth of new social regulation (e.g., EPA, OSHA, EEOC)
Late 1970s	Demise of Old Economic Regulation (e.g., airlines, trucking, banking)
1980s	Debate about industrial policies

It also has been controversial. Politicians were divided about how much involvement and what type of involvement the United States should encourage.[34] Some politicians cherished the competitive system and its individual freedom and feared a powerful state. Others welcomed concentrated state power. They believed the exercise of state power was essential for economic growth.

First Stirrings of Regulation

At about the time that the federal government passed the first national regulatory legislation, the 1887 Interstate Commerce Act (initially targeting price fixing and other abuses in the railroad industry), it also passed the Sherman Antitrust Act (1890), which was designed to prevent monopoly and promote free markets (see Exhibit 11–5). During the 1912 national elections, Theodore Roosevelt's Progressive party argued for centralized policies. Roosevelt hoped that the government would establish national regulation and have the power to control most aspects of commerce. It would fix prices. It would force companies to publish detailed accounts of their transactions, control security issuance, and investigate business activities. It also would control hours, wages, and the other conditions of labor.

In opposition to Roosevelt stood the Democratic party of Woodrow Wilson, which continued to adhere to its Jeffersonian origins. Wilson argued that it was not appropriate for government to try to dictate to businesses.

Influential political commentators like Walter Lippman criticized Wilson's ideas as appealing to the "planless scramble of little profiteers." Lippman favored big business over entrepreneurs. According to Lippman, the country did not need antitrust policies that would break up industries and restore the economy to "primitive competitive-like conditions."[35]

The controversy between Wilson and Roosevelt focused on the purposes the nation's antitrust legislation would serve. In 1914, the Clayton Act and the Federal Trade Commission Act were offered as extensions to the Sherman Act. Under Wilson's economic

New Freedom Woodrow Wilson's program to promote individual freedom by enhancing antitrust protection and increasing investigation of unfair business practices.

program, called the **New Freedom,** the purpose of these laws would be to specify which business practices were unfair and uncompetitive and to give a new antitrust commission wide powers to investigate and prosecute.

A Stronger Federal Role

This battle was won by Wilson, but the proponents of a stronger federal role had other chances to implement the policies they favored. During World War I, the War Industries Board (WIB) gained sweeping control over the national economy. Headed by financier Bernard Baruch, its purpose was to give business leaders the chance to benefit from "combination, cooperation, and common action with their natural competitors."[36]

This philosophy of business combination later flourished under the leadership of Secretary of Commerce, and later President, Herbert Hoover. Hoover encouraged businesses under his theme of **associationalism** to form trade and professional societies that would work in close cooperation with government. He used the FTC to implement his associationalist ideas. Business leaders would meet, ostensibly for the purpose of outlawing or suppressing unscrupulous forms of business practice. In reality, the codes devised under FTC authority often fostered collusion in fixing prices and restricting output. They failed to protect consumer interests. Ironically, Hoover associationalism became the model for postwar European reconstruction in Europe. French statesman Jean Monnet (the founder of the Common Market) called it "indicative planning" and tried to apply it throughout the European Community.

associationalism Formation of business trade and professional alliances that work closely with government to pursue common economic goals.

Planning under the New Deal

During the Great Depression, another effort to engage in business planning took place in the United States. The New Deal of Franklin Roosevelt was skeptical of the individualism of the past, which it blamed for the country's distress. It therefore sought increased collective action to turn around the nation's ailing economy.

One of the first initiatives of the New Deal was the National Industrial Recovery Act, which Congress passed in 1933. Under this legislation, the federal government set up the National Recovery Administration (NRA). It established industry codes that covered output, prices, wages, working conditions, investment, and trade practices. By 1934, the NRA had written 450 codes that extended to 5 million companies and 23 million employees.[37]

Although consumer and labor interests were represented on the NRA, business was the dominant group. Through its powerful trade associations, it was able to cast the NRA codes as it wanted. Labor was given increased wages in exchange for industry's right to raise prices and restrict output. Consumers received the promise of economic recovery. Small business was also underrepresented on the NRA and complained bitterly.

In 1935, the Supreme Court declared the NRA unconstitutional, effectively abolishing it. Supreme Court judges Louis Brandeis, a former adviser to Woodrow Wilson, and Felix Frankfurter opposed consolidated state power. They did not want the party of Jefferson to suppress the individualism for which it always had stood.[38]

Regulating Particular Sectors

With the passing of the NRA, the New Deal lost its capacity to comprehensively regulate economic activity. It regulated prices and entry in particular sectors instead. Separate regulatory agencies were established in a number of important emerging industries. In effect, protection against competition was afforded to the high-tech, infant industries of the period: aviation (Civil Aeronautics Board), communications (Federal Communications Commission), and natural gas (Federal Power Commission).

The deregulation movement of the late 1970s terminated the protection of these industries. They were now mature, and the agencies that had been set up during the New Deal to promote them stifled innovation and prevented dynamic adaptation to new competitive conditions.[39]

Business Cycle Management

After World War II, the government was expected to play an active role in smoothing the business cycle. Through the use of fiscal and monetary policies it could gain effective control over rates of growth, employment, and prices and prevent another depression.

The Council of Economic Advisers (CEA) was created to assist the president in devising appropriate macroeconomic policies to influence overall economic activity. The Employment Act of 1948 gave the federal government the responsibility to maintain economic growth, keep employment up, and assure that price levels were stable. President Kennedy's tax cuts, inspired by CEA director Walter Heller, helped start the longest continuous period of growth in American history.

When Richard Nixon assumed the presidency, economists believed the basic economic problem—business cycle instability—had been solved.[40] They felt that the "level of misery" in society, that is, the combined unemployment and inflation rates, was constant. Thus, fiscal and monetary policy tools simply gave partisan administrations a choice between tolerating more unemployment or more inflation: tight-money Republicans tolerated more unemployment while Democrats had to worry about a working-class constituency and favored less unemployment.[41] In 1970, no one anticipated that both the unemployment rate and the inflation rate could increase simultaneously, or that the economy again would get so out of control.

The New Social Regulation

Another government activity that gained ground in the post-World War II period was protecting people from unintended by-products of business activities, including environmental degradation, erosion of health, and exclusion of minorities. A new type of regulation, called social regulation, rose in importance (see Exhibit 11–6). It was far less acceptable to business than the old economic regulation, because it often involved government control over production and the quality of goods and services, not just government control over prices and entry.[42]

The new social regulation differed from earlier regulation in two other ways. First, the new agencies often had lengthy, specific laws rather than vague statutes. The Environmental

EXHIBIT 11–6 Selected Federal Regulatory Agencies

New Social	Old Economic
1964: Equal Employment Opportunity Commission (EEOC)	1887: Interstate Commerce Commission (ICC)
1970: Environmental Protection Agency (EPA)	1920: Federal Power Commission (FPC)
1970: Occupational Safety and Health Administration (OSHA)	1933: Federal Deposit Insurance Corporation (FDIC)
1972: Consumer Product Safety Commission (CPSC)	1934: Federal Communications Commission (FCC)

Protection Agency (EPA), for example, had precise pollution reduction targets and timetables, which allowed little room for discretion. In contrast, the Federal Trade Commission, which had no specific timetable for eliminating unfair methods of competition, had great latitude for discretionary behavior. In addition, the new agencies were often organized along functional lines. The EPA, for example, regulated the pollution of all firms, unlike the FCC or the ICC, which were limited to a particular industry. The new agencies, as a result, were less likely to have sympathy with those they regulated. They were more resistant to domination by forces within a single industry.

According to Murray Weidenbaum, who served in the Reagan administration as head of the CEA, these changes signified a "second managerial revolution." The first revolution had involved a shift in decision-making power from the formal owners of business corporations to professional managers. The second revolution shifted power from corporate management to government planners and regulators, who influenced and controlled key managerial tasks. The distinction between private power and public power was becoming "increasingly blurred."[43]

Growth in the new social regulation, however, must not be confused with government growth in general.[44] It constitutes less than 3 percent of all federal spending and employment. Defense expenditures, entitlements, transfers to state and local governments, and interest payments on the federal debt dwarf the amount of money spent on regulation.

Government Support for Industries in Other Nations

Today, the debate about government's role concerns industrial policies, which are meant to improve a country's international competitive position by fostering the growth of "strategic" industries.[45] These policies rely on the government to offer incentives and impose constraints. Incentives cause transactions that would not occur if market forces alone were operating. Constraints prevent deals that would take place if these forces operated by themselves. The proponents of industrial policies argue that the American economy, which has been threatened by energy shortages, inflation, unemployment, and economic stagnation, is in decline. The Japanese, along with other international rivals, support their industries. Therefore, the United States has no choice but to do so also.

General or nonselective industrial policies, which can be distinguished from sector-specific industrial policies, are available to all industries. An example of a sector-specific policy is the government's long-term effort to shape the development of American agriculture through production quotas, prices, and income policies. Another example is its use of price controls, taxes, direct regulation, and research and development to shape energy development. On the other hand, the bailouts of Lockheed, Boeing, Continental Illinois, and other companies, are examples of short-term, firm-specific policies.

These policies raise two separate but related issues: the economic issue of whether it is possible in the United States to select strategic sectors that are worth promoting, and the political issue of whether it is possible to administer a national policy designed to help these sectors.

Have Government Policies Helped Industries in Other Nations?

Opponents of industrial policies maintain that the extent to which they have actually helped economic development in other countries is exaggerated.[46] For instance, in Japan, MITI tried but failed to coordinate firm behavior in industries such as cotton spinning, automobiles, and computers. These industries remain intensely competitive despite efforts by MITI to limit competition. It is even possible that MITI's policies inadvertently spurred competition as firms entered the market in anticipation of earning cartel-like profits.

In industries where Japan had the most domestic competitors (e.g., pocket calculators) it was the most successful. In industries where MITI was active (e.g., shipbuilding), Japan confronted overcapacity. MITI helped downsize these industries.

In the early stages of industrialization, when a nation is building heavy industry and infrastructure, centrally coordinated industrial policies may be effective, but in later stages, when a nation is involved in worldwide competition in high-tech areas such as integrated circuits and microprocessors, relying on government-coordinated industrial policies may be a disadvantage. In this stage, industries must be prepared for rapid change. They have to be sensitive to market signals and cannot take orders from slow-moving government bureaucracies whose orientation is as much political as economic.

Industrial Policy Making in France. The French government takes an active role in planning industrial policy. Its indicative planning model, borrowed from Hoover's associationalism, had as its purpose to "construct a series of national champions" that would compete in international markets.[47] The French believed strongly that those policies were needed because the scale and efficiency of French industry were not adequate for world competition. A group of elite civil servants, trained in the most prestigious institutions of higher learning in France, implemented the policies. Insulated from political pressures, their mission was to regulate competitive forces without input from trade unions, consumer groups, small businesses, or farmers, all of which were excluded from their forums.

French industrial policies came together in national plans after World War II, when the French economy, along with that of other nations, flourished. The fifth and sixth plans, formulated in 1968 and 1970, involved comprehensive efforts at resource allocation, including incomes policies for labor and specific investments for business, but they were not completely implemented. Neither business, government, nor labor was willing to cooperate fully. Notable flops were the plans to build an internationally competitive computer industry and a commercially viable supersonic aircraft, the Concorde, in cooperation with Great Britain.

U.S. Policies Affecting Industry

Critics have argued that American industries suffered because the policies of the U.S. government were inconsistent and lacked order. There was little overall coordination or sense of purpose.[48] For instance:

- Import restrictions mainly aided the steel, textiles and apparel, and motor vehicle industries (see Chapter 9);
- Federally subsided loans mainly helped the home construction industry and agriculture.
- The federal government financed roughly one-half of U.S. research and development (R&D), but much of it went to defense-related businesses and a high proportion to the aerospace industry.

The patchwork of federal policies, created incrementally over time in response to specific contingencies, reflected the influence of lobbyists and special-interest groups.

Outcomes of the policy-making process were unstable. What one Congress or administration did was undone by another. Laws were amended and reamended in rapid succession. Changes in party, administration, and intellectual fashion brought new policies to the forefront; with them came new conditions with which business managers had to contend. For example, regular overhauls of the tax system meant that business managers could not be certain that today's tax policies would remain in place tomorrow. The investments they made might not pay off when the political environment was different.[49]

Government Responsibility for Declining Competitiveness

According to the critics, government's responsibility for declining competitiveness was in two main areas:[50]

stop-and-go macroeconomic policies Alternating stimulatory and deflationary policies used by the government to deal with stagflation (high unemployment and inflation).

1. Contradictory, Stop-and-Go Macroeconomic Policies. President Lyndon Johnson's guns-and-butter spending policies were not matched by tax increases. He conducted the War on Poverty at the same time that the United States was engaged in the Vietnam War. Strong inflationary pressures already were present at the time of the 1973 Arab oil embargo. The transfer of huge amounts of money to oil-exporting nations weakened the economy further.

The efforts by presidents Nixon, Ford, and Carter to deal simultaneously with high inflation and unemployment—stagflation—were largely ineffective. Existing macroeconomic theory was not designed to cope with these conditions. It had good remedies for only one problem at a time. With both problems present, successive administrations waffled between stimulatory policies to end the recessionary conditions and deflationary policies to put a brake on high prices.

President Reagan took new initiatives. He cut taxes to spur consumer spending and increased government spending on defense. The Federal Reserve Bank, under the leadership of Paul Volcker, tightly controlled the money supply, bringing the rapidly accelerating inflation of the late 1970s to a halt. The cost, however, was a massive recession; weak economic growth quickly depleted government revenues.

The combined effects of these policies yielded a federal debt that nearly doubled. The interest payments on the debt accelerated. Government demand for money to finance the deficit crowded out private investment, which in turn hurt lagging U.S. competitiveness.

With the demand for money high, U.S. interest rates were greater than interest rates in other nations. Foreign money was attracted to the United States, raising the value of the dollar. With the dollar highly valued, American manufacturers had difficulty selling their goods abroad and foreign producers found it easy to sell their goods in the United States.

2. Inconsistent Industrial Policies and Ineffective Trade Policies. Macroeconomic difficulties took place at the same time that the government failed to develop consistent industrial or effective trade policies. To many people in the business community, federal tax, credit, spending, and trade policies were inefficient, random, and confusing. The tax system, for instance, rewarded real estate investments but discriminated against investments in manufacturing. The assistance provided to the chemical and aerospace industries was greater than that given to paper products and pharmaceuticals. The reasons for the differences were not apparent; federal policies neither created an "even playing field" nor did they marshal resources in an effective manner to assist targeted growth industries.

Business Responsibility for Declining Competitiveness

These arguments about government's responsibility for lagging American competitiveness were matched by arguments placing the responsibility squarely on business.[51]

- American managers had a short-term time horizon, where the emphasis was almost exclusively on return on investment and share price increases rather than market share and new products (see Exhibit 11–7).
- They did not pay sufficient attention to product quality and costs.
- They were bureaucratic and indecisive, and slow in introducing new technologies, manufacturing processes, and products.
- They were more interested in financial manipulation and short-term cost reductions than in achieving long-term competitiveness and market share.
- They set high return-on-investment (ROI) targets, so that many potentially worthy projects were not undertaken.
- Their preoccupation with selling and buying assets kept them from focusing on production; and caused unnecessary labor-management friction.
- Their investments in real estate and commerce, speculative activities, and interest in takeovers sacrificed long-term competitiveness and markets for short-term results.

Exhibit 11–7 Corporate Objectives: U.S. and Japanese Managers[52]

U.S. Managers	*Japanese Managers*
1. Return on investment	1. Market share
2. Share price increase	2. Return on investment
3. Market share	3. New products
4. Product portfolio	4. Rationalize production and distribution

Critics maintained that foreign managers had different goals and time frames (compare the order of priorities of U.S. and Japanese managers in Exhibit 11–7). The goals and timetables of foreign managers matched those of their governments. While U.S. managers sought short-term profitability and shareholder wealth maximization, foreign managers pursued long-term growth, competitive viability, and stable employment, precisely the goals needed for sustained success in the international marketplace.

Why Carrying Out Policies to Assist U.S. Industries Is Difficult

The critics missed an important point about why it is difficult to effectively carry out policies to assist industries in the United States. National crises, like war, may be able to temporarily unify the American people, but the Constitutional system is built on checks and balances and divided power.

The American Political Tradition

Three characteristics of the American system make it difficult to carry out industrial policies:

1. *A profusion of interest groups*. The founders of the American republic embraced the idea that numerous interests should exist. Diversity reflects the different backgrounds of the American people and the dynamic character of U.S. society. The existence of many interests dilutes the strength of any particular one. Indeed, no single organization represents business or labor in the United States as it does in other countries. Thus, policies favored by one business group are likely to be opposed by another business group.

2. *The accessibility of political institutions*. No one ever seems to permanently lose a political battle in the United States. Frustrated interests always have appeal to other governmental units. State and local governments exist alongside the federal government. The three branches of the federal government are not unified in any coherent and logical way. The executive branch has departments that represent diverse interests—business and labor, environmentalists and developers, and so on. Congress is divided into numerous committees and subcommittees. Even after it has enacted a law, there is no assurance that the law can be effectively carried out because the bureaucracy, which is charged with implementing the legislation, must face an array of competing interests.

3. *The absence of a neutral administrative elite*. No trusted, professionally based, neutral civil service exists in the United States on the scale that it exists in such European nations as France or Great Britain. The U.S. bureaucracy, particularly at its upper reaches where the appointments are almost all political, is more partisan. An impartial bureaucracy is needed to make industrial policy decisions.

These obstacles do not mean that industrial policies cannot be carried out in the United States. They simply mean that the U.S. political system has not been designed to make it easy to do so. An enduring sense of national peril would be necessary if private groups were to permit the government to exercise the kind of authority needed to carry out industrial policies effectively.

The Need Still Exists

The proponents of industrial policies grant that these obstacles exist. Nevertheless, they hold that industrial policies are still necessary.[53] They point to four reasons:

1. The federal government already is extensively involved in making these policies. It is playing a role in a variety of ways, but the role it is playing is inadvertent and lacks coherence. For instance, the U.S. tax code favors some industries over others. Federal R&D constitutes nearly half the R&D conducted but federal R&D policies lack clear priorities and were formulated without careful consideration of their overall effects. At a minimum, the U.S. government should coordinate the many policies it already has.

2. The nature of international competition is such that other nations are providing assistance to their industries through subsidies, favorable exchange rates, low-interest loans, and in other ways. Thus, the U.S. government also needs to provide help.

3. When industries ask for trade relief, the government needs to have criteria to evaluate the claims. It cannot engage in ad hoc policy making. In exchange for the relief it grants, it must demand concessions that will force industries to modernize and compel them to reduce excess capacity, invest in new plant and equipment, lower wages, and change work rules.

4. As some industries lose competitiveness and others gain competitiveness, the government should play a role in easing the transition. It should follow the lead of Japan, which provides for the retraining of displaced workers who might otherwise have trouble finding new jobs.

Institutional Arrangements to Implement These Policies

The proponents of industrial policies believe that institutional arrangements have to be created to implement these policies. They imagine a Council on Industrial Competitiveness in the White House, which would function like the Council of Economic Advisers. Just as the CEA coordinates the federal government's macroeconomic decisions, the Council on Industrial Competitiveness would coordinate the microeconomic decisions.

For proponents of industrial policies, federal government involvement in macroeconomic matters is insufficient. Since the government is already involved in microeconomics, proponents say, it should be more careful about what it is doing. Given the realities of international competition, it has to coordinate its efforts.

Opponents of industrial policies believe that additional government bureaucracies are unnecessary and unwarranted, that they extend the scope of government far beyond what can be defended in economic theory. Even if coordinated industrial policies have facilitated economic growth in other nations, they would not necessarily succeed in the United States with its special political traditions.

In carrying out industrial policies, four problems stand out:

- Changing market perceptions about the relative costs and benefits of a policy.
- Division within government (e.g., between prodevelopment and antidevelopment forces or between politicians with different views of the proper role of government).
- Industry disagreement (e.g., whether a program should exist and how extensive it should be).
- Lack of consensus about the appropriate means to achieve policy goals.

These factors suggest difficulties likely to affect any effort to initiate and carry out long-term, strongly interventionist industrial policies.

An Agenda to Restore U.S. Competitiveness

Some things that the United States might consider doing to help restore its competitiveness include increasing savings and investment while keeping consumption at a fixed share of the GNP and cutting military expenditures by eliminating the causes of war.[54] Like Great Britain before it, the United States is finding it difficult to combine high domestic consumption with substantial military commitments. A number of other suggestions are:[55]

- Open foreign markets to U.S. exports.
- Provide managers with the incentive to take a long-term perspective.
- Elevate technically sophisticated individuals to top management positions.
- Remove incentives for financial manipulation and paper profits.
- Raise educational standards.
- Strengthen incentives for environmental protection and energy conservation.
- Reform the system of product liability.

Conclusions

This chapter has looked at arguments that the U.S. economy is in decline. It has examined how well the country is doing compared with its major international rivals, stressed the issue of productivity, discussed the decline in services and manufacturing, and noted weaknesses in high-tech areas such as supercomputers and semiconductors.

The U.S. government has provided practical assistance to American businesses in many ways. Its policies affect the size and structure of markets and the costs of doing business. Government policies are of strategic importance to all firms.

Among the most important changes in the role of government in the post-World War II period has been its involvement in fiscal policy management, its expanded role in social regulation, and its diminished role in economic regulation. In the 1980s, the debate about government shifted: Given the realities of the new international competition, what should it do? Proponents of industrial policies maintained that the U.S. government should play an active role. Opponents held that the U.S. government was incapable of playing a larger role. This chapter ends with several suggestions to enhance U.S. competitiveness.

Discussion Questions

1. What are some of the trends in the U.S. economy? How strong is the U.S. economy? What are some of its weaknesses?
2. Give some examples of what governments do to promote business. Should the United States carry out similar policies?
3. How would you distinguish the views of Jefferson and Hamilton on the role of government in economic development? Has the United States evolved in a more Jeffersonian or more Hamiltonian direction?
4. Give examples of the way the U.S. government influences business. What strategic importance do these influences have?
5. Describe the controversy surrounding the passage of the 1914 FTC Act.
6. Explain why you would or would not agree with the statement that the Democrats always have been the party of big government and the Republicans always have been the party of small government.
7. What was the NRA? What was it designed to accomplish? Why was it declared unconstitutional?
8. Distinguish between the new social regulation and the old economic regulation.
9. Discuss the major innovations in U.S. government policy toward industry after World War II.
10. To what degree is the U.S. government responsible for declining U.S. competitiveness?
11. To what extent is business responsible for declining U.S. competitiveness?
12. Why is it so difficult to formulate policies to aid the competitiveness of U.S. industries?
13. What can the United States do to enhance its competitiveness? What policies should a major business group like the Business Roundtable propose to the U.S. government?
14. In your opinion, should the United States have industrial policies? If yes, what kind of industrial policies should it have?

Endnotes

1. Paul Kennedy, "The (Relative) Decline of America," *Atlantic*, August 1987, pp. 29–38; P. Kennedy, *The Rise and Fall of the Great Powers* (New York: Vintage Books, 1987).
2. P. G. Peterson, "The Morning After," *Atlantic* 260 (1987), pp. 43–69.
3. L. C. Thurow, "How to Get Out of The Economic Rut," *New York Review of Books*, February 14, 1985, pp. 9–10.
4. "U.S. Competitiveness in Manufacturing," Case No. 9–386–133, Harvard Business School, 1986.
5. *The Reindustrialization of America* (New York: McGraw-Hill, 1982); I. M. Destler, *American Trade Politics: System under Stress* (Washington, D.C.: Institute for International Economics, 1986).
6. R. Z. Lawrence, *Can America Compete?* (Washington, D.C.: Brookings Institution, 1984); J. S. Nye, *Bound to Lead* (New York: Basic Books, 1990); J. E. Schwarz, *America's Hidden Success: A Reassessment of Public Policy from Kennedy to Reagan* (New York: W. W. Norton, 1988); J. E. Schwarz and T. J. Volgy, "The Myth of America's Economic Decline," *Harvard Business Review*, Sept.–Oct. 1985, p. 101.
7. D. B. Yoffie, "Note on Free Trade and Protectionism," Working Paper no. 383–174, Harvard Business School, 1983.
8. President's Commission on Industrial Competitiveness, *Global Competition: The New Reality*, vol. 1 (Washington, D.C.: U.S. Government Printing Office, 1985).
9. "U.S. Competitiveness in Manufacturing," Case 9–386–133, Harvard Business School, 1986; New York Stock Exchange, Office of Economic Research, *U.S. International Competitiveness: Perception and Reality*, August 1984.
10. Robert Reich, "Making Industrial Policy," *Foreign Affairs*, Spring 1982, pp. 852–82.
11. Ibid.
12. Central Intelligence Agency, *Handbook of Economic Statistics*, (Washington, D.C.: U.S. Government Printing Office, 1991), p. 11.
13. "Can America Compete?" *Business Week*, Aug. 6, 1990, p. 14.
14. Thomas Steward, "U.S. Productivity," *Fortune*, Oct. 19, 1992, pp. 54–57.
15. Andrew Kupfer, "How American Industry Stacks Up," *Fortune*, March 9, 1992, pp. 30–46.
16. "America's Investment Famine," *The Economist*, June 27, 1992, pp. 89–90.
17. E. F. Denison, *Trends in American Economic Growth, 1929–1982* (Washington, D.C.: Brookings Institution, 1985); "U.S. Competitiveness in Manufacturing," Case no. 9–386–133, Harvard Business School, 1986; Council of Economic Advisers, *Economic Report of the President*, 1984.
18. "Why Services Are Different," *The Economist*, July 18, 1992, p. 67.
19. *The Economist.*
20. Central Intelligence Agency, *Handbook of Economic Statistics.*
21. *The Economist.*
22. Louis Richman, "How Capital Costs Cripple America," *Fortune* Aug. 14, 1989, pp. 50–54.
23. "U.S. Competitiveness in Manufacturing," Harvard Business School; C. Rappoport, "Why Japan Keeps Winning," *Fortune* 124 (1991), pp. 76–88.
24. Rappoport, "Why Japan Keeps Winning," pp. 76–88.
25. Ibid.
26. W. Ouchi, *The M-Form Society: How American Teamwork Can Recapture the Competitive Edge* (Reading, Mass.: Addison-Wesley, 1984).
27. Michael Hawthorne, "High Technology Economic Policy: Some Thoughts on Sematech," paper presented at the Annual Meeting of the American Political Science Association, Sept. 1991.
28. Rappoport, "Why Japan Keeps Winning."
29. Adam Smith, *The Wealth of Nations* (New York: Modern Library, 1965), p. 650.

30. K. Prewitt and S. Verba, *An Introduction to American Government* (New York: Harper & Row, 1974).
31. J. Gale, R. A. Buchholz, and A. A. Marcus, *Achieving Competitive Advantage through the Political Process: Business Strategy and Legitimacy,* Discussion Paper No. 75, The Strategic Management Research Center, The University of Minnesota, 1987; J. Gale and R. A. Buchholz, "The Political Pursuit of Competitive Advantage: What Business Can Gain from Government," in *Business Strategy and Public Policy,* ed. A. A. Marcus, A. M. Kaufman, and D. R. Beam (Westport, Conn.: Greenwood Press, 1987), pp. 31–41.
32. M. E. Porter, "The Competitive Advantage of Nations," *Harvard Business Review,* March–April 1990, p. 28.
33. M. Friedman and R. Friedman, *Free to Choose: A Personal Statement* (New York: Avon Books, 1980).
34. A. Kaufman, L. S. Zacharias, and A. Marcus, "Managers United for Corporate Rivalry: A History of Managerial Collective Action," *Journal of Policy History* 2 (1990), pp. 56–97; T. K. McCraw, "Mercantilism and the Market: Antecedents of American Industrial Policy," in *The Politics of Industrial Policy*, ed. C. E. Barfield and W. A. Schammbra (Washington, D.C.: American Enterprise Institute, 1986), pp. 33–62; J. C. Miller, T. F. Walcott, W. E. Kovacic, and J. A. Rabkin, "Industrial Policy: Reindustrialization through Competition or Coordinated Action?" *Yale Journal on Regulation* 2 (1984), pp. 1–37.
35. Cited in Miller et al., "Industrial Policy."
36. Ibid., p. 124.
37. Kaufman et al., "Managers United for Corporate Rivalry"; Miller, et al., "Industrial Policy."
38. T. K. McCraw, *Prophets of Regulation: Charles Frances Adams, Louis D. Brandeis, James M. Landis, Alfred E. Kahn* (Cambridge, Mass.: Harvard University Press, 1984)
39. A. Marcus, "Business Demand for Regulation: An Exploration of the Stigler Hypothesis," *Research in Corporate Social Performance and Policy* 7 (1985), pp. 25–46; A. Marcus, "Airline Deregulation, Business Strategy, and Regulatory Theory," in *Public Policy and Economic Institutions* (Greenwich, Conn.: JAI Press, 1990); A. Marcus, "Airline Deregulation: Why the Supporters Lost Out," *Long Range Planning* 20, no. 1 (1987), pp. 90–98; B. Mitnick, *The Political Economy of Regulation* (New York: Columbia University Press, 1980).
40. J. D. Gwartney and R. L. Stroup, *Economics: Private and Public Choice* (New York: Harcourt Brace Jovanovich, 1987).
41. A. Marcus and B. Mevorach, "Planning for the U.S. Political Cycle," *Long Range Planning* 21 (1988), pp. 50–56; P. Young, A. Marcus, R. S. Koot, and B. Mevorach, "Improved Business Planning through an Awareness of Political Cycles," *Journal of Forecasting* 9 (1990), pp. 37–52.
42. W. Lilley and J. C. Miller, "The New Social Regulation," *Public Interest,* Spring 1977, pp. 49–62; P. Weaver, "Regulation, Social Policy, and Class Conflict," *Public Interest,* Winter 1978, pp. 45–64; A. A. Marcus, *The Adversary Economy: Business Responses to Changing Government Requirements* (Westport, Conn.: Quorum Books, 1984).
43. M. L. Weidenbaum, "The Future of Business/Government Relations in the United States," in *The Future of Business: Global Issues in the 80s and 90s,* ed. M. Ways (New York: Pergamon Press, 1979), pp. 48–76.
44. A. A. Marcus, *The Adversary Economy: Business Responses to Changing Government Requirements* (Westport, Conn.: Quorum Books, 1984).
45. F. G. Adams and C. A. Bollins, "Meaning of Industrial Policy," in F. G. Adams and L. R. Klein, eds., *Industrial Policies for Growth and Competitiveness* (Lexington, Mass.: D.C. Heath, 1983); C. S. Allen, and H. Rishikoff, "Tale Thrice Told: A Review of Industrial Policy Proposals," *Journal of Policy Analysis and Management,* 1985, p. 4; J. L. Badaracco and D. B. Yoffie, "'Industrial Policy': It Can't Happen Here," *Harvard Business Review,* November–December 1983, pp. 97–105; C. E. Barfield and W. A. Schammbra, eds., *The Politics of Industrial Policy* (U.S.A.:

American Enterprise Institute, 1986), pp. 187–205; A. T. Denzau, *Will an 'Industrial Policy' Work for the United States?* formal publication No. 57, Center for the Study of American Business, Washington University, 1983; A. A. Marcus and A. M. Kaufman, "Why It Is Difficult to Implement Industrial Policies: Lessons from the Synfuels Experience," *California Management Review* 28 (1986), pp. 98–114; P. Norton, "A Reader's Guide to Industrial Policy," in *The Politics of American Economic Policy Making,* ed. P. Peretz (Armonk, NY: M. E. Sharpe, 1987), pp. 126–27; K. Phillips, *Staying on Top: The Business Case for a National Industrial Strategy* (New York: Random House, 1984); C. L. Schultze, "Industrial Policy: A Solution in Search of a Problem," *California Management Review* 25 (1983), pp. 5–15.

46. G. Gilder, "A Supply-Side Economics of the Left," *Public Interest,* Summer 1983, pp. 29–43; A. Etzioni, "The MITIzation of America," *Public Interest,* Summer 1983, pp. 44–51.
47. S. S. Cohen, S. Halimi, and J. Zysman, "Institutions, Politics, and Industrial Policy in France," in *The Politics of Industrial Policy,* ed. C. E. Barfield and W. A. Schammbra (Washington, D.C.: American Enterprise Institute, 1986), pp. 106–27; D. C. Mueller, ed., *The Political Economy of Growth* (New Haven: Conn.: Yale University Press, 1983).
48. R. Reich, "An Industrial Policy of the Right," *Public Interest,* Fall 1983, pp. 3–17; R. B. Reich, *The Next American Frontier: A Provocative Program for Economic Renewal,* (Harrisonburg, Va.: R. R. Donnelley, 1983).
49. A. A. Marcus, "Policy Uncertainty and Technological Innovation," *Academy of Management Review* 6 (1981), pp. 443–48.
50. U.S. House of Representatives, Committee on Banking, Finance and Urban Affairs, Industrial Competitiveness Act, April 1984; "U.S. Competitiveness in Manufacturing," Case No. 9–386–133, Harvard Business School, 1986.
51. Denison, *Trends in American Economic Growth;* C. W. L. Hill, M. A. Hitt, and R. E. Hoskisson, "Declining U.S. Competitiveness: Reflections on a Crisis," *The Academy of Management Executive* 2 (1988), pp. 51–60; U.S. House of Representatives, Committee on Banking, Finance and Urban Affairs, Industrial Competitiveness Act, April 1984; "U.S. Competitiveness in Manufacturing," Harvard Business School; Robert Reich, "The Next American Frontier," *Atlantic Monthly,* 1983, pp. 53–57.
52. George Cabot Lodge, *Comparative Business Government Relations* (Englewood Cliffs, N.J.: Prentice Hall, 1990), p. 26.
53. S. E. Eizenstat, "Reindustrialization through Coordination or Chaos?" *Yale Journal on Regulation* 2 (1984), pp. 39–51.
54. R. Rosecrance, *America's Economic Resurgence: A Bold New Strategy* (New York: Harper & Row, 1990).
55. Compare with Michael Porter, *The Competitive Advantage of Nations* (New York: Free Press, 1990).

Case 11–A
U.S. Memories: Global Competition in the Semiconductor Industry[1]

The way I describe it is, we finally after a lot of years of bickering with one another found a common motivator. It was called fear . . . The CEOs discovered they were in deep trouble. They honestly understood that it was not likely that they could turn [the U.S. DRAM industry] around on their own and that something needed to be done or they would have difficulty surviving as companies.

Sanford Kane, CEO, U.S. Memories, April 1992

It was late Friday afternoon on a sunny July day in Cupertino, California, in 1989. John Smith returned to his office at Apple Computer after a long management team meeting to find a thick envelope with a business plan for a new semiconductor manufacturing consortium called U.S. Memories. The president of Apple was asking John to evaluate the plan and present his recommendations to the board. John had to decide whether or not Apple should join seven other firms, including IBM, Hewlett-Packard (HP), and Digital Equipment Corporation (DEC), and become a member of U.S. Memories.

U.S. Memories' goal was to become a major DRAM (pronounced *DEE-Ram*) producer. DRAMs, or dynamic random access memory chips, are the most common type of semiconductor chip, representing approximately 14 percent of the total market. For the past two years, these memory chips had been extremely expensive and difficult to obtain. DRAM prices began to rise in mid-1987 after a series of trade disputes between the United States and Japan. These disputes culminated in the 1986 U.S.–Japanese Semiconductor Trade Agreement (SCTA), which was followed by the imposition of sanctions on Japanese semiconductor manufacturers for failure to comply with the agreement (see Case 9-B on Motorola).

During this time, semiconductor and computer systems manufacturers, numerous politicians, and policy makers were extremely concerned that Japanese firms produced approximately 90 percent of the world's DRAMs. U.S. Memories' principal goal was to assure a stable, American-made supply of DRAMs for its member companies. In addition, the consortium sought to double the world market share of American DRAM producers and to restore domestic DRAM production.

Smith knew Apple had lost a lot of money buying DRAMs in 1988 and 1989 when prices were high and supplies tight. Though the idea of a stable, domestic DRAM supply was indeed attractive, Smith needed to carefully evaluate the proposed venture.

Buying DRAMS

In 1984, world chip consumption began to slow; the next year demand for DRAMs collapsed. Chip makers were hit with tremendous losses due to excess capacity. They responded by cutting prices. Aggregate DRAM prices per bit fell by nearly 80 percent. Unable to compete in the face of overcapacity and rapidly falling prices, U.S. DRAM manufacturers pressured the government for trade protection against Japanese rivals. The government responded with the Semiconductor Trade Agreement and imposition of trade sanctions. These sanctions came shortly after DRAM prices had bottomed out. During the next two years, DRAM prices surged to unprecedented levels. Price increases and tight supplies had not been experienced before by computer systems manufacturers.

Apple and the other systems manufacturers were extremely concerned about the volatile DRAM market conditions of the late 1980s. A combination of unique events made DRAM market signals difficult to interpret. First, there was the almost complete shift in global market share from the United States to Japan. This brought with it considerable suspicion and mistrust of Japanese firms by U.S. manufacturers. Second, the introduction of the 1Mb chip in 1986 brought new technological challenges for semiconductor manufacturers, as the use of new materials in the production process made initial reject rates as high as 90 to 95 percent in some cases. Chip prices stayed high longer than usual in the early stage of this generation because new manufacturing systems had to be developed. Third, higher DRAM prices after 1987 were partly the result of an upsurge in demand for personal computers and workstations packed with as much as four times the memory of previous models. The increased demand for personal computers drove up demand for chips, but DRAM suppliers had cut their production in response to the soft demand of 1984–1985. This meant that demand outstripped supply for a short period while chip makers rushed to increase capacity. Moreover, a short supply of older generation chips, such as the 256K, was in part caused by manufacturers shifting too much capacity too quickly to the newer generation chips. Finally, the sanctions levied against Japan for failure to comply with the SCTA added yet another element of uncertainty to the price surge of 1987.

In addition to high prices and tight supplies, rumors began to surface in the industry that some Japanese chip manufacturers had begun using controversial "tying practices," that is, pressuring U.S. DRAM consumers to buy other unwanted products as a precondition for being allowed to purchase DRAMs.[2] The Semiconductor Industry Association (SIA) charged that Japanese firms were using the SCTA and trade sanctions as a convenient cover for their coordinated attack on the U.S. computer manufacturing industry. Indeed, Apple Computer and other U.S. computer systems manufacturers depended on Japanese firms for their DRAM supplies. The vertically integrated Japanese DRAM manufacturers, however, competed directly with Apple in downstream computer markets. This strange dependence was uncomfortable at best and a serious strategic threat at worst.

In the past, Apple had been accustomed to regular price and supply cycles over each chip generation and maintained a policy of buying its chips from a wide range of suppliers from around the world. The turbulent DRAM market conditions of 1987–1989 had eroded Apple's leverage with its chip suppliers. Apple had lost money buying expensive DRAMs for two years in a row. It was unclear whether high DRAM prices and tight supplies were transitory phenomena or permanent structural changes in the international semiconductor industry. If permanent structural changes were indeed occurring, perhaps a stronger domestic industry would be the answer to the problems Apple faced.

By 1989, all but three U.S. companies (Micron, Texas Instruments, and Motorola) had left the DRAM business, and those remaining did not have nearly the capacity to satisfy the DRAM needs of Apple and other U.S. systems manufacturers. If the unprecedented price surge and tight supplies were the result of a calculated attack by Japanese firms, management would need to take some action to secure a stable supply of DRAMs.

Concerns about the Domestic DRAM Industry. The volatile state of the DRAM market in the late 1980s reinforced the need for domestically owned production capabilities. Industrial policy advocates and large computer systems manufacturers such as IBM emphasized the need to protect and nurture vital domestic industries such as DRAMs. The loss of these industries would be detrimental for the following reasons:

1. Users of DRAMs became dependent on foreign suppliers.
2. Semiconductor equipment manufacturers—companies providing machines and materials used in making DRAMs and other semiconductors—had their customer base weakened.
3. Spillovers resulting from the design and production of DRAMs, such as the diffusion of technological know-how, were not realized.
4. National security could be jeopardized.

U.S. Memories was meant to be an important first step in restoring the domestic DRAM industry through active industry and government intervention.

DRAM Users

By the late 1980s, computer systems manufacturers faced technological dependence on foreign firms that were their direct competitors in many downstream markets. Japan's main DRAM manufacturers—NEC, Mitsubishi, Fujitsu, Hitachi, Toshiba, and Oki—were vertically integrated into downstream products such as computer systems, laser printers, and business machines. U.S. computer systems manufacturers such as IBM, HP, and DEC competed with them in many markets and relied on them for DRAMs. Japanese firms had captured more than 80 percent of the worldwide DRAM market and more than 90 percent of the most advanced 1Mb DRAM market by 1987. With only three domestic DRAM manufacturers remaining, U.S. computer makers had few domestic supply options.

U.S. systems manufacturers were hurt by escalating DRAM prices that raised their production costs. For example, the price of 256K DRAMs was $1.99 in late 1986. This price rose to as much as $3.50 in late 1988. Faced with rising costs, computer systems manufacturers had to increase prices, difficult for systems manufacturers since demand for computers is highly price-elastic. A small price increase leads to a much larger decline in demand. Price hikes and supply interruptions caused several U.S. computer systems manufacturers to ration memory chips and to delay the introduction of new products. In a business like computers, where R&D and innovation are vital to survival, such delays seriously weakened competitiveness.

Higher costs hurt the competitive position of U.S. computer systems manufacturers in both domestic and global markets. This provided Japanese systems manufacturers, who made their own DRAMs, with the opportunity to penetrate computer markets in which U.S. firms had held a dominant position.

Semiconductor Equipment Manufacturers. Supporters of U.S. Memories warned that the failure of the U.S. DRAM industry would weaken the semiconductor materials and equipment manufacturing industry. IBM was particularly concerned about this issue. Even though it made most of the DRAMs it needed, IBM did not make the equipment used to manufacture DRAMs. IBM worried that unless U.S. semiconductor firms produced enough memory chips to keep U.S. equipment makers healthy, these firms would fall into Japanese hands or go out of business due to the erosion of their domestic customer base. That could leave IBM and other U.S. firms dependent on Japanese companies for critical semiconductor process technologies.

Spillovers. Another consideration associated with a domestic DRAM industry is the preservation of skills and know-how obtained from producing these chips. DRAMs are considered technology drivers, that is, high-volume products that allow a firm to hone its manufacturing skills and improve its production processes. Since DRAMs are produced in such large volumes, firms have a continuous opportunity to learn about and improve their complex production technologies. This valuable knowledge can drive innovation and improvements in more sophisticated, higher-margin chips like microprocessors.

In addition to the spillovers created in the manufacturing process, domestic production created human capital benefits. DRAM production required trained engineers, technicians, and designers. When they left these companies, they started new businesses or went to other firms, taking with them and diffusing their know-how and expertise.

National Security. The loss of semiconductor manufacturing know-how also concerned defense planners. With components playing an increasingly important role in advanced weapons systems, these developments posed the risk of losing access to essential know-how. Depending solely on foreign firms for sourcing of military components was an added concern.

The Birth of U.S. Memories

The idea for U.S. Memories was born out of the conviction on the part of the U.S. electronics industry that the presence of U.S. companies in the worldwide DRAM market was critical. When it became clear in early 1989 that no single U.S. semiconductor company could take on that challenge alone, the concept of a collective effort was developed.

The collective effort resulted in U.S. Memories, a joint venture of U.S. semiconductor manufacturers and electronics systems manufacturers. The reason for U.S. Memories was to provide its investors and others with a large, stable, and assured supply of DRAMs while providing a real return on investment. U.S. Memories intended to become a long-term, leading player in the industry.

On June 21, 1989, the Semiconductor Industry Association (SIA) announced the formation of U.S. Memories. The new company was to be an independent, for-profit, self-sustaining corporation with initial funds provided by its semiconductor and computer systems members. For computer systems manufacturers (IBM, HP, and DEC), joining the consortium meant a reliable supply of DRAMs and technological independence from Japanese competitors. For semiconductor manufacturers (Intel, National Semiconductor, LSI Logic, and Advanced Micro Devices), many of whom had exited the DRAM market several years earlier, joining U.S. Memories meant being able to offer their customers a complete line of chips. This would reduce their vulnerability to Japanese chip makers. Selling a broader product line was considered a marketing advantage because it enlarged the chip maker's customer base and allowed "one-stop shopping."

In addition to U.S. Memories' seven original members, more participants were needed to finance the venture. The up-front capital costs to start production were enormous; having more members meant that those costs could be spread out over a larger base of investors. Even with a larger membership base, the initial equity investment per member would be large: at the very least, a total equity investment of $100 million. If additional members could not be persuaded to join, U.S. Memories would have trouble getting off the ground. With this in mind, U.S. Memories' CEO Sandy Kane—a charismatic and persuasive 27-year IBM veteran—launched a bold effort to attract other members such as AT&T, Compaq, Apple, Sun, and Tandy. Because the addition of more members would increase administrative costs, the corporation required members to take at least a 1 percent equity position. This meant that only larger companies could afford to join, and smaller companies would not be considered for potential membership.

All consortium members would be required to buy a share of the output of U.S. Memories and would have the option of purchasing additional output if desired. U.S. Memories would begin by manufacturing 4Mb DRAMs, the newest technology licensed from IBM.

Sandy Kane believed that it was vital to secure the necessary funds and build the new plant as quickly as possible; the rapid pace of technological change made early production of 4Mb DRAMs essential. This would enable U.S. Memories to move down the learning curve, increase yields, lower costs, and gain market share. Conversely, any delays in launching the venture could result in competitive disadvantage. If Japanese firms began production earlier than U.S. Memories, they would benefit from moving down the learning curve first and would capture market share at the expense of U.S. Memories. Furthermore, Kane wanted to preserve the sense of excitement and momentum that accompanied the announcement of the creation of U.S. Memories. Computer and semiconductor industry executives, journalists, and politicians watched the progress of the venture with great interest.

The original business plan required a $1 billion investment—50 percent equity-financed by member companies and 50 percent debt-financed, for which Kane hoped to secure low-interest government-guaranteed loans. Member companies also would purchase collectively at least 50 percent of U.S. Memories' output with the remaining output be offered first to members and then sold on the open market. Consortium members were guaranteed their committed chip allotment at no more than competitive market prices.

Four semiconductor manufacturing facilities (fabs) would be built over approximately four years. The first three fabs would produce 4Mb chips at different stages of the generation life cycle. Plants would be built and commence production in a staggered process, and each would be shut down in the same fashion to retool for the next generation. The fourth plant, the last to be built, would produce only 16Mb chips, the next DRAM generation.

The four-fab plan was extremely risky. Since the fabs were to be constructed in a staggered process over the course of the 4Mb generation, timing was crucial. Even a one-month delay could make the difference between success or failure. If the second or third fab commenced production too late relative to the market introduction of the 16Mb generation, much of the output of these plants would be superfluous.

Member companies complained about the output share they were required to purchase. Until the late 1980s, systems manufacturers had enjoyed considerable leverage over their suppliers and chafed at the idea of being committed to buy a fixed share from U.S. Memories. This aspect of the business plan was vital to the success of U.S. Memories, however, since it would save marketing expenses and buffer the consortium from fluctuations in demand. In the DRAM industry, which was frequently beset by overcapacity and cyclical demand patterns, the assurance of a stable customer base would be a great advantage.

After receiving much criticism on the business plan from members and prospective members, Kane was forced to make modifications. A wait-and-see approach was taken with respect to the second fab, and the third fab was to be eliminated altogether. Depending upon the success of Fab 1 and general market conditions, members would decide whether to construct Fab 2. Cost and timing considerations led to almost universal agreement on eliminating Fab 3. Rather than having four manufacturing facilities as originally planned, U.S. Memories would eventually have only two or three.

The second modification to the business plan involved increasing the output members were required to buy. Initially, members had to buy an output share equal to half of their committed investment percentage. This meant that if a member had a 10 percent investment commitment, it would have to purchase 5 percent of the output. The revised plan asked members to buy an output percentage up to their investment percentage. If a member's investment commitment was 10 percent, it would now be required to buy a 5 to 10 percent share of output. Finally, the initial equity requirement was reduced from $500 million to $100 million and the debt/equity ratio would be changed from 50–50 to 60–40.

Considerations and Recommendations

In deciding whether to join the consortium, Apple Computer had many issues to consider. First, the capital requirement was significant, and the rate of return on the investment in U.S. Memories was low—much lower than what could be obtained through alternative investments. But, as Kane made clear, an investment in U.S. Memories was not principally a financial investment. Acquiring a stable supply of DRAMs was potentially a strategic investment in Apple's long-term survival.

The Market. On the other hand, if the price and supply conditions in the market were simply a "temporary blip" as opposed to real structural market changes, then the advice of T. J. Rodgers—the flamboyant CEO of Cypress Semiconductor who was an ardent opponent of U.S. Memories—"be brave, do nothing" would have been warranted. In this case, the best strategy would be to ride out the rough DRAM market conditions and to wait for supplies to loosen up and for prices to fall.

Relations with Japanese Suppliers. Another consideration in joining U.S. Memories involved Apple's relationships with its Japanese suppliers. If Apple announced its decision to join the consortium, it would have to wait two years for U.S. Memories to start production to buy its share of DRAMs. During this time, it would still be dependent on its Japanese suppliers. DRAMs were already difficult to obtain. If its present suppliers learned that Apple intended to cut them off in the future, they could retaliate. On the other hand, if its present suppliers were currently holding back on DRAM supplies in order to erode Apple's position in the computer market, Apple had to do something to stay competitive.

Viability of U.S. Memories. Apple also needed to assess the viability of U.S. Memories itself. At the time the consortium was formed, the only remaining American DRAM producers were Texas Instruments (TI), Micron, and Motorola, which had a combined global market share of 10 to 15 percent in 1988. One of the objectives of U.S. Memories was to double the worldwide market share of U.S. DRAM producers. It was assumed this could be done without hurting existing U.S. firms and that U.S. Memories would only take market share away from Japanese manufacturers. This assumption was challenged by TI, Micron, Motorola, and by T. J. Rodgers. Existing DRAM manufacturers reflected the controversy. James Peterman, vice president of the Semiconductor Group at Texas Instruments said that while U.S. Memories represents a welcome initiative, "We don't really see any way we can participate. [The new consortium will manufacture DRAMs, and] that's what our business is. We have to view it as a competitor. We have a lot invested in this business—not only assets, but in the tough times we had in 1985–86 when we lost money."

Government Support. A related issue involved the types of government support U.S. Memories hoped to get. First, the founders of U.S. Memories hoped that the Semiconductor Trade Agreement (SCTA), due to expire in 1991, would be extended. To be price competitive, U.S. Memories was counting on maintaining the controversial system of fair market values (FMVs) that had been established to prevent dumping by Japanese firms. FMVs allowed firms like TI, Micron, and Motorola (along with all the Japanese DRAM producers) to reap huge profits from DRAM production in the late 1980s.[3] At the same time, the FMVs proved extremely damaging to Apple and other systems manufacturers who found themselves suddenly faced with significantly higher DRAM prices. This situation was paradoxical: on the one hand, the FMVs were a form of trade protection that U.S. Memories needed to be viable; on the other hand, they raised the price of DRAMs to the detriment of the U.S. systems manufacturers, some of whom were members of U.S. Memories. These price increases put U.S. computer systems manufacturers at a competitive disadvantage vis-à-vis their Japanese competitors.

The second type of government support U.S. Memories required was an exemption from antitrust laws. Although U.S. Memories did not appear to be in violation of federal antitrust laws, it could still be sued by a third party (e.g., another semiconductor manufacturer). According to existing antitrust law, firms participating in anticompetitive activities that harm other firms are liable for treble damages—three times their profits. If some members were unable to pay their share, the remaining members would have to assume the additional burden. In an extreme case, a single member could be liable for the entire amount of the treble damages.

Finally, U.S. Memories hoped to receive a $500 million low-interest government-guaranteed loan as a source of debt capital. This was a great point of contention for opponents of U.S. Memories. Presumably, the low-interest government loan would level the financial playing field with respect to Japanese chip makers. However, it would also give U.S. Memories an advantage over domestic chip makers such as the small, entrepreneurial firm of Micron Technologies, which did not have access to government loans of the type U.S. Memories hoped to receive. With access to cheaper capital, U.S. Memories would have a competitive edge over other domestic firms and could potentially pose a threat to domestic as well as foreign competition.

What Should Apple Do?

To answer the question of what Apple should do—Should it become a member of U.S. Memories or not—certain factors had to be reviewed: (1) What is a DRAM? (2) What is the market for DRAMs? (3) What is the state of U.S.-Japan trade relations? (4) What is the composition of the U.S. computer systems' industry? (5) How has cooperation worked in the past in this industry? (6) What were Apple's interests?

1. What Is a DRAM? Dynamic random access memory chips, or DRAMs, are the most common type of semiconductor chip. Invented by Intel in 1971, DRAMs have the paradoxical property of being both technologically sophisticated and a common commodity. Their status as a commodity has earned DRAMs the nickname of "jellybeans" by semiconductor manufacturers. DRAMs are almost perfectly standardized from one to another and require little specialized marketing and distribution. Price is the primary criterion that systems makers use to choose one DRAM over another. DRAMs are distributed in several ways. Most of the larger systems manufacturers buy DRAMs directly from chip makers. Smaller DRAM customers often buy through distributors, who purchase chips from DRAM makers.

The most common use of DRAMs is in computer systems; they form the backbone of a computer's random access memory (RAM). This memory controls "short-term" computer operations such as what types of software applications to use; how many applications can be open at the same time, and the speed with which a computer is able to process applications currently in use. Random access memory is different from the type of memory that governs the storage size of a computer's hard disk. The two types of memories—random access and storage—are roughly analogous to short- and long-term memory.

An important attribute of DRAMs is their historic position as technology drivers. The mass production of these highly complex devices generates "learning" about complex production processes that can be applied to a much wider range of other device types produced by a company in lower volume. Such high-complexity, high-volume technology drivers are widely viewed as a prerequisite to remaining competitive in semiconductors over the long term. Since low manufacturing costs are crucial to success in DRAM production, chip makers seeking to lower their costs do so through increased yields and improved manufacturing. The emphasis on manufacturing creates skills and knowledge in production processes which can spill over onto many other higher-value semiconductor products such as microprocessors. It is precisely for these reasons that Japanese companies and industrial policymakers believed that Japan's initial entry into the semiconductor industry should begin with DRAM production.

DRAMs come in generations, occurring at intervals of approximately three to four years. A new generation will have four times the memory capacity of the one it replaces, and will often require radically different manufacturing processes from the previous generation. Tremendous expense is involved in retooling plants for a new chip generation; in extreme cases, entirely new plants may have to be constructed. From the standpoint of the computer systems manufacturers, switching costs are fairly low across DRAM generations because computers, unlike microprocessors, do not need to be assembled with the latest DRAM technology. Increasing the amount of older DRAMs in a PC has roughly the same effect as using a DRAM with a higher memory capacity. Thus, systems manufacturers have the luxury of waiting until prices drop and technologies standardize to switch to the new generation.

When a new generation is introduced, unfamiliarity with the new manufacturing processes will frequently result in low yields and extremely high chip prices. At this stage in the life cycle of a new chip, computer systems manufacturers continue to purchase the previous chip generations. They do not buy the new chip until the price per bit on the two generations roughly equalizes. The point at which systems manufacturers adopt the new generation chip is referred to as the "crossover." Since the new generation will have four times the bit capacity as the one it replaces, the crossover will occur when the new chip costs approximately four times the price of the older one. At this price level, the per-bit price for the old and new chips are equal.

Because of short product life cycles and extremely high up-front R&D costs in developing new chip generations, margins on DRAM production are low to nonexistent. Since demand for DRAMs is extremely price sensitive, chip makers will often use forward pricing on a new generation to encourage early crossover. This type of pricing strategy is common in industries where economies of scale in production are important. Firms that use forward pricing set initial prices below costs in order to move down the learning curve in production. This allows chip makers to produce and sell greater volumes than would be possible if they priced DRAMs at or above cost. Large-volume production enables chip makers to lower their costs and gain market share.

For systems manufacturers, the most unpredictable aspect of buying DRAMs is the cyclical nature of DRAM prices and supplies. As mentioned previously, chip supplies may be tight and chip prices high in the early stages in a new chip generation. When the crossover occurs, systems makers will frequently order higher-priced chips from their suppliers or distributors in order to assure a supply of the new generation chip. In response to orders from customers and distributors, chip makers will increase capacity and flood the market with DRAMs. Because the price of DRAMs is still falling at this stage, systems makers may cancel the orders they made when prices were higher and demand lower prices from their suppliers. Systems manufacturers may also cancel orders if demand for computers slows. After flooding the market, chip makers will be left with excess capacity. They are often forced to sell DRAMs at below cost. To avoid incurring further losses, chip makers will cut production.[4]

2. The DRAM Market. Since its invention by Intel in 1971, the DRAM market has had a turbulent history. Throughout the 1970s, DRAM manufacture was dominated by U.S. firms, which were the unrivaled leaders in technology, engineering, and manufacturing of all semiconductor products.

At approximately the same time as the invention of the DRAM came the invention, also by Intel, of the microprocessor. The semiconductor industry would thereafter be split into high-volume commodity chips such as DRAMs and EPROMs (erasable programmable read-only memory) and lower-volume, more technologically advanced chips such as microprocessors. As chip technology became increasingly sophisticated, U.S. firms began concentrating on higher-end chips at the expense of commodity chips. Short product life cycles for memory chips brought smaller returns and necessitated enormous R&D expenditures.

The late 1970s was perhaps the most eventful period in the history of the semiconductor industry. Price competition was intensifying, and the industry began to experience cyclical demand swings which, combined with the proliferation of small, upstart semiconductor firms, would lay the groundwork for the stormy and antagonistic relationship between semiconductor producers (called the "cowboys" of Silicon Valley by computer makers) and systems manufacturers. This buyer-supplier ill-will would characterize the U.S. industry for many years to come.

The mid-1970s also brought increasing industry globalization as U.S. firms moved more of their operations offshore, European firms began to enter the market, and Japanese firms emerged as world-class competitors. Japanese competition caused the market share of U.S. firms to decline rapidly. From 1974 to 1988, U.S. firms lost market share at about 6 percentage points per year. By 1989, only three U.S. firms continued to make DRAMs, and most of their production was located offshore. As the dynamic memory market matured, Japanese DRAM manufacturers commanded increasingly larger shares of the global market with each successive chip generation, peaking at close to 90 percent of the advanced 1Mb market in late 1989.

Although Japan's domination of the DRAM market seemed only to be increasing throughout the 1970s and 1980s, industry globalization continued to bring new players into the market. By the late 1980s, firms from Korea (Samsung and Hyundai) were growing rapidly and were among the largest DRAM manufacturers in the world. Additionally, the governments of Hong Kong and Taiwan were making commitments to manufacture DRAMs as a part of their industrial policies.

3. U.S.-Japanese Semiconductor Trade Issues. Industry globalization, low chip prices, and declining U.S. market share in DRAMs brought inevitable trade frictions between the United States and Japan. U.S. firms contended that Japan made it difficult for them to enter the Japanese semiconductor market and accused Japanese semiconductor manufacturers of dumping in the United States and the markets of other countries. A series of dumping complaints culminated in 1986 with the U.S.-Japan Semiconductor Trade Agreement (SCTA). The three objectives of the SCTA were to open the Japanese market to foreign semiconductor manufacturers, to prevent Japanese semiconductor manufacturers from dumping chips in the United States, and to prevent Japanese semiconductor manufacturers from dumping chips in third country markets.

Dumping, or selling goods at less than their fair value, was made illegal in the United States in 1921 with the passage of the Antidumping Act. This act provides for a duty to be imposed on certain imported foreign merchandise to make it unprofitable for foreign manufacturers to sell goods on U.S. markets at prices below cost. The Department of Treasury must inform the International Trade Commission (ITC) that goods are being sold in the United States at less than their fair market value.

To determine dumping, the Department of Commerce constructs quarterly fair market values (FMVs) for DRAMs with a formula made up of the sum of the following parts:

1. Material costs, including some R&D for materials.
2. Fabrication costs.
3. General sales and administrative expenses, including some R&D for other purposes (not less than 10 percent of the above two costs).
4. Profit (not less than 8 percent of the above two costs).

This formula is applied on a company-by-company basis using proprietary cost information to determine the minimum price of each company's products. Real-time fabrication cost data is used in determining FMVs.

As discussed earlier, semiconductor prices tend to fall rapidly as firms move down the learning curve within a given chip generation. This rapid price decline, combined with tremendous up-front R&D costs and the use of forward pricing, makes the determination of a "fair" price at any given point on the life cycle extremely difficult. For this reason, the system of FMVs is highly controversial in the semiconductor industry.

Despite the SCTA, chip prices remained low through 1986, and American DRAM manufacturers were unable to gain access to the Japanese market. This prompted the Reagan administration to impose sanctions on Japan in March 1987. Following the imposition of sanctions, chip prices began an unprecedented surge.

4. The Computer Systems Industry. In 1989, computer systems manufacturing was an estimated $250 billion a year industry worldwide. In the United States alone, revenues totaled $150 billion a year, making it the third largest industry after automobiles and petroleum.

Historically, the computer manufacturing industry had been segmented into three broad product classifications: mainframes, minicomputers, and microcomputers. *Mainframe computers,* usually priced between $500,000 and $14 million, are centrally located computers designed to handle the large-scale computing needs of up to 128 concurrent users. These computer systems are typically accompanied by custom software applications which are tailored to meet the data-processing demands of an entire organization. IBM has dominated the mainframe market for the past 30 years and held 70 percent of the $30 billion worldwide market in 1989.

Minicomputers are smaller, somewhat more decentralized versions of mainframes. These computer systems, capable of supporting 64 concurrent users, are aimed at satisfying the information processing needs of small organizations or large departments. These computers range in price from $100,000 to $500,000. DEC, the traditional leader of the minicomputer market, has recently been challenged by IBM.

Microcomputers were initially designed as single-user, stand-alone systems aimed at satisfying an individual's unique computing needs. It was not until the late 1970s, when Intel introduced its 8088 microprocessor, that these desktop computer systems became widely available. The 8088 microprocessor was eventually replaced by the 80286 ("286") chip which fueled the popular IBM PC AT computers.

By the mid-1980s, more powerful and less expensive semiconductors and microprocessors radically altered the structure of the global computer industry. The long-standing distinctions between the three major industry classifications became less clear as computer makers were increasingly able to build machines with superior price/performance capabilities. Furthermore, advances in hardware, software, and peripheral systems eventually led to the creation of new types of computers like PCs and workstations which were less easily classified. These product innovations put mainframe and minicomputer manufacturers into competition with PC and workstation manufacturers who were capable of putting more affordable computing power into smaller machines.

The 1980s ushered in other significant structural changes in the global computer industry. In the early 1980s, hardware manufacturers were able to sell nearly all the goods they could produce. The industry reaped enormous profits regardless of economic conditions. All of this changed in the mid-1980s when markets had become saturated. Buyers had purchased enough hardware and only needed to replace computer equipment as it became worn-out. Demand for computers became increasingly sensitive to price, and firms could no longer increase their revenues and earnings regardless of economic conditions. In 1985, a severe downturn hit the entire industry and threatened the survival of many firms.

Further structural changes resulted from buyer demands for open systems that were completely compatible with each other. Compatibility of systems made computers more standardized and lowered barriers to entry; this forced manufacturers to shift the focus of competition from differentiated product features to price, and industry profit margins declined. To cope with the new competitive environment, computer manufacturers concentrated on shortening the transition between design and manufacture, and attempted to locate low-cost sources of reliable components.

Increasingly, competition in the computer industry became a race to reduce the time to market. Since barriers to entry by way of imitation decrease rapidly after a new product's introduction, profit margins are highest at the beginning of the product's life cycle. Companies that beat rivals to market with a new product stood to gain considerably more than their slower competitors.

The trend towards open systems also resulted in a proliferation of computer manufacturers, many from Japan and South Korea, which took advantage of the freely available technological know-how. By 1988, more than 200 companies manufactured IBM-compatible PC clones in a fiercely competitive product market.

The rise of Japanese companies as major players in the computer industry caused further structural change. Bolstered into action by a large industry-government cooperative venture during the late 1970s, Japanese companies made staggering advances into semiconductors and computers. The four largest Japanese computer producers—Fujitsu, NEC, Hitachi, and Toshiba—are also the largest semiconductor makers. By 1982, Japan reached parity with the United States in bilateral computer trade, and it achieved a surplus of more than $4 billion in 1987. At the same time, the share of U.S. firms in the Japanese market steadily declined.

5. Cooperation between the Computer and Semiconductor Industries. Despite the difficult relations between semiconductor manufacturers and computer systems makers, the two industries have a long history of cooperation in both the United States and Japan. Indeed, the kind of multifirm cooperative venture after which U.S. Memories had been modeled had existed for more than six years in the United States and dated back to the 1970s in Japan. Many of these consortia involved cooperative research rather than production, since it was believed that technological economies of scope existed across the computer and semiconductor industries. Most of the well-known

U.S. ventures such as the Microelectronics and Computer Technology Corporation (MCC), Sematech, and the Semiconductor Research Corporation involved many of the same companies that eventually became members of U.S. Memories.

MCC. The Microelectronics and Computer Technology Corporation (MCC) was founded in 1983 by 10 computer systems and semiconductor manufacturers. Conceived as a response to Japan's Fifth Generation Computer Project, MCC was the first research consortium of its kind in the United States. Its goal was to conduct cooperative research in four main areas—advanced computer architecture, computer-aided design, computer software technology, and microcircuitry—and to pioneer the technologies necessary to keep the United States ahead in the global computer race. Since many firms with varied skills can pool both their knowledge and financial resources, cooperative research consortia like MCC were believed to be an important component of success in technology industries like computers and semiconductors and had been widely used in Japan. Moreover, since 1984 cooperative research consortia have been permitted under U.S. antitrust laws and do not face the same potential scrutiny as multifirm production ventures.

Six years after its inception, MCC's record was mixed. It had serious problems from the beginning such as the refusal of IBM—the dominant force in the computer industry—to join due to worries about giving away trade secrets. Many of the companies that did join had similar fears about secrecy and either remained suspicious of each other or were reluctant to provide any proprietary data to benefit cooperative research projects. Because many of the research projects undertaken by MCC were at least a decade away from product development, member companies were generally dissatisfied with the return that they got on their financial contributions to the consortium. In spite of these problems, however, MCC did produce numerous practical successes in a diverse range of areas such as integrated circuits (semiconductors) and artificial intelligence. If member companies did gain access to MCC technologies, it often proved to be worth their while. Even T. J. Rodgers, ardent critic of U.S. Memories, was one of the technology beneficiaries.

Sematech. Started four years after MCC, Sematech was also conceived as a response to a Japanese alliance—the Very Large Scale Integration (VLSI) project which promoted leading-edge research in DRAM technology. Unlike MCC, Sematech was able to recruit most of the leading companies in both semiconductor and computer systems manufacture including IBM, AT&T, Intel and Motorola. Fourteen companies joined at the outset, almost all of which were large due to the high ticket price of membership. Another key difference between Sematech and MCC was the Defense Department (DOD) participation in the former. Indeed, since its inception, Sematech has received hundreds of millions of dollars from DOD appropriations, which has attracted severe criticism from nonmember firms. Small companies that could not afford to join accuse large companies of ganging up together with government support to create a "Club of Big Boys" to hurt smaller, more innovative rivals. In one instance, Sematech was even accused of holding back technology from other American manufacturers who were not members of the consortium.

Sematech learned much from MCC's mistakes. Its goals were clearer and its research was less abstract. Its stated objective was to provide U.S. chipmakers with "domestic capability for world leadership in manufacturing," and to make Sematech the "manufacturing driver." In spite of its focus on manufacturing, Sematech would not actually manufacture anything. It hoped instead to create the same technologies that Japanese companies obtain naturally by doing high-volume manufacturing. These goals met with mixed success and were later redirected toward supporting the semiconductor equipment manufacturing industry.

Like MCC, Sematech's overall record has been varied. Some members were dissatisfied with the way Sematech's resources were being allocated and with the types of research being undertaken. Several companies ultimately quit. Some companies like Texas Instruments objected to Sematech's initial goal of focusing on DRAM manufacturing, fearing it would compete with their own DRAM business. Others, like Intel, remained strong supporters: "we [at Intel] think the success of Sematech is critical to the success of America's high-technology sector."

Multinational Joint Ventures. In addition to the multifirm ventures in the United States, some semiconductor and computer systems manufacturers formed multinational joint ventures involving, in some cases, research. In others, the intent was to secure DRAM supplies. Texas Instruments, one of three U.S. DRAM makers, launched such a venture with Acer, a Taiwanese computer maker. In return for an up-front investment from Acer, Texas Instruments agreed to build a DRAM manufacturing plant in Taipei. The output of the new plant would be split between the two partners.

6. Apple Computer, Inc. Founded in a California garage in the mid-1970s, Apple Computer began as one of the most revolutionary companies in the United States. Its initial product was the company's entire reason for being—the Macintosh computer, which set a new standard for user-friendliness. Known for its graphical user interface that represented information with icons and symbols, its consistency of use across different software applications, and its introduction of the mouse, the Macintosh offered high-end graphics capabilities in desktop publishing applications.

Apple's founders, Steven Jobs and Steve Wozniak, also revolutionized a uniquely Californian atmosphere at the new company. In return for their devotion, enthusiasm, and willingness to put in frequent work weeks of up to 90 hours, employees were rewarded with a casual but stimulating environment that fostered creativity and respect. This environment was a great source of pride to Apple's founders who rebelled against the ossified culture of larger, established rivals like IBM.

Apple's culture did not come without a price, however. Its innovative products required large and continuous investment in R&D, but the original company engineers and executives refused to be burdened by thinking about money. Moreover, the company had been so "stuck" on the Macintosh product that it did not really forge plans for its future direction. Finally, its casual corporate environment frequently resulted in considerable inefficiencies.

By 1985, Apple was no longer the small company it once was. It was hit hard by the downturn in the computer market in the mid-1980s and was forced to lay off 20 percent of its workforce. Amid these changes, Apple brought in John Sculley, president and CEO of Pepsi-Cola, to craft a new direction for the company.

Apple's initial marketing strategy had differed from that of its rivals. Instead of focusing on systems managers at large corporations and government institutions, Apple's sales staff pitched the Macintosh to ordinary individuals in corporations and to the educational market. By 1988 Apple had captured 12 percent of the office and professional market sector.

Sculley ushered in a more mainstream corporate environment along with a host of strategic and marketing changes. In the future, Apple would concentrate more on high-end business machine sales and its new products would be less revolutionary. To meet this objective, Apple introduced the second-generation Macintoshes in 1987. The company would expand the efforts to make its systems "talk" to other computers, such as IBM PCs and DEC systems, and strengthen its established position in office networking, the computing wave of the future. Finally, Apple hoped to increase its presence in computer peripheral products and software.

Following the downturn of the mid-1980s, Apple's performance was stellar. Its profits increased 41 percent in 1987 and 84 percent in 1988 ($400.3 million on revenues of $4.1 billion). Its 1988 ROE was 40 percent, nearly three times that of IBM. Corporate goals were to reach a 20 percent share of the business PC market in the next few years and to double the company's revenue to $10 billion by the early 1990s. At the upper management level, however, infighting ensued and many of the original Apple members, including Steven Jobs, left the company.

In mid-1989, Apple faced two important threats to its position. First, IBM had teamed up with Microsoft, to give IBM's new PS/2 line of computers the same easy-to-use graphics that were the

Mac's biggest selling point. While experts still believed the PS/2 to be inferior to the Mac in ease of use, the gap was narrowing. Apple had to do something more striking to forge to the lead.

The second threat to Apple was the DRAM crisis and the mistakes Apple had made in responding to it. Rather than cut production of Macintoshes, Apple bought chips on the spot market at twice the normal price. Instead of swallowing its higher costs, Apple increased the price of its Macs by as much as $800 at a time when computers were getting cheaper. Sales fell off sharply. The increased costs of memory components adversely affected the company's operating results during the second half of 1988, resulting in a 51.5 percent gross margin decline in the third quarter and 49.2 percent in the fourth quarter. The impact of higher DRAM costs continued during the first half of 1989, as the gross margin further declined to 49.1 percent in the first quarter and 46.2 percent in the second quarter. To make matters worse, Apple led Wall Street to believe that its earnings would come to about $.65 per share, but in January 1989 it announced that they would be closer to $.35 per share. The market reacted violently and nearly 10 percent of Apple shares were sold that day—the biggest one-day sell-off in Nasdaq history, and Apple's market value fell by 10 percent in one day alone.

Apple's annual reports reflected the severity of the DRAM crisis:

> 1988
> In 1988, gross margin was positively affected by improved operating efficiencies related to increased sales volumes, by increased sales of higher-margin products as a proportion of net sales, and by the overall favorable effect of foreign currency exchange rates on revenues earned overseas. These favorable effects, however, were offset by the increasing cost of certain key purchased part components, particularly DRAMs, of which a worldwide shortage continues to exist . . . The continuing industry wide shortage of DRAM devices has resulted in increased prices for these components. This situation may have an adverse impact on gross margin, to the extent the Company is unable to procure DRAMs at relatively favorable prices.

> 1989
> The most significant factor affecting Apple profits was pressure on our gross margin caused by our increased cost of goods—most notably the DRAM . . . It was a product cost increase that the U.S. computer market did not absorb.

Discussion Questions

1. What are the dominant economic characteristics of the DRAM industry?
2. What are the forces driving change in the DRAM industry?
3. What is competition like in the DRAM industry? Is this industry attractive?
4. What should Apple Computer do? Should it become a member of U.S. Memories or not? Discuss the arguments for and against joining U.S. Memories.
5. If Apple does not join U.S. Memories, what alternatives does it have for obtaining DRAMS?
6. Should U.S. industries in advanced technological areas combine in associations like U.S. Memories, and should they be encouraged to do so by the U.S. government to meet foreign competitive challenges?

Endnotes

1. This case was prepared by Susan Feinberg, Bill McEvily, and Stefanie Lenway.
2. Rumors of tying practices appeared in the press, in SIA publications, and in interviews with Sandy Kane, Andy Procassini (president of the Semiconductor Industry Association), and Craig Stacey (manager of All American SemiConductors, a semiconductor distributor). Stacey recalled that in the late 1980s, DRAM manufacturers were asking their distributors to sell memory chips in "packages" with more advanced chips. Stacey considered this packaging of chips extremely unusual.

3. After the imposition of sanctions against Japan in mid-1987, U.S. semiconductor firms experienced profits for two reasons. First, an unprecedented chip shortage led to higher DRAM prices. Second, the SCTA called for Japanese DRAM manufacturers to raise prices on DRAMs to the fair market value. American DRAM manufacturers also benefited from these price increases. For example, Micron Technologies, of Boise, Idaho, which lost $34 million in 1986 and $23 million in 1987, *earned* $98 million in 1988!
4. An extreme example of this "futures-like" aspect of the DRAM market was described by Craig Stacey, a semiconductor distributor. Stacey had sold DRAMs to a customer at the prevailing market price. Several days later the market price fell, and the customer attempted to return the chips and repurchase them at the lower market price. Semiconductor distributors who purchase DRAMs when the price is declining are often forced to sell them at prices below costs. Distributors try to avoid this situation by maintaining small inventories.

Case 11–B
Initial Position: Chrysler and Honda[1]

Lee Iacocca, Chrysler's chairman, wanted to understand the success of his competitors in the automobile industry better.[2] While his company again was in decline, some of the competitors had made major advances. Iacocca was most interested in understanding the success of Honda Motor Company. From 1976 to 1986, it grew more rapidly than any auto company. The Accord model became the best-selling car in the United States, and Honda surprised everyone with its successful entry into the luxury car market.

Iacocca posed the following questions to his staff:

- Based on Honda's distinct history and culture, how can its strategy be understood?
- Based on the strategic moves it has made in the past, what are its tendencies? What initiatives is it likely to take in the future?
- What can Honda's U.S. competitors do to counter these moves?
- What can Chrysler learn from Honda's way of behaving? Which aspects of Honda can be imitated, and which cannot, by a U.S. company like Chrysler?

Chrysler's Position in 1990

Iacocca admitted that Chrysler was in serious trouble.[3] One of its biggest mistakes had been diversification. It became involved in aerospace and defense industries, which diverted management attention from making cars. It had made other mistakes, such as joining Italy's Maserati in an aborted effort to produce a new luxury coupe.

An important issue was the effort to slash costs. Even though Chrysler had shut down a third of its assembly plants in three years (in the past 10 years Iacocca had shut down 20 plants and laid off over 100,000 people), it had too many levels of management. As the fifth largest car seller in the United States—behind General Motors, Toyota, and Ford—it could not afford to have a top-heavy structure based on a holding-company model.

To break even, Chrysler had to sell 1.9 million vehicles a year. This was up from a breakeven point of only 1.1 million vehicles just a few years ago. Chrysler had the capacity to make 2.3 million vehicles annually. Sales in 1990, however, plunged 17 percent, compared with the overall industry decline of 5 percent. Chrysler's stock price dipped to $12 a share on September 14, 1990. The company could be bought for $2.8 billion. No other company in the United States with revenues and sales as high could be purchased so cheaply. Many expected a foreign automaker that needed a U.S. distribution network (perhaps Fiat) to make a bid for Chrysler.

The company needed new and attractive products, but the money for product development was unavailable. A project to create a small minivan was dropped because of a shortage of cash; the introduction of a new midsized family sedan was delayed; and a new Jeep model, scheduled for introduction in 1992, might not be ready on time. Chrysler was having trouble finding new products to match the hits it achieved in the 1980s—the Dodge Caravan and Plymouth Voyager minivans and to a lesser extent the LeBaron convertible. It had to avoid the mistakes it had made with the now discontinued Omni and Horizon lines.

Costs had to be cut and vehicles brought online when some of the company's best talent was leaving. With bonuses and perks reduced, layoffs taking place and more expected, some of the company's best managers sought employment elsewhere. Gerald Greenwald, second in command, left to become CEO at another company. A group of highly talented tailpipe engineers went to work for Ford, a marketing person took a job with an ad agency that did business with Ford, and another talented engineer went back to teaching.

The Acquisition of AMC. Chrysler gained from its earlier acquisition of American Motors (AMC); however, important mistakes were made:

- The decision to move the Omni/Horizon assembly operations to a former AMC plant in Kenosha, Wisconsin, which Chrysler then shut down 15 months later.
- The agreement to produce a midsized sedan, AMC's Premia, because of an obligation to Renault.
- The inability to match Ford's price on the Explorer sport-utility vehicle, which competed directly with the Jeep Cherokee.

Chrysler could not successfully market the Premia, but was obligated to pay Renault more than $100 million because it was producing fewer Premias than the merger required. The purchase of the Jeep Cherokee was the main reason for the AMC deal since it was the best-selling four-door sport-utility vehicle. However, when Ford introduced the less-expensive Explorer, sales of the Cherokee plunged by 22 percent.

Employees also didn't like Iacocca's decision to build a new $1 billion technical center and possible headquarters 30 miles north of Detroit. They called the complex the "Taj Mahal." Iacocca had to hold a series of "town hall" meetings with them to discuss this and other moves the company had made.

Employees often asked Iacocca's opinion of Honda, especially after a series of advertisements in which he proclaimed that a survey suggested that Americans preferred buying Chryslers to Hondas. Douglas Fraser, retired president of the United Auto Workers, called Iacocca's ads ridiculous.[4] The facts were that one in four American buyers chose a Japanese-made car, while only 1 in 11 chose a Chrysler-made vehicle.

Honda's Rise

In contrast to Chrysler's demise, the ascendance of the Japanese manufacturer Honda was truly remarkable.[5] Honda only came into existence in 1948. Founded by an unschooled, feisty, and temperamental Japanese mechanic, Sochiro Honda, its first product was a motorcycle conversion kit for bicycles. Mr. Honda bought cheaply and retooled small engines the Japanese Army had used for communication purposes. They were in great demand during the postwar occupation as people often had to travel long distances to buy bread and other necessities.

Sochiro Honda, the son of a blacksmith, left the small village where he was born in 1922. Always a maverick who spoke his mind, he had a razor-sharp temper and cultivated a "David versus Goliath" image.[6]

Sochiro Honda was a brilliant mechanic who loved working with machines. He understood that he lacked the business sophistication to be successful, so in 1949 he took on a partner, Takeo Fujisawa, to add needed financial and marketing expertise to his fledgling company. Honda described Fujisawa as someone who had "lofty ideas," but "translated thoughts into actions . . . If he had been a man who did nothing but chase dreams, I would not have been impressed."[7]

A Full-Scale Motorcycle Producer. After Fujisawa came aboard, Honda became a full-scale motorcycle producer, but it was a late entrant to the industry. Its manufacturing capabilities were limited, and it had no standardized drawings, procedures, or equipment. The best it could do was to keep abreast of recent technological developments, persuade distributors to carry it as a second line, and engage in direct advertising to consumers.

In the early 1950s, the company was floundering. Therefore, to demonstrate the firm's technical prowess and enhance its reputation, Sochiro Honda concentrated on winning international motorcycle racing events. His success came from developing a new combustion chamber configuration that doubled the horsepower of the engine and halved its weight.

Fujisawa set the company the challenge of designing a safe, inexpensive motorcycle, one that could be driven with one hand to make it easier to transport packages. Such a motorcycle was needed to facilitate the movement of goods and services among Japan's densely crowded commercial enterprises. Thus, the Honda 50cc Supercub was born. Soon, it constituted more than 60 percent of Honda's sales. The company set up an automated plant with a 30,000-unit-per-month capacity, and it distributed directly to retailers (mostly bicycle shops) on a cash-on-delivery basis.

The next challenge was to sell in the United States. Two Honda executives arrived in the United States in 1958 with no other strategy than to make some sales. According to Kihachiro Kawashami, one of the executives: "It was a new frontier, a new challenge, and it fit the 'success against all odds' culture that Mr. Honda cultivated."[8]

Kawashami did not foresee a large U.S. market. His first impression was that everyone drove large, powerful, and luxurious cars. There were less than a half million motorcycle registrations in the United States and about 60,000 European imports in 1958. Kawashami's goal, simply, was to compete with the European imports; he would be satisfied with about 10 percent of the import market.

Kawashami started small in the Los Angeles market where there was year-round sunshine, a growing population, and a Japanese immigrant community. Early sales, however, were threatened when the cycles Honda manufactured started to leak oil and have clutch failures. They were driven faster and harder in the United States than they were in Japan, and Honda's test facility in Japan had to work 24 hours a day until it solved these problems.

Kawashami soon noticed that Honda's smaller cycles were being bought by normal Americans and not by "black leather jacket" motorcycle enthusiasts. Sporting goods stores wanted to sell them, not motorcycle dealers that catered to the enthusiasts. This observation presented a dilemma. If Honda focused on the Americans who bought its bikes, it risked alienating the enthusiasts, who would buy premium motorcycles at high prices. The company could not be a wimp in an industry where Harley Davidson set the standard and characters that Marlon Brando and Lee Marvin played in *The Wild Ones* were role models. That strategy defied all logic and common sense.

Nevertheless, as an outsider, Honda took the risk. Its advertising campaign stressed the kinder, gentler aspects of motorcycle riding. The theme it adopted was "You Meet the Nicest People on a Honda." The campaign theme originally came from an undergraduate at the University of California at Los Angeles. Tapping a new cycle market that did not previously exist, Honda captured almost 50 percent of U.S. motorcycle sales by 1964.

Shifting Attention to Cars. With the retirement of its founders, Honda was ready to shift its attention to cars. Its first lightweight truck and sports car had been introduced in 1962. These products were followed by the Honda Civic, with its revolutionary compound vortex controlled combustion (CVCC) engine that it brought to the market in 1971. The Civic was the first car to comply with the U.S. Clean Air Act. It also got EPA's highest rating for fuel economy—by 1983, 51 miles per gallon for highway driving.

Then, when the Japanese were considered the masters of the small, economy car, Honda came out with the midsized Accord. This car helped move the Japanese manufacturers beyond the image of producing only basic, no-frills transportation. It was not only larger than the typical Japanese car, but it also had quality features that rivalled those of Mercedes-Benz, BMW, and Porsche.

Honda started to manufacture Accords indistinguishable from those made in Japan in Marysville, Ohio, in 1982, thus becoming the first Japanese auto manufacturer to successfully set up a facility in the United States. It was actually exporting Accords made in Ohio to Japan. By 1989, the Accord was the top-selling car in the United States, and Honda was the fastest-growing automaker in the world. It had made a phenomenal entry into the U.S. luxury car market with the Accura and was competing head-to-head with U.S. manufacturers in all segments of the market. According to the J. D. Power and Associates Customer Satisfaction Index, the Accura was the world's most satisfying car to own.[9]

In 1991, Honda announced a new Civic engine that could get 50 miles per gallon in the city and 65 on the highway, thus improving existing auto efficiency by 10 to 25 percent and creating additional challenges for U.S. automakers. It also added a station wagon to its line of Honda Accords.[10]

Honda's Philosophy. In marketing automobiles, Honda was guided by a philosophy that had certain basic principles.[11]

1. *Create new markets*. Honda was trying to create new markets. It was not interested in competing in industries where existing markets already had been created. To create new markets it had to think about styling and comfort, as well as technology. For instance, the Supercub motorbike's configuration made it easier for women to ride. However, it was also necessary to be on the leading edge technologically. Thus, Honda established an independent research and development center early in its existence and took seriously the ideas of the people who worked there. All of the presidents who followed Sochiro Honda came from the research department.

2. *Employee participation in management*. Honda encouraged employee participation in management. Employees had to learn to trust management. They had to be instilled with a sense of common purpose. They had to believe that management and labor stand on common ground. Sochiro Honda insisted that the division of labor "not deprive people of their right to think." Only if everyone thinks about improvements can the industry prosper. These principles are carried out in a number of ways.

- Honda does not have separate cafeterias for white- and blue-collar workers.
- Everybody wears the same white cotton shirt and green and white baseball cap.
- Workers have voluntarily banded together to create quality circles that consider topics like employee welfare and recreation in addition to production efficiency.
- Honda hires people not simply on the basis of their abilities and willingness to cooperate. It will, unlike other Japanese manufacturers, tolerate outspoken mavericks like its founder. Its third president, Tadashi Kume, fought a vigorous battle against Sochiro Honda to have the CVCC engines be water-cooled rather than air-cooled. Kume won despite Honda's opposition.[12]

- Employees are asked to keep diaries of their ideas so that they, not their supervisors, gain full credit for their creative activities.
- There are two promotion systems: one for advancement in rank as a manager and one for advancement in rank as an expert.

Honda stated that the workplace "is no battlefield." It is not a place "where the winner smiles and the loser cries." His emphasis is on cooperation and trust, the essential factor in a successful manufacturing strategy.[13]

3. *International orientation and close community ties*. Honda's international orientation is matched by close ties to the community where it locates new plants. It recognizes that successful international operations depend on these ties. Honda was the first Japanese company to set up manufacturing facilities in the United States. Part of the reason was that its annual import quota (under the voluntary guidelines) to the United States of about 350,000 cars was less than the 500,000 for Toyota and 450,000 for Nissan. Thus, it could only expand U.S. sales by creating U.S. production facilities. However, it has never been reluctant to move its plants overseas. After World War II, it was the first Japanese company to establish a manufacturing facility abroad, setting up a motorcycle plant in Belgium in 1962. Honda now had more than 50 plants in over 30 countries. It carried out this localization strategy to remain close to the customer.[14]

4. *Unique approaches*. Honda used unique approaches to solving problems. It sought to distance itself and set itself apart from other companies. It wanted to be free from customs, routines, precedents, and conventional ways of doing things. It relished the role of being the maverick in the industry, since its competitors could not predict what it was likely to do. For instance, during the economic boom of the 1950s in Japan, rather than increasing production to boost profits, Honda reduced costs, improved production methods, and raised the technical level of employees. It did not build a larger, bulkier rod for a racing engine to avoid its collapse, but made the engine smaller, lighter, and sturdier, in accord with the Japanese saying that "a large tree cannot stand against powerful winds, while the slender and more flexible bamboo can."[15] Importantly, Honda decided against using catalytic converters to clean up auto pollutants; instead, it developed a new engine design, the CVCC, which did not need the converters.

Some Statistics on the Automobile Industry

In 1989, Japanese companies captured a record 26 percent of U.S. auto sales. Japanese transplants accounted for 22 percent of the cars built in the United States. The bulk of GM and Ford profits came from their operations in Europe, not the United States. The Japanese, however, were establishing assembly plants in Great Britain and on the Continent where they promised to be a strong threat to the United States. Chrysler had already sold its European holdings.

While GM needed 5 workers a day to build a car, Chrysler 4.4 workers, and Ford 3.4 workers, the typical Japanese manufacturer needed less than 3. The Japanese were able to design, engineer, and launch new cars more than twice as fast as U.S. automakers.

With respect to quality, in 1980, the average Ford car had 6.7 defects, GM 7.4, and Chrysler 8.1 compared with the Japanese average of 2 defects per car. By 1990, Ford was down to 1.5 defects per car, GM to 1.7, and Chrysler to 1.8, but the Japanese had reduced their defects to 1.2 per car.

The Japanese cost advantage had been more than $2,000 per car a decade ago. In 1990, it was under $600 per car.[16]

Iacocca's Choices

Lee Iacocca had some tough choices to make. After considering the Honda experience, he was wondering what, if anything, Chrysler could do to catch up and emulate Honda's success?

Iacocca wondered where Honda would move next. Could it continue to innovate now that it was getting so much bigger *and* more bureaucratic? Would it remain a dynamic force in the auto industry?

How could Chrysler counter competitive moves from Honda? Was there any way Chrysler could regain its position in the U.S. market or stake out a new position as a global competitor on the scale of Honda?

Chrysler was issuing $720 million in new equity to help ensure that it had the financial strength to launch new products in 1992. It had plans to spend $16.6 million on plant, equipment, and products through 1995.[17] What could Chrysler learn from the Honda experience to make sure that this money was well spent? How should Chrysler allocate this money to assure that this would happen?

Discussion Questions

1. What mistakes did Chrysler make? Why did it make these mistakes?
2. Why was Honda successful?
3. What could Chrysler learn from Honda?
4. What type of long-term competitor was Honda likely to be in the U.S. auto market?
5. What should Chrysler do? How should it restructure itself so that it could compete in the world auto market?

Endnotes

1. This case was written by Alfred Marcus.
2. Bradley Stertz, "Detroit's New Strategy to Beat Back to Japanese Is to Copy Their Ideas," *The Wall Street Journal*, Oct. 1, 1992, p. 1, A10; Alex Taylor, "Iacocca's Last Stand at Chrysler," *Fortune*, April 20, 1992, pp. 62–73.
3. P. Ingrassia and B. A. Stertz, "With Chrysler Ailing, Lee Iacocca Concedes Mistakes in Managing," *The Wall Street Journal*, September 17, 1990, p. 1.
4. Ibid.
5. R. T. Pascale, "Honda (B)," Harvard Business School case, 1983.
6. D. E. Sanger, "Sochiro Honda, Auto Innovator, Is Dead at 84," *New York Times*, August 6, 1991, p. 1.
7. T. Sakiya, *Honda Motor* (Tokyo: Kodansha International, 1982), p. 66.
8. Pascale, "(Honda (B)," p. 4.
9. A. Taylor, "Who's Ahead in the World Auto War?" *Fortune*, November 9, 1987, p. 78.
10. "Honda, Mitsubishi Redesign Gas-Saver Engine for Compacts," *Minneapolis Star Tribune*, August 3, 1991, p. 1M; J. Gilbert, "Honda Accord Adds Wagon Utility without Trading Off Sporty Manners," *Minneapolis Star Tribune*, August 3, 1991, p. 1M.
11. Sakiya, *Honda Motor*, pp. 20–21.
12. Taylor, "Who's Ahead in the World Auto War?" p. 88.
13. Sakiya, *Honda Motor*, p. 104.
14. H. S. Stokes, "Honda the Market Guzzler," *Fortune*, February 20, 1984, p. 106.
15. Sakiya, *Honda Motor*, p. 113.
16. P. Ingrassia, "Auto Industry in U.S. Is Falling Relentlessly into Japanese Hands," *The Wall Street Journal*, February 16, 1990, p. A1.
17. B. Stertz, "Chrysler to Issue $720 Million in New Equity," *The Wall Street Journal*, August 18, 1991, p. A3.

CHAPTER

12

GLOBAL COMPETITION

Since 1973, economic growth in Western countries has slowed in terms of all relevant measuring rods. The phenomenon has been strikingly general, persistent, and large.

Angus Maddison, "Growth and Slowdown in Advanced Capitalist Economies"[1]

Introduction and Chapter Objectives

What accounts for differences in the economic performance of nations? Economic theory stresses labor and capital. Consumers and markets also are important as the examples of the formerly centrally planned economies of the Soviet Union and Eastern Europe show. France, South Korea, and Taiwan demonstrate the importance of international market exposure. The ability to incorporate the latest technology into high-quality low-cost goods also plays a role. The United States, strong in product innovation, has lagged behind in production capabilities. Product innovation has to be matched by production strength. The Japanese lag behind in introducing new products, but excel at making products others have originated.

Differences between the U.S. and Japanese economies are discussed in this chapter. The British sociologist Ronald Dore argues that the U.S. economy is built on a contract model that emphasizes individual rights, while the Japanese economy is built on a community model that emphasizes loyalty and long-term attachments. The continued success of Japan is questioned by some who see a "hollowing out" as Japan becomes more involved in finance and investment abroad than manufacturing at home. Reasons for Japan's recent economic problems are given. The prospects for the European Union (EU) are discussed, with an emphasis placed on Germany's pivotal role, along with the challenges the EU faces in dealing with the former communist countries of Central and Eastern Europe.

This chapter concludes with a discussion of the comparative place of the United States in the world economy. It provides evidence for a U.S. comeback and gives some reasons why it is taking place. In exploring these matters, the focus is placed on the reasons for the varying economic performance of nations.

Economic Competitiveness

From 1580 to 1820, the Netherlands was the world's economic leader; its average annual growth in domestic product (GDP) per worker was .2 percent. From 1820 to 1890, the United Kingdom (U.K.) was the leader with an average annual growth in GDP per worker of 1.2 percent. The United States took over the leadership from 1890 to 1989, when its average annual increase in GDP per worker was 2.2 percent. By 1990, Japan had surpassed the United States; from 1950 to 1990, its average annual growth rate had averaged 7.7 percent, while the U.S. average was 1.9 percent. The average annual income per Japanese worker in 1950 was $1,230; in 1990 it was $23,970, an economic performance unsurpassed by that of any other nation since the end of World War II.[2]

All nations in the world increased their economic welfare in the postwar period. In general, however, countries initially rich had greater increases in wealth than countries initially poor. Countries like Japan were the world's development miracles, but other countries were development disasters (see Exhibit 12–1). Differences in the distribution of wealth among nations did not change much between 1960 and 1985. The wealthiest countries remained 29 times richer than the poorest. The United States, the wealthiest country in the world in 1985, had a per capita income 43.3 times greater than the per capita income of the poorest country, Ethiopia.[3]

Since the end of World War II, the pace of economic change in the world accelerated. Starting in 1780, it took the United Kingdom 58 years to double its real income per person. Beginning in 1839, the United States accomplished this feat in 47 years. Postwar Japan did the same in only 34 years. South Korea doubled its wealth in 11 years since

EXHIBIT 12–1 Statistics on Selected Developing Nations, 1990

	GDP (% real growth)	*Per Capita Purchasing Power ($)*	*Population (millions)*
Thailand	10.0	1,410	56.6
South Korea	9.0	5,560	42.8
Singapore	8.3	12,810	2.7
Taiwan	5.2	7,390	20.4
Pakistan	5.0	380	114.6
India	4.5	300	852.7
Zimbabwe	4.2	550	10.4
Mexico	3.9	2,650	88.0
Columbia	3.7	1,300	33.1
Hong Kong	2.5	11,000	5.8
Philippines	2.5	700	64.4
Egypt	1.0	700	53.2
Zaire	−2.0	190	36.6
Argentina	−3.5	2,560	32.3
Brazil	−4.6	2,560	152.5

SOURCE: Adapted from Directorate of Intelligence, Central Intelligence Agency, *Handbook of Economic Statistics* (Washington, D.C.: U.S. Government Printing Office, 1991), p. 30.

1966, and China did so in less than 10 years starting in 1985.[4] With rapid communication and diffusion of technologies, catching up was taking less time than it had in the last century.

The next 30 years offered unprecedented opportunity for many nations, as they adopted market-friendly economic reforms and linked their economies to the rest of the world through trade and investment. Though the outlook for Russia and much of Africa remained troubled, many people living in Asia, Latin America, and Eastern Europe had the potential to enjoy much higher living standards.[5] If China, India, and Indonesia were to have average annual growth rates of 6 percent, by the year 2010, they would have 700 million consumers with living standards comparable to those of present-day Spain. The resurgence of India and China reflect a return to the past, because for most of history these nations had the world's largest economies. As late as 1830, more than 60 percent of the world's manufacturing output was centered in these nations. Their rapid growth could have an immensely positive effect on the world economy, stimulating the economic growth of all nations and providing many opportunities for market development and investment.

The Post-1973 Slowdown

Though the future looked bright, the Arab oil embargo of 1973 had inaugurated a slowdown in world economic growth; average annual growth during 1973–1985 was only 1.4 percent compared with 2.9 percent during 1960–1973. As economic growth leveled off, many nations had difficulties they had not experienced previously. The U.S. decline in average annual growth from 3.7 to 2.3 percent was not exceptional. Japan could not be happy with a mere 3.8 percent average annual growth rate after having enjoyed rates of more than 10 percent during the 1960s.[6] Japan's percent decline during the 1970s was the greatest among industrialized nations (see Exhibit 12–2).

Many factors contributed to the post-1973 slowdown: the oil price shocks of 1973–1974 and 1979–1980 (see Chapter 13), the movement from a fixed to a floating monetary system, and worldwide recessions in 1974–1975 and 1980–1981. Perhaps, the rate of

EXHIBIT 12–2 Average Annual Growth Rates in Major Industrial Nations
Real Gross National Product per Capita

	1961–70	*1971–80*	*1981–85*	*1986–90*
Japan	9.4	3.4	3.2	5.1
France	4.4	3.0	1.0	2.4
West Germany	3.6	2.6	1.3	2.8
Canada	3.3	3.3	1.9	2.3
United States	2.5	1.7	1.8	2.0
United Kingdom	2.2	1.8	1.7	2.4

SOURCE: Adapted from Directorate of Intelligence, Central Intelligence Agency, *Handbook of Economic Statistics* (Washington, D.C.: U.S. Government Printing Office, 1991), p. 59.

growth in the period after World War II simply was unusual, and the world was regressing toward a more normal and sustainable growth rate.

The reasons for the post-1973 slowdown were not readily apparent nor was it clear why some countries and some regions of the world fared better than others. The extent to which government policies contributed to country performance also was uncertain. In any case, with the slowdown came changes in relative competitive advantage. Among developing nations, some performed better than others.[7] The gap between the United States and other countries was shrinking. So-called follower nations were catching up with the leader.

Labor and Capital

Economists use labor and capital productivity to account for differences in national growth rates (see Exhibit 12–3).[8] Labor input consists of weekly working hours while capital input equals increments in investment less depreciation. Labor input can be augmented by improvements in educational quality and work intensity that partially offset a decline in working hours.

The average Japanese worker, for instance, continued to work more hours per year (2,149) than the average West German (1,676), American (1,632), French (1,554), or British (1,518) worker.[9] The main reason for this difference was that the Japanese workweek was six days, while employees in other countries worked only five days. Other differences had to do with vacation, sick time, and lost time due to occupational accidents, strikes, and so forth.

EXHIBIT 12–3 The Contribution of Labor, Capital, and Technology to Economic Growth

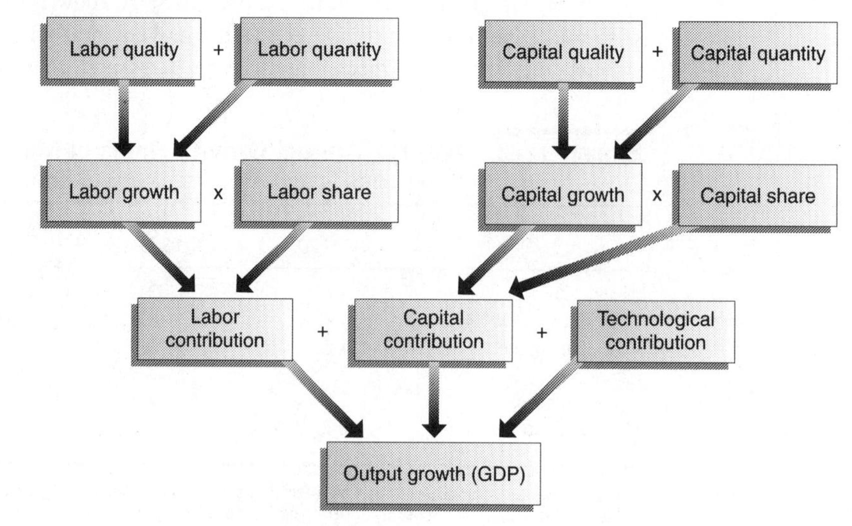

Educational Quality and National Competitiveness

Differences in the educational quality of the workforce also played a role in national competitiveness.[10] Germany, for instance, has long been noted for its highly skilled workforce and its high-quality scientific and technical education and specialized training. It had a distinctive industrial apprenticeship system that was unmatched by most countries. Along with its world-class research capabilities and good management-labor relations, these qualities resulted in high labor productivity.

Japanese workers also were known for their skills in subjects such as mathematics, and for their discipline, willingness to work hard, and group orientation. Japan had a large pool of well-trained engineers and its in-house company training programs were excellent. Japan's strengths in elementary and secondary education, private tutoring, and company training more than compensated for weaknesses in its colleges and universities.

The United Kingdom had a truly outstanding upper tier of people who were noted for their creativity, inventiveness, and independent thinking and for their capabilities in pure scientific research. However, the overall workforce was poorly skilled and poorly motivated. The educational system lagged behind that of other countries, with access to the best education primarily only to the elite. Technical colleges had a very low status and industry had no well-developed apprenticeship system. Humanities and pure science were valued above practical pursuits like engineering. Managers generally had their origins in the lower middle class and frequently lacked higher education; company training, which was not particularly strong, did not compensate. A high degree of labor-management antagonism existed, breeding narrow definitions of responsibility and an unwillingness to change traditional practices.

The eroding quality of human resources in the United States long has been a topic of discussion.[11] The country possessed very high quality schools at the top, but the standards of the average German university were higher than the standards of the average American university, and the percentage of students with technical majors in U.S. universities was lower. Public elementary and high schools had low educational standards and weak discipline and provided poor training in the sciences, mathematics, and languages compared with many other countries (see Exhibit 12–4).

EXHIBIT 12–4 Education Expenditures in Industrialized Countries, 1985
As a Percentage of Gross Domestic Product

	K-12	*Higher Education*	*All Levels*
Canada	4.0	1.8	6.3
France	3.9	.7	5.5
United States	3.8	2.5	6.2
Japan	3.1	1.0	4.8
United Kingdom	2.3	.9	4.8
West Germany	2.2	.9	4.1

SOURCE: Adapted from United Nations Educational, Scientific, and Cultural Organization, *Statistical Yearbook* (Paris: UNESCO, 1988).

Though spending was high, American schools were weak. Their weakness often was cited as being a major reason for declining U.S. competitiveness. Functional illiteracy was said to exist among a high proportion of the workforce. Neither a significant apprenticeship system nor a well-developed vocational school system existed to compensate for this weakness. Recommendations for improvement ranged from better teacher training to providing prenatal and preschool programs for disadvantaged youngsters. A key element in providing an effective workforce in the future was to properly educate children from low-income families. Educationally disadvantaged youth, who constituted more than a third of the country's young people, were more than three times as likely to drop out of school as students from middle- and high-income families.[12]

Capital Augmentation

A country's capital as well as its labor had to be improved if its economy was to grow. Capital could be augmented by replacing older factories, machines, buildings, and equipment with newer ones. New capital would embody the fruits of technical progress (e.g., investments in R&D); thus, investing in new factories and machines should be the surest way to realize economic gains.[13] Some augmentation of capital also is achieved by employees from the experience and knowledge they gain on the job and from recombining and retrofitting existing capital rather than replacing it.

Beyond Capital: The Importance of Markets

Analyses done on developing countries show that capital accumulation (measured by investment to GDP) is the most significant reason for economic development.[14] However, economists recognize that emphasizing capital without paying attention to markets is insufficient. For instance, Porter has emphasized the importance of markets by noting that Japanese demand for compact, portable, quiet, light, multifunctional products comes from the crowded living conditions and small plants, offices, and warehouses that exist in that country. These conditions have led to innovations in the use of materials, energy, and logistics. They have resulted in the production of compact and space-efficient goods and innovations in short production lines, the avoidance of unnecessary storage space and inventory, and combined production operations. Pioneering in space-saving and just-in-time production has been necessary to meet the demands of sophisticated home buyers who have limited room.[15] **Sophisticated domestic consumers** who are quality conscious can force a nation's firms to be more innovative and to produce to more exacting standards, generating competitive advantage when those firms face global markets.

sophisticated domestic consumers
Buyers who force a nation's firms to be more innovative and produce to more exacting standards, thereby increasing competitive advantage.

Centrally Planned Economies

Centrally planned economies like the former Soviet bloc nations were not subject to this kind of market discipline (see Exhibit 12–5). Although they possessed attributes needed for economic growth, including a well-educated workforce, technically trained and guaranteed life-time employment, and a government bureaucracy with a long-term planning horizon and a willingness to sacrifice today's consumption for tomorrow's growth, their

EXHIBIT 12–5 Average Annual Growth Rates of Formerly Centrally Planned Economies
Real Gross National Product per Capita

	1961–70	*1971–80*	*1981–85*	*1986–90*	*Population*	*Per Capita Purchasing Power ($)*
Soviet Union	3.5	1.5	.9	.2	290.9	9,140
Czechoslovakia	2.4	2.3	1.0	.5	15.7	8,100
Hungary	3.1	2.5	.6	−.2	10.6	6,100
Poland	3.3	3.0	1.0	−1.8	37.8	4,400
Romania	4.2	3.5	−.6	−3.3	23.3	3,200

SOURCE: Adapted from Directorate of Intelligence, Central Intelligence Agency, *Handbook of Economic Statistics* (Washington, D.C.: U.S. Government Printing Office, 1991), pp. 29, 38.

economic performance was so dismal during the 1980s that it pushed them into a massive crisis.

These nations were closed economies, which were not exposed to world economic conditions. They built up their human and physical capital without responding to market demand. Their workforces were generally skilled and capable; human resources were not a major problem. Their leaders made long-term capital commitments; indeed, they had sacrificed the present for the future and forced people to save by literally confiscating their possessions. But the lack of innovative activity and the tendency of the system to produce low-quality goods that fell far short of world standards and consumer needs severely hindered development.[16]

The former Soviet bloc nations were battered by their inability to compete successfully in increasingly competitive world markets. The problem of quality in their goods had a number of dimensions: (1) an abundance of low-quality goods that consumers were forced to accept because there were no alternatives; (2) goods that were several generations behind those available in the rest of the world; and (3) low-quality services (e.g., in retailing and transportation) upon which manufacturers and consumers rely.

In a centrally planned economy, planners, not producers or consumers, made the important decisions. The planners could not always anticipate what producers or consumers wanted. Producers experienced serious bottlenecks in making goods, and consumers endured shortages in the goods they valued. While store shelves remained full of goods they shunned, there were long waiting lines for the goods they wanted.

The socialist ideology also hindered development. Its dedication to income equality and job security took away incentives people need to excel.[17] Since few opportunities were open and the chances of advancement were limited, people made few serious efforts to succeed. Apathy reigned among workers and dissatisfaction was high.

A final problem was the desire of central planners to maintain price stability.[18] Prices were not used to adjust the economy to changing competitive conditions. Market signals needed to bring change into motion were missing. The system was static, rigid, and closed to competitive forces emanating from domestic consumers and the world economy.

International Market Exposure

In contrast to the former Soviet bloc nations, the economic successes of such nations as France, South Korea, and Taiwan were built upon exposure to international market conditions and consumer demand. The experience of these countries, however different, shows the importance of such exposure.

France

Contrary to the myth that French economic development is mainly a result of central planning, the underpinnings of French success are in its international market exposure.[19] The strategy France employed after World War I, political isolation and economic exploitation of its traditional adversary Germany, had failed.

France's goal after World War II was instead to integrate as much as possible with its European neighbors to prevent war and to enhance its own prosperity and that of all of Europe. France became a charter member of the General Agreement on Tariffs and Trade (GATT) in 1947 (see Chapter 9). In 1948, it joined the Organization for European Economic Cooperation (OEEC). It was committed in principle, if not always in practice, to the doctrine of free trade. The OEEC had great trouble at first in liberalizing trade, and some of the earliest problems, such as the timing of compliance for the loosening of quotas, involved France.

Nonetheless, in 1950 France called for the creation of a European common market for coal and steel. The Treaty of Paris established the European Coal and Steel Community, six of whose members then agreed in 1957 to extend the scope of their agreement into the European Economic Community (EEC), which became known as the Common Market. The EEC prohibited tariffs, quotas, and subsidies that restricted or distorted trade between member states. The Common Market now has 12 members and since 1994 has been called the European Union.

Meanwhile, France lost its colonies and focused more on developed nations. The share of exports that France's former colonies absorbed declined from 42 percent in 1952 to about 10 percent in 1962, when most of them had achieved independence.[20]

The French, like the rest of the EEC nations, became heavily exposed to foreign direct investment. It served to increase the competitive vigor of the markets in which French companies competed. Overall, it is probable that the salutary effects of international exposure rather than government planning largely explain French success in the post-World War II period.

South Korea

South Korea's growth also has involved exposure to international markets stimulated by the government's strong proexport policies and by the economy's ability to take over Japanese markets as the yen appreciated.[21] After the Korean War ended, South Korea tried to compete with Japan as a low-cost producer; it relied on its low labor rates to enter the world cotton textile market. However, it lacked certain Japanese advantages—group control over industry, large manufacturing units, shipping subsidies and low transportation costs, bulk purchases of raw materials, and efficient marketing of finished products. In addition, low wage rates imposed domestic costs in the form of low consumer spending, purchasing power, and productivity.

Currency manipulation did not provide a way out of this dilemma. Devaluations, which were intended to make South Korean exports cheaper and increase sales abroad, instead made the raw materials and capital goods South Korea needed more expensive. Exchange rate fluctuations, other than accounting for increased volatility, appear to have had little impact on real economic growth and national competitiveness. The cure for South Korea's problem was productivity growth, not devaluation.

To achieve this growth, the South Korean government imposed itself on the economy. It assumed control over the private sector with the purpose of expanding exports significantly. First, it used the Law for Dealing with Illicit Wealth Accumulation to confiscate assets from profiteers. Then it forged alliances with these profiteers and provided them with the incentives to become legitimate businesses so long as they were willing to lay the groundwork for export-led growth.

The government provided the newly formed firms with incentives to offset some of Japan's advantages. Barriers were imposed on imports and firms were allowed to inflate their returns on domestic sales. The government nationalized the banks, and it offered long-term capital at favorable rates to targeted firms and industries willing to invest heavily in foreign trade. A strong interventionist state made exports a compulsion rather than a choice for South Korean companies.[22]

Other factors helped. Inflows of foreign credit came to South Korea from financial institutions like the World Bank and International Monetary Fund. South Korea, located on the border of the Communist world, was considered a strategic asset. The loans allowed South Korea to purchase modern plant and equipment. Learning by doing aided in the rapid productivity enhancements. Synthetic fibers reduced the need for expensive imported raw materials. When Japan's wage levels rose, South Korea was ready to take Japan's place as a low-cost producer of textiles.

The emphasis on export-led growth means that no other industrial power, including Japan, has such a high dependence on foreign trade as South Korea. Only Hong Kong, Singapore, and Taiwan are comparable.[23]

The government-orchestrated strategy of export-led growth helped make the South Korean economy strong in an extremely short period of time. The South Korean story illustrates how important an emphasis on export-led growth can be. Investments, however, must be based on the existence of a market for the manufactured goods. The South Korean example goes against the argument that central planning can have little effect on strengthening a country's export potential.

Comparing Taiwan's and South Korea's Paths to Prosperity

Both Taiwan and South Korea made enormous strides in the post-World War II period. The progress they achieved is instructive because it can be directly compared to the backwardness of their Communist neighbors, the People's Republic of China and North Korea, both of which started at similar levels but did not go nearly as far.

Social welfare and equality in both Taiwan and South Korea are at all-time highs. The unemployment rate in Taiwan is consistently below 2 percent. In South Korea it has not exceeded 4 percent in the last 20 years.[24]

EXHIBIT 12–6 South Korea's Chaebol, 1990

	Sales (in billions $)	*Net Profit (in millions $)*
Samsung	$35.6	$348
Hyundai	31.8	445
Lucky-Goldstar	22.8	308
Daewoo	15.8	217
Sunkyong	10.6	90
Ssangyung	7.2	159
Kia	6.1	100
Lotte	4.9	142

SOURCE: Adapted from *The Economist,* June 8, 1991, p. 76.

Both countries have few resources, little arable land, and high population densities. Both have pursued export-led growth policies, but they have done so in different ways. Taiwan has been less aggressive in protecting domestic industry. The South Korean government has been more interventionist in rewarding companies for some activities and punishing them for others.

Taiwan has relied more on the free market and a highly educated, technically trained (more than a third of Taiwanese students in higher education study engineering), and enterprising workforce. It has let interest rates rise to their market level, encouraging savings and investment and creating a very atomized industrial structure. Taiwan's companies are financed through equity markets; they are lightly leveraged and small. In 1981, more than 80 percent of the country's firms had fewer than 20 employees.[25]

In comparison, South Korea's companies are highly concentrated and very heavily leveraged. They have received low-interest loans from government planners. Some of these firms grew into the South Korean giants known as the *chaebol*. In 1984, the sales of the top 10 *chaebol* represented about two-thirds of South Korea's GNP (see Exhibit 12–6).

There is much controversy about which country's economy will be stronger in the future. While the South Korean *chaebol* have some admirable strengths, including people, persistence, agility, and financial clout, they also have notable weaknesses including bureaucracy, lack of focus, and lack of creativity.

Technology

Global market exposure was an important factor in spurring economic growth. Another important factor was technology.[26] Expanded markets were insufficient if the goods produced did not incorporate the latest in technology. High-quality, low-cost goods required technological innovation.

The Austrian economist Joseph Schumpeter argued that new capital replaces old capital in waves ("creative destruction") as particular sectors (e.g., textiles, steel, railroads, automotive, chemicals, pharmaceuticals, telecommunications, computers, biotechnology) dominate the world economy at certain intervals. Thus, technical change and the ability to generate innovations are critical for economic growth (see Chapter 16).[27]

R&D spending by corporations is an important part of this process. U.S. companies lost market share in 12 of 15 critical industries from 1960 to 1986. This drop in market share is connected to lower R&D spending by American firms. Corporate R&D, not government-sponsored R&D, spurs competitiveness, and U.S. firms fund R&D at a rate lower than firms in other countries. The large, diversified American company, organized into separate profit centers and dominated by professional managers, is likely to be risk-averse and invest less heavily in R&D than firms that are functionally organized and operating to maximize returns to investors.[28]

Product versus Process

When a group of Europeans rated the 50 best people in the world in nine technologies, U.S. scientists and engineers rated best in five instances, they were tied for first twice, and they were second twice. However, Japan was number two in every case where the United States was number one, and it was number one in the two cases where the United States was number two.[29] The gap between the United States and countries such as Japan has been narrowing. More U.S. patents were going to foreigners, especially the Japanese, than ever before.

While the United States was spending about the same on R&D as a percentage of GNP as Japan and West Germany—about 2.7 to 2.8 percent—only 1.7 to 1.8 percent of U.S. spending was for civilian research and development.[30] The United States spent a much higher percentage of its GNP on defense (see Exhibit 12–7). Virtually all Japanese and West German spending was on civilian research and development. Military spin-offs to the commercial sector, once common (e.g., the jet aircraft), had become infrequent. Instead, the U.S. commercial sector often developed technologies that were "spun into" the military (e.g., the semiconductor).

The Japanese in particular excelled at process technologies (e.g., robotics). The U.S. decline in this area was directly related to the slump in productivity growth.[31] U.S. manag-

EXHIBIT 12–7 Defense Expenditures of Major Industrialized Nations
As a Percentage of GNP

	1965	*1975*	*1985*	*1988*
United States	7.2	5.6	6.5	6.1
United Kingdom	5.9	4.9	5.2	4.3
France	5.2	3.8	4.0	3.9
Canada	3.0	1.9	2.2	2.1
West Germany	4.3	3.6	3.2	2.9
Japan	1.0	.9	1.0	1.0

SOURCE: Adapted from Directorate of Intelligence, Central Intelligence Agency, *Handbook of Economic Statistics* (Washington, D.C.: U.S. Government Printing Office, 1991), pp. 29, 38.

ers have thought that the highest returns on investment came from new products, not from building old products better. First-rate people went into new-product development, not process technologies. However, the Japanese discovered that it was unnecessary to invent new products. By manufacturing existing products cheaper and better than the people who invented them, they could capture the profits.

Americans, for instance, invented the video recorder, but could manufacture it only at a unit cost of $100,000. The Japanese lowered the costs of manufacturing so that they could sell VCRs at a unit cost of $300. No VCRs are now manufactured in the United States. Instead, the Japanese have made enormous profits selling this product to Americans.

The Japanese approach to managing the R&D process involved the deliberate creation of excess information and its sharing by different groups that were linked horizontally and vertically in the firm and outside it. Project teams in Japan had cross-sectional diversity, which was supposed to produce ideas of higher quality and quantity. Every member involved in a project was given a part in creating or suggesting solutions to problems regardless of the position they held in the organization. Vendors and subcontractors also were consulted about project needs. Different phases in project development were overlapped to speed entry into the market and gain rapid information from consumers. The Japanese aim was to gain insights from consumers about product improvements while at the same time maintaining their existing customer loyalty.[32]

The Japanese Economy

Managers, politicians, academicians, and others have been fascinated by the growth of the Japanese economy. Much has been written to explain this success and to show how the factors behind it can be transferred to other countries.[33] As analyses of the Japanese economy proliferated, however, there was a tendency for writers to find in Japan what they already valued. Few analysts saw the Japanese economic miracle as an aggregate, focusing instead on a particular area. Thus, Japanese success was variously attributed to low defense spending, easy access to capital, a high educational level, low levels of unionization, labor-management cooperation, lifetime employment, decision making by consensus, quality circles, industrial policies, trade protection, or any of a number of other factors. In the discussion that follows, three features of the Japanese economy will be stressed: a high level of savings and investment, a high level of equity held by banks, and the importance of business alliances in the Japanese economic system.

High Levels of Savings and Investment

Japanese firms enjoyed a competitive advantage over U.S. firms because they could secure funds at low rates of interest. What made this possible was that Japan had an excess of savings over investment. Individuals were encouraged to save through many means, including tax incentives, and they paid no taxes on capital gains (up to a certain high amount) and interest on savings. Unlike Americans, however, the Japanese had to save money to buy a house because there were no tax deductions for the interest on mortgage payments. They also had to save for old age, since Japanese social security benefits were small by U.S. standards.

Since the Japanese government was averse to running fiscal deficits, the bulk of the savings was invested in industry. The Bank of Japan and the Ministry of Finance played an important role in this process. The government was able to direct capital flows into industries targeted for development, and industry received numerous tax incentives and depreciation allowances to encourage investment and export.

Comparative studies of U.S. and Japanese firms in the semiconductor business showed significantly lower costs of debt financing in Japan.[34] During the mid-1970s recession, U.S. semiconductor manufacturers were forced to cut back on capital spending, but NEC, Hitachi, and Toshiba did not face the same constraint (see Case 11–A on U.S. Memories). They continued to invest heavily in new production capacity, so that when the recession ended they had the capacity to supply a growing market. Since the mid-1980s, however, the situation for Japanese firms changed somewhat as companies used substantial cash inflows to lower their debt burdens and to invest heavily in equities.

Equity Held by Banks

Japanese banks were permitted to hold equity in companies. U.S. banks have not been allowed to do so; the Glass-Steagall Act of 1933 separated the activities of trust departments and commercial banking. In the United States, banks legally must have an arm's length relationship with the companies to whom they lend money. They have not been allowed to take an active role in managing a company's affairs under pain of losing their legal status of lender and becoming a shareholder with all the limitations that entails (the last to be paid back in case of bankruptcy).

Japanese banks can assume managerial responsibilities, including not only the rescheduling of loan payments and the granting of emergency loans but also taking active control by extending advice about which assets to liquidate, business opportunities to pursue, managers to hire or fire, and reorganizations to be carried out.[35] However, the control of a company's policy and the selection of managers was not a function that banks readily aggrandized. The threat of extensive intervention existed only when a company found itself in very serious financial difficulty.

Some analysts have argued that the close ties between Japanese firms and banks meant that the former could obtain loans at a higher debt to equity ratio than U.S. firms. Banks made large loans at low interest rates because they had more power and regularly obtained good information on how a company's divisions were doing. They relied less on annual accounting data and more on their intimate knowledge of the firm's management, customers, and progress in product development. However, some analysts disputed the significance of the good information ties and resultant high debt to equity ratio. They claimed that most loans were secured by assets (e.g., property), and that accounting practices in Japan were more conservative than in the United States.[36]

As world capital markets became more open, Japanese savers were attracted by higher rates of return outside Japan. They purchased large amounts of assets (e.g., real estate and U.S. Treasury bonds) on international markets. Similarly, foreign firms were attracted by the low rates of interest offered by Japanese banks and sought to obtain loans from them. Thus, Japanese banks have become the largest in the world and, with the free flow of capital across international boundaries, the distinctive advantages of Japan's banking system have receded.

Business Alliances

Company ownership in Japan also has been more concentrated than in the United States. In a sample of 585 U.S. companies, only about half had individuals who owned 5 percent or more of the shares of stock. In a sample of 135 Japanese firms, all but six had a single shareholder with this kind of holding. Whereas the large owner in the United States was likely to be a founding family, in Japan it was likely to be an interlocking group of banks, insurance companies, and manufacturing concerns called a ***kereitsu.*** Typically, about 20 to 30 percent of the common stock was controlled by the *kereitsu* with the understanding that these long-term holdings were not to be traded. As a result, only about 25 percent of the shares listed on the Tokyo Stock Exchange were available for trading; takeovers and other types of corporate restructuring were extremely rare.[37]

kereitsu
An interlocking group of Japanese banks, insurance companies, and manufacturers in which controlling interests of stock are held by management and other members of the enterprise group.

Kereitsu evolved out of a system of longstanding cooperation among Japanese firms that distinguished them from U.S. firms. Believing that funds and managerial skills were limited, the *kereitsus* pooled resources. A corporation lacking experience overseas and needing natural resources from abroad would join the group. The Mitsubishi Bank, for instance, owned significant portions of Mitsubishi Trust Bank, Tokyo Marine, Mitsubishi Heavy Industries, Mitsubishi Corporation (the trading company), Mitsubishi Electric, Asahi Glass, Kirin Beer, Mitsubishi Chemical, and NYK. These companies in turn owned more than a quarter of Mitsubishi Bank's stock.[38]

zaibatsu
Pre-World War II Japanese business alliances, often family controlled, which were pyramid-like structures that held other businesses, subsidiaries, and affiliated firms.

Earlier enterprise groups were called ***zaibatsu.*** They were pyramid-like structures, run by autocratic leaders, in which a family-held business in turn controlled other businesses, which also controlled subsidiaries and affiliated firms. After World War II, the *zaibatsu* were reconstituted and renamed *keiretsu*. The dominant ones are Mitsui, Mitsubishi, and Sumitomo and the Fuji, Sanawa, and Dai-ichi Kang banks.

The *zaibatsu* derived their power from their commercial might. They were large trading companies particularly good at helping Japanese businesses penetrate foreign markets. Today's *keiretsu* obtain their power from the financial clout of the large banks and insurance companies around which other companies are organized. Member companies in the *keiretsu* have much more independence than the *zaibatsu*. They carry on much less of their commerce (typically less than 30 percent) with other members of the *keiretsu*. Goods are bought from nonmember companies when they are offered at lower prices.

Still, members of the *keiretsu* are highly interconnected. They own each other's stock, which contributes to the stabilization of stock prices, have various kinds of financial relations, and sometimes share or exchange top managers. The easy availability of funding during Japan's rapid economic growth was advantageous to *keiretsu* members. The sharing of managerial know-how helped an economy in which employees did not move from firm to firm. Companies could obtain information about technology and markets that otherwise might not be available to them.

Cooperative ventures primarily were in importing energy resources, introducing new technologies, launching new businesses, and the export of large projects. However, high-technology companies just starting up generally found the *keiretsu* stifling and did not become heavily involved with them. The *keiretsu* mainly have large, capital-intensive businesses that rely on substantial economies of scale. Such cooperation among American firms is prohibited by antitrust laws.[39]

A Hollowing Out

hollowing out Process by which a country achieves manufacturing superiority and becomes more involved in finance, investment, and manufacturing abroad, but faces the possibility of losing its capacity for domestic productivity gains.

Is Japan going through a predictable cycle of decline with the **hollowing out** of its industry whereby the country engages more in finance, investment, and manufacturing abroad and produces less at home? Its mercantile period lasted from 1945 to 1980, during which the government promoted exports, restricted imports, and manipulated incentives for the formation and use of capital. The Japanese focused initially on labor-intensive, low-technology industries such as textiles. The dominance of heavy industry like steel was next, followed by high value-added products such as electronics. Japanese successes yielded very large current account surpluses that provided it with the means to make the transition from an industrial economy concentrating on trade to an investment-oriented economy.[40]

Though the Japanese were able to consume more, they did not do so. They maintained their frugal saving habits, which provided them with even more funds for foreign investment. Early Japanese investments were in low-tech industries and raw material sources in Asia and elsewhere. Japanese foreign direct investment then moved to manufacturing. Foreign direct investment in raw materials declined from 60 percent in 1980 to 28 percent in 1985. Total foreign investment was up from $0.4 billion in 1960 to $38.5 billion in 1985, paralleling the rise in Japan's trade surplus. Much of the new investment was destined for manufacturing in the United States and Asian nations.[41]

With U.S. trade restrictions in place, the only alternative the Japanese had for an expanding market share in the United States was to expand their manufacturing base in that country. With labor costs reaching levels near to those of the United States and Europe, the Japanese also had to rely on low-cost Asian manufacturing. This investment in manufacturing abroad led to declines in domestic productivity growth. The existence of an easy income source abroad distracted industrial producers from the dynamic and innovative pursuit of productivity at home. When production experience moved overseas, organizational learning, which was often tacit, was not easily transferred back to Japan. As a consequence, Japan was losing some of its manufacturing excellence.[42]

Bursting of the Bubble

In 1989, the Tokyo Stock Exchange was valued at $3.6 trillion, three times the value of all listed U.S. companies on the New York Stock Exchange. Land prices in Tokyo were so high that the grounds of the Imperial Palace were reputed to be worth more than all the land in California.[43] In 1982, the Japanese yen fell to record low levels compared with the dollar. The U.S. trade deficit swelled and the industrial nations of the world started a campaign to bring down the value of the dollar. To slow the process, the Bank of Japan drove up the money supply, making credit cheap and easily available. Manufacturing firms borrowed not only to acquire new capital but to buy assets in other companies and to invest abroad. These conditions led to a speculative bubble; borrowers expected that land and equity values would keep rising, so they used rising asset values as collateral to borrow more. Property values skyrocketed, and the average family could no longer afford a simple apartment. Speculators made vast amounts of money, threatening the egalitarian character of Japanese society.

Meanwhile, the Japanese government began to fear inflation. Labor shortages were common and foreign workers were recruited to work in Japanese factories. The Bank of Japan, under veteran bureaucrat Yasushi Mieno, believed that the situation was intolerable. To restore Japan's social cohesion and stop inflation, he tightened monetary policy. He also intended to limit the use of foreign workers, punish speculators, and make property more affordable for the typical family.

The result of the Bank of Japan's policies was a collapse in asset prices, a massive contraction in household and corporate wealth, and a fall in demand that drove many businesses to bankruptcy. Banks suffered because the land and equity they held as collateral were now worth less than the loans extended against them. People feared that the bad debts would bring down the banking system. Japan's banks, the world's largest, had little money to loan to the rest of the world, which contributed to the worldwide recession of the early 1990s.

The Japanese economy, however, continued to be cushioned from the worst of this economic shock by a widening trade surplus with the United States. This occurred despite the growing value of the yen. Also, Japan continued to have relatively large government budget surpluses, which it could use to stimulate the economy. The controversy over how to stimulate the economy (tax cuts or increased public spending), however, helped to end political stability and contributed to the downfall of the Liberal Democratic party.[44]

Effects on the Automobile Industry. Japan's automakers suffered under these changing conditions (see Cases 12–A and 12–B on the automobile industry). In 1980, they exceeded U.S. manufacturers in worldwide production and started to dominate the world industry with their manufacturing and product development skills. They changed the domain of competition with high productivity, low-cost production, quality, workmanship, and rapid product change and technological innovation. While U.S. and European firms took an average of 65 months to introduce a new car, Japanese manufacturers could do so every 42 months. They relied on close ties with their suppliers and relatively independent project teams in contrast to in-house suppliers and functional departments.[45]

By the early 1990s, however, Japanese society was in gridlock. The production system was not working well in congested urban areas where poor roads and massive pollution existed. A shortage of well-trained blue-collar workers who could be given broad responsibilities made it less easy to do rapid setups and frequent product changes, and inadequately trained foreign workers introduced quality problems. With so many model changes, automotive recycling became an issue. Only so many old cars could be sold to the rest of Asia.

The weakness of Japanese banks and the stock market collapse also contributed to the problems of the auto companies. The bursting of the bubble meant that money was not as available to finance rapid model changes. Japanese companies had to become more like companies in other countries—focused more on profit and less on growth. In any case, the best U.S. plants had successfully copied Japanese methods. They now were achieving near parity in efficiency and quality. Competitive domains in the industry were shifting to materials, innovative products, skillful overseas management, and styling. Whether the Japanese companies would be able to maintain dominance was uncertain (see Case 12–A, "Reversal of Fortune: Honda and Chrysler").

Other Problems. Japan had several other problems with which to contend:

1. Consumers were aware that despite their wealth they did not enjoy comparable living standards with Americans. Over time, the Japanese would be more likely to consume and less inclined to save.
2. Japan's population was aging, which was also likely to suppress savings. The cost of capital could go up, interest rates rise, and investment might fall.
3. The political consensus was breaking down. The Liberal Democratic party lost power because of corruption and a failing economy.
4. As Japan lost the advantage of catching up, its skill in adopting foreign technology could no longer be the main engine of its growth. It had to be creative.

All these factors put new strains on the distinctive form of capitalism that had served Japan so well in the past.

Special Feature

The Community Model

Ronald Dore, the British sociologist, who lived for long periods of time in Japan and wrote extensively about Japanese society, argues that a sense of fairness explains Japan's success. He believes that Japanese capitalism is practiced according to a "community model" which distinguishes it from the "company law" model of capitalism in the United States and the United Kingdom. In the community model, managers are senior members in the firm, and shareholders are one of many stakeholder groups that have to be satisfied. In the company law model, on the other hand, the firm is the property of shareholders, and managers act as their agents seeking to maximize shareholder wealth and to minimize expenses.

For the community model to flourish, the participants must feel that the system is fair. They must practice "restraint in the use of market power" out of consideration for the interests of their bargaining partners and adversaries. This sense of fairness is fostered by many elements:[47]

1. Government:
   a. *The size of government in Japan is relatively small.* Both the United States and United Kingdom absorb more of national income in taxes than does Japan. The U.S. tax code is more burdensome than Japan's.
   b. *The Japanese value and honor public service.* Government ministries are able to recruit some of Japan's most talented people into the civil service, which is considered a prestige career. Ministries like MITI thus have the respect of the business community. The official economic White Papers and "Visions" that it issues are influential in mobilizing and unifying public opinion on economic issues.
   c. *By contrast, the Japanese do not much honor politicians, whose role in running the economy is small.* This eliminates, for the most part, destabilizing swings in policy caused by changes in party control

of government. The *Liberal Democratic party* maintained power for over 30 years. Politicians have less economic influence than ministry officials.

2. Labor:
   a. *The Japanese work not only hard, but well.* Although yearly working hours are greater than in the United States or Britain, the crucial difference behind product quality and innovation in Japan is that the Japanese managers and engineers work well together. Institutional and cultural characteristics account for their dedication to hard work in teams.
   b. *The Japanese are well educated.* The educational quality of the workforce is high: over 90 percent of each age group stays in school until the age of 18, 40 percent go on to college and 50 percent of all master's degrees are in engineering.[48]
   c. *The Japanese work cooperatively in large corporations.* Decision-making processes emphasize widespread and slow consultation and diffusion of responsibility, yet swift execution of agreed decisions. Decisions may take longer to make, but implementation proceeds rapidly because of the commitment earned during the decision-making process. Specific features of the employment system—lifetime employment as the norm, representation of employee interests, and predictable tracks of promotion by merit with minimum-seniority thresholds—are thought to foster cooperation.
   d. *The Japanese maintain a constant emphasis on quality.* Since Japan became aware in the mid-1950s that the rest of the world perceived its goods as shoddy, its view has been that quality improvement is a constant battle. While American managers blame workers for quality gaps and have relied on end-of-the-line inspections to eliminate defects, Japanese firms stress process improvements and the constant redesigning and upgrading of products to enhance quality.[49]
   e. *Japanese workers have a sense of ownership.* The Japanese payment system is based on bonuses to employees for profitability gains rather than straight salaries that are paid regardless of how well the firm has done. Japanese workers therefore feel a sense of ownership in the businesses that employ them.
   f. *Japan has an effective form of union-management relations.* All Japanese companies conclude bargaining arrangements with unions at the same time. Pay raises start at the same date (April 1).
3. Capital:
   a. *Japan has a high savings rate and low interest rates, and corporate investment is very high.* Japanese culture values prudence and a willingness to defer gratification. Its weak natural-resource position also has contributed to the high savings rate.
   b. *Equity often is held by banks that finance the loans.* As discussed, a high proportion of corporate capital has been in the form of bank loans rather than equity. Creditors and owners are not separate as in the United States. The close working relationships between banks and corporations foster long-term relationships. They allow Japan to have a managerial, production-oriented capitalism, not a shareholder-dominated form of capitalism.
   c. *Japanese corporations are good at forming alliances with each other.* Also, as discussed, Japan has an impressive array of industry associations that foster close cooperation between corporations.

Toward a Single European Market

With Japan hurting, would Europe, with its tremendous potential, be able to fill the void? In 1985, the European Economic Community made the decision to create a single market by 1992. Its reasons were that continuing fragmentation harmed consumers and prevented businesses from effectively competing against the United States and Japan.[46]

The problems with fragmentation were numerous:

1. European companies had to have additional engineers on staff to design products for the different standards that prevailed in each European country. Philips Industries, for instance, employed an additional 70 engineers to make the seven types of television sets needed for different European countries. The cost to Philips was over $20 million a year.
2. Long truck lines at European borders meant that truckers had to wait an average of 80 minutes before the paper work was cleared. These delays cost the European economy an estimated $10 billion a year.

The all-European market was designed to:

- Harmonize regulations and standards.
- Liberalize the movement of capital, people, and services.

There would be baseline essential standards in such areas as health, safety, and environmental protection; deregulation of the transportation and insurance industries; and mutual recognition of professional qualifications. Some border controls would have to continue to check for narcotics, terrorism, and illegal immigration. No one expected to achieve the goal of equalizing taxes, and differences in value-added and excise taxes would remain because high-tax countries would lose too much money and low-tax countries would have to raise taxes if tax rates were harmonized. Many high-tech businesses in the United States were concerned about the implications of a possible "fortress-like" Europe, which would impose specific conditions that U.S. firms would find hard to accept.

Planned Expansion of the European Union

Treaty of Maastricht Set the terms for the creation of a single European government, where all European nations would have a common currency, foreign and defense policies, and citizenship.

The European Community aimed to expand beyond the 12 member states it had in 1985. These nations were Belgium, Denmark, France, Germany, Greece, Ireland, Italy, Luxembourg, Netherlands, Portugal, Spain, and the United Kingdom. They encompassed 350 million people. The European Community wanted to add 13 more countries so that it would have a market of more than 450 million people by the year 2000. When the European Community officially became the European Union (EU), after its member nations ratified the **Treaty of Maastricht,** it first chose new members from the countries in the European Free Trade Association—Austria, Finland, Iceland, Liechtenstein, Norway, Sweden, and Switzerland. With 35 million people, these countries had the world's most affluent consumers. Following the breakup of the Soviet bloc, the East European countries were eager to join the EU. While the EU had special trading arrangements with some of these countries—the Czech Republic, Hungary, Poland, and Slovakia—it refused to consider them for full membership until the end of the century.

The EU realized that Central and Eastern Europe could be an important growth market in the future, adding as much as 1 to 2 percent to the EU's growth rates, but it was reluctant to open up its markets rapidly, because these nations had cheap labor and inexpensive agricultural products, with which the EU nations would have trouble competing. For instance, an average Czech factory worker earned $2,500 a year in 1990, while an average German worker took home $23,000. An engineer in Hungary was paid $7,000 that year, while one in the EU received more than $50,000. The production of milk in Central Europe cost half what it cost in the EU. Potatoes produced in Central Europe were one-third as expensive as potatoes produced in the EU. In sum, the EU feared immediate entry of the former Soviet bloc nations because its own workers and farmers would be threatened.

Germany's Pivotal Role

A newly united Germany was expected to play the pivotal role in developing ties with Central European countries. Germany had invested more in these nations than any other country. However, the bulk of its investments were used to meet the challenges of reunification. The unification of West Germany and East Germany proved to be more complex and time-consuming than anyone imagined. Germany's public debt jumped to 33 percent of GNP between 1991 and 1994, peaking at 59 percent of GNP.[50]

The Germans feared runaway inflation because it had helped destroy the fledgling democracy of the Weimar Republic in the 1920s and made it possible for extremists like Hitler to rise to power. But the Deutsche Bank, under the leadership of Hans Tietmeyer, kept interest rates high to prevent inflation from getting out of control. With the currencies of the EU linked, Germany's policy depressed economic growth throughout the European Union and created tensions among the European nations.

As tensions rose and the economies of the former Communist bloc countries stalled, a vast migration of people to Germany took place. Capital that Germany might have spent in the East was diverted toward paying for the absorption of millions of new immigrants. Many ethnic Germans living in Poland, Yugoslavia, Romania, and Russia exercised their right under Germany's constitution to return to Germany. Germany also accepted many non-German political and economic refugees from the former Soviet bloc. It provided them with housing, training, and welfare, raising government deficits even further. The large numbers of immigrants created social tensions in Germany. The neo-Nazi revival, racism, and riots threatened the country's political stability.

Despite these challenges, the German economy remained strong. Its pluses were its high level of investment, quality of life, and the peculiar form of capitalism, called ***Mitbestimmung* (codetermination),** that had evolved. This form of capitalism allowed for a great deal of worker participation, by which workers had extensive consultative powers. Company boards in Germany were run almost like constitutional democracies with trade unions playing a substantial role.

Mitbestimmung (codetermination) The extensive consultative powers that German workers and trade unions have on the boards of major corporations.

Like the Japanese, the Germans had created an alternative form of capitalism. Germany's was based on the idea that completely free markets were damaging when they extended to workers competing for jobs in the labor market. Workers should not be treated like goods that customers bought in consumer markets. While the German system provided for great continuity and stability, it also had its negatives. One of them was immobility in the labor market. Another was overregulation; there was a regulation for nearly everything in Germany. The German system was both heavy-handed (because of so many regulations) and expensive. Social insurance for the unemployed, by U.S. standards, provided extremely generous benefits. For the employed, wages were high and holidays were long. An employer could not easily lay off its workers.

Capital markets were as rigid as labor markets. It was hard to start a new business in Germany. The expansion of the welfare state, the resistance to change, and the veto power of affected interests made it difficult for the German economy to adjust to new conditions. Germany could not easily compete globally on the basis of providing low-cost goods. With the type of capitalism it had created, its comparative advantage was high-cost, precision-built, value-added products.

Germany had a secure place, along with the United States and Japan, as one of the world's economic superpowers. Some nations in the EU, however, expressed bitterness toward Germany. They resented its anti-inflation stand, which held back their own growth and prolonged the European recession.

Central and Eastern European Privatization

With credit in Germany in tight supply, there was not enough cash for investment in Central and Eastern Europe. Unlike the fast-growing economies of Asia, the likelihood was slim that the nations of this arca could pay for their own development through high domestic savings and strong export growth. Economic growth was slow after years of decline, and hopes faded for a quick transition to fully functioning market economies.

No precedent existed for the vast privatization programs of the Central and Eastern European economies. The building of full market economies with their many rules and institutions was an immense undertaking. A whole new system had to be created: property and contract laws, accounting and bankruptcy rules, administrative bodies and courts to enforce these rules, labor laws and tax codes, and banks and financial institutions.[51]

big bang approach The attempt by some former Communist countries to hand over their economy at once to private investors.

Poland tried the **"big bang" approach** of privatizing all at once: by 1991, more than 40 percent of its economy had been turned over to private hands. However, in the Czech Republic, while government officials allowed 85 percent of prices to be set by market conditions, private business constituted only 2 percent of GDP in 1991. In Hungary, only about 33 percent of the economy was in private hands. In Romania and Bulgaria, progress in freeing prices and creating a private sector was very slow.

Many of the formerly state-owned firms in Central and Eastern Europe were worthless. They had been propped up by low oil prices, caused massive pollution, and consumed more than they produced. No one wanted to buy or own them. It was estimated that up to 25 percent of the businesses in these nations had no real value.

Downturn in the European Union's Popularity

The difficulties Europe was experiencing, especially in integrating formerly Communist Central and Eastern Europe put a strain on the EU. In the early 1990s, the popularity of the EU declined and new tensions came to the surface. The United Kingdom expressed its dissatisfaction with EU social policies such as granting part-time workers the same benefits as full-time workers and providing full-time workers four weeks of guaranteed vacation. Poor nations like Spain and Greece pressured the rich nations for more subsidies. The rich nations lacked funds because of their high unemployment. The Norwegians, when given the chance to join the EU, voted against it.

Big countries had more votes in the EU Council of Ministers, which functions like a legislature (the European Parliament is largely symbolic). Small countries were protected by a system of weighted voting. With additional states joining the EU, there was a great deal of discussion about redefining voting rules.

Many Europeans resented the EU's civil servants, who were perceived as technocrats far removed from popular needs and aspirations. The Maastricht Treaty, which was supposed to create for Europe a single government with a common foreign and defense policy, a common currency (the ecu), and a common citizenship, was in trouble. Europeans in favor of the EU, however, were optimistic that in the long run and despite setbacks, the gains that the EU had brought to member countries would be expanded. While not realizing all the goals its leaders had set for it, the EU would remain a very important force.

The United States' Renewal

Compared with Europe and Japan, to what extent was the United States in a serious and irreversible decline?[52] First, the United States continued to have advantages other countries did not have. Its military prowess could be matched by no other country (see Case 12–C on Alliant Techsystems). It remained an immigrant country that was constantly being revitalized by the entrepreneurial talents and energies of its newcomers (see Exhibit 12–8).

Japan, the world's second largest economy, was tied to the U.S. economy, its major overseas market. If the United States declined, Japan would suffer. It was in Japan's interest to see continued American prosperity. Europe's resources were impressive—twice that of Japan's. The continent played a larger role in world trade than Japan, and its armed forces, if combined, outnumbered those of the United States. However, the issue of political cohesiveness remained a stumbling point. Moreover, the immobility of labor and capital showed the European economy to be less dynamic than the U.S. economy. In the early 1990s, there were signs of renewed American competitiveness, while the economies of Japan and Europe were struggling.

To a greater extent than either Japan or Germany, the United States in the 1990s was growing faster, creating more jobs, and keeping inflation in check. It still held an absolute lead in productivity and was making gains there, too. In the postwar period, it was unusual to see the United States outperforming Japan and Germany in GNP growth and productivity improvement.[53]

EXHIBIT 12–8 A Comparison of Immigrant Skills with Those of U.S. Population, 1988

	Immigrants Entering U.S. (percentage)	*U.S. Population (percentage)*
College education	22.7%	19.9%
Engineers	2.9	1.5
Teachers	3.4	3.8
Medical doctors	0.6	0.5
Skilled blue-collar workers	10.2	12.1

SOURCE: Council on Competitiveness, based on data from Immigration and Naturalization Service, Labor Department, and Census Bureau.

Exploring the reasons for the renewed U.S. competitiveness requires consideration of the role of: capital, technology, and labor; management and organization innovations; environmental standards and energy prices; and new government policies.

Fluid Capital. In a period of vast global transformation, countries with fluid capital like the United States and the United Kingdom were outperforming countries with systems of dedicated capital like Germany and Japan. Fluid capital was transient and transaction driven; it involved outside owners, fragmented stakes, and a relatively limited flow of information. Dedicated capital, in contrast, was relationship driven; it involved significant stakes with great owner influence, inside information, and extensive information flow.

Throughout the 1980s, the conventional wisdom was that dedicated capital was superior to fluid capital. A reliance on fluid capital was frequently given as a reason for the comparative economic decline of the United States. However, fluid capital provides benefits that may be better suited to the dynamic economic changes of the 1990s. For example, it has allowed businesspeople to enter new fields and to recognize and exploit emerging opportunities. In systems of dedicated capital, businesspeople are more apt to stick with an investment through ups and down in order to realize a long-term gain. On the other hand, small business growth in the United States has been phenomenal even as large business downsized and reduced its workforce.

Technology. In technology, the United States had the lead in the number of personal computers per worker but it had not translated this advantage into productivity gains because, most economists believed, organizational adjustments had not been made and workers were not adept at using the software that was available. New studies, however, indicated that the U.S. lead in computers per worker was beginning to pay off.

While the United States showed weakness in process technology, it had an enormous capacity to introduce new products. In a period of rapid economic transformation, this capacity was more important than a capacity to manufacture existing products more cheaply. U.S. creativity produced gains because of the transition to new products and technologies.

Labor. The gap between the performance of U.S. students and those of other nations on standardized tests was going up. Nonetheless, the United States remained a haven (through immigration) for talented scientists and technical workers from around the world (the "brain drain"), which compensated for a relatively weak educational system. Moreover, it might not be the competence and intelligence of the workforce that makes a difference, but the variety and diversity of talents and skills that the workforce brings to bear on its tasks. In workforce variety and diversity, the United States had a clear lead over its major rivals.

Management and Organization

Management also was important. Around 1900, Russia, Australia, and Argentina were the equal of the United States in raw materials per capita. A highly educated and trained workforce, innovative and capable of technical invention was found to a greater extent in Great Britain and Germany. What the United States did possess that no other country had—and that helped assure its economic ascendancy—was the large modern corporation. The separation of management from ownership in the corporation, the capacity to raise vast funds of money and to serve large markets, with a managerial system run by a professional, educated managerial class divided into functional areas of expertise (e.g., marketing, finance, production, etc.) was unique.[54]

Starting in the 1980s, the United States borrowed various aspects of the Japanese system (e.g., just-in-time inventory systems, quality circles, defect-free production).[55] The massive experimentation in new managerial forms that was taking place (e.g., corporate reengineering) was purely American, and other countries were trying to catch up. This willingness to experiment and adjust to new conditions was lacking in other capitalist nations (Germany and Japan) that were more frozen in their old managerial and organizational forms.

Environmental Standards and Energy Prices

Exacting environmental standards in the United States also forced innovations in the use of raw materials and the elimination of waste, which may have had positive effects on productivity (see Chapter 15). U.S. environmental pressures had the potential to be "good for business" because they:

- Spurred technological change such as the reformulation of fuels and new designs for zero-emission vehicles.
- Stimulated the growth of an environmental protection business sector made up of consultants, products, recyclers, and nonprofit specialty firms.
- Helped build an industry devoted to the export of environmental products and services.
- Motivated the reduction of waste (e.g., pollution prevention), which in turn increased business efficiency.
- Gave an advantage to those companies that advertised environmental friendliness as a product attribute.

Ultra-low U.S. fossil-fuel prices also may have provided a temporary advantage. The price of energy in the rest of the world was approximately four times that in the United States (primarily owing to taxes). In the short run, low-cost energy provided U.S. businesses with lower costs in the U.S. market. In the long run, this advantage might dissipate as U.S. companies lagged in introducing the efficiency-enhancing changes that high-price energy demands.

Government Policies

The U.S. government actually was more successful than many foreign governments in keeping its budget deficit in check. It also started to move from an emphasis on basic R&D to one of commercial application (e.g., the transformation of the Defense Advanced Research Program into a commercial program). It began to convert its extensive laboratory systems—20 percent of all U.S. scientists and technical employees work in government labs—to commercial uses. Under the Omnibus Competitiveness Act of 1988, the Commerce Department set up an advanced technology program of direct government funding for a select group of technologies that showed commercial promise (see Chapter 16). This department also had a program of assistance to small and midsized businesses with the purpose of manufacturing for commercial use some of the advanced technologies developed in government labs. This federal program was matched by numerous local and state government assistance programs designed to protect and create jobs. Finally, the government stretched its laws to permit Japanese-like business alliances in many fields (see Case 11–A on U.S. Memories).

Understanding Comparative Economic Performance

In sum, to understand the comparative economic performance of nations, many factors have to be considered:

1. *The catch-up phenomenon*. Other countries started to catch up with the United States. They copied U.S. technology and improved upon it without having to bear the large initial costs associated with its development. Thus, they enjoyed the opportunities of backwardness, which began to wither away as the economies of the United States and other countries converged.

2. *The foreign trade bonus*. Loosening of foreign trade restrictions gave other nations in the world the advantages of a huge world marketplace, which the United States had enjoyed on a more exclusive basis. Large markets meant economies of scale and efficiencies that could not otherwise be realized.

3. *Government policies*. Other nations used government policies to advance their economic interests. These policies might be inwardly oriented and protective of domestic industries, however inefficient they were, or outwardly oriented and export-led, fully exposing economies to world economic competition. They could be used to raise savings, lower interest rates, and increase investment. They could be employed, alternatively, to devalue and appreciate the domestic currency to make domestic goods cheaper on international markets or to make imported raw materials and capital cheaper. Political stability and the social solidarity that governments created also were important. For example, it was hard to imagine rapid economic development in the nations of the Middle East because of the civil discord and political tension that prevailed.

What Managers Can Do

Economic growth and international competitiveness were complex phenomena composed of many elements, and only some factors were under direct managerial control. What could managers do to advance their companies' interests?

This question has to be focused on the kinds of matters managers are best able to address:[56]

- Facilitating innovation through research and development.
- Aligning ownership patterns to take a long-term view.
- Forging alliances so as to combine different firms' strengths.
- Instilling an awareness of product quality and safety among employees.
- Changing organization structures to acknowledge different international market conditions.
- Diversifying their companies with long-run competitiveness in mind.
- Generating employee commitment to improved productivity.
- Effectively managing business cycle changes.
- Effectively managing the political risk of operating in different conditions throughout the world.

A more inclusive list of some of the elements involved in enhancing a nation's economic performance is provided in the special feature that follows.

Special Feature

Elements that Enhance a Nation's Economic Performance

1. Labor productivity:
   - *a.* Value of leisure time.
   - *b.* Work intensity.
   - *c.* Educational quality.
   - *d.* Experience and knowledge gained on the job (learning by doing).
   - *e.* Employment contracts (short-term versus lifetime).
   - *f.* Payment schemes (straight salary versus salary + bonus).
   - *g.* Unions and relative wages.
   - *h.* The work ethic.
   - *i.* Cultural factors (e.g., Confucianism/the Protestant ethic).
2. Capital accumulation and innovation:
   - *a.* Extent of investment increments.
   - *b.* Age of capital:
     - (1) Replacement of old with new (modernization).
     - (2) Investment in short-lived versus durable.
     - (3) Recombination and retrofitting of existing capital.
   - *c.* Ability to innovate in use of capital:
     - (1) R&D spending in the firm.
     - (2) R&D spending in society as a whole.
     - (3) Extent of engineers in the population.
     - (4) Technical education.
     - (5) Ability to exploit scale economies from large-scale projects.
     - (6) Development of an entrepreneurial/managerial class with the requisite motivations and skills to start projects and sustain economic development.
   - *d.* Risk-taking propensities in population (e.g., availability of venture capital opportunities).
   - *e.* Requisite flexibility in use of capital: capability of managers to shift resources to most profitable applications:
     - (1) Skill development among managers.
     - (2) Training and awareness.

3. The cost of capital:
   a. Ability of firms to generate retained earnings.
   b. Savings.
      (1) Government programs to expand savings.
      (2) Individual propensity in population to delay gratification.
   c. Debt:
      (1) Availability and use of domestic financing and government saving.
      (2) Availability and use of foreign financing, foreign aid, and assistance from the World Bank and IMF.
      (3) Conditions imposed by banks in financing and refinancing loans.
      (4) Types of financial institutions (bank/nonbank):
         (a) Expansion of these institutions.
         (b) Their soundness.
         (c) Government ownership and direction.
         (d) Legal climate for lending.
         (e) Acceptance of equity ownership by banks.
   d. Equity market and bond market development: pressures exerted by these markets for short-term payoffs.
   e. Return on investment (actual/expected) needed for loans and capital market investment.
4. Resource/sectoral factors:
   a. Energy intensity.
   b. Natural resource intensity.
   c. Sectoral elements (industrial versus service sector versus specialization in primary and secondary products).
   d. Emphasis on labor-intensive or capital-intensive industries.
5. Government factors:
   a. Industrial policies:
      (1) Inward orientation or export-led.
      (2) Aggressive/nonaggressive.
      (3) Sector-specific/neutral.
      (4) Responsiveness to market signals/nonresponsiveness.
      (5) Government control of financial sector (e.g., benefits offered exporters).
      (6) Government control of trade policy and other instruments.
         (a) Import barriers.
         (b) Import substitution targets.
   b. Extent and type of government regulation.
   c. Government commitment to private sector and extent of privatization.
   d. Extent and type of government ownership.
   e. Ratio of government expenditures to GDP.
   f. Extent of government deficits.
   g. Willingness to use deficits for countercyclical purposes.
   h. Political stability:
      (1) Social solidarity/political cohesion.
      (2) Distribution of income.
      (3) Extent of democratization.
   i. Skills of economic policymakers (e.g., existence of people with perception, artfulness, imagination, and skill in leadership class and bureaucracy).
6. World market orientation of firm and economy of which firm is a part:
   a. Closed/open character of economy.
   b. Government protection of infant industries/promotion of exports.
   c. Knowledge of foreign markets and language capabilities among managers needed to enter foreign markets.
   d. Extent of involvements in foreign markets:
      (1) Import intensive (raw materials).
      (2) Export intensive (finished products).
   e. Imitation capabilities:
      (1) Introduction of foreign technology.
      (2) Absorption of foreign know-how.
      (3) Abilities to take over markets opened by others.
   f. Exchange rate influences:
      (1) Availability of foreign exchange.
      (2) Competitive devaluations/inflation.

Conclusions

This chapter has argued that when considering rates of growth among countries in the world, examining only labor and capital is insufficient. A host of other factors are important. This chapter focused on international market exposure, technological innovation, and a sense of fairness that is reinforced by other conditions in the economy. Specific country examples have been given to illustrate how these elements play a role in economic development. The strengths and weaknesses of the world's major economic powers have been compared.

Some reasons for the revival of the U.S. economy in the mid-1990s have been suggested. To what extent will the United States continue to perform well? There is good reason to believe that the fluid capital system in place in the United States can outperform the dedicated capital system in place in Japan and Germany, because fluid capital is more capable of redeploying assets and adjusting to change. The American penchant for experimentation is helping the United States to retake the lead. U.S. managers move from one management fad to the next at a dizzying pace. This innovation frenzy is a powerful contributor to unfreezing systems no longer workable in a world of change. In many ways, the U.S. system is more flexible than the systems of its global competitors, a factor that needs to be better incorporated into theories of comparative economic performance.

Discussion Questions

1. How have different national economies evolved historically?
2. What happened to the world economy after 1973?
3. What role do labor and capital play in economic development?
4. How can labor's input be augmented?
5. What role does educational quality play in national competitiveness?
6. Why aren't labor and capital sufficient to explain economic growth? What other factors have to be considered?
7. Why did the formerly socialist economies of Central and Eastern Europe fall apart?
8. What has to be done now to get these economies to work?
9. What explains the success of the French economy in the post-World War II period?
10. What explains the success of the South Korean economy?
11. Compare the South Korean and Taiwanese economies.
12. What role does technology play in economic development?
13. What is the difference between product innovation and process innovation? Which country (the U.S. or Japan) excels at product innovation? Which country excels at process innovation? Why do these differences exist?
14. What theme does sociologist Ronald Dore use to explain Japanese economic success? Do you agree with his analysis? Why or why not?
15. What is the future of Japan's economy? Is hollowing out going to have a negative effect? Why or why not?

16. Why did the Japanese bubble burst?
17. How have changes in the Japanese economy affected the Japanese automobile industry?
18. What are some of the factors retarding European integration? Discuss.
19. What factors have hindered privatization of the Central and Eastern European economies? Discuss the strengths and weaknesses of these economies.
20. What unique advantages does the United States bring to global competition? What disadvantages? Should one be optimistic or pessimistic about the future of the U.S. economy? Why?
21. What should managers do to make their companies more competitive? What are your recommendations?

Endnotes

1. A. Maddison, "Growth and Slowdown in Advanced Capitalist Economies," *Journal of Economic Literature*, 1987, p. 649; R. L. Bartley, "The Great International Growth Slowdown," *The Wall Street Journal*, July 10, 1990, p. A18, 30; G. Bombach, *Postwar Economic Growth Revisited* (New York: North-Holland, 1985).
2. Stephen Parente, "Changes in the Wealth of Nations," Federal Reserve Bank of Minneapolis, 1993, pp. 3–16; Richard Kirkland, "What if Japan Triumphs?" *Fortune*, May 18, 1992, pp. 60–67; CIA, Directorate of Intelligence, *Handbook of Economic Statistics:* (Washington, D.C. U.S. Government Printing Office, 1991), p. 30.
3. Wealth disparities among nations were much larger than wealth disparities among U.S. states. Connecticut, the richest state, was 1.8 times wealthier than Mississippi, the poorest. The disparities among U.S. workers, on the other hand, matched the disparities among nations; incomes of the highest paid U.S. workers were about 30 times the incomes of the lowest paid.
4. Michael Porter, "The Competitive Advantage of Nations," *Harvard Business Review*, 1990, pp. 73–93; "Asia: A Billion Consumers," *Economist*, 1993, pp. 3–22; "When China Wakes," *Economist*, 1992, pp. 3–18; "Indonesia: The Long March," *Economist*, 1993, pp. 3–18.
5. "Helping Russia," *Economist*, Dec. 21, 1992–Jan. 3, 1993, pp. 101–104; Louis Kraar, "Korea's Tigers Keep Roaring," *Fortune*, May 4, 1992, pp. 108–10.
6. Maddison, "Growth and Slowdown in Advanced Capitalist Economies," pp. 649–98; *World Development Report* 1987 (New York: Oxford University Press, 1987).
7. K. Dervis and P. Petri, "The Macroeconomics of Successful Development," *NBER Macroeconomics Annual*, 1987, pp. 211–62.
8. K. Choi, *Theories of Comparative Economic Growth* (Ames, Ia.: Iowa State University Press, 1983); Maddison, "Growth and Slowdown in Advanced Capitalist Economies."
9. Maddison, "Growth and Slowdown in Advanced Capitalist Economies."
10. G. S. Becker, *Human Capital: A Theoretical and Empirical Analysis, with Special Reference to Education*, 2nd ed. (Chicago: University of Chicago Press, 1975); M. Porter, *The Competitive Advantage of Nations* (New York: Free Press, 1990), pp. 69–131; M. Porter, "Determinants of National Competitive Advantage," *The Competitive Advantage of Nations*, (New York: Free Press, 1990), pp. 69–131. "Education: Trying Harder," *Economist*, 1993, pp. 3–18. J. Pencavel, "The Contributions of Higher Education to Economic Growth and Productivity," Stanford Center for Economic Policy Research, 1990, pp. 1–48; R. Sturm, "How Do Education and Training Affect

a Country's Economic Performance" (Santa Monica, Calif.: Rand Institute, 1933); A. Heidenheimer, "Aligning Global and Parochial Concerns in Education Policy," Washington University Department of Political Science, 1990; Clark Kerr, "Education and the Decline of the American Economy: Guilty or Not?" University of Minnesota Industrial Relations Center Distinguished Lecture, 1989.

11. "Human Capital: The Decline of America's Work Force," *Business Week*, September 19, 1988; Kerr, "Education and the Decline of the American Economy."
12. "Human Capital."
13. Maddison, "Growth and Slowdown in Advanced Capitalist Economies."
14. Dervis and Petri, "The Macroeconomics of Successful Development"; Yuan-li Wu and Hung-chao Tai, "Economic Performance in Five East Asian Countries," in *Confucianism and Economic Development* (Washington, D.C.: Washington Institute, 1989), pp. 38–55.
15. Porter, "Determinants of National Competitive Advantage."
16. P. Gumbel, "How Gorbachev's Plan Has Left Soviet Union without Much Soap," *The Wall Street Journal*, November 20, 1989, p. A1; E. A. Hewett, ed., *Reforming the Soviet Economy: Equality versus Efficiency* (Washington, D.C.: Brookings Institution, 1988); E. A. Hewett, "Soviet Economic Performance: Strengths and Weaknesses," in *Reforming the Soviet Economy*, ed. E. A. Hewett (Washington, D.C.: Brookings Institution, 1988), pp. 31–94.
17. Hewett, "Soviet Economic Performance."
18. Ibid.
19. W. J. Adams, "A New International Environment," in *Restructuring the French Economy*, ed. W. J. Adams (Washington, D.C.: Brookings Institution, 1989), pp. 120–206.
20. Adams, *Restructuring the French Economy*.
21. A. H. Amsden, *Asia's Next Giant: South Korea and Late Industrialization* (New York: Oxford University Press, 1989), pp. 55–79.
22. Ibid.
23. Ibid.
24. "Taiwan and Korea: Two Paths to Prosperity," *Economist*, July 14, 1990, pp. 22–29; E. Hartfield, "The Divergent Economic Development of China and Japan," in *Confucianism and Economic Development* (Washington, D.C.: Washington Institute, 1989), pp. 92–115; Porter, "Determinants of National Competitive Advantage."
25. "Taiwan and Korea: Two Paths to Prosperity."
26. Lester Thurow, "An American Game Plan," *MIT Management*, Spring 1992, pp. 33–48.
27. Porter, "Determinants of National Competitive Advantage."
28. L. G. Franko, "Global Corporate Competition: Who's Winning, Who's Losing, and the R&D Factor as One Reason Why," *Strategic Management Journal* 10 (1989), pp. 449–74; C. L. Hill and A. A. Snell, "External Control, Corporate Strategy, and Firm Performance in Research-Intensive Industries," *Strategic Management Journal* 9 (1988), pp. 577–90; R. E. Hoskisson and M. A. Hitt, "Strategic Control Systems and Relative R&D Investment in Large Multiproduct Firms," *Strategic Management Journal* 9 (1988), pp. 605–21.
29. R. H. Hayes and W. J. Abernathy, "Managing Our Way to Economic Decline," *Harvard Business Review*, July–Aug. 1980; L. C. Thurow, *Technology Leadership and Industrial Competitiveness* (Minneapolis: Center for the Development of Technological Leadership, University of Minnesota, 1988).
30. Ibid.
31. Thurow, *Technology Leadership and Industrial Competitiveness*.
32. Nonaka, "Redundant, Overlapping Organization," pp. 27–38.
33. J. C. Abegglen and G. Stalk, *Kaisha: The Japanese Corporation* (New York: Basic Books, 1985); A. Murray and U. C. Lehner, "U.S., Japan Struggle to Redefine Relations as Resentment

Grows," *The Wall Street Journal*, June 13, 1990, p. A1; R. T. Pascale and A. G. Athos, *The Art of Japanese Management: Applications for American Executives* (New York: Simon and Schuster, 1981); D. Garvin, "Quality Problems, Policies, and Attitudes in the U.S. and Japan: An Exploratory Study," *AMJ*, Dec. 1986, pp. 653–74; D. Encarnation, "Cross-Investment: A Second Front of Economic Rivalry," *California Management Review*, Winter 1987, pp. 20–49; D. Dunphy, "Convergence/Divergence: A Temporal Review of the Japanese Enterprise and Its Management," *AMR*, July 1987, pp. 445–59; M. Olson, *The Rise and Decline of Nations*, 1982.

34. W. Ouchi, *The M-form Society: How American Teamwork Can Recapture the Competitive Edge* (Reading, Mass.: Addison-Wesley, 1984).
35. Ibid.
36. Abegglen and Stalk, *Kaisha: The Japanese Corporation;* "Japan's Troublesome Imports," *Economist*, Jan. 11, 1992, p. 61; Abegglen and Stalk, *Kaisha*.
37. "Capitalism: In Triumph, in Flux," *Economist*, May 5, 1990, special section, "Punters or Proprietors?" p. 6.
38. Lester Thurow, ed., *The Management Challenge: Japanese Views* (Cambridge, Mass.: MIT Press, 1985); P. Sheard, "The Economics of Interlocking Shareholding in Japan," Stanford Center for Economic Policy Research, 1991, pp. 1–44.
39. R. Komiya, "Structural and Behavioristic Characteristics of the Japanese Firm" [in Japanese in *Gendia Chugoku Keizei: Nicchu no Hikaku Kosatsu (The Contemporary Chinese Economy: A Comparative Study of China and Japan)*] (Tokyo: University of Tokyo Press, 1989), pp. 97–145; M. Aoki, "Toward an Economic Model of the Japanese Firm," *Journal of Economic Literature* 28 (1990), 1–27; 5.63; W. C. Kester, "Capital and Ownership Structure: A Comparison of U.S. and Japanese Manufacturing Corporations," in A. M. Spence, ed., *International Competitiveness* (Cambridge, Mass.: Ballinger, 1988).
40. E. J. Lincoln, *Japan: Facing Economic Maturity* (Washington, D.C.: Brookings Institution, 1988); Maddison, "Growth and Slowdown in Advanced Capitalist Economies," pp. 649–98; Young Kwan Yoon, *The Irony of Plenty: Japanese Foreign Direct Investment and Productivity*, APSA paper, 1987, pp. 1–36; G. S. Hansen and B. Wernerfelt, "Determinants of Firm Performance: The Relative Importance of Economic and Organizational Factors," *Strategic Management Journal* 10 (1989), pp. 399–411; W. S. Kim and E. Lyn, "FDI Theories and the Performance of Foreign Multinationals Operating in the U.S.," *Journal of International Business*, 1990, pp. 41–54; K. Miller and P. Bromiley, "Strategic Risk and Corporate Performance," *Academy of Management Journal* 33 (1990), pp. 756–79.
41. Yoon, *The Irony of Plenty;* K. Gartrell, "Innovation, Industry Specialization, and Shareholder Wealth," *California Management Review*, 1990, pp. 87–101; J. E. Butler, "Theories of Technological Innovation as Useful Tools for Corporate Strategy," *Strategic Management Journal* 9 (1988), pp. 15–29; B. Mascarenhas, "Domains of State-Owned, Privately Held, and Publicly Traded Firms in International Competition," *Administrative Science Quarterly* 34 (1989), pp. 582–97; R. Osborn and C. C. Baughn, "Forms of Interorganizational Governance for Multinational Alliances," *Academy of Management Journal* 33 (1990), pp. 503–19.
42. Yoon, *The Irony of Plenty;* P. Bromiley and A. Marcus, "The Deterrent to Dubious Corporate Behavior: Profitability, Probability, and Safety Recalls," *Strategic Management Journal*, 1989, pp. 233–50; N. Rose, "Profitability and Product Quality: Economic Determinants of Airline Safety Performance," *JPE*, 1990, pp. 943–61.
43. "Japanese Finance," *Economist*, May 30, 1992, p. 84.
44. Andrew Pollack, "Japanese Deficit to Grow Sharply," *New York Times*, Feb. 20, 1995, p. C1.
45. M. Cusumano, "The Limits of Lean," *Sloan Management Review*, 1994, pp. 27–33.
46. "Europe: The Deal Is Done," *Economist*, Dec. 14, 1991, pp. 51–52; Shawn Tully,"Europe 1992," *Fortune*, Aug. 24, 1992, pp. 135–42; Shawn Tully, "Now the New Europe," *Fortune*, Dec. 2,

1991, pp. 136–56; "The Business of Europe," *Economist*, Dec. 7, 1991, pp. 63–64; "What Are the Costs and Benefits of an Enlarged European Community?" *Economist*, Oct. 17, 1992, p. 75; "Europe's Two Trade Areas," *Economist*, Oct. 26, 1991, pp. 81–82; Commission of the European Communities, *The Competitiveness of the Community Industry* (Luxembourg, 1982); "The European Community: An Expanding Universe," *Economist*, July 7, 1990.

47. R. Dore, *Taking Japan Seriously* (Stanford, Calif.: Stanford University Press, 1987).
48. Ibid.
49. R. E. Cole, "U.S. Quality Improvement in the Auto Industry: Close but No Cigar," *California Management Review*, 1989, pp. 71–85.
50. Carla Rapoport, "Why Germany Will Lead Europe," *Fortune*, Sept. 21, 1992, pp. 149–54; Paul Hofheinz, "How Germany Is Attacking Recession," *Fortune*, June 14, 1993, pp. 132–34; "Germany: The Shock of Unity," *Economist*, May 23, 1992, special report; "Is Germany's Treuhandanstalt a Good Thing?" *Economist*, March 21, 1992, p. 71; Craig Whitnew, "Bonn Politicians Vow a Crackdown Against Violence," *The New York Times*, Oct. 9, 1992, pp. 1, A7.
51. "Pioneers of Capitalism," *Economist*, April 4, 1992, pp. 79–80; "Business in Eastern Europe," *Economist*, Sept. 21, 1991, special report; "Eastern Europe: The Old World's New World," *Economist*, 1993, pp. 3–22; "Poland: Souls in a New Machine," *Economist*, 1994, pp. 3–22; N. Healey, "The Transition Economies of Central and Eastern Europe," *Columbia Journal of World Business*, 1994, pp. 62–72; A. Shama, "Management Under Fire: The Transformation of Managers in the Soviet Union and Eastern Europe," *Executive*, 1993, pp. 22–36; "Russia: The Sixth Wave," *Economist*, 1992, pp. 30–36; "Ukraine: The Birth and Possible Death of a Country," *Economist*, 1994, pp. 1–18; D. Rondinelli and M. Fellenz, "Privatization and Private Enterprise in Hungary: An Assessment of Market Reform Policies," *Business and the Contemporary World*, 1993, pp. 75–88; K. Obloj and M. Kostera, "Polish Privatization Program," *Industrial and Environmental Crisis Quarterly*, 1993, pp. 7–22; R. Rottenburg, "From Socialist Realism to Postmodern Ambiguity: East German Companies in Transition," *Industrial and Environmental Crisis Quarterly*, 1993, pp. 71–92; D. Holt, D. Ralston, and R. Terpstra, "Constraints on Capitalism in Russia: The Managerial Psyche," *California Management Review*, 1994, pp. 124–42; M. King, "The Challenge of Accounting in Eastern Europe," *Business and the Contemporary World*, 1994, pp. 112–22.
52. J. S. Nye, *Bound to Lead* (New York: Basic Books, 1990); J. E. Schwarz, *America's Hidden Success: A Reassessment of Public Policy from Kennedy to Reagan* (New York: W. W. Norton, 1988); J. E. Schwarz, and T. J. Volgy, "The Myth of America's Economic Decline," *Harvard Business Review*, Sept.–Oct. 1985, p. 101; J. Erceg and T. Bernard, "Productivity, Costs, and International Competitiveness," Federal Reserve Bank of Cleveland, November 15, 1988.
53. Alfred Marcus, "Explaining the Renewed Competitiveness of the U.S. Economy," *Business and the Contemporary World*, 1994, pp. 29–34; Sylvia Nasar, "The American Economy, Back on Top," *New York Times Business*, Feb. 27, 1994, p. 1, 6.
54. Alfred Chandler, "Organizational Capabilities and Industrial Restructuring," Harvard Business School, 1992.
55. Jeremy Main, "How to Steal the Best Ideas Around," *Fortune*, Oct. 19, 1992, pp. 102–6.
56. W. G. Egelhoff, "Strategy and Structure in Multinational Corporations," *Strategic Management Journal* 9 (1988), pp. 1–14; S. Ghoshal and N. Nohria, "Internal Differentiation within Multinational Organizations," *Strategic Management Journal* 10 (1989), pp. 323–37; J. M. Geringer, P. W. Beamish, and R. C. deCosta, "Diversification Strategy and Internationalization: Implications for MNE Performance," *Strategic Management Journal* 10 (1989), pp. 109–19; W. C. Kim, P. Hwang, and W. P. Burgers, "Global Diversification Strategy and Corporate Profit Performance," *Strategic Management Journal* 10 (1989), pp. 45–57; P. C. Earley, "Social Loafing and Collectivism," *Administrative Science Quarterly* 34 (1989), pp. 565–81; I. Harpaz, "The Importance of Work Goals: An International Perspective," *Journal of International Business*, 1990, pp. 75–93;

B. Mascarenhas and D. A. Aaker, "Strategy over the Business Cycle," *Strategic Management Journal* 10 (1989), pp. 199–210; C. Y. Kwok and L. D. Brooks, "Examining Event Study Methodologies in Foreign Exchange Markets," *Journal of International Business*, 1990, pp. 189–224; R. Johnson, V. Srinivasan, and P. Bolster, "Sovereign Debt Ratings: A Judgmental Model Based on the Analytic Hierarchy Process," *Journal of International Business*, 1990, pp. 95–117.

Case 12–A
Reversal of Fortune: Honda and Chrysler[1]

The 1991 recession struck all the world's automakers hard including Honda. Its sales dropped and for the first time it had to park 2,000 unsold Hondas on a storage lot outside its plant in Ohio. Its traditional no-discount policy had to be changed and it offered dealer rebates of $900 per car. Its earnings plunged 26 percent in the first quarter of 1991, but Honda remained profitable while U.S. automakers reported record losses.[2]

Honda's sales were down 18.3 percent in the first quarter of 1993, while Mazda's declined 16 percent and Toyota's fell by 7 percent. Among Japanese automakers, only Nissan made gains because it introduced the new U.S.-made Altima. The total Japanese share of the U.S. market, including transplants, fell by 27 percent compared with 30 percent a year earlier. Accord sales fell by 40 percent to ninth place, after having been the best-selling car in the United States from 1989 to 1991. Taurus beat it in 1992 only when Ford lured customers with $50 million in rebates.[3]

To overcome these problems Honda's president Nobuhiko Kawamoto (see Appendixes 1 and 2) considered major changes: (1) moving Honda out of Formula One auto racing, where its engines dominated, and redirecting resources to environmental research and fuel economy; and (2) dismantling some of the slow, collegial-style of company decision making and assigning more individual responsibility. Young engineers apparently were frustrated by the long meetings and the lack of agreement.

Kawamoto also was thinking about what Honda could learn from Chrysler. Japanese automakers were always eager to adapt practices from other companies. Chrysler now presented itself to Kawamoto as an example of successful corporate revitalization. Kawamoto wanted to know what factors accounted for Chrysler's change and if any of them had relevance for Honda.

The Decline in Japanese Car Sales

Price was the main reason for the decline in Japanese car sales. The $2,500 per vehicle advantage they enjoyed at the start of the 1980s had vanished. With the yen up more than 10 percent to 114 per dollar, Japanese automakers were having trouble competing. Even Japanese cars made in the United States were affected because they relied so heavily on Japanese components. An Accord with air bags and antilock brakes cost $19,030, while an equivalently equipped Olds Cutlass Supreme went for $16,445. The Japanese minivan experienced a big price escalation after the Japanese lost an antidumping suit and agreed to restrict sales by raising prices 20 percent rather than accept punitive tariffs. The Mazda minivan sold for $5,000 more than Chrysler's.

Quality was the other reason for the rebound of U.S. manufacturers. In learning to copy the Japanese way of making cars, they had reduced the quality gap. The transplants showed that managers could successfully introduce techniques such as teamwork, lean manufacturing, and personal responsibility for quality control among U.S. workers.

Chrysler's Success

In 1994, Chrysler was the most profitable U.S. carmaker. It had record earnings and had issued large profit-sharing checks. Chrysler had picked up a 1.4 percent market share in North America (up to 14.4 percent), while Ford gained .7 percent (up to 25.4 percent), and GM lost .6 percent (down to 33.1 percent). Chrysler built its revitalization strategy around two features: striking design and Japanese-like product management teams.[4]

Rather than please all customers Chrysler was seeking to provoke intense love-and-hate reactions. Only this type of reaction would stop customers from continuing to think of Chryslers as "toasters on wheels." Thus, the strategy Chrysler forged was to make a leap in design that would take other companies years to match. The strategy depended on hiring many new, young designers who were given the liberty to make "extravagant" mistakes. Rather than allowing its cars to be dominated by pragmatic engineering considerations that would squelch innovation, Chrysler was looking for a dramatic appearance. It was seeking bold hard-to-manufacture curves, that would leapfrog over the competition.

Chrysler wanted to be known as the industry leader in styling. This meant:

1. Expanding passenger space.
2. Lavishing attention on the interior with a low-gloss, quality-fit finish on the exterior.
3. Increasing the driver's sense of control by thrusting the cabin out over the front of the wheels.
4. Placing the wheels to the corner of the car to provide driver and passenger with a greater sense that the car clings to the road.

Chrysler's strategy was to develop designs that would make its cars as striking as possible because it believed that design adds value faster than it adds cost. Customers were won over by the LH (facetiously called "last hope") midsize cars—Concorde, Eagle Vision, and Intrepid; the Grand Cherokee and Dodge Ram full-size pickups; and the Neon, which was competing with GM's Saturn and the Honda Civic. Chrysler was hoping that customers would be equally won over by the new Stratus and Cirrus models which would compete directly with the Accord, Camry, and Taurus.

The new process for vehicle development came from copying Japanese methods, the result of Chrysler's long and painstaking study of how the Japanese did things. Chrysler divided its workers into teams who produced the new models on a common budget rather than allowing separately financed departments to perform a different aspect of development in sequence. Some of the teams were huge, up to 700 people. They were brought together in a design center in the new headquarters building in Auburn Hills, Michigan, so that they could constantly interact. In the past, Chrysler designers had opposed the use of teams because they produced lowest-common-denominator cars, but the new teams proved to be very innovative. Engineers, manufacturing specialists, accountants, marketing, and salespeople and suppliers reviewed designs and solved problems that might previously have been seen as intractable (e.g., with the cab so far forward it was necessary to pack the engine, cooling system, airbags, etc., into a much smaller space).

Chrysler took the risk that a U.S. automaker could profitably build a small car. It invested about $1.3 billion in the Neon's development costs, a very low amount for a totally new car line. Development costs were kept low by getting suppliers to contribute to the development costs in return for long-term contracts. Chrysler also brought together workers, engineers, body designers, and marketing experts early in the process. Therefore, the designers would not be in a position to say what the car would look like, only to be contradicted by production engineers who would argue that the car could not be built that way or marketing people who would claim that the car would not sell. The Neon was brought to market in the astoundingly brief time of 30 months, which is about half the time it takes to bring a car like it to the market. The Neon, moreover, was designed to be built inexpensively with very low labor input. Thus, Chrysler was able to hold down the sticker price and still make a profit of $3,000 to $4,000 on each car it sold to the dealer. Though Chrysler was way ahead of its domestic rivals in its capacity for striking design and use of teams, it still lagged in product defects, which might threaten its newly won success.

Honda's Attempt to Reform Itself

Since the departure of Honda's founders, the company had been governed by what company officials called the "republican system." All 30 senior executives spent most of their days gathered around conference tables at headquarters. They carried out their activities in a single unpartitioned office that was about the size of a small gym. The company's top executives sat so close to each other that if they wished to speak they could tap each other on the shoulder. Kawamoto was considering eliminating some of the group decision making, setting up private offices, assigning individuals specific duties, and holding them accountable. These proposed changes were unprecedented for Honda.

What was most troubling to Kawamoto was Honda's decline in the Japanese market. It went from a third-place tie with Mitsubishi in 1989 to a fourth-place finish in 1990, barely staying ahead of Mazda. Honda executives believed that the company's decline in the Japanese market was caused by Honda's becoming too cautious and overly bureaucratic. It was choosing conservative styling more appropriate to the mass market than the niche markets to which it appealed in Japan. Its cars were perceived as competent, but dull. In Japan, only about 4,000 Accords a month were sold as opposed to projected sales of 7,000 cars. Jazzier versions of the Accord—Vigor and Inspire—were selling at a combined rate of 10,000 a month, about three times more than expected. The main difference was one of image not performance, but in style-conscious Japan, image had become critically important. Whimsically styled cars with sporty names like Figaro and Diamante manufactured by Nissan and Mitsubishi gained ground on Honda's more conservative offerings.

The new Accord Honda introduced in the fall of 1993 was built according to entirely different principles than those of the past. Instead of bottom-to-top management, it was made with a top-to-bottom approach. Previously hands-off directors asserted greater control over front-line operators. A single person took charge of car development. Middle managers agreed to follow guidelines and employees had clear job responsibilities; their pay was based partly on how well they met their goals. Use of the *waigaya* (noisy-loud) system of consultation was restricted. Policy no longer was made by middle managers and senior managers in informal brainstorming sessions. All meetings had to have clear leaders.

Kawamoto played a greater role in decision making. No longer did he delegate critical design and production decisions to the company's Japanese engineers. He wanted them to work together with marketing, sales, and manufacturing—and with U.S. engineers, who had been brought to Japan for two-to-three-year periods to help with design and cost-cutting.

The new Accord sold with antilock brakes and dual air bags at $19,030, the same price as the old model. It was a wider, sportier car with a pronounced wedge shape that gave the appearance of being lower in the front and higher in the rear. The car had a quiet, smooth, ride. Its four-cylinder engine had been completely redone and was slightly more fuel-efficient than the old one. Honda had great hopes for this car. It believed it would do very well against the similarly equipped Taurus, which sold for $17,433, and Camry, which sold for $21,433.

The reforms needed to redesign the Accord, however, had not been easy to carry out since they amounted to a denial of so many of the methods that had been perfected by the company's founder, Mr. Honda. Kawamoto was unsure how to proceed. Should he transform the company further along the lines he had started or bring the company back in line with its original principles? What should he learn from Chrysler's recent success?

Appendix 1: Excerpts from Remarks Made by Nobuhico Kawamoto, President of Honda, at a 1990 Press Conference in Detroit

. . . our focus is on the importance of the individual . . . this is . . . expressed as the three joys . . . joy to buy and use our product . . . joy to produce and . . . joy to sell our products . . . It is important to view our industry within the context of society . . . We must think more broadly than transportation. We are really in "the mobility industry." . . . Mobility is the link between one individual and another. Our business is to support the efforts of individuals to link together . . .

The 1990s . . . will be a decade of challenges, including such social issues as the environment and safety . . .

Our constant challenge is to improve the basic performance of the . . . vehicle; running, turning, and stopping. Honda's product development efforts seek out two additional areas . . . "human fitting" and "social fitting." Human fitting is to make the car more user-friendly for the driver and passengers—easy to drive, comfortable, and safe . . . Social fitting is to bring the car more into harmony with society and the environment.

Appendix 2: Excerpts from an Interview with Shoichoro Irimajiri, Former President of Honda North America

Ensuring employee involvement in decision making and the way we do things is a concern as we grow larger (79,000 associates in 1990) and get too bureaucratic . . . The most critical factors in the competitive battles of the 1990s will be the speed with which auto companies can launch new products . . . given its size, Honda has the strongest R&D capability in the industry, is very good at engineering, and, because of the Honda Way, has very flexible well-trained workers . . . Our new product development cycle is already . . . the fastest in the industry . . .

In the year 2000, there probably will be four dominant players in the worldwide auto scene: one U.S. company, one European, and two Japanese. The other companies will slip behind . . . or be merged out of existence . . . Honda's challenge is to ensure that by the end of the century, it will be one of the front runners at the head of the pack.

Discussion Questions

1. Why had Honda slipped?
2. What should it do to make a turnaround?
3. What could it learn from Chrysler?

Endnotes

1. This case was written by Alfred Marcus.
2. C. Chandler and P. Ingrassia, "Just as U.S. Firms Try Japanese Management, Honda Is Centralizing," *The Wall Street Journal*, April 11, 1991, p. A1; "Honda Loses Its Way," *Economist*, Sept. 14, 1991, pp. 79–80.
3. "Japan Spins Off," *Economist*, April 17, 1993, pp. 61–62; Michael Williams and Krystal Miller, "Redesign of Honda's Management Faces First Test," *The Wall Street Journal*, Sept. 1, 1993, p. B1–B2.
4. Robert Simison, Douglas Lavin, and Jaqueline Mitchell, "With Auto Profits Up, Big Three Get a Major Opportunity, *The Wall Street Journal*, May 4, 1994, pp. A1, A6; Alex Taylor, "A U.S.-Style Shakeup at Honda," *Fortune*, Dec. 30, 1991, pp. 115–20; Ralph Sorenson, "Honda Motor Company (B)," Harvard Business School, Nov. 16, 90; Kathryn Graven and Joseph White, "Honda Gets New Driver for the 90's," *The Wall Street Journal*, May 11, 1990, p. B1; James Bennet, "The Designers Who Saved Chrysler," *New York Times* Business Section, Jan. 30, 1994, pp. 1, 6.

Case 12–B
Ford Motor Company's Global Strategy[1]

Ford and the other U.S. auto companies tried to stop the loss of market share to Japanese producers by improving quality, reducing costs, and keeping prices lower than foreign automakers. Though the Japanese auto companies continued to be under stress, they remained tough competitors despite the deep Japanese recession and the yen's increase in value relative to the U.S. dollar. With additional production capacity on board in their U.S. plants they had good 1994 results. In the first eight months of the year, Honda's unit sales increased by 15 percent, Nissan's by 8 percent, and Toyota's by 4 percent.

Slow Rebound from the Recession

With 5 of the 10 best-selling cars from 1982 to 1992, Ford was the most successful U.S. automaker, picking up 5 percent in domestic market share. However, in the early 1990s it became apparent that Ford's rising market share was not generating the kind of profits it expected. During recessions, the company lost money and the 1990–1991 downturn was no exception. Its profitability was slow to recover, and Chrysler's earnings came back much faster.[2]

Ford's lackluster earnings growth can be explained by three key factors:

1. The long recession in most of Western Europe where Ford had over 30 percent of its sales.
2. Heavy expenditures (more than $6 billion) on the introduction of a new "world car," the Mondeo, far outstripped those for the Taurus a few years back. Many observers felt the Mondeo would not generate the revenues to justify the investment. Coordinating development on a worldwide basis had been more complicated than Ford had anticipated.
3. As 25 percent owner of Mazda, Ford suffered deep losses in Japan totalling more than $300 million in 1994. In the 1980s, Mazda had expanded rapidly introducing many sporty, streamlined models including the highly profitable Miata, but in the 1990s global demand was weak and Mazda had too much capacity. It also had to contend with the fact that it was virtually impossible for Mazda to lay off workers in Japan. A huge new plant never operated at capacity. Mazda cancelled plans to bring out a luxury line (the Amati) to compete with Toyota's Lexus and Nissan's Infiniti. Its search for cash forced it to sell a 50 percent interest in another manufacturing facility. Ford responded by asserting more control, increasing its representatives on Mazda's board from four to seven and relocating its board members to Japan where they could take a direct role in management.[3]

A Global Focus

Many of Ford's challenges had to do with its worldwide operations.[4] It was the most global of the U.S. auto producers. In a mature, highly competitive, and capital-intensive industry, management had its hands full. Ford's 1994 annual report declared:

> The old rules no longer apply for many businesses. National borders are disappearing. We need to improve our competitive standing despite the enormous complexities and pressures of this new economic order. Ford has been an international company almost from the day it started. But in today's world, development of truly "global" vehicles—cars that minimize duplication and maximize resources across continents—is becoming essential.[5]

Ford's vision of global opportunities extended to Asia and developing countries where auto demand was on the rise. Between 1987 and 1991, Malayasia's demand for cars grew 290 percent. The 1992–2002 projections for the Asian market were twice as strong as those for the North American market, which in turn was expected to expand at almost three times the rate of Western Europe (see the Appendix). Kenneth Courtis, the Deutsche Bank's chief economist in Tokyo, predicted that in the decade starting in 1995, non-Japanese Asia would account for two-thirds of the world's increase in car sales. Up to 16 car factories would be built in Asia, each with an average annual capacity of 200,000 cars. Unless challenged by other world automakers, 10 of the new factories were likely to be Japanese.

China — Number One Market Target

Ford was determined to exploit the newly emerging Asian market for its own benefit. Its number one new market target was China. In 1994, Japanese firms already sold 27,000 cars in China; projections showed that by 1999, they would be able to sell more than a half million. Since Deng Xiaoping opened up the country in 1978, real GNP growth had been 9 percent per year. For the past 14 years, China's GNP had accelerated 6.5 percent faster than that of the United States. By the year 2002, the size of the Chinese economy was expected to be eight times greater than it was in 1978, and by 2010, it was likely to be the world's largest. Up to one-third of its 1.2 billion people would have disposable incomes equal to the developed world's average in 1995. That would mean that for the first time the Chinese could afford consumer items such as refrigerators, television sets, and cars.

Seeking to build on the lead it already had in total vehicle sales in Taiwan and Australia, Ford set up its first 10 independent franchised dealerships in China in 1993 and began to sell vehicles built in North America. It adapted five of its models to run on leaded gasoline, the only kind available in China. It named a senior executive to run a new group to pursue joint ventures and started negotiations for the manufacture of components and auto glass. Two component operations with a Chinese partner already had been established and a third was nearly ready. Vehicle assembly, although much more complicated, was a distinct possibility in the not-so-distant future. Chinese labor was cheap labor (30 cents an hour in 1994) and skilled in manufacturing for world markets.

The Threatened Unraveling of Ford's Chinese Relations. Ford's application with the Chinese government to become a legally recognized entity was put on hold in January 1995, when a growing trade rift between the United States and China developed. The United States was demanding that the Chinese immediately stop pirating copyrighted U.S. computer software, movies, and music and putting phony U.S. labels on consumer products. Trade representative Mickey Kantor said the United States would impose stiff tariffs on Chinese goods if an agreement was not quickly achieved. The Chinese maintained that they had made good efforts to accommodate the Americans and had shown great flexibility, but that new U.S. demands made agreement impossible.

The 1988 Omnibus Trade and Competitiveness Act permitted the United States to impose "special 301" sanctions—in this case 100 percent tariffs—on some Chinese exports, which would double the price U.S. consumers had to pay for consumer electronics, toys, and clothing, the likely targets.

In the past, the Chinese failed to keep their word on preventing the illegal pirating of U.S. computer software. They also had not come through on promises to President Clinton when he had decided in the spring of 1994 to renew their "most favored nation" (MFN) trading status. In granting MFN to the Chinese, Clinton had reversed a campaign promise. He claimed that he had been swayed by arguments from U.S. businesses, Ford among them, that the trade benefits would be good for them. Clinton also had been swayed by Chinese arguments that the rights of dissidents would be protected; nevertheless, the Chinese had continued their crackdowns against dissidents.

Meanwhile, the U.S. trade deficit with China had ballooned. In 1994, it was $30 billion, second only to the $60 billion deficit with Japan. While Chinese markets remained closed to many U.S. goods, U.S. markets were wide open to Chinese goods. With so much at stake, a trade war seemed to be detrimental to the interests of both the United States and China. The Chinese said that they did not want a trade war, but they were perfectly prepared for one if necessary. If the United States imposed the 301 sanctions, the Chinese would retaliate with sanctions of their own.

Ford's plans for Asia could be affected by these developments. It was committed to opening up China and integrating it further into the world economy. It had favored the market opening agreement reached by the Chinese and the United States in October 1992, which called on the Chinese to clean up their opaque regulations, lift the quantitative barriers that obstruct imports, and take steps to make their currency convertible. Ultimately, Ford hoped that these steps would prepare the way for China's early admission to GATT. A trade war with China over copyright laws was not the direction of U.S.-Chinese relations that Ford wanted.

Ford communicated to the trade negotiators that it hoped they would quickly resolve the copyright issue. Meanwhile, it tried to figure out its stake. In transferring technology from parent to subsidiary, it exercised strict control. Nothing short of 100 percent ownership of a foreign subsidiary was permitted. In the 1930s, Henry Ford had said no to a request to establish production in China because the land title would have to be held in the name of a Chinese national. Today's Chinese were mainly interested in Western technology, and they seemed willing to give Western companies the right to operate only if they shared this technology completely. Japanese automakers were therefore reluctant to enter China for fear of losing their technology to the Chinese. The issue of copyright protection was a complicated one and Ford could see arguments on both sides.

3M — A Model for Global Operations. The 3M Company (see Case 16–B) was a model for Ford's worldwide operations. Globally diversified, 3M was sensitive to the slightest changes in the world economy. It had subsidiaries in 56 countries and sold its wares in more than 200. In 1992, 3M's international production exceeded domestic production for the first time; international sales surpassed U.S. sales in 1993. 3M started its businesses in Asia in the 1950s and 1960s. It learned about the markets and built relationships, carefully nurturing locally hired staffs. Since 1987, annual growth rates had exceeded 25 percent in Asia (excluding Japan). By the end of the decade, 3M was likely to triple its sales in the region. The need for infrastructure—roads, telecommunications, power—was large, and 3M was active in these markets. It was very good at adapting its products to local needs and had become better at coordinating its operations across national boundaries.

3M was the first U.S. company to establish a wholly owned venture in China. The company had operated a sales office in Shanghai since 1984. Over the past few years, it had opened a second sales office there as well as offices in Beijing and Canton. New sales offices were being opened in Chengdu, Shenyang, and in the Xiamen/Fuzhou area. With China's economy growing at double-digit rates, 3M saw wide-open market opportunities for its products. It had built a new $12.5 million, 80,000-square-foot plant, and was the only U.S. company to have sole ownership of a manufacturing operation. High on its political agenda was the development of close and friendly trading ties between the United States and China and the maintenance of China's MFN trade status.

Ford had to decide how to respond to the changes occurring in U.S.–Chinese relations. It was watching the copyright issue closely and with apprehension. What were the implications for Ford? How should Ford respond politically, in alliance with other companies, or by itself? How should it respond strategically? Should it retreat in any way from its ambitious business plans in China? What policies should it promote to maintain its competitive position?

Appendix: A Billion Asian Consumers

By the year 2000, more than half the world's people would be Asian. Half the growth in the world's products between 1990 and 2000 would come from Asia. The number of desperately poor in Asia fell from 400 million to 180 million between 1970 and 1990, while the population grew by two-thirds. One billion Asians would be able to buy basic goods, like televisions, refrigerators, and motorbikes, and 400 million would have disposable incomes equal to the developed world's average.[6]

The rapid growth and absolute size of the Asian middle class should create immense business opportunities in an area that in the first 25 years after World War II suffered constant warfare and enormous instability. Asian economic prospects were viewed at the time as dim. Then a manufacturing revolution and export-led growth began in Japan and spread to South Korea, Singapore, Taiwan, and Hong Kong. In the 1970s, comparable economic growth was achieved in Thailand, Indonesia, Malaysia, and China. Eight of the 13 developing countries most successful in raising real incomes during 1965–1990 were in Asia. These Asian nations were growing three times as fast as nations in the developed world excluding Japan. The fast growth was combined with greater income equality.

Not all Asian countries shared in this growth. North Korea, Vietnam, and Burma were failures; the Philippines and India lagged to some extent, but were catching up. Ironically, in the 1940s North Korea and Vietnam had been the richest non-Japanese Asian nations. It was not inevitable of course that all of Asia would continue to advance to the point where it would develop income levels compared to Western developed nations. Growth spurts at the beginning of the 20th century by Russia, parts of the Austro-Hungarian Empire, and South America had not been sustained.

The key factors explaining Asia's growth were labor, capital, growing efficiency, government, and openness to foreign influences.

Labor. The human capital policies that produced growth were huge government investments in primary and secondary education (higher education in the most rapidly developing Asian nations was comparatively slight). The productivity of the average laborer in light manufacturing thus increased. The investment in education yielded greater income equality and consumer spending, which further stimulated economic growth. Latin American nations, which invested primarily in higher education that was enjoyed by the elite, did not fare as well. The strong education provided Asian women, as much as men, had an added positive benefit in helping to lower the birth rates. Women, who were systematically excluded from the workforce in Japan, became, in effect, at-home teaching mothers.

Capital. Saving rates throughout Asia were immense. In the mid-1960s, Asian nations were saving about 16 percent of their GDP; by the early 1990s, they were saving 36 percent. They were investing about as much as they saved—35 percent of their GDP compared with 20 percent in 1965. Two-thirds of this investment came from the private sector compared with about 50 percent in the rest of the world.

Efficiency. Unlike the countries in Central and Eastern Europe and the former Soviet Union, which had a similar record of accumulating physical and human capital, Asian investments were very efficient. The former Communist countries made finished products that were less valuable than the raw materials from which they were produced. The productive combination of labor and capital by means of managerial techniques and ideas acquired from around the globe was critical to the Asian success story. Moreover, the Asian economies were very good at moving up the value chain; that is, they did not continue to do more of the same but actively sought out new and more profitable products and businesses.

Government. Most governments got out of the way of this growth, allowing free market pricing of labor, capital, and goods. They allowed highly competitive domestic markets to grow and provided for macroeconomic (i.e., inflation, interest rates, and exchange rate) stability to the extent possible. They also tried to channel funds from government-controlled banks into favored industries that had export potential. Banks were extremely influential, since most of the financing came from banks, not capital markets.

Openness to Foreign Influences. Another major difference between the Asian and former communist societies of Europe was openness to foreign influences. For instance, as soon as the Chinese economy opened itself to foreign influences, it began to take off.

Four key factors could put an end to Asian growth, however. The first and most important was a trade war. Others were a worldwide credit crunch, resource constraints (in particular, high energy prices because of rapidly rising demand), and environmental limits (see Chapters 13–15).

Discussion Questions

1. Why were international operations critical to Ford's strategy?
2. What threat did a trade war between the United States and China pose for Ford?
3. What should Ford do to avoid such a war?
4. What could Ford learn from 3M?
5. What opportunities presented themselves to Ford in the Asian market?
6. How could Ford best take advantage of these opportunities?

Endnotes

1. This case was written by Alfred Marcus.
2. Rick Haglund, "Ford Might Be in Need of a Major Tuneup," *Minneapolis Star Tribune,* July 6, 1993, p. 5B.
3. James Sterngold, "Mazda Gives Ford Motor More Control," *New York Times,* Dec. 28, 1993, p. D1.
4. Kevin Done, "Europe to Handle Smaller-Sized Cars," *Financial Times Weekend,* April 24, 1994, p. 11.
5. Ford Motor Company, *1994 Annual Report.*
6. "Asia: A Billion Consumers," *Economist,* 1993, pp. 3–22.

Case 12–C
Alliant Techsystems Inc.
Downsizing a Defense Contractor[1]

Alliant Techsystems Inc., a defense contractor and supplier of armaments and ordnance to the United States military, finds itself at an interesting crossroad in its brief life. Recently spun off from Honeywell, Alliant is faced with the potential of declining sales and profits.

Economic and political events beyond its control are exacerbating an already severe federal budget deficit, resulting in demands for sizable cuts in Pentagon expenditures. As Alliant relies on the military for 85 percent of sales, the implications of this policy are significant. Alliant must choose a course of action: Should it remain in business as primarily a defense contractor? Or should it attempt to broaden its economic base by diversifying into other markets?

The Company

Alliant has been supplying defense products and systems to the United States and its allies for 50 years. Alliant was formerly Honeywell's Defense and Marine Systems Business (DMSB), Test

Instruments Division and Signal Analysis, and it was launched as an independent company in September 1990.[2]

Honeywell's progeny had a difficult birth. A casualty of corporate restructuring, DMSB was offered for sale in October 1989. The sale proved difficult. Buyers were leery of projected declines in Defense Department expenditures. Honeywell's board rejected the few offers submitted as being inconsistent with the subsidiary's true value.[3] Ultimately, DMSB was spun off as a separate entity, with Honeywell shareholders receiving one share of stock in the new company for every four shares they held in Honeywell. Although a somewhat unwanted child, Alliant Techsystems was born.

Alliant is a leader in each of its business areas: precision armament, ordnance (munitions), marine systems, and information storage. Its major programs include the design and manufacture of the 120 millimeter shells for the M-1 Tank, the Mark 48 torpedo, cluster bombs, mines, various "smart" weapons, antisubmarine missiles, and graphic recorder products. With a workforce of 8,300 employees and 1990 sales of $1.4 billion, it is the 15th largest direct supplier to the U.S. Department of Defense. Alliant's sales have remained flat for the past four years, with net income ranging between $13 and $46 million.

Approximately 85 percent of Alliant's business is with the U.S. Defense Department. An additional 8 percent is with U.S. allies. The balance, approximately 7 percent, represents commercial accounts.[4]

Macroenvironment

A significant portion of Alliant's sales is associated with long-term U.S. government contracts and programs that have significant inherent risks. U.S. government contracts entered into by Alliant are, according to their terms, subject to government termination either for the government's convenience or through default by Alliant. In addition, many government contracts are conditioned upon the continuing availability of Congressional appropriations. Because the U.S. government provides, directly and indirectly, approximately 85 percent of Alliant's revenue, the loss of a significant portion of this business would have a materially adverse effect on Alliant's operations and profitability.

Unfortunately, the economic reality of severe budgetary constraints is forcing Washington to revaluate the wisdom of ever increasing defense expenditures.

The 1980 federal "on budget" deficit was $72.7 billion.[5] It will be an estimated $374.4 billion in 1991. To control this soaring deficit spending, the administration is proposing defense outlays of $295.2 billion for fiscal 1992.[6] This marks the first time in 10 years that the White House has proposed an actual year-to-year reduction in military expenditures (see Exhibit 1). Significantly, when adjusted for inflation, defense spending will fall 11.3 percent, the sixth real decline in a row.[7]

Political realities are propelling the U.S. administration into proposing even larger cuts for future defense budgets. The Warsaw Pact has collapsed. Russia is refocusing its energies away from the West and towards its internal troubles. In addition, the United States and Russia are negotiating several arms agreements which seek to reduce current levels of armaments. In the wake of Operation Desert Storm, the United States finds itself uniquely secure in the world. Recognizing the changing political landscape, and responding to congressional demands for a "peace dividend," the secretary of defense has proposed slashing the Pentagon's budget to $283 billion by 1996. In real terms, this means a cumulative 34 percent decline in appropriations since 1985. At a projected 3.6 percent of GNP, military spending in 1996 would be at its lowest since 1939.[8]

In practical terms, the impact could be immense. The plan envisions cutting the size of the army by 25 percent, slashing the navy's fleet of combat ships nearly that much, and retiring more than 400 fighters and bombers in the air force. Nearly all military construction is proposed to be frozen in fiscal 1993, and nearly 100,000 employees, or 10 percent of the Pentagon's civilian workforce, are slated to be off the payroll by the end of calendar 1996.[9]

EXHIBIT 1 Defense Budget, 1980–1992 (in $ billions)

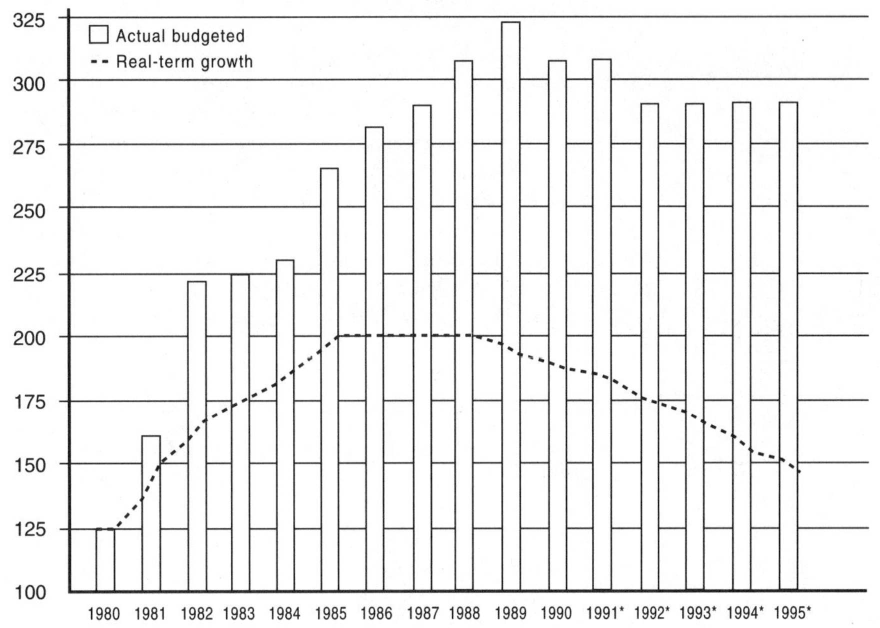

*Estimated.

SOURCE: Council of Economic Advisers, *Economic Index—January 1991.*

Ramifications for Alliant

These proposals to reduce Pentagon spending have serious ramifications for Alliant. Specifically, by canceling existing programs and by changing government procurement policies through the reduction of "sole-source" contracting, the government is taking steps that threaten several of Alliant's major military contracts. As a result, the company's financial health and existence are challenged.

In an effort to control defense expenditures, the administration proposed to eliminate or curtail several programs that directly affect Alliant. Production of cluster bombs is scheduled for termination after 1992. As sole-source provider of this weapon, Alliant will lose $125 million in annual revenues. In addition, the defense secretary proposes to eliminate production of the M-1 tank. As primary supplier of the tank's 120 millimeter shells, Alliant estimates a loss of up to 25 percent of the $250 million in annual revenue that this program generates. Together these programs represent a potential yearly revenue loss of $190 million.[10]

Curtailing sole-source contracting by the Defense Department will also harm Alliant. Under this form of contracting, a manufacturer agrees to develop a product for the military, with the right to be the only, or sole, source for that product.[11] The Defense Department now requests that contracts be "dual source," requiring a sharing of the technology among firms and competitive bidding for shares of the total contract amount. The idea is that "the guy that's got the best price gets the biggest share [of the contract]."[12] The burden, in the form of lower sales and profits and in the loss of proprietary rights, falls upon the military contractor.

This issue is of critical importance to Alliant. The company is currently the sole-source provider for the Navy's Mark 46 torpedo. At $300 million in yearly revenue, or almost 21.4 percent of sales, the Mark 46 is the largest of Alliant's defense contracts. However, the Mark 46 program is scheduled for termination and will be superseded by a new torpedo, the Mark 50. Developed as a dual-source contract with Westinghouse, the Mark 50 contract will be awarded on a competitive-bid process. Under a worst-case scenario, Alliant could lose this entire contract. Typically, however, the contract is split. The company with the low bid receives the majority of the contract, with the balance going to the competitor. Significantly, the addition of competitive bidding into the contracting process will almost certainly reduce profit margins. As one defense industry analyst put it, the loss of the Mark 50 program would make Alliant's future "pretty grim."[13]

The loss, cancellation, or "dual-sourcing" of these contracts underscores the seriousness of Alliant's condition. In a worst-case analysis the company could lose $490 million of its major contract business, an almost 35 percent reduction in sales. Depending on how deeply the defense budget is cut, other contracts between the company and the Pentagon could also be canceled or reduced.

Opportunities

While political and economic realities have created significant challenges for Alliant, they have also created opportunities such as export markets and the projected explosion in so-called smart weaponry.

A direct result of Operation Desert Storm has been an increased demand for U.S. weaponry and defense technology. Defense analysts estimate that Egypt and the Middle Eastern kingdoms will spend upwards of $25 billion over the next five years to rebuild their armies and upgrade their defense capabilities.[14] The U.S. defense industry, with weaponry fresh from victory over its Soviet counterparts in Iraq, is the beneficiary of this buildup. Thus, Alliant, as supplier of precision armament and ordnance, should directly benefit.

In addition, the success of technologically sophisticated weaponry in the Gulf War has refocused congressional attention on smart weapons.[15] The trend of the future for the defense industry is development of ever more discriminating weapons, those that pinpoint and attack enemy targets while distancing combatants ever farther from the field of battle.

Alliant is attempting to shift its market to take advantage of these opportunities. Predicting growth markets in the Middle East, Alliant has set a goal to increase exports from 8 percent of sales in 1991 to 15 to 20 percent by 1995. In addition, the company is continuing its research into third-generation smart weapons. Development of the Mark 50 torpedo, surface-ship torpedo defense systems, smart artillery-delivered anti-tank ordnance, and "autonomous underwater vehicles" demonstrates Alliant's continuing attempts to diversify through technology.[16]

The Brink

Despite these opportunities, Alliant appears to be a company poised on the brink of a precipice, balancing to keep from plunging into the abyss of declining sales and earnings. Toby Watson, chairman of Alliant, indirectly acknowledges this through his own conservative financial forecasts. His optimal projection is for a decline in defense spending of 2 percent per year, in real terms, through 1996; with a maximum real-term decline of 20 percent. Based on these numbers, he projects company sales to remain flat, at $350 million to $400 million a year. As a result, he expects that Alliant will continue its no-dividend policy for the foreseeable future.[17]

This analysis is far from optimistic. Projected sales and earnings are flat, despite the inclusion of expanding export markets and the introduction of new weaponry. In addition, the analysis underestimates projected real-term declines in Pentagon spending through 1996, 20 percent versus the administration's proposed 34 percent.

The financial markets also discount Alliant's opportunities. In fact, Honeywell's failure to sell DMSB had been a direct result of market pessimism towards the future profitability of the company, including both domestic and international sales. In its prospectus Alliant conceded that

> the impact of these various [political and economic] developments is likely to be a sizeable decrease in the defense spending, which despite being concentrated in particular program areas, may cause a contraction of the defense industry as a whole. . . No assurance can be given that the general slowdown in the defense industry will not have a material adverse effect on the Company's business or that the Company will be profitable in future years.[18]

This was an acknowledgement that Alliant did not have a significantly broad base to weather downturns in defense spending. With 85 percent of its sales currently with the Department of Defense and an additional 8 percent with foreign governments, Alliant finds itself hostage to political and economic conditions outside its control. In a period of enormous federal deficits and uncertain political alliances, defense spending must suffer. So will Alliant's sales and profits.

Employee morale has been very low. A survey of 231 nonunion personnel showed that most were bitter about management's performance.[19] More than 1,700 workers have been laid off. The remaining workforce numbers only 7,200. A profit-conscious corporate culture has been imposed on staff by means of a series of consolidations and reorganizations of people and facilities. Employees also resent the expenditure of more than $1 million to remodel corporate offices, while more than $7 million has been spent closing facilities and relocating workers.

Diversification

The difficulty of diversifying Alliant's product line into the consumer market is summed up in comments by Watson: "It's very difficult to imagine [our] machines making lipstick cases."[20] Other companies in the defense industry, however, have tried to enter businesses that can take advantage of their core competencies—McDonnell Douglas, selling coal slurry; Grumman, buses; Kaman Aerospace, guitars; and Teledyne Tyan Aeronautical, coffins. For Alliant, dual-use technology opportunities include medical products, airport noise monitoring, drug enforcement, automobile emissions testing, vehicle electronics, and underwater mapping. However, it is problematic to find a consumer market in which Alliant can transfer its expertise in munitions and armaments, while at the same time generating a respectable profit. Two possibilities will be discussed. The question is to what extent either fits into an overall plan for Alliant's revitalization.

Small-Caliber Munitions. One product that does lend itself to Alliant's unique abilities is that of small-caliber munitions. This industry manufactures, markets, and distributes cartridges for handguns, shotguns, and rifles to a broad range of users; including the police, sportsmen, and recreational shooters. It is an industry that is compatible with its existing business, it is profitable, it is easy to enter, and it has a history of successful defense industry involvement.

A significant advantage of entering this market is the compatibility with Alliant's existing businesses. The only practical difference between manufacturing a 120 millimeter shell for the M-1 tank and a bullet for a 22-caliber hunting rifle is the diameter of the shell. Beyond that, their basic elements are similar: a casing, a primer, a charge, and a projectile. Alliant could utilize these similarities to achieve economies of scale, transferring production of small-caliber munitions to its existing ordnance plants. In effect, Alliant gains an outlet to the consumer market without significantly altering its product mix.

The small-caliber munitions industry also has the sales volume and profitability to support

Alliant. With 9,000 + employees, the industry reported combined 1989 sales of $910 million, with net profits of slightly over $50 million. The market for consumer ordnance is expected to remain stable, with industry revenues and earnings expected to grow at 5 percent annually.[21]

In addition, the consumer ordnance market is an easy market to enter. With 77 manufacturers the market is still relatively segmented. Many manufacturers serve one particular market segment or one specific geographical region, but only 17 are considered major players, indicating a national presence. The degree of segmentation provides a number of candidates for acquisition, as well as offering an opportunity to subsequently increase market share through consolidation.[22]

History has shown that a large defense contractor can successfully and profitably integrate a consumer ordnance manufacturer. Olin Corporation, a direct competitor with Alliant in the government munitions market, is the parent corporation of Winchester, one of the largest munitions and armament manufacturers in the consumer market. With over $3 billion in sales, Olin does not break out the sales and earnings of Winchester into its munitions and armaments divisions. However, its annual report states that the consumer ordnance division made significant contributions to its 1990 earnings.[23] While not guaranteeing success for Alliant, it does indicate that the defense and consumer ordnance industries are compatible.

The inherent difficulties of consolidating a defense contractor with a consumer products firm do not seem insurmountable. For example, unfamiliarity with the consumer market, including marketing, distribution, and contracting, can be avoided by acquiring an existing, profitable concern. Ultimately, the industries have more similarities than differences.

Global Demilitarization. Another opportunity for Alliant is to enter the global demilitarization market.[24] Alliant has a great deal of experience dismantling conventional weapons. Only weapons manufacturers have the expertise and qualifications to take apart weapons systems that they build. In Russia, the Ukraine, and Belarus, there are 1.4 million tons of munitions. Tanks, rockets, guns, and ammunition have to be destroyed, dismantled, and recycled. The ultimate disposition of these weapons is of international importance. If the matter is not handled properly, it can create significant problems.

Sales of surplus weapons create the chance for both internal and external security problems in Russia and the other nations of the old Soviet bloc. External buyers for Russia's advanced weaponry are countries such as Iran and China. Terrorists can easily get their hands on these weapons and create havoc throughout the world. Internal buyers have the potential to cause civil unrest and discord. If these weapons find their way into the hands of opponents of the existing governments, anarchy could result.

Destruction of the weapons is not simple. Enormous environmental hazards are involved in countries already suffering from immense environmental degradation. Outmoded weapons used to be buried, detonated, or simply dumped into the ocean, solutions that today are unacceptable. The nations of the former Communist empire are not capable of dismantling the weapons in an environmentally sound manner. They have never had to deal with so many weapons that must be taken *out* of service. Unlike the United States, these countries have no standard procedures or regulations for handling this task.

If Alliant enters this market, it must design its operations to meet the unique characteristics of the task. Flexibility is a key element in any equipment investments it makes and in the reclamation process it develops. The company's goal must be to generate profits in hard currency, something that cannot be assured because of the uncertain condition of the economies of the countries of the former Communist bloc.

Alliant will have to form close partnerships with the ministry of defense in any country requesting demilitarization service because this ministry is responsible for the legal title to the weapons, transportation to the site of operation, and access to the local workforce. Alliant would be responsible for the capital equipment and the technical and business expertise. After an operation is completed, the partners split the profits. The U.S. government does not have to approve demilitarization operations because they are considered nonmilitary trade. Alliant needs only to procure an export license and a technology assistance license from the Commerce Department.

On the capital equipment side, Alliant has developed flexible modular factories that can disassemble many weapons at factory production scale and speed. However, there are over 8,000 different types of conventional munitions and each location is likely to house a different mix. Furthermore, the individual weapons sites are highly dispersed throughout the former Soviet bloc. Alliant's demilitarization "factories" are a series of trailers which can be hooked up to trains. Alliant can minimize costs by deploying only the required modules to each location. Once the equipment is on-site, the weaponry has to be reviewed and sorted by type. Disassembly is performed by pulling the pieces apart mechanically or cutting them apart with high-pressure water jets. The casings are separated from the explosives and the propellants. These items then are sold for hard currency. The casings have a high commercial value since they are constructed with good-quality brass, steel, aluminum, and copper. The explosives have potential commercial uses in mining and construction. They also can be processed and converted into agricultural fertilizer.

The problem for Alliant is that the Germans and Japanese are very strong in the demilitarization industry. German companies like Messerschmitt-Boelkow-Blohm and Diehl are experienced and equally as capable as Alliant. Alliant will have to work hard to expand its range of contacts in the former Soviet bloc and to gain the trust of the new governments and their people.

Another problem is that the governments of these states are highly unstable. At a critical moment in the negotiation or implementation process, they could change direction or fall from power. Moreover, ownership of the weapons and control over them are often in doubt. The weapons often were deployed by the Soviet Union in far-flung areas and regions. Today, it is unclear whether ownership of the weapons lies with Russia or with the country where the weapons are located. Though the people of Russia and the other former Soviet bloc countries desperately need assistance in cleaning up their excess munitions, ultimately they may lack the political will and financial means to do so. Alliant has excellent expertise to offer, but the extent to which this expertise can be used is not clear. The degree to which Alliant should commit itself to this endeavor is uncertain.

Other Strategic Thrusts Other strategic thrusts the corporation can make is to form partnerships with former competitors. If two defense contractors join forces, major defense programs are in less danger of being terminated. Combined technologies strengthen the program and the two companies can better defend it than one.

An example is "sense and destroy armor" (SADRAM). Alliant used to compete for the production of this program with Aerojet, a California company, but now it has joined forces with it. Rather than a winner-take-all project, the Defense Department awarded the contract to Aerojet, which employs Alliant as a subcontractor. The two companies will share the $4.5 billion award over the next decade through a joint-venture agreement.

Alliant has developed similar joint-venture agreements with four European weapons firms to develop weapon systems and to seek weapons contracts. Canada, the Netherlands, Turkey, and Japan all buy Alliant's MK46 Torpedo. The U.S. government will pay Alliant $150 million to replace cluster bombs used in the Gulf War, and there is potential to sell this weapons system internationally.

What Should It Do?

What should Alliant do? Should it diversify into consumer sectors, commit itself to demilitarization, continue to cut back its operations, examine possible acquisition targets, develop partnerships with other weapons' manufacturers, or look for markets overseas? How can it take advantage of its technological prowess, given the new federal budget circumstances?

Discussion Questions

1. What factors threaten Alliant's future?
2. What can Alliant do to influence these factors?
3. What strengths does Alliant have?
4. How should Alliant realign itself to current market conditions? To what extent should it remain mainly a military company? To what extent should it explore other options?
5. If Alliant were to explore other options, how would it go about doing so?
6. What civilian markets have real potential? Could Alliant succeed in these markets?
7. To what extent is the demilitarization market a real option that Alliant should pursue?

Endnotes

1. This case was written by Jon Bogen, Paul Ness, Tom Rectenwald, and Paul Rutzen. Celeste Daly, Linda Gordon, Paula Gritzmacher, and Josh Yuen contributed to this revised version.
2. *Information Statement* (Minneapolis, Minn.: Alliant Techsystems Inc., October 1, 1990), p. 9.
3. Ibid.
4. Ibid., p. 15.
5. The term *on budget* reflects actual deficit spending before any budgetary reserves are added. It is a truer reflection of deficit spending than the frequently quoted off-budget figures.
6. Council of Economic Advisers, *Economic Index—January 1991* (Washington, D.C.: U.S. Government Printing Office, 1991), pp. 32–34.
7. *The Wall Street Journal*, March 5, 1991, p. A14.
8. Ibid.
9. *The Wall Street Journal*, Feb. 11, 1991, p. A3.
10. *St. Paul Pioneer Press*, Oct. 1, 1990, pp. 7, A14.
11. *Washington Post*, February 12, 1989, p. 41.
12. *St. Paul Pioneer Press*, Oct. 1, 1990, p. 6.
13. *St. Paul Pioneer Press*, Oct. 1, 1990, p. 1; *Information Statement*, p. 33.
14. "NBC Nightly News with Tom Brokaw," March 5, 1991.
15. S. L. Kirsch, "How Defense Will Change," *Fortune* 123, no. 6, p. 58.
16. Dow Jones Wire Service, Sept. 28, 1991, 5:21 P.M., p. 3; *Minneapolis Star Tribune*, Sept. 17, 1990, p. 7d.
17. *Minneapolis Star Tribune*, Sept. 17, 1990, p. 7d.
18. *Information Statement*, p. 14.
19. S. Gross, "More Changes Lie Ahead for Alliant," *Minneapolis Star Tribune*, June 24, 1991, p. 10D.
20. *St. Paul Pioneer Press*, October 1, 1990, p. 5.
21. "Ordnance and Accessories," in *1990 Census of Manufacturers* (Washington, D.C.: Department of Commerce, 1990), p. 3; *Value Line*, February 8, 1991, p. 1255.
22. *1990 Census of Manufacturers*, p. 1; *Value Line*, p. 1256.
23. *1990 Annual Report*, Olin Corporation, p. 16.
24. Gross, "More Changes Lie Ahead for Alliant," p. 1D, 10D; Alliant Techsystems, *1994 Annual Report*; C. Daly, L. Gordon, P. Gritzmacher, and J. Yuen, "Strategic Decision Making in a Time of Turbulence: Alliant Techsystems, Inc.," University of Minnesota Business School student paper, 1993; Terri Peterson Smith, "Disarmingly Simple," *Corporate Report Minnesota*, Feb. 1993, pp. 67–69.

PART

IV

Energy and the Environment

CHAPTER

13

From Nature

Energy Policies

If it is very easy to substitute other factors for natural resources, then there is in principle no (energy) "problem." The world can, in effect, get along without natural resources, so exhaustion is just an event, not a catastrophe.

Robert Solow, "The Economics of Resources or the Resources of Economics"[1]

Introduction and Chapter Objectives

Natural resources must be available for businesses to make the goods and provide the services that people need. Their availability depends on market forces (the laws of supply, demand, and price), technical capabilities, and government policies. In the long run, smooth transitions from the use of one set of resources to another should take place if markets are to function without unnecessary government interference and if technological change takes place in response to market signals. In the short run, however, there can be unexpected price hikes and resource scarcity. Severe economic problems and adjustment difficulties accompany these conditions. Governments make the situation worse when they try to cushion people from the effects of higher prices; doing so leads to inappropriate long-run decisions that prolong the crisis (e.g., decisions to purchase energy-inefficient capital equipment).

Major energy price shocks shook the world in 1973 and 1979. With the decline of the Cold War, energy policy issues, with their focal point in the Persian Gulf, are an important factor that managers should consider. This chapter focuses on these issues.[2]

The Crisis in the Persian Gulf

The following headline appears in your morning newspaper: "Iraq Takes Control in Kuwait: Bush Embargoes Trade."[3] Your heart sinks as you wonder what this development will

Exhibit 13–1 Evolution of the Gulf Crisis, 1990

July 17	President Saddam Hussein of Iraq accuses Persian Gulf countries that exceed their oil production quotas of "stabbing his country in the back."
July 18	Tarez Aziz, Iraqi foreign minister, denounces Kuwait to Arab League nations claiming that it has "stolen" $2.4 billion worth of Iraqi oil.
July 24	Iraq, maintaining that oil prices should rise to $25 a barrel, deploys thousands of troops on the Kuwaiti border.
July 25	Iraq, refusing to give assurances that it will not attack Kuwait, demands payment of $2.4 billion in compensation from Kuwait.
July 27	While Iraq continues to demand that Kuwait meet its "legitimate rights," the Organization of Petroleum Exporting Countries (OPEC) agrees to increase oil prices to $21 a barrel.
August 2	Iraq, unsatisfied, sends its troops and tanks into Kuwait, launching an attack on that country.

mean (see Exhibit 13–1). Between them Iraq and Kuwait control nearly 20 percent of the world's proven oil reserves (see Exhibit 13–2).

Declining U.S. Production

In the spring of 1990, U.S. production of crude oil was falling and alternative production methods and technologies, while offering some promise, were not ready to take up the slack. The United States was distracted by changes in the Soviet Union and looming budget battles that were only peripherally related to the energy problem. Output from Alaska's North Slope had peaked at about 2 million barrels a day in 1988 and production of domestic crude oil, 7.6 million barrels a day, was at a 26-year low. In 1989, only 542 exploratory wells had been dug, a decline from 2,334 in 1984. Because of restrictions on offshore drilling and drilling in Alaska wildlife reserves, the drilling that did take place occurred in areas where less oil was likely to be discovered.

The implications were serious. By 1989, the cost of imported oil in the United States had increased by 28 percent. This hindered efforts to close the trade deficit; nearly $50 billion of the trade deficit, or about 45 percent, was spent on foreign oil.

The United States imported 46 percent of the oil it consumed in 1989, substantially more than the 31.5 percent it imported in 1985 and very near the 1977 record of 47.7 percent. The Department of Energy estimated that by the year 2000 domestic production would fall to less than 6 million barrels a day and that the bill for imported oil would increase to more than $100 billion annually in constant dollars if oil prices increased as anticipated to nearly $28 a barrel. The United States would be importing over 75 percent of the oil it consumed. For a nation that imported very little petroleum prior to 1970, this change was remarkable.

Exotic alternatives to imported oil did not show much promise, so the long-term prospects for the United States to get away from heavy dependence on foreign oil were not particularly good. The ultimate example of an exotic alternative was cold fusion, the possibility of extracting vast sums of energy from the forging together of subatomic material.[4] The commercial prospects for cold fusion lay only in the distant future. Still, it might

EXHIBIT 13–2 Proven Oil Reserves and Production, 1990

	Proven Reserves (billions of barrels)	*Production (millions of barrels per day)*
Saudi Arabia	255.0	4.9
Iraq	100.0	2.8
Kuwait	94.5	1.6
Iran	91.5	2.9
Soviet Union	58.4	11.6
United States	34.1	7.6
Rest of Middle East	117.9	4.1
All others	259.0	28.1
World total	1,012.0	63.6

SOURCE: Adapted from *BP Statistical Review of World Energy, 1990.*

have promise for offering cheap and abundant power that would help eliminate world dependence on petroleum from unstable regions.

Where then was American energy going to come from in the future? Oil companies were trying to revive old domestic petroleum fields by expanding the use of horizontal drilling, which would enable them to capture oil that could not be reached by conventional methods. Though the costs of horizontal drilling were about twice the costs of drilling a conventional well, production rates could be four to five times as great, enabling the companies to rapidly recover the expenses (in the best of cases within a year). The 1989–1990 market for horizontal drilling equipment had increased 18 times from what it had been the year before. Independent oil companies such as Oryx Energy, Union Pacific Resources, and Burlington Resources were taking the lead in using this new method while some of the large integrated companies like ARCO, Amoco, and Texaco used it to a lesser extent. Horizontal drilling had the potential to revive moribund fields in Colorado, North Dakota, and Wyoming. The payoff would be an increase in U.S. proven reserves, considered to be about 27 billion barrels, by several billion barrels.

Nevertheless, an increase in American oil reserves by several billion barrels did not put the United States anywhere near the capability of the Persian Gulf powers to supply the world with oil. There was no doubt that American oil vulnerabilities, which began when the United States first imported substantial amounts of foreign petroleum, were rising.

A Proposal for a Broad-Based Energy Tax

The Bush administration was considering a broad-based energy tax as one means of reducing the budget deficit. This tax would affect nearly every energy source—gasoline, oil, natural gas, nuclear power, and hydroelectric power. It would mean an increase of about 5 to 6 cents on a gallon of gas, an addition to the existing federal gas tax of 9 cents a gallon. It would bring in an additional $20 billion to the Treasury, or about 40 percent of the funds needed to reduce the budget deficit.

At the time, the energy tax did not seem out of line, since the fuel cost of a mile's driving in the United States had plunged from 4 cents per mile in 1979 to 2 cents per mile in 1989. U.S. gasoline prices were about one-third what they were in other nations, chiefly because of lower U.S. gasoline taxes.

The energy tax had an additional benefit: by discouraging energy use, it helped the environment. The biggest cause of pollution is energy use, which contributes to oil spills, acid rain, smog, and greenhouse warming. Some Democrats favored the energy tax because it encouraged conservation and the development of alternative fuels and technologies, but other Democrats bitterly resisted it, claiming that the tax burden would fall most heavily on the poor.

The Organization of Petroleum Exporting Countries (OPEC)

To understand the role of energy in the international economy, it is important to examine actions of the major producers. They belong to the Organization of Petroleum Exporting Nations (OPEC), which came into existence in 1960 following decisions by the multinational oil companies to reduce the price of oil.[5] From 1970 to 1973, the already dominant position of OPEC in terms of world oil production and reserves (three-fourths of the world's oil discoveries between 1945 and 1973 had been in OPEC countries) grew. OPEC was supplying over 80 percent of the free world's exports. The five founding members (Saudi Arabia, Iran, Iraq, Venezuela, and Kuwait) were operating close to maximum sustainable capacity (see Exhibit 13–3).

EXHIBIT 13–3 Selected Statistics of OPEC Nations, 1990

	Crude Oil Production (thousands of barrels per day)	*Share of Oil in GNP (%)*	*Population (millions)*	*Per Capita Purchasing Power ($)*	*Trade Balance (billions)*
Saudi Arabia	6,436	54	14.1	6,430	6.6
Iran	3,076	20	57.0	1,400	1.8
Venezuela	2,103	22	19.7	2,150	10.1
United Arab Emirates (UAE)	2,062	40	2.3	11,870	2.1
Iraq	1,948	50	18.8	1,940	4.0
Nigeria	1,779	42	118.8	310	1.7
Libya	1,350	45	4.2	5,860	−0.1
Indonesia	1,249	9	190.1	490	5.7
Kuwait	1,222	31	2.1	9,700	5.2
Algeria	765	25	25.4	2,130	1.3
Qatar	385	30	.5	13,200	0.9
Ecuador	285	15	10.5	920	0.9
Gabon	280	40	1.1	3,1000	

SOURCE: Adapted from Directorate of Intelligence, Central Intelligence Agency, *Handbook of Economic Statistics, 1991* (Washington, D.C.: U.S. Government Printing Office, 1991), p. 32.

Massive Price Increases

The first massive price increase followed the outbreak of the Arab-Israeli War in October 1973. The Organization of Arab Petroleum Exporting Countries (OAPEC), consisting of Saudi Arabia, Abu Dhabi, Libya, Algeria, Kuwait, Bahrain, Qatar, and Dubai, curtailed production by 10 percent and did not permit oil shipments to the United States. However, after 1977 substantial increases in production from Mexico, the North Sea, and Alaska, and increases in non-OPEC production alleviated the pressure on oil prices. As markets became weaker, OPEC's share of world crude production went down.

At the time of the Iranian revolution, real oil prices actually had started to fall. Between 1979 and 1980, however, petroleum prices again doubled. Iranian oil production dropped off because of the revolution. Various countries, led by Japan, tried to take precautions against a possible decline in the flow of oil out of Gulf, and additional pressure on prices came from a buildup in stocks by these countries in 1979 and 1980.

Decline in Demand

World oil demand reached a peak in 1979. Demand fell thereafter because of energy savings and interfuel substitution, non-OPEC supplies, including natural gas liquids from the Soviet Union, and the deep worldwide recession of 1980–1982.[6] In response to these changes, mistrust among the OPEC nations grew. They were unable to meet in November 1980 in Baghdad because of differences about the Iran-Iraq War. OPEC's radical camp—consisting of Iran, Algeria, and Libya—vehemently opposed the United States and favored short-run OPEC revenue maximization. The Gulf Cooperation Council (GCC), a moderate faction led by Saudi Arabia (see Exhibit 13–4) sought a less restrictive pricing policy leading to long-run revenue maximization. An independent group consisting of the remaining OPEC members frequently altered its position.

The first price reduction in the 23-year history of OPEC occurred at the March 1983 London meeting when prices were reduced from $34 to $29 a barrel. Individual OPEC countries resorted to separate deals with consuming nations to maintain their market shares. The cartel began to unravel. It lost control of the oil market during 1985–1986

EXHIBIT 13–4 Members of the Gulf Cooperation Council, 1989

	Oil Reserves (billions of barrels)	*Population (millions)*	*GDP per Capita ($)*	*Armed Forces*
Saudi Arabia	255.0	14.1	6,400	65,700
UAE	97.7	1.6	15,200	43,000
Kuwait	94.5	2.1	11,250	20,300
Qatar	4.5	0.4	14,700	7,000
Oman	4.3	1.5	5,900	25,500
Bahrain	0.1	0.5	7,200	3,350

SOURCE: *Oil and Gas Journal,* Institute for Strategic Studies.

because its members could not enforce an acceptable market-sharing scheme.[7] Under these circumstances, the Saudis and some of their Gulf neighbors decided that they had to increase their share of the world oil market to maintain revenues. The Saudis were able to sell at low prices without suffering substantial revenue losses because price declines were offset by production increases. In taking the actions it did, Saudi Arabia risked hostile retaliation from the OPEC radicals—Iran, Iraq, and Libya (see Exhibits 13–5 and 13–6).

Why Most Cartels Fail

cartel
Producers' groups, with control over critical commodities, that come together to restrict supply in order to raise prices.

Like OPEC, numerous other **cartels,** formed to control the price and supply of a commodity, have existed on international markets, but most ultimately failed.[8]

In theory, cartels have within them the seeds of their own destruction because in response to higher prices, people search for alternative suppliers, reduce their use, and try to locate substitutes. When the market for a cartel's product diminishes, the problems it faces in continuing collusion grow. If everyone in the cartel sells at a discount, the cartel rapidly disintegrates. When the cheating becomes rampant, cartel members abandon further cooperation.[9]

The Gulf War and Oil

This state of affairs within the oil producers cartel of which Iraq was a part, was not to the liking of Saddam Hussein, who needed cash to rebuild his country's war-torn economy. It serves as the background for his invasion of Kuwait.

EXHIBIT 13–5 Major Oil Exporters, 1970–1990
Hundreds of Thousands of Barrels per Day

	1970	*1975*	*1980*	*1985*	*1990*
OPEC					
Saudi Arabia	3.6	6.8	9.3	2.6	6.1
Iran	3.5	4.9	.9	1.7	2.2
Venezuela	3.4	2.0	1.8	1.2	2.0
UAE	.8	1.7	1.7	1.0	2.2
Iraq	1.5	2.1	2.5	1.2	1.7
Nigeria	1.1	2.7	2.0	1.3	1.2
Libya	3.3	1.5	1.8	1.0	1.3
Indonesia	.7	1.1	1.2	.7	.9
Kuwait	2.8	2.0	1.6	.9	1.2
Algeria	1.0	.9	.9	.5	1.0
Non-OPEC					
Soviet Union	1.9	2.6	3.2	3.3	3.2
Mexico	0	.1	.8	1.6	1.3

SOURCE: Adapted from Directorate of Intelligence, Central Intelligence Agency, *Handbook of Economic Statistics, 1991* (Washington, D.C.: U.S. Government Printing Office, 1991), p. 87.

EXHIBIT 13–6 Oil Revenues of OPEC Nations and the Soviet Union, 1975–1990
Billions of U.S. Dollars

	1975	*1980*	*1985*	*1989*	*1990*
Saudi Arabia	27	99	26	24	45
Iran	19	13	15	11	16
Venezuela	8	18	13	9	14
UAE	7	19	12	11	17
Iraq	8	25	11	15	9
Nigeria	7	24	12	9	14
Libya	6	23	10	6	10
Indonesia	4	13	12	6	8
Kuwait	8	19	9	9	6
Algeria	4	15	13	6	9
Qatar	2	6	3	2	3
Ecuador	1	2	2	1	1
Soviet Union	8	28	34	30	27

SOURCE: Directorate of Intelligence, Central Intelligence Agency, *Handbook of Economic Statistics, 1991* (Washington, D.C.: U.S. Government Printing Office, 1991), p. 32.

Exploiting Oil Vulnerabilities

At the end of the 1980s, Iraq began to lay the groundwork for exploiting oil vulnerabilities. It held direct talks with the Iran aimed at resolving the remaining issues in the decade-long hostility between the two nations. Iraq and Iran then agreed on the decisions that it wanted OPEC to make. Both wanted higher oil prices and lower production levels to earn more foreign currency to help rebuild their economies. To accomplish these purposes, they believed Saudi Arabia's power must be diminished within the region and in OPEC. Iraq and Iran felt that the Saudis, with the world's largest oil reserves, had acted in concert with the United States to keep oil prices low.

The next turn of events was the plummeting of oil prices from $22 a barrel in January 1990 to $16 in July 1990. OPEC producers added nearly 3 million extra barrels of oil a day into inventories in the second quarter of 1990. Prices for low-grade crude briefly slipped below $10 a barrel. The 13-member states of OPEC reported declining revenues at a rate of $100 million a day. Iraq claimed that it lost a billion dollars a year for every one-dollar reduction in the price of a barrel of oil. There were fears among the OPEC nations that prices would go down even more, to as low as $7 a barrel.

Iraq, along with Venezuela and Indonesia, placed the blame for the weak petroleum markets on Kuwait and the United Arab Emirates (UAE), whom they accused of cheating on their production quotas. Iraq had little faith in Saudi Arabia, which was trying to mediate the situation. Saudi Arabia was searching for a new strategy that would get Kuwait and the UAE to cut back their production. Reflecting the uncertainty, the futures price of crude oil crept up—by 11 cents a barrel—to $16.58 on the New York Mercantile Exchange.

Iraq's debt from the war with Iran was an immense $80 billion, and it wanted to see oil prices go up to $25 a barrel so it could pay off the debt and fund its military expansion. Kuwait, on the other hand, had diversified investments in the West and did not want to see the world economy, already tottering on the edge, slip into recession. Kuwait sought continued stability of world oil prices at about $14 a barrel. The dispute between the nations over oil prices opened an old rift between them. Lacking what it regarded as a suitable outlet to the sea, Iraq had been demanding that Kuwait lease to it Bubiyan Island, an empty sandbank, at the top of the Persian Gulf. The territorial dispute was only part of the reason that the two nations were at odds. At a more fundamental level, the Baathist ideology of the ruling clique committed Iraq to a form of pan-Arabism that does not recognize the territorial integrity of neighboring Arab states.

In response to the Iraqi-inspired demands, OPEC agreed to a new oil price ceiling of $21 a barrel, which was based on a production limit of 22.5 million barrels. Iraq, however, was still not satisfied even though an increase in the price to $21 a barrel would have been difficult in the summer of 1990 because of large petroleum inventories and lagging consumption worldwide. Worldwide consumption had increased by only 1 percent in 1990 and it had actually declined by 2 percent in the United States, the world's largest consumer of energy. Kuwait responded to the situation by affirming its acceptance of the OPEC oil production quota and agreeing to negotiate its border dispute with Iraq, but to no avail. When Iraqi troops moved to the Kuwaiti border, the Gulf sheikhdoms looked to the United States for protection. Neither Kuwait nor its GCC allies could defend themselves in a military confrontation with Iraq. Using the pretext of long-standing disagreements with Kuwait, Saddam Hussein invaded the nearly defenseless neighbor and quickly overwhelmed it.

World Response to the Iraqi Invasion

With Kuwaiti reserves representing about 10 percent of the world total and Iraqi reserves another 10 percent, Iraq controlled more than 20 percent of the world's oil. It threatened the oil resources of the remaining Gulf states, which together constituted nearly 70 percent of the world's oil. The United Nations condemned Iraq and imposed an economic boycott. This condemnation brought together nations that previously had been adversaries, including the United States and the Soviet Union. It united the moderate Arab states of Egypt and Saudi Arabia with hard-line and intransigent Syria, Iraq's traditional foe.

Certainly, Iraq faced difficult economic circumstances at home: an inflation rate estimated at 22 percent in 1988, a decline in the GDP of 4 percent, and huge foreign debts that were the legacy of Iraq's 10-year war with Iran. In attacking Kuwait, however, Saddam Hussein threatened the economic security of all nations. The Persian Gulf region powered the world's automobiles and factories by supplying more than a quarter of the world's daily need for oil. Forty-seven percent of the oil used in Europe came from this area, and 63 percent of the oil used in Japan. If Iraq became the master of the Gulf, it would be virtually free to determine how much of this oil was to be supplied, to whom, and at what price.

World oil prices skyrocketed to $27 a barrel the day after the August 2, 1990, invasion. Each $4 increase in the cost of a barrel of crude raised U.S. gasoline prices by about 10 cents a gallon. The airline, chemical, and steel industries, which were heavy users of petroleum and petroleum by-products, would suffer. For each penny change in the price of a gallon of jet fuel, United Airlines's annual expenses went up by $22.5 million. American

EXHIBIT 13–7 Major Consuming Nations, 1960–1990
Hundreds of Thousands of Barrels per Day

	United States	*Japan*	*West Germany*	*France*	*United Kingdom*	*Canada*
1960	9.8	.6	.7	.6	1.0	.8
1970	14.7	4.0	2.6	2.0	2.0	1.5
1980	17.1	5.0	2.6	2.3	1.6	1.8
1985	15.7	4.3	2.3	1.8	1.6	1.4
1990	16.9	5.3	2.4	1.8	1.8	1.7

SOURCE: Directorate of Intelligence, Central Intelligence Agency, *Handbook of Economic Statistics, 1991* (Washington, D.C.: U.S. Government Printing Office), pp. 85, 87.

automobile manufacturers—in the midst of a movement toward larger, more powerful, and less fuel-efficient cars, and spurred on by relatively low gas prices since 1986—were likely to lose ground to Japanese competitors. While Japanese manufacturers consistently achieved average fuel efficiency standards of more than 30 miles per gallon, U.S. car manufacturers appeared to be stuck at about 27 miles per gallon. According to Environmental Protection Agency (EPA) estimates, 9 of the 10 most fuel-efficient model cars in 1991 were made in Japan; the tenth was not an American car, but the Volkswagen Jetta.

Japan's Preparation

Japan was in many ways better prepared to deal with the Gulf War crisis than the United States. Since 1973, energy policy had been one of its highest domestic political priorities.[10] Now, in 1990, the Japanese government darkened hallways in government buildings and turned down office air conditioners. Japan's Ministry of Trade and Industry (MITI) required drivers not to exceed 50 miles per hour and buildings to be no cooler than 28° Celsius (82.4° F). MITI reaffirmed its commitment to the conservation programs it had initiated following the 1979 oil price hike. Since 1979, it had kept close tabs on the energy consumption of nearly 5,000 factories by requiring from 1 to 10 energy conservation engineers on selected factory floors. The engineers had to spend up to a year studying for an exam that 80 percent would fail. Those who passed sent regular reports about energy use to MITI. The engineers devised plans and took steps to make Japanese factories more energy efficient. By means of energy conservation and industrial restructuring, Japan had reduced its energy use to the point where it was producing 2.24 times the real output for the same energy input as in 1973 (see Exhibit 13–7). While nearly 80 percent of Japan's energy supplies in 1973 came from oil, this figure had dropped to less than 58 percent by 1990.

With the goal of reducing demand and diversifying resources, Japan developed cooperative technical and economic agreements with most of the OPEC and many non-OPEC producers. It made numerous investments in the development of industry and infrastructure in the Persian Gulf, and the Gulf states in turn purchased large amounts of Japanese securities.[11] To finance the energy price increases that occurred (see Exhibit 13–8), Japan expanded exports.

EXHIBIT 13–8 The Costs of Oil Imports, 1980–1990
Billions of Dollars

	United States	*Japan*	*West Germany*	*France*	*United Kingdom*
1980	$76.9	$58.9	$35.1	$30.7	$14.0
1985	51.4	40.6	24.1	18.8	10.5
1990	64.5	33.4	19.0	14.8	15.1

SOURCE: Directorate of Intelligence, Central Intelligence Agency, *Handbook of Economic Statistics, 1991* (Washington, D.C.: U.S. Government Printing Office, 1991), p. 89.

Production in the basic materials industry, particularly aluminum and petrochemicals, was stagnant because world economic growth was weak and the competitiveness of these segments of Japanese industry, given higher energy prices, declined. Japanese economic growth took place in processing and assembly industries and in the expanding service sector, which were less energy-intensive.

Energy Rationalization Law The basis for Japan's extensive energy conservation efforts.

The **Energy Rationalization Law** of 1979 was the basis for Japan's energy conservation efforts. It provided for the financing of conservation projects and for a system of tax incentives. It has been estimated that over 5 percent of total Japanese national investment in 1980 went for energy-saving equipment.[12] In the cement, steel, and chemical industries the figure was more than 60 percent of total investment. Japanese society shifted from petroleum to a reliance on other forms of energy including nuclear power and liquefied natural gas (LNG). By 1995, oil provided less than 60 percent of Japan's energy needs. Nuclear power provided 14 percent and LNG 12 percent, both up from 7 percent in 1982.

The main reduction in energy use took place in industry. Many companies invested heavily. Nippon Steel Company installed a $5.6 million coke dry quencher that reduced consumption by 25 percent. Asahi Glass rebuilt production equipment and redesigned production processes to cut energy use by 40 percent in a decade. Japan's northern subway system recycled heat from engines for use in air-conditioning to save energy. Hino Motors added switches to its machine tools so that they would not idle when not in use. It recycled machine oil and reduced shop lighting and air-conditioning. Tokyo Electric Power Company converted to nuclear power, cutting its use of oil by two-thirds. In 1990, Japan's 38 nuclear power plants supplied 9 percent of the country's total energy needs, an increase from almost nothing in 1973.

MITI also encouraged companies to switch from oil to more plentiful coal and natural gas, which could be obtained from politically stable nations. It allowed oil and gas companies and the utilities that supplied electricity to keep their prices artificially high so long as they diverted the excess profit to energy research. In essence, the permission to do so created an energy tax which had many important benefits. The tax stimulated energy research and discouraged energy use. In 1987, the tax revenues provided more than $830 million for energy research that helped Japan develop advanced solar-cell technology, new means for transporting and storing liquid natural gas, and better methods for producing electricity from gasified coal and sea water.

Geographic compactness, population density, and superior public transportation provided Japan with advantages that the United States did not have. Japan benefited from a movement away from energy-intensive heavy industry toward financial services and consumer electronics, which used less energy. Japan, which already was more energy efficient than the United States in 1973, improved its efficiency by one-third. Japanese conservation efforts following the oil shocks of 1973 and 1979 insulated it to a greater extent than other countries from energy price hikes. The share of oil in total Japanese energy demand declined from 77 percent in 1973 to 57 percent in 1987. This decline took place despite the increasing wealth of individual Japanese consumers, who bought more television sets, refrigerators, air conditioners, and other appliances. The Japanese also drove more and bought more cars in the interim. Between 1973 and 1987, Japanese economic output more than doubled, but its reliance on oil imports fell by 20 percent. American reliance on foreign imports increased during this period from 36 percent to 43 percent of total oil consumed.

Oil Price Shocks and Recession

All but one of the eight post–World War II recessions in the United States had been preceded by an oil price increase. At the outset of the Gulf War, consumer confidence was down and factory orders were declining. If the Federal Reserve Board increased the money supply and lowered interest rates, it risked exacerbating inflation. This happened in the 1970s after the first oil price shock when loose monetary policies helped raise inflation to double-digit levels. The Dow-Jones Industrial Average tumbled 183 points in the three days following the Iraqi invasion of Kuwait. Some analysts estimated that oil prices would climb to $50 or $60 a barrel.

The United States, which was dependent on foreign supplies for almost 50 percent of its oil, obtained only about 6.6 percent of it from Iraq and about 1.5 percent from Kuwait. Its largest foreign suppliers were Venezuela, Nigeria, and Canada. The Japanese, 99 percent dependent on foreign oil, imported about 12 percent of it from Iraq and Kuwait.

Oil, nonetheless, was a pervasive part of the American economy. U.S. fuel and oil costs constituted from 4 to 8 percent of all shipping costs. These in turn affected food prices and the prices of nearly all goods bought and sold. Petroleum-based liquid asphalt constituted about half the costs of road resurfacing. Raw materials used in adhesives, coatings, and similar products contained petroleum derivatives. Other products with petroleum derivatives were trash bags and precision plastic parts used in computers. Chemical companies were heavy users of petroleum derivatives. For businesses, the cost increases of the petroleum price hikes varied widely depending on the products they made, where these products fell in the crude-oil production chain, and how much petroleum-based material the products contained.

During the Arab oil embargo between October 1973 and January 1974, the price of oil jumped from $3 to $13 a barrel. This caused the inflation rate in industrial nations to nearly double from 7.9 percent in 1973 to 14 percent in 1974 and the GNP growth rate to fall about 1.75 percent. From the end of 1978 to the end of 1979, oil prices again spiked upward, this time from $13 a barrel to $39 a barrel. Inflation rates grew from 7.8 percent at the end of 1978 to 13.6 percent in the first half of 1980. The GNP started to decline in 1979 and did not come back until 1983 when the developed countries, determined to fight inflation, let the unemployment rate slip to 8.5 percent.

Differences from Earlier Price Hikes

As much as the situation in 1990 was similar to earlier price hikes, it also was different. In 1973, when Arab oil producers refused to ship oil to the United States and other Western nations, Saudi Arabia was the instigator of the boycott. This time, with the United Nations, by virtue of a 13–0 Security Council vote, deciding to impose widespread trade restrictions on Iraq, the Saudis were supporting the effort by promising to provide 2 million extra barrels of oil a day to replenish world supplies. The 2 million extra barrels of oil a day represented about half of what the world needed to completely make up for the loss of 20 percent of its supply from Iraq and Kuwait.

Other differences between 1990 and earlier oil shocks existed. U.S. dependence on OPEC oil was now greater (28 percent in 1990 compared with about 13 percent in 1974). However, the industrialized nations had succeeded in diversifying their sources of energy. In 1974, about half of the world's oil came from OPEC countries; in 1990 only about a third came from OPEC. Additional production potential had been developed in the meantime on the North Slope of Alaska, the North Sea, Mexico, and elsewhere. Industrial nations had learned from earlier oil crises how to improve the efficiency with which they used petroleum—in 1990 they used 40 percent less oil to produce one dollar of real GNP.

The United States and other nations had also accumulated large oil reserves that could last as long as 200 days. The United States had a 590-million-barrel reserve, the Japanese a 140-million-barrel reserve, and the Germans a 100-million-barrel reserve, which cushioned these nations against a supply shortage. The reserves could be used to stabilize oil markets. The main problem with the reserves was whether they could be used as anticipated. Two-thirds of the petroleum reserve in the United States consisted of a "sour" variety unsuitable for many U.S. refineries. It had not been tapped in the past and analysts were uncertain who would buy the oil, what they would do with it, and if there would be hoarding and speculation.

Finding Alternative Supplies

Over the long term, conservation in conjunction with technological innovation would drive down oil prices; high prices could not be sustained. The problem was in the short term, when alternative supplies were needed but not necessarily easy to find.

Pemex The publicly owned oil company of Mexico.

Mexico. In the long term, Mexico was a supplier of great potential. The true extent of its oil resources, ranging anywhere from 45 billion barrels of oil to 260 billion, could not be properly estimated. However, Mexico was ill-prepared to provide the world with extra petroleum. Since the debt crisis of 1982, investment in **Pemex,** its publicly owned oil company, had plummeted. The decline in drilling for oil in Mexico had been extreme. In 1989, only about half the number of exploratory wells were opened as in 1987.

tar sands
Mixture of clay, water, bitumen, and oil that is found in abundance in western Canada.

Canada. Once considered a country whose oil reserves had great potential, Canada was having difficulty exploiting these reserves. Its proven reserves were estimated at about 4.2 billion barrels, but it was believed to have vast untapped reserves in its Northwest Territories. However, this oil was not easily accessible and it was extremely expensive to develop. Canada also had huge deposits of **tar sands** in its western provinces, but these deposits, a mixture of clay, water, and bitumen, had to be refined before they could be used. The refining process was not only expensive and capital-intensive, but also it could be extremely damaging to the environment.

Russia. Russia, which produced 20 percent of the world's oil, could not be called on for additional production because political disruption and outdated technology had ground its oil industry to a halt. Russia's oil industry suffered from declining exports and chronic shortages of basic equipment such as pipes and valves. Although Russia had 60 billion barrels of oil reserves (more than twice the amount of the United States) and the world's largest proven natural gas reserves (about 45 percent of the world's total), it was not likely to add much in the way of new energy production, because it lacked the capability to efficiently produce and market either oil or natural gas.

United States. The U.S. oil industry, too, was in the doldrums in 1990. After a century of high production, no vast pools of undiscovered oil existed in the United States. Worse still, the infrastructure needed for oil exploration and production had been deteriorating. For instance, the capability to build pipelines and manufacture drill bits had declined to about 50 percent of what it had been 10 years earlier. Skilled professional engineers, scientists, and oil-field workers were needed to enhance production from existing wells and to find new oil. Many had retired after the last oil boom of the 1970s and, with low oil prices in the 1980s, they had not been replaced. With its constant booms and busts, the oil industry was no longer as attractive to scientists or blue-collar field workers who did the hard work of getting the oil out of the ground. Non-OPEC producers such as Mexico, Canada, Russia, and the United States could be expected to produce at most an additional 200,000 to 400,000 barrels per day.

Other Nations. Besides Saudi Arabia, which was able to take up about half the slack of the oil lost from Iraq and Kuwait, the world could rely on Venezuela for approximately 600,000 barrels a day and on the UAE for another 800,000 barrels, leaving a shortfall of about 500,000 barrels. As oil prices rose, demand fell and a variety of producers, notably Nigeria, Indonesia, and Libya, made up the difference. As a result, this supply interruption, unlike others in the past, did not involve real shortages of oil.

The Need for an Energy Policy

Clearly, the United States needed an energy policy to reduce its dependence on foreign oil. It had made substantial progress between 1976 to 1986, when it cut its ratio of energy use to GNP by 2.8 percent per year, but by 1987 this progress had come to a halt. Much of the improvement came about because the United States had eased out of energy-intensive heavy industries, by investing money overseas and building plants abroad, and had replaced them with service industries that used less energy. Progress also took place because automobiles obtained 50 percent more miles per gallon than they had in 1973. However, the improvements in automobile efficiency were reversing themselves as post-1985 gasoline prices dipped to inflation-adjusted lows. With cheaper driving possible, people were driving more.

Americans on average used more gasoline than people in other countries with comparable standards of living. They consumed about 350 gallons per person in 1989, while Germans consumed only about 150, not just because the Germans had more efficient vehicles, but because Americans drove more miles and had more cars. In the United States as well as the rest of the world, the ratio of cars per person was rising.

At the time of the Gulf War, however, the U.S. government resisted the idea of mounting a major effort to establish a new energy policy. The Bush administration did not want people to be reminded of the sacrifices they had been asked to make during the Carter years. In a famous gesture designed for direct comparison with the Carter administration, President Bush continued to use a gas-guzzling speedboat during his summer holiday in Maine.

The Bush administration's first stab at devising a policy relied solely on voluntary cooperation. It put inflating automobile tires to their proper pressure at the head of a list of conservation measures. An admittedly weak and ineffectual gesture, the administration claimed it would save 100,000 barrels of oil a day if drivers carried it out. Another measure advocated was more car and van pooling; 20 percent more ride-sharing would save another 90,000 barrels of oil a day. The administration also called on people to observe speed limits, thus saving 50,000 barrels a day, and to drive the most energy-efficient car (if there was a choice), saving 40,000 barrels a day.

To increase the oil supply, administration officials asked oil companies to extract additional oil from Alaska's North Slope. They also considered reopening for exploration Alaska's Arctic National Wildlife Refuge, which had been closed in the aftermath of the *Exxon Valdez* oil spill. The Energy Department indicated that it would be willing to mediate a dispute that prevented oil production from the ocean floor along the California coast. A Chevron-led consortium could pump up to 100,000 barrels a day from platforms built near Santa Barbara, but state and local authorities denied permits on environmental grounds.

gasohol
A blend of gasoline and ethanol (corn alcohol).

The Energy Department also announced that it would switch its own vehicles to **gasohol**—a blend of gasoline and 10 percent ethanol—and would encourage ethanol producers to produce at full capacity. The administration called upon industries to switch from petroleum to more plentiful natural gas whenever possible. Overall, these programs were designed to increase the oil supply by 270,000 barrels a day.

On August 31, 1990, the administration announced that it would support the first national advertising campaign in a decade to promote conservation. It was also considering a tax credit designed to stimulate the recovery of hard-to-get oil from existing fields and a plan to expedite the processing of permits for oil exploration in the Beaufort Sea near Alaska. President Bush went so far as to declare that the United States "must never again enter any crisis—economic or military—with an excessive dependence on foreign oil." But he went no further, and he refused to back up his words with additional actions.

Reluctance to Do More

The U.S. government was reluctant to do more for a variety of reasons. These reasons included the Bush administration's free-market ideology, public opinion polls indicating the unpopularity of other options, and domestic political interests, already agitated about the budget deficit, which were ready to exact a high price for steps the Bush administration might take. On the grounds that the government should not intervene in energy markets, the administration opposed an auto fuel efficiency bill introduced by Senator Richard Bryan, Democrat from Nevada, that would have forced auto manufacturers to improve fleet fuel efficiency standards to 40 miles per gallon by the year 2001.

The bill, first designed as an environmental measure, would have saved 2.8 million barrels of oil per day by the year 2005, more than all the oil the United States had been importing from the Persian Gulf. Energy Secretary James Watkins admitted that two-thirds of the oil burned each day in the United States came from transportation, with the largest share from 171 million private cars and trucks; but he pointed out most automakers opposed fuel economy legislation on the grounds that the public was demanding larger, that is, "safer," cars, which would be impossible to build if the bill took effect.

The administration supported the auto industry's claims with studies asserting that the proposal would result in additional highway accidents and deaths. William Reilly, head of the EPA under Bush, came out against the fuel efficiency standard. On September 25, 1990, supporters of this proposal lost a procedural vote in the Senate, ending hope for passage in 1990.

According to a Gallop poll, 80 percent of Americans favored tougher conservation measures, but 62 percent were opposed to higher gasoline taxes designed to encourage conservation. Despite public opposition, congressional Democrats reintroduced the idea of a tax on energy consumption into the budget talks. The 9 cents per gallon tax they proposed was supposed to enhance revenues, but this purpose would be defeated if people actually curtailed their driving. Republicans ultimately accepted this proposal and it became part of the budget agreement.

Congress, however, refused to consider taking the broader step of gradually increasing American gasoline taxes to levels normally found in other industrialized countries. In France, the United Kingdom, Germany, and Japan, motorists routinely spent $45 to $50 for 12 gallons of gas to fill their tanks. More than 75 percent of this expense was tax. However, the idea of adjusting markets to reflect the true social costs of petroleum use was not one that was accepted by either Congress or the administration.

The American public expressed other opinions that made it difficult for the government to develop a more elaborate energy policy. Fifty-seven percent of Americans, despite the Persian Gulf crisis, continued to oppose the construction of more nuclear power plants, and only 48 percent favored easing restrictions on offshore oil drilling. Tax breaks to stimulate the oil industry were out of the question with enormous budget deficits and the windfall earnings of the oil industry from high petroleum prices. Solar power obtained a boost with a 30 percent increase in research funding sponsored by Congress and endorsed by the administration, but this increase appeared insignificant compared with the funding for solar power in countries such as Japan. The Bush administration considered a tax credit for alternative energy investments, which was supported by environmentalists, but administration economists warned that such measures would not result in sufficient additional revenues to justify the budgetary costs.

Long-Term Energy Alternatives

In the long run, the United States—or any country—has a number of promising options, if the country is willing to take advantage of them. Perpetual heavy reliance on imported oil from unstable regions is neither necessary nor inevitable.

Natural Gas

With 4,000 trillion cubic feet of gas reserves under the ground in the United States, Canada, and other countries, natural gas is far more plentiful than oil (see Exhibit 13–9). From an environmental perspective, natural gas is cleaner burning and less polluting. However, additional conversion of industries in the United States from oil to natural gas had been limited to the equivalent of about 160,000 barrels of oil a day.

The extent to which natural gas is an attractive automobile fuel replacement depends on its price and whether it can be adapted for use in internal-combustion engines. As oil prices rise, natural gas prices also go up. Existing cars can run on natural gas only if engine modifications are made and a compressed-gas storage tank is added. If natural gas prices rise too rapidly, however, the conversion of existing autos will not be worth the expense.

Another disadvantage of natural gas over regular fuel is that it is more difficult to store and transport. It is not yet a practical replacement for gasoline. Mobil Corporation developed an advanced process at its New Zealand subsidiary which could convert natural gas directly into gasoline at a cost of just under $35 a barrel. The New Zealand plant produced 15,000 barrels of gasoline a day, providing for one-third of New Zealand's needs.

Energy Conservation

An even better alternative than natural gas from an environmental perspective is conservation. Historically, people used 2 percent less oil for every 10 percent rise in fuel prices.

EXHIBIT 13–9 U.S. Primary Energy Production by Type
Thousands of Barrels per Day Oil Equivalent

	1970	*1980*	*1990*
Coal	7,359	9,785	11,989
Crude oil	11,380	10,170	8,825
Natural gas	10,686	9,838	8,814
Hydroelectric/nuclear	1,394	2,774	4,525

SOURCE: Adapted from Directorate of Intelligence, Central Intelligence Agency, *Handbook of Economic Statistics, 1991* (Washington, D.C.: U.S. Government Printing Office, 1991), p. 84.

A 30 percent drop in consumption following the last energy price hike took place because people cut the amount of energy they used in response to the higher prices.

The potential for conservation is great. People had increased the amount of energy they used during the 1980s because energy prices had fallen. On average, Americans drove 1,000 more miles per year than they did in 1980. Since 1987, the cars they used have become 7 percent heavier, 10 percent more powerful, and one-half mile per gallon less fuel efficient. Reversing these trends could mean savings of 200,000 barrels of oil a day.

An increase in oil prices would compel U.S. airlines to lower consumption. Next to labor, jet fuel is the second biggest expense for the airlines. Jumbo jets average less than half a mile per gallon. In 1990, the average fuel cost of a flight from New York to Los Angeles was $7,000, and these fuel costs pushed the airlines toward record losses of over $1 billion. To cut energy consumption, they called on pilots to fly at higher altitudes where the air is thinner. They warned the pilots to take the most direct route between locations even if the flight was choppier for passengers. A light touch on the throttle, once the plane was at cruising speed, was also recommended. In addition, pilots were asked not to keep engines idling at airports, even if it meant shutting off air conditioners and annoying passengers.

Immediately after the Iraqi invasion, high fuel prices along with a looming recession depressed energy consumption in industrial countries. The flattening of world oil demand delayed shortages that might have arisen from the Persian Gulf crisis.

Price increases also have stimulated technological innovation such as the energy-saving fluorescent light bulb. The bulb costs about $15, screws into standard sockets, and has about the same color and intensity as a regular 60-watt bulb, but it uses only 15 watts of electricity and lasts 10 times longer. With greater sales volume, the price of the new bulb might come down to $10. If 25 percent of the power generated in the United States came from fluorescent light bulbs instead of incandescents, the need for new capital-intensive power plants, which burned conventional fuels or relied on nuclear power, would decline.

Many utilities and, more importantly, many of the public utility commissions that regulated them accepted the idea of rewarding the utilities for marketing such efficiency-enhancing mechanisms. Boston Edison offered the fluorescent bulbs to customers for $3 a piece, going door to door and installing them to make sure that they would be used.

Good at innovation, entrepreneurs can design and deliver a package of new energy-saving technologies to industrial users. To do so, they have to be in close touch with their customers. It takes about 35 steps, for example, to change industrial motors and their components. The changes could yield savings of roughly half the energy the motors consumed with the payback arriving in about one year. But to design and carry out the changes, the entrepreneurs have to address many areas, including consumer education, the selection and installation of the equipment, financing, and maintenance. They might have to offer a performance guarantee through an insurance company, stating that if the savings were not realized the entrepreneurs would absorb a percentage of the shortfall.

Coal

Conservation and natural gas are the best alternatives to petroleum, but the most abundant alternative is coal. Proven coal reserves in the United States are large enough to last another three centuries at current consumption levels. Unfortunately, coal is dirty. It contributes carbon dioxide to the atmosphere when burned, which may lead to global warming. Safety, too, is a matter of concern, especially in the mining of coal. Few opportunities are left for coal use; 57 percent of the electricity produced in the United States comes from coal-fired generating plants, while oil supplies only 5 percent.

Coal could replace gasoline as a vehicle fuel, but only to a limited extent and at a very high price. South Africa, which could not rely on other nations to supply it with petroleum when sanctions had been imposed for its apartheid policy, had converted coal for this purpose for many years. However, the process of making coal into gasoline is dirty and expensive, and the South African government was forced to heavily subsidize it.

Tar Sands

Canadian tar sands are another alternative. An estimated 300 billion barrels of oil are recoverable from the Athabasca region in northern and western Canada. Syncrude Canada Ltd., a partially owned subsidiary of Exxon, converted tar sands into 180,000 barrels of oil a day. Suncor, Inc., a unit of Sun Company of Philadelphia, produced 60,000 barrels of oil a day from tar sands. Oil prices only have to remain substantially higher than $25 a barrel for these ventures to be commercially viable. Venezuela also is capable of producing a superheavy crude from tar sands found in its Orinoco Belt, but without the addition of water, the product is difficult to transport.

Oil Shale

oil shale
Petroleum deposits trapped in rock commonly found in the western United States.

Another alternative is **oil shale**. The United States has proven reserves of 600 billion barrels of shale oil, about the same as all of OPEC's proven reserves. However, the costs of extracting usable oil from shale are estimated to be as high as $100 for an equivalent barrel of oil. The extensive process used to break up and crush the rock to capture the small residues of trapped oil is extremely expensive and damaging to the environment. An operating shale oil plant is highly capital-intensive and would require immense government subsidies. Even with vast government subsidies, Unocal's Parachute Creek plant lowered costs only to the equivalent of $40 a barrel of imported oil.

Ethanol

During the 1970s, the United States had turned to gasohol, a mixture of gasoline and grain alcohol (ethanol), in the hope that this product would expand the market for corn, reduce pollution, and lessen American dependence on foreign oil. Adding ethanol to gas raises the octane level and causes gasoline to burn more cleanly. In midwestern farm states (e.g., Minnesota), gasohol sales peaked at nearly 33 percent of the auto fuel market in 1985. Since then, the sale of gasohol declined to less than 10 percent. Rumors circulated that gasohol could destroy carburetor seals, hurt engine valves, and erode the paint from car surfaces. Although these rumors were untrue, the real problem with gasohol remained its price. At about $1.50 a gallon, it simply is not competitive with gasoline.

Propane

Yet another option is propane, a fuel used in more than 300,000 vehicles despite its never having benefited from government subsidies. Very low in pollution, especially ground-level pollution that plagues big cities, 85 percent of propane is derived from domestic oil and natural gas production as a by-product. The remaining 15 percent comes from non-OPEC countries such as Canada and Mexico. Mostly used for heating, propane is a much neglected fuel for motor vehicles. It could, with existing supplies, propel up to 3.5 percent of the vehicles on American roads with little difficulty. The problem is obtaining additional supplies.

Solar Power

Solar power also might play a role in reducing U.S. dependence on foreign energy supplies. Solar power comes in many forms. Rapid technological advances have made photovoltaic prices competitive in limited applications (see Case 13–A on ARCO Solar). Another solar option is a trough-like collector that can be used to produce electricity in very sunny climates. In Southern California, solar collectors had been manufactured successfully by Luz International, Ltd. The price of a kilowatt hour of solar-generated power fell from 24 cents in 1980 to 8 cents in 1990. Another decline of 2 cents per kilowatt hour would make solar-generated power competitive with other forms of electric generation. The potential for replacing foreign petroleum with solar power, however, is small, because the utilities in the sun-drenched regions of the Southwest, which would buy solar power, use little petroleum to generate electricity.

Geothermal Power

geothermal power Energy trapped in coastal areas where the earth's crust has created unique geologic conditions.

Geothermal power, created where the earth's crusts have established perfect geologic conditions of heat, temperature, and pressure, also can play a role in reducing U.S. energy dependence. Unocal Corporation has reserves off the coast of Southern California which were the equivalent of 216 million barrels of oil. The company plans to spend millions of dollars exploring for additional geothermal energy off the Pacific coasts of California, the Philippines, and Indonesia. Geothermal power, however, has major limitations. First, it cannot be transported but must be consumed near its source. Generating electricity with geothermal energy is very expensive; the cost is about 9.5 cents per kilowatt hour from Unocal's Salton Sea facility compared with 4.5 cents to 7.5 cents from more conventional sources.

Nuclear Power

While nuclear power was once a promising option for the United States, no new construction of nuclear plants is planned; and some older U.S. plants are being decommissioned. Growth in sales of new nuclear plants is mostly confined to Asia. Safety and waste storage issues, along with greatly diminished public acceptance, makes nuclear power a less viable option than it was in the past.

Confined to generating electricity, nuclear power has been incapable of direct applications in the transportation sector. Nonetheless, researchers have made progress in advanced nuclear power plant prototypes, and a comeback of this power-generating source is possible if technological progress occurs and air pollution issues (e.g., sulfur dioxide and greenhouse gas emissions) become severe.

A Tax on Energy

A tax on energy use would not only stimulate innovation and energy-saving behavior but also make the alternatives more competitive with oil and thus more attractive. It would reduce the payback period for all types of conservation measures and stimulate alternative production. The market, not the government, would choose which alternative to emphasize based on a host of factors of concern to users, including cost and convenience.

However, no U.S. administration was willing to seriously consider such a tax. If the price of gasoline in the United States had risen as fast as other items on the Consumer Price Index during the 1980s, by 1990 Americans would have been paying $2 a gallon for gasoline, a figure much closer to what people in other countries were paying. The higher price would have encouraged Americans to drive fewer miles in smaller cars and to take other energy-saving measures. Instead, the relatively low price for American gasoline was sending the exact opposite message.

Energy Supply and Demand in the Future

In the long run, a number of scenarios were possible. On the one hand, oil resources would remain heavily concentrated in the Persian Gulf region, and no cheap, clean, and plentiful alternative would come to the forefront. Prospects for continuing expansion of non-OPEC production would remain limited. U.S. production would be below its 1970 peak even with high prices. Without Alaska, U.S. output would have been 25 percent less than it was in 1985. The only substantial non-OPEC discoveries in the post-1973 period, despite heavy exploration, had been in Mexico, but Mexico had only about 10 percent of the world's reserves. U.S., Canadian and North Sea oil would be depleted after three decades of production at current levels, while Persian Gulf producers could sustain current output levels for more than a century. A different scenario saw energy prices, like all resource prices, falling over time. The premise of a fixed stock was mistaken. Natural resources had to be seen as inexhaustible, nonbinding constraints on production. Although humans tended to exploit the cheapest stock of natural resources first, diminishing returns were more than offset by increasing knowledge about how to obtain new stock and how to utilize the existing stock more efficiently. In 1945, it appeared impossible that more oil could be discovered in the United States. The country was more "drilled up" than any other, it was claimed, and remaining reserves were then estimated to be only 20 billion barrels of oil. Nonetheless, the United States, excluding Alaska, produced over 100 billion barrels of oil over the next 40 years. Efforts by any nation or group of nations to withhold production were not likely to work in the long run because of the varied interests of the nations holding petroleum reserves. This also put downward pressures on long-term oil prices.

Breaking the Connection between Energy Consumption and Economic Growth

A key challenge is to break the connection between energy consumption and economic growth,[13] but the feedback effects between energy and the economy are very complicated.[14] Consumption of energy is both necessary for economic growth and a consequence of it. Different nations have different energy-to-GNP ratios. There is a substantially higher energy consumption pattern in the former Communist bloc countries than in Western Europe. Per capita consumption of energy in the United States is greater than in other industrialized nations; the U.S. ratio of energy to output far exceeded that in France, Germany, and Sweden, which have similar per capita income and output. The explanations for the different ratios among countries are complex. They include different pricing policies, the extent to which the countries are import-dependent, their product mix, and the state of their technology. The composition of GNP, exchange rates, climate, and geography play a role as do environmental, demographic, and sociological factors. The people in countries with lower ratios of energy to output than the United States appear to have a greater willingness to change lifestyles and to substitute other economic goods for energy.

Stages in economic development are significant. Underdeveloped countries typically have low energy-to-GNP ratios. As they became more developed, their energy-to-GNP ratios increase, becoming greater than those of developed countries. When economic growth slackens in developed nations, the energy-to-GNP ratio tends to fall.

Historically, growth rates in energy usage in the United States closely paralleled growth rates in the GNP.[15] Earlier in the 20th century, U.S. growth rates for energy consumption and GNP were nearly identical, 3.2 percent and 3.3 percent, respectively. For industrial nations, a 1 percent annual increase in energy usage paralleled a 1 percent annual increase in gross domestic product (GDP) from 1960 to 1973. Between 1973 and 1981, however, when GDP grew at an average annual rate of 2.3 percent, consumption of total primary energy grew by mere .2 percent per year. This decline in energy intensity reflects structural changes in the use of energy, responses to policies and prices, and cyclical effects. Intensity of energy use is lower, which has made a substantial dent in the link between economic growth and energy consumption.[16]

Conclusions

The world economy requires energy from highly unstable regions of the globe. In the long run, the availability of energy is assured, as long as lower-grade resources exist and labor and capital substitutions can take place. The market will work to raise prices so long as imperfections in the market do not exist and governments do not take inappropriate actions that prevent adjustment. In the long run, the U.S. and world economies have changed from more intensive to less intensive energy use. In the long run, energy scarcity is not an important problem. Even in the short term, as long as major wars or some other cataclysmic event do not cause widespread disruption of energy shipments, shortages are not likely to occur.[17] If a country does not have adequate domestic supplies, it can import the resources it needs by offering to pay a sufficiently high price. The real problem in the short term is unexpected price shocks caused by large-scale, unanticipated curtailments in supply, which increase prices. The world experienced two oil price shocks in 1973 and 1979 and very nearly experienced a third at the time of the Gulf War.

This chapter has looked at energy shortages and their causes and effects. The focus was on the crisis surrounding the Gulf War. The role of major producing (OPEC) and consuming nations has been analyzed. OPEC's near collapse in the mid-1980s was discussed, and the factors that permitted it to continue to function have been analyzed. Why most cartels fail in the long run has been addressed, and the long-term prospects for energy supply and demand in the world have been assessed.

Discussion Questions

1. Describe U.S. oil vulnerabilities at the outbreak of the Gulf War.
2. Why did some Democratic politicians oppose a broad-based energy tax? Is this position correct?
3. What countries are members of OPEC? What factions exist in the cartel? What are some different interests of these factions?
4. Why was OPEC forced to accept lower oil prices during the 1980s?
5. Why didn't Iraq want lower oil prices? Why were lower prices not wholeheartedly supported by Saudi Arabia and Kuwait?
6. What caused the Gulf War?
7. Discuss Japanese energy policies. How have they differed from U.S. policies?
8. Why didn't the Gulf War cause rapidly escalating oil prices similar to those of 1973 and 1979?
9. Where are alternative petroleum supplies likely to be found?
10. What kind of energy policy should the U.S. government have?
11. What are the long-term alternatives to petroleum? Assess their practicality.
12. Construct alternative scenarios of future demand and supply for energy. What do you think is likely to happen?

Endnotes

1. R. Solow, "The Economics of Resources or the Resources of Economics," *American Economic Review*, 1974, p. 10; quoted in V. K. Smith, ed., *Scarcity and Growth Reconsidered* (Baltimore: Johns Hopkins University Press, 1979).
2. Much of this chapter is adapted from Alfred Marcus, *Controversial Issues in Energy Policy* (Beverly Hills, Calif.: Sage Press, 1992).
3. G. Brooks and T. Horwitz, "Gulf Crisis Underscores Historical Divisions in the Arab 'Family,'"

The Wall Street Journal, August 13, 1990, p. A1; G. H. Anderson, M. F. Bryan, and C. J. Pike, "Oil, the Economy, and Monetary Policy," *Economic Commentary*, Federal Reserve Bank of Cleveland, November 1, 1990; "Iraqi Invasion Raises Oil Prices, Threatens U.S., Other Economies," *The Wall Street Journal*, August 3, 1990, p. A1: A. Murray and D. Wessel, "Iraqi Invasion Boosts Chances of Recession in the U.S. This Year," *The Wall Street Journal*, August 6, 1990, p. A1; "Oil's Economic Threat Is Less Than in '70s," *The Wall Street Journal*, August 20, 1990, p. A1; "Rising Oil-Import Bill Will Slow Trade Gains," *The Wall Street Journal*, March 5, 1990, p. A1; C. Solomon and R. Gutfeld, "Petroleum Reserve Has Lots of Oil, but Using It Could Be a Challenge," *The Wall Street Journal*, September 5, 1990, p. A1; C. Solomon, "Sudden Impact: Prices at U.S. Gas Pumps Soar," *The Wall Street Journal*, August 6, 1990, p. B1; A. Sullivan, "Gasoline Exports Rise Despite Concern over Supplies," *The Wall Street Journal*, September 17, 1990, p. B1; A. Sullivan, "It Wouldn't Be Easy, but U.S. Could Ease Reliance on Arab Oil," *The Wall Street Journal*, August 17, 1990, p. A1; A. Sullivan, "OPEC May Face Long Wait to See Higher Oil Prices," *The Wall Street Journal*, July 30, 1990, p. A4; J. Tanner, A. Murray, and B. Rosewicz, "Crude-Oil Prices Fall as Saudis and Others Plan to Boost Output to Offset Shortages," *The Wall Street Journal*, August 9, 1990, p. A3; J. Tanner, "Crude-Oil Prices Register Sharp Drop on Worries of Possible Glut in Supply," *The Wall Street Journal*, April 6, 1990, p. C6; J. Tanner, "Petroleum Use Starting to Fall, Agency Reports," *The Wall Street Journal*, October 5, 1990, p. A3; J. Tanner, "OPEC Adds Capacity, Easing Risk that Cost of Oil Will Soar in '90s," *The Wall Street Journal*, November 22, 1990, p. A1; J. Tanner, "Supplies of Oil Start to Shrink, Firming Prices," *The Wall Street Journal*, September 6, 1990, p. A3; J. Tanner, "Surge in Oil Output Could Lead to a Glut Even if Persian Gulf Standoff Drags On," *The Wall Street Journal*, November 12, 1990, p. A3; J. Taylor, A. Q. Nomani, and S. W. Angrist, "Hedgers Enjoy an Edge as Oil Prices Swing," *The Wall Street Journal*, August 29, 1990, p. B1; "How Big an Oil Shock?" *The Economist*, August 11, 1990, pp. 12–13; M. Wald, "America Is Still Demanding a Full Tank," *New York Times*, August 12, 1990, p. E3; M. L. Wald, "Effect of Fall in Soviet Oil Output," *New York Times*, September 6, 1990, p. D1; A. Murray and D. Wessel, "Iraqi Invasion Boosts Chances of Recession in the U.S. This Year," *The Wall Street Journal*, August 6, 1990, p. A1.

4. "The Fusion Thing," *Economist*, Feb. 8, 1992, pp. 85–86.
5. M. V. Samii, "The Organization of the Petroleum Exporting Countries and the Oil Market: Different Views," *Journal of Energy and Development* 10 (1985), pp. 159–73.
6. D. Gately, "The Prospects for Oil Prices Revisited," *Annual Review of Energy* 11 (1986), pp. 513–88; D. Gately, "Lessons from the 1986 Oil Price Collapse," in *Economic Activity*, 2nd ed., W. C. Brainard and G. L. Perry, eds. (Washington, D.C.: Brookings Institution), pp. 237–87.
7. W. Lowinger, G. Wihlborg, and A. Willman, "An Empirical Analysis of OPEC and Non-OPEC Behavior," *Journal of Energy and Development* 11, no. 2 (1986), pp. 119–41; Gately, "The Prospects for Oil Prices Revisited"; Gately, "Lessons from the 1986 Oil Price Collapse."
8. D. J. Teece, "Assessing OPEC's Pricing Policies," *California Management Review* 26 (1983), pp. 69–87; H. Tsai, *The Energy Illusion and Economic Stability: Quantum Causality* (New York: Praeger, 1989).
9. Gately, "The Prospects for Oil Prices Revisited," pp. 513–88; Gately, "Lessons from the 1986 Oil Price Collapse," pp. 237–87; Lowinger et al., "An Empirical Analysis of OPEC and Non-OPEC Behavior," pp. 119–41; Tanner, "OPEC Adds Capacity."
10. E. Ramstetter, "Interaction between Japanese Policy Priorities: Energy and Trade in the 1980s," *Journal of Energy and Development* 11, no. 2 (1986), pp. 285–301.
11. Ibid.
12. B. Mossavar-Rahmani, "Japan's Oil Sector Outlook," *Annual Review of Energy* 13 (1988), pp. 185–213.

13. Central Intelligence Agency, Directorate of Intelligence, *Handbook of Economic Statistics, 1991* (Washington, D.C.: U.S. Government Printing Office, 1991), p. 84.
14. U. Erol and E. Yu, "On the Causal Relationship between Energy and Income for Industrialized Countries," *Journal of Energy and Development* 13, no. 1 (1988), pp. 113–39; Tsai, *The Energy Illusion and Economic Stability;* Y. Wang and W. Latham, "Energy and State Economic Growth: Some New Evidence," *Journal of Energy and Development* 14 (1989), pp. 197–221.
15. J. Darmstadter, J. H. Landsberg, H. C. Morton, and M. J. Coda, *Energy, Today and Tomorrow: Living with Uncertainty* (Englewood Cliffs, N.J.: Prentice Hall, 1983); E. Kanovsky, "The Coming Oil Glut," *The Wall Street Journal*, November 30, 1990, p. A14; S. H. Schurr, ed., *Energy in America's Future: The Choices before Us* (Baltimore: Johns Hopkins University Press, 1979).
16. Tsai, *The Energy Illusion and Economic Stability.*
17. R. Pindyck and J. Rotemberg, "Energy Shocks and the Macroeconomy," in Alm and Weiner, eds., *Oil Shock*, 1984, pp. 97–121; R. S. Pindyck, ed., *Advances in the Economics of Energy and Resources* (Greenwich, Conn.: JAI Press, 1979).

Case 13–A
ARCO Solar Inc.[1]

In early 1988, top management at Atlantic Richfield (ARCO) had an important decision to make concerning the future of the company's solar energy division. (Financial statements are shown in Exhibits 1 and 2.) The wholly owned subsidiary, ARCO Solar Inc., was a world leader in photovoltaic cell production (photovoltaics are semiconductors that produce electricity directly from sunlight), yet in the 11 years since ARCO had purchased the company, it had never turned a profit.[2] ARCO instituted a restructuring plan in 1985 that called for the company to divest itself of operations unrelated to its core oil, gas, chemicals, and coal businesses; yet, the solar technologies being developed by ARCO Solar seemed within a few years of profitability. At the same time, ARCO enjoyed a reputation as a model of good corporate citizenship for continuing to support photovoltaic research and development for so long.

ARCO: A Brief History

Atlantic Richfield was originally incorporated in 1870 as the Atlantic Refining Company and, until the 1960s, was exclusively an oil and gas business. The company was renamed when it merged with the Richfield Oil Corporation in 1966. In 1961, ARCO expanded into the chemicals and plastics business, and by 1977 was well established in the coal business. By 1988, ARCO was one of the largest integrated petroleum enterprises in the industry. ARCO subsidiaries conducted oil and gas exploration, production, refining, transportation, and marketing. The chemicals, plastics, and coal operations along with the oil and gas businesses constituted the core of ARCO's business.[3]

ARCO expanded into nonpetroleum businesses with limited success. In 1967, ARCO bought the Nuclear Materials & Equipment Company, a producer of uranium- and plutonium-bearing fuels, which it sold in 1971. ARCO also, at one time or another, owned a newspaper, an air-conditioning company, a plant cell research institute, and a building products operation. All were eventually sold.

The 1970s were a turbulent time for the petroleum industry. The energy crises of 1973–1974 and 1979 precipitated a national search for energy alternatives to petroleum. One of the most attractive alternatives was solar energy. The supply was not controlled by foreign countries and it was a clean

EXHIBIT 1 Atlantic Richfield: Consolidated Balance Sheet (in $ millions)

	December 31	
	1987	*1986*
Assets		
Current assets:		
Cash	$ 174	$ 122
Short-term investments	3,761	2,275
Marketable equity securities	758	0
Accounts receivable	709	348
Notes receivable	57	246
Refundable income taxes	0	764
Inventories	801	779
Prepaid expenses and other current assets	204	209
Total current assets	6,464	4,743
Investments and long-term receivables:		
Affiliated companies accounted for on the equity method	898	920
Other investments and long-term receivables	289	338
	1,187	1,258
Fixed assets:		
Property, plant, and equipment, including capitalized leases	26,663	26,175
Less accumulated depreciation, depletion, and amortization	12,258	11,325
	14,405	14,850
Deferred charges and other assets	614	753
Total assets	$22,670	$21,604
Liabilities and Stockholders' Equity		
Current liabilities:		
Notes payable	$ 1,373	$ 872
Amounts payable for securities purchased	626	0
Accounts payable	1,147	957
Taxes payable, including excise taxes	243	225
Long-term debt and other obligations due within one year	422	874
Accrued interest	229	356
Other	427	466
Total current liabilities	4,467	3,750
Long-term debt	6,028	6,661
Capital lease obligations	286	307
Deferred income taxes	3,641	3,562
Other deferred liabilities and credits	2,254	2,065
Minority interest	216	0
Stockholders' equity:		
Preference stocks	2	2
Common stock ($2.50 par value: shares issued—1987, 217, 484, 404; 1986, 217, 279, 037 shares outstanding—1987, 177, 686, 928; 1986, 177, 510, 339)	544	543
Capital in excess of par value of stock	1,034	1,073
Retained earnings	6,683	6,173
Treasury stock, at cost	(2,438)	(2,445)
Foreign currency translation	53	(87)
Total stockholder's equity	5,878	5,259
Total liabilities and stockholders' equity	$22,670	$21,604

EXHIBIT 2 Atlantic Richfield: Consolidated Statement of Income and Retained Earnings (in $ millions except per share amounts)

	1987	1986	1985
Revenues:			
Sales and other operating revenues, including excise taxes	$16,829	$14,993	$22,492
Interest	308	283	176
Other revenues	471	498	412
Total revenues	17,608	15,774	23,080
Expenses:			
Costs and other operating expenses	10,760	9,495	14,770
Selling, general, and administrative expenses	1,107	1,223	1,295
Taxes other than excise and income taxes	702	629	1,114
Excise taxes	547	506	769
Depreciation, depletion, and amortization	1,661	1,646	1,762
Interest	985	972	622
Unusual items	0	0	2,303
Total expenses	15,762	14,471	22,635
Income from continuing operations before gain in issuance of stock by subsidiary	1,846	1,303	445
Gain from issuance of stock by subsidiary	322	0	0
Income before income taxes, minority interest and discontinued operations	2,168	1,303	445
Provision for taxes on income	932	688	112
Minority interest in earnings of subsidiary	0	0	0
Income from continuing operations	1,224	615	333
Discontinued operations—net of income taxes:			
Loss from operations	0	0	(21)
Loss on disposal	0	0	(514)
Net income (loss)	$1,224	$ 615	$ (202)
Earned per share:			
Continuing operations	$6.68	$3.38	$1.55
Net income (loss)	$6.68	$3.38	$(0.97)
Retained earnings:			
Balance, January 1	$6,173	$6,264	$8,782
Net income (loss)	1,224	615	(202)
Cash dividends:			
Preference stocks	(4)	(5)	(8)
Common stock	(710)	(701)	(766)
Cancellation of treasury stock	0	0	(1,542)
Balance, December 31	$6,683	$6,173	$6,264

source of energy. It was also abundant: the sunlight striking the earth in a year contains approximately 1,000 times the energy in the fossil fuels extracted in the same time period.[4] With gasoline and heating-oil prices rising beyond anything previously experienced, there was a great deal of public enthusiasm for solar power.

The enthusiasm seemed justified. Photovoltaic (PV) cells, which produce electricity directly from sunlight, were invented in 1954, and were first used to power U.S. satellites at a cost of over $1,000 per peak watt (a measure of a cell's output at maximum sunlight). By 1974, the price had dropped to $50 per peak watt; by 1977 it was $17 and was continuing to decline as the cells were improved.[5]

ARCO initiated a study of the potential of the solar energy field in 1972. By 1976, with oil apparently on the way out and solar power a promising energy source for the future, the company's studies culminated in a decision to enter the solar field. ARCO did so in 1977 with the purchase of Solar Technology International, Inc., a tiny Chatsworth, California, operation with eight employees. Solar Technology was renamed ARCO Solar Inc.

ARCO Solar Inc.

Solar Technology International was founded in 1975 by an engineer, J. W. (Bill) Yerkes, with $80,000 he pulled together by mortgaging his home and obtaining loans from relatives. The company produced PV panels that powered microwave repeater stations, corrosion-prevention systems in pipelines, navigational aids, irrigation pumps, electrified livestock fences, and trickle chargers for batteries on boats and recreational vehicles. When Yerkes sold the company to ARCO in 1977 for $300,000, he stayed on as ARCO Solar's first president.[6]

In 1979, the company bought a 90,000-square-foot building in Camarillo, California, and built the world's first fully automated production line for PV cells and panels. By 1980, the company was the first to produce panels generating more than a megawatt of power in a year. Sales had more than doubled from the previous year.

To interest electric utilities in photoelectric power generation, the company constructed demonstration projects where PV's potential for supplying large amounts of energy could be proven. In 1981, the company installed a prototype power generation facility on the Navajo reservation in Arizona and New Mexico that was large enough to power 200 homes. The project was judged a success, and the company moved from a largely research mode into a marketing stage.

An even larger demonstration project was conceived, and by the end of 1982, the company had constructed a PV power facility three times larger than the biggest such plant then in existence. The $15 million, one-megawatt plant near Hesperia, California—large enough to power 400 homes—was constructed on 200 acres of high desert, an area with no strong winds that might blow sand on the panels, thereby blocking sunlight and wearing down the mechanisms.[7]

The power at Hesperia was generated by 108 "trackers," double-axis computer-controlled structures that turn to follow the sun. Each tracker had 265 one-by-four-foot 40-watt PV modules, each of which were made of 35 individual single-crystal silicon cells. The trackers' ability to follow the sun boosted their power output by 40 percent over what a stationary panel could generate.[8] The electricity generated by the plant fed into the Southern California Edison grid and was purchased by the utility.

The plant was constructed in six months, a record for a power plant. Even more impressive, the plant was completed under budget, an uncommon occurrence for a new power-generating facility.

Encouraged by the success of the Hesperia project, the company began construction of a 16-megawatt plant on the Carissa Plain, near Bakersfield, California. The six-megawatt first phase of the project, completed in early 1984, occupied 640 acres. The project utilized several technical improvements in the PV module and tracker construction, which increased each tracker's peak power output by 50 percent, reducing the number of trackers needed. As in Hesperia, a utility bought the power generated by the plant, thus avoiding the cost of generating power from its most expensive fuel, gas or oil. This rate (around 6 cents/kwh) was less than what it cost ARCO Solar to generate the power, but a 37 percent federal and state tax credit for the solar installation brought the cost down enough to justify it as a demonstration of PV's potential.[9]

Meanwhile, ARCO Solar took the industry by surprise by announcing it would begin selling thin-film amorphous silicon products in 1984, much earlier than industry analysts had thought possible. "Genesis," a one-square-foot amorphous silicon cell, was the first use of thin-film technology beyond the tiny cells used in calculators and watches. Developed by a 100-person ARCO Solar research team whose existence had been kept secret, the five-watt module had a 6 percent conversion efficiency and a 20-year design life. It sold to distributors for about $45. Genesis generated enough electricity to maintain batteries in recreational vehicles, cars, and boats, or to power security systems or other low-power remote applications.[10]

Genesis made ARCO Solar the world leader in the race to commercialize thin-film technology. The company's sales doubled again in 1984, and its international network of distributors continued to expand. By 1986, the company was selling 400 Genesis modules per month.[11]

ARCO Solar increasingly turned its attention to thin-film technology. The efficiencies of the thin-film cells steadily improved: by 1985 the company's researchers had a thin-film cell with a record 13.1 percent efficiency, and were predicting 20 percent efficiencies by 1990. Sales volume continued to climb due to the success of the Genesis modules.

In 1986, the company entered into joint ventures with a Japanese company (Showa Shell Sekiyu) and a German firm (Siemens) to manufacture and market ARCO Solar products in the Pacific and Europe. ARCO Solar was now the largest manufacturer of PV products in the world.[12]

But even though sales continued to climb, the company still remained unprofitable. Research and development continued to require a large commitment (35 to 40 percent of sales revenues), and though ARCO Solar's products had improved greatly, the market for PVs, due to the oil glut, was not growing as the company had hoped.

The PV Industry

When ARCO entered the industry in 1977, it was only one of a number of oil industry giants investing in the infant industry. Exxon had become involved in 1969, Shell in 1973, Mobil in 1974, and Amoco in 1979. Chevron, Union Oil of California, Occidental Petroleum, Phillips, Sohio, Gulf, Sun, and Texaco were also funding PV research.

These oil companies, flush with profits from the rising price of oil, were interested in expanding into new businesses that showed promise. In the late 1970s, solar energy seemed to be the energy source of the future.

As an energy source, PVs competed directly with fossil fuels. With oil prices rising and the equivalent price of PV electricity falling, the new technology's future looked promising. Worldwide sales of PV products rose rapidly, from around $11 million in 1978 to an estimated $150 million in 1983. Industry analysts forecasted a billion-dollar PV industry by 1990 and PV electricity at half the equivalent price of oil. The government's 1976 "Project Independence" goal of PV electricity at 50 cents per peak watt seemed achievable in the not-too-distant future.[13]

However, things began to sour for the industry in the early 1980s. By 1982, the price of oil began to fall (see Exhibit 3). As the nation learned to conserve energy, the demand for electricity fell below projections in many areas, and utilities, not needing new capacity, lost interest in PV demonstration projects. The oil glut that developed in the 1980s made fossil fuels plentiful again, and it made renewables like PVs appear unnecessary. The utilities that needed to expand wanted an established, uninterruptable source of power, and were unwilling to invest in an unproven technology.

EXHIBIT 3 World Crude Oil Prices, 1977–1987

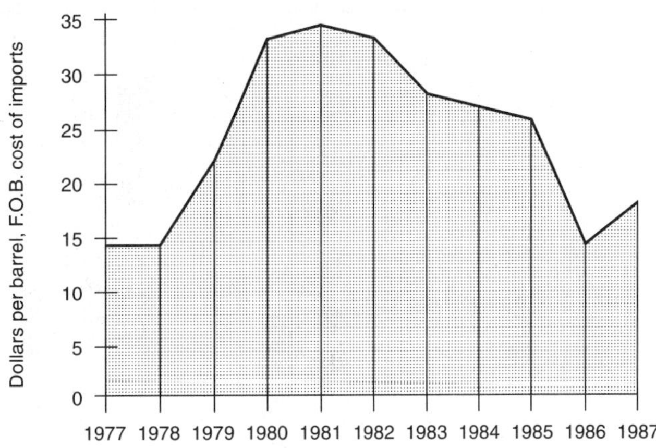

SOURCE: Solar Energy Industries Association.

Another threat to PVs arose in the early 1980s: a severe cutback in the federal government's commitment to solar energy research and development (see Exhibit 4). President Ronald Reagan, elected to the White House by a landslide and committed to slashing federal nonmilitary spending, cut heavily into the funding that facilitated much of the progress in PV technologies. Federal funding for solar energy, which rose from $2 million in 1972 to $2 billion in 1978, was cut by more than half in 1982 from its 1981 level. With two exceptions, federal funding continued to drop every year for the rest of the decade.[14] In 1987, the imposition of the Gramm-Rudman-Hollings budget cuts reduced the PV research budget to the lowest level ever. The burden of financing solar energy research, of which the federal government had shouldered 75 percent in 1980, fell increasingly on industry alone.

Besides cuts in research funding, the federal tax credits that encouraged consumers and business to invest in solar technologies expired in 1985. The 40 percent residential tax credit and 15 percent tax credit for industrial, commercial, and agricultural installations, had helped the solar industry's sales to rise rapidly. While the commercial tax credits were extended in 1986 after an intensive lobbying effort by the solar energy industry, the residential credits were not renewed when they expired in 1985.[15]

By the mid-1980s, the decline in crude oil prices was forcing the oil industry to slash capital spending and lay off employees. Several oil companies, particularly those that were forced to sell service stations and refineries, took a hard look at their portfolios, and some decided to get out of the solar energy business. Exxon's Solar Power Company, for example, ceased operations in 1983. Standard Oil wrote off its investment in 1986. By 1988, ARCO and Amoco were the only major U.S. oil companies that still played a significant role in the PV industry.[16]

Competition in the PV Market

In addition, foreign competition grew tougher throughout the decade. While U.S. government R&D funding fell throughout the 1980s, this was not true of some foreign governments. By 1985, the Japanese government was spending 19 percent more on PV R&D than the U.S. government.

EXHIBIT 4 Federal Appropriations for Photovoltaic Research and Development, 1977–1987

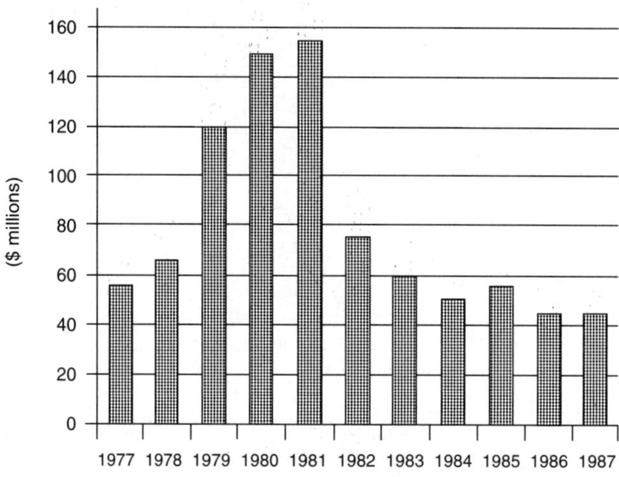

SOURCE: Solar Energy Industries Association.

In 1988, for the first time, both the West German and Japanese governments spent more on PV research than the United States.[17] And their investments were paying off; the U.S. companies' share of the world PV market fell from 80 percent in 1981 to 60 percent in 1983 to about 35 percent in 1987. In 1985, only 5 of the top 20 PV firms in the world were located in the United States, though ARCO Solar was number one worldwide. At the same time, the market itself seemed stagnant. After growing rapidly in the late 1970s and early 1980s, world PV sales stalled at the $125 million to $150 million level in the mid-1980s. With all its promise, solar power still accounted for only 0.1 percent of the electricity generated each year.[18]

As they had in other industries, the Japanese showed their expertise in taking an existing technology and commercializing it. In the late 1970s, most attention in the PV industry was directed toward developing cheaper, more efficient single-crystal cells. These cells had the highest conversion efficiencies of any of the PV technologies, but they were also very expensive.

The Japanese, however, used a new type of cell (amorphous silicon), which was much less efficient than the single-crystal cells (3–5 percent efficiency versus 15–20 percent or more efficiency) but much cheaper to produce. They used amorphous silicon cells to power small consumer electronic products like calculators. By 1985, the Japanese were selling 100 million amorphous-silicon-powered calculators and other small electronic products per year. Their experience in amorphous silicon cell production gave them the early lead in PV manufacturing technology, along with economies of scale and lower production costs. In 1985, the Japanese manufacturers shipped seven megawatts of amorphous silicon, almost all of it in consumer products, compared to 0.5 megawatts by U.S. producers.[19]

The most lucrative markets for PVs, though, was utility or grid power generation. In 1987, PVs were economical in grid systems only for what is known in the utility industry as "peaking power," more costly power sources that are used only during peak load periods.

The other major potential market was in providing power for areas without grid systems. Three-

EXHIBIT 5 Cost of a Solar Cell per Peak Watt of Electricity Generated

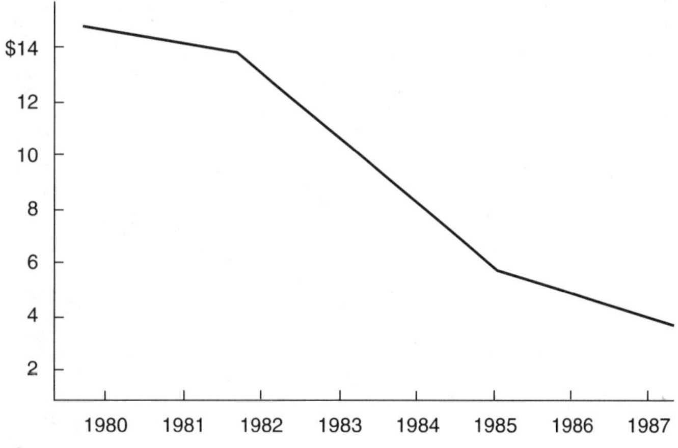

SOURCE: Solar Energy Industries Association.

quarters of the world's population are without grid electricity, yet many people live in areas where sunlight is abundant and intense. Thousands of small, solar energy systems were already operating in these areas and the potential market seemed huge. The Department of Energy estimated that the potential market was 10 to 20 times the current sales level.[20]

Most of the U.S. producers' attention was directed toward developing a cell that could generate electricity at a price competitive with fossil fuels. The price of PV electricity was falling, but whereas electricity from coal cost about 4 to 8 cents per kilowatt-hour (kwh) and oil or natural gas 5 to 10 cents/kwh, PV electricity cost about 25 to 30 cents/kwh (see Exhibit 5).[21]

By the mid-1980s, thin-film technologies, like amorphous silicon, seemed to hold the most promise. These technologies, which used a fraction of the material required to produce single-crystal cells and less labor, were continually being refined to yield more efficient cells. By 1986, thin-film technologies had been developed to the point where they seemed to be within a few years of reaching 7 to 8 cents/kwh, which would make PVs competitive with fossil fuels and nuclear power (see Exhibit 6).

There was another reason for optimism. By 1988, the search for new energy sources began to regain the momentum it had in the 1970s, though for a different reason. The threat posed by global warming had begun to draw attention. Experts warned that consumption of fossil fuels had to be reduced significantly to address the problem. Also, the Three Mile Island and Chernobyl nuclear accidents severely damaged the nuclear power industry's credibility and chances for a large role in the future of electricity generation appeared unlikely. Hydroelectric power, while clean and safe, had limited expansion potential. Solar energy's potential was once again apparent.

ARCO, the Industry Leader

By 1988, ARCO Solar was the undisputed world leader in the PV industry, with 20 percent of the $150 million market (see Exhibit 7). The company was leaner than it had been, with 350 employees, half the number in 1983, and sales forecasts were optimistic; the company had a growing backlog of

EXHIBIT 6 Efficiencies of Experimental Amorphous Silicon Cells

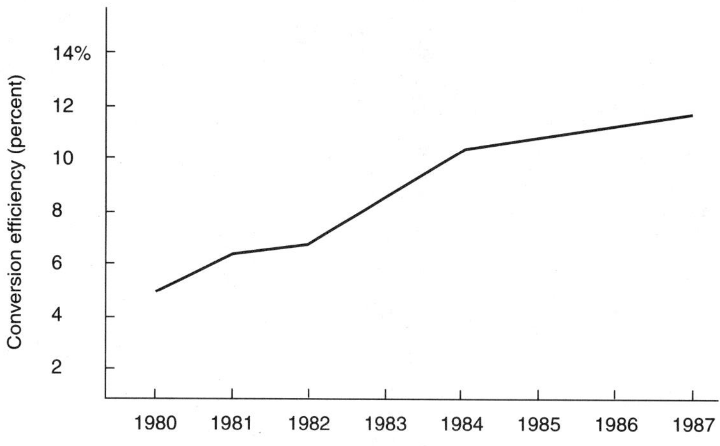

SOURCE: Department of Energy, "National Photovoltaic Program: 1987 Program Review."

orders. The company's research labs had made advances in a new type of thin-film material, copper indium diselenide (CIS), which promised nondegradability and had even better efficiencies than amorphous silicon. The company was four to five years ahead of the competition in CIS technology, and a line of CIS cells was planned.[22]

Though ARCO Solar was the world's leading producer of PV cells, it had never made a profit. Its $30 million in annual revenue was matched every 15 hours by its parent company. Though ARCO Solar's president was confident the company could stand on its own feet within two or three years, some analysts believed that the $200 million ARCO had invested in its solar subsidiary had hurt the parent company's status on Wall Street.[23]

Other criticisms began to surface in the press. Bill Yerkes, the founder and first president of the company, told the *Los Angeles Times* that "the company was screwed up two years after [ARCO] bought it. We went from making cells for $10 a watt and selling them for $15 to making cells for $32 a watt and selling them for $5."[24] Other former employees cited additional examples of instability: the company's headquarters had shifted five times, and six men had been president in 12 years (three presidents in the first 3 years alone).

What Should ARCO Do?

In 1985, ARCO underwent a restructuring that signaled a shift in corporate strategy. Anticipating continued low oil prices, the company cut costs by $500 million, repurchased 24 percent of its outstanding common stock, and wrote off $1.5 billion in losses on the sale of assets and the expenses incurred by personnel reductions. The chairman of the board retired and the CEO stepped down.

The new CIS thin-film technology showed promise of being the basis of a line of PV cells that would be truly competitive with fossil fuels for utility-scale power generation in the next few years. Given the rising concern over global warming, an economically competitive PV cell for large-scale power generation could be a bonanza.

ARCO also enjoyed its reputation as a socially responsible corporation for continuing to support

EXHIBIT 7 U.S. Photovoltaic Shipments (in Megawatts)

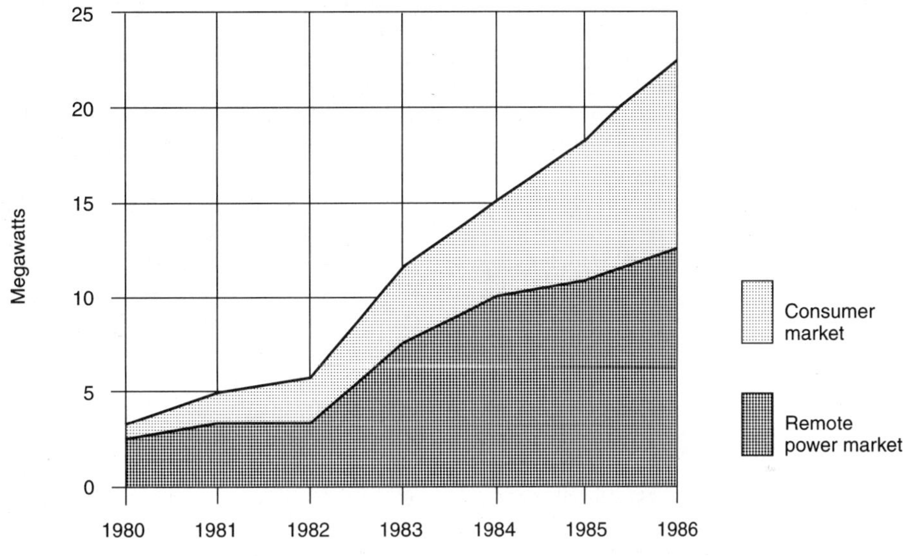

SOURCE: Department of Energy, "National Photovoltaic Program: 1987 Program Review."

solar energy when so many oil companies had dropped out. Although critics had claimed in the late 1970s that the oil companies were buying up the solar technology in order to suppress it, "Big Oil," with its deep pockets, was now generally acknowledged as being good for the PV industry. ARCO was a hero of sorts in the renewable-energy community.

Should ARCO sell ARCO Solar? Top management had a difficult decision to make.

Appendix: How Photovoltaic Cells Work

A photovoltaic cell produces electricity directly from sunlight. When the sunlight strikes the surface of the semiconductor material of which the cell is made, it energizes some of the semiconductor's electrons enough to break them loose. The loose electrons are channeled through a metallic grid on the cell's surface to junctions where they are combined with electrons from other cells to form an electric current.

The electrons from different semiconductor materials are broken loose by different wavelengths of light. Some wavelengths of sunlight reach the earth's surface with more intensity than others. Consequently, much of the effort of photovoltaic research has been to find semiconductor materials that are energized by the most intense light wavelengths and have the potential to provide the most energy.

Single-crystal silicon cells were the first type widely used, powering satellite radios as early as 1958. These cells are energized by some of the most intense sunlight wavelengths, and have achieved conversion efficiencies (percentage of light energy converted to electricity) of more than 20 percent. Other, nonsilicon, single-crystal cells have achieved efficiencies of more than 27 percent.[25]

While efficient, these single-crystal cells are also expensive to produce and the crystals are difficult to grow. Much of the crystal is wasted when sawed into pieces for individual photovoltaic cells.

Because they cost so much, their use has been limited mainly to applications where electricity is necessary and there are no other alternatives, such as in the space program.

To reduce production costs, researchers began to search for ways to fabricate silicon into cells that did not require the expensive and wasteful single-crystal techniques. One result of their efforts are *polycrystalline silicon cells*, which sacrifice some efficiency in return for cheaper manufacturing methods. The most efficient polycrystalline cells to date achieve better than 15 percent efficiencies. Together, single-crystal and polycrystalline cells account for two-thirds of those sold.[26]

Perhaps the most promising PV technologies are the "thin-film" techniques, in which cells as large as four square feet—as opposed to crystalline cells which are approximately 1/4 inch in diameter—are produced by depositing a film of PV material less than one-hundredth the thickness of a crystalline cell on a suitable base, or substrate. These cells are only about half as efficient as single-crystal cells, but because they can be produced for about one-fourth the cost or less, they offer the greatest potential for large-scale use.

Thin-film silicon cells (called *amorphous silicon*) accounted for 37 percent of the world market for photovoltaics in 1987. One drawback to amorphous silicon cells, however, is that they typically lose about one-sixth of their power output in the first few months of use. Certain other thin-film materials, such as the promising copper indium diselenide (CIS) and cadmium telluride (CdTe), may not suffer from this light-induced degradation.

The world leader in CIS technology is ARCO Solar. The company has developed a four-square-foot CIS cell with a 9 percent conversion efficiency, demonstrating that large-scale applications of thin-film technology are feasible. A Texas company, Photon Energy, has developed an inexpensive, simple process for applying CdTe to panels as large as ARCO's, achieving a 7 percent efficiency. The company has managed better than 12 percent efficiencies in the laboratory and expects to do even better in the near future.

Besides improving conversion efficiencies by developing new photovoltaic compounds, researchers have been breaking efficiency records by "stacking" cells; these "mechanically stacked multijunction" (MSMJ) cells are actually two cells pasted together. The top cell extracts the energy from one part of the light spectrum, and the lower cell uses the energy from a different part. An MSMJ cell composed of a single-crystal gallium arsenide cell and a single-crystal silicon cell achieved a better than 30 percent efficiency in the late 1980s, and researchers believe that a three-layer cell with a 38 percent efficiency is possible.[27] Efficiency improvements via stacking of more economical thin-film cells are also being investigated.

The continuing improvements in conversion efficiencies are especially remarkable considering that in 1982, theoretical physicists believed that the maximum achievable efficiency of a solar cell was only 22 percent; at that time, the highest efficiency achieved was 16 percent. Theoreticians now estimate that 38–40 percent is the limit, although the physics of thin-film technology is not completely understood.

Other Sun-Powered Energy Sources. Photovoltaics are not the only way of utilizing the sun's energy.[28] They are not even the major producer of electricity from sunlight, a distinction that belongs to solar thermal technologies. Solar thermal systems work by using the heating rays of the sun to warm air, water, or oil for space heating or thermal power generation. Luz International of Los Angeles is the world's largest producer of solar thermal electric plants. The company's seven plants in California's Mojave Desert produce 90 percent of all solar-generated power in the world. Company officials estimate that solar thermal plants occupying just 1 percent of the Mojave could supply all of Southern California Edison's peak power requirements. Solar thermal facilities, which on sunny days can achieve conversion efficiencies twice that of some PVs, generate power at a cost equal to late-generation nuclear plants, and the cost is dropping.

Biomass technologies focus on developing fast-growing plants that can be burned to extract the solar energy the plants store. A promising biomass technique involves growing certain types of algae in shallow ponds located in the desert. The algae produce an oil that can be extracted and used as fuel.

Ninety percent of the wind-generated electricity in the United States is produced by wind turbines located in three mountain passes in California. These three passes have been credited with having 80 percent of the world's usable wind supply, though experts estimate that under the right conditions, wind power could generate up to 5 percent of the nation's electricity. The California turbines accounted for 1 percent of California's electrical production in 1989. Production of new wind-powered facilities has been sluggish since tax credits for such construction ended in 1985 and because wind power is not competitive with fossil fuels at current prices.

Hydroelectric power, the cheapest power source, is the largest generator of electricity among the renewables. It has limited potential for further expansion, though, since all the most convenient rivers have already been dammed.

Altogether, renewables (solar, biomass, wind, hydro, and geothermal) account for about 9 percent of the electric power generated in the United States.

Discussion Questions

1. In deciding what to do about ARCO Solar, what factors should the company consider?
2. What is the potential of ARCO Solar's products?
3. Even if the products proved to be very promising, should ARCO sell its solar division? Why or why not?
4. What role should long-term energy price factors play? What role should social responsibility play?

Endnotes

1. This case was written by Mark C. Jankus with the editorial guidance of Alfred Marcus and Gordon Rands, both of the Curtis L. Carlson School of Management, University of Minnesota.
2. Donald Woutat, "Atlantic Richfield Plans to Sell ARCO Solar Unit, Cites Poor Prospects for Growth," *Los Angeles Times*, February 25, 1989, p. IV–1.
3. ARCO Annual Reports, 1977–1989.
4. "Waiting for the Sunrise," *Economist*, May 19, 1990, p. 95.
5. Solar Energy Industries Association, *15 Years in Business with the Sun* (Washington, D.C.: SEIA, 1989).
6. Bruce A. Jacobs, "Bill Yerkes—The Sunshine King," *Industry Week*, July 8, 1985, p. 66; James Bates, "Sale of ARCO Unit Casts Shadow on Future of Solar Energy Venture," *Los Angeles Times*, March 7, 1989, p. IV–1.
7. "1-MW Solar Facility Planned in California," *Electrical World*, May 1982, p. 25.
8. Don Best, "PV Power Goes On-Line in Hesperia," *Solar Age*, April 1983, p. 37.
9. "Solar Plant Is Largest," *Engineering News-Record*, April 7, 1983, p. 16; Alyssa A. Lappen, "Solar Lives!" *Forbes*, August 15, 1983, p. 104.
10. Don Best, "ARCO Goes Amorphous," *Solar Age*, November 1983, p. 15.
11. Karen Berney, "Why the Outlook Is Dimming for U.S.-Made Solar Cells," *Electronics*, September 23, 1985, p. 32; Bill Yerkes, "Big Oil's Future in Photovoltaics," *Solar Age*, June 1986, p. 14.
12. Don Best, "ARCO Solar Enters Joint Venture with Japanese Firm," *Solar Age*, May 1986, p. 20.
13. Kenneth R. Sheets, "Solar Power Still the Hottest Thing in Energy," *U.S. News & World Report*, May 2, 1983, p. 45.
14. Solar Energy Industries Association, *15 Years in Business with the Sun*.
15. Berney, "Why the Outlook Is Dimming for U.S.-Made Solar Cells," p. 32.

16. Matthew L. Wald, "U.S. Companies Losing Interest in Solar Energy," *New York Times*, March 7, 1989, p. 1.
17. Ibid.
18. Barbara Rosewicz, "ARCO is Trying to Sell Solar-Panel Unit, Reversing Move into Alternative Energy," *The Wall Street Journal*, February 27, 1989, p. B–3; Best, "ARCO Solar Enters Joint Venture with Japanese Firm," p. 20; Lad Kuzela, "Days are Sunny for Jim Caldwell," *Industry Week*, October 13, 1986, p. 75; "Waiting for the Sunrise," *Economist*, p. 95.
19. Berney, "Why the Outlook is Dimming for U.S.-Made Solar Cells," p. 32.
20. Department of Energy, "National Photovoltaics Program: 1987 Program Review," April 1988.
21. David E. Carlson, "Low-Cost Power from Thin-Film Photovoltaics," in T. B. Johansson, ed., *Electricity: Efficient End-Use and New Generation Technologies, and Their Planning Implications* (Washington, D.C.: American Council for an Energy Efficient Economy, 1989).
22. Mark Crawford, "ARCO Solar Sale Raises Concerns Over Potential Technology Export," *Science*, May 26, 1989, p. 918.
23. Bates, "Sale of ARCO Unit Casts Shadow," p. IV–1.
24. *Los Angeles Times*, March 7, 1989, p. IV–11.
25. Neelkanth G. Dhere, "Present Status of the Development of Thin-Film Solar Cells, *Vacuum* 39, nos. 7–8, p. 743.
26. "Waiting for the Sunrise," *Economist*, p. 95.
27. Dana Gardner, "Solar Cells Reach Efficiency Highs," *Design News*, April 24, 1989, p. 38.
28. Information in this section is adapted from James R. Chiles, "Tomorrow's Energy Today," *Audubon*, January 1990, p. 58.

CHAPTER

14

To Nature

Environmental Philosophy and Economics[1]

The Second Law of Thermodynamics states that there is always a waste byproduct of any process. It is the Law of Entropy, of irrevocable dissipation, not only of energy but of matter. The ultimate fate of the universe is chaos. All kinds of energy are gradually transformed into heat, and heat becomes so dissipated that humans cannot use it.

Adapted from Nicholas Georgescu-Roegen, "Energy and Economic Myths"[2]

Introduction and Chapter Objectives

Environmental and pollution problems are transforming the world economy. They not only drive technological innovation but also help shape the legal and economic context of management in the United States and abroad. This chapter introduces environmental issues and discusses the challenges that they pose to managers.

Three environmental challenges are addressed. The first is a philosophical challenge emanating from the ethical viewpoints of environmentalists, which is increasingly understood and appreciated by broad segments of the public but which is at odds with some of the tenets of business philosophy. The second challenge is in the area of public policy, where economic approaches have been developed and applied to pollution problems. They attempt to balance the costs and benefits of environmental protection. Their strengths and weaknesses need to be better understood by managers. The third challenge relates to the adequacy of scientific information for resolving thorny environmental issues. Ultimately, it is the adequacy of this information that determines how capable public officials are of resolving environmental disputes.

Waste Production as a By-Product of Business Activity

Businesses produce waste in the process of extracting raw materials from nature, transforming the raw materials into useful products, and transporting the finished products to markets. These essential business activities yield by-products which have undesirable qualities that have to be absorbed by nature. Thus, the physical environment not only provides goods and materials to the economy (see Chapter 13), but the goods and materials flow back again to the environment as wastes or residuals.[3]

In making business decisions, managers need to keep the costs and risks of waste generation in mind. They also need to be aware that preventing and managing wastes provide opportunities for business gain. Managers are in a position to profit from handling society's wastes creatively.

People have long recognized that nature is of critical importance as a source of material inputs to economic activity, but they have been less aware that the environment also plays an essential role as a receptacle for society's unwanted by-products. A simple materials balance model illustrates the relationship between the economy and the environment (see Exhibit 14–1). The production sector, which consists of mines and factories, extracts materials from nature and processes them into goods. Transportation and distribution networks move and store the finished products before they reach the point of consumption. The environment provides the material inputs needed to sustain economic activity and carries away the wastes generated by it.

Energy conversion supports materials processing by providing electricity, heating, and cooling services. It also aids in transportation and distribution. The environment provides essential elements for materials processing, including air and water, fossil fuels, agricultural products and timber, and minerals. The numerous by-products of these processes must be absorbed or assimilated by the environment. The by-products include air pollutants such as hydrocarbons, carbon monoxide, sulfur dioxide and particulate matter; solid wastes such as bottom and fly ash from combustion; radioactive wastes; and noise.

The useful energy from energy conversion helps make food, forest products, chemicals, petroleum products, metals, and structural materials such as stone, steel, and cement. The processes by which these materials are made, however, produce wastes, noise, and rubbish. Some waste materials are recovered by recycling, but most are absorbed by the environment. They are dumped in landfills, burned in incinerators, and disposed of as ash. They end up in the air, water, or soil.

EXHIBIT 14–1 From Nature to Nature: The Flow of Materials

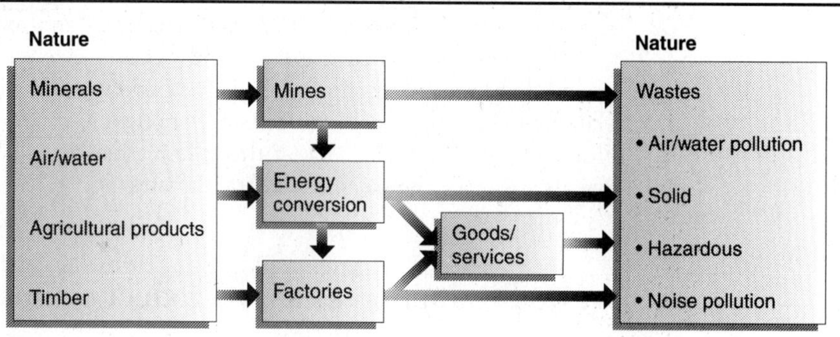

SOURCE: A. Freeman, R. Myrick, A. Haveman, and V. Kneese, *The Economics of Environmental Policy* (New York: John Wiley, 1973).

Through this process, households have useful products to consume, but households also generate waste, a large portion of which is discarded as garbage. All wastes find their way back to nature.

The law of the conservation of energy dictates that the material inputs and energy that enter the economy cannot be destroyed.[4] But they do change form, finding their way back to nature in a disorganized state as unwanted and perhaps dangerous by-products. The ultimate limits to economic growth—the splendid affluence achieved in developed countries—does not simply come from the availability of raw materials in nature. Nature's limited capacities to absorb wastes set a limit on how much an economy can produce.

Environmental Philosophy and the Environmental Movement

The environmental movement has made people conscious of the environmental degradation caused by production. At the start of the 1990s, the worldwide movement was showing strength and vitality that it had not been shown since the 1970s.[5] One of its primary attractions was that it provided a political alternative to the traditional ideologies of laissez-faire capitalism and socialism. People of different political persuasions could unite behind environmental causes. A New York Times/CBS poll in 1989 found that 79 percent of the American population agreed that "environmental improvements must be made regardless of cost." In 1981, when the same question was asked, only 45 percent accepted this statement (see Exhibit 14–2).

Labeled the Earth Decade, the 1990s were supposed to spawn a "new environmentalism" with features different from the "old." The new environmentalism also gained expression in the request made of companies to subscribe to the Principles of CERES (Coalition for Environmentally Responsible Economics). CERES is a coalition of leading social investors like the Calvert Social Investment Fund, environmental groups like the Sierra Club, public pension bodies including the states of New York and California, labor organizations, and other public interest groups. Started in the wake of the *Exxon Valdez* oil spill

EXHIBIT 14–2 Emerging Public Consensus on the Environment

- Americans believe the condition of the environment is worsening and consider the environment a top priority.
- Most believe that business, government, and consumers have not done enough to protect the environment.
- Most believe that creating a cleaner environment can actually create jobs and help the economy.
- Despite the recession, nearly three fourths of the public favor protecting the environment even at the risk of slower economic growth.
- Most have taken some personal action to improve the environment and consider themselves environmentalists.
- Trend-setting environmental consumers have changed their personal economic behavior to protect the environment.

SOURCE: Environment Opinion Study; also see *The Environment: Public Attitudes and Individual Behavior,* a study conducted by the Roper Organization, July 1990, New York.

EXHIBIT 14–3 Coalition for Environmentally Responsible Economics: Environmental Principles

Protection of the biosphere: Minimize the release of pollutants that may cause environmental damage.

Sustainable use of natural resources: Conserve nonrenewable resources through efficient use and careful planning.

Reduction and disposal of waste: Minimize the creation of waste, especially hazardous waste, and dispose of such materials in a safe, responsible manner.

Wise use of energy: Make every effort to use environmentally safe and sustainable energy sources to meet operating requirements.

Risk reduction: Diminish environmental, health, and safety risks to employees.

Marketing of safe products and services: Sell products that minimize adverse environmental impact and are safe for consumers.

Damage compensation: Accept responsibility for any harm the company causes the environment; conduct bioremediation, and compensate affected parties.

Disclosure of environmental incidents: Public dissemination of accidents relating to operations that harm the environment or pose health or safety risks.

Environmental directors: Appoint at least one board member who is qualified to represent environmental interests; create a position of vice president for environmental affairs.

Assessment and annual audit: Produce and publicize each year a self-evaluation of progress toward implementing the principles and meeting all applicable laws and regulations worldwide. Produce and distribute annual environmental audits to the public.

SOURCE: *Chemical Week,* September 20, 1989; CERES Coalition Handbook.

in 1989, CERES published its principles, which asked companies to reduce their wastes, use resources prudently, market safe products, and take responsibility for past harm (see Exhibit 14–3). Among the most prominent companies to subscribe to these principles are General Motors and Sun Oil (see the Case 14–A about General Motors at the end of this chapter).

The philosophy out of which the new environmentalism springs is an amalgam of diverse sources and ideas that combines numerous points of view. Some of the key aspects of this philosophy are noted in a sketch of the history of the movement as reflected in the ideas of some of its influential thinkers.[6]

Conservation versus Environmentalism

The conservation movement, which predates the environmental movement, has been anthropocentric (human- as opposed to nature-centered), technologically optimistic, and chiefly concerned with the efficient use of resources. It adheres to the tenets of scientific management; that is, it seeks to avoid waste by promoting the rational and efficient use of nature's riches and maximizing long-term yields, especially of renewable resources. Moreover, the leaders of the conservation movement as a whole have not generally questioned the system of political authority or the character of the economic system.

The environmental movement, in contrast, following the lead of George Perkins Marsh (1801–1882), has shown that the unintended negative effects of human economic activities on the environment are often greater than the positive effects. There are links, for example, between forest cutting and soil erosion and between the draining of marshes and lakes and the decline of animal life. Other early environmentalists such as John Muir (1838–1914) and Aldo Leopold (1886–1948) argued that humans are not above nature but a part of it. Nature is to be revered for the spiritual experience it provides. Humans should preserve nature not simply for its economic use but for its own sake—that is, what humans can learn from it.

The environmental movement has stressed technological limitations. Humans should neither control nor dictate to nature. The political and ideological dimensions of the antitechnological attitude have led to a questioning of the logic of private investment decisions, production, expansion, and economic growth. Environmentalism is often ascetic in its orientation: human beings should live simply, without display, excess, or ostentation.

Science and the Environment

Rachel Carson's best-selling *Silent Spring* helped ignite the modern environmental movement by alerting the public to the dangers of unrestricted pesticide use. She discussed the accumulation of insecticide residues in the fatty tissues of fish and birds that eat fish, the resistance insects develop to the toxins, the dispersion of the toxins far from their source, and the interaction of the toxins in the human body. Carson brought together the findings of toxicology, ecology, and epidemiology in a form accessible to the public. Melding scientific, moral, and political arguments, she made the connection between environmental politics and values and scientific knowledge.

Barry Commoner's *Science and Survival* continued in this vein,[7] but he explicitly expanded the scope of ecology to include everything in the physical, chemical, biological, social, political, economic, and philosophical worlds.[8] All these elements fit together, and they had to be understood as a whole. The symptoms of environmental problems are in the biological world, but their source is in economic and political organizations, and the solutions are political.

This combination of science and environmental politics has not been an easy one.[9] Many in the scientific community have opposed it, and many in the environmental community have been hostile to what science has had to offer. Scientists generally feel that they are obligated to improve the material condition of humanity. Environmentalists, on the other hand, often question whether additional material progress is necessary. Some environmentalists interpret the ecological perspective to mean that nature establishes immutable limits to human progress.

The distinction between engineering and the physical sciences on the one hand, and biology and the life sciences on the other, is important. Engineers and physicists generally have had greater faith in technology than biologists and life scientists, who are more sensitive to nature's limitations. Environmentalists generally criticize the "linear, non-integrated, hyper-specialized" character of engineering and the physical sciences as being responsible for many environmental problems. They hold that the narrowness of these disciplines means that environmental consequences and costs are not considered when human interference with natural processes takes place.[10]

Economics and the Environment

Environmentalists also tend to criticize businesses for their notions of efficiency and emphasis on economic growth. For example, environmentalists argue that managers often do not adequately consider the unintended side effects of growth. Managers need to supplement estimates of the economic costs and benefits of growth with estimates of effects that cannot be measured in economic terms. According to environmentalists, the burden of proof should rest with proponents of the new technologies. The new technologies should not be implemented simply because they advance material progress. In affluent societies, mere economic expansion is insufficient.

E. J. Mishan, an economist who contributed to the development of cost-benefit analysis, criticized society's obsession with growth.[11] Growth is promoted for many reasons—to restore the balance of payments, to make the nation more competitive, to create jobs, to reduce the deficit, to provide for the old and sick, and to lessen poverty. The public is encouraged to focus on statistics of productivity, balance of payments, and growth, while ignoring the obvious costs. The goal of many environmentalists is a **steady-state economy**, where population and per capita resource consumption stabilize. Herman Daly defines a steady-state economy as one in which "constant stocks of people and artifacts [are] maintained at some desired level . . . by the lowest feasible flows of matter and energy"[12] (see Exhibit 14–4).

steady-state economy One that maintains a constant level of people and goods with the lowest possible use of matter and energy.

The environmentalist Paul Hawken foresees "the next economy" as one based on products that last longer because they have been better designed. These products should

EXHIBIT 14–4 Business and Environmental Viewpoints Compared

	Business	*Environmentalists*
Imperative	Preservation of the organization	Preservation of natural systems
Key stakeholders	Shareholders, employees, customers	Natural systems, future generations
Basis for decisions	Short- to moderate-term return on investment	Long-term preservation of natural systems
View of natural resources	Means to achieve ends Use efficiently based on cost	Ends unto themselves Use only if needed and with proper safeguards in place
Regulating mechanisms	The market	Natural systems Government
View of economic growth	Desirable, depends on increased resource consumption	Not desirable when it requires resource consumption or pollution above sustainable limits

be lighter, stronger, and easier to repair; they also should consume less energy; and they will be traded again and again.[13]

Human services do not require much energy or material throughput and yet contribute to economic growth. Environmental cleanup and energy conservation also contribute to economic growth while having a positive effect on the environment. Environmentalists maintain that growth can continue, but only if the forms of growth are carefully chosen.

Free time would have to be a larger component of an environmentally acceptable future economy. Free time removes people from potentially harmful production. It also provides them with the time needed to make alternative production processes and techniques work, including organic gardening, recycling, public transportation, and home and appliance maintenance for the purposes of energy conservation.

The problem with reducing the rate of economic growth, as many environmentalists admit, is what it might do to the aspirations for economic mobility by the poor. Rising output satisfies the demands of the poor and middle class for better living conditions without challenging the privileges of the wealthy. Without economic expansion, the struggle for economic advancement might lead to social disorder.

Another requirement of an environmentally acceptable economy, then, is that people accept a "new frugality," a concept that also has been labeled "joyous austerity," "voluntary simplicity," and "conspicuous frugality."[14] (See the special feature, "Amory Lovins: The Soft Energy Path," about how environmentalists deal with trade-offs between energy and environmental requirements.)

The Warnings of Environmentalists

Environmentalists believe that the earth is in great danger. They see a catastrophe coming soon. The earth cannot tolerate the additional contaminants of industrial civilization. Environmentalists project current resource use and environmental degradation into the future to demonstrate that civilization is running out of critical resources[15] (see the special feature, "The Radical Environmentalism of Bill McKibben"). Human intervention, in the form of technological innovation and capital investment complemented by substantial human ingenuity and creativity, is insufficient to prevent this outcome unless drastic steps are taken soon. Numerous civilizations have been destroyed because they abused the environment.

Environmentalists use the laws of physics (the notion of entropy) to show how society systematically dissipates low-entropy, high-concentration forms of energy by converting them to high-entropy, low-concentration waste that cannot be used again except at very high cost. They also rely upon the laws of biology (the notion of carrying capacity) to show that the earth has a limited ability to tolerate the disposal of contaminants. They draw on engineering and management concepts to argue that exceedingly complex and dangerous technologies cannot be managed by humans without disastrous consequences for humanity and the environment.

Their philosophy does not blend in easily with the optimistic tenets of management theory and the materialistic beliefs of businesses. Environmentalists point out that nearly every economic benefit has an environmental cost, and that the sum total of the costs in an affluent society often exceeds the benefits.

Special Feature

Amory Lovins: The Soft Energy Path

For some environmentalists, the energy price shocks of 1973 and 1979 necessitated a reformulation of environmental values. This reformulation was guided by the theories and conclusions of Amory Lovins, a physicist whose books and writings on the "soft energy path" (SEP) were highly influential.[16]

After the 1973 oil embargo, environmentalists were on shaky ground. They opposed offshore oil drilling, the Alaskan pipeline, and additional coal burning, and favored auto emission reductions that had the potential to decrease automotive fuel efficiency. Their views appeared to increase U.S. vulnerability to OPEC. Lovins answered the criticism by proposing policies for an alternative energy future based on renewable resources and energy efficiency. His program promised to reduce pollution and at the same time increase economic growth.

Lovins argued that environmental problems were mainly problems of energy. Human beings had a choice between the so-called hard energy path (HEP) of the past and the soft energy path (SEP) of the future. HEP involved capital-intensive, nonrenewable energy sources that threatened the environment. SEP was based on the efficient use of energy in housing design and other areas. It also was based on obtaining increasing amounts of energy from renewable sources such as sunlight, geothermal energy, wood stoves, wind, water, waves and tides, plants, alcohol, and solar photovoltaics, which promised to be the ultimate soft technology. Lovins struggled against the presumption that the more energy people used, the better off they were. Another part of his analysis concerned the diseconomies of scale in distributing energy from central sites to dispersed consumers. Thus, the SEP was socially more decentralized in character.

Lovins was a major critic of nuclear power, which he opposed because of potential malfunctions, accidents on a scale not found in any other industry, radioactivity, and problems linked to reprocessing, terrorism, sabotage, and theft. Safety in the nuclear industry required a corps of highly trained, dedicated personnel. Alvin Weinberg, one of the founders of the nuclear power program in the United States, referred to this group as a "technological priesthood."[17] The managers of nuclear production in the United States had to be experts who stood apart from the rest of society and maintained rigorous standards to prevent accidents. Extensive psychological testing might be required to recruit these experts; to control them, it might be necessary to monitor their personal, psychological, and financial affairs. Capital punishment might be imposed for crimes committed by nuclear personnel. Lovins therefore believed that nuclear power could only succeed in centrally planned economies where control over individuals was greater and where bureaucratic power could override economic limitations.

Ultimately, it was the economic weaknesses of nuclear power that Lovins stressed. Nuclear power simply was not competitive in the free market. The basic premise of his position was that conservation and renewable resources would win in the marketplace only if the competition was fair.[18] Fair competition meant that the full social and environmental costs of a technology had to be included in the price consumers paid for energy. Lovins advocated what economists had proposed for the electric utilities, that is, marginal cost pricing that would charge users the full cost of new supplies. He also advocated flat or inverted rate structures, which would require large users to pay as much or more per unit of energy as small users.

Lovins's basic approach was in harmony with economic values. Price signals emanating from the marketplace would provide people with the incentives they needed to adapt and conserve. Environmentally benign alternatives to fossil fuel would be introduced in the context of a free market. The role of the government was to remove economic and political barriers and allow creative individuals to find solutions.

The noninterventionist approach of Lovins to economic policy was in contrast to that taken by most environmentalists. It was more in line with a theory of business management in which the market, not government, was sovereign. Lovins, however, provided managers with a major challenge. Implementing SEP meant replacing or substantially modifying virtually the whole capital stock of society—appliances, autos, housing, and highways. OPEC and SEP provided an impetus for environmentalists to accept new technologies and emerging industries, such as telecommunications, computers, and information processing that appeared environmentally benign. It also freed them from a politics of negativism and confrontation with the organized forces of society.

Not all environmentalists were happy with this approach.[19] They had technical disagreements; for instance, they pointed out that there would be competition between using biomass (plant material) for fuel and using it for food under the soft path. Further, even if the entire U.S. corn crop were converted to alcohol, it could provide only about 7.5 percent of the nation's need for motor fuel and only a little more than 1 percent of the total energy needed.[20] Environmentalists also pointed out that coastlines and mountain tops would have to be cluttered with windmills, and that endless acres of land would have to be devoted to biomass-derived fuels. Some environmentalists even argued that Lovins was wrong, and that the use of some nuclear power was benign because it produces large amounts of energy on a relatively small amount of land.

Public Policy and Economic Approaches

Public policy and economic approaches to environmental issues counter claims made by the environmentalists. They argue that limits to growth can be overcome by human ingenuity, that benefits afforded by environmental protection have a cost, and that government programs to clean up the environment are as likely to fail as the market forces that produce pollution.[21]

Overcoming the Limits to Growth

The traditional economic view is that production is a function of labor and capital. In theory, resources are unnecessary since labor and/or capital are infinitely substitutable for resources. Impending resource scarcity results in price increases that lead to technological substitution of capital, labor, or other resources for those that are in scarce supply. Price increases also create pressures for efficiency in use, which leads to reduced consumption.[22]

Thus, resource scarcity is reflected in the price of a given commodity. As resources become scarce, their prices rise accordingly, and price increases induce substitution and technological innovation.

People turn to less scarce resources that fulfill the same basic technological and economic needs provided by the resources no longer available in large quantities. To a large extent, the 1973 price shock induced by the Arab oil embargo and the 1979 price shock following the Iranian Revolution were alleviated by higher prices leading to the discovery of additional supplies and by conservation. By 1985, energy prices in real terms were lower than they were in 1973 (see Chapter 13).

People respond to signals about scarcity and degradation. They respond not only to price signals and not only in economic terms, but also in political, sociological, and psychological terms.[23] Governments express people's collective sentiments and start programs

Special Feature

The Radical Environmentalism of Bill McKibben

In Bill McKibben's best-selling book *The End of Nature*, the reverence for nature and resentment of intrusions from human technologies is absolute.[24] His concern is that technology and businesses have made everything on earth "manmade and artificial." Nature is being completely "crowded out" by human interference. McKibben expresses a sense of sadness and loss because "nature's independence" has been destroyed.[25] Humility toward nature is what he offers because nature is spiritually superior to human beings. McKibben believes that nature has rights over which human beings have no intrinsic authority. Humans should be prevented from doing whatever they want to nature. They should be stopped from exercising their dominion over nature for the sake of material progress.

What is surprising about McKibben is the extremism of his ideas, his willingness to sympathize with the notion that "individual suffering—animal or human—might be less important than the suffering of species, ecosystems, the planet."[26] For much of history, most humans have not experienced nature as kind and gentle but as harsh and dangerous, and therefore human beings have felt compelled to subordinate nature in order to protect themselves.

McKibben's extremism is partially a consequence of his desperation. As he sees it, there can no longer be "personal solutions." A person cannot escape from industrial society by "moving to the woods" because the woods are no longer inviolate. The solutions McKibben believes are necessary could entail infringements on individual rights that differ from the market-based solutions proposed by some environmentalists.

to counter the impending scarcity and degradation. Social movements begin to affect people's expectations and lifestyles. People's attitudes and values change. These feedback loops, which are expressive of human change in the face of information about natural resource scarcity and environmental degradation, are inadequately factored into the simple deterministic models.

Extrapolating past consumption patterns into the future without considering the human response is likely to be a futile exercise. As far back as the late 18th century, Thomas Malthus made pessimistic predictions about the limits to growth, but the lesson of modern history is one of technological innovation and substitution in response to price and other societal signals, not one of calamity brought about by resource exhaustion. In general, the prices of natural resources have been declining despite increased production and demand. Prices have fallen because of discoveries of new resources and because of innovations in the extraction and refinement process.[27]

Policy analysts and economists also question the motives and intentions of environmentalists. For example, the interests of the well-to-do are served by arguing that the prospects for additional growth are limited, thus closing channels for those who are less well off. The argument that growth is limited is also in the interests of those who want to manage humankind toward sustainability. According to some economists, a triad of the affluent—"members of the leisure class, intellectuals, and professionals"—may increase social tension and decrease the prospects for peaceful and democratic settlement of national and international conflicts because of their antigrowth pronouncements.[28]

Balancing the Costs and Benefits

Environmentalists might believe that total elimination of risk is possible and even desirable, but economists and policy analysts argue that the benefits of risk elimination have to be balanced against the costs.

Measuring risk is itself very complicated. It involves determining the conditions of exposure, the adverse effects, the levels of exposure, the level of the effects, and the overall contamination. Long latency periods, assessing the implications for human populations of laboratory studies of nonhuman animal species, and the impact of background contamination complicate these efforts. Simple cause-and-effect statements are out of the question.[29]

The most that can be said is that exposure to a particular contaminant *is likely* to have caused a particular disease. Risk has to be stated in terms of probabilities, not certainties, and it has to be distinguished from safety, which is a societal judgment about how much risk society is willing to bear. When comparing technological systems, different types of risks (e.g., from mining, radiation, industrial accidents, and climate impacts) have to be compared.[30] This type of comparison further complicates the judgments that have to be made.

Reducing risk involves asking the extent to which the proposed methods of reductions are likely to be effective, and how much they will cost. In theory, decision making could be left to the individual. Society could provide people with information (e.g., warning labels) and each person would then decide what to do—whether to purchase a product or service depending upon the environmental and resource consequences. However, relying upon individual judgments in the market may not adequately reflect society's preference for something of value such as air quality. Thus, social and political judgments are needed.

However much science reduces uncertainty in making social and political judgments, gaps in knowledge remain.[31] Scientific limitations open the door for political and bureaucratic biases that may not be rational. In some instances, politicians have framed legislation in ways that seriously hinder, if not entirely prohibit, the consideration of costs (e.g., the Delaney Amendment and the Clean Air Act). In other instances (e.g., the Presidents' Regulatory Review Council), they have explicitly forced cost factors to be considered. Moreover, cost factors can be considered in various ways. Analysts can carry out cost-effectiveness analysis in which they attempt to figure out how to achieve a given goal with limited resources, or they can carry out more formal risk-benefit and cost-benefit analyses in which they have to quantify both the benefits and the costs of risk reduction.[32]

Qualitative Judgment in Cost-Benefit Analysis

Economists and policy analysts are the first to admit that formal, quantitative approaches to balancing costs and benefits do not eliminate the need for qualitative judgments. Cost-benefit analysis was initially developed for water projects in which the issues were much less complicated than those society now faces.[33] For example, today we must determine the value of a magnificent vista obscured by air pollution or the loss to society if a plant or animal species becomes extinct. We ask what the opportunity costs are of spending vast sums on air pollution—sums that could have been invested in productivity enhancement and global competitiveness.

Equity issues, both interpersonal and intergenerational, cannot be ignored when doing cost-benefit analysis. The costs of air pollution reduction may have to be borne disproportionately by the poor in the form of higher gasoline and automobile prices. The costs of water pollution reduction, on the other hand, may be borne to a greater extent by the rich because these costs are financed through public spending. Regions dependent on dirty coal may find it in their interests to unite with environmentalists in seeking pollution-control technology. Pollution-control technology might save coal-mining jobs in West Virginia and the Midwest where the coal is dirty but impede the development of the coal-mining industry in the West where large quantities of clean-burning coal are located.[34]

intergenerational equity
Concern that interests of future generations will be ignored because they are not currently represented in the market.

Intergenerational equity also plays a role. Future generations have no current representatives in the market system or political process. To what extent should current generations hold back on their own consumption for the sake of posterity? Should Bentham's "achieving the greatest good for the greatest number" be modified to read "sufficient per capita product for the greatest number over time?"[35]

These questions are particularly poignant given the fact that most people living on earth today do not have "sufficient per capita product." Achieving moral consensus is extremely difficult in a worldwide community where there are many differences in cultural values. The extent to which political coercion should play a role in achieving global standards on such matters as consumption and procreation must be considered. Neither economics nor policy analysis has simple answers to these ethical issues, which require choosing an appropriate ethical rule.

Market and Government Failures

Most policy analysts and economists accept that markets ordinarily are the superior means for fulfilling human wants. In a market, transactions are made between consenting adults only when both, or several, parties feel they are likely to benefit. Society as a whole gains from the aggregation of individual transactions that take place because of the calculations individuals make about their own welfare. The wealth of a society grows by means of the invisible hand that offers spontaneous coordination with a minimum of coercion and explicit central direction. The intervention of government may be justified only under special circumstances (e.g., if markets are not perfectly competitive, market participants are not fully informed, or property rights are not appropriately assigned).

The lack of appropriately assigned property rights serves as a major justification for government intervention for the sake of natural resource and environmental protection. Since nature lacks a discrete owner, its rights may be violated by market exchanges between consenting parties. As a "common property resource," it is subject to overuse and degradation. Lacking a discrete owner, it is inadequately protected from transactions affecting it unless government is empowered to intervene.

externality
Imposition on society of costs that have not been incorporated into the price system.

Policy analysts and economists view this degradation of nature stemming from the lack of specific property rights as a type of **externality,** that is, the imposition on society of costs that have not been incorporated within the price system. The costs to society are costs to the nonconsenting third parties whose interests in nature have been violated. The parties consenting to the deal inflict damage without compensating the third parties because, without clear property rights, no entity will stand up for the rights of violated nature.

Nature's owners are a collectivity that is hard to organize. They are a large and diverse group that cannot easily pursue remedies in the legal system. In attempting to gain compensation for the damages done to nature, they suffer from the "free-rider" problem, which makes collective action difficult. The **free-rider problem** can be understood as, "Let someone else take care of it." No member of the group has a sufficient interest in the damage to pursue the matter further. Each only has a small amount to gain. Thus, only government intervention can protect the ownership rights of the collectivity in the natural world from harm.

free-rider problem
Enjoying the benefits, without paying the cost, of someone else's activities; applied to the damages done to nature, it means that collective action on nature's behalf is difficult to organize because no single member of a group has a significantly large interest.

Policy analysts and economists, however, point out that although collective action problems provide a rationale for government involvement, government involvement will not necessarily be effective in addressing the problem. Just as the market can fail so can the government.

Politicians may receive inadequate signals from concerned citizens. Voters may not understand the issues well enough to formulate coherent options to present to politicians. Political decision making also may be dominated by interest groups and biased information, partisanship, ideology, personal deals and arrangements, and financial constraints. In addition, the laws are carried out by civil servants who may not succeed because the goals of the legislation are too diverse or other problems exist that prove unmanageable: insufficient resources, overwhelming political opposition, higher priority for other issues, or sabotage caused by bureaucratic infighting.[36]

Economists and policy analysts speak of the "deadweight costs" of any government program that must be balanced against the proposed benefits. The term *internalities* describes these inefficiencies in public decision making.[37]

The Burden on Scientific Information

Policymakers face the burden of insufficient or inadequate scientific information. The political process puts an immense burden on science to give definitive answers to such questions as the potential for generating energy from exotic technologies like fusion and solar power and the risks to exposed populations from various chemicals. Science rarely stands up fully to this challenge.

Society needs all kinds of knowledge. It needs to know the true extent of resource limitations, the risks from environmental contaminants, and the expense of cleaning up these contaminants. It also requires knowledge about the strengths and weaknesses of solutions inside and outside the government to environmental problems. Unfortunately, many uncertainties persist.

How Scientific Knowledge Is Generated and Used

residual risk
Decisions made with partial knowledge where some element of risk is not completely understood.

Environmental issues compel consideration of how scientific knowledge is generated and used in public policy debates. Most important choices are made under conditions of "**residual risk**" or limited knowledge: complete knowledge is not available, but the decisions are not the result of mere guesswork either. Even if total knowledge were available, the appropriate actions to take based on this knowledge would not be apparent. Moreover,

Real-World Example

The Catalytic Converter Controversy

An example of the burden that scientific information puts on the political process is the catalytic converter controversy. To understand this controversy, it is necessary to go back to President Nixon's statement in 1970 about the Environmental Protection Agency (EPA), in which he stressed the need to merge pollution control programs so as to manage the environment "comprehensively." Nixon argued that energy and environmental issues should be considered together, but his plan for comprehensive environmental management was never realized.

At the time EPA was created in 1990, Senator Edmund Muskie, Democrat from Maine and head of the powerful Senate Subcommittee on Air and Water Pollution, was searching for "handles" that would force the automobile industry to achieve air quality goals by a specific date. He addressed a problem of regulatory administration that scholars have called "vague delegation of authority."[38] According to this doctrine, the typical regulatory statute has indefinite provisions. In effect, Congress says to the bureaucracy, "Here is the problem—deal with it." The regulatory agency, however, lacks the binding authority needed to coerce industry into complying with statutory requirements. The remedy for problems attributable to vague and ill-formed legislation is to draft statutes that have clear goals and explicit means of implementation.

Clean Air Act. The 1970 Clean Air Act mandated that auto manufacturers achieve a 90 percent reduction in hydrocarbon and carbon monoxide emissions by 1975, and a 90 percent reduction in nitrogen oxide emissions by 1976. Similar legislation passed in 1992 by California required that 2 percent of a car company's sales in that state have "zero emissions" by 1998 and that 10 percent have "zero emissions" by 2003 (see Case 14–A).

The air quality goals in the 1970 Clean Air Act, however, were "based on incomplete data and large margins of safety."[39] The required 90 percent reductions were taken from calculations of the highest levels of carbon monoxide emissions ever recorded in Chicago, the highest levels of nitrogen oxide emissions ever recorded in New York, and the highest level of hydrocarbon emissions ever recorded in Los Angeles.

Meanwhile, President Nixon warned the American people about the possibility of energy shortages. In 1973, he said that the United States had only 6 percent of the world's population, but it used one-third of the world's energy. Then, the Syrian and Egyptian armies launched their surprise attack on Israel, and the Arab oil-producing nations imposed an oil embargo. U.S. consumers experienced long waits in line for gasoline, truck drivers blockaded highways to protest fuel shortages and price increases, and the National Guard in some states had to be called out to maintain order.[40]

Extending Deadlines. President Nixon urged Congress in 1974 to modify the Clean Air Act, saying that the interim 1976–1977 auto emission standards should be extended so that manufacturers could concentrate on fuel economy. The automobile emission deadlines already had been extended once before, in 1973. Congress passed a law extending emission deadlines for another year, and the auto manufacturers were given the right to ask for still another one-year extension.[41]

To meet the emissions standards then in effect, auto makers had retuned existing engines. The problem was that the retuning reduced fuel economy by about 10 percent. EPA officials believed that if auto companies used catalytic converters, there would be no fuel penalty. The National Academy of Sciences backed up the EPA. Its studies showed that 90 percent reductions were possible in cars equipped with catalytic converters with no fuel penalty.[42]

Acid Emissions. The Ford Motor Company then asked for another extension, because sulfuric acid emissions had been discovered in catalytic converter discharges. John Moran, a health effects researcher located at Research Triangle Park—EPA's scientific complex near Durham, North Carolina—held an unauthorized press conference in the fall of 1973, alerting the public to the danger. He made public a study showing that although catalytic converters reduced hydrocarbons and carbon monoxide, they emitted significant amounts of sulfuric acid with probable adverse effects on public health. Moran's study pointed out that the converter, which was supposed to eliminate the health hazards caused by air pollution, caused a health problem. The acid emissions were minute, but in regions of high traffic density, they could be dangerous.

Moran's statements were attacked by EPA staff. They held their own unauthorized press conference and accused Moran of leaking information about health risks because he wanted EPA headquarters to continue funding his emissions-testing program. They claimed that only at sufficiently high concentrations were adverse health effects associated with sulfuric acid, but these concentrations were too small to make a difference and unlikely to occur anyway.

In 1975, Congress held hearings on amendments to the Clean Air Act. All the participants in the debate—environmentalists, industry, representatives of the administration, and experts—used the language and rhetoric of science to advance their positions and buttressed their arguments with some form of scientific study.[43] Ultimately, catalytic converters were allowed, but not without substantial delay in implementing the Clean Air Act. Predictably, environmentalists were disappointed, but General Motors, surprisingly, was also upset. It had spent hundreds of millions of dollars on catalyst research, built an expensive plant for fabricating catalytic converters, and signed long-term contracts to obtain the precious metals used in the converters—all steps that its U.S. competitors, Ford and Chrysler, had not taken (see Case 14–A, "Environmental Pressures and New Product Development at General Motors).

existing knowledge changes over time, allowing uncertainties to develop that make it more difficult to know what to do.[44]

Choices about policy and implementation are thus made and remade in response to a sorting-out process of what is known and unknown. This process depends on the imperfect capabilities of individuals, groups, and organizations to perceive risk and to act on the basis of their perceptions. Implicit in the process is an evaluation of "societal negligence." Derived from the classic formulation of Judge Learned Hand, **Hand's rule for assessing societal negligence** postulates that in evaluating risk, a "reasonable" person considers (*a*) the probability of injury, (*b*) the gravity of the injury should it occur, and (*c*) the burden of taking adequate precaution. Judge Hand argued that if the expected injury (probability × gravity) exceeds the costs of precaution and the defendant takes no action, then the defendant is negligent.[45]

Hand's rule for assessing societal negligence
In evaluating risk, a reasonable person considers the probability of injury times the gravity should it occur compared with the costs of precaution.

Extended to society at large, the costs of precaution should be balanced against the probability of harm times the costs of harm. Environmentalists are likely to emphasize the probability and costs of harm while downplaying the burdens of precaution. When the expected danger is great, the movement's prevailing philosophy of more government involvement, slower growth, and simpler living can be implemented. In contrast, corporations are likely to focus on the burdens of precaution, since these burdens fall disproportionately on them and have far-reaching implications for their products and how these products are made.

The government should be guided by rational and scientific judgments, but because the uncertainties are great, both elected officials and bureaucrats are swayed by the viewpoints of environmentalists and business. Environmentalists and business groups contribute information to the debate, and they sponsor studies and interpret existing studies in accord with their point of view. Neutral experts also contribute information to the debate. In the end, public officials are caught in the middle, having to make binding decisions based on uncertain information.

Conclusions

Waste products are made when businesses produce any good or service. These waste products have to be disposed of properly. The capacities of natural systems to absorb this waste are an ultimate limit on the economic expansion a society can achieve.

This chapter has described different approaches to environmental problems. Environmentalists emphasize the limits of nature's capacity to absorb waste. Public policy analysts and economists show how these limits can be overcome by the price system and government; they admit that regulation is needed in some instances but warn that the value of regulation has to be balanced against the costs. Cost-benefit analysis is the way policy analysts/economists prefer to deal with environmental issues, but cost-benefit analysis, as public policy analysts and economists will admit, has qualitative components. It does not get around important normative considerations that play a critical role.

The knowledge that public officials have about environmental issues is also important. This chapter concludes with a discussion of the scientific and other uncertainties encountered in implementing environmental policies.

Discussion Questions

1. Describe the flow of materials from nature to nature. What effect does this flow have on economic growth?
2. Describe the major tenets of the conservation movement. Compare its tenets with those of environmentalism.
3. What contributions did Rachel Carson and Barry Commoner make to the environmental movement?
4. How do environmentalists view economic growth? How are their views on this topic different from the views of economists?
5. What is the soft energy path? How does it differ from the hard energy path?
6. What if the price system was fixed as Lovins advocated? Would energy choices made by society be different? Why or why not?
7. How do you view the environmentalism of Bill McKibben? Does nature deserve absolute respect?
8. According to policy analysts/economists, how are limits to growth to be overcome?
9. What are some of the arguments for and against cost-benefit analysis? What are the appropriate uses for cost-benefit analysis?

10. What do the deadweight costs of any government action have to do with solving environmental problems?
11. What does the regulatory problem "vague delegation of authority" refer to? How does the 1970 Clean Air Act approach this problem?
12. In 1975, when Congress held hearings on the Clean Air Act, what should General Motors have done? What kind of arguments should it have made? What types of analysis should it have used to support its arguments?
13. What does the term *residual risk* suggest? How important is it in describing environmental issues?
14. What is Judge Learned Hand's rule? To what extent is it helpful in determining if society has been negligent?

Endnotes

1. I would like to acknowledge the assistance of the following students in my course on business and the environment who contributed to parts of Chapters 13 and 14. Dan Batterman, Jose Blando, Therese Bodine, Chris De Vanes, Franz Hofmeister, Rob Hogg, Pat Keran, Debora Knops, Brent Korengold, Carin Peterson, Gregory Steininger, Mark Van Wie, Rosemary Ward, and Warren Winkelman. My teaching assistant Gordon Rands has made a substantial contribution to the ideas expressed here.
2. N. Georgescu-Roegen, *Energy and Economic Myths* (New York: Pergamon, 1976).
3. A. Freeman, R. Myrick, H. Haveman, and A. V. Kneese. *The Economics of Environmental Policy* (New York: John Wiley, 1973); A. V. Kneese, *Economics and the Environment* (New York: Penguin Books, 1977).
4. Georgescu-Roegen, *Energy and Economic Myths.*
5. D. Kirkpatrick, "Environmentalism: The New Crusade," *Fortune*, February 12, 1990, pp. 44–55; R. Irwin, "Clean and Green," *Sierra*, November/December 1985, pp. 50–56; J. Crudele, "Environmental Issues Could Be Hot Item of '90s," *Minneapolis Star and Tribune*, March 18, 1990, p. 2D; R. Buchholz, A. Marcus, and J. Post, *Managing Environmental Issues: A Case Book* (Englewood Cliffs, N.J.: Prentice Hall, 1990).
6. R. Carson, *Silent Spring* (Cambridge, Mass.: Houghton-Mifflin, 1962); R. Paehlke, *Environmentalism and the Future of Progressive Politics* (New Haven: Yale University Press, 1989), pp. 13–41, 76–143; R. Nash, ed., *The American Environment* (Reading, Mass.: Addison-Wesley, 1968); R. Revelle and H. Landsberg, ed., *America's Changing Environment* (Boston: Beacon Press, 1970); L. Caldwell, *Environment: A Challenge to Modern Society* (Garden City, N.Y.: Anchor Books, 1971); J. M. Petulla, *Environmental Protection in the United States* (San Francisco: San Francisco Study Center, 1987).
7. B. Commoner, *Science and Survival* (New York: Viking Press, 1963).
8. B. Commoner, *The Closing Circle: Nature, Man and Technology* (New York: Bantam Books, 1971).
9. Paehlke, *Environmentalism and the Future of Progressive Politics*, pp. 13–41, 76–143.
10. Ibid.
11. Cited in Paehlke, *Environmentalism and the Future of Progressive Politics.*
12. Ibid., p. 130.
13. P. Hawken, J. Ogilvy, and P. Schwartz, *Seven Tomorrows: Toward a Voluntary History* (New York: Bantam Books, 1982); Paehlke, *Environmentalism and the Future of Progressive Politics.*

14. Paehlke, *Environmentalism and the Future of Progressive Politics*, p. 136.
15. D. Mann and H. Ingram, "Policy Issues in the Natural Environment," in *Public Policy and the Natural Environment*, ed. H. Ingram and R. K. Goodwin (Greenwich, Conn.: JAI Press, 1985), pp. 15–47.
16. A. B. Lovins, *Soft Energy Paths: Toward a Durable Peace* (New York: Friends of the Earth International, 1977).
17. Paehlke, *Environmentalism and the Future of Progressive Politics*.
18. Ibid.
19. J. R. Emshwiller, "Energy-Efficient Guru Sees Fertile Field for Start-Ups," *The Wall Street Journal*, October 30, 1990, p. B2.
20. Paehlke, *Environmentalism and the Future of Progressive Politics*.
21. A. Nichols and R. Zeckhauser, "The Perils of Prudence," *Regulation*, November/December 1986, pp. 13–25; J. F. Morrall, "A Review of the Record," *Regulation*, November/December 1986, pp. 25–35; Buchholz, Marcus, and Post, *Managing Environmental Issues: A Case Book*.
22. A. Kneese, "The Economics of Natural Resources," in *Population and Resources in Western Intellectual Traditions*, ed. M. Teitelbaum and J. Winter (Washington, D.C.: The Population Council, 1989), pp. 281–309.
23. Mann and Ingram, "Policy Issues in the Natural Environment."
24. B. McKibben, *The End of Nature* (New York: Random House, 1989).
25. D. Kevies, "Paradise Lost," *New York Review of Books*, December 21, 1989, pp. 32–38.
26. Cited in Kevies, "Paradise Lost," p. 35.
27. Kneese, "The Economics of Natural Resources."
28. W. Rostow cited in Mann and Ingram, "Policy Issues in the Natural Environment," pp. 146–48.
29. W. Lowrance, "Choosing Our Pleasures and Our Poisons: Risk Assessment for the 1980s," in *Technology and the Future*, ed. A. Teich (New York: St. Martins Press, 1990), pp. 180–207.
30. Mann and Ingram, "Policy Issues in the Natural Environment."
31. A. A. Marcus, "Risk, Uncertainty, and Scientific Judgment," *Minerva* 2 (1988), pp. 138–52.
32. L. Lave, *The Strategy of Social Regulation* (Washington, D.C.: The Brookings Institution, 1981).
33. Kneese, "The Economics of Natural Resources."
34. Mann and Ingram, "Policy Issues in the Natural Environment."
35. Ibid.
36. A. Marcus, *Controversies in Energy Policy* (Beverly Hills, Calif.: Sage Press, 1992).
37. Mann and Ingram, "Policy Issues in the Natural Environment," p. 41; J. Q. Wilson, *American Government: Institutions and Policies* (Lexington, Mass.: D. C. Heath, 1980).
38. See R. Noll, *Reforming Regulation: An Evaluation of the Ash Council Proposals* (Washington, D.C.: Brookings Institution, 1971); and T. Lowi, *The End of Liberalism* (New York: W. W. Norton, 1969).
39. Ibid., p. 30.
40. Ibid., p. 91.
41. *Energy Supply and Environmental Coordination Act of 1974*, Public Law 93–319 (88 Stat. 248) 1974.
42. *Report on Automotive Fuel Efficiency* (Washington, D.C.: EPA February, 1974); J. Quarles, *Cleaning Up America* (Boston: Houghton Mifflin, 1976), p. 194; and Committee on Motor Vehicle Emissions, *Semi-Annual Report* (Washington, D.C.: National Academy of Sciences, February 12, 1973).
43. Public Law 91–604 (84 Stat. 1676), December 31, 1970. See S. Hays, "Clean Air: From the 1970 Act to the 1977 Amendments," *Duquesne Law Review* 17, no. 1 (1978–79), p. 40.
44. Marcus, "Risk, Uncertainty, and Scientific Judgment."
45. R. Cooter and T. Ulen, *Law and Economics* (Glenview, Ill.: Scott, Foresman, 1988).

Case 14–A
Environmental Pressures and New Product Development at General Motors[1]

The companies in the automobile industry are facing product development and strategy challenges in response to environmental pressures.[2] How will these challenges affect new product development? How should the companies respond? General Motors (GM) policy board, the most important decision-making body at the company (see Case 2–A) has asked your consulting group A-LINEMENT to prepare an analysis.

The environmental pressures the automobile companies confronted could be seen in narrow terms: a tailpipe emissions problem. The solutions were improved catalytic converters and the use of reformulated gasoline (methanol or ethanol; see Case 15–B, "Archer Daniels Midland and Ethanol," following the Chapter 15). The pressures also could be seen in broad terms: issues such as global warming, oil dependence, and national security. The solutions involved taking away the subsidies for driving, taxing gasoline, restricting motor-vehicle traffic, and providing incentives for public transportation. The strategic implications for the automakers in response to these challenges covered many facets of their business from products, markets, competition, R&D, and strategic alliances to corporate politics.

The Evolution of U.S. Policy

The evolution of U.S. environmental policy from 1970 to 1990 was based on the principle that vague delegation of administrative responsibilities would not work. Without Congress mandating specific timetables to force technological change, the automobile companies would not budge. Thus, the 1970 Clean Air Act required that automakers achieve a 90 percent reduction in motor-vehicle emissions by 1975–1976. They could ask for a single one-year delay based on economics, which they sought and obtained in 1973. In 1974, Congress again deferred implementation of the 90 percent reductions for a year because of a possible conflict between reducing energy use and lowering emissions. Arguments by the automobile industry that it could not meet the deadlines and concerns about possible "acid emissions" led Congress to pass in 1977 amendments to the Clean Air Act which again postponed implementation. The auto companies had until 1982–1983 to achieve the original 90 percent reductions.

By 1990, they had made substantial progress: 95 percent reductions in emissions of carbon monoxide and hydrocarbons and 75 percent reductions in emissions of nitrogen oxides. However, most major urban areas in the United States failed to meet air quality standards for some period of time during a typical year. Los Angeles, for instance, exceeded these standards for 146 days in 1990. While each vehicle emitted less pollution, more vehicles were on the road, traveling additional miles, and often improperly maintained. Vehicles miles traveled had more than doubled since 1970, and they were going up at a rate of 3 percent per year.

New Technology Forcing Standards

Under pressure from federal authorities, the California Air Resources Board (CARB) established new technology forcing standards in 1990. It mandated a phase-in of low-emission, ultralow-emission, and zero-emission vehicles. By 1997, 25 percent of the new cars sold in the state would have to be low-emission vehicles (LEVs) and 2 percent ultralow-emission vehicles (ULEVs).[3] By

EXHIBIT 1 California's Vehicle Emission Goals for 2001 and 2003
(percentage of all cars that must meet goals)

	LEVs	*ULEVs*	*ZEVs*
2001	90%	5%	5%
2003	75	10	10

1998, 48 percent would have to be LEVs, 2 percent ULEVs, and 2 percent zero-emission vehicles (ZEVs). California's goals for the years 2001 and 2003 are listed in Exhibit 1.

California represented 14–18 percent of the U.S. new car market, and 10 percent of the market for new cars sold worldwide. U.S. automakers originally opposed the California standards. When New York and Massachusetts issued rules for adopting the California program and other northeastern states, Illinois, and Texas considered similar moves, the auto companies issued a warning: With unproven technology, to meet these standards on a third of all new vehicles sold in the United States was too big a risk. The auto companies tried unsuccessfully to prevent the EPA from approving the state plans. They maintained that the costs were too high and that tailpipe standards should be given a chance to work.

An Electric Vehicle (EV) Industry

The only viable way to meet the requirement to sell a car that had zero emissions at the source (a ZEV) was with an electric vehicle (EV). The standards in effect in California and other states would create a potential market for 1.3 million EVs by the year 2003 (see Exhibit 2).

Because they emitted no exhaust at the source, electric vehicles (EVs) were the only technology that seemed able to achieve the zero emissions goal.[4] Other promising technologies such as hydrogen cars appeared to be too early in the development stage.

Advantages of EVs. EVs had the following advantages over conventional cars that were powered by internal combustion engines (ICEs)[5]:

1. *Eliminate almost all air pollution*. More than 60 percent of the air pollution in the United States was produced by motor vehicles with ICEs. Air pollution contributed to high health care costs, the destruction of plant and animal life, and the degradation of ecosystems. EVs produced a 10th of the emissions produced by ICEs, even after taking into consideration the electric power generation needed for recharging. An Electric Power Research Institute (EPRI) study showed that EVs would bring about a 99 percent reduction in carbon monoxide, a 98 percent reduction in hydrocarbons, and a 92 percent reduction in nitrogen oxides in California. Using offpeak power, more than 20 million EVs could be charged without building more power plants. If the power for recharging came from solar, wind, or other renewable energy sources, there would be virtually no pollution.

2. *Reduce U.S. dependence on foreign oil*. EVs could reduce U.S. dependence on petroleum from unstable Middle Eastern countries. The U.S. consumed more than 70 million barrels of oil a day, acquiring a huge trade deficit. Huge military expenditures were required to protect the oil sources. With less need for foreign oil, fewer environmental disasters such as the oil spills off the coasts of Alaska and Scotland would be likely to occur.

3. *Eliminate noise pollution*. EVs produced no noisy exhaust, valve-train clatter, or knocking. They made for a more serene urban setting less disrupted by incessant traffic noise.

EXHIBIT 2 The Potential Electric Vehicle (EV) Market in the U.S.

	ZEVs as Percent of Market	Number of ZEV's in California	Number of ZEVs in 12 Northeastern states
1998	2%	40,000	100,000
1999	2	40,000	100,000
2000	2	40,000	100,000
2001	5	100,000	250,000
2002	5	100,000	250,000
2003	10	200,000	500,000
		520,000	1,300,000

SOURCE "Why Wait for Detroit?" South Florida Electric Auto Association.

4. *Energy efficient*. EVs did not waste energy when stopped in traffic. On a typical battery charge costing a dollar, an EV could travel between 50 and 100 miles. In contrast, a typical gasoline-powered passenger car could go only 25 miles on one dollar's worth of gasoline. In Europe and Asia, where gasoline costs three to four times more than in the United States, the cost advantage was even greater.

5. *Safety*. EVs were safe. Highly flammable fuel, leaking from fuel tanks, did not pose a risk. Moreover, another common cause of highway accidents, belt and hose failures, could not happen because EV motors were much simpler than ICEs. They had only one moving part.

6. *Eliminate costly maintenance*. EV engines did not require the extensive maintenance necessary with an ICE. The engines did not have points, plugs, exhaust pipes, air filters, fuel injectors, radiators, chokes, head gaskets, valve grinds, rings, manifolds, mufflers, hoses, pistons, caps, rotors, distributors, crankcases, head gaskets, or catalytic converters. Tune-ups, spark-plug replacements, oil changes, and other costly maintenance activities were entirely eliminated.

Disadvantages of EVs. The disadvantages of EVs also were significant. The most significant objection was that EVs cost substantially more than conventional vehicles. U.S. automakers estimated that in the first few years of production, new EVs built from the ground up, would cost at least $21,000 more than similar gasoline-powered vehicles. Converting existing vehicles to electric power, however, could be achieved for as little as $5,000. Many small companies in the United States and Europe already made conversions or offered conversion kits to consumers. Conversions of VW Rabbits by Herb Adams V.S.E. cost $19,000; it sold conversion kits for $7,000. Sebring Auto Cycles of Florida did conversions of Dodge Colts for $16,000. The Solar Car Corporation offered electric retrofits of Ford Festivas with regenerative braking, built-in battery chargers, and solar-assisted charges for $25,000.

Purpose-built EVs, however, had many advantages over conversions. AC Propulsion, Inc., of San Diego built high-performance EV drivetrains that gave performance as exciting as a sports car. Denmark's Kewet Motors made a small neighborhood car for picking up groceries or doing household errands. In France, Renault had joined forces with media conglomerate Matra to produce a futuristic, bubble shaped, electric minicar called the Zoom. This car was so small that it could be parked with its head facing the curb.

The designers of a purpose-built car had the opportunity to integrate the latest in custom-built EV components into the vehicle. For example, they could mount efficient, high-speed AC (alternating current) motors on the wheels or another optimum location; use superlight, rigid high-tech composite materials for the body; install energy-saving high-pressure tires; and put in advanced charging devices that could reduce charging time by as much as 90 percent while tripling battery life. A purpose-built EV would be smaller, lighter, and sleeker than a converted vehicle; it would have better handling characteristics and might have the same amount of passenger space and power.

Calstart (a consortium of California aerospace and high-tech companies, electric utilities, environmental groups, labor unions, and research institutions) had built a one-of-a-kind, showcase vehicle, which cost more than $1 million (see Exhibit 3). This vehicle combined some of the best features developed by EV component suppliers. With large production runs, manufacturing costs undoubtedly would fall. Daniel Rivers, the manager of light-duty electric vehicles for Hughes Electronics, estimated that a $4,000 AC drive motor would fall in price to $500 or lower with production runs of 5,000 to 10,000. An EV needed six heavy-duty bipolar transistors that converted direct battery current into alternating current. These transistors cost $325 a piece, but they would drop in price below $100 with larger production runs.

Relying on Conversion Vehicles. Conversion vehicles had many disadvantages, not the least of which were poor driving characteristics. A writer for *Popular Science* described the sensation of driving a converted Mazda Miata:

> They perform well enough to serve as functional cars . . . Gasoline-engine vibrations are missing, and the throaty exhaust note is replaced by the soft, high-pitched whine of an electric motor. But initial pleasure begins to fade . . . at 3,350 pounds, it's more than one and a half times the weight of the production Miata. Even with power-assist steering, maneuvering . . . becomes an arm-tiring exercise . . . Acceleration is a chore for the engine and taxing for the driver . . . quick response and taut handling . . . is negated by . . . weight.[6]

Most of the world's automakers, however, did not believe that sufficient time was available for the design, development, and testing of an entirely new EV vehicle. To keep costs at a reasonable level, they planned on conversions for their first offerings.

Rather than a totally redesigned car, GM considered a converted Geo Prizm.[7] Chrysler decided to convert to electric some of its next generation of minivans.[8] Ford considered an electric version of the Taurus or some other popular model. Honda would convert Civics, and France's PSA decided to introduce 10,000 electric Peugeots and Citroëns by 1995.

Mercedes and BMW were taking a different route. They had combined with the Swiss watchmaker, Swatch, to produce a prototype city car called the Swatchmobile, which would be available for purchase in 1997.

The aim of Japanese automakers was to have 200,000 EVs in operation by the year 2000. Both Toyota and Nissan had prototype electric vehicles that used nickel cadmium, as opposed to lead-acid, batteries. The Japanese companies, however, were silent about their specific plans.

Range and Refueling Times

Another objection to EVs was the unacceptability of their range of only 50 to 70 miles per seven-hour charge time. Drivers were accustomed to up to 400 miles of uninterrupted driving before refueling. They could fill up a gasoline-powered vehicle in less than five minutes. Battery-powered vehicles could not match this performance.

For 1997, the technology of choice remained lead-acid batteries, currently found in the majority of cars. Researchers were getting better range with advanced lead-acid batteries. Their cost of $1,500–2,000 a pack was relatively cheap. Their weight was going down. Electrosource of Austin, Texas, for example, had succeeded in coating the lead onto woven glass fibers instead of casting it.

Electronic Power Technology of Atlanta had made a major advance in charging times. Its pulse-charging systems were able to charge lead-acid battery systems in 10 to 15 minutes and triple the

EXHIBIT 3 Features of Calstart's Showcase Vehicle

Feature	*Supplier*	*What the Component Does*
Bipolar lead-acid batteries	Trojan Battery	Offers increased vehicle range, greater acceleration, and rapid recharging
Brushless DC motor	I Won Motronics	High efficiency, lightweight, low-cost brushless motor, superior low-speed torque, cool-running, multiphase design
Energy management system	Amerigon	Extends and predicts range by controlling charging and optimizing energy flow to electronic systems
Motor controller	Delta Tau Delta	Maximizes efficiency and enhances acceleration and stopping on inclines through motor current feedback
Semiconductors	International Rectifier	High-voltage, high-current switches for motor controller, battery charger, electric brakes, etc.
Regenerative energy braking system	Dowty Aerospace	Extends driving range by using energy lost during braking to charge batteries
Inductive charging system	Hughes Power Control Systems	Efficient, safe battery charging through electromagnetic, plastic-coated coupler connection
Aluminum frame	Kaiser Aluminum	Lightweight, recyclable frame suitable for cost-effective, low-volume manufacture
Underbody assembly	Fairchild Manufacturing	Recyclable, lightweight panel reduces vehicle drag; removable portions allow easy access
Formidable finish	Avery Deninson	Dry paint film for plastic parts produces smooth, high-gloss surfaces, applied in pollution-free, safe manner
EV tires	Pirelli Armstrong	New tread design and sidewall compounds offer 30% less rolling resistance and 15% lower weight

SOURCE: Calstart Showcase Electric Vehicles.

life of the batteries. An average battery system might last 45,000 miles or more instead of only 15,000 miles, and it would need to be replaced far less frequently.

Another objection was the lack of an infrastructure for refueling. However, California had started work on building a network of charging systems. The U.S. government had given Calstart $20 million to develop an EV infrastructure, and it was putting in place the needed charging outlets in houses and garages.

Other Battery Types. Japanese and European consortia were spending vast sums of money on battery research. The Department of Energy and U.S. automakers also tried to match this spending.

They formed an Advanced Battery Consortium, a $260-million, four-year project to do research on battery technology. Many battery types, other than lead-acid, were under investigation. The Japanese had developed lithium polymer and nickel-metal-hydride batteries for consumer products and were attempting to scale them up for electric cars. They had a large lead on U.S. companies. Hydro-Quebec and 3M had a version of the lithium polymer battery that could get three times the performance of lead-acid batteries. GM was working with Ovonic Battery in Troy, Michigan, on a metal hydride battery similar to that found in laptop computers.[9]

Mercedes and BMW backed the sodium-nickel-chloride battery. Like metal hydride, it had double the energy of the lead-acid battery, but current flowed out of it slowly, making it difficult to accelerate or climb hills. Usually, a battery that released electrons rapidly was good at climbing hills and acceleration, but poor at long-range storage. Israel's Electric Fuel had a zinc-air system that had excellent performance on both dimensions, but part of the battery had to be replaced during recharging. Asea Brown Boveri, the Swiss engineering company, experimented with a sodium-sulfur battery, developing a prototype vehicle with a range of 160 miles. During recharging, however, the vehicle caught fire, raising safety concerns. The main problem with any new battery system was scaling up to large production runs. No one had yet figured out how to solve the difficulties of mass producing a new battery type.

The quest for a workable EV had also stimulated research on other power sources including fuel cells, which consumed hydrogen without combustion; flywheels, which stored energy in rapid disk rotation; and charge-storing capacitors.[10] Besides their costs, a problem with fuel cells was their emission of small amounts of air pollutants, which might disqualify them as zero-emission vehicles. For fuel cells to be viable, this problem had to be overcome.

A Hybrid Vehicle

A hybrid vehicle that merged systems and techniques from different technologies was likely to generate the best overall product. Rosen Motors of Los Angeles, founded by the same family of venture capitalists that started Compaq Computer, was committed to a lightweight hybrid EV with a gas-turbine engine. Volvo's Environmental Concept Car was based on the same idea. It had both an electric and a supplemental diesel engine. It was a roomy family car, big enough for four adults and a child. It was lightweight and very aerodynamic. With a turbine engine and high-speed generator for onboard recharging, it had a cruising range of more than 400 miles, yet could operate in cities exclusively on batteries.[11]

Ford had a similar hybrid vehicle. The Double Action Cruiser was based on the Escort Wagon. It had an electric motor powered by a nickel-cadmium battery pack that provided a 30-mile range for city driving. When the car accelerated to 40 miles per hour, the gas engine automatically took over. When an extra surge was needed to pass another car, the electric motor became active again and joined the gasoline engine in propelling the vehicle.[12]

The Impact Prototype. General Motors had an early lead in EV technology. Its Impact prototype exhibited in the late 1980s was capable of going from 0 to 60 miles per hour in 60 seconds. Fast and nimble, the Impact's light plastic body and custom-made suspension were well designed to handle the heavy weight of the batteries.

> The motor . . . provides something more akin to thrust than acceleration; it's a stepless, nearly noiseless sensation of motion that is always instantly on tap . . . The ride is superb, the handling well-mannered, and the brakes feel solid underfoot . . . the Impact could stick with any sports sedan on the road today . . . the car leaves the impression, not so much as a surprisingly good electric car, but as possibly the best-handling and best-performing small car that GM has ever turned out.[13]

Twenty-seven 12-volt lead-acid batteries weighing 1,100 pounds were needed to provide the Impact with its power (its total curb weight was 2,910 pounds). The Impact had regenerative brakes to convert the mechanical energy generated by the slowing of the wheels into usable electricity to power the motor. The batteries had to be replaced every 20,000 to 30,000 miles at a cost of $2,000.

Hughes Aircraft came up with a solution for charging time: a 220-volt charging stand that looked like a parking meter. An inductive-charged coupler plugged into a charging port between the headlights. After a 90-mile drive, it took only two hours to fully recharge the batteries.

However, GM decided not to go through with production plans when it concluded that the Impact was too small, cost too much, and did not go far enough on a charge (only about 80 miles) to sell. Currently, all U.S. automakers believed that there was no real market for EVs. They would have to price EVs well below cost and then charge more on ICE vehicles to make up the difference, a tactic that was bound to alienate consumers. Therefore, automakers might be tempted to pay a fine of $5,000 for every vehicle that fell short of their quota. Another possibility was that they might decide to buy credits from start-up companies that made EVs, rather than to offer many vehicles on their own.

Start-up companies like U.S. Electricar welcomed the provision in California's mandate that allowed the automakers to trade for EV permits. Electricar already had a deal with Hughes Aircraft to buy advanced motor and electronic control systems to produce electric-powered Chevy S-10 trucks and Geo Prizms. It was trying to obtain engineless vehicles from GM in return for the EV credits it would earn from their sale. It had targeted fleet sales to organizations like the Postal Service, rather than individual buyers.[14] Other EV start-up companies like Solectrica Corporation of Massachusetts, which was begun by MIT-trained engineers, were aiming to become suppliers and developers of parts for the automakers.

Delaying Implementation of EV Mandate. U.S. automakers, however, were trying to delay implementation of the electric car mandate. In February 1994, they accelerated their efforts to convince regulators in California and the Northeast to postpone the 1998 deadline. In separate announcements, GM President John Smith and Ford Chairman Alexander Trotman claimed that without a better battery the auto industry could not meet the deadline. Trotman was very aggressive in his stand, but Smith took a softer position: "As proud as we are of the Impact and all the rave reviews it has received, we think we can make the electric vehicle more practical and less costly if given more time."[15]

GM was lending out 50 Impacts for two-week test trials around the country. It thought that consumers would not be interested in a car that cost considerably more than a gasoline-powered vehicle and which went less than 100 miles before it needed recharging. The company was surprised when 9,300 people in California and 14,000 people in New York made requests to test-drive the vehicle.

Meanwhile, regulators in California, 12 northeastern states, and the District of Columbia, despite intense industry lobbying, reaffirmed their commitment to the 1998 deadline. A 1994 CARB report maintained that the technology to meet the standards was here. Governor Pete Wilson of California appeared ready to stand behind the deadline. With the failure of their lobbying, the automakers sought new ways to collaborate to meet the deadline. Negotiations held in 1993 broke down because of different views held by the three companies.

The oil industry, meanwhile, was beginning to show its opposition. It quietly financed what appeared to be a grass-roots, consumer campaign against proposed utility company investments in electric vehicle infrastructure. The campaign was run by Woodward & McDowell, a California public relations firm. A mailing to 200,000 California ratepayers did not acknowledge oil company financing. The utility companies, in opposition, formed an alliance with environmentalists and labor and called the oil industry's campaign a "dirty trick."

Partnership for a New Generation Vehicle (PNGV)

In 1993, the Clinton administration announced that the government's national laboratories and the domestic automobile companies would collaborate on a program to produce an 80-mile-per-gallon vehicle to be ready in 10 years. The EPA concluded that to stabilize U.S. fuel consumption in the early 21st century, fuel economy must be tripled. Growth in future U.S. gasoline demand would coincide with an exponential increase in the number of vehicles worldwide, especially in rapidly growing Asian countries. The new generation vehicle initiative received impetus from Vice President Gore's often repeated warnings about global warming.

In 1992, GM had already unveiled an Ultralite concept car that got 65 miles per gallon in a traffic-free environment. It used a two-stroke engine and extremely light carbon-fiber materials in its body. The car weighed slightly under 1,400 pounds; unfortunately, the materials used in its construction cost about $18 per pound compared with about 50 cents per pound for steel.

Switching to a car capable of 80 miles per gallon would require more than a light body and changes in electronic engine controls and transmission, better tires, and improved aerodynamics. A complete reassessment of the vehicle's drive system was needed. It might be necessary to try a hybrid concept, combining fuel cells and flywheel storage.

Lovins's Vision. Amory Lovins, the energy-efficiency expert, maintained that the hypercar of the future would not be an electric car running on batteries that had to be recharged by plugging them into utility-generated electricity, but a hybrid, which used electric wheel motors but made the electricity onboard from fuel cells and stored excess power in flywheels. This offered "the advantages of electric propulsion without the disadvantages of batteries."

The key was the use of composite materials which were made by embedding glass, carbon, polyaramid, and other ultrastrong fibers in special moldable plastics. With a hybrid propulsion system, a four-seat passenger car might then weigh under 850 pounds, yet be as safe as a steel car because composites could absorb as much force per pound as steel.

Moldable synthetic materials already were in the boatbuilding industry and were rapidly coming to dominate aerospace construction. While their costs were 40 times those of steel, they could be fashioned into lightweight, easy-to-handle parts that would vastly simplify assembly. Rapid model changes and continuous improvements in product design and market responsiveness were possible. To meet the needs of niche markets, small design teams could do tiny production runs in a short amount of time. Tooling costs would be lower because fewer parts were needed. Moldable plastics eliminated painting, the most pollution-causing part of making a car. No recycling was necessary because the composite materials lasted almost forever without rusting, denting, or chipping.

Lovins urged U.S. automakers to employ a leapfrog strategy to the hybrid fuel cell, flywheel car made of composite materials, but he doubted that auto executives were ready for it: "All this is alien to the thinking of most (though not all) automakers today. Theirs is not a composite-molding/electronics/software culture but a diemaking/steel-stamping/mechanical culture." At a minimum, Lovins suggested that the California Air Resources Board should allow ultralight, composite cars to be considered as zero-emission vehicles (ZEVs). Rigid adherence to an EV strategy was, in his opinion, a clear mistake.[16]

A Moderate Point of View. While not as sanguine as Lovins that a car could get hundreds of miles per gallon, John DeCicco and Mark Ross argued that raising gas mileage to 46 miles per gallon was possible. It would cost about $800 per vehicle and eliminate 2,100 gallons of fuel over a typical 12-year vehicle life span. The savings would be worth $2,500 even if fuel prices did not increase.

DeCicco and Ross advocated methods for achieving these gains that were somewhat similar to those of Lovins. They suggested that composite material made less vehicle mass possible; with less vehicle mass, less power was required. A smaller, more efficient drivetrain and motor could be installed without sacrificing comfort, safety, or performance. These analysts differed from Lovins in the kind of drivetrain and motor they thought could be reasonably installed. The authors saw a lean-burning two-stroke engine as the next important advance, not some type of fuel-cell, flywheel hybrid. Like Lovins, they claimed that cleaner air and reduced oil imports could be achieved without resort to a battery-powered electric vehicle.[17]

GM's Role

Despite the opposition, a global electric vehicle industry appeared to be emerging. Countless individuals, firms, and organizations had been affected by the emergence of this industry. Those affected included not only automobile manufacturers, but electric utility companies, automotive parts suppliers, and oil companies and service stations. General Motors had to decide what role it should play. Whatever it did, it had the opportunity to be a major force in the newindustry.

Since the electric vehicle industry was arising in response to regulatory change, federal, state and local governments were involved. Their multifaceted interventions included much more than simply driving technological change by enacting strict environmental legislation. Indeed, a vast network of federal and regional governmental agencies were encouraging the creation of new multifirm organizations such as the U.S. Advanced Battery Consortium and Calstart to develop clean-vehicle technologies and create markets for electric vehicles through direct government purchases and consumer incentive plans (see Case 11–A on U.S. Memories). To determine the position it would take, GM needed a political as well as a business strategy.

Discussion Questions

1. To what extent could General Motors count on delay in implementing California's auto emission standards? What difference would delay make for its strategy?
2. Should GM produce its own vehicles, buy credits from other manufacturers, or be willing to pay fines to meet the California standards?
3. Should GM go with a conversion electric vehicle or a purpose-built model?
4. Compare the advantages and disadvantages of different vehicle concepts such as the ultralight vehicle propelled by an internal combustion engine, by batteries, or by flywheel and fuel cells.
5. What should GM do to respond to this challenge?

Endnotes

1. This case was written by Alfred Marcus.
2. "The Car Industry," *Economist*, Oct. 17, 1992, special report.
3. Michael Parrish, "State Is Driving Force Behind Emission-Free Cars," *Los Angeles Times*, Aug. 9, 1993, pp. 1, A15; "Electric Cars," *Business Week*, May 30, 1994, pp. 104–12.
4. Donald Nauss, "Drivers, Plug in Your Engines," *Los Angeles Times*, Aug. 8, 1993, p. 1, A16; Richard Ernsberger and Myron Stokes, "Hop In—And Step on the Electricity," *Newsweek*, Oct. 25, 1993, pp. 36–37.
5. *Buyer's Guide to Electric Vehicles*, Dec. 31, 1993.
6. "We Drive the World's Best Electric Car," *Popular Science*, January 1994, pp. 52–58.
7. General Motors, *Environmental Report 1994*.
8. Chrysler Corporation, *Environmental Programs 1992*.

9. Mathew Wald, "In Quest for Electric Cars . . ." *New York Times*, March 6, 1994, p. 12F; Mathew Wald, "Battery Makers Are Betting on Lithium Polymer Cells," *New York Times*, Oct. 30, 1994, p. 8F.
10. P. J. Skerret, "Fuel Cell Update," *Popular Science*, June 1993, pp. 89–91, 120; Dan McCosh, "Emerging Technologies for the Supercar," *Popular Science*, June 1994, pp. 95–101.
11. "Volvo's Environmental Turbine Car," *Popular Science*, January 1994, p. 48.
12. "Ford's Double Action Cruiser," *Popular Science*, January 1994, p. 51.
13. Ibid., p. 57.
14. Michael Parrish, "Clean Machines: Deal with Hughes . . . ," *Los Angeles Times*, June 24, 1993, pp. D1, D6.
15. Mathew Wald, "GM Putting Its Electric Car on Road . . . ," *Minneapolis Star Tribune*, Feb. 5, 1994, p. 1M; Oscar Suris, "Detroit Steps Up Push for Delay . . . ," *The Wall Street Journal*, Feb. 7, 1994, p. 4.
16. Amory Lovins and L. Hunter Lovins, "Reinventing the Wheels," *Atlantic Monthly*, January 1995, pp. 75–86.
17. John DeCicco and Marc Ross, "Improving Auto Efficiency," *Scientific American*, Dec. 1994, pp. 52–60.

CHAPTER

15

Worldwide Environmental Issues

The . . . principle of ecology is holism . . . The biosphere is a unity . . . Following immediately from this . . . principle is the fact of interdependence. Everything within any ecosystem . . . can be shown to be related to everything else; . . . there are no linear relationships; every effect is also a cause in the web of natural interdependence; . . . ecologists . . . convey this sense of pervasive community and interrelationship [with] . . . "You can never do just one thing."

William Ophuls, *Ecology and the Politics of Scarcity*[1]

Introduction and Chapter Objectives

Both environmental problems and corporate activities are worldwide in character. To compete on a global level, U.S. managers need to understand how pollution problems manifest themselves outside the country. This chapter discusses the environmental movement in Western Europe, one of the major trading areas for the United States. It examines two key issues, solid wastes and atmospheric pollution, which are among the most pressing issues confronting businesses in the 1990s. Some of the practical steps managers can take to constructively cope with environmental problems are discussed in the final section of this chapter.

The Greening of Western Europe

Environmental problems vary in different countries and regions of the world. Managers must be savvy about the nuances of these problems if they are to be successful.[2] This section focuses on Western Europe. Environmentalism has been a strong force in that part of Europe. In the Soviet bloc, communist governments focused on production. The consequences of their nearsighted actions were disastrous, as those who must clean up the rivers, towns, forests, and even the soil after the fall of communism can testify.

American companies need to understand that there is a large growth market in Europe for environmentally friendly products. The German government has stamped more than 3,000 products with the Blue Angel insignia, indicating environmental approval. In the United Kingdom, John Elkington's *Green Consumer Guide*, a review of ecologically safe products, was on the best-seller list for nine months in 1990–91. Procter and Gamble, an American company, has adapted to the situation in the United Kingdom by marketing diapers that have been pulp-bleached without toxic chlorine gas.

The West European environmental movement started somewhat later than the American movement, but in important respects (e.g., the sale of environmentally safe products and electoral politics) it has gone much further than its American counterpart (see Exhibit 15–1 comparing pollution control expenditures). For U.S. firms doing business in Western Europe in the 1990s, environmental concerns are increasingly important.

The Consequences of Activism

In 1985, the European Community (now the European Union) changed its governing legislation to give it specific authority in the area of environmental protection (see Exhibit 15–2). The 12 member states had to create or amend their own legislation in accord with community directives to standardize environmental policies and prevent the creation of pollution havens in the poorer countries.

The European Community (EC) took major environmental initiatives in a number of areas.[3] Strict limits on emissions from new power plants, for example, signified increases in capital investment and production costs for business. Regulations for the release of toxic substances by chemical plants into waterways were also expected.

The EC's activism had some interesting consequences. For example, it put limits on the British government's program of privatization. The United Kingdom's Water Authorities were unable to meet the EC's water quality standard. The government had to comply with the standards before it could sell $11 billion in shares of the Water Authorities to the public.[4]

Another consequence comes from the 1985 EC law affecting automotive emissions. Initially the EC applied U.S.-style standards that called for expensive three-way catalytic

EXHIBIT 15–1 Pollution Control Expenditures in EC and Non-EC Countries: 1990
(in 1980 U.S. Dollars per Capita)

European Community Nations		Non-European Community Nations	
Netherlands	$1,170	Japan	$1,260
West Germany	1,110	Canada	1,260
France	740	United States	800
United Kingdom	650		
Italy	120		

SOURCE: Adapted from Directorate of Intelligence, Central Intelligence Agency, *Handbook of Economic Statistics, 1991* (Washington, D.C.: U.S. Government Printing Office, 1991), p. 28.

EXHIBIT 15–2 The European Union (EU)

Purpose: Single market, free movement of goods

Council of Ministers
Legislative body: 1 member from each state

European Commission
Advisory body of 17 commissioners, appointed to 4-year terms
Specific portfolio of policy areas:
Proposes new legislation to Council of Ministers
Regulations: Directly enforceable in member state
Directives: Instructions to member states to adopt laws.
Makes sure member nations enforce regulations and directives

European Parliament
Popularly elected representatives from all states
Expanded powers under 1987 amendments to force Council of Ministers to accept legislation aimed at harmonizing European laws

European Court of Justice
Can institute action against member states for failure to implement all European laws

Treaty of Rome of 1987
Expressly authorized legislation on environmental matters
100 environmental laws adopted
Unanimity not necessary; member state implementation still can differ in timing, content, intensity of enforcement

converters only on large cars. Small cars could meet the requirement by having lean-burn engines. At the time, the West German government provided tax breaks to customers who bought cars with the converters, and the EC decided to move toward the U.S. standard by 1993, when all cars are required to have catalytic converters. This decision provides competitive advantage to GM, which had been anticipating the change in the standard, and was a blow to companies like Fiat, Renault, Peugeot, and Ford, which had been specializing in the lean-burn engines.[5]

The EC decision on auto emission standards also provided a boost to manufacturers of auto emissions equipment. A subsidiary of Allied Signal, an American company that supplies catalysts, expanded production capacity in northern France to meet anticipated demand. Cars with catalytic converters require special injection systems that feed the engine precisely mixed doses of fuel, and Robert Bosch of Germany, the world's largest producer of fuel injection systems, planned to spend $500 million to expand its plants in Germany, France, and Belgium.[6]

The Environment and Trade

European activism also affected Coca-Cola and Pepsi, the large American beverage companies, which saw Europe as a huge growth market. The average European drinks less than a third the volume of soft drinks of the average American. U.S. companies rely almost exclusively on aluminum cans and plastic bottles that are less expensive, lighter, and more transportable than glass bottles. In the United Kingdom, France, Spain, and Italy, cans and plastic gained acceptance, but Germany, Denmark, Switzerland, and the Netherlands relied mostly on reusable bottles. Denmark went so far as to ban cans and plastic bottles; the West German government was *considering* a quota system that would limit them to 20 percent of the soft drink and 10 percent of the beer market. In these countries, environmentalists allied themselves with local bottlers to prevent the introduction of alternative packaging.

According to the European Court of Justice, these countries had the right to limit or ban cans and plastic bottles because the measures protected the environment, which was a mandatory requirement under the Treaty of Rome, 1987. The treaty committed the EC to "harmonious and balanced development of economic activities, sustainable and noninflationary growth, respecting the environment." Restrictions on trade between member nations were prohibited with the exception, among other things, of the "protection of life or health of humans, animals, or plants." The treaty stated that the environment could not be used as an "arbitrary discrimination, or a disguised restriction on trade." Nonetheless, the European Court allowed member nations to set high environmental standards, so long as they did so in a consistent fashion.[7]

Ideally, the European Union (EU) would like to move toward common standards in all member nations, but over the years it increasingly recognized the differences among individual countries on environmental matters. For instance, the German government imposed very harsh restrictions on the import of products treated with pentachlorophenols (PCPs), which were used as a disinfectant and preservative in a great number of industries. Since German regulations in effect banned PCP throughout the EU, member states argued that Germany was preventing free trade. The European Court, despite EU rules on harmonization, allowed the German standards to stand. In general, the court's tendency was to permit countries to have their own environmental standards so long as these standards did not openly flout free trade.

The European Environmental Movement

The European environmental movement was different in many ways from the environmental movement in the United States. Europeans opposed to nuclear power had fought pitched battles with the police, and many people were injured and some killed. The German Greens, a political party, were an explosive mixture of pacifists, antinuclear activists, feminists, and proponents of alternative lifestyles. The Greens arose as political parties in nearly all the Western European countries. They won 28 seats in the West German Bundestag (Lower House of the German Parliament) in 1983. Four years later, they won 8.3 percent of the popular vote and elected 44 deputies to this body. The Greens used the quasi-legislative European Parliament to forge greater cohesiveness and discipline among different national movements. They increased their representation in the European Parliament from 11 in 1984 to 27 in 1989. As the movement switched to the electoral arena, conflict intensified between its moderate and militant factions.[8]

As in the United States, local issues often dominated the agenda: declining forests in Germany, expansion of France's superfast railways in Belgium, opposition to hunters in

Italy, and preservation of historic sites from the ravages of pollution in Greece and Ireland. Overall, European environmentalists proved successful in halting many projects.[9]

The Greens had a strong moralistic tone and borrowed economic ideas from all shades of the political spectrum. Many were apolitical and hostile to the traditional left (i.e., socialists). They were divided chiefly over the question of growth, which remained a core value of worker parties throughout Europe. The Greens favored sustainable development and quality of life which permitted less room for improvement in the plight of the lower classes. Extreme right-wing parties, also seeing a resurgence in Europe, borrowed themes and slogans from the Greens including romanticism about nature and nostalgia for the allegedly simpler times of the past. The conservatives and social democratic parties also used their ideas when they considered it appropriate. No party in Europe could ignore them.[10]

The Effects of the Recession

The slowing of economic growth and continued high levels of unemployment since 1990 dampened some of the enthusiasm for the environment in Europe. Recent developments in Germany, the United Kingdom, and France are sketched.[11]

Germany. The environment, on the top of national opinion polls as the issue of main interest to German voters throughout the 1980s, slipped to third place behind unemployment and crime in 1994. Environmental research lost a third of its national funding. Nonetheless, Germany proceeded with a number of innovations. These included the world's most advanced recycling law, which makes manufacturers responsible not only for the return of the packaging used in consumer goods from automobiles to hair dryers, but also for the material used in production, which should be environmentally benign.

During the hot summer of 1994, two German states temporarily introduced speed limits on the autobahns, an unprecedented move in a nation that had had no speed limits since Hitler abolished them in 1934. The government continued to push forward with trail blazing transportation technology for the world's first magnetic levitation trains, which are scheduled to begin operation in 2005.

Germany's main political parties supported the principle of an **ecological-social market,** in which the environment was considered part of the economy. Those who caused pollution had the responsibility of paying for it. The government stood behind the goal of reducing carbon dioxide emissions by 30 percent by the year 2005.

ecological-social market
Market that integrates the natural world and the economy, and requires those responsible for pollution to pay for it.

United Kingdom. The brutal summer of 1994 also affected attitudes toward the environment in the United Kingdom. In southern England, numerous asthma sufferers were admitted to hospital emergency rooms. People from all sides of the political spectrum from Earth First to the Confederation of British Industry agreed that former Prime Minister Margaret Thatcher's vision of a "Great Car Economy" was unworkable. The government introduced new restrictions on driving and on vehicles that caused excessive pollution. Rail subsidies were increased, incentives for alternative fuels introduced, and a voluntary initiative called the Greener Car Forum started. This forum brought together groups from automobile and oil companies, government officials, and environmentalists to consider an "ecostar" label for vehicles.

The government's imposition of a value-added tax (VAT) on domestic fuels generated substantial opposition from groups concerned about the effects of this tax on older people and the poor. Recycling was stalled, but the country was making rapid progress in water treatment. Corporate environmentalism (see the last section of this chapter) also was advancing rapidly. British firms were noted for their voluntary acceptance of environmental quality standards, **eco-auditing**, open corporate reporting on environmental issues, and strong Green support for their products.

eco-auditing Independent examination and assessment of a company's environmental practices for conformance to company procedures, state laws, and regulations.

France. The Greens commanded only 7 percent of the total popular vote in the 1994 parliamentary elections, but a poll showed that 80 percent of the French considered environmental protection an urgent problem, up from 59 percent six years earlier. In 1994, France passed a comprehensive law aimed at increasing public participation in environmental decisions, minimizing risk, preventing pollution, and managing waste disposal. The law called for the creation of a national commission to publicly debate environmental issues and a substantial increase in the tax on dumping waste.

The business community formed a new association, Enterprises for the Environment, which tried by means of seminars, training sessions, and publications to persuade small businesses to be aware of their environmental duties.

A Comparison with the United States

Most U.S. environmental initiatives attempted to address the adversarial nature of U.S. regulation.[12] **President Clinton's Council on Sustainable Development** (PCSD) brought together representatives from business, government, and environmental groups to make policy recommendations on ways to simultaneously promote environmentalism and economic growth. The PCSD included five cabinet members, representatives of the Environmental Defense Fund, the Natural Resources Defense Council, the National Wildlife Federation, and the Sierra Club as well as companies such as Ciba-Geigy, Dow, Georgia-Pacific, Chevron, and S. C. Johnson. The Ecoefficiency Task Force of the PCSD started demonstration projects on environmentally responsible printing, automobile painting, chemical product stewardship, and ecoindustrial development.

President Clinton's Council on Sustainable Development Brings together representatives from various interest groups to develop methods to benefit the environment and the economy.

The EPA and Energy Department worked with the Eco-Efficiency Initiative of Business for Social Responsibility, an association representing 800 companies, to implement the Clinton administration's Climate Change Action Plan. The goal was to keep global warming gases at 1990 levels by the year 2000. This business-government partnership relied on voluntary programs to achieve its goal. It helped develop new relations between companies and their suppliers on the one hand, and new electric utility company programs on the other, to stimulate energy efficiency.

Carol Browner, head of the EPA in the Clinton administration, also created a partnership program with business. The Common Sense Initiative was an ambitious effort to change environmental enforcement. Instead of focusing on individual pollutants, the initiative tried to examine the overall impact that pollution reduction requirements had on entire industries such as the pulp and paper industry. The intent was to promote a comprehensive approach toward environmental policy making rather than to respond to particular incidents. The purpose also was to give industry the flexibility to respond in a more cost-effective way.

In general, the U.S. government was trying to move away from a legalistic, adversarial approach to regulation and to create dialogue between environmentalists and business. The Clinton administration, however, supported no new environmental initiatives. Under pressure from industry, it did not give its approval to legislation that would have reduced chlorine discharges into U.S. waterways. Chlorine breaks down into dioxin and other toxic chemicals which, through fish in the waterways, end up as food people eat. The administration's concern was that the compound was basic to 15,000 chemicals sold in the United States and supported 1.3 million jobs.

The election of Albert Gore, a noted environmentalist, to the vice presidency generated hopes among environmentalists, but other issues such as health care, welfare, and international tensions claimed the Clinton administration's attention. However, when the Republican majority in the new Congress of 1995 passed a moratorium on new federal regulation and called for further risk-benefit and economic-impact analysis, Carol Browner and other administration officials came to the defense of existing programs. The ongoing struggle over environmental policies in the United States and the rest of the world continued to generate uncertainties in the business community as each nation pursued a separate course.

Two Important Issues: Solid Wastes and Atmospheric Pollution

Two important environmental issues illustrate the slogan "Think Globally and Act Locally." Solid wastes are primarily a local issue but they have global implications. Atmospheric pollution is a global issue but it has its origins, like many environmental problems, in personal consumption decisions made at the local level.

Solid Wastes: Overview

Americans generated 160 million tons of trash each year, which was roughly equivalent to 3.5 pounds of solid waste per person per day (see Exhibit 15–3). The volume of this waste was 80 percent greater than it was in 1960, and by the year 2000 it was expected to increase another 20 percent. There was no sign that this volume of waste would decrease. Currently, it would take 1,000 football fields 30 stories high to store the waste generated annually by Americans.[13]

Landfills. The three main methods of disposing of municipal solid waste were landfills, incinerators, and recycling. Eighty percent of the solid waste in the United States goes into landfills, which have a designated life span of only 10 years. More than two-thirds of the nation's landfills have closed since the 1970s.[14]

While modern sanitary techniques and lined landfills greatly reduce the risk of envi-

EXHIBIT 15–3 Estimates of the Annual Waste Generated in the United States and Other Countries in the Late 1980s

	Municipal Waste (Thousands of Metric Tons)	Industrial Waste (Thousands of Metric Tons)	Nuclear Waste (Heavy Metal in Metric Tons)
United States	208,800	760,000	1,900
Japan	48,300	312,300	770
W. Germany	20,230	61,400	360
United Kingdom	17,700	50,000	900
France	17,000	50,000	950

SOURCE: Directorate of Intelligence, Central Intelligence Agency, *Handbook of Economic Statistics, 1991* (Washington, D.C.: U.S. Government Printing Office, 1991), p. 174.

ronmental contamination, many existing landfills were built without these precautions and are little more than holes in the ground. Moreover, many were built on or near wetlands; it was believed that the water would wash away and purify the wastes. However, now it is generally recognized that the waste material contains inks, paints, dyes, and a host of chemicals that can leach into the groundwater and cause serious drinking-water contamination.[15]

Advances in sanitary landfilling are meant to mummify the wastes to prevent leaching. However, mummification has its own set of problems. For example, biodegradable plastics are meant to break down and may be harmful because of the complexity of their construction. They simply degrade to smaller pieces without reducing the amount of space in the landfill that they occupy. Plastics constitute less than 10 percent of the total volume of material finding its way into landfills, paper is 37.1 percent, and yard waste another 20 percent (see Exhibit 15–4).[16]

NIMBY ("not in my backyard") Opposition from local people to placing hazardous wastes or other environmental risks in their communities.

Finding new landfill space is difficult in the United States because of the **NIMBY ("not in my backyard")** syndrome. In the Northeast, finding a site for a new landfill is virtually impossible. Alternatives to operating landfills have to be found.

Incineration. One alternative to landfills is incineration, which can reduce the volume of waste by 90 percent. Other alternatives are recycling and source reduction, which prevent wastes from permanently entering the waste stream. In Germany and Japan, about 50 percent of the waste is recycled, and almost all of the rest is burned in incinerators. However, the United States has had trouble moving from a system that relies on landfilling to one that relies on incineration and recycling.[17]

To what extent is incineration a viable option in the United States? Originally billed as a panacea for landfill overcrowding, groundwater contamination, and alternative energy generation, it has met with many obstacles. During the 1970s, incineration was synonymous with terms such as "resource recovery" and "waste to energy." Energy prices rose throughout this period, making previously uneconomical power sources appear reasonably priced. Thus, energy-generated revenues associated with incineration played a major role in justifying construction. Incinerator developers and their financial supporters estimated that the energy generated and sold eventually would amount to over half of the revenue

EXHIIBIT 15–4 Materials Discarded into the Municipal Solid Waste Stream
(In Millions of Tons)

	1970		1984		2000*	
Materials	*Tons*	*Percent*	*Tons*	*Percent*	*Tons*	*Percent*
Paper and paperboard	36.5	33.1%	49.4	37.1%	65.1	41.0%
Glass	12.5	11.3	12.9	9.7	12.1	7.6
Metals	13.5	12.2	12.8	9.6	14.3	9.0
Plastics	3.0	2.7	9.6	7.2	15.5	9.8
Rubber and leather	3.0	2.7	3.3	2.5	3.8	2.4
Textiles	2.2	2.0	2.8	2.1	3.5	2.2
Wood	4.0	3.6	5.1	3.8	6.1	3.8
Other	—	0.1	0.1	0.1	0.1	0.1
Food wastes	12.7	11.5	10.8	8.1	10.8	6.8
Yard wastes	21.0	19.0	23.8	17.9	24.4	15.3
Miscellaneous inorganics	1.8	1.6	2.4	1.8	3.1	2.0
Totals	110.3	100.0	133.0	100.0	158.8	100.0

*Estimated

SOURCE: Adapted from Franklin Associates, EPA, Office of Solid Waste, *Characterization of Municipal Solid Waste in the United States, 1960–2000,* PB-178323, 1986.

needed to cover the costs of incineration. The Public Utilities Regulatory Policies Act of 1978 offered a guaranteed market for the energy produced.

In the 1980s, however, energy prices plummeted, ending hopes that the energy produced would make a major difference in covering the costs of incineration. The Tax Reform Act of 1986 ended incentives such as investment tax credits (which had financed up to 10 percent of construction costs), accelerated depreciation allowances, and favorable financing policies for industrial revenue bonds.[18] Thus, incineration in the late 1980s was faced with decreasing economic justification as well as growing public opposition.

Public opposition was based chiefly on environmental and health considerations. Incinerators emit many pollutants, both toxic and nontoxic, including dioxins, DDT, lead, mercury, arsenic, and benzene. People in the vicinity of incinerators absorb these chemicals through breathing, eating, and drinking the contaminated substances.[19]

Public opposition to incineration also was based on reports of operational problems, mechanical failures and shutdowns, and cost overruns in construction. Hidden costs of construction included water sewer lines and surface roads that had to be constructed to accommodate the increased traffic to and from incinerators. Another concern was the ash left after combustion. If it was categorized as hazardous, disposal costs would increase from 5 to 10 times.[20]

In addition, opponents of incineration claim that municipality guarantees to provide the needed waste for incineration are a deterrent to starting effective recycling and waste-reduction programs. After the huge financial commitment to incineration has been made, they assert local officials will be loath to do anything to threaten the success of incineration. If insufficient waste is available, an incinerator is likely to be a financial failure.

Proponents of recycling also claim that while incineration generates a small amount of energy, recycling saves much more. For instance, recycling aluminum saves about 90 percent of the energy needed to make aluminum from virgin materials. Recycling paper saves about half the energy needed to make new paper.[21]

Recycling. Recycling programs in the United States have met with moderate success. The passage of the Resource Recovery Act in 1970 gave symbolic recognition to the public's interest in recycling, but recycling rates in the United States in the 1970s never exceeded 5 to 7 percent of the waste generated, and by the end of the 1980s amounted only to about 10 percent of the nation's total waste stream.[22]

Some solid waste professionals claim that up to 80 percent of the nation's wastes can be recycled; however, the exact amount is difficult to determine due to lack of precise information about the composition of the waste stream. Recycling rates vary from material to material; up to 80 percent of the nation's aluminum is recycled but virtually none of the wet garbage (e.g., organic material like table wastes) is recycled.

Recycling requires a high degree of coordination among consumers, business, and government. Consumers need to provide waste material and to separate it. They then need to buy products made from recycled, or **secondary materials.** Although consumers express a willingness to buy recycled products, this willingness has not been reflected in increased product sales. In addition, the amount of recycling has been limited by consumer disdain for paper that is not pure white and other materials that are less attractive when made from secondary materials.

secondary materials
Recycled goods that consumers and manufacturers would have to buy if recycling is to succeed.

For recycling to succeed in a major way, businesses too would have to choose secondary materials over virgin materials. They would also have to develop products for secondary materials and processes for handling them. However, recyclable materials are often highly dispersed, and the cost of collecting them can be labor-intensive and expensive. Moreover, they often are of low grade and contain impurities, factors that raise the costs of preparation for remanufacture.

Most manufacturing facilities are set up to use virgin materials; they cannot use secondary ones. Thus, companies would have to make expensive new capital investments if they were to use recycled materials. These investments would have to compete with other business opportunities for corporate funds.

As long as current markets for secondary materials are limited, recycling programs will have difficulty gaining ground. There is only so much demand for cereal boxes made from recycled newsprint. The capital investment to develop equipment and processes for recycled materials is high. Also, the volatility of the secondary materials market discourages many companies from entering it; the flow of materials is often unpredictable and price can be alternately depressed or greater than that for virgin materials.

Recycling will take off only if manufacturers believe that it is profitable. For example, many companies recycle high-grade computer paper because it fetches high prices and saves the **tipping fees** of landfill disposal. Recycling even low-grade office waste, which contains multiple materials, yields a decent price and avoids tipping fees.

tipping fee
The price charged to dispose of waste material in a landfill or incinerator.

Government can promote community recycling efforts, fund R&D, and buy recycled products. It also can promote recycling by removing the tax advantage that virgin materials have. Mining, timber, and energy companies are given depletion allowances of between 5 to 22 percent of the value of the minerals produced. They also have capital gain advantages that lead to investment in virgin materials production. The social costs of depleting nonrenewable resources, on the other hand, are not included in the price of the virgin materials.

The federal government's role in recycling is largely symbolic. EPA, for instance, is committed to a 25 percent recycling goal, but spends only 1 to 2 percent of its budget on recycling programs.[23]

source reduction Attempt to eliminate waste before it is generated.

Source Reduction. The purpose of **source reduction** is to eliminate waste before it is generated; it is unique because it is not an end-of-the-pipe solution. The actual potential for source reduction is unknown. Businesses can modify their production processes to be less wasteful, and many have done so when it appears profitable. 3M for example has a highly successful "Pollution Prevention Pays" program.[24]

Businesses can modify their products to use less material and packaging. Consumers too can change their lifestyles in many small but meaningful ways. They can shop for goods that contain less packaging and use nondisposable alternatives whenever feasible. Since recycling brings with it environmental problems (processing already used materials, transporting them to markets, and reusing them), source reduction is a better solution to the waste problem (see Exhibit 15–5). But source reduction is very threatening to an acquisitive society that thrives on convenience.

Special problems are posed by beverage bottles and diapers. They were once reused,

EXHIBIT 15–5 Waste Management Hierarchy

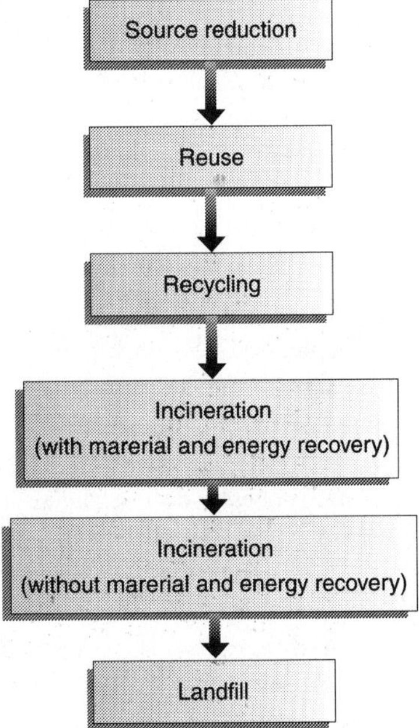

SOURCE: L. Blumberg and R. Gottlieb, *War on Waste* (Washington, D.C.: Island Press, 1989).

EXHIBIT 15–6 How CFCs Contribute to Ozone Depletion

Application	*Percentage*
Aerosol propellants and other miscellaneous uses	5%
Solvent cleaning of metal and electronic parts	12%
Sterilization of medical equipment and instruments	4%
Production of plastic foam insulation products	28%
Mobile air conditioners	19%
Refrigeration and space air conditioning	9%
Unallocated production	22%

SOURCE: Adapted from U.S. EPA, 1986; see Daniel Dudek et al., "Business Responses to Environmental Policy: Lessons from CFC Regulation" (Washington, D.C.: Environmental Defense Fund, 1989).

but now are commonly thrown out. Wholesalers and retailers do not want the bother of handling reusable bottles. Many working mothers, hospitals, and day care centers would find it unthinkable to give up plastic diapers and other throwaway baby products.[25]

Manufacturers have created whole systems around throwaway products and packaging, and Americans have become accustomed to their convenience. Certainly, though, if the amount of garbage is reduced at the source, less of it would have to be processed at landfills and incinerators.[26]

Atmospheric Pollution: Overview

The pollutants historically regulated by the government are hydrocarbons, nitrous oxides, carbon monoxide, sulfur dioxide, and particulate matter. Emitted from automobiles and smokestack industries like steel, chemical, and petroleum refining, these pollutants mainly threaten human health. Sensitive individuals are likely to suffer increased incidence of cardio-pulmonary diseases such as asthma under conditions of high exposure. However, the threats to the atmosphere from ozone depletion and carbon dioxide buildup are somewhat different and more serious.

CFCs (chlorofluorocarbons) Chemicals used in aerosol propellants, coolants, solvents, and foaming agents that destroy the earth's ozone cover.

Ozone Depletion. Scientific evidence strongly supports the theory that **chlorofluorocarbons (CFCs)** are destroying stratospheric ozone (see Exhibit 15–6). Other naturally occurring and manufactured agents such as carbon dioxide produced by decaying vegetation and nitrogen-based fertilizers also contribute to the phenomenon. Still other agents and natural processes counteract ozone depletion, increasing the complexity of the issue. The methods used to validate the theory and to measure the amount of ozone being depleted by CFCs suggest that a multitude of relevant agents are responsible, but primarily implicate CFCs.[27]

Invented in 1930 to be used as cooling agents for the Frigidaire division of General Motors, CFCs are chemically stable, low in toxicity, and nonflammable. For many years they were believed to be completely safe and hundreds of applications for them were found. Sold under trademarks such as Freon (made by Du Pont), CFCs are used as aerosol propellants, coolants in refrigerators and air conditioners, cleaning solvents for electronic

EXHIBIT 15–7 Economic Scope of CFC Application in the United States

Use	*Value (Billions of Dollars)*	*Employment (Thousands)*
Refrigeration	$ 6.0	52
Air-conditioning	10.9	125
Mobile air-conditioning	2.0	25
Cooling servicing	5.5	472
Plastic foam	2.0	40
Food freezing	0.4	<1
Sterilants	0.1	<1
Totals	$26.9	715

SOURCE: Adapted from Alliance for a Responsible CFC Policy, 1986. See Daniel Dudek et al., "Business Responses to Environmental Policy: Lessons from CFC Regulation" (Washington, D.C.: Environmental Defense Fund, 1989).

components, and foaming agents in the manufacture of furniture and mattresses, styrofoam, and building insulation. Despite the fact that the United States has banned CFCs for use in aerosol propellants, about one-third of all CFCs in global use are produced and consumed in the United States for these other uses (see Exhibit 15–7).

Substantial evidence indicates that CFCs are harming the ozone layer of the stratosphere, the upper atmosphere between 15 and 30 miles above the Earth. Stratospheric ozone, which acts as a shield by absorbing radiation from the sun, allows only safe levels of ultraviolet (UV) rays to reach the earth's surface. Even conservative estimates raise serious concerns about increased levels of surface radiation as the earth's protective shield of ozone is reduced.

Estimates of the actual percentage of ozone depletion range from a low of about 4 percent to a high of over 31 percent. A five- to sevenfold increase in skin cancer is expected for every percentage point decrease in ozone. Other potential harmful effects from the destruction of the ozone layer include increased incidence of cataract formation, reduction in crop yields, elimination of marine life, and the weakening of materials, including plastics.[28]

Significant actions are underway in the United States and around the world to reduce the risks of CFC-related ozone depletion (see Case 15–A, "Dupont and the Clean Air Act of 1990"). They include EPA regulations and international agreements, such as the Montreal and London Protocols, to reduce and monitor CFC production, use, and disposal, and develop safe substitutes for CFCs (See Exhibit 15–8). Ultimately, CFC use is slated to be phased out in the United States and throughout the world by the year 2000, and substitutes are being developed.[29]

Carbon Dioxide Buildup. Human activities of the past hundred years also are altering the composition of the atmosphere, threatening a global warming trend. Many scientists already are convinced that warming has started and that it will get worse through the next century. Since 1900, scientists estimate a warming trend of between 0.5 and 2 degrees centigrade per year.[30]

EXHIBIT 15–8 CFC Alternatives and Consequences of Their Use

Application	*Substitute*	*Trade-Offs*
Refrigeration and air conditioning	Ammonia	Toxic, explosive
	Sulphur dioxide	Combustible, less efficient
Plastic foams	Pentane	Flammable, smog precursor
	Methylene chloride	Suspected carcinogen
Food freezing	Cryogenic systems	Less energy efficient

SOURCE: Adapted from Alliance for a Responsible CFC Policy, 1986. See Daniel Dudek et al. "Business Responses to Environmental Policy: Lessons from CFC Regulation," (Washington, D.C.: Environmental Defense Fund, 1989).

greenhouse effect Warming of the earth caused by the buildup of carbon dioxide and other gases that trap infrared energy, or heat, in the stratosphere.

Global warming is caused by the **greenhouse effect,** the trapping of infrared energy, or heat, in the stratosphere by carbon dioxide and other greenhouse gases. These gases are transparent to sunlight, thus letting the energy penetrate the earth. Absorbing most of the sunlight, the earth converts the light energy into heat. Unabsorbed light is reflected back into space as heat. As it rises from the earth, it strikes the carbon dioxide and other greenhouse gases. Some heat is reflected back toward the earth, causing the warming effect. (The effect is the same as that of a greenhouse where the panes of glass allow higher energy light waves to enter easily, but do not allow the heat of lower energy waves to escape through the glass.)

Major emphasis is placed on carbon dioxide, which is 50 percent of the problem. Carbon dioxide is measured in the atmosphere at approximately 344 parts per million (ppm). This amount is large considering that only 100 years ago the concentration was only 293 ppm. Thus, an increase of about 15 percent has occurred in the last 100 years.

The major reason for the increase in carbon dioxide is the burning of fossil fuels—oil, coal, and gasoline. Scientists tend to be pessimistic about reducing the use of fossil fuels (see Exhibit 15–9).

The other gases contributing to the greenhouse effect are methane, CFCs, nitrous oxides, and ozone (see Exhibit 15–10). The atmosphere contains 100 percent more methane than it did during glacial periods. This increase is caused by the harvesting of rice paddies, the use of landfills, and the flaring of natural gas wells. CFCs emitted from the earth are found in the atmosphere at one part per billion. Nitrous oxides in minute traces are found in the atmosphere because of the use of fertilizers, natural processes (the emittances of soil microbes), and the burning of fossil fuels. The last major gas that contributes to the greenhouse effect is ozone. Even though the ozone layer provides ultraviolet protection at high levels in the atmosphere, it is dangerous at lower levels, where it is more commonly known as smog.

There are a number of natural processes that counteract the greenhouse effect. For instance, carbon dioxide is absorbed by the oceans and by tropical rain forests and other forms of vegetation, and it is reflected back into space by the clouds. The oceans are considered to be the major sink for carbon dioxide which is readily dissolved into seawater and where aquatic plants absorb it and hold on to it. The quantity of carbon dioxide absorbed by the oceans, however, is unknown. Because of the vastness of the oceans, scien-

EXHIBIT 15–9 CO² Emissions, Auto Registrations, and Energy Consumption: Major Industrial Nations

	United States	Canada	West Germany	United Kingdom	Japan	France
CO² emissions (metric tons per capita)	5.34	4.58	3.00	2.67	2.20	1.56
Auto registrations (units per thousand persons)	571	448	462	353	241	395
Energy consumption (barrels of oil equivalent per capita)	57	61	32	27	24	29

SOURCE: Adapted from Directorate of Intelligence, Central Intelligence Agency, *Handbook of Economic Statistics, 1991* (Washinton, D.C.: U.S. Government Printing Office, 1991), p. 28.

tists find it difficult to estimate the exact quantities of carbon dioxide plants absorb and oxygen they produce through photosynthesis.

The rate of absorption by terrestrial plants is estimated to be 500 billion tons of carbon dioxide annually worldwide, but this estimate is also uncertain. Because of deforestation, it could be decreasing rapidly.

Unlike the oceans and the rain forests, clouds naturally counteract heat retention not by absorbing carbon dioxide but by reflecting sunlight back into space. If the infrared light from the sun does not reach the earth, heat cannot be created, and if the heat on the earth's surface does not go up, the greenhouse effect cannot occur. However, when infrared light does reach the earth, clouds reflect the heat back toward the earth, thus warming it.

Major uncertainty exists about the role of clouds in counteracting the greenhouse effect. Ultimately, this matter is extremely complicated because it depends on subtle distinctions about cloud thickness and structure.

Impact of the Greenhouse Effect. The greenhouse effect can have many impacts on the world. Some of the major predicted consequences are listed below. These predictions assume that the levels of carbon dioxide and the other greenhouse gases will be emitted at the present rate:[31]

- In Greenland and the North Pole, some of the permafrost and ice will melt, causing the oceans to rise and threatening floods of coastal areas.
- The midwestern United States will be hit hard by drought conditions; the warmer weather will increase evaporation and cause drier soils.
- With the increased evaporation, river levels will lower, causing a shortage in water supplies, lower generation of power, and a disruption in agricultural irrigation.
- The nations of Central and Eastern Europe and Russia will gain approximately 40 days in their growing season, which could make them net exporters of grain to the rest of the world.
- The increased temperatures will cause a wider area of rain forest growth, moving

EXHIBIT 15–10 Contributors to the Greenhouse Effect

Gases Contributing to Greenhouse Effect		Human Activities Contributing to Greenhouse Effect	
Gas	*Percent*	*Activity*	*Percent*
Carbon dioxide	50%	Energy use and production	57%
Methane	20	Use of CFCs	17
CFCs	15	Agricultural products	14
Nitrous oxide	10	Deforestation	9
Ozone	5	Other industrial practices	3
	100%		100%

the African rain forests north and bringing rain to Chad, Sudan, and Ethiopia, breaking their prolonged dry spell.

- An increase in snow and frigid rain in Antarctica would create a thicker ice level, which would help counteract some of the greenhouse effect by reflecting more sunlight and counteracting the rise in sea level.

Canada and the United States have the highest emission levels of greenhouse gases per capita among the developed nations. The highest level of greenhouse gas emissions per capita in the world, however, is found in what was formerly East Germany. Brazil and the Ivory Coast have the highest levels of emissions per capita among developing countries. Per unit of GNP, the emissions of greenhouse gases in Brazil and India surpass the levels found in the United States. Contributions by country are shown in Exhibit 15–11.

Limiting Carbon Dioxide Buildup. A first approach to limiting carbon dioxide buildup is to make energy supply and use more efficient. Examples of available technology for conservation are efficient light bulbs in commercial buildings, better insulated buildings, and vehicles that obtain more miles per gallon. A fleet average of 40 miles per gallon, with no increase in miles driven, would cut U.S. auto-related carbon emissions in half.[32]

Another option to reduce the use of fossil fuels is to use different sources of energy. Alternatives such as nuclear power, hydropower, solar technologies, and natural gas produce far less carbon dioxide.

Methanol has been proposed as an alternative motor-vehicle fuel. Methanol made from biomass (primarily wood, organic wastes, or agricultural produce) would not contribute to greenhouse emissions as long as the biomass feedstock was replaced. (See Case Study 15–B, "Archer Daniels Midland (ADM) and Ethanol" at the end of this chapter.)

Hydrogen fuel cells appear to be a good long-term alternative for motor-vehicle propulsion if the serious technical difficulties can be overcome. A hydrogen-based fuel cell would emit only water vapor and nitrous oxides, the latter at significantly lower levels than fossil fuels. A big problem, however, is tank storage. Smaller tanks must be devised so that the driving range of hydrogen cars is not sacrificed. Another problem with the fuel tank is safety (see Case 14–A, "Environmental Pressures and New Product Development at General Motors").

A final method to reduce carbon dioxide buildup is to put a stop to the deforestation

EXHIBIT 15–11 Sources of Greenhouse Gasses

Country	*Percent of Total*
United States	21%
Former Soviet Union	14
European Union	14
China	7
Brazil	4
India	4
Others (total)	36

of the world's rain forests. The burning of the rain forests emits an estimated one billion tons of carbon dioxide a year; at the same time the earth loses one of its major sinks to absorb carbon dioxide. Encouraging the reforestation of areas denuded of natural tree cover is a gesture of important symbolic significance, but it cannot make a significant dent in carbon dioxide buildup.[33]

The Need for an International Treaty

An international treaty on global greenhouse gases, modeled on that of the Montreal and London accords for CFCs, was needed. However, the circumstances that produced these accords were much different than the circumstances surrounding the buildup of greenhouse gases.

First, the Montreal and London accords were reached amid growing international recognition of the scientific basis for the ozone depletion theory. Negotiations gathered momentum after scientists observed a rapidly growing ozone hole over the Antarctic. With respect to global warming, however, great uncertainties remained. Firm evidence was needed to convince people in all nations to take climate change seriously. But the evidence might appear too late. According to the adage, throw a frog into a cauldron of boiling water and it will jump out to save its life, but boil it gradually and it will stay put until it dies.

The second difference between the circumstances surrounding ozone depletion and carbon buildup was that many companies favored a worldwide agreement to limit CFC production. They did so not only because of a sense of corporate social responsibility but because, as manufacturers of expensive CFC substitutes, they stood to gain from new products, methods, and substances.[34] If regulation was inevitable, these manufacturers preferred that it be uniform in coverage and enforceable, so that no company could cheat and offer cheap CFCs as competition to the higher-priced alternatives and so they could plan for a transition to the new era.

Carbon dioxide buildup, however, was unlikely to see a convergence of scientific recognition and industry support. The industry situation was very different. CFCs were produced by a relatively small number of companies and had a relatively narrow range of uses. In comparison, fossil fuel producers and the uses of their products were numerous. Moreover, fossil fuels were very hard to replace.[35]

Implementing the Rio Climate Change Treaty of 1992

Rio Framework on Climate Change
The 1992 treaty establishing long-term goals on stabilizing greenhouse gases at safe levels for humans.

The 1992 Rio Framework on Climate Change, signed by 159 nations, established a *long-term* goal of stabilizing greenhouse gases at levels safe for humans. Eventually, these emissions would have to be cut by 60 to 80 percent. In the short term, nations were expected to list existing emissions and adopt national climate plans. The Europeans and Japanese wanted a freeze at 1990 levels, to which the Bush administration was adamantly opposed, preferring instead a wait-and-see attitude because more study was needed.

Most of the national plans adopted after the Rio treaty were modest: the funding of energy efficiency projects, R&D, and work on renewable energy. No nation in the world had passed a carbon tax, though the European Union considered one that began at a $3 a barrel oil equivalent and would go up to $10 a barrel in seven years. No agreement was reached, however, on how to distribute the tax burden among member states, and the proposal was affected by many conflicts.

Since countries with growing economies like Greece, Spain, Portugal, and Ireland forecast inevitable increases in emissions, the expectation was that Germany, Belgium, the Netherlands, and Denmark would have to compensate them. The United Kingdom, which had only recently raised its energy taxes, did not support the tax. The governing institutions of the EU were not unanimous about a carbon tax either: the Environment Commission favored it, but the Economic and Financial Affairs Commission, concerned about jobs and the competitiveness of European industry, and the Customs Union, which already felt overburdened by the need to harmonize tax policies among EU member nations, opposed it.

Economic analysis showed that the tax, if it did not involve increased government revenues, would have little impact because energy constituted only 2 percent of industrial costs. However, in energy and energy-intensive industries, such as iron, steel, clay, and glass, the impact would be very high. Trade groups in those industries made emotionally charged arguments against the tax. Environmentalists and the energy-efficiency and renewable-energy industries did not have the capacity to counter these forces. Ultimately, passage of a carbon tax in the EU was made conditional on the introduction of a carbon tax in competitor nations: the United States, Japan, and the newly industrialized nations of Asia.

In principle, the EU remained committed to using taxes for environmental purposes.[36] In practice, this idea met with many difficulties. A European Commission report in 1995, *Economic Growth and the Environment*, argued for a shift to taxes from regulation. Taxes and environmental charges, the report maintained, were the best means to make an economy sustainable. They conformed to the move from government to the marketplace and sent a clear message to businesses and other economic actors. Less hemmed in by bureaucratic rigidities, businesses would be free to respond to market signals.

Implementing a tax system, however, remained a formidable challenge. Revenues from environmental charges would decline as companies reduced their pollution to avoid payment. The use of taxes might make it more difficult to integrate the economies of Central and Eastern Europe. The EU would have to answer the question of how to use the revenues: Should they be used to subsidize R&D and smooth the transition toward new and cleaner industries?

What Companies Can Do

Pollution and environmental problems posed numerous challenges for business. These challenges occurred at the highest levels in the firm: business strategy and organization. They also affected corporate staff in the public affairs and legal departments and influenced people in traditional functional areas such as operations, marketing, accounting, and finance.[37]

Environmental considerations must be part of companywide decision making from the beginning; they are not something to be considered only at the end. Companies may have to think long term even if profits suffer in the short term. Management support at the highest level is essential because changes of the magnitude called for by environmental issues cannot be accomplished without it.

Companies such as DuPont, 3M, and Pacific Gas & Electric have made well-regarded responses to environmental expectations in the past.[38] Their responses may have relevance for other companies. Based on these responses, a list is provided of actions companies can take.

Strategy and Organization. Companies can take the following actions:

1. *Cut back on environmentally unsafe operations*. Du Pont, the leading producer of CFCs, has announced that it will voluntarily pull out of this $750 million business by the year 2000, if not sooner.
2. *Carry out R&D on environmentally safe activities*. Du Pont has announced that it is spending up to $1 billion on the best replacements for CFCs.
3. *Develop and expand environmental cleanup services*. Building on the expertise gained in cleaning up its own plants, Du Pont has formed a safety and environmental resources division to help industrial customers clean up their toxic wastes. The projected future revenues are $1 billion by 2000.
4. *Compensate for environmentally risky endeavors*. Applied Energy Services, a power plant management firm, donated $2 million in 1988 for tree planting in Guatemala to compensate for a coal-fired plant it was building in Connecticut. The trees were meant to offset emissions that might lead to global warming.
5. *Make structural changes*. The CERES Principles call on companies to appoint an environmentalist to the corporate board and to conduct an annual public audit of the company's environmental progress. The environmental auditing movement has taken off, and many companies now routinely, if for no other reason than to prevent liability, conduct audits.[39]

Public Affairs. Companies can take the following actions:

1. *Avoid losses caused by appearing insensitive to environmental issues*. A cost to Exxon of an apparent lack of concern about the *Exxon Valdez* oil spill was that 41 percent of Americans said that they would consider boycotting the company.
2. *Attempt to gain environmental legitimacy and credibility*. Edgar Woolard, the chairman of Du Pont, has been vocal in his support for environmental protection and regularly delivers speeches on corporate environmentalism. Cosponsors of Earth Day have included

Apple Computer, Hewlett-Packard, Shaklee, and the Chemical Manufacturers Association. McDonald's has shown that it is a proponent of recycling.

3. *Collaborate with environmentalists*. Du Pont and PG&E executives meet with environmental groups. PG&E rented a computer model from the Environmental Defense Fund (EDF) that shows the relationship between conservation and electricity costs.

The Legal Area. Companies can take the following actions:

1. *Prevent confrontation with state or federal pollution control agencies*. W. R. Grace faces expensive and time-consuming lawsuits from its toxic dumps, and Browning-Ferris, Waste Management, and Louisiana-Pacific confront violations that have damaged their reputations.

2. *Comply early*. Since compliance costs only increase over time, the first companies to act will have lower costs. This enables them to increase their market share and profit and win competitive advantage.

3. *Take advantage of innovative compliance programs*. Instead of source-by-source reduction, EPA's bubble policy allows a factory to reduce pollution at different sources by different amounts provided that the overall result is equivalent. 3M therefore has installed equipment on some production lines and not on others at its tape manufacturing facility in Pennsylvania, thereby lowering its compliance costs.[40]

Operations. A company can take the following actions:

1. *Promote new manufacturing technologies*. Louisville Gas and Electric has taken the lead in installing smokestack scrubbers, Consolidated Natural Gas in using clean-burning technologies, and Nucor in developing state-of-the-art steel mills. PG&E has agreed to rely on a combination of smaller-scale generating facilities like windmills or cogeneration plants, along with aggressive conservation efforts. It has canceled plans to build large coal and nuclear power plants.

2. *Encourage technological advances that reduce pollution from products and manufacturing processes*. 3M's "Pollution Prevention Pays" program is based on the premise that it is too costly for companies to employ add-on technology and that they should attempt instead to eliminate pollution at the source.[41] Add-on technology is expensive because it takes resources to remove the pollution, the pollution removal then generates new wastes, and more resources are needed to remove the additional waste.

3. *Develop new product formulations*. 3M's rapid-fire agent to extinguish petroleum fires did not meet EPA requirements. Thus, the company had to develop a new formulation, which was 40 times less toxic but equally effective and less expensive to produce.

4. *Modify production equipment and change manufacturing operations to achieve source reduction*. Besides new product formulations, 3M also has modified its equipment and changed operations. Its Kenlevel metal-plating process does not require the use of cyanide, is up to 50 percent more energy efficient, and creates a competitive advantage.

5. *Eliminate manufacturing wastes*. With fewer wastes, add-on equipment becomes less necessary. 3M's philosophy is to invest in reducing the number of materials that trigger regulation. It has, for example, replaced volatile solvents with water-based compounds,

eliminating the need for costly air-pollution equipment. Amoco and Polaroid have similar pollution-reduction programs.

6. *Find alternative uses for wastes.* When Du Pont halted ocean dumping of acid iron salts, it discovered that the salts could be sold to water treatment plants at a profit.

7. *Recycle wastes.* Firms with active recycling programs are 3M, Safety-Kleen (solvents and motor oil), Wellman (plastic), Jefferson Smurfit (paper), and Nucor (steel).

Marketing. A company can take various actions in this area:

1. *Cast products in an environmentally friendly light.* A 1989 Michael Peters Group survey found that 77 percent of Americans say that a company's environmental reputation influences what they buy.[42] Companies such as Procter & Gamble, ARCO, Colgate-Palmolive, Lever Brothers, 3M, and Sun Oil have tried to act on the basis of this finding. Wal-Mart has made efforts to provide customers with recycled or recyclable products. The number of new green products introduced in the United States has increased, and many new product introductions have green features.[43]

2. *Avoid being attacked by environmentalists for unsubstantiated or inappropriate claims.* British Petroleum claimed that a new brand of unleaded gasoline caused no pollution, a claim that it had to withdraw after suffering much embarrassment. The degradable-plastics controversy should provide producers with another warning about the perils of unsubstantiated or inappropriate claims. The Body Shop, a London-based chain of skin and hair care stores that provides literature on ozone depletion and global warming to its customers and has collected signatures on a petition to save the rain forests, is a third example. Companies have to be honest with their customers and have to educate them without charges of fraud.

Accounting. A company can take the following actions:

1. *Demonstrate that antipollution programs pay.* 3M's experience is that pollution-prevention programs must pay so that companies will be motivated to carry them out successfully. Environmental pressures force American companies to spend large sums of money that they could otherwise use for capital formation, new product research and development, and process improvements that raise productivity. Thus, every company should use a minimum of resources to reduce pollution and at the same time encourage innovation.

2. *Show the overall impact of the pollution-reduction program.* Companies have an obligation to account for the costs and benefits of their pollution reduction programs. By 1989, 3M reported that it had reduced wastes by 50 percent and had saved the company over $4 million. Its pollution-prevention program added almost 6 cents a share or $13 million to the company's profits. This figure does not include the value of reused material or savings coming from reduced disposal costs.

Finance. The actions that a company can take in this area include the following:

1. *Gain the respect of the socially responsible investment community.* Socially responsible rating services and investment funds try to help people invest with a "clean conscience."[44]

Their motto is that they can do well while they are doing good. Socially responsible investments can be profitable in the long run because companies that can deal creatively with pollution, safety, and employment problems are likely to be innovative in other areas as well (see Chapter 4).

2. *Recognize true liability*. Smith Barney, Kidder Peabody, and other investment houses have environmental analysts who search for a company's true environmental liability. They looked closely at ITT's $30 million charge against earnings for a plant in Georgia that made creosote-soaked railroad ties and telephone poles. The land on the plant site had been damaged and would have to be cleaned up.

3. *Recognize business opportunities*. Smith Barney's indexes of solid waste stocks rose 59 percent and hazardous waste stocks more than 42 percent in 1989 while the overall stock market rose only 27 percent. In the long run, the prospects for solid waste companies (e.g., Waste Management, Laidlaw Industries, and Browning Ferris) are supposed to be very good because of a scarcity of landfill in some parts of country, and because cities like New York have no alternative ways to get rid of their garbage. In the short run, these companies were having some difficulties.[45] Their prospects ultimately will improve as the federal defense and energy departments and individual companies will have to clean up toxic wastes sites they have created.

Environmental Service and Technology Companies

Business should get better, especially abroad, for environmental service and technology companies. The worldwide market is estimated to be growing to $300 billion annually. However, development of this industry has not been easy because regulatory barriers, cultural differences, and other factors have affected market access. The Asian Pacific region offers the greatest opportunities, with a market of $40 to $50 billion annually and a growth rate of 15 to 20 percent. The region's largest economy, Japan, however, has proved hard to penetrate, so the best accessible markets are Taiwan, Hong Kong, Singapore, Australia, and New Zealand.[46]

Latin America also offers good opportunities with a growth rate estimated at 15 to 20 percent per year. Current spending, however, is only $4–5 billion and lax regulatory enforcement remains a problem.

Eastern and Central Europe have the greatest demand for environmental services and technology. Annual growth rates in spending of 20 to 30 percent are possible, but base spending in 1995 is estimated to be only $6–7 billion. Therefore, much of the funding must come from international organizations.

Annual spending increases in Western Europe are estimated to be between 7 and 10 percent compared with 4 to 6 percent in North America. The estimated annual expenditures in 1995 for environmental services and technologies were $60 to 70 billion in Western Europe and $90 to 110 billion in North America.

In sum, firms have many opportunities, covering all aspects of their business, to meet the challenge posed by pollution and environmental problems. In time, the environmental service and technology sector is bound to take off and become an important force in solving the world's environmental problems.

Conclusions

This chapter has tried to make the following points:

1. Pollution problems are worldwide, and businesses operate in settings throughout the world where environmental conditions, environmental movements, and environmental laws vary. Managers must be aware of the differences because awareness may provide them with opportunities for gain and the potential to avoid liabilities.

2. Two of the most pressing pollution problems affecting the globe are solid-waste disposal and atmospheric pollution. Solid-waste disposal is a local problem. By creating programs to reduce and recycle wastes, companies can do something about it now. Atmospheric pollution is a global problem with long-term consequences. International treaties are needed to deal with problems like the hole in the ozone layer and global warming. Companies require long-term plans for these uncertain contingencies.

3. The actions companies can take to cope with environmental problems extend from strategy making and organization to marketing, finance, accounting, and operations. Efforts to reduce pollution are in accord with various other efforts to enhance quality, lower costs, and introduce new products and technologies. They fit into a strategic approach to problem solving where companies provide value to customers through low-cost (waste minimization) and differentiated (green) products. Companies should prune their product portfolios and stress pollution-reducing alternatives to take advantage of the opportunities and avoid the inevitable risks. The future of the world's environment is in their hands.

Discussion Questions

1. Discuss environmental policies in the European Union. What have been some of the consequences of these policies for business?
2. In what ways is the European environmental movement different from the environmental movement in North America? What are the consequences of these differences for business?
3. To what extent does the United Kingdom provide fertile ground for the expansion of U.S. firms experienced in the technologies and know-how of environmental protection?
4. What other countries in Europe might provide fertile ground for the expansion of experienced U.S. firms.
5. What are the three main methods of disposing of solid wastes? What are the advantages and disadvantages of each?
6. What business interests are represented by the different methods of waste disposal? What public policies would these different business interests tend to favor? What challenges do they face in building their business?
7. Why hasn't recycling been more successful?
8. What are the prospects for source reduction? What special problems and opportunities does it offer business?

9. What are the public risks posed by ozone depletion? What are the challenges to business? Will business be able to meet these challenges?
10. What risks are posed to the world by carbon dioxide buildup? What must businesses do to confront this issue? What should government officials do?
11. Why has it been so difficult for the EU to introduce a carbon tax?
12. Environmental issues pose numerous challenges to business. Discuss actions that companies can take in different functional areas.
13. Which of the environmental actions that companies can take are most important? Which are the easiest to take? Which are companies least likely to take? Why? Have any examples of company actions been left out of this chapter?
14. As a practicing manager, what kind of environmental policy would you draw up for your company? How would you ensure that the company carries out this policy?
15. Define strategic environmental management. How can companies convert environmental challenges into opportunities for business expansion and profit?

Endnotes

1. W. Ophuls, *Ecology and the Politics of Scarcity* (San Francisco: W. H. Freeman, 1977), pp. 21–22.
2. R. Buchholz, A. Marcus, and J. Post, *Managing Environmental Issues: A Case Book* (Englewood Cliffs, N.J.: Prentice Hall, 1992).
3. Shawn Tully, "What the 'Greens' Mean For Business," *Fortune*, October 23, 1989, pp. 159–64.
4. Ibid.
5. Ibid.
6. Tully, "What the 'Greens' Mean for Business," pp. 159–64; S. McMurray, "Chemical Firms Find that It Pays to Reduce Pollution at Source," *The Wall Street Journal*, June 11, 1991, p. A1.
7. Martin Wright, "Environmental Law: Free Trade," *Tomorrow*, Oct.–Dec. 1994, p. 98.
8. Roger Cans, "Les Saga des Verts Europeans," *Le Monde*, June 1, 1989, p. 1; H. de Bresson, "La Tentation du Pouvoir," *Le Monde*, June 1, 1989, p. 9.
9. Ibid.
10. Ibid.
11. Theresa Waldrop, Martin Wright, and Martha Johnston, "The Way Ahead for Germany, Britain, and France, *Tomorrow*, Oct.–Dec. 1994, pp. 82–92.
12. Joel Makower, "Friend of the Earth?" *Tomorrow*, Oct.–Dec. 1994, pp. 46–52.
13. "Buried Alive," *Newsweek*, November 27, 1989, pp. 66–76; Louis Blumberg and Robert Gottlieb, "The Growth of the Waste Stream," in *War on Waste*, ed. Louis Blumberg and Robert Gottlieb (Washington, D.C.: Island Press, 1989), pp. 3–26.
14. Directorate of Intelligence, Central Intelligence Agency, *Handbook of Economic Statistics, 1991* (Washington, D.C.: U.S. Government Printing Office, 1991), p. 174.
15. Blumberg and Gottlieb, "The Growth of the Waste Stream."
16. William Rathje, "Rubbish!" *Atlantic Monthly*, Dec. 1989, pp. 99–109; Blumberg and Gottlieb, "The Growth of the Waste Stream."
17. Louis Blumberg and Robert Gottlieb, "The Resurrection of Incineration" and "The Economic Factors," in *War on Waste*, ed. Louis Blumberg and Robert Gottlieb (Washington, D.C.: Island Press, 1989), pp. 26–58 and pp. 123–55.
18. Ibid.

19. Jeffrey Stevens, "Assessing the Health Risks of Incinerating Garbage," *EURA Reporter*, Oct. 1989, pp. 6–10.
20. Ibid.
21. Blumberg and Gottlieb, "The Resurrection of Incineration" and "The Economic Factors."
22. Louis Blumberg and Robert Gottlieb, "Recycling's Unrealized Promise," in *War on Waste*, ed. Louis Blumberg and Robert Gottlieb (Washington, D.C.: Island Press, 1989), pp. 191–226.
23. Ibid.
24. David Brunner, Will Miller, and Nan Stockholm, "3M Company: Creating Incentives Within the Individual Firm," in *Corporations and the Environment: How Should Decisions Be Made*, ed. David Brunner et al. (Stanford, Calif.: Stanford Business School, 1981), pp. 97–110.
25. Louis Blumberg and Robert Gottlieb, "The Squeeze on Reuse Strategies," in *War on Waste*, ed. Louis Blumberg and Robert Gottlieb (Washington, D.C.: Island Press, 1989), pp. 226–58; C. Lehrburger, "The Disposable Diaper Myth," *Whole Earth Review*, Fall 1988, pp. 60–66; F. Lyman, "Diaper Hype," *Garbage*, Jan.–Feb. 1990, pp. 36–40.
26. Kirsten Oldenburg and Joel Hirschhorn, "Waste Reduction," *Environment*, March 1987, pp. 16–20, 39–45; Azita Yazdani, "Waste Reduction," *Environment*, Nov. 1989, pp. 2–4.
27. F. Sherwood Rowland, "Chlorofluorocarbons and the Depletion of Stratospheric Ozone," *American Scientist*, Jan.–Feb. 1989, pp. 36–45.
28. S. Fred Singer, "My Adventures in the Ozone Layer," *National Review*, June 30, 1989, pp. 34–38; Joseph Morone and Edward Woodhouse "Threats to the Ozone Layer," in *Averting Catastrophe*, ed. Joseph Morone and Edward Woodhouse, (Berkeley: University of California Press, 1986), pp. 76–96.
29. Forest Reinhardt, "Du Pont Freon Products Division," in *Managing Environmental Issues: A Casebook*, eds. R. Buchholz, A. Marcus, and J. Post, (Englewood Cliffs, N.J.: Prentice Hall, 1992), pp. 261–86; Daniel Dudek et al., "Business Response to Environmental Policy: Lessons from CFC Regulation" (Washington, D.C.: Environmental Defense Fund, 1989); Stuart Gannes, "A Down to Earth Job: Saving the Sky," *Fortune*, March 14, 1988, pp. 137–41.
30. Anthony Ramirez, "A Warming World," *Fortune*, July 4, 1988, pp. 102–7.
31. "A Cool Look at Hot Air," *The Economist*, June 16, 1990, pp. 17–20; Gordon MacDonald, "Scientific Basis for the Greenhouse Effect," *Journal of Policy Analysis and Management* 3 (1988), pp. 425–44; Irving Mintzer, "Living in a Warmer World: Challenges for Policy Analysis and Management," *Journal of Policy Analysis and Management* 3 (1988), pp. 445–59; Lester Lave, "The Greenhouse Effect: What Government Actions Are Needed?" *Journal of Policy Analysis and Management* 3 (1988), pp. 460–70; Peter Brown "Policy Analysis, Welfare Economics and the Greenhouse Effect," *Journal of Policy Analysis and Management* 3 (1988), pp. 471–75.
32. William Chandler, Howard Geller, and Marc Ledbetter, *Energy Efficiency: A New Agenda*, American Council for an Energy Efficient Economy, 1988, pp. 19–65; Jose Godemberg et al., "An End-Use Oriented Global Energy Strategy," *Annual Review of Energy*, 1985, pp. 613–88; Janet Marinelli, "Cars—The Technology Already Exists to Make Cars that Get 50+ MPG," *Garbage*, November/December 1989, pp. 28–37; Steven Plotkin, "The Road to Fuel Efficiency in the Passenger Vehicle Fleet," *Environment*, July/August 1989, pp. 19–20, 36–42; Robert Whitford, "Fuel Efficient Autos: Progress and Prognosis," *Annual Review of Energy*, 1984, pp. 375–408.
33. Roger Sedjo, "Forests Might be Able to Moderate or Postpone the Buildup of Atmospheric Carbon," *Environment*, Jan.–Feb. 1989, pp. 15–20; Robert Repetto, *The Forest for the Trees? Government Policies and the Misuse of Forest Resources* (Washington, D.C.: World Resources Institute, 1988), pp. 1–43; Buchholz, *Managing Environmental Issues*.
34. Reinhardt, "Du Pont Freon Products Division."
35. "A Cool Look at Hot Air."

36. Martin Wright, "The EU's Market Instrument Vision," *Tomorrow,* March 1995, p. 78.
37. Frank Friedman, "Implementing Strong Environmental Management Programs," in *Practical Guide to Environmental Management,* ed. Frank Friedman (Washington, D.C.: Environmental Law Institute, 1988), pp. 27–57; William Petak, "Environmental Management: A System Approach," *Environmental Management* 3 (1981), pp. 213–24; Charles Priesing, "A Framework for the Environmental Professional in the Chemical Industry," *The Environmental Professional* 4 (1982), pp. 299–315; Buchholz, *Managing Environmental Issues.*
38. David Kirkpatrick, "Environmentalism: The New Crusade," *Fortune,* February 12, 1990, pp. 45–55.
39. Reinhardt, "Du Pont Freon Products Division,"; Kirkpatrick, "Environmentalism: The New Crusade,"; "Olin Corporation's Regulatory Audit Program," in *Current Practices in Environmental Auditing* (Cambridge, Mass.: Arthur D. Little, 1984), pp. 13–33; Report to U.S. Environmental Protection Agency, "Allied Corporation's Health, Safety, and Environmental Surveillance Program" in *Current Practices in Environmental Auditing* (Cambridge, Mass.: Arthur D. Little, 1984), pp. 33–53; Christopher Duerksen, *Environmental Regulation of Industrial Plant Siting* (Washington, D.C.: The Conservation Foundation, 1983), pp. 17–49, 79–109; Friedman, *Practical Guide to Environmental Management,* pp. 85–97 and pp. 133–43.
40. Brunner, "3M Company: Creating Incentives Within the Individual Firm," pp. 97–110; A. Mazur, "Controlling Technology," in *Technology and the Future,* ed. Allan Teich (New York: St. Martin's Press, 1990), pp. 207–20; Michael Greenberg et al., "Network Television News Coverage of Environmental Risks," *Environment,* March 1989, pp. 16–43; Deborah Stone, "Casual Stories and the Formation of Policy Agendas," *Political Science Quarterly,* Summer 1989, pp. 281–301.
41. Brunner, "3M Company: Creating Incentives Within the Individual Firm."
42. Kirkpatrick, "Environmentalism: The New Crusade."
43. Marketing Intelligence Service.
44. R. Irwin, "Clean and Green," *Sierra,* Nov.–Dec. 1985, pp. 50–56.
45. Bill Birchard, "Waste Disposal Industries Are Suffering, While Pollution Prevention Firms Are Thriving," *Tomorrow,* March 1995, pp. 59–62.
46. Terry Rothermel and Douglas Shooter, "Where to Go and What to Know," *Tomorrow,* Oct.–Dec. 1994, pp. 52–55.

Case 15–A
Du Pont and the Clean Air Act of 1990[1]

By the time Congress recessed for the 1990 Memorial Day holiday, it was clear that new clean air legislation would soon be passed, legislation that would have a greater impact on Du Pont than any legislation ever had.[2] Both the House of Representatives and Senate had passed amendments to the nation's Clean Air Act. After the holiday, lawmakers would reconvene in a conference committee to reconcile the two versions and to accommodate the Bush administration's concerns.

As one of the 10 largest companies in the United States and, according to government reports, the nation's fifth-largest polluter, E. I. du Pont de Nemours & Company had more at stake than perhaps any other company (Exhibit 1 shows a financial statement). Nearly every type of atmospheric pollution identified in the proposed legislation was generated by a Du Pont subsidiary. Du Pont's main substitute for chlorofluorocarbons (CFCs) would be banned under the new legislation a decade sooner than the company had hoped. Provisions designed to address the acid rain problem

EXHIBIT 1 Du Pont's Financial Performance, 1987–89

Industry Segments (in millions)	Sales			After-Tax Operating Income		
	1989	1988	1987	1989	1988	1987
Industrial products	$ 3,702	$ 3,082	$ 2,636	$ 629	$ 355	$ 319
Fibers	5,966	5,465	5,012	729	676	601
Polymers	5,581	5,423	4,783	455	531	475
Petroleum	12,314	10,995	10,560	538	391	277
Coal	1,818	1,757	1,770	223	226	157
Diversified business	6,153	5,638	5,170	307	275	271
Total company	$35,534	$32,360	$29,931	2,881	2,454	2,100
Interest and other corporate expenses:						
Net of tax				(401)	(264)	(314)
Net income				$2,480	$2,190	$1,786

(dollars in millions except per share amounts)	1989	1988	1987
Sales	$35,534	$32,360	$29,931
Net income	2,480	2,190	1,786
Earnings per share	3.53	3.04	2.46
Dividends per share	1.45	1.23⅓	1.10
Net return	15.7%	14.6%	12.9%

SOURCE: Adapted from Du Pont's 1989 annual report.

would threaten parts of Du Pont's coal operations. Operating costs for the company's chemical division would rise significantly if the law's new requirements concerning toxic air emissions survived the conference committee in their strictest form. And Conoco, Du Pont's gasoline subsidiary, would be affected by provisions mandating cleaner-burning gasoline.

The question now facing Du Pont was how to respond to the legislation.

The Clean Air Act of 1970

The Clean Air Act (CAA) of 1970 was intended to protect people and property from the ill-effects of air pollution.[3] The three titles of the law dealt with pollution from both stationary (industrial plants, buildings, and factories) and mobile sources (cars, trucks, buses, and airplanes). The CAA originally required the nation's air to be clean by 1975. However, this proved impossible, and the law was amended in 1975 and 1977 to allow more time for industry either to comply or to deal with newly discovered pollutants and ambiguities in the law. By 1982, most of the nation's air quality control regions had met the established limits for four of the six major pollutants: lead, nitrogen oxides, particulates, and sulfur oxides. Ozone and carbon monoxide proved more intractable, and some parts of the country had failed to attain the standards set for these pollutants by the end of the decade. However, progress had been made overall. The EPA reported that between 1978 and 1987, the level of carbon monoxide dropped 32 percent, lead by 88 percent, nitrogen dioxide by 12 percent, ozone by 16 percent, particulates by 21 percent, and sulfur dioxide by 35 percent.

Environmentalists, however, were dissatisfied with this progress, citing the threats that airborne pollutants posed to forests, waterways, and wildlife when precipitated out of the atmosphere in the form of so-called acid rain. But their efforts to amend the CAA in the 1980s failed, largely because of the deregulation ideology of the Reagan administration. By 1990, however, the political situation had changed. The Senate finally passed a clean air bill in April 1990 and the House completed voting on its version in late May.

The administration estimated that the bill would cost U.S. industry—already spending $33 billion a year on air pollution control—at least another $21.5 billion annually, more than General Motors, General Electric, Ford Motor, IBM, and Exxon collectively earned in 1989.[4] The amendments designed to combat acid rain could mean double-digit electricity rate increases for the heavily industrialized Middle West. Thousands of the nation's coal miners could expect to lose their jobs. Antipollution equipment could raise the price of a new car by $600. On the other hand, the estimated expected benefits were also significant because air pollution was contributing to the premature deaths of over 50,000 people per year and costing the nation $10 billion to $25 billion annually in health care.[5]

In the ranks of industry there certainly would be winners and losers. For each company that would have to spend some of the $20 billion or more that the CAA was supposed to cost, several other companies would win substantial dividends as the recipients of that spending.[6]

Du Pont and the New Clean Air Act

The new legislation would have profound consequences for Du Pont. The corporate giant, founded in the early 19th century as an explosives manufacturer, had $35.5 billion in sales in 1989, 10 percent higher than in 1988. The company had made a name for itself by harnessing science for commercial purposes. Du Pont's laboratories were the birthplace of nylon, Teflon, Orlon, Dacron, Lycra, and Kevlar. Du Pont helped General Motors develop Freon and became the first producer of the ubiquitous chemical. The company produced a wide range of products, from pesticides to biomedical equipment.

The new CAA had economic implications for most of Du Pont's businesses, but the chlorofluorocarbon, chemical, coal, and gasoline businesses were particularly affected.

Chlorofluorocarbons

Chlorofluorocarbons (CFCs) are a group of chemical compounds prized by industry for their wide range of uses, stability, economy, and nontoxicity. Du Pont's Freon Products division is the largest producer of CFCs in the world, supplying half the U.S. demand and 25 percent of worldwide demand. Though CFC sales are significant (Du Pont's are about $750 million), their future is limited because of the threat they pose to the earth's stratospheric ozone layer, which protects the planet from harmful ultraviolet radiation. In 1974, a wave of concern following the discovery of this threat led to a ban four years later on the use of CFCs as aerosol propellants. Concern waned again until 1985 when the "ozone hole" over Antarctica was discovered. Stratospheric ozone measurements showed that the ozone layer was being depleted faster than had been predicted. Political leaders from around the world agreed to a phaseout of CFCs in the Montreal Protocol in 1987. The Protocol calls for a 50 percent reduction in production by 1998.

In 1988, Du Pont vowed to completely end production of CFCs in the year 2000. The company shifted its attention to developing a marketable substitute, spending $5 million in 1985, more than $30 million in 1988, and planning to spend more than $1 billion on the effort by 2000. Known substitutes like propane, carbon dioxide, or pentane were dangerous, inferior, or more expensive. A promising possible substitute that Du Pont called 132b had to be scrapped when it was discovered the compound caused sterility in male rats.

By early 1990, the company rested its greatest hopes on a class of chemicals called HFCs and HCFCs. These chemicals performed many of the same tasks as CFCs, but because their molecular composition allowed them to break down before they reached the upper atmosphere, they had either zero (HFCs) or only 2 to 10 percent (HCFCs) of the ozone-depleting capacity of CFCs. Though more expensive, these compounds were not prohibited under the Montreal Protocol and appeared to be the most viable alternative. Unfortunately for Du Pont, the new House and Senate bills would freeze production of most HCFCs in 2015 and ban nearly all production in 2030. Both dates were decades earlier than the 2030–2050 timeframe Du Pont had deemed reasonable.

This posed a serious obstacle to Du Pont's plans for the substitute chemical. Customers would be hesitant to adapt to a substitute that would itself be phased out. For example, HCFC-22 could be used in automobile air-conditioning systems, but only if the systems were substantially redesigned to handle the higher operating pressures necessary to use HCFC-22. General Motors executives estimated the necessary retooling would cost their company $600 million.

In March 1990, citing competitive issues, the company sent a letter to its Freon customers urging them to contact their congressmen to protest the legislation for an earlier-than-planned phaseout of HCFCs. Publicly, Du Pont executives were silent about how the company would respond. But even before Congressional debate on the issue began, Du Pont had designed its first new HCFC plant to produce small quantities of the chemical.

Du Pont managers were now faced with hard decisions about where to focus the CFC and CFC-substitute division's energies. How hard should it lobby Congress to end the early ban on HCFCs? To what extent should it redirect its research and development efforts to other possible substitutes?

If Du Pont was going to redirect its corporate development strategy, it needed an assessment of the scientific and technical issues that was clear, understandable, and definitive. However, the state of scientific and technical knowledge was in such a state of flux that reaching such an understanding would not be easy.

Chemicals

Two major provisions of the proposed CAA legislation had substantial implications for Du Pont's chemical operations. Du Pont was the largest U.S. chemical company and had 80 or more plants around the country that could be affected.

First, the Senate bill would require chemical plants to stop production unless they could reduce toxic emissions to the point where people living near the plant faced no more than a 1-in-10,000 risk of getting cancer from them. Several Du Pont plants in Texas and Louisiana, which emitted carcinogens like carbon tetrachloride (which is used to produce synthetic rubber), had been cited by the EPA for posing an unacceptable cancer risk to nearby residents. Some of these cited plants already controlled their toxic emissions through state-of-the-art technology; additional safety measures to further reduce emission levels would be very expensive.

Achieving the Senate risk level would be very difficult, but even more difficult would be proving that it was achieved—risk analysis itself is a tricky business. Experts practicing it use different assumptions, which can be contested not only in the legal system but in the court of public opinion, where estimates of risk raise emotions and arouse public controversy.

Unlike the Senate bill, the House bill did not specify an acceptable level of risk, relying instead on the EPA to conduct further risk-assessment studies and make recommendations to Congress. These studies could take years to complete and digest, time that Du Pont could use to plan for the needed changes. Du Pont favored the House bill, but the company feared that too close an identification with the House's position might backfire; environmentalists would use industry backing as a tactic to obtain more stringent regulations from Congress.

The second major provision affecting chemical operations was contained in both versions of the bill; it required that every production line nationwide install the best available emission control technology. The measure was designed to reduce toxic fumes by 90 percent. If companies on their own could not meet the 90 percent reduction, the EPA would set standards for them, defining the best available control technology and requiring the companies to install it.

Toxic fumes are blamed for 2,700 potential cancer cases annually (0.2 percent of all reported cases) as well as other health problems. The cost to industry of the best-technology requirement was pegged at $5 billion per year. However, Du Pont, acting on its own initiative, had already begun spending hundreds of millions of dollars to reduce its emissions voluntarily to 60 percent of their 1987 levels by 1993. This effort was in addition to the company's ongoing reductions in air pollutants, which it had tracked since the early 1970s. If Du Pont were to continue with its own plan, it might be able to meet the 90 percent reduction guideline that would exempt it from EPA-specified emission-control measures. On the other hand, if the company failed to satisfy the reduction requirement, it would have spent millions of dollars on control equipment only to find that the EPA might require different equipment. Whether to continue with its own plan or wait for the EPA regulations to be clarified was a key issue for the chemicals division.

Coal

After a decade of debate, Congress and the administration were ready in 1990 to combat acid rain. Formed when sulfur and nitrogen oxides precipitate out of the atmosphere, acid rain damages forests and lakes, particularly those in the Northeast. A major culprit in the formation of acid rain is the high-sulfur coal used by some coal-burning energy utilities and industrial plants. Du Pont's Consolidated Coal subsidiary is one of the two biggest high-sulfur coal producers in the country, with high-sulfur coal accounting for 60 percent of its production.

Congress and the administration were largely in agreement on the provisions that would address the acid rain problem: Utilities would be forced to cut sulfur dioxide emissions by 10 million tons annually by the year 2000, at a cost of about $4.1 billion per year. The president's proposal included an innovative pollution-trading system, which would allow utility companies that cut their emissions by more than the required amount to sell their unused pollution "rights" to utilities that could not meet the standards.

Because many utilities would find it cheaper to buy low-sulfur coal than to invest in costly emission-control technology, Consolidated Coal executives estimated that $40 million to $50 million in annual revenue would be lost, 750 to 800 company coal miners would lose their jobs, and perhaps two of the company's four high-sulfur coal mines would be forced to close starting in 1995. Again, it was unclear what Du Pont should do. Protesting to Congress at this late date was likely to be futile. There had to be some opportunity for creative adjustment to this change in government policy.

Gasoline

The proposed CAA amendments that dealt with gasoline seemed to offer a business opportunity to Du Pont's Conoco subsidiary. The opportunity stemmed from the fact that a gasoline meeting the standards proposed for the mid-1990s had not yet been developed. Both the Senate and House versions of the legislation would require that cleaner burning gasoline be sold in nine of the nation's smoggiest locations: Los Angeles, New York City, Houston, Chicago, Milwaukee, Baltimore, San Diego, Philadelphia, and much of Connecticut.[7] Together, these areas comprise 25 percent of the U.S. gasoline market, but a very small portion of Conoco's market. The Senate version specified what the reformulated gasoline should contain, while the House version allowed refineries more leeway as long as they met the minimum performance standards.

If the oil industry failed to persuade lawmakers to change the reformulation requirement, there would be a large market for any company that came up with an acceptable, working formulation. Conoco researchers started working on the problem shortly after President Bush unveiled his clean air proposal requiring cleaner fuels.

After being caught off-guard when the Senate passed the reformulation amendment, industry trade groups and companies undertook an unprecedented, multimillion-dollar lobbying effort to defeat a similar amendment in the House.[8] Conoco neither contributed to this lobbying effort nor initiated its own effort. A $1 million newspaper ad campaign attacked both the gasohol lobby, which was pushing for the reformulation provision, and Congressman Bill Richardson (Democrat, New Mexico) who sponsored the provision. Several oil companies set up 800 telephone numbers, encouraging their shareholders to call or to send prepaid mailgrams to Congress protesting the amendment. The oil companies also urged their employees and dealers to deluge Congress with mail on the subject. The American Petroleum Institute (API), an industry trade group, circulated API-financed research that discounted the benefits of reformulated gasoline.

The lobbying blitz backfired. According to an environmental lobbyist involved with the legislation, not only did the oil industry lack credibility, but House members were irritated by its heavy-handed tactics. The barrage of mail and attention on the issue confirmed the belief of many lawmakers that Congress needed to define exactly how gasoline should be reformulated rather than leave it to the oil industry to decide.

What Next?

The CAA amendments in their final form would substantially determine how Du Pont would spend its environmental-equipment budget, which was slated to be $500 million by 1991. But other costs would also increase as a result of the legislation (e.g., the company's electric bill). By some calculations, Du Pont—which uses about 0.5 percent of all the electricity generated in the United States—could expect to spend up to $40 million more per year in energy costs alone. There were opportunities as well. Du Pont's fledgling environmental services business was projected to expand tenfold during the 1990s, up to $1 billion per year. Though management had to consider how to approach the legislation in the short term, how to prepare for its implementation in the long term was more serious. With new clean air legislation virtually sure to pass (see the appendix for a summary of the major provisions of the Clean Air Act of 1990), Du Pont would have to respond.

Its basic business strategy would be affected in at least six ways:

1. How could Du Pont contain costs so as to continue to bring value to customers and remain competitive? What advantage was to be won from an aggressive pollution prevention program in its core chemical businesses?
2. Could Du Pont innovate fast enough in areas like CFC substitutes and reformulated gasoline to move ahead of the competition and capture new markets?
3. Would Du Pont have to rethink its portfolio of business products, deciding that some were not worth further investment or keeping for the long term because they had substantial pollution problems and posed the risk of significant environmental liabilities?
4. What kind of reorientation in corporate strategic thinking was required? How should Du Pont present itself to the public?
5. What kind of company was Du Pont going to be? How should it explain the reorientation to employees concerned about their jobs and their future?
6. What long-term political strategy would Du Pont have to adopt to achieve its goals?

Appendix: Major Provisions of the Clean Air Act of 1990[9]

Toxic Emissions. Only seven chemicals have been regulated since 1970, but over the next 10 years the majority of polluting plants must use the best technology available to reduce their emissions of 189 toxic chemicals by 90 percent.

For any remaining cancer risks, the EPA is required to set health-based standards that produce ample margins of safety (e.g., a cancer risk of not more than 1 in 10,000) for people living near factories. Coke ovens are eligible for extensions until 2020 if they made extra-stringent reductions in the first round.

The alternative fuels program should significantly reduce toxic emissions from vehicles. Additional cuts from cars or fuel will be required after an EPA study. Benzene and formaldehyde must be controlled.

Acid Rain. In the first phase, the 111 dirtiest power plants in 21 states must cut sulfur-dioxide emissions by a total cut of 5 million tons in 1995. Two-year extensions can be given to plants that commit to buy scrubbing devices that allow continued use of high-sulfur coal.

In the second phase, more than 200 additional power plants must make sulfur-dioxide cuts by the year 2000, for a total nationwide cut of 10 million tons. This deadline can be extended until 2004 for plants that use new clean-coal technology.

An innovative trading system is created in which utilities that make extra-deep pollution reductions get credits, which can be sold or swapped to utilities that want to increase their emissions. Bonus pollution credits are awarded to dirty utilities that install scrubbers and to power plants in high-growth and extremely low-polluting states in addition to the hard-hit Middle West.

A nationwide cap on utility sulfur-dioxide emissions is imposed after the year 2000.

Utilities must cut nitrogen-oxide emissions by 2 million tons a year, or about 25 percent, beginning in 1995.

No help is provided for ratepayers beyond changes in the trading system. Coal miners and others put out of work because of clean-air rules may qualify for extra weeks of unemployment pay under a $250 million, five-year job assistance program.

Smog. Some 96 areas missed the deadline for meeting health standards for ozone, a main ingredient of smog. The new bill requires that all but nine areas comply by November 1999, except for Baltimore, and New York, which must comply by 2007, and Los Angeles, which must comply by November 2020. Areas that are moderately polluted or worse must cut smog 15 percent within six years. After that, areas with serious pollution must make 9 percent improvements every three years until they meet the standards.

Tougher tailpipe standards for automobiles are phased in, starting with the 1994 models, to cut nitrogen oxides by 30 percent and hydrocarbons by 40 percent. Even deeper cuts are required for the year 2003 models if the EPA finds they are cost-effective and needed (see Case 14–A). These standards have to be maintained for 10 years or 100,000 miles.

Warranties on pollution-control equipment must last eight years or 80,000 miles for catalytic converters and electronic diagnostic equipment, and two years or 24,000 miles for other pollution gear.

Special nozzles are required on gasoline pumps in almost 60 smoggy areas. Also, fume-catching canisters are to be phased in on all new cars, starting in the mid-1990s. Gauges are also required on cars to alert drivers to problems with pollution-control equipment.

Industrial polluters that emit as little as 10 or 25 tons of smog-forming chemicals a year may have to make cuts, depending on the severity of smog in their areas. The present law sets the limit at 100 tons a year. Another 43 categories of smaller pollution sources, including printing plants, are also regulated.

Alternative Fuels. Beginning in 1995, all gasoline sold in the nine smoggiest cities must be cleaner-burning, reformulated gasoline that cuts emissions of hydrocarbons and toxic pollutants by 15 percent (see Case 15–B). By the year 2000, the reductions must equal 20 percent.

Starting with 1998 car models, fleets of 10 or more cars in the two dozen smoggiest cities must run 80 percent cleaner than today's autos while trucks must be 50 percent cleaner. Requirements could be delayed three years if clean vehicles are not available.

By the model year 1996, automakers must begin producing at least 150,000 superclean cars and light trucks annually under a California pilot program designed to launch vehicles that can run on nongasoline fuels, such as natural gas and methanol. By the year 2001, even cleaner models must be produced.

Discussion Questions

1. What should Du Pont's strategy be toward the proposed legislation?
2. What types of changes in Du Pont's business strategy will the Clean Air Act of 1990 signify?
3. What opportunities do you see for Du Pont in the Clean Air Act?
4. How will the passage of the bill affect Du Pont compared with its competitors?

Endnotes

1. This case was written by Mark C. Jankus under the editorial guidance of Alfred A. Marcus, Curtis L. Carlson School of Management, University of Minnesota. See R. Buchholz, A. Marcus, J. Post, *Managing Environmental Issues: A Casebook* (Englewood Cliffs, N.J.: Prentice Hall, 1992).
2. Barbara Rosewicz and Richard Koenig, "How Clean Air Bill Will Force Du Pont into Costly Moves," *The Wall Street Journal*, May 25, 1990, p. A1.
3. *The Clean Air Act: A Primer & Glossary*, pamphlet, Clean Air Working Group.
4. Barbara Rosewicz and Rose Gutfeld, "Clean Air Legislation Will Cost Americans $21.5 Billion a Year," *The Wall Street Journal*, March 28, 1990, p. A11.
5. David Wessel, "Air Bill's Cost-Benefit Data Look Very Foggy Close Up," *The Wall Street Journal*, May 25, 1990, p. A7.
6. Rose Gutfeld, "Firms, Environmentalists Gear Up for Crucial Round," *The Wall Street Journal*, May 25, 1990, p. A7.
7. Allanna Sullivan and Rose Gutfeld, "Bill Would Require Oil Companies to Sell Advanced Fuel," *The Wall Street Journal*, May 25, 1990, p. A7.
8. Jil Abramson, "Big Oil May Have Misfired in Heavy Lobbying Drive," *The Wall Street Journal*, May 25, 1990, p. A6.

Case 15–B
Archer Daniels Midland (ADM) and Ethanol[1]

In her third assignment (see Cases 1–A and 5–A), Joanne Magnuson, new analyst for Alliance Capital, was asked to give her opinion of Archer Daniels Midland (ADM) as an investment risk. An institutional investor had held more than $500,000 worth of stock in ADM for the past five years. This investor was considering whether to up its stake in ADM, reduce it, or keep it steady. It was concerned with ADM's involvement in the alternative energy industry, specifically the risks the company had taken to become the world's largest producer of ethanol. This case first performs a detailed analysis of ADM's financial position and then analyzes the ethanol issue. The question for Joanne Magnuson was the bearing that the ethanol controversy would have on ADM's stock market performance.

Company Description

ADM's sales in 1994 were $11.2 billion and its profits were $484 million.[2] It employed 14,168 people. Its main competitors were (total sales given in parentheses) American Maize Products ($539 million), Conagra ($23.5 billion), and CPC International ($6.74 billion).

ADM is able to procure grain as cheaply as any company in the world. It buys it from farmers and resells it to exporters and processors. It transports, stores, and trades agricultural products such as corn, wheat, soybeans, peanuts, cottonseed, sunflowers, barley, flaxseed, rice, and canola around the world.[3] In the United States, it owns 140 grain elevators. Lead by the 73-year-old Dwayne Andreas and a cost-conscious, shareholder-oriented management team, ADM has a complex of elevators, barges, and rail cars that are regarded as the world's finest grain collection and transport system.

Strategically, ADM is not simply an agricultural commodity dealer, but has placed itself between the farmer and the consumer, processing agricultural commodities into valuable products for food, feed, and industrial use. It makes crops into food and feed ingredients like high-fructose corn syrup (HFSC) and vegetable oil. It produces ethanol, animal feeds, pasta, and malt. It also shells peanuts. For most of its major products, it is the low-cost producer.

ADM's foreign sales represent about 25 percent of its total, but these sales have been affected by the credit limits of large buyers in Central and Eastern Europe whose needs for grains are great, but who do not have the financing to maintain imports.

Main Products

HFSC. HFSC (corn syrup) is ADM's most important product. Demand typically has increased by about 2 percent per year, but recently it has grown to more than 6 percent annually as the beverage industry has expanded its product lines with New Age beverages, sports drinks, and iced tea. HFSC costs are about 10 cents a pound less than cane and beet sugar, which makes it the low-cost caloric sweetener for the beverage and food industries. If the United States and the European Union were to eliminate price supports for sugar, ADM believes that the price advantage would increase and demand for HFSC would grow.

Bioproducts. An area of great promise for ADM has been bioproducts, which are food and feed additives such as vitamins, amino acids, and flavor enhancers derived from corn and soybeans rather than petrochemicals. Along with its citric acid business, ADM acquired the fermentation technology needed to make such products from Pfizer, the pharmaceutical company. Among the products ADM offers are lysine, lactic acid, xanthan gums, monosodium glutamate (MSG), sorbitol, biological insecticides, and milk from soy protein. ADM also has aggressively marketed veggie burgers, hamburgerlike analogues sold under the brand name of Harvest Burgers. Recently, ADM added tryptophan and threonine to the group of bioproducts that it sells. These amino acids have annual growth potential of greater than 40 percent. Bioproducts, moreover, have greater margins than ADM's other products, and as their use grows their profitability helps offset the weak showing of the ethanol business.

Ethanol. With 68 percent of the U.S. market, ADM is the world's largest producer of ethanol, a corn-based fuel. Demand for ethanol first started to expand in the late 1970s. Because ethanol is a domestic product made of distilled grain, it was viewed as a promising alternative to imported oil. (U.S. dependence on foreign crude oil approaches 50 percent.) Ethanol also gained in attractiveness when lead was phased out as an octane enhancer in gasoline. Ethanol keeps gasoline from burning as fast and reduces engine knock. It is one of the few products that can be used as a substitute for lead.

Financial Performance

Operating Margins. ADM's 1994 operating margins were 10.0 percent, a rapid improvement from about 5.6 percent in 1984 and down only slightly from a high of 11.9 percent in 1990. Earnings per share followed suit and increased at an average compound annual rate of nearly 28 percent. Earnings have since flattened out as operating margins have declined to an estimated level of 10 percent. Management cannot be entirely satisfied with ADM's operating margins compared with those of its competitors. Aside from Conagra, the company's margins have not only been consistently lower than those of CPC, but also they have been lower on average than American Maize, a much smaller competitor in the corn products business. Some of the flattening in margins can be attributed to the cost-price squeeze ADM has experienced in the ethanol business. Ethanol, used as a gasoline additive or substitute, is priced according to the price of gasoline while costs are determined by the price of corn. High corn prices and low gasoline prices produced the 1994 squeeze.

Net Profit Margin or Return on Sales. In 1994, ADM's net profit margin was 4.4 percent. Until the ethanol price squeeze caused the net profit margin to drop from 5.4 percent in the fiscal year ending in June 1993, ADM maintained the second highest margin level among its competitors. The company was aided by low tax rates and relatively low depreciation.

Return on Total Capital. In 1994, ADM's return on total capital was 8.0 percent. ADM ranked a consistent third among its competitors. Only American Maize was lower. Return on capital was in a nice uptrend during the growth period from 1983 to 1990, but has steadily declined from a peak of over 12 percent since then.

Market Valuation

ADM's price-earnings ratio relative to the Value Line Universe in 1994 averaged 0.94. Except for fiscal years 1983–1984, when earnings were depressed, ADM has not had an average relative P/E greater than 1 since 1978–1980, a period of high inflation favorable to commodities. After hitting a new high of nearly $29 at the end of 1991, its stock has been stuck in a trading range between $20 and $26.

The EPA Ruling on Renewable Energy

ADM may stand to benefit from an EPA ruling that requires an increased role for ethanol in reformulated gasoline. Though Andreas is a generous contributor to both political parties, the ruling is being contested by several groups and the outcome is uncertain.

Motor vehicle pollution is responsible for more than half the carbon monoxide, more than one-third the nitrous oxides, and more than one-quarter the carbon dioxide in the nation's air. A wintertime oxygenate program started in 1992 required that additives be put in fuel during the winter months, November through February, in the 40 some metropolitan areas in the United States that exceed carbon monoxide standards. This program was subsequently expanded to include October

Exhibit 1 Ethanol Production Capacity
(in thousands of gallons per year)

	Operational Capacity	*Under Construction*	*Total*
ADM	867,000		867,000
Cargill	30,000	80,000	110,000
Pekin Energy Company	100,000		100,000
New Energy Co. of Indiana	75,000		75,000
South Point Ethanol	65,000	10,000	75,000
Midwest Grain Products	12,000	60,000	72,000
High Plains Corporation	20,900	50,000	70,900
Others	226,400	93,000	319,400
Total	1,404,300	294,000	1,698,300

and March. Although the EPA does not require the use of ethanol in this program, ethanol captured a very high percentage of the market in the Middle West and West, but not the East. The Clean Air Act of 1990 also required that gasoline that exceeded federal ozone (smog) standards in nine regions must have at least 2 percent oxygen to make it burn cleaner.

The Case for and against Ethanol After ADM and other companies participated in negotiations to write the new clean air rules, they announced more than 500 million gallons in planned or potential ethanol expansion. By 1992, however, ADM was no longer certain that the growth in demand would take place.[4] On March 27, it announced that it would not follow through on plans for a large increase in ethanol capacity. Since U.S. regulations were likely to mean less potential for the product, ADM would not add another 150 million gallons to its existing capacity. Cargill, the big Minnesota grain dealer and an ADM competitor, continued with its plans to add a 30-million-gallon refinery to a corn-processing plant, but it was uncertain about whether to continue with its additional planned capacity increases (see Exhibit 1).

Despite indications that regulations arising from the Clean Air Act would be "fuel neutral," the initial rules covering the smog problem favored MTBE (methyl tertiary butyl ether), a mixture of natural gas, petroleum, and/or wood products, although MTBE also can be made from decomposing garbage in landfills. For example, California, a leader in air-emission regulation, drafted rules that favored MTBE over ethanol. This made some politicians upset because about 30 percent of MTBE was produced abroad, mainly in the Middle East.

Ethanol's opponents, largely from oil marketing and refiner trade groups (the American Petroleum Institute and the National Petroleum Refiners Association), discounted the planned scale-back in expansion. They argued that the purpose was to apply political pressure in Washington. They pointed to the high profile of ADM Chairman Dwayne Andreas, a financial backer of both Republican and Democratic candidates.

Ethanol long had been favored by politicians.[5] Produced domestically, it had enjoyed a federal gasoline excise tax exemption of 54 cents per gallon since the early 1980s, when pure ethanol was blended with gasoline. Many states and localities also gave gasoline tax waivers for ethanol blends. Nebraska, for instance, has a production-incentive program that amounts to 20 cents per gallon, and Kansas has one that amounts to 10 cents per gallon. Because ethanol costs substantially more to refine than gasoline, producers required these subsidies to keep the price competitive.

ADM, however, argued that the subsidy went to the petroleum companies (the blender) and not to itself (the ether producer). In addition, it contended that the tax treatment of ethanol yielded

EXHIBIT 2 Reid Vapor Pressures of Ethanol and Methanol

Ethanol	18.0 psi
Methanol	8.5 psi
Regulatory maximum for reformulated gas	
Northern climates	8.1 psi
Southern climates	7.2 psi

positive gains to the U.S. Treasury. Citing a General Accounting Office report, ADM held that increased ethanol production reduced farm subsidies, which produced net savings to the federal government of between $488 and $608 million per year.

The reason EPA and California favored MTBE over ethanol was that while ethanol works well at reducing carbon monoxide emissions, it has less effect than MTBE in cutting ozone, the main cause of urban smog. Chicago, for instance, is on EPA's ozone nonattainment list, but its carbon monoxide levels are rated satisfactory. Ozone is produced when the chemicals emitted from gasoline combine in sunlight with nitrogen oxides to form volatile organic compounds. Reid vapor pressure measures the tendency of a fuel to break down and form volatile organic compounds: the higher the vapor pressure, the more likely this will happen (see Exhibit 2).

Ethanol has about twice the propensity of methanol to break down and form these compounds. Its vapor pressure characteristics tend to aggravate ozone problems in the summer and in warm weather at other times of the year.

Large U.S. environmental groups tended to favor MTBE for this reason. They opposed ethanol because they believed its production was energy-intensive and thereby highly polluting. From the tractors used in the fields to the processing plants, ethanol did more harm to the environment than MTBE.

At first, the EPA sided with the environmentalists and refused to support a vapor pressure waiver for ethanol. Farm state legislators urged the EPA to grant such a waiver, maintaining that they had helped draft the Clean Air Act and that the EPA misinterpreted their intentions. Those arguing for a waiver maintained that although ethanol increased ozone problems in warm weather, overall it had a positive effect on air quality. MTBE had caused health problems, they argued, particularly in Alaska's cold climate. Ethanol blends, despite higher vapor pressure than MTBE blends, reduced the amount of unburned hydrocarbons, and therefore were acceptable in high ozone areas. More complex models, which considered the particles evaporating into the air from the fuel itself, showed that ethanol might decrease nitrogen oxide emissions, whereas earlier models had shown that it tended to increase them. In any case, refined gasoline was in no sense standard. It varied from refinery to refinery and from season to season, and more regions (49) had carbon monoxide problems than ozone problems.

Instead of a vapor pressure waiver for ethanol, the Clinton administration urged that the EPA adopt a rule that 30 percent of the additives in reformulated gasoline should come from renewable sources. The administration justified its position in terms of heavy U.S. dependence on finite fossil fuels imported from unstable areas of the globe. The EPA announced that it would support this rule. The rule that would go in effect in 1995 would reserve for renewables 15 percent of the market share for gasoline additives. In 1996, this requirement would increase to 30 percent. Theoretically, MTBE made from wood products or garbage was a renewable fuel. The EPA hoped that the renewable additive ultimately would be distilled from several possible sources, not only corn-based ethanol. At present, however, the only commercially viable renewable oxygenates were ethanol and ETBE, a product made from ethanol.

The EPA requirement would affect up to 65 percent of the U.S. gasoline supply. Normal growth in addition to the mandate would double demand for ethanol by the year 2000. Reformulated gas would have to be used in nine U.S. regions that have severe ozone problems: New York, Los Angeles, Baltimore, Chicago, Hartford, Houston, Milwaukee, Philadelphia, and San Diego. Eleven northeastern states, Texas, Kentucky, and the District of Columbia also joined the program. Their commitments meant that a third of the gasoline consumed nationwide would have to be reformulated.

Subcommittees in the Senate voted down EPA's proposed mandate and voted against providing tax incentives for ethanol, and the petroleum industry sued in the U.S. Court of Appeals for the District of Columbia to block the rule. Charles DiBona, president of the American Petroleum Institute claimed that the EPA was motivated by a "shameful, unlawful abuse of power"; it was catering to politically powerful agribusinesses and had no authority to specify which fuel had to be used. The petroleum industry believed that the decision should be left to the marketplace to determine, not the politicians. If this were done, ethanol would be the preferred alternative in the Middle West because transportation costs were cheap. Since ethanol cannot be transported through existing pipelines (condensation in the pipelines can destroy it unless it is further refined), it must be transported by truck or rail. In the West and the East, ethanol was not a practical choice. MBTE was the preferred alternative.

A third option was ETBE, an ether made from ethanol and isobutylene. It was also an octane enhancer, and since it was partially made from ethanol, it enjoyed federal tax exemptions (36 cents per gallon compared with 54 cents per gallon for the pure ethanol blend exemption). Moreover, ETBE had the lowest vapor pressure of the three fuels, only 4.0 psi, and could be shipped through pipelines without any problems. What inhibited ETBE from consideration was that production capacity was low and it was sold in very small commercial quantities.

On September 14, 1994, the federal appeals court blocked the EPA ruling. It held that the EPA had not made a convincing case when it gave preference to ethanol. The court stated that the EPA was not ruling on the merits of the case. It delayed its decision till both sides could present their arguments. This decision was viewed as a victory for the oil industry over the agricultural interests that had lobbied for the ethanol requirement, but the same issue again would be debated by the court early in 1995.[6]

An important development was the rising price of MTBE. Prices almost tripled in 1994 because of concerns about tight oxygenate supplies under the reformulated gasoline program. The gap between ethanol and MTBE pricing had narrowed, making ethanol use more attractive from an economic standpoint. A related matter was that it took almost twice as much MTBE as ethanol to reformulate one gallon of gasoline. The oxygenate requirement for MTBE was 11.0 percent, while it was only 5.7 percent for ethanol. With spot market prices at $1.05 a gallon for MTBE and $1.40 a gallon for ethanol (and a tax credit for ethanol), the net cost to the refiner of ethanol was 5.3 percent lower than that for MTBE. Even small changes in prices would have enormous impacts with a program that was expected to affect the nearly 60 billion gallons of gasoline consumed annually in the United States. Ultimately, an additive market worth several billions of dollars was at stake.

Discussion Questions

1. What should Joanne Magnuson recommend? Should the investor increase its stake in ADM, reduce it, or keep it at the same level?
2. How do you see the scientific evidence on ethanol versus MTBE? Which has more environmental risks associated with it?
3. Given budget deficit in Congress, how likely was Congress to cut its subsidy to ethanol?
4. How was the judge likely to decide the ethanol question?
5. What impact would the judge's decision have on ADM as an investment risk?

Endnotes

1. This case was written by Alfred Marcus and Donald Geffen.
2. Bonnie Wittenburg, "Archer Daniels Midland," *Dain Bosworth Research Capsule*, May 2, 1994; Bonnie Wittenburg and David Thickens, "Archer Daniels Midlands High Plains Corporation," *Dain Bosworth Update Research*, Sept. 14, 1994.
3. Archer Daniels Midland Company, *Annual Report* 1993.
4. Adam Lashinsky, "ADM Pares Back Ethanol Plan," *Crain's Chicago Business*, March 30, 1992, p. 3.
5. Bonnie Wittenburg and David Thickens, "High Plains Corporation," *Dain Bosworth Research Report*, June 22, 1994; Bonnie Wittenburg and David Thickens, "High Plains Corporation," Dain Bosworth Research Capsule, July 1, 1994.
6. "Court Puts Stay on EPA Ethanol Requirement," *Minneapolis Star Tribune*, Sept. 14, 1994, p. 9A; Sharon Schmickle, "Oil Industry Wants Court to Block EPA Ethanol Rule," *Minneapolis Star Tribune*, July 14, 1994, p. 7A.

PART

V

The Social and Legal Effects of Technology

CHAPTER

16

The Promise of Technology

Economic Growth and Prosperity

Our decisions to do something positive, the full consequences of which will be drawn out over many days to come, can only be taken as a result of animal spirits — of a spontaneous urge to action rather than inaction, and not as the outcome of a weighted average of quantitative benefits multiplied by quantitative probabilities . . . Thus, if the animal spirits are dimmed and the spontaneous optimism falters, leaving us to depend on nothing but a mathematical expectation, enterprise will fade and die . . . [and] individual initiative will only be adequate when reasonable calculation is supplemented and supported by animal spirits, so that the thought of ultimate loss which often overtakes pioneers, . . . is put aside as a healthy man puts aside the expectation of death.

John Maynard Keynes, *General Theory of Interest, Employment, and Money*[1]

Introduction and Chapter Objectives

This chapter is about the contributions that technology can make to economic growth and prosperity. The roles played by entrepreneurs, innovative companies and products, investors, and government are discussed. Technological forecasting is important particularly for managers. Why do some technologies succeed, while others fail? Key technologies of the future and technological developments in Japan are considered. This chapter concludes with a description of the innovation process, emphasizing the important social role of technology.

The Importance of Technology

Economic growth—the capacity of a nation to produce the goods and services its people desire—depends on an array of factors including the quantity and quality of labor and natural resources; capital, machines and equipment; management; and values that encourage hard work, diligence, and thrift. Other elements critical for economic growth are a high level of technology and the knowledge to convert the factors of production into goods and services. Technology leads to increasing mechanization and gives rise to an efficient division of labor, which improves productivity and permits the accumulation of capital.

Technology is both the cause of many of the world's environmental problems (see Chapters 14 and 15) and the best hope for their cure. All the classical economists of the late 18th and early 19th centuries, including Adam Smith, David Ricardo, and John Stuart Mill, stressed technology as a critical component of economic development.[2] Thomas Malthus's pessimism that runaway population would lead to increasing misery as the world's population expanded more rapidly than the food supply was based on the premise that technological developments would fall behind population growth.

Technological pioneers often are stubborn dreamers who stick tenaciously to their vision despite the odds against their succeeding. Since few new ideas bear fruit, it sometimes takes foolhardy optimism to overcome a natural inclination toward caution. For innovation to work, at least five elements are needed: entrepreneurs, innovative companies and products, investors, government, and the determination to overcome the many obstacles that inevitably arise.

Entrepreneurs

Small companies employing less than 500 employees have accounted for a large proportion of U.S. job growth since 1988. A new breed of entrepreneur has played an important role. Many entrepreneurs are refugees from large corporations where they gained the solid business experience that results in their success. The rule that a majority of businesses fail in the first five years did not apply to the early 1980s; close to 80 percent of the companies started during that time were still functioning in the early 1990s.[3] The difficulties of being an entrepreneur today—health costs, taxes, government regulation, access to capital, competition, and acquiring a workforce—deterred many from the task. Those who did inaugurate new businesses tried to avoid the risks. Thus, they would commence with a niche in a business they already knew, take on experienced partners, perhaps start with a franchise, and make adjustments quickly when their efforts were not working.

Besides corporate refugees, the new breed of entrepreneurs consisted of many women. A high percentage of the new firms also were started by traditional inventors who were not interested in managing a large enterprise; they lacked people skills and, when they had achieved success, quickly sold out to larger companies. Other entrepreneurs were well-connected individuals who had access to investment bankers and venture capitalists.

Innovative Companies and Products

Two companies known for their innovative products are 3M (see Case 16–A and Case 16–B at the end of this chapter) and Sony (see the next Real-World Example). 3M's innovations extend from low-tech Post-It notes to futuristic synthetic ligaments.[4] More than 30 percent of its revenues came from the 200 or more new products introduced each year during 1985–1990, when 3M's net income doubled. During the recession of the early

1990s, it was careful to limit layoffs of employees and to continue spending 6.6 percent of its total sales on research, about double the U.S. industry average. 3M modernized its factories to cut manufacturing costs and expanded its product line.

Because 3M was a major supplier to the auto industry, many of its products were vulnerable to the recession, and the company faced stiff price competition on its computer diskettes from Japanese companies such as Sony. 3M's products in less recession-prone businesses, like health care, also faced challenges as the United States moved toward cutting these costs. 3M tried to address the needs of other companies during the recession by offering products that would be perceived as cost-saving devices. It tried to speed up product development cycles by getting its design, production, and marketing teams to work more closely together.

Throughout the recession, 3M continued overseas expansion. Its businesses in the Far East enjoyed average yearly growth rates of 20 percent and more (see Case 12–B, "Ford Motor Company's Global Strategy"). In Europe, however, 3M faced serious difficulties; to save money, it consolidated operations there, linked customers to subsidiaries by computers so that orders could be processed more quickly, and established four large warehouses to replace 17 minidistribution centers. To reduce customer complaints it focused on the smallest details of its businesses. For instance, it reduced the time to process complaints in its medical products division by having sales representatives carry preaddressed, postage-paid labels.

Investors

In the early 1990s, venture capital investments declined by about a half from $4.2 billion in 1987 to slightly over $2 billion in 1991.[5] Investments became concentrated in fewer deals. Initial public offerings of stock replaced venture capitalists as the financial supporters of the ablest entrepreneurs. Venture capitalists too often tended to have arm's length relationships with those they funded, watching only the financial aspects of the business and not offering strategic guidance or practical help. Those venture capitalists who had money during the recession became more specialized and demanding, and they gave more careful scrutiny to the deals they made.

Public offerings were the main alternative to venture capital. Wall Street investors supported the biotechnology industry although the biotech firms were slow to develop new products and few earned profits. Given that it takes a decade or more to move a product from the laboratory to the marketplace, the patience of the backers of biotechnology was remarkable. Without collateral, banks found it impossible to extend loans to finance this type of development.

Government

Government's role in technological innovation was important because the payoff to society was greater than it was to the individual company or investor. Without government, innovation would be underfunded. Rational companies and individuals would forgo the advantage of being first as the innovator and produce imitations instead, because copying was almost always cheaper than innovation. Though innovation benefited all of society, it was not in the interest of a specific group other than government to provide for it.[7]

Real-World Example

Sony

Like 3M, Sony has been a consistently innovative company,[6] producing many high-technology successes from the transistor radio to the camcorder, compact disk player, Trinitron television, and Walkman. The company also has had its share of failures, including the Beta Max videocassette recorder. Sony's repeated success at innovation differentiates it from companies like Atari, which invented the videogame, but had no successful follow-ups. Unlike companies like Casio, Samsung, and Sanyo, which try to copy products made by others and sell them cheaply, Sony's goal is to release 1,000 new products per year, 800 improved ones, and 200 that open entirely different markets.

Among its workforce of 112,000, Sony employs more than 9,000 scientists and engineers. It spends 5.7 percent of its revenues on product research and development, and like 3M, its corporate research department organizes an annual exposition, which is open only to employees, where scientists exhibit what they are doing. Sony also wants its products to have a distinct character, so it employs many artists as well as engineers in a strong design center.

The company founder, Masaru Ibuka, articulated the company's vision as "never to follow others." However, while Sony follows typical Japanese practices of lifetime employment, company slogans and attire, long hours, and a rigid pay ladder, it also makes a point of not relying on specialists. Sony employees are supposed to be open-minded and optimistic and have wide-ranging interests. The company moves them from one product group to another and tries to instill in them the ambition to create new products. Talented young people are given key positions in new product development teams. These newcomers have the freshness of vision to create entirely new products, while experienced engineers find better ways to manufacture existing products.

Sony always has concentrated on the consumer market, which was largely ignored by U.S. electronics firms that worked on military and space applications. Its distinctive capacity was to package the latest technology into small, inexpensive items that consumers found easy to use. Sony continues to bring out numerous new products, including the Palmtop pocket-sized notepad computer that reads writing and keeps track of appointments, addresses, telephone numbers, and personal memos; and the Data Discman, a portable, paperback-size electronic book that displays text and graphics and has audio output.

Sony has not had unbroken successes, however. Its move into the U.S. entertainment industry through the acquisition of Columbia Pictures was an uncharacteristically big risk that brought Sony unaccustomed difficulties.

All major industrial nations had technology policies. The post–World War II technology policy of the United States was based on government support for basic research, which it was hoped, would benefit society at some point in time. The U.S. government was a leader in financing many discoveries, but it lagged behind other nations in applying the research to commercialize products.[8] For that reason, Congress has shown less willingness to pay for it. Instead, it has promised increased financing for civilian technologies. Seven hundred national labs were eager to get involved, and they formed more than 1,000 cooperative R&D arrangements (CRADAS) with private companies. The National Institute of Standards and Technology (NIST) started an Advanced Technology Program (ATP), which gave grants to companies developing promising but risky technologies. ATP did not single out industrial sectors for help (e.g., silicon technologies versus steel) nor did it emphasize generic technologies (e.g., advanced material processing or high performance computing). The amounts APT gave were relatively small and the companies it considered for grants had to convince NIST that their ideas had technical merit, practicality, and commercial prospects. Among the 1992 winners were optical computers and advanced plastics for automobiles (see Case 14–A). In addition, the Commerce Department developed a strategic partnership initiative, in which companies that produced new technologies had the opportunity to meet people from the companies that might use it.

The Pentagon remained the largest financial backer of research in the United States. At first, it gave its support almost exclusively to its suppliers, who were largely sheltered from the civilian market. Increasingly, however, it came to rely on innovations from the civilian economy. Defense Advanced Research Products Administration (DARPA) funding for **dual-use technologies** (military and commercial) was very successful. Germany, Switzerland, and Japan mostly had market-driven technology policies, while the technology policies of the United States, the United Kingdom, and France were more government-directed and military-driven.

dual-use technologies Technologies with military and civilian applications.

Overcoming Obstacles to Innovation

It was not easy to build competitive advantage on the basis of scientific advances alone. U.S. scientists were as good as any in the world, but the United States was not a leader in making their inventions into commercial successes.[9] At least eight reasons explain why innovation is hard to accomplish:

1. Companies that come up with the discoveries do not always profit from them. The EMI scanner was an enormous scientific discovery—as large as anything since X rays—but EMI suffered great losses in developing it and sold the rights to the technology at a cut-rate price.

2. Companies that make discoveries do not always use them. Drug companies exploit their own inventions, but relatively small engineering companies routinely make discoveries, such as the bar code readers at supermarket checkout counters, that others use. Suppliers originate many new ideas for their customers.

3. Innovation rarely is instantaneous. Technologies improve in reliability, quality, and flexibility as they diffuse. In a series of small steps and refinements, they develop an evolving range of applications.

4. Innovation usually starts as a solution to a narrow problem. The innovators rarely know all the ramifications. Thomas Watson at IBM, for instance, thought the computer would be of limited use. He believed that the single computer his company made in 1947 would solve scientific problems, but it would have limited commercial application.

5. Diffusion is very uneven. It follows the classic S-shaped curve. The first to adopt new technology are daring; the great mass of people are much slower to change.

6. Large firms in rapidly growing industries sometimes make innovations first because of their financial strength and access to information, but this is not always true. Some innovators are small unknown firms, like Microsoft, that rapidly rise to the pinnacles of success. The early market for innovation cannot be easily established, and it is not easy to tell in advance who will dominate this market.

7. The expectation that prices for a new product will fall retards adoption. People

wait to buy because they believe further technological progress will drive prices down—think of the market for personal computers! Meanwhile, the inventors and developers who have endured most of the risk may not have staying power. Their inventions are then exploited by the **second and third movers,** those companies that later enter an industry.

second and third movers
Imitators who do not bear the cost but enjoy the benefits of commercially exploiting new technologies.

8. Developers frequently do not profit from the commercial application of their ideas. Since imitators face lower costs, the incentive to create is not large. Patent protection does not always help.

In short, the path to successful innovation is strewn with many obstacles.

Waves of Innovation

The Russian economist Nikolai Kondratiev (1892–1938) expounded a theory that economic progress was not linear but took place in long waves, each of them lasting about half a century.[10] Each wave had periods of prosperity, recession, depression, and recovery. Joseph Schumpeter, the Austrian economist, connected these waves of growth to technological innovations. The first period (1782–1845) saw major innovations in steam power and textiles; the second (1845–1892) in railroads, iron, coal, and construction; and the third (1892–1948) in electrical power, automobiles, chemicals, and steel.[11]

Technological change, according to Schumpeter, is like a "series of explosions" with innovations concentrating in specific sectors, or leading-edge industries that provide the momentum for growth. These leading sectors propel the economy forward; without them, economic growth is not possible.

Entrepreneurs, seeing the opportunities for profit, vigorously exploit the new technologies. The pioneers are followed by a swarm of imitators. The combined activity of the pioneers and followers generate boom conditions. Soon, however, there are so many imitators that prices fall and an economic bust follows. This process is one of "**creative destruction**" in which lagging sectors fall behind. Their time passes; they wither and die or are kept afloat by government subsidy and bailout. To spur a revival, new innovation is needed.

creative destruction
Process that replaces old technologies with new ones.

Alternative Futures

The prosperity of the post–World War II period was built on innovations in semiconductors, consumer electronics, aerospace, pharmaceuticals, petrochemicals, and synthetic and composite materials (see Exhibit 16–1). A dynamic growth phase existed shortly after World War II. The middle to late 1960s was a period of consolidation. This was followed by a period of maturity beginning at the end of the 1960s, when many markets were saturated.

As markets stagnated, unemployment in manufacturing grew. Many companies lowered production costs by making incremental manufacturing improvements and exporting jobs to foreign countries where labor costs were lower. After 1973, growth rates declined worldwide (see Chapter 12), and the post–World War II boom lost its momentum.

EXHIBIT 16–1 Waves of Innovation

1782–1845	Steam power, textiles
1845–1892	Railroads, iron, coal, construction
1892–1948	Electrical power, automobiles, chemicals, steel
1948–1973	Semiconductors, consumer electronics, aerospace, pharmaceuticals, petrochemicals, synthetic and composite materials

SOURCE: R. Rothwell and W. Zegveld, *Reindustrialization and Technology* (Armonk, N.Y.: M. E. Sharpe, 1985); J. A. Scumpeter, *Business Cycles* (New York: McGraw-Hill, 1939).

Postindustrial Society

Sociologist Daniel Bell constructed the model of a postindustrial society to explain the diverse changes that were occurring in society.[12] A postindustrial society differed from an industrial society in five ways:

1. The economic sector changed from producing *goods* to producing *services*.
2. A *professional and technical class* became dominant in society.
3. *Theoretical knowledge* became the central source of innovation.
4. The *control of technology* and *technological assessment* became primary activities.
5. *New intellectual technologies* (modeling, simulation, cybernetics, decision theory, and systems analysis) influenced decision making.

"The Powers of the Mind." The popular writer George Gilder extended Bell's vision of postindustrial society. He claimed that "wealth in the form of physical resources" was losing value and importance to "the powers of the mind," which were gaining the upper hand "over the brute force of things." Economic activity in earlier periods centered on physical labor, natural resources, and capital. Today, ideas and technology, not material resources, are the hallmark of ascendant nations and corporations.[13]

Electronics, computer software, and telecommunications relied upon human creativity. They emancipated human beings from their dependence upon the physical world. The microchip, according to Gilder, symbolized this "worldwide shift of the worth of goods from materials to ideas" as the material costs of the product constituted only about 2 percent of the total costs of production.[14] The most valuable part of the microchip was the idea for its design (see Case 11–A on U.S. Memories). The rise of the mind as a source of wealth that spanned industries was among the most important forces in the 21st century.

Technological Forecasting

These trends suggest that managers need to forecast technological change and anticipate breakthroughs early when response times are long and they are in a better position to take advantage of them. Technology is dynamic and has many important implications for business expansion and contraction. An estimated 25 percent of existing technology is replaced every year. Managers can understand these changes through simple trend analysis, monitoring expert opinion and other sources of information for indications of changes, and constructing alternative scenarios.[15]

Trends

Trends in one area often lead to the forecasting of trends in another (e.g., military jet speeds foretell commercial jet speeds). The number of components needed to manufacture one product can help managers to estimate the number needed to manufacture a similar product. But trends must be analyzed with caution. Simple extrapolation can be deceiving if it does not take into account the impact of one trend on another, ignores how the human response can change the direction of a trend, and leaves no room for surprises. Economic forecasts are good at predicting the future based on the past so long as the future resembles the past in important ways, but radical breaks that no economist can predict may take place (e.g., the 1973 Arab oil embargo).

Experts

Expert opinion can be used, but experts make mistakes. The British Parliament established a committee of experts at the end of the 19th century to investigate the potential of Thomas Edison's incandescent lamp. It found the idea "unworthy" of attention. During World War II, a panel of experts selected by the federal government did not believe that an intercontinental ballistic missile could accurately deliver its payload 3,000 miles away. The Rand Corporation, a think tank in Southern California, devised the "Delphi method" to aggregate the beliefs of experts about particular issues. Each expert is asked to predict important events and to clarify the reasons why he or she believes the event is likely to occur. Successive requestioning in light of the answers helps to sharpen the results.[16]

Alternative Scenarios

When the future is uncertain, managers can construct alternative scenarios. They can create a series of possible sequences of future events that take into account the uncertainty (see Chapter 2). In 1972, Shell Oil forecast and assessed the implications of three different energy scenarios: immediate (2 years), middle range (10 years), and long range (25 years). This exercise forced Shell's managers to think through what they would do if unfavorable circumstances should arise and provided them with the opportunity to better manage future contingencies should they occur.[17]

Managers need to monitor the environment for signals that may be the forerunners of significant changes. To do so, they have to clarify their ideas about which indicators to follow. Then they have to understand how to put the information together and interpret it for the purposes of decision making. In a free society, the amount of information produced is immense. Professional conferences, technical papers, and the media yield data that vie for a manager's attention. What to focus on and what to ignore is a perpetual problem.

The Next Wave of Innovation

For economic growth to take off, a new wave of innovation is needed. Where will it come from? The following technologies may play an important role.[18]

- *Artificial intelligence*. Computer use will continue to expand into areas where human intelligence formerly was applied. The computers will be able to carry out such activities as learning, adapting, recognizing, and self-correction.
- *Genetic engineering*. The genetic code of living organisms will be mapped, restructured, and remodeled to enhance or eliminate certain traits. This potential will allow scientists to predict and correct genetic diseases. It should allow them to create crops that are resistant to pests and drought.
- *Advanced computers*. Evolving chip technologies open up the promise of the development of faster and more powerful computers. Sarnoff chips, which contain 100 or more tiny lasers, have been used to create the first functional optoelectric integrated circuit. They could be used in powerful new desktop computers in the future.
- *Bioelectricity*. Damaged or dysfunctioning nerves, muscles, and glands can be stimulated to promote their repair and restore their health so they function properly. Currently, this technique can be used in humans with severed bones and defective hearts and lungs. It speeds the healing rates of wounds and is an alternative to addictive painkillers.
- *Multisensory robotics*. Robots can be made that can perform more than simple, repetitive tasks. Useful service robots, such as smart shopping carts and mobile helpers for factory and personal use, are in the works.
- *Parallel processing*. This technique permits many computers to be used simultaneously in solving a problem. It greatly enhances computer power and performance and thereby increases the complexity of the scientific and technical tasks that can be handled.
- *Digital electronics*. Information from audio, video, and film sources can be digitized for more rapid retrieval. The use of optical memory systems such as optical disks, film, and bar code readers is likely to be expanded.
- *Lasers*. Lasers are light amplified by the stimulated emission of radiation. They permit holography (3-D imagery), which may become more common in advertising. Microwave scalpels equipped with lasers have already begun to replace the old metal scalpels used in surgery.
- *Fiber optics*. Fiber optics carry up to four signals at once (television, telephone, radio, and computer). They promise to greatly improve and expand communications.
- *Microwaves*. New applications are being developed beyond the wireless digital information sent on satellite dishes and used on heating devices such as the microwave oven. Possibilities also include microwave clothes dryers and cancer treatment systems.
- *Advanced satellites*. As more countries send satellites into orbit, satellites will be

used for new purposes including oil and mineral exploration and pinpoint surveillance and mapping.

- *Solar energy*. Photovoltaic cells convert sunlight to energy (see Case 13–A on ARCO Solar). New uses will be developed beyond pocket calculators and remote power applications. Solar technologies also can be used for rural electrification projects in the developing countries and as alternatives to automobile and jet fuel.
- *Microtransistors*. A quantum transistor 100 times smaller and 1,000 times faster than current transistors has been developed. If mass-produced, it would revolutionize the electronics industry.
- *Molecular design*. Supercomputers can design new materials molecule by molecule and atom by atom. Tailor-made enzymes for industrial use have been developed. Additional products made in this way promise to move out of the laboratory.
- *New polymers*. Lighter, stronger, heat-resistant, and able to conduct electricity, new polymers can be used in many products ranging from garbage bags to army tanks, ball bearings, moldable batteries, and running shoes.
- *High-tech ceramics*. These materials promise to be resistant to corrosion, wear, and high temperatures and will be used to create lighter-weight cars and cleaner-running engines. They open up the possibility of a new, more efficient engine design that creates less pollution.
- *Fiber-reinforced composites*. These lightweight and noncorrosive composite materials often are stronger than steel, and they can be used in the construction of buildings, bridges, and aircraft.
- *Superconductors*. These materials carry electricity without loss of energy. They make possible less expensive but more advanced magnetic resonance imaging (MRI) machines for hospitals. They can be used in TV antennas and faster computer circuits. New developments in superconductors could permit the construction of trains with magnetic levitation.

All of these technologies have a wide variety of uses, from telecommunications and computers to health and transportation. They rely on new materials and manufacturing processes for their realization. They promise to extend human sensory capabilities and intellectual processes. By making machines capable of imitating the functioning of the human brain, a computer could process many types of information simultaneously. Mathematical data could be processed at the same time the computer received spoken commands in English or a foreign language.[19]

Obstacles to Adopting Promising Technologies

innovation
Putting an idea created in a laboratory into practical and widespread use.

In theory, these technologies are very promising, but formidable obstacles stand in the way of their widescale adoption and use. A promising idea, commonly referred to as an invention, is not the same as an innovation.[20] An invention is merely the creation of the idea in the laboratory. It is the test of a certain principle, an act of technical creativity that describes a concept that may be suitable for patenting. By contrast, **innovation** puts this idea into widespread use; commercial exploitation assures broad application. The following sections describe some of the obstacles that have been encountered in commercializing two of the technologies previously listed.

Artificial Intelligence

The marketplace applications of artificial intelligence have been very disappointing. Many companies established in the mid-1980s have ceased to exist, and others have shrunk in size and cut back their workforces. Sales that were supposed to reach into the billions of dollars did not exceed $600 million in 1990. Much of the venture capital funding and many of the talented technical people who were attracted to the field abandoned it.[21]

Artificial intelligence (AI) allows computers to mimic ordinary human intelligence. It includes systems that help machines in factories "see," that enable computers to analyze aerial photographs, and that permit language recognition for translation or dictation. Security applications for guarding warehouses have been developed, but AI's greatest promise is in expert systems—software packages that can imitate the reasoning and decision processes of specialists in various fields based on the rules of thumb they use and the data they have available.

The American Express Company successfully applied artificial intelligence in its credit authorization department. It developed a program to review cardholder requests for money to make big purchases. The customer's credit history was reviewed in an instant; if problems existed, they were identified immediately for employees to investigate.

Despite the promise of this type of application, the developers of artificial intelligence have not understood potential markets. For instance, Applied Expert Systems tried to sell a $50,000 software package to professional financial planners. The company claimed that the computer could produce a better financial plan than the planners. Understandably, the professional planners felt threatened by this claim and refused to buy the package. Applied Expert Systems next tried to sell it to banks and insurance companies, which were less threatened.[22]

Another artificial intelligence program, called LISP, was simply too expensive. LISP Machine Inc., Xerox, and Texas Instruments all had workstations that used LISP, but the cost of at least $100,000 was more than most customers were willing to pay.[23]

The problems in the artificial intelligence industry may have been the lack of a good sense for market forces on the part of its founders, many of whom were researchers. Initially, they were very well funded and spent money freely without a sense of the limits of either time or budgets which are needed to make a commercial success.

Genetic Engineering

Genetic engineering companies fared somewhat better than the artificial intelligence companies. The technology was very seductive; entrepreneurs and scientists alike hyped the chances of its success. However, scientists not only had trouble focusing on the products they would make, but they frequently misjudged the time required to prove that the products worked and to obtain regulatory approval. For example, Liposome Company believed that fatty, water-filled membranes could be used to deliver drugs more effectively through the membranes. But to figure out five diseases where this would work, it had to screen more than a million possibilities and then develop a method of delivering the drugs. Finally, it required large-scale manufacturing methods.

Federal regulators, too, have been an obstacle to the commercialization of biotechnology products because five federal agencies each have some jurisdiction and guidelines are not clear. Many companies have had to maintain manufacturing facilities that they could not run at full capacity and sales forces that could not market a product while they waited for regulatory acceptance. To get around the regulatory process, biotechnology companies have looked for applications of their products that need little or no regulatory approval. They also have allied themselves with large drug and chemical companies that are experienced at obtaining approval. Large manufacturers also help them shoulder the risks and furnish marketing capabilities.

Large manufacturers that have entered the biotechnology business on their own have not always been successful. Monsanto, for instance, made a huge investment in biotechnology research.[24] It developed a bovine growth hormone (BGH) to boost the milk production of cows. BGH is a protein similar to the one cows make naturally. It is injected into the cows twice a month and increases milk yields by 10 to 20 percent. However, Monsanto's product was banned by the governor of Wisconsin after opposition from dairy farmers who supposedly would be the product's main customers. Farmers feared that a milk glut would lower prices. Consumer anxieties about artificial foods and the fears of giant grocery chains that people would not buy milk from cows injected with BGH initially prevented the product from being widely used.

Monsanto has also been criticized by environmentalists about another genetically engineered product—a new strain of cotton and soybean plants that can withstand spraying from Monsanto's herbicide Roundup. Environmentalists wonder why Monsanto cannot work on pest-resistant crops rather than crops that resist pesticides.

Biotechnology has great promise. It might be possible to use plant cells to make valuable substances in large quantities that plants make in small quantities.[25] Genetically manufactured products such as melanin could offer protection from skin cancer. Other genetically manufactured products would modify or enhance the flavor of fruits and vegetables, help in the petroleum refining process, and protect people inadvertently exposed to radiation. However, these products can only be developed if they can overcome the regulatory hurdles and gain public acceptance.

Why Technologies Fail

However promising, many ideas fail to find widescale application (see Exhibit 16–2). Only a small percentage of projects succeed depending on the industry and the circumstances. After a commercial launch has occurred and less-attractive R&D projects and proposals have been weeded out, the success rate is higher. Still, failure is common, and managers have little control over it: it is hard to pick winners.[26]

risk
Conditions where the odds of economic success are known with certainty, as opposed to uncertainty, where the odds of success are unknown.

Economists distinguish between conditions where the odds of success are known with certainty (e.g., flipping a coin), which they call **risk,** and conditions where the odds of success are unknown, which they call *uncertainty*. Classification is a question of degree.

EXHIBIT 16–2 Obstacles to the Commercialization of Technologies

Artificial intelligence	Failure to understand potential markets
Genetic engineering	Unclear regulatory responsibilities
	Consumer anxieties
	Environmental criticism

The art of assigning statistical probabilities is just that—an art. Better management does not easily reduce the failure rate, nor can managers always manipulate the situation to their liking or produce the results they desire. After the fact, it may be easy to say why success or failure occurs, but it is not easy to know what to do beforehand.[27]

Technical and Commercial Feasibility

Most managers have powerful reasons to keep risk to a minimum. In deliberating whether to undertake a particular project, they have to consider technical and commercial feasibility. They have to estimate:

1. Probable development, production, and marketing costs.
2. The approximate timing of these costs.
3. Probable future income streams.
4. When the income streams are likely to develop.

All of these calculations are fraught with uncertainty. The only way to reduce uncertainty is to undertake safe projects. Thus, managers tend to be biased toward innovations where success is easy—simple, well-tread areas where fundamental research and invention is not necessary.[28]

Managers establish new generations of existing products, introduce new models, and differentiate a product further rather than create different products and new product lines. They reduce uncertainty by licensing other people's inventions, imitating other people's product introductions, modifying existing processes, and making minor technical improvements. An automobile with a new type of engine, for instance, is less likely to be introduced than an auto with simple modifications of an existing engine.

Optimistic Bias. Managers must have an optimistic bias to launch a new product. Without it, the contemplation of failure overwhelms the inclination to proceed. An optimistic bias affects all types of investment decisions; innovations are no different. If the actual chances of success were based on entirely sober and realistic assessments, fewer innovations would occur. Engineers, for instance, make optimistic estimates of development costs, but actual costs and the probabilities of technical success are hard to determine.[29]

Predicting Market Success. It is also difficult to predict market success. Market launch and growth in sales are distant in time, and future conditions vary. No one knows what the reaction of competitors will be to the threat of new products. Not only is it difficult

Exhibit 16–3 Technical Uncertainty

- Whether product will work
- Performance under different operating conditions:
  Before product reaches market
  In early stages of promising commercial launch
  After product introduction

to achieve an advance understanding of the costs, given changing economic circumstances, but also it is hard to know in advance how long a product will be on the market and how dominant, given the threat of technical obsolescence, it will be.

The empirical evidence confirms that "early estimates of future markets have been wildly inaccurate."[30] The successful developers of computers thought that fewer than 4,000 would be sold in the United States by 1965. They did not dream that over 20,000 units would be sold in the United States by 1965 and that the potential market was unlimited.

Even with sophisticated techniques for estimating project success, companies make flagrant errors. For instance, no firm was more experienced than Du Pont with new product introductions, yet the company has lost large sums with some products before it withdrew them from the market. Three types of uncertainty that affect new product development—technical, business conditions and the market, and government—have to be considered.

Technical Uncertainty

After prototype testing, pilot plant work, trial production, and test marketing, technical uncertainty is likely to exist in the early stages of introducing products (see Exhibit 16–3). The question typically is not whether a product will work but one of degree—of standards of performance under different operating conditions and of the costs of improving performance under these conditions. Unexpected problems can arise before a product reaches the market, in the early stages of a promising commercial launch, and after product introduction, as the examples below illustrate.

Before a Product Reaches the Market. Unexpected problems affected the pharmaceutical company Syntex even before it got a new product on the market. Syntex's patent on its major money-maker, Naprosyn, an anti-inflammatory drug, was about to expire. The company created a new ulcer drug, Enprostil, which not only eased the pain of ulcers but also lowered cholesterol. With about 23 million people worldwide suffering from ulcers, drugs that treat the problem, like SmithKline Beecham's Tagamet and Glaxo Holdings' Zantac, yielded substantial profits. However, the principal researcher who pioneered Enprostil's development spotted evidence of dangerous blood clots that might produce new ulcers or pose a risk of heart attack or stroke. Enprostil failed to win FDA approval and was not a commercial success.[31]

The Early Stages of Production. Serious setbacks can also occur in the early stages of a promising commercial launch. For instance, Weyerhaeuser Company sought to become an important player in the disposable diaper market with its Ultrasofts product. Ultrasofts had superior features—a clothlike cover and superabsorbent pulp material woven into the pad designed to keep babies dry. Consumer tests showed that parents favored it two to one over competing brands. The advertising and promotion campaign offered coupons saving parents $1 per package to try the product. Procter & Gamble and Kimberly-Clark, which together controlled 85 percent of the $3.8 billion baby diaper market, came back with aggressive cost cutting and promotion campaigns to keep customers loyal. Meanwhile, manufacturing problems occurred in Weyerhaeuser's Bowling Green, Kentucky, plant. The system that sprayed the superabsorbent material into the diapers started to break down and a fire broke out. Weyerhaeuser had to raise prices to retailers by 22 percent to cover the unexpected expenses. The retailers refused to give the product shelf space, and Weyerhaeuser was forced to withdraw the product from the marketplace.[32]

After a Product Is on the Market. Serious setbacks also take place when a product is on the market. At General Electric (GE), the appliance division's market share and profits had been falling. Its cumbersome 1950s technology took three times as long to make compressors as it took Japanese and Italian manufacturers. The compressor, a pump that creates cold air in a refrigerator, is as crucial to it as an engine is to a car. GE committed $120 million to building a factory to manufacture a newly designed compressor that had parts made of powdered metal instead of hardened steel. Powdered metal was more easily fabricated to the extreme tolerances that were needed and it was cheaper than steel. Evaluation engineers, however, told the designers that powdered metal had not worked in air conditioners. Designers discounted their views, test data showed no failures, and a technician's observation of excessive heat was ignored. Field testing was limited to about nine months instead of the usual two years, because managers wanted the product on the market immediately. GE scrapped its old compressors and proudly declared that an American company could still take the lead in world manufacturing. Consumers bought the refrigerators with the new compressor in record numbers, with GE increasing its market share by 2 percent, its best showing in years. However, some compressors began to fail after about a year on the market, and GE, which had sold the refrigerators with five-year warranties, decided to recall and replace them.[33]

General Business Uncertainty

General business uncertainty also affects the introduction of new products. It had a negative effect on General Motors efforts in bringing Saturn to the market. Saturn's introduction at a time of poor economic conditions and overcapacity in the industry meant initially disappointing sales. GM was hurt by the changing business conditions of the early 1990s when Saturn was introduced.[34]

The Role of Customers. Pioneering new technologies carries great uncertainties in knowing what consumers want and providing it to them in a timely fashion. Having a good idea is not enough. Models of innovation that start with scientific and technological advances miss the important role that customers play both in the adoption decision and in subsequent refinements.

For example, Motorola's excellence as an engineering company is widely recognized. Still, it has been unable to keep its customers from defecting to such rivals as Intel, Sun Microsystems, and Mips Computer Systems. Motorola's obsession with technological excellence—its engineers had to create the best-designed, fastest, and highest quality product possible—prevented it from meeting market needs in a timely fashion. While competitors were already shipping products to customers, Motorola was still making revisions. IBM chose Intel's chip to be the standard in personal computers, not because Motorola's was technically inferior, but because Intel was more responsive to its needs. Motorola did capture nearly 80 percent of the market for microprocessors used in workstations, but this market was much smaller than the personal computer market. Transferring technology from the laboratory to the market is not easily accomplished when technology-oriented managers dominate.[35]

Uncertain Government Support

New products also can be hurt by uncertain government support. For instance, high-definition television (HDTV) was once a favorite among politicians and business lobbyists in Washington, D.C. Sharp images, perfect sound, and the convenience of large, thin screens had great appeal. The consumer market was estimated at more than $100 billion. Government and business officials met to map out a strategy for developing a new technology to compete with Japan and other foreign nations. However, the Bush administration did not cooperate because it believed that support for research that had commercial potential should come only from the private sector. It cut government support for HDTV. The only American firm willing to take on the risks by itself was Zenith. All other companies backed out because the government would not subsidize the high costs of development.[36]

Striving for Constant Innovation

These examples illustrate the lesson that an innovator cannot afford to rest on its laurels. Past success does not guarantee success in the future. Firms must strive for constant innovation.

For instance, SmithKline Beckman scored a great success with Tagamet, the ulcer medicine it introduced in 1976. For years the biggest problem the company faced was meeting demand. However, Glaxo Holdings, developed a competing drug, Zantac, with fewer side effects. SmithKline, meanwhile, was unable to come up with new blockbuster drugs despite spending vast sums on research.[37] In retrospect, it is easy to say that SmithKline did not act quickly enough to build up a world-class research capability. However, in the pharmaceutical industry, luck may play as much of a role as talent and organization and SmithKline's management could do only so much. Still, the lesson is this: to maintain technical and market leadership, a firm has to strive for constant innovation.

Technology Push and Market Pull

The "technology-push" model of innovation starts with discoveries in basic science and engineering. From these discoveries new goods and services come to the marketplace. However, numerous empirical studies and descriptions of innovation demonstrate the importance of a clear perception of market needs. Successful innovations need both scientific/technical advances and market appeal (see Exhibit 16–4).

Von Hippel shows that the amounts of innovation from scientific/technical people and from manufacturers and users are about equal. Frequent interactions between these groups are important. Users must be sophisticated enough to make technically relevant recommendations and be able to purchase and use the products that incorporate their suggestions.[38]

The challenge innovators face is to match technological opportunity with market need. For managers, this means bringing together the different in-house functions (such as marketing, R&D, and manufacturing) that have a knowledge of consumer needs and scientific and technical developments. Exclusively, technology-push or **market-pull** models are now viewed as atypical examples of a more general process in which constant interaction takes place between market requirements and scientific achievement.[39]

market pull
Theory that consumer demand, not new discoveries in science and engineering, drive innovation.

Although more R&D does not necessarily result in more innovation, market need alone may yield such simple, incremental innovations that they do not add up to much in the long run.[40] In the end, different types of innovation, science and technology-based and market-driven, exist at different stages in the product life cycle.

Japanese Innovation

Japanese innovation—more of the market-pull variety—had relied on imitation, purchase, and copy of foreign technology. Its improvements have been incremental and involved modest, but commercially extremely important, refinements of inventions made elsewhere, most often in the United States.[41]

EXHIBIT 16–4 Evaluating New Products: The Commercial and Technical Screen

		Technical Potential	
		High	*Low*
Commercial promise	*High*	Sure success	Need technical breakthrough
	Low	Need market acceptance	Sure failure

Buying Western Technology

From 1950 to 1980, Japan bought Western technology through more than 30,000 licensing and technology importing agreements for which it paid more than $10 billion.[42] The videotape recorder, for instance, was an American invention, created by Ampex Corporation for television productions. Sony made the changes necessary in video recording to appeal to a mass consumer market.

Japan has excelled in this type of applied research. However, it has been trying in recent years to go beyond applied research and the adaptation of Western technologies. The nation's leaders realize that it needs to be able to achieve the kinds of scientific and technical breakthroughs that can create new industries and transform an entire economy. Spurred by a desire for self-reliance and national pride, the leaders have been trying to shift Japanese research priorities toward basic science and research.[43]

Obstacles to Ascendancy in Basic Research

Creativity is necessary for success in basic research. The emphasis in Japanese education, however, has been on rote learning and brute memorization, which are designed to give students the skills to pass rigorous standardized tests. The Japanese have succeeded in lifting their average student above the educational levels generally found in the United States. Thus, the average Japanese blue-collar and salaried worker is better educated and more disciplined than the average blue-collar or salaried worker in the United States. However, American elites are probably more skilled than those in Japan. Japan has had few Nobel Prize winners in the sciences while Germany has had 4 times as many, Great Britain 10 times as many, and the United States 30 times as many.[44]

Since Japanese culture stresses consensus and conformance to group norms, intellectual dialogue and confrontation are not as common. The individual genius who shows disdain for what others do and succeeds despite breaking all the rules is not accepted in Japanese society. In areas where creativity is called for, such as computer software, Japan is lagging behind the United States and other Western nations.

The number of graduate students in Japan is about 3 percent of the total student population compared with about 12 percent in the United States.[45] Most Japanese research is carried out in corporations, not universities, and the corporations emphasize finding practical, commercial applications and solving real-world problems, not basic research.

The Japanese, however, understand that to maintain economic leadership they will have to extend their technical competence beyond incremental innovations. They will have to emphasize basic discoveries. The Japanese also realize that they can no longer live off Western technology; to succeed in the long run they will have to export original ideas.

The Japanese have begun to make great strides. About half the patents filed worldwide now come from Japanese corporations.[46] Japanese technological advances are mostly in hardware areas and they show the continued Japanese genius for manufacturing. Nevertheless, the Japanese have not caught up with the United States and other Western nations in the creative industries of movies, records, and pharmaceuticals.

Product-Focused Research

Japan has more technical and scientific workers per capita than any nation in the world (5,000 per million of population compared with 3,500 in the United States and 2,500 in Germany), and it spends as much on research and development as a percentage of GNP as the United States and more than any single European nation.[47] While U.S. research directed toward military needs is likely to decline somewhat under budgetary restraints and the end of the Cold War, Japan's research has long been more product oriented. Japan also has the capital derived from a high rate of savings to spend on new factories to manufacture the new products. It is beginning to export much of the manufacturing technology to other countries in the Pacific Rim where labor costs are cheaper than in Japan.

Japan's successes in technology are based on many factors (see Exhibit 16–5):

fusion factor The ability to blend incremental improvements from sometimes alien fields to create a product with entirely new features.

1. *Fusion factor.* The ability to blend incremental improvements from sometimes alien fields to create a product with entirely new features is known as the **fusion factor.** The heavy investment by Japanese industrial groups (*keiretsu*) in each other's companies facilitates this process.

2. *Linking innovations.* The Japanese recognize that making a fundamental breakthrough is by itself insufficient. To be really successful at innovation, it is necessary to devise a better way to manufacture and help customers use the product. For instance, Corning Glass, a U.S. company, first developed fiber optics, but Japanese companies solved the practical problems that prevented customers from using this product—they fell apart too easily and the messages sent were often lost during transmission. Robots with various forms of "soft automation" have given the Japanese great advantages in easily redesigning their production facilities in response to changing consumer preferences. Japanese engineers also consider cost and manufacturability from the beginning while American engineers are more concerned about the technical feasibility of a project.

3. *Less reliance on rate-of-return criteria.* Japanese managers do not rigidly adhere to rate-of-return criteria in assessing new projects because they believe that one successful innovation is likely to breed another and that waves of innovation cannot be predicted by conventional rate-of-return techniques. For example, a new optical chip fashioned from gallium arsenide could promote new tools for chip manufacture and solve remaining problems in developing high-definition television (HDTV), thereby speeding innovations in both areas.

4. *Speed in marketing a product.* The Japanese believe that speed in getting a product to the market is critical. Even if the product is not perfect, it is better for customers to buy

EXHIBIT 16–5 Characteristics of Japanese Innovation

- Fusion—a blend of incremental improvements from different fields.
- A recognition that marketing and manufacturing innovation have to go hand in hand with product innovation.
- Less reliance on conventional rate-of-return criteria and belief in waves of innovation.
- Insistence on speed in getting a product to market in effort to obtain feedback from customers.
- Persistence and refusal to accept failure.

the product and get used to it. This process enables companies developing the product not only to earn needed income but also to receive invaluable feedback about what the next generation of the product should be like. This feedback cannot be obtained from conventional marketing studies. U.S. scientists at MIT developed a machine capable of recognizing over 400 words, but they had no plans to bring this machine immediately to the market. In contrast, the Japanese telecommunications giant Nippon Telegraph and Telephone developed a machine that recognized only 32 words, but the company already was working on a commercial application.

5. *Refusal to accept failure.* Japanese engineers do not know the meaning of failure. They push on to success regardless of the obstacles. Studies of the working habits of Japanese and American engineers show that after a hard day of work, American engineers go home to their families. Japanese engineers are more willing to stay on the job and continue what they are doing; to retreat or give up would be accompanied by great shame.

As U.S. scientists become more reluctant to share their technology with the Japanese, the Japanese will have to build their success on an indigenous capability for invention.[48] Nonetheless, they have developed many important and unique qualities that have led to technological successes, and these qualities are likely to persist.

The Innovation Process

New ideas rarely are carried out as expected, product gestation periods are often longer than anticipated, and R&D costs are often underestimated while markets are overestimated. After analyzing numerous innovations, Van de Ven and his colleagues concluded that the innovation process typically consists of the following stages:[49]

1. The gestation period of an invention, which lasts for many years, after which seemingly coincidental events occur that set the stage for the innovation to be initiated.
2. Internal or external shocks to an organization often get things going; without them the level of apathy is great.
3. Dissatisfaction is needed to move people from the status quo.
4. The plans submitted by the developers of an invention to the "resource controllers" are in the form of "sales pitches," not realistic assessments of the costs and the obstacles.
5. Once development begins, those involved usually disagree and have a lack of clarity about what the innovation is supposed to entail.
6. Ideas about what should be done proliferate, making the challenge of managing the innovation extremely difficult.
7. Continuity among innovation personnel is broken as people come and go for many reasons including frustration with the process or alternative career opportunities.
8. Emotions run high and frustration levels build as normal setbacks are encountered, mistakes made, and blame apportioned.

9. At first, schedules are adjusted and additional resources are provided to compensate for the unanticipated problems, but as the problems snowball, the patience of the resource providers weakens.
10. The goals of the resource providers and innovation managers begin to diverge and a struggle for power emerges about project goals and evaluation.
11. Resources tend to get tight and run out before the dreams of the developers are fulfilled.

Innovations often are terminated because new resources are not forthcoming. The ideas continue to show promise, but the resource providers lose patience. The ability to see a project to the end is critical to the successful completion of an innovation.

No project evaluation technique has been developed to make this process smoother or to resolve the difficulties inherent in it. Advanced portfolio methods created by statisticians and management consultants typically are not used.[50] Elements of critical success include the enthusiasm and commitment of a project leader, the skills and abilities of the people involved, unanticipated spin-offs from and to other projects, relationships forged by the innovators with customers and resource providers, and intangibles that cannot be assessed with certainty beforehand.

Hunches and Persistence

Hunches and persistence, the elements most feared by cautious investors, are also needed for innovations to succeed. The acceptance of a high degree of uncertainty associated with an innovation usually is confined to special cases: small entrepreneurs willing to take a big gamble, large firms with a portfolio of innovations where one major success or many small ones can compensate for inevitable failures, large firms with substantial resources and few constraints on their use, large and small firms persuaded by the enthusiasm of inventors and product champions to overlook the sober assessments of financial analysts, and government-subsidized research that is allowed to proceed despite financial risks because of some pressing need such as national security.[51]

The social importance of technology, even with all the problems in its development, remains high. Technology promises to aid the visually impaired with products such as a closed-circuit television device that enlarges print up to 60 times its normal size, to produce a safe and effective birth control pill that can terminate an unhealthy pregnancy up to seven weeks after the last onset of menstruation, to make plastics more recyclable, to help doctors predict who will get cancer, to repair the stagnant economies of Eastern Europe, and to do much more.[52]

Conclusions

Economic progress occurs in stages that are driven by new technologies. At present, it is unclear which technologies will drive economic growth and which will prevail in the future.

The technical, economic, and political obstacles that stand in the way of the development of new technologies are substantial. These obstacles affect the entire development process. Evaluating the promise of a technology requires careful assessment of both the technology's maturity and the market potential, which work together in its successful launching.

Japanese innovation is distinguished by the ability to fuse incremental improvements from many fields, the attention paid to manufacturing and marketing as well as new product development, the disregard for strict rate-of-return assessments, the rush to put products on the market, and the drive to succeed at all costs. This chapter has stressed the many difficulties in developing new technologies, the social importance of technology, and the need for creative entrepreneurs to play their hunches and be persistent despite the odds against success.

Discussion Questions

1. Why is technology important?
2. What five factors drive technological innovation? Discuss the role of each.
3. Describe Schumpeter's theory. What current relevance does it have?
4. What are the arguments of the technological pessimists? What are the arguments of the optimists? What does Daniel Bell say? What do you believe?
5. What are the differences between simple extrapolation, expert advice, and scenario building in forecasting the future?
6. Select a technology that has promise (e.g., cellular communications, biotechnology). Chart what has been accomplished in bringing this technology to market and what must still be accomplished. Give your estimate of the technology's potential.
7. What kind of estimates do developers of technology have to make? Why are these estimates inherently uncertain? What kind of system would you set up in a company so that better estimates could be made?
8. What problems did Enprostil encounter? What problems did Ultrasofts encounter? What problems did GE encounter with its refrigerator compressor? What could have been done to avoid these problems?
9. Analyze Motorola's problems in the chip market.
10. Will the United States be competitive in the market for HDTV? Why or why not?
11. Why do firms have to strive for constant innovation?
12. Which is dominant in innovation—the technology-push or market-pull models? Why?
13. What are Japan's strengths and weaknesses as an innovator?
14. What role do hunches and persistence play in innovation?

Endnotes

1. John Maynard Keynes, *General Theory of Employment, Interest and Money* (New York: Macmillan, 1936), cited in C. Freeman, *The Economics of Industrial Innovation*, 2nd ed. (Cambridge, Mass.: MIT Press, 1982), p. 156.
2. James D. Gwartney and Richard L. Stroup, *Economics: Private and Public Choice* (New York: Harcourt Brace Jovanovich, 1987).
3. Ronald Henkoff, "Where Will the Jobs Come From?" *Fortune*, Oct. 19, 1992, pp. 58–64; Kenneth Labich, "The New Low-Risk Entrepreneurs," *Fortune*, July 27, 1992, pp. 84–92; "On Birth and Business," *Economist*, Oct. 5, 1991, p. 71.
4. "3M Run Scared?" *Business Week*, Sept. 16, 1991, pp. 60–62.
5. "Venture Capital," *Business Week*, Dec. 2, 1991.
6. Brenton Schlender, "How Sony Keeps the Magic Going," *Fortune*, June 18, 1991, pp. 76–84; "Sony," *Economist*, May 30, 1992, p. 67.
7. Stephen Sacks, "Science and Technology Industrial Policy," paper delivered at the Annual Meeting of the American Political Science Association, 1991.
8. "American Technology Policy," *Economist*, July 25, 1992, pp. 21–23.
9. "Innovation," *Economist*, Jan. 11, 1992, pp. 17–19.
10. Nikolai Kondratiev, "The Major Economic Cycles," *Voprosy Konjunktury* 1 (1925), pp. 28–79; English translation reprinted in *Lloyd's Bank Review*, no. 129, 1978.
11. I. M. Kirzner, *Perception, Opportunity, and Profit: Studies in the Theory of Entrepreneurship* (Chicago: University of Chicago Press, 1979); J. A. Schumpeter, *Business Cycles: A Theoretical, Historical and Statistical Analysis of the Capitalist Process* (New York: McGraw-Hill, 1939).
12. Daniel Bell, *The Coming of Postindustrial Society: A Venture in Social Forecasting* (New York: Basic Books, 1973).
13. George Gilder, "The World's Next Source of Wealth," *Fortune*, August 28, 1989, pp. 116–20.
14. Ibid.
15. G. Starling, *The Changing Environment of Business*, 3rd ed. (Boston: PWS-Kent Publishing, 1988).
16. Ibid.
17. R. E. Willis, *A Guide to Forecasting for Planners and Managers* (Englewood Cliffs, N.J.: Prentice Hall, 1987); P. Wack, "Scenarios: Uncharted Waters Ahead," *Harvard Business Review*, Sept.–Oct. 1985, pp. 89–99; M. Magnet, "Who Needs a Trend-Spotter?" *Fortune*, Dec. 9, 1985, pp. 51–56.
18. D. A. Burrus, "A Glimpse of the Future: Twenty New Technologies That Will Alter the Career Paths of the Class of '91," *National Business Employment Weekly*, Spring 1991, p. 6; "A Survey of Artificial Intelligence," *Economist*, March 14, 1992, special report.
19. "White Collar Computers," *Economist*, Aug. 1, 1992, pp. 57–58.
20. W. M. Bulkeley, "Bright Outlook for Artificial Intelligence Yields to Slow Growth and Big Cutbacks," *The Wall Street Journal*, July 5, 1990, p. 81.
21. Ibid.
22. Ibid.
23. Ibid.
24. R. Koenig and R. Smith, "Drop in Tagamet Sales Is Putting SmithKline in Danger of Takeover," *The Wall Street Journal*, Jan. 13, 1989, p. A1; A. Newman, "Biotech Shares May Soon Fulfill Profit Promise," *The Wall Street Journal*, Oct. 8, 1990, p. C1.
25. Bylinsky, 1988; Freeman, *The Economics of Industrial Innovation*.
26. Frank Knight, *Risk, Uncertainty, and Profit* (New York: Houghton Mifflin, 1921).
27. Knight, *Risk, Uncertainty, and Profit*; Freeman, *The Economics of Industrial Innovation*.

28. Ibid.
29. Ibid.
30. Ibid., p. 155.
31. M. Chase, "Did Syntex Withhold Data on Side Effects of a Promising Drug?" *The Wall Street Journal*, Jan. 8, 1991, p. A1.
32. A. Swasy, "Diaper's Failure Shows How Poor Plans, Unexpected Woes Can Kill New Products," *The Wall Street Journal*, Oct. 9, 1990, p. B1.
33. T. F. O'Boyle, "GE Refrigerator Woes Illustrate the Hazards in Changing a Product," *The Wall Street Journal*, May 7, 1990, p. A1.
34. J. B. White and M. G. Guiles, "GM's Plan for Saturn, to Beat Small Imports, Trails Original Goals," *The Wall Street Journal*, July 9, 1990, p. A1.
35. R. Rothwell and W. Zegveld, *Reindustrialization and Technology* (Armonk, N.Y.: M. E. Sharpe, 1985); S. K. Yoder, "Motorola Loses Edge in Microprocessors by Delaying New Chips," *The Wall Street Journal*, March 4, 1990, p. A1.
36. B. Davis, "High-Definition TV, Once a Capital Idea, Wanes in Washington," *The Wall Street Journal*, June 1, 1990, p. A1.
37. Koenig and Smith, "Drop in Tagamet Sales"; R. Koenig, "Rich in New Products, Monsanto Must Only Get Them on Market," *The Wall Street Journal*, May 18, 1990, p. A1.
38. Schumpeter, *Business Cycles;* J. Schmookler, *Invention and Economic Growth* (Cambridge, Mass.: Harvard University Press, 1966); M. Betz, *Managing Technology: Competing through New Ventures, Innovation, and Corporate Research;* E. Von Hippel, *Appropriability of Innovation Benefit as a Predictor of the Functional Locus of Innovation*, working Paper 1084–79, Sloan School of Management, MIT, Cambridge, Mass., 1979; E. Von Hippel, "The Dominant Role of Users in the Scientific Instrument Innovation Process," *Research Policy* 5 (1976); E. Von Hippel, "Users as Innovators," *Technology Review* 80 (1978).
39. D. C. Mowery and N. Rosenberg, "The Influence of Market Demand upon Innovation: A Critical Review of Some Recent Empirical Studies," *Research Policy* 8 (1978).
40. R. H. Hayes and W. J. Abernathy, "Managing Our Way to Economic Decline," *Harvard Business Review*, July–Aug. 1980.
41. E. Mansfield, "Industrial R&D in Japan and the United States: A Comparative Study," *Innovation and Change in Japan and the United States* 2 (1988), pp. 223–28; S. Lehr, "The Japanese Challenge: Can They Achieve Technological Supremacy?" *New York Times Magazine*, July 8, 1984, pp. 18–23; "Thinking Ahead," *Economist*, Dec. 2–8, 1989.
42. "Thinking Ahead."
43. Lehr, "The Japanese Challenge."
44. Ibid.
45. "Thinking Ahead."
46. Ibid.
47. Ibid.
48. A. Murray and U. C. Lehner, "What U.S. Scientists Discover, the Japanese Convert—Into Profit," *The Wall Street Journal*, June 25, 1990, p. A1.
49. A. H. Van de Ven, H. L. Angle, and M. S. Poole, eds., *Research of the Management of Innovation* (N.Y.: Harper & Row, 1989).
50. Freeman, *The Economics of Industrial Innovation*.
51. U. Gupta, "Watching and Waiting: Biotechnology Holds Great Promise, but Investors Are Still Waiting for the Payoff," *The Wall Street Journal*, Nov. 13, 1989, p. R32; Freeman, *The Economics of Industrial Innovation*.
52. S. C. Bakos, "Abortion Pill Ready for Use in Five Countries," *Minneapolis Star Tribune*, Oct. 2, 1988, p. 1E; Chase, "Did Syntex Withhold Data on Side Effects of a Promising Drug?"; A. K.

Naj, "GE Pushes to Develop Recyclable Plastic," *The Wall Street Journal*, Aug. 13, 1990, p. B5; R. Brenner, *Betting on Ideas: Wars, Inventions, Inflation* (Chicago: University of Chicago Press, 1985); M. Waldholz, "A Genetic Discovery Helps Doctors Predict Who Will Get Cancer," *The Wall Street Journal*, Oct. 31, 1989, p. A1; R. Ricklefs, "Firms Introduce Products Aimed at Visually Impaired," *The Wall Street Journal*, Sept. 28, 1988, p. B25.

CASE 16–A
HEARING FOR THE PROFOUNDLY DEAF
Cochlear Implants[1]

In granting approval for the commercial sale of one of 3M (Minnesota Mining and Manufacturing) Company's cochlear devices in the United States in November 1984, the U.S. Food and Drug Administration (FDA) announced that this was the first time one of the five human senses had been replaced by an electronic device. Cochlear implant technology appeared to be an extraordinary innovation that would transform the traditional hearing-aid industry, which in the past had served only individuals with residual hearing, not the profoundly deaf.

Cochlear implants are biomedical devices that allow profoundly deaf people to discriminate sound through the electrical stimulation of the cochlea in the inner ear (see Exhibit 1). The concept of using electricity to bring hearing to the deaf goes back 200 years to the experiments of the Italian scientist, Alessandro Volta, who first studied the effects of electrical stimulation of the ear. Research in the field since the mid-1970s had led by 1985 to a proliferation of different cochlear implant technologies with commercial potential.

By late 1985, however, sales of the 3M cochlear implant device were not reaching projected levels. When 3M recalled it because of technical defects, the whole industry seemed in danger of being permanently derailed. The management of 3M had to decide whether to go ahead with its plans to develop and market this promising new technology, or to scrap it.

Cochlear Implant Technology

An implant can be extracochlear, meaning that the device's electrodes do not enter the cochlea (inner ear), or intracochlear; it can be a percutaneous plug, where the inner ear is reached by a direct channel through the cranium, or intracaneus, where access to the inner ear is made through magnetic couplings. Devices were already available in single-channels while multiple channel devices of 4, 8, or 22 channels were in various stages of development in 1984. The FDA had approved 3M's single-channel cochlear implant device. Surgery was necessary to install the device; some danger to the patient's inner ear was possible during the surgery and after the device had been installed.

Implanting a device was not cheap; the average cost exceeded $20,000. In addition, it was not easy to diagnose whether a patient would benefit. People had many different hearing defects. Physicians at the University of California, San Francisco (UCSF) had developed a measuring instrument for the evaluation of profound deafness, the "minimum auditory capability" battery. However, the criteria used for cochlear implant patient selection and evaluation continued to vary. The existence of the nerve fiber needed for stimulation could not be guaranteed regardless of the method of diagnosis used.

Even after a device was implanted, patients required substantial rehabilitation. Formerly deaf people who had the capacity to be helped by cochlear implants simply did not hear in the

EXHIBIT 1 Illustration of a Cochlear Implant Device

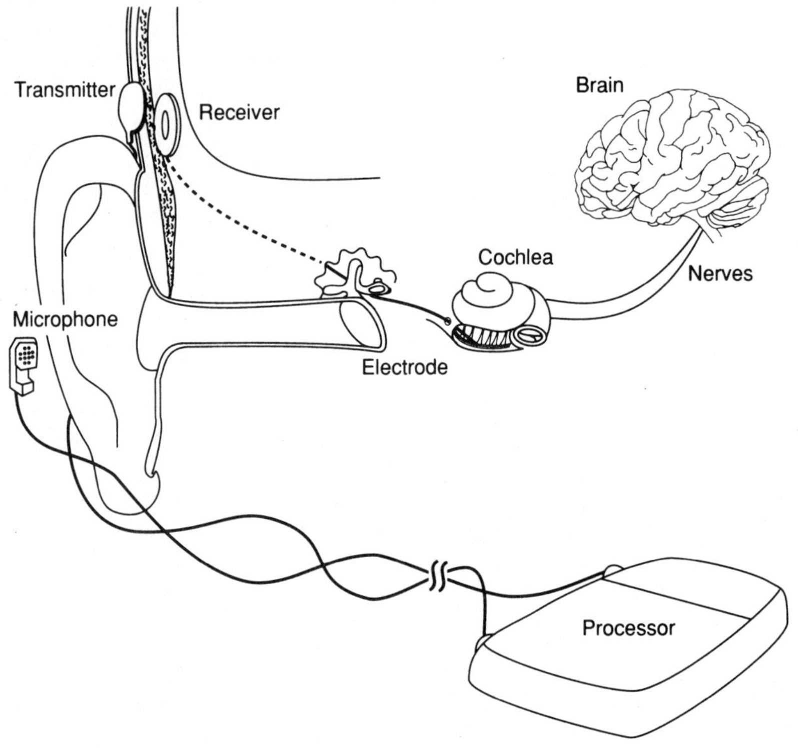

same manner as people with normal hearing. Audiologists, speech and language pathologists, psychologists, and otologists (specialists in the science of the ear) had to work with patients to get them to recognize and interpret the sounds that they heard.

Many deaf people, moreover, had adapted quite well to living in a world without sound. They relied on sign language and, through extensive involvement in schools, social activities, and other institutions, they grew accustomed to deafness. Firms in the industry had to think about creating both the diagnostic capabilities to identify people who would benefit and the rehabilitation services needed to get them to take full advantage of the opportunity.

The 3M Company

Starting as a relatively small sandpaper business, 3M had evolved into a worldwide provider of goods and services. It had more than 60,000 products and over 40 product lines. Best known for making and distributing tapes, the company had manufacturing plants in more than 30 states and did business in more than 63 countries. Twenty-six of its manufacturing facilities were international and more than 50 percent of its revenues came from its international operations.

3M's growth rate of 10 percent per year was based primarily on the introduction of new products and the penetration of markets throughout the world. While its growth rate in the United States had stalled, its growth rate outside the country continued at a rapid pace. 3M was prepared to take advantage of approaching European unity and had established joint ventures with Japanese companies in Asian markets.

While 3M had return on investment and dividend objectives, its main goal was to reap 25 percent of its sales from products that had not been on the market five years earlier. It was known worldwide as a technological innovator with a heavy emphasis on research. Its new products included familiar items such as Post-It notes. It also had created new uses for and modifications of existing products.

Indeed, 3M was one of the most successful companies in the United States in introducing new products. More than 6 percent of its total sales went into R&D in order to create products that had commercial applications. 3M was working on new products in digital image processing, retroflection, optical recording, and supergravity. Its corporate culture was unique in the degree to which it fostered innovation and provided employees opportunities to realize their ideas.

3M's existing product lines included its core businesses based on abrasives and adhesive manufacturing technologies. 3M extended basic coating methods used in making sandpaper to such items as audiovisual tapes. Another 3M product line was chemicals that could be coated on fabrics to make them resistant to stains or dust (e.g., Scotchguard). Still another product area was nonwoven material used in medical masks, tapes, and floormats.

3M also had a medical products area that developed pharmaceuticals and medical devices. It was this group that reviewed the cochlear implants device.

The Development of Cochlear Implants

The basic research in cochlear implant technology had been carried out by physicians and researchers from around the world. They were associated with universities and teaching clinics instead of commercial companies. None of the researchers had been working exclusively on cochlear implants. Most of their work was dedicated to furthering basic knowledge on the science of hearing. Breakthroughs in many different disciplines had to take place before a workable cochlear implant device could be made.

In 1935, researchers reported for the first time that electrical stimulation of the auditory nerve led to hearing. Experiments involving such stimulations were conducted by French researchers in the late 1950s. The first cochlear implant in the United States was performed in 1961 by a clinical physician, William House, who was founder of the House Ear Institute in Los Angeles.

House's energy and dedication as a champion of the cochlear implant technology was needed to bring different innovations together and overcome the obstacles that existed to creating a workable device. The extended gestation period for the technology lasted about 40 years (1935–1976) during which time the basic research to develop it was accomplished. Financing came mainly from universities and the government; no private company engaged in or funded the basic research.

Cochlear implant technology was first recognized as possessing commercial promise at an international conference on the electrical stimulation of the acoustic nerve in 1973. However, it was not until 1983 that the American Medical Association gave it official endorsement. The American Speech, Language and Hearing Association then created a special ad hoc committee on cochlear implants, and in 1985 the American Academy of Otolaryngology–Head and Neck Surgery endorsed cochlear implants, an important first step for the granting of Medicare coverage.

Private Firm Involvement

Private firms did not become actively involved in cochlear implant development until the late 1970s when corporations such as 3M, Storz, Symbion, Nucleus, and Biostem initiated proprietary R&D activities to develop new businesses in cochlear implants. Efforts to establish cooperative relations among these firms did not work out because each firm had ties with different academic institutions

EXHIBIT 2 Key Events in the Development of 3M's Cochlear Implant (CI) Technologies

1977	University of Melbourne approaches 3M for joint venture. 3M decides to pursue CI program by itself.
1978	3M collaborates with Robin Michelson of University of California, San Francisco (UCSF).
1979	3M and William House begin cooperative R&D; 3M takes up initial research of the House device.
1980	Separate CI program set up at 3M.
1981	Agreement between 3M and Austrian researchers. 3M begins R&D work on Austrian device. Clinical trials initiated for House device. 3M initially educates FDA about CI.
1982	3M initiates training program for physicians. UCSF-3M relationship terminated. Marketing activities initiated for House device.
1983	3M convinces third-party payers to cover House device. 3M promotes Austrian device at a training program. 3M submits first PMA for House device.
1984	3M establishes pilot plant at St. Paul and manufacturing facilities. 3M receives PMA approval for House device. 3M commences clinical trials for Austrian device.
1985	Six training programs initiated by 3M. 3M starts servicing the House device. FDA grants IDE approval for Austrian device. 3M recalls its House device from the market. FDA does not accept 3M's PMA application for children. Formation of industry council consisting of 3M, Cochlear Corporation, Storz, and Symbion.

and teaching clinics. These ties provided access to the basic scientific knowledge needed to carry out an applied R&D program, but each firm followed a different technological path and became a rival of the others.

3M's cochlear implant program progressed in stages, beginning with an exploration of the technology's business potential and leading eventually to the formal creation of a separate cochlear implant program in 1980. The 3M cochlear implant program generated the resources needed to develop proprietary products and competencies solely from within the company. In contrast, Nucleus, 3M's major competitor in the industry, raised resources internally and from outside sources, including private investors.

In 1977, 3M was approached by the University of Melbourne in Australia, which was interested in commercializing the cochlear implant technology (see Exhibit 2). The relationship between the university and 3M, however, never went beyond the negotiation stage. The University of Melbourne later entered into an agreement with Nucleus, which became 3M's main competitor.

Between 1978 and 1982, 3M collaborated with Dr. Robin Michelson of UCSF to develop a multichannel implant. The 3M-UCSF relationship produced a cochlear device that was subsequently implanted in several individuals during 1980 and 1981. When 3M ended the partnership in 1982, UCSF went on to license its technology to Storz, another start-up business, in 1983.

3M entered into licensing agreements with the House Ear Institute and with researchers in Austria in 1981. Symbion and Biostem, two other firms in the fledgling cochlear implant industry, entered into relationships with cochlear implant research programs underway at the University of Utah and at Stanford University, respectively, in 1983.

FDA Approval

All medical products, including cochlear devices, are subject to review and approval by the FDA. Before clinical tests can be conducted on humans, an "investigational device exemption" (IDE) must be obtained from the FDA based on clinical tests on animals. Next, each of the clinical sites must obtain an "institutional review board" clearance to certify its capability to conduct clinical tests on humans. After test results indicate that a minimum level of safety and effectiveness has been achieved, the device must be submitted to an FDA panel for premarket approval (PMA). If the FDA determines that the device is safe and effective, and establishes that the company engages in "good manufacturing practices," it approves the product for commercial sale. The whole FDA approval procedure may take from three to five years.

In 1981, when 3M applied for IDE status for its first cochlear implant device, the FDA said it did not know enough about the technology to evaluate the application. The FDA requested that 3M prepare additional documents about cochlear implants and related safety issues. The FDA subsequently granted a number of approvals for clinical investigation and commercial marketing.

In November 1984, the FDA approved the 3M-House single-channel device for commercial sale, the first cochlear device to win FDA approval. 3M trumpeted the achievement in its 1984 annual report, estimating the market for the device at more than 400,000 persons and several billion dollars worldwide. In October 1985, the FDA granted Nucleus approval to market commercially in the United States its multichannel device, considered by many otologists to be superior to House's single-channel device. The otologists believed that once a single-channel device was implanted, the ear would not be suitable for a multichannel system. Thus, they opposed using the single-channel system because it would foreclose the use of further options. However, technological and scientific uncertainties as well as an absence of common comparison criteria made it difficult to compare the efficacy and safety of the different technologies. It was not sufficiently clear which system, single- or multichannel, was better in the short term and which showed more promise in the long term.

A major challenge to 3M took place in 1985 when the U.S. Office of Health Technology Assessment (OHTA) claimed that the implantation of its device in children could result in inner-ear damage. The FDA stated its concerns about limited research on cochlear implants for children and the potential for damaging a child's cochlea "thereby eliminating the patient from consideration for future cochlear implants with improved technology."[2]

More Problems for Cochlear Implants

Although the FDA's approval of the 3M and Nucleus devices meant that cochlear implants could be sold commercially in the United States, the market for the devices did not develop as quickly as the manufacturers had hoped. Potential beneficiaries were reluctant to believe cochlear implants had anything to offer them. Many were accustomed to living in a world of deafness and feared entering a world of sound and the demands it might put upon them.

Hearing aids, which work on the principle of amplification of sound, had not helped profoundly deaf people in the past. Vibrotactile devices, which transmitted pressure pulses through the skin and were poor substitutes for the real sensation of sound, offered only limited benefits. Little, if any, marketing infrastructure was in place to help the deaf understand the potential benefits of cochlear implants. To compensate, 3M encouraged physicians to promote cochlear implants.

Marketing cochlear implants was further complicated by the high degree of technological uncertainty about their safety and efficacy. Unlike hearing aids and vibrotactile devices, cochlear implants could cause damage to the inner ear during implantation surgery. Moreover, once implanted, the devices' electrodes could not be replaced easily without further risk to the cochlea. This meant that patients who already had the device implanted might not be able to take advantage of improved electrode technologies. For these reasons, the FDA limited further research on children and many physicians were reluctant to promote cochlear implant technologies.

These safety and efficacy ramifications posed a marketing dilemma for 3M and other firms. It was important for a company to project a realistic picture and not make exaggerated claims, but—with research still in an early stage and no way for the public to judge the authenticity of the claims that were being made—there was widespread perception that exaggeration took place. This hurt the credibility of the product and made marketing difficult.

Another problem for the industry was that Medicare coverage did not cover the costs of the devices and their implantation. Third-party reimbursement, unique to the biomedical industry, was essential for the success of any new product. The cost of $20,000 or more per patient was too high for the average deaf person to bear without third-party reimbursement. An industry analyst reported that "third-party payers were capricious in their coverage of implant costs, with payment policies varying from state to state and from patient to patient."[3] Thus, many patients were effectively cut out of the market for the cochlear implant device. In 1983, 3M was successful in obtaining coverage for its first single-channel cochlear device from some third-party insurers, but wider coverage by private insurance companies and by Medicare was still not a reality at the end of 1985.

A Struggling New Technology

Because of these problems, the commercial viability of the cochlear implant industry was uncertain. Symbion and Storz announced that they would reduce their commitments to their cochlear implant programs because they did not perceive the market to be growing rapidly enough. In late 1985, the industry was struck another blow when 3M, following FDA product recall guidelines, voluntarily withdrew its 3M-House device from the market because of technical difficulties. Realizing that the recall might irreparably tarnish the image of the new technology, 3M initiated discussions with other firms in the industry to devise a strategy to minimize the negative impact of the recall.

The 3M managers who had worked on development of the technology were not ready to give up. They still believed that the cochlear implants had promise: to extend the House device for implantation in children, to create an advanced single-channel device in collaboration with the Austrian researchers, and to carry out an in-house program leading to the development of a better multichannel device. But 3M needed to rethink its strategy for making the device a success. It needed to come up with new ideas, perhaps in collaboration with other members of the industry.

Discussion Questions

1. What had gone wrong in the development of the cochlear implant technology?
2. What could 3M do to salvage its investment in this technology? Develop a plan of action.
3. How can this action plan be sold to 3M management?
4. Should 3M abandon its cochlear implant program?

Endnotes

1. This case was adapted by Mark Jankus and Alfred Marcus from Raghu Garud and Andrew H. Van de Ven, "Technological Innovation and Industry Emergence: The Case of Cochlear Implants," in A. H. Van de Ven,

Harold L. Angle, and Marshall Scott Poole, eds., *Research on the Management of Innovation* (New York: Harper & Row, 1989), pp. 489–532.

2. Garud and Van de Ven, p. 497.
3. Ibid., p. 498.

Case 16–B
Product Innovation at 3M[1]

In her fourth assignment (see Cases 1–A, 5–A, and 15–B), Joanne Magnuson, new analyst for Alliance Capital, was asked to give her opinion of 3M as an investment risk. An institutional investor had held more than $500,000 worth of stock in 3M for the past five years. This investor was now considering whether to up its stake in 3M, reduce it, or keep it steady. It was concerned about 3M's capacity to continue to innovate, given the increasing pressures coming from Wall Street to boost earnings. This case performs an analysis of 3M's financial position and business strategy. Joanne Magnuson had to consider whether these new pressures and other changes in 3M's operating environment would affect the company's capacity to introduce new products.

Company Description

3M, a globally diversified manufacturer with nearly 90,000 employees, sells more than 60,000 products and services (1.5 employees per product).[2] Its expertise is centered in surfaces and films, but its products range from Scotch tape to sandpaper, adhesives, coatings, sealants, abrasives, floor coverings, fabric and paper protectors, Post-it notes, Scotchguard fabric protector, computer floppy disks, reflective road-sign coatings, and laser images. The company makes stethoscopes, dental crowns, fire-fighting agents, electrical connectors, insulating and conducting materials, and even bingo supplies.

3M's total sales in 1993 were $14.02 billion on which it earned profits of $1.26 billion. Thirty percent of the company's revenues came from products introduced within the past five years. 3M spent a high percentage of its revenues on R&D. Foreign sales in 1993 represented 50 percent of total sales. No company in the world was quite like it. Perhaps its uniqueness made for its continued success. It competed for only a small fraction of each of its many competitors' product lines. In scientific, photographic, and control equipment, 3M's competitors were Eastman Kodak, Xerox, Fuji, Baxter, Johnson Controls, Honeywell, Konica, and Siebe. Its competitors in business supplies were Comdisco, Sensormatic Electron, Pitney Bowes, Deluxe, Avery Denison, Alco Standard, and Xerox.

Performance Comparison

In assessing 3M's performance, the following firms are used as points of reference (total sales for 1993 in parentheses): Avery Dennison Corp. ($2.61 billion), Eastman Kodak Company ($16.36 billion), Fuji Photo Film Company ($10.16 billion), and Xerox Corporation ($14.44 billion). 3M's 1993 operating margins were 21.6 percent. Among these firms, it had alternated since 1983 with Fuji Photo for highest margins. Its net profit margins or return on sales in 1993 were 9.0 percent, the highest in this group, but these margins had stabilized and improved only slightly since 1991. Its earnings on total capital in 1993, 17.5 percent, were the best in this group. However, its market valuation (its price earnings ratio relative to the Value Line universe) averaged just 1.09 in 1993, which was in the middle of the pack. Moreover, its market valuation using this measure had been steadily declining for the past 16 years.

3M's low market valuation could be attributed to the fact that its growth in earnings was not keeping up with its growth in sales. Though heavy R&D spending kept generating new products, Wall Street analysts regarded 3M as a mature company with limited potential for high profits.[3]

Pressure on Earnings

3M's earnings had been flat since 1990 (see Exhibit 1), reflecting weakness in the Japanese and European economies (30 percent of 3M's business) even as the U.S. economy rebounded and sales growth in the rest of Asia and Latin America surged. Negative currency translations dampened its earnings growth. The most troubled business sector was magnetic media—audio- and videocassette tapes (roughly 5 percent of 3M's sales) where prices dropped by 10 percent in 1993. Demand for medical products also softened, particularly in expensive items such as heart-lung machines and medical software systems, reflecting uncertainty over U.S. health care reform. However, the company had good growth in reflective sheeting, commercial graphics, safety and security systems, and pharmaceuticals.

Breast Implant Settlement

Another challenge for the company was the breast implant settlement. 3M faced numerous lawsuits over silicone breast implants sold by its McGhan Medical subsidiary from 1977 to 1984. 3M acquired McGhan to gain access to technology to develop intraocular lenses, which are implanted in the eye for the treatment of cataracts. 3M sold McGhan in 1984. Lawyers initially sought between $500 million and $713 million in damages from 3M. The money would be paid over three decades. Suits were filed after January 1992, when the Food and Drug Administration (FDA) banned the sale and use of implants. In 1993, a Houston court verdict cost the company $14 million in punitive damages, plus a share of $12.9 million in compensatory damages, split among three companies. The suit involved leaking, not ruptured, implants, which the jury ruled led to health problems including nerve damage and lupus, and it charged 3M and the other companies with conspiracy to avoid responsibility. The suit in Houston was the first involving breast implants to go against 3M. A 1991 suit filed in Hawaii resulted in no assessment of damages against the company.

3M was appealing the Houston verdict and held that its implants were safe. It did not believe

EXHIBIT 1 3M's Sales, Profits, and Employment Since 1984

Year	*Sales (in $000s)*	*Income (in $000s)*	*Employees*
1984	$ 7,947	$ 733	89,179
1985	8,117	664	88,093
1986	9,056	779	84,489
1987	10,004	918	85,144
1988	11,323	1,154	85,569
1989	11,990	1,244	87,584
1990	13,021	1,308	89,601
1991	13,340	1,154	88,477
1992	13,883	1,233	87,292
1993	14,020	1,263	86,168

that the scientific evidence supported the jury's conclusion that the illnesses described by the plaintiffs were caused by silicone breast implants. Nonetheless, it agreed to contribute $325 million over three years to a settlement fund, joining other large manufacturers of breast implants (Dow Corning, Bristol-Myers Squibb, Baxter, Union Carbide). The product liability settlement of $4.3 billion was the largest in U.S. history.[4]

As approved by a Federal district judge in Birmingham, Alabama, the settlement would end most lawsuits. Under the terms, women received payments of $200,000 to $2 million for diagnosis, treatment, and removal of implants. An estimated one to two million American women had such implants. The women had the right to participate or withdraw from the settlement and pursue their own suit, if they wished. Likewise, 3M had the right to withdraw if not enough claimants took part.

If it held up, the settlement was likely to put additional pressure on profits and 3M might be forced to become more cautious about introducing new products. The settlement meant that 3M would have to cut costs and rapidly move ahead with its plans to increase productivity.

New Product Strategy

3M's strategy was to compete in developing new and useful products. Until 1993, the goal was that 25 percent of its products should be no more than five years old. In that year, it raised the goal to 36 percent being no more than four years old. The purpose of these goals was to encourage high levels of R&D productivity.

Among the products introduced in 1994 were *odorless sponges* (O-Cel-O brand) and *sweat-proof bandages* (Active Strips). These products competed directly with Johnson & Johnson's famous Band-Aid brand for a part of the annual $500 million consumer bandage market. Designed for people with "active lifestyles," the bandages adhered to the skin, even when it was wet. The flexible foam strip stretched to stay put on moving fingers, knuckles, knees and elbows. The pads on the bandages did not stick to wounds and the adhesive strip formed a seal to help protect against dirt and contaminants. The price was competitive with other bandages.[5]

Another product inaugurated in 1994 was *optical recording disks*, which store digital information. The new 3M minicartridge could hold up to 555 megabytes (mb) of user data without data compression. Data compression of 2:1 resulted in more than 1 gigabyte of storage capacity. The new media/drive combination provided capacity and performance in an economical package for essential backup/restore operations.[6]

Another recent product was *Scotch-Brite(TM) Never Scratch(TM) Wool Soap Pads*. It was the first soap pad to effectively clean delicate surfaces, including nonstick cookware, glassware and stovetops, without scratching. It was introduced after the 1993 launch of Scotch-Brite Never Rust Wool Soap Pads for heavy-duty cleaning, the company's first incursion into the $100 million wool soap pad market. Never Rust pads achieved approximately 20 percent of the market share. 3M used its knowledge of abrasives, resins, and adhesives to create these products. Like Never Rust pads, the Never Scratch pads resembled steel wool, but they did not rust or splinter. The fibers of both pads were made from recycled plastic beverage bottles. The packaging was made from 100 percent recycled paper. The detergents used were biodegradable and phosphorous-free. Nearly three-fourths of all cookware sales were nonstick, double the amount in 1987, for which an effective soap pad had not been developed: consumers used steel wool, even though it scratched the surfaces. Never Scratch pads also worked well on countertops, tile walls, floors, bathroom fixtures, and virtually any surface that could be scratched during cleaning.[7]

Business Partnerships

In pursuing the goal of new product development, 3M typically formed partnerships with businesses and other entities. For instance, it teamed up with Hydro-Quebec and Argonne National Laboratory to develop the prototype for *a high-powered, lithium polymer battery* that would be one-eighth the weight of the lead acid batteries used today (see Case 14–A). The contract was the largest awarded by the United States Advanced Battery Consortium (USABC), a division of the United States Council for Automotive Research, an alliance of U.S. automakers and the Department of Energy. In 1993, USABC awarded 3M a $32.9 million, two-year contract to develop a battery to make electric-powered cars more practical and affordable. The battery consisted of multiple layers of foil and other material coated with polymers that functioned as electrodes. The layers were rolled into a cylindrical shape that could fit anywhere in a car. 3M provided the expertise in applied coatings and manufacturing.[8]

3M also formed a business alliance with Dow Corning Corporation to sell and develop *"firestopping" products* used in the building construction and renovation industry. It had agreed to increase its investment in HEARx Ltd. from $5.5 million to $6.5 million. HEARx was the nation's largest network of independent *auditory vestibular rehabilitative centers*, operating at 46 locations in New York, Florida, Georgia, South Carolina, Virginia, and Oregon. It had comprehensive state-of-the-art facilities offering a full range of diagnostics and rehabilitative services. 3M also teamed with Research Triangle Institute to develop an inexpensive synthetic *diamond coating process* for use in precision electronics and machine tools. The agreement was the first time the not-for-profit research consortium had entered into a commercial research transaction so early in a product's development. The coating, which had all the properties of diamonds—hard, durable and highly conductive—could be used in abrasives and machine tools, optics, and electronics.[9]

Productivity

3M's emphasis on new product development was matched by a growing emphasis on boosting productivity. Though domestic sales had grown 6 to 7 percent per year, prices had declined about 3 percent. As margins slipped, 3M was under pressure to cut costs, but Wall Street analysts claimed the company was too slow in doing so. The goal now was to increase productivity, measured by sales per employee, 8 per cent annually, and to increase companywide margins by 3 percent by 1995.

So far the company had reduced worldwide employment by more than 5,000 and consolidated European operations. Currently, it was assessing the capabilities of all departments, with special attention to waste in procurement.[10]

Downsizing

At a time when many companies had reduced their workforces, 3M had kept employment virtually flat. It avoided large-scale cutbacks with demanding hiring policies and targeted contractions. The company encouraged early retirements in struggling divisions by providing severance pay, bridge payments (in the amount the person would obtain from Social Security at age 62), and "preretirement leave." People in a shrinking business who were too young to retire went into an "unassigned pool" where they had six months to find another company job (about 70 percent are placed). By the year 1995, 3M expected that up to 7,000 employees would leave the company, and only about a third would be replaced. Companywide, 3M employment dropped by about 1,125 workers in 1993. Employment was down by about 3,650 people worldwide over three years, giving the hope that the goal of a 5,000 reduction would be met earlier than expected.

To increase operating margins, 3M made a sweeping reorganization of its European businesses switching from country-led units to business-centered ones and consolidating manufacturing, warehousing, and data processing operations. It made the changes in anticipation of a unified European market. Instead of running subsidiary companies within individual countries, 3M companies operated across Europe. It established 18 business centers on the Continent, each responsible for one or more companies. Europe also was split into eight economic regions that reflected the diversity of the area. These changes lowered employment in Europe. Down about 8 percent over the past three years, it meant that the breakeven point of the European operations had been significantly reduced.[11]

The campaign to boost margins now was moving to the United States. The newly appointed senior vice president for finance, Giulio Agostino, came from the Italian subsidiary, where he had reduced the number of employees by 26 percent while doubling business volume. At headquarters, Agostino went through each department area by area, looking for ways to meet the company's productivity goals. Selling and administrative expenses were cut $22 million, reversing four years of annual increases. He also centralized procurement operations.

International Operations

3M was sensitive to the slightest changes in the global economy. It had subsidiaries in 56 countries and sold its products in more than 200. In 1992, international production exceeded domestic production for the first time; international sales surpassed U.S. sales in 1993. With 3M's largest international markets, Europe and Japan, only at the threshold of a slow recovery from the economic downturn, its expectation of higher 1994 earnings depended on growth in the U.S. economy and in Asia.[12]

3M started doing business in Asia in the 1950s and 1960s; it was the first U.S. company to establish a wholly owned venture in China (see Case 12–B). It had also remained in South Africa during the period of U.S. sanctions against that country for its racial policies; this was likely to give 3M an edge as racial reconciliation and nation-building began. It was branching out, setting its sights on all of sub-Sahara Africa, a potential market of 400 million people, 10 times the size of South Africa. A new 3M division was scheduled to open in Egypt, providing market coverage from Cape Town to Cairo. On the other hand, 3M had applied the brakes to expansion in Russia because of economic concerns. It still saw plenty of opportunities in the former Communist countries of Hungary, the Czech Republic, and Poland.

Discussion Questions

1. Should Joanne Magnuson advise the investor to change its investment in 3M? If so, by how much?
2. What impact was the breast implant settlement likely to have on the company?
3. To what extent did environmental pressures drive product development at 3M? What would be the effect if government policies shifted or public sentiment changed?
4. What is your assessment of the way 3M handled corporate cutbacks? Were its productivity gains rapid enough, or was it placing too much emphasis on product introductions?
5. How will 3M's international operations affect its future financial performance? Was the company overexposed to foreign risk?

Endnotes

1. This case was written by Alfred Marcus and Donald Geffen.
2. Dale Dauten, "3M Proves to Be an Innovative Place of Wonder," *Minneapolis Star Tribune*, Jan. 19, 1994, p. 2D; Tom Peters, "The Most Valuable Player Awards: 3M Just Does It," *Minneapolis Star Tribune*, Jan. 4, 1994, p. 2D.
3. "Despite Better U.S. Results, 3M's Third-Quarter Earnings Slip," *Minneapolis Star Tribune*, Oct. 28, 1993, p.

5D; John J. Oslund, "De Simone Says New Products, Foreign Expansion are among Keys to 3M's Future Financial Success; But Shareholders Are Happy to Get Some Old Products," *Minneapolis Star Tribune*, May 11, 1994, p. 1D; Susan E. Peterson, "3M Reports Slight Drop in 4th-Quarter Earnings," *Minneapolis Star Tribune*, Jan. 28, 1994.

4. John J. Oslund, "Pre-Tax Charge for Breast-Implant Suites Pulls 3M 1st-Quarter Earnings Down 7%," *Minneapolis Star Tribune*, April 28, 1994, p. 5B; "3M Will Pay $325 Million to Settle Implant Suits," *New York Times*, April 12, 1994, p. 8C; Steve Alexander, "3M, Four Others Add to Breast Implant Settlement," *Minneapolis Star Tribune*, April 12, 1994, p. 1D; Susan Feyder, "3M Co. Assessed $14 Million in Punitive Damages by Jury," *Minneapolis Star Tribune*, March 4, 1994, p. 1D; "3M Gets $5 Million, Stock to Settle Suite," *Minneapolis Star Tribune*, Jan. 7, 1994, p. 3D.
5. Susan E. Peterson, "3M Decides to Stick It to Band-Aid," *Minneapolis Star Tribune*, Feb. 10, 1994, p. 1D.
6. Larry Teien, "3M Unveils High-Performance DC2555 Minicartridge for New TEAC ME-01F Tape Backup Drive," *Minneapolis Star Tribune*, Feb. 14, 1994, sec. 1, p. 1.
7. Deborah S. Johnson, "3M Continues to Revolutionize Soap Pad Category," UMI/Data Courier; PR Newswire; Business Dateline 1994, Sec. 1, p. 1; John R. Engen, "Scotchbrite Prospects in Asia," *Corporate Report Minnesota*, Oct. 1993.
8. Josephine Marcotty, "3M Wins Contract to Develop Battery Prototype to Power Electric Vehicles," *Minneapolis Star Tribune*, Dec. 16, 1994, Business sec.
9. Ellen M. McPartlan, "Dow Corning, 3M Announce Business Alliance for Fire Protection Products," PR Newswire; Business Dateline, Dec. 8, 1993, Sec. 1, p. 1; Paul A. Brown, "3M Agrees to Increase Investment in HEARx Ltd," Business Wire 1993, Dec. 3, 1993, sec. 1, p. 1; Jennifer Toth and Bob Wiliams, "RTI, 3M Team Up in Research Deal," *News & Observer*, Aug. 26, 1993, Business sec.
10. Frank Wright, "3M Co. Sticks to It," *Minneapolis Star Tribune*, May 12, 1994, p. 1D; John J. Oslund, "Hiring, Retiring: Rigorous Control of Employment Policies Has Let 3M Avoid Downsizing," *Minneapolis Star Tribune*, May 9, 1994, p. 1D.
11. Tom Fredrickson, "3M Unifies Its Empire in Europe," *City Business/Twin Cities, Inc.* 1993 11, no. 10 (Aug. 13, 1993), p. 1.
12. Pam Berry, "3M's Export Innovation," *Corporate Detroit Magazine* 10, no. 8 (July 1993), sec. 1, p. 42.

CHAPTER

17

The Impact of Technology

Who Might Be Harmed

Time and time again warnings are ignored, unnecessary risks taken, sloppy work done, deception and downright lying practiced . . . Better organization will always help any endeavor. But the best is not good enough for some risks that we have decided to pursue . . . There is no technological imperative that says we must have power or weapons from nuclear fission or fusion, or that we must create and let loose upon the earth organisms that will devour our oil spills.

Charles Perrow, *Normal Accidents*[1]

Introduction and Chapter Objectives

Some technologies are inherently dangerous. Even under the best conditions, they are difficult to manage. They have catastrophic potential and may be prone to disaster. This chapter considers how society manages these inherently dangerous technologies. It looks at the risks of everyday life, rational risk assessment, and the question of how safe is safe. Risk and uncertainty in economics are compared with risk and uncertainty in science and engineering. The chapter considers the requirement that managers make judgments with imperfect knowledge and analyzes the psychological misperceptions and organizational biases that managers can bring to these judgments. The critical question of how much is a human life worth is considered in this wide-ranging discussion of technological risks.

Normal Accidents

Technologies such as nuclear power plants, chemical plants, aircraft and air-traffic control, ships, dams, nuclear weapons, space missions, and genetic engineering may be inherently dangerous. They pose potentially catastrophic risks to operators, passengers, innocent bystanders, and even future generations. They have the capacity to take the lives of many people at once and do irreparable harm to humans and to the environment.

Charles Perrow, a sociologist and organizational theorist, maintains that no matter how effective management practices are, these technologies are likely to fail. Better operator training, safer designs, more quality control, and more effective regulation cannot eliminate the risk. These technologies suffer from complexity and tight coupling.[2]

Complexity means that technologies have many components (i.e., parts, procedures, and operators) that interact in unexpected ways. Failure can take place in more than one component simultaneously (e.g., a fire will start and the fire alarm will be silent). Given the interaction of multiple failures, the causes of the failure will be incomprehensible to operators for a critical period of time, during which time the operators will neither be able to figure out what has gone wrong nor what to do.

Slack, if available, would help overcome the problem of not knowing what to do. Slack is the time and resources needed to figure out what has happened and how to fix it. However, some systems do not have sufficient slack; they are very *tightly coupled*. They work very fast, their parts cannot be isolated from each other, and they cannot be quickly or easily shut off. In addition, many of the interactions that take place within these systems are not directly observable by operators, so that it is very hard for them to know what is really going on.

Because of complexity and tight coupling, management of these technologies is difficult (see Exhibit 17–1). The two features are contradictory. With complexity, operators have to be able to take independent, creative action when faced with unexpected contingencies. With tight coupling, the actions of operators must be carefully monitored and controlled. Operators cannot afford to make mistakes, so they are not given freedom of action. It is these organizational contradictions that make it so hard to manage high-risk technologies. According to Perrow, "the systems cannot be both decentralized and centralized at the same time; they are organizational Pushmepullyous, straight out of Dr. Doolittle stories, trying to go in opposite directions at once."[3]

Does Risk Taking Enhance Safety?

In *Searching for Safety*, Aaron Wildavsky, prolific author and University of California (Berkeley) political scientist, takes the opposite view to Perrow. He believes that risk tak-

EXHIBIT 17–1 Problems in Managing Dangerous Technologies

	Catastrophic Potential	*Inconsistent Management Principles*
Complexity	Many components: Unexpected interactions. Causes of failure incomprehensible for critical period.	Prepare for unexpected: Operators have to be prepared to take independent, creative initiative.
Tight coupling	Systems interconnected: Work fast Parts cannot be isolated. Systems cannot be easily or quickly shut off.	Can't afford mistakes: Operators have to be carefully monitored and controlled.

ing has enhanced the safety, health, and well-being of society. Well-being is a function of how wealthy society is, and the wealth of a society increases in proportion to its willingness to take risks.

Entrepreneurial risk taking in capitalist societies is reflected in a willingness to court technological dangers. For example, bridges, natural gas lines, and commercial air travel appeared to be very dangerous when first introduced. As early as 1830, William Huskisson, British politician and advocate of free trade, died after his leg was severed by a train at the celebrations marking the opening of the Liverpool and Manchester Railway. Today, these technologies are accepted and commonplace, but accidents still occur. By recognizing and dealing with the problems, society has learned how to cope with the residual danger.[4]

trial-and-error learning Hypothesis testing, feedback, and the discovery and correction of error.

Trial-and-error learning increases the welfare of society. It consists of hypothesis testing, feedback, the discovery of error, and the incremental correction of this error. In the process, dangers to humans and the environment gradually decrease. Entrepreneurs in capitalist societies engage in this activity in a decentralized, flexible way, unimpeded by government interference. Government interference slows the discovery of danger and impedes its correction, according to Wildavsky. Risk-averse government officials prevent error correction. The government's centralized, slow, planned, simulated trial-and-error learning makes for a rigid system that sets limits on what can be tested. A rigid system puts constraints on innovation, learning, and the correction of error.[5]

The goal should be to increase total safety, so that more people are better off over a period of time. The marketplace, not government, advances this goal. It does so by giving people the right to experiment by trial and error and risk taking instead of risk aversion. According to Wildavsky, "encouraging trial and error promotes resilience—learning from adversity how to do better—while avoiding restrictions that encourage the continuation of existing hazards."[6]

Perrow, in contrast, believes that learning from events, such as nuclear power accidents or chemical plant explosions, is neither tolerable nor possible:

> In the past, designers could learn from the collapse of a medieval cathedral under construction, or the explosion of boilers or steamboats, or the collision of railroad trains on a single tract. But we seem to be unable to learn from chemical plant explosions or nuclear plant accidents.[7]

Perrow believes that learning about the operation of high-risk technologies quickly reaches a plateau where the learning curve becomes flat. Wildavsky, however, vigorously disputes the notion that conducting trials involving error is too risky and that the only alternative is trial without error. He maintains that "increasing the pool of general resources, such as wealth and knowledge, secures safety for more people than using up resources in a vain effort to protect against unperceivable, hypothetical dangers."[8]

The Risks of Everyday Life

Everyday life indeed is risky. Each year about 2.3 million Americans die. This means that the average person in the United States faces about a 9 in 1,000 risk of dying each year. The 10 leading causes of death in 1993 were heart disease, cancer, stroke, lung diseases, accidents, pneumonia and flu, diabetes, HIV virus, suicide, and homicide, in that order.

EXHIBIT 17–2 The Risks of Dying

• At age 80:	83 in 1,000
• From participating in air shows/air racing	5 in 1,000
• From smoking	3 in 1,000
• From heart disease	3 in 1,000
• From cancer	2 in 1,000
• At age 40:	2 in 1,000
• From a mountaineering accident	0.6 in 1,000
• From accidents	0.5 in 1,000
• From working in mines	0.5 in 1,000
• From a boxing accident	0.5 in 1,000
• From working in construction	0.4 in 1,000
• From a hang-gliding accident	0.4 in 1,000
• At age five:	0.3 in 1,000
• From suicides and homicides	0.1 in 1,000
• From all occupations	0.1 in 1,000
• From being struck by a lightning bolt	.00005 in 1,000

SOURCE: Adapted from J. F. Morrall, "The Perils of Prudence," *Regulation,* Nov.–Dec. 1986, pp. 25–39.

Nearly three-quarters of a million Americans die each year from heart disease and 740,000 from cancer, while 31,000 are suicides and 25,000 are homicide victims (see Exhibit 17–2).

As people age, their risk of dying goes up. In 1986 the annual risk of death from all causes for a five-year-old child was .3 in 1,000, at age 40, the risk increases to about 2 in 1,000, and at age 80 the risk goes up to 83 in 1,000. Sports such as mountaineering, boxing, and hang gliding are extremely risky, but the risk of death from smoking is greater than any of those sports; more than 300,000 Americans die annually from this activity. A heavy smoker who smokes 10 times as many cigarettes as an occasional smoker faces more than 10 times the risk, and cigarette smokers face two to four times the risk of dying of a heart attack as nonsmokers.[9]

The risks of dying from cancer are 2 in 1,000 and from dying in an accident .5 in 1,000. Most federal regulations are designed to reduce the risk of dying from cancer and accidents, but the extent to which cancer deaths can be reduced is difficult to ascertain. Scientists have only a partial understanding of the disease, the scientific community disputes where to look for causes and cures, and cancer exists in many forms and each appears to have a different origin. The disease mainly affects people in old age and appears to be related to a person's genetic endowment. A study by the Congressional Office of Technology Assessment traced 35 percent of all cancers to diet, 30 percent to smoking, and 6 percent to occupational and environmental exposures. The ability of the government to affect these factors is limited.[10]

Similarly, the ability of the government to reduce accidents may be limited because the factors (e.g., reckless driving) that cause accidents are beyond the government's control. Accidents claim almost 90,000 American lives annually, with motor vehicle accidents accounting (in 1993) for over 40,000 deaths annually, down from 54,000 deaths in 1970.[11]

Some occupations have more risk associated with them than others. The annual risk of a work-related death in all occupations is .1 in 1,000, but the risk of driving to work is greater than the chances of dying on the job. Compared with all occupations, however, miners face five times the average risk and construction workers four times the average risk.[12]

Rational Risk Assessment

rational risk assessment Rational ordering of scientific and technical risks as opposed to risk management driven by fearful citizens, self-promoting politicians, and outraged columnists.

Rational risk assessment calls for a more rational dealing with risks in terms of a person's chances of being harmed and what society can do to prevent that harm. The funds for risk reduction are not limitless and the costs keep mounting. By the year 2000, an estimated 3 percent of the GNP will go to environmental cleanup alone. Instead of falling under the influence of fearful citizens, self-promoting politicians, and outraged columnists, risk management should be viewed in a more detached and analytical way.[13]

Polls suggest that Americans worry most about dangers such as oil spills, acid rain, pesticides, nuclear power, and hazardous wastes, but scientific risk assessments show that these are only low- or medium-level dangers. Greater hazards come from radon, lead, indoor air pollution, and fumes from chemicals such as benzene and formaldehyde. Radon, the odorless gas that seeps up naturally from the ground and is found in people's homes, causes as many as 20,000 deaths from lung cancer each year while hazardous waste dumps cause at the most 500 cancer deaths. Nonetheless, the Environmental Protection Agency (EPA) has spent over $6 billion a year to clean up hazardous waste sites and only $100 million a year for radon protection. To test a home for radon costs about $25; to clean up a contaminated house costs $1,000. To make the entire national housing stock free from radon would cost several billion dollars. In contrast, spending to clean up hazardous waste sites is likely to exceed $500 billion even though only 11 percent of them pose a measurable risk to human health.[14]

Greater rationality means that less attention would be paid to some risks and more attention to others. For instance, scientific risk assessment suggests that sizable new investments will be needed to address the dangers of ozone depletion and greenhouse warming (see Chapter 15). Ozone depletion is likely to result in 100,000 more cases of skin cancer by the year 2050. Global warming has the potential to cause massive catastrophe.[15]

For businesses, risk assessment provides a way to allocate costs efficiently. They are increasingly using it as a management tool. In December 1984, dangerous gas escaped from an insecticide plant owned by Union Carbide in Bhopal, India. Some 2,500 people were killed and thousands more suffered side effects and disruption of their lives. (see Case 17–A). To avoid another accident like Bhopal, Union Carbide set up a rating system of "safe," "made safer," or "shut down" for its plants.[16] Other chemical companies are taking steps to manage risks better.

Environmentalists, on the other hand, generally see risk assessment as a tactic of powerful interests that use it to prevent regulation of known dangers or permit building of facilities where there will be known fatalities. Even if the chance of someone contracting and dying of cancer is only one in a million, that one person still will perish, a statistic documented by risk assessors. The environmentalists want society to be concerned about the fate of these individuals. Among particularly vulnerable groups of the population (e.g.,

EXHIBIT 17–3 Analyzing Risk

1. Magnitude
- Nature, potency, distribution of hazard
- Number of people exposed
- Means by which one exposed
- Adverse health effects at different exposure levels

2. Management
Action based on
- Public health
- Environmental goals
- Legislation
- Legal precedent
- Values
- Financial considerations
- Social considerations
- Organizational factors

allergy sufferers) the risks are likely to be as much as one fatality for every 100 persons.[17] Thus, environmentalists argue that risk assessors present their findings in too conservative a fashion. By treating everyone alike, they overlook the real danger to particularly vulnerable people. Risk assessment should not be an excuse for inaction.

How Safe Is Safe?

Efforts to define, identify, and reduce risks to the public are impeded by a dearth of scientific data, a lack of resources, and the intrusion of political and ideological considerations into the legislative and regulatory processes. Regulators have trouble answering the basic question of how safe is safe.[18] Since absolute safety is impossible and some degree of risk is inevitable, deciding what constitutes "acceptable" risk is difficult. Regulators and business managers have to balance a number of competing social and financial considerations and health and safety factors (see Exhibit 17–3).

The first step in analyzing risk is to assess its magnitude. This means analyzing information about the nature, potency, and distribution of hazardous substances; the number of people exposed; the means by which they are exposed; and the adverse health effects at various levels of exposure. The second step is to manage the risk. This means taking action based on the goals of public health and environmental protection, relevant legislation, legal precedent, and the application of social, economic, and political values.

Uncertainties are associated with both steps. Risk assessment, for instance, is plagued by the problem of extrapolating results from animal studies to humans, while the principles that apply to risk management are often contradictory or unclear. The clean air and water acts require that pollution be reduced to the lowest achievable level consistent with an adequate margin of safety, while the pesticide and consumer protection laws require that the costs of regulation be balanced against the benefits. Also, courts can intervene later to overturn agency decisions. The Supreme Court demanded a cost-benefit analysis from OSHA about its benzene standard, and OSHA had to change an earlier decision to make it more lenient.

Judgment is critical to this process. Regulators usually consider risks greater than one in a million to be significant, but mitigating circumstances may present themselves in a particular situation. For instance, the risk of lung cancer to the residents near an Idaho nuclear processing plant operated by the Department of Energy may be 1 in 1,000; however, few people live near the plant. Only one additional cancer case may occur every 13 years, and the costs of lowering this figure may be as high as $78 million for each cancer death averted. In a case like this, the EPA may decide not to promulgate a regulation.

Government officials and business managers have great responsibility. While an individual may be willing to take a risk where the likelihood of death is high (1 in 20,000), regulators and managers decide for large populations that have no real choice about voluntarily accepting such a risk. As a consequence, they have to live up to very high standards of decision making.

Risk Uncertainty, and Managerial Judgment

Managers face troubling dilemmas concerning the risks of the technologies they control. The decisions they make often depend on "answers to questions which can be asked of science and yet which cannot be answered by science."[19]

The introduction of new pesticides illustrates the difficulty science has of resolving the conflict between increased agricultural productivity and health and environmental damage. To reach a confidence level of 95 percent about safety, scientists must test huge numbers of experimental animals, but even with the large numbers of animals the scientists can only say that no effect is probable.[20] It is impossible in many technologies to identify every failure mode, and it is extremely costly and utterly impracticable to build full-scale prototypes and to test them under every conceivable circumstance.

Limitations of time and money and incomplete knowledge mean that some scientific and technological questions cannot be definitely resolved. In these cases, both individual and collective judgments play a role. While confrontation between individuals of opposing positions is desirable, adversary procedures cannot resolve with scientific certainty issues that are on or beyond the boundaries of what is scientifically known.

Human beings behave rationally in simplified situations where they have full knowledge, but these conditions are not characteristic of the real world. The German sociologist Max Weber's conception of organizations as reliable means for achieving desired ends depends on having knowledge available that is adequate to the organizations' tasks. However, this conception is too simple; it ignores conditions where knowledge is partial, limited, and contested.[21]

Insufficient knowledge is, however, not the only source of organizational failure. Negligence or failure to attend to what is known is also a source of failure. Negligence brings about breakdowns. Investigations into the accidents at Three Mile Island, Bhopal, Chernobyl, the *Exxon Valdez,* and the *Challenger* started with the search for technological deficiencies and concluded with an emphasis on individual negligence and organizational insufficiency. In each of these cases, early warnings had been issued but were not heeded. There was evidence that people in the organization knew what was likely to happen but had taken no action.

Risk and Uncertainty in Economics

In economics, decision making under uncertainty has been reserved for a particular class of people, entrepreneurs (see Chapter 18). The economist Frank Knight made the distinction between risk, where the "distribution of the outcome of a group of instances is known," and uncertainty, where "it is impossible to form a group of instances" because the situation is highly unique. When probabilities are known (flipping a coin), you have risk. To the extent that knowledge of probabilities is certain, probabilities may be based on deduction from assumed principles, scientific knowledge, empirical observations, and individual judgments.[22]

All economic activity involves choice between rewards, some of which are small and can be anticipated with confidence while others are large and cannot be anticipated with confidence. The larger the expected reward, the greater the uncertainty that the entrepreneur faces and the greater the expected reward. The prospect of the reward induces the entrepreneur to take the risk. Society resolves the issue of economic uncertainty by passing on the burden to entrepreneurs, the risk-bearers for society. They estimate future demand and the results of proposed activities in meeting this demand, however uncertain. Although entrepreneurs strive to reduce the uncertainty, they may admit that this objective is unattainable.

Involuntary Risks

Uncertainty about the impact of technologies cannot be resolved by allocating the costs to a specific group. Only some risks (e.g., those ascribable to motorcycling and sky diving) are voluntarily undertaken; that is, the individuals involved have chosen to accept these risks. Some risks are **involuntary risks**—that is, individuals have not agreed to accept them—such as the risks of living or working near a nuclear power plant or inhaling smoke emitted by people in public places or by factories owned by others.

involuntary risks Risks that people have not agreed to accept, such as the risks connected with proximity to a nuclear power plant or from inhaling secondary smoke.

The risk that a person will be harmed by a technology is a statistical likelihood. Ranging from local phenomena to global hazards, the risks are usually not reliably known by those exposed to them or by those who bring about the exposure. People exposed to unknown risks are in no position to make a rational decision about what to do. Ultimately, it depends on how they obtain the benefits and how they weigh the benefits against the risks, but people cannot rationally weigh the benefits against the risks if they do not have a complete rendering of the risks. In some instances, groups in the population that bear a particular risk are unknown in advance. Moreover, some hazards have irreversible and intergenerational effects; in these cases, the individuals who must bear a large portion of the burden, including the unborn, have no choice.[23]

Gaining knowledge that will reduce risk may be too costly. In the case of reactor safety, it may be unacceptable to learn or advance by the usual trial-and-error manner practiced in engineering because of the incalculability of widespread human casualties and environmental damage that would result from a major mishap.[24] Entrepreneurial failures, in contrast, mainly affect individuals who have voluntarily accepted the possibility that their ventures might not succeed. Unlike the failures of complex, dangerous technologies, entrepreneurial failures usually do not have catastrophic potential for many people in society.

Risk and Uncertainty in Science and Engineering

When engineers assess the risks of a new technology, they are not concerned about scientific principles. Instead, their concern is technical: Will the system function as designed? Scientific uncertainty reflects a lack of fundamental knowledge about the behavior of the physical and biological world. Technical uncertainty reflects uncertainty, for example, about a backup safety system: Will it work under conditions of stress when it must do so to prevent loss of life? It does not really matter to the engineer what theories are used to explain the behavior of the backup system; what matters is that the system works. On the basis of engineering principles and informed conjecture, the engineer tries to calculate the likelihood that the backup system will fail and how many fatalities and injuries will occur. The engineer analyzes potential accidents and their consequences, such as those arising from the explosion of a chemical plant, with this in mind. The engineer then represents the results as a probability, which then becomes the measure used to describe the risks of the technological installation.

If this probability could be reliably determined (i.e., adequately estimated on the basis of assumed principles and actual experience), understanding the risk would be complete. There would be no residual uncertainty. However, because tacit assessments and informed judgment play a role in constructing the model, understanding the risk is incomplete and the probability itself is uncertain.

The uncertainty can be reduced by more testing and better understanding of principles, but it cannot be eliminated. Wolf Haefele wrote that an element of "residual risk" always remains.

> We can always improve our knowledge about contingent conditions, but we can never make it complete . . . The risk can be made smaller than any small but predetermined number which is larger than zero. The remaining risk . . . opens the door . . . to . . . hypotheticality.[25]

Of course, better knowledge can reduce residual risk, but it takes time and money to generate a more complete understanding and both time and money are scarce.

Furthermore, even if knowledge of the risks improves, that alone does not solve the problem of weighing the anticipated benefits against the costs. That problem is not a scientific problem, however, but one which requires value judgments by society at large or its representatives. Society must decide how far it wishes to remain committed to a product or technology once it has weighed the costs and the benefits.

Judgment with Imperfect Knowledge

Under conditions of perfect ignorance (i.e., complete uncertainty), choices about risks necessarily would be random. Under conditions of complete ignorance, consequences cannot be linked reliably to alternatives because any outcome is equally probable. If the results conform to expectations, that is merely a matter of chance. On the other hand, conditions of perfect knowledge would permit decisions to be fully rational. Between the extremes of perfect knowledge and perfect ignorance lie virtually all relevant problems of risk and uncertainty that affect society.

When some evidence is available, but uncertainty still exists, subjective estimation of probabilities plays an important role. Consider the process of evaluating the risk of a particular chemical substance. The process starts with the identification of the hazard where the aim is to characterize the potential adverse effects on health of exposure to the chemical substance; for example, whether the substance can cause an increase in the occurrence of cancer and birth defects.[26]

However, the knowledge available is wholly reliable in only a few cases. Risk assessment often requires extrapolation from animals to human beings; the aim is to prevent the need to develop human data because of a catastrophe like that which occurred with birth defects in infants caused by the mothers' taking the drug thalidomide during pregnancy. Determinations, therefore, are made on the basis of the effects of the chemical on experimental animals.

Animal Study Inferences

Inference from animal studies to human beings is necessary, but in some cases these inferences have been ambiguous or uncertain. For instance, consistently positive results in both sexes and in several strains and species and higher incidence at higher doses constitute the best evidence of oncogenic (relating to tumors) effects. However, more often than not such consistent observations are unavailable and experimental data leading to a positive finding barely reach a threshold of statistical significance. Also, the experimental data frequently involve diseases that have a tenuous relation to human diseases.

Moreover, interpretation of animal data may be difficult. Typically, a given percentage of test animals have the disease, a smaller percentage in the control group have the disease, and it is up to the analyst to decide whether the difference is statistically significant or attributable to chance. One group of animals is usually given the highest dose that can be tolerated, a second group may be exposed at half that dose, and a control group may be unexposed. The highest dose that can be tolerated is used for a number of reasons. First, if a small dose is used, it might not induce a sufficient quantity of disease in a small group of experimental animals to be statistically significant. Tests on 10 animals, for example, might fail to detect tumors affecting 37 percent of the population, and tests on 100 animals might fail to detect tumors affecting 4.5 percent of the population. In a population of over 200 million human beings, that is equivalent to nearly 10 million cases of cancer. Second, under experimental conditions, individuals are exposed not to a single pathogen but to numerous pathogens that may act concurrently with each other.

However, scientists have challenged the testing of animals at very high doses, arguing that the high doses may overwhelm normal defense mechanisms, that this method is unrealistic given the lower doses to which individuals are actually exposed, and that people differ in important ways from laboratory animals.[27] The acceptance of data from laboratory animal studies by the legal and regulatory system was long controversial and gained greater legitimacy only in the mid-1970s.

Psychological Misperceptions

Psychologists have taught that human beings are prone to make fundamental mistakes when confronted with decisions under uncertainty.[28] For example, some individuals tend to consider themselves personally immune from hazards (e.g., those arising from the use of automobiles, motorcycles, power mowers, and toxic substances) that other individuals would readily acknowledge. Some individuals also have difficulty imagining events of low probability but severe consequences (e.g., airplane crashes, tornadoes, earthquakes, and nuclear power accidents) happening to themselves.

Another common finding is that the risks of involuntary activities such as exposure to nuclear energy are more unacceptable than the risks arising from voluntary activities such as motorcycle driving.

People also tend to underestimate the error and unreliability inherent in small samples of data. They have unreasonable expectations about the replicability of early results and undue confidence in these results. In addition, they judge the probability or frequency of events on the ease of retrieving information about similar events from recent memory, and they also rely on the saliency of events in their evaluations.

Judgment is further biased by direct experience with a lethal event and exposure to reporting about the event on television and in the press. No matter what the implications of additional evidence, natural starting points, or "anchors," act as aids in judgment, and there is a tendency to believe that past performance is a valid indicator of future occurrences. Human beings also tend to be overconfident about their estimates.[29]

While most people rely on vague impressions in making judgments about unfamiliar subjects, experts are trained to rely on computational tools, theories, specific observations, and their experience to estimate risk. These methods also have limitations. For example, experts assign the same weights to hazards that take many lives at once as they do to hazards that take many lives one at a time. They tend to lump voluntary and involuntary hazards together and to underestimate possible pathways to disaster.

In recent years, experts have failed on a number of occasions to consider adequately the extent to which human deficiency or negligence affects technological systems. Among the most prominent of these cases were the Three Mile Island nuclear power accident, Chernobyl, the *Challenger*, and Bhopal. Experts also tend to be insensitive to how a system functions as a whole. And they have been known to be slow to detect chronic, cumulative environmental effects, such as acid rain and the gradual accumulation of carbon dioxide in the environment.

Collective Risk Decisions

Collectively shared attitudes and conceptions of risk are of considerable importance because most risk decisions are made by groups of people, not by individuals. However, groups working on these decisions may develop an illusion of invulnerability and the suppression of doubts. Such attitudes are affected by the consensus within the group, the insulation of the group from external criticism, and the active promotion of a dominant individual to the exclusion of the views of others.[30]

On the other hand, shared information in groups can lead to greater realism in the perceptions of risk. New information and rationally persuasive arguments can be introduced into discussions within a group, and better use can be made of existing information. Thus, rational discussions in a group can increase the prospects for realistic judgment, depending on factors such as the size, composition, and values of the group.[31]

EXHIBIT 17–4 Models for Analyzing Organizational Factors

Outcomes are the result of these models:

1. **Rational actor**—Rational decisions by individuals.
2. **Bureaucratic**—Organizational procedures, routines, and standard operating procedures.
3. **Political**—Bargaining and negotiation among institutional leaders.

SOURCE: Graham Allison, *Essence of Decision: Explaining the Cuban Missile Crisis* (Boston: Little, Brown, 1971).

Three Models of How Organizations Affect Decisions about Risk

Graham Allison has proposed the use of three models in analyzing the influence of organizational factors on decisions about risk (see Exhibit 17–4). Model I is the "rational actor model" in which outcomes are the result of rational choices by individuals. Allison believes that this model has the least explanatory power. Model II is the "bureaucratic model" in which outcomes are the result of the parochial preferences, perceptions, and procedures of managers. Lower-level managers, for example, distort factual information and report only facts that support their position.[32] Organizational objectives, capacities, and interests have a limiting effect on rational decision making. Model III is the "political model"; outcomes are the result of conflict among formal institutional participants with conflicting interests and accounts of the situation. For example, in the government, appointive heads of agencies with temporary tenure, outside experts, and permanent civil servants have different motivations, knowledge, and outlooks. Yet they all participate in decisions.[33]

Probabilistic knowledge is not likely to satisfy the needs of organizational decision makers who require precise and unequivocal knowledge. They confront many sources of information that vary in completeness, pertinence, and reliability. To understand, use, and recall the information is difficult, especially for individuals whose experience may be in practical affairs and who cannot ordinarily aggregate or organize diverse bits of probabilistic technical information according to clear principles. Under these conditions, critical information might be ignored or suppressed and only congenial information might be recalled and emphasized.[34] Organizational and political factors may dominate.

The Manipulative Use of Information

Scientific information in organizations is often used for other purposes than establishing the truth. It has manipulative or propagandistic value in promoting group interests. The manipulative use of information is well-known. Environmental associations often take exaggerated and aggressive positions on issues because voluntary organizations have to attract and keep members and obtain the necessary monetary support.[35]

In industry, the tendency is to underestimate risks.[36] For example, in the 1960s after the Corvair was on the market for a few months, it was clear to motor car experts and General Motors managers that the car was difficult to control; indeed, it would go out of control without warning. Why did the managers wait so long to make the necessary changes? One answer is economic: the redesign and production of a new suspension system would have cost too much money. Another answer is the managers' disregard of relevant information. They believed that the Corvair's safety record was in line with that of other small cars of the time. The Volkswagen Beetle, for example, had a far worse record. Consequently, GM managers disregarded the rapid changes in public expectations and legislation that were taking place.

With the Corvair precedent at rival GM, one wonders why managers of the Ford Motor Company waited so long when problems occurred with the Pinto. Public opinion had changed, and stiff new laws governing safety had been enacted. One reason Ford waited was that the car had one of the shortest production schedules in the history of the automobile industry. The Pinto rapidly became a success. Demands for its recall went unheard and unheeded for years after the car had been introduced and its product and design managers had been rewarded for meeting manufacturing schedules at a low cost. At their level of management, broader and longer-term concerns about the company's reputation and its liability for suits seemed unimportant (see Case 18-A "Auto Safety Policy at Ford: Revisiting the Pinto").

Government Agencies

Government agencies also play an important role in evaluating risk. They display many styles in making decisions about risk. For example, different agencies using the same evidence can arrive at very different conclusions about the same chemical. After a report in 1979 from the Chemical Industry Institute of Toxicology showed that formaldehyde causes cancer in rats, the Consumer Product Safety Commission decided to ban the substance while the Environmental Protection Agency and the Occupational Safety and Health Administration took no action.[37]

The different reactions come about because agencies are governed by different statutes, have different standards, and use different procedures. There is no single or uniform federal cancer policy, for example, and at least 10 different laws and four different agencies regulate cancer-causing substances, including the Food and Drug Administration, the Occupational Safety and Health Administration (OSHA), the Environmental Protection Administration (EPA), and the Consumer Product Safety Commission. Moreover, the EPA has developed somewhat different policies for cancer under each of its separate statutes that deal with air, water, drinking water, solid waste, hazardous waste, toxic substances, and pesticides.

Various government agencies also have different procedures for dealing with risk. Some rely more on outside contractors and experts; some are more careful about separating the functions of hazard identification and policymaking; and some use outside scientific review panels or some kind of formal or informal peer review. Other government agencies may not do any of these things or do them to a lesser degree. Moreover, each agency has somewhat different principles for making inferences about risk to human beings from animal studies, and the agencies' guiding principles differ with respect to their comprehensiveness, detail, completeness, and flexibility.

How federal agencies view risk can be seen in the differing values they assign to human life. Mandated cost-benefit analyses carried out on all major regulatory initiatives and reviewed by the Office of Management and Budget in the White House show that

OSHA values a life at $2 million to $5 million, EPA at $1 million to $7.5 million, and the Federal Aviation Administration (FAA) at $650,000.[38] The agencies justify the differences by claiming that their regulations protect different types of people with different risk preferences. The agencies have opposed efforts to impose a single figure (see the special feature, "How Much Is a Life Worth?"). The methodologies used for computing what a human life is worth range from net present value calculations of lifetime earnings to a **willingness-to-pay criteria**. There is no single best methodology for making this sensitive judgment.

willingness-to-pay criteria
Method for determining the value of a human life based on subjective survey questions; for example, how much would you pay to have an ambulance in your neighborhood?

Informal Rules of Choice

Informal rules of choice play an important role when people are confronted with complex technologies where the degree of risk is highly uncertain. As the tasks people face call for judgments that are too complicated to be entirely reduced to formulas, they have a large zone of discretion in which their individual skills and professional traditions can play a significant role.[39]

Most people cope with the unknown limits to their knowledge by simplifying their tasks. They put limits on the amount of information they will receive and analyze, and they confine themselves to a small range of responses.

Toxicologists in the EPA's pesticide division illustrate the informal rules of decision that government officials use. Demands on their time grew at a rapid pace during the 1970s. A program of reregistering the more than 50,000 substances already in use had been initiated. The number of new applications from industry increased, as did the required data submitted in support of these applications.

Expectations were also raised about the level of sophistication of the scientists' reviews. The pressure to deal with a mounting backlog increased during the Reagan administration, but the additional demands were not met by additional funding for the appointment of more scientists. Rather, appropriations for the pesticide program fell from $70.5 million in 1980 to $50.7 million in 1983. The number of persons employed in the division dropped from 829 to 537, but the number of registrations handled by each employee increased.[40]

Some of the government reviewers coped with this situation by routinely copying verbatim the summary statements accompanying safety and health studies submitted to the agency by industry. They accepted without question the accuracy and thoroughness of the industry's interpretations of experimental results. This was not a consequence of their having insufficient scientific knowledge, but one of accepting unaccredited statements as valid or of negligence in judging the information needed—information that was perhaps readily available. Of 578 randomly selected applications reviewed by the scientific staff, one-third contained some evidence of "cut and paste," 29 reached scientifically challengeable conclusions, and 5 actually failed to report major health effects because they relied on descriptions contained in the data submitted by the company.[41]

On the other hand, some of the government officials coped with the demand for rapid decision making under conditions of uncertainty by using a number of shortcuts or rules of thumb. These officials tended to rely on summaries to flag positive results, and to use past actions taken by the agency, reviews of the literature, or their general knowledge and

Special Feature

How Much Is a Life Worth?

The question of how much a life is worth may appear repellent and absurd since human worth cannot be truly captured in monetary terms; nonetheless, it is important to determine the value for risk reduction purposes. The costs of reducing a risk often are immediate and apparent, while the benefits are far off and hard to determine. Thus, it is important to try to develop an approximate value of the benefits that often involve the saving of human life.

A humanitarian would spend money on all worthy endeavors to eliminate risk, but resources are limited and choices must be made about where to maximize return. Rational assessments of how much to spend on a new medical technology, highway design, or air pollution policy require estimating the value of human life. It is necessary to know the dollar value of human suffering that would be avoided.

Until the late 1960s, society had a simple answer to the problem of how much a human life was worth.[42] A person was valued according to the net present value of his or her expected lifetime earnings. Calculations in 1986 dollars showed that an American man in his late 20s was worth about $500,000 and a woman about $350,000. Clearly, this approach had problems. Not only were women valued less than men; minorities had less value than the majority, old people had less value than the young, and people without employment and without the prospect of working had no worth at all.

An alternative was to use a **willingness-to-pay criteria.** People were asked questions on surveys: How much would you be willing to pay to have an ambulance in your neighborhood? (This could reduce the number of deaths by heart attack.) How much would you have to be paid to join a group of 10,000 persons, one of whom would be chosen at random for execution? How much would you pay to buy back various numbers of bullets in a Russian roulette game? Given the artificiality of the questions, none of the answers was entirely believable. Depending on the types of questions asked, the estimates for the value of a human life ranged from a low of $75,000 to a high of $2 million in 1986 dollars.

In response to these limitations, economists tried to derive the value of a human life on a more objective basis. For example, a study examined people's willingness to pay extra for homes in areas with little pollution and came up with a 1986 $600,000 to $900,000 price tag for a human life. A study of risk-time trade-offs among seat-belt users and nonusers calculated the worth of a human life at about $625,000 in 1986 dollars. Labor market studies of the interaction of job safety and pay among workers concluded that the value of a human life was between $650,000 and $3 million in 1986 dollars, depending on individual risk preferences.

A major point of contention has been what to do about slow-developing diseases that are likely to kill people only in the future. Should a future life be discounted so that money is available to save a life now? Also, it is conceivable that some medical breakthrough will take place during the next 30 years, which will eliminate the threat to the person's life.

Another issue is the discrepancies in the value of a human life in different cultures. U.S. juries often award sums in excess of $10 million for wrongful death. In India, the typical award would be no more than a few hundred dollars. It is not surprising that the relatives of victims involved in the Bhopal disaster wanted the case tried in the United States, while Union Carbide wanted it tried in India (see Case 17–A). The National Council of Churches and other secular groups have expressed their indignation about this legal double standard for the valuation of a human life, which they find morally unacceptable.

feeling for the substance. Officials would contract out pieces of the work they did not feel competent to perform. They relied on the general reputation of particular laboratories or toxicologists who did the studies, or looked for common and easily detectable shortcomings to enable them to discover abuses. They tried to find missing information and were alerted by numbers that did not quite add up or by data that looked too good. They made conservative judgments based on their scientific background to establish a position from which to bargain with the applicants.

All officials were trying to cope, given the limitations and considerable strain under which they had to work. Some were loyal, conscientious, and constructive, responding with scientific, technical, organizational, and other solutions.

In contrast, one prominent official became a whistle-blower, tipping off the media to the cut-and-paste activities in the agency. Principle, not politics, is often thought to motivate whistle-blowers. What is missing in such accounts, however, is the extent to which whistle-blowers are guided not only by the dictates of moral conscience but by professional standards. Whistle-blowers may have greater commitment to professional ethics than they do toward the organization for which they work.

Officials who failed to exert themselves to use their best knowledge were neither loyal to their organization nor committed to professional standards. As the pressure intensified, they fell short of their responsibility to use their knowledge in the assessment of risks. In the face of great stress, they became demoralized. They remained in their jobs because, in a government bureaucracy, it was difficult to dismiss or otherwise penalize or discipline them for perfunctory work.

New Skills

Many scientists and engineers believe that their education and training are inadequate for making decisions about policies that might contain considerable risks to human life. They were trained in experimental methods in disciplines where one can frequently find simple yes and no answers.

In making assessments in the grey and ambiguous area of risks to human beings, however, discretionary judgment is required. Under these circumstances, even vigorous conventional scientific and engineering training might be of little assistance.

Scientists and engineers who are appointed to deal with problems involving risk cannot always rely on their expert knowledge derived from narrow, traditional disciplinary training. Risk assessment often requires scientific knowledge that goes beyond disciplinary boundaries. The scientists and engineers must have an understanding of a wide variety of disciplines and the ability to employ advanced statistical techniques that require subtle and discriminating evidence.

To function effectively in this setting, accomplished scientists and engineers often need to acquire new skills, especially those that facilitate clinical judgment. This is a slow and laborious process.

Error Correction

The lack of preparation for making intelligent risk assessments is not simply a matter of insufficient knowledge. Managers often do not make sound use of the knowledge they already possess. Because of the pressures of time, they may be constrained to select solutions before all the information has been considered. Even if they used all the information they had, it might be difficult to decide among the alternatives.[43]

Since overlap and duplication sometimes compensate for error, it might be desirable to maintain or create organizational redundancies when assessing risk under conditions of uncertainty. While special units might be useful for monitoring and review, they tend to separate their members from the problems that front-line managers have to address. This separation can breed resentment and uncooperativeness between managers and those who assess their work.[44]

Indeed, those who work in special monitoring units often face considerable hostility and resentment. After the Three Mile Island accident, for example, safety review groups at nuclear power plants found that at several plants the nuclear power plant personnel responsible for the identification of risk did not have the authority to change the situation, even after they had identified the risks. While members of safety review groups perceived many problems and made numerous recommendations for change, the production managers ignored these recommendations because they interfered with production.[45]

Prompt error correction is not easily accomplished even when errors and remedies have been discovered by the most reliable methods. Investigations of some of the worst disasters show that warnings from various sources have been ignored (for example, O-rings in the case of the *Challenger*) because those with authority had difficulty distinguishing "true signals" from the "noise."[46] Management may recognize error slowly because their training leads them to discard prevailing knowledge only when it clearly is defective. It may be reluctant to admit error because of fear of blame. The warnings of public interest groups may be dismissed because the crudity of their accusations makes it easy to refute their assertions.

Evidence about mistakes is almost always ambiguous. More often than not, at least some of the evidence will be discarded. The correction of error depends not only on recognizing the error but also in having someone with enough power to do something about it. In this sense, a strategy of embracing error and rewarding those who admit to their mistakes cannot be readily carried out. As in all practical activities, it requires both knowledge and power to correct errors.

Decisions with Incomplete Knowledge

Probably not a single technology exists about which complete knowledge is available and hence complete certainty about the risks. Where the knowledge is incomplete, however, managers' assessments of technological risks are critically important for present and future generations. The norms for making these decisions—in organizational and social settings where the decisions can be highly controversial and the scientific information ambiguous—are not very well established. Managers may choose from many approaches, but they must not take actions that have critical consequences for society until they have undergone reflective and conscientious self-examination.[47]

As decision makers, managers will face contentious issues that can draw them into the adversary process. They will tend to suppress awkward aspects of the evidence and to state a case even more strongly than the evidence can support. However, it is important that they admit where uncertainty exists and acknowledge limitations in the current state of knowledge. However profound the achievements of science and technology, a great deal about its impacts is unknown.[48]

Conclusions

This chapter has discussed the controversy about normal accidents. Some believe that accidents cannot be avoided, so certain technologies must be abandoned; others maintain that trial-and-error learning applies to risky as well as nonrisky technologies, and that society over time improves its capabilities to handle dangerous technologies.

The major causes of death in the United States and the extent to which government can affect these causes have been reviewed. The concept of rational risk assessment and actual decision making by managers were discussed and analyzed. Managers face situations where they either have insufficient knowledge or are unable to take advantage of the knowledge they do have. In the tragedy at Bhopal, managers had knowledge they did not use.

This chapter distinguished between risk and uncertainty in economics and in science and technology. It introduced the concept of residual risk to describe scientific and engineering risk. It discussed society's needs for making risk assessments based on inferences from animal studies.

This chapter also considered psychological, group, and organizational limits on decision making. It looked at the ways environmentalists, business people, and government officials view technological risk, the criteria society applies in evaluating the value of a human life, and some of the steps managers should take to improve risk decision making.

Discussion Questions

1. Why do normal accidents occur? Can they be avoided?
2. To what extent can trial-and-error learning apply to risky technologies? Who is right about learning in risky situations—Perrow or Wildavsky? Why?
3. What are the major causes of death in the United States? To what extent can government regulatory agencies help reduce the cause of death?
4. What does the term *rational risk assessment* mean? To what extent would society be better off if risks were assessed more rationally?
5. What difficult dilemmas do managers face when introducing a new pesticide?
6. Insufficient knowledge is the main source of organizational failure in risky technologies. To what extent do you agree or disagree with that statement?
7. Distinguish between risk and uncertainty in economics. Who bears the burden of uncertainty in economic theory? How does this differ from risky technologies?
8. What does Haefele mean by the term *residual risk*?
9. In assessing risk, is anything wrong with making inferences from animal studies? Does society have a choice about relying on animal studies?

10. What are some psychological misperceptions that bias people's risk perceptions? How significant are these biases?
11. To what extent do groups improve risk decision making?
12. In what ways do organizations bias risk decision making?
13. Why do businesses underestimate risk? Why do environmentalists overestimate risk?
14. What affects the way government agencies view risk?
15. Name some of the criteria society has used to evaluate the worth of a human life. How good are these criteria? Can you think of better criteria?
16. What is meant by an informal decision rule, a shortcut, or a rule of thumb as a means for evaluating risk?
17. What difference does it make in evaluating risk if managers have clinical skills in addition to scientific skills?
18. What can society do to improve its risk-assessment capacities?

Endnotes

1. Charles Perrow, *Normal Accidents* (New York: Basic Books, 1984), pp. 10–11.
2. Ibid.
3. Ibid.
4. Aaron Wildavsky, *Searching for Safety* (New Brunswick, N.J.: Transaction Press, 1988), pp. 125–47.
5. Ibid.
6. Ibid.
7. Perrow, *Normal Accidents*, p. 12.
8. Wildavsky, *Searching for Safety*.
9. John F. Morrall, "The Perils of Prudence," *Regulation*, Nov.-Dec. 1986, pp. 25–39; National Center for Health Statistics, U.S. Dept. of Health and Human Services, cited in *World Almanac and Book of Facts 1995* (Mahwah, N.J.: World Almanac, 1994), pp. 957, 959.
10. Morrall, "The Perils of Prudence," pp. 25–39.
11. National Center for Health Statistics, U.S. Dept. of Health and Human Services; The National Safety Council, cited in *World Almanac 1995*, pp. 959, 964.
12. Morrall, "The Perils of Prudence," pp. 25–39.
13. J. Main, "The Big Cleanup Gets It Wrong," *Fortune*, May 20, 1991, pp. 95–101.
14. Main, "The Big Cleanup Gets It Wrong"; Richard Morgenstern and Stuart Session, "Which Are the Largest Problems EPA Might Tackle? Which Are the Smallest?" *Environment*, July-Aug. 1988, pp. 15–17, 35–39.
15. Morgenstern and Session, "Which Are the Largest Problems EPA Might Tackle?" pp. 15–17, 35–39.
16. Ibid.
17. Morgenstern and Sessions, "Which Are the Largest Problems EPA Might Tackle"; P. Shabecoff, "Tangled Rules on Toxic Hazards Hamper Efforts to Protect Public," *New York Times*, November 27, 1985, p. A1.
18. L. B. Lave, *How Safe Is Safe Enough? Setting Safety Goals*, formal publication no. 96, Center for the Study of American Business, Washington University, January 1990; Shabecoff, "Tangled Rules on Toxic Hazards."
19. Alfred Marcus, "Risk, Uncertainty, and Scientific Judgment," *Minerva* 2 (1988), pp. 138–52; Alvin Weinberg, "Science and Trans-Science," *Minerva* 10 (April 1972), pp. 209–22.

20. David Whiteside, "Note on the Export of Pesticides from the United States to Developing Countries," in *Ethics in Management* (Boston: Harvard Business School, 1984), pp. 121–36.
21. Paul Slovic and Baruch Fischoff, "Cognitive Processes and Societal Risk-Taking," in *Cognitive Social Behavior* (Hillsdale, N.J.: Lawrence Elbaum Associates, 1976); Vincent Covello, "The Perception of Technological Risks: A Literature Review," *Technological Forecasting and Social Change* 23, no. 4 (1983), pp. 285–98; Milton Weinstein and Robert Quinn, "Psychological Considerations in Valuing Health Risk Reductions," *Natural Resources Journal*, June 1983, pp. 659–73; Max Weber, *The Theory of Social and Economic Organization* (New York: Free Press, 1947).
22. Frank Knight, *Risk, Uncertainty, and Profit* (New York: Houghton Mifflin, 1921).
23. Knight, *Risk, Uncertainty, and Profit*, p. 233; also see S. Lippman and R. Rumelt, "Uncertain Imitability," *Bell Journal of Economics* 13 (1982), pp. 418–38.
24. Andrew Sage and Elbert White, "Methodologies for Risk and Hazard Assessment: A Survey and Status Report," *IEEE Transactions on Systems, Man, and Cybernetics*, Aug. 1980, pp. 425–41.
25. Wolf Haefele, "Hypotheticality and the New Challenges: The Pathfinder Role of Nuclear Energy," *Minerva* 12 (July 1974), p. 313.
26. William Lowrance, *Of Acceptable Risk* (Los Altos, Calif.: William Kaufmann, 1976); and National Research Council, *Risk Assessment in the Federal Government: Managing the Process* (Washington, D.C.: MAS, 1983).
27. William Havender, "Ruminations on a Rat: Saccharin and Human Risk," *Regulation*, March-April 1979, pp. 17–24.
28. B. Fischoff, S. Lichtenstein, P. Slovic, S. Derby, and R. Keeney, *Acceptable Risk* (Cambridge, England: Cambridge University Press, 1983); see also P. Slovic, B. Fischoff, and S. Lichtenstein, *Perceived Risk*, paper presented at General Motors Symposium, Warren, Michigan, Oct. 9, 1979.
29. Covello, "The Perception of Technological Risks," p. 30.
30. Irving Janis, *Groupthink: Psychological Studies of Policy Decisions and Fiascoes*, 2nd ed. (Boston: Houghton Mifflin, 1982).
31. A. Vinokur, "Review and Theoretical Analysis of the Effects of Group Processes upon Individuals and Group Decisions Involving Risk," *Psychological Bulletin*, Oct. 1971, pp. 231–41.
32. Graham Allison, *Essence of Decision: Explaining the Cuban Missile Crisis* (Boston: Little, Brown, 1971); Morton Halperin, *Bureaucratic Politics and Foreign Policy* (Washington,D.C.: Brookings Institution, 1974).
33. James Q. Wilson, *The Politics of Regulation* (New York: Basic Books, 1980); and A. Marcus, *Promise and Performance: Choosing and Implementing an Environmental Policy* (Westport, Conn.: Greenwood Press, 1980).
34. Paul Shrivastava and Ian Mitroff, "Enhancing Organizational Research Utilization: The Role of Decision-Makers' Assumptions," *Academy of Management Review* 9 (1984), pp. 18–26; Kenneth Hammond et al., "Fundamental Obstacles to the Use of Scientific Information in Public Policymaking," *Technological Forecasting and Social Change* 24 (1983), pp. 287–97.
35. Mary Douglas and Aaron Wildavsky, *Risk and Culture* (Berkeley: University of California Press, 1982). Douglas and Wildavsky say that environmental organizations "survive only through attack."
36. See Alfred Marcus, *The Adversary Economy: Business Responses to Changing Government Requirements* (Westport, Conn.: Greenwood Press, 1984).
37. Bill Keller, "Federal Agencies Set Varying Cash Value on Workers' Lives," *Minneapolis Star and Tribune*, Oct. 27, 1984, p. 12A; N. Ashford, W. Ryan, and C. Caldart, "Law and Science Policy in Federal Regulation of Formaldehyde," *Science*, Nov. 25, 1983, pp. 894–900; see also H. Sapolsky, ed., *Consuming Fears: The Politics of Product Risks* (New York: Basic Books, 1986).
38. Lave, *How Safe Is Safe Enough?*
39. See Alfred Marcus, "Professional Autonomy as a Basis of Conflict in an Organization," *Human Resources Management*, Fall 1985.
40. House Committee on Agriculture, Subcommittee on Department Operations, Research, and Foreign Agriculture, *Regulations of Pesticides, Vol. III: Appendix to Hearings* (Washington, D.C.: U.S. Government Printing Office, 1983).

41. Elliot Marshall, "EPA Ends Cut and Paste Toxicology," *Science*, Jan. 27, 1984, pp. 379–80.

42. M. Geyelin, "Dollar Valuation of Life Pleasures Set Back," *The Wall Street Journal*, March 27, 1991, p. B6; L. Dyer, "Environmental Policy and the Economic Value of Human Life," *Journal of Environmental Management*, 1986, pp. 229–43; J. Leape, "Quantitative Risk Assessment in the Regulation of Environmental Carcinogens," *Harvard Environmental Law Review*, 1980, pp. 86–117; D. Seligman, "How Much Money Is Your Life Worth?" *Fortune*, March 3, 1986, pp. 26–27.

43. See John Steinbruner, *The Cybernetic Theory of Decision* (Princeton, N.J.: Princeton University Press, 1974).

44. Martin Landau, "On the Concept of a Self-Correcting Organization," *Public Administration Review*, Nov.-Dec. 1973, pp. 532–42; Daniel Metaly, *Error Correction in Bureaucracies*, doctoral dissertation in political science, University of California, Berkeley, 1978.

45. Aaron Wildavsky, "The Self-Evaluating Organizational," *Public Administration Review*, Sept.-Oct. 1972, p. 519; Alfred Marcus and Richard Osborn, *Safety Review at Nuclear Power Plants: A Review Assessment*, prepared for U.S. Nuclear Regulatory Commission (Seattle, Wash.: Battelle Human Affairs Research Centers, 1984).

46. David Faust, *The Limits of Scientific Reasoning* (Minneapolis: University of Minnesota Press, 1984).

47. Edward Shils, "Science and Scientists in the Public Arena," *American Scholar*, Spring 1987, pp. 185–202.

48. See R. V. Jones, "Temptations and Risks of the Scientific Adviser," *Minerva* 10 (July 1972), pp. 441–52; R. V. Jones, "The Obligations of Scientists as Counsellors," *Minerva* 10 (Jan. 1972), pp. 107–58.

Case 17–A
The Bhopal Disaster

Implications for Investments in Developing Countries[1]

John Brown asked his secretary to hold his calls and settled back in his chair to prepare for the conference he would attend the next week on investing in the world's developing countries or, as they are sometimes called, Third World or less developed countries (LDCs). To compete in the increasingly global economy, corporations had to be prepared to take advantage of expansion opportunities in foreign countries. The risks of expansion, however, had been highlighted for all business people by the industrial accident that had occurred at a Union Carbide plant in Bhopal, India, the year before. The accident had killed more than 2,000 people and injured thousands more.

No industry was more concerned than chemical manufacturing with the implications of the accident for foreign operations. The worst industrial accident in history had drawn critical attention to the industry. The U.S. Congress and federal agencies had proposed tougher laws and regulations governing how the industry should conduct its business. Numerous stories in the media had documented the events leading up to the accident and the horrible consequences it had for the impoverished Indians who lived near the plant where the accident occurred.

American chemical companies had begun to make changes in their safety policies and procedures to prevent a repeat of the disaster. Brown's employer, W. R. Grace & Company, was one of many companies reevaluating its policies for investing in LDCs.

W. R. Grace and Company

W. R. Grace & Company was a diversified conglomerate, which in 1984 operated chemical, energy production and services, retailing, restaurant, and other types of subsidiaries in 47 states and 42 countries. The company's specialty and agricultural chemicals divisions accounted for 42 percent of its $6.73 billion in sales and 65 percent of its $322.6 million in income in 1984. At that time Grace employed thousands of workers in Latin America, the Far East, and other less developed regions. The chemical operations in those regions accounted for 10 percent of the chemical division's sales and 20 percent of its profits.

In some countries where Grace operated plants, the government held the majority interest, much as India controlled Union Carbide's Bhopal plant. For example, the Trinidad government owned 51 percent of Grace's anhydrous ammonia facility in Trinidad and the company owned 49 percent. The company was continuing to expand its operations in the LDCs, opening a silica gel production plant in Brazil in 1984.

John's supervisor, the company's vice president for plant operations and facilities affairs, asked him to develop for the conference, among other things, a list of guidelines for conducting business in LDCs. John opened the folder of background materials the research staff had prepared and began to read.

The Role of Chemicals in Feeding the World's People

American chemical companies had much to offer developing countries. The fertilizers and pesticides that W. R. Grace produced were a vital part of the Green Revolution that had increased food production dramatically in the poorer nations where additional food was so vital.

Experts estimated that up to a quarter of the world's population was chronically malnourished, and the number was growing every year. It was necessary to increase food crop yields if everyone was going to be fed, since there was little unused land left to be cultivated in the developing countries. According to Norman Borlaug, the Nobel Peace Prize-winning agricultural scientist, increases in world food supply required the use of pesticides. Pesticide use had increased the average yield of corn crops grown in the tropics on research plots from 30 bushels per acre to 440 bushels per acre. Pesticide use also helped protect the crops after harvesting, when they were in storage and vulnerable to rodents and insects. Experts claimed that about 25 percent of the worldwide harvest would be lost without pesticide use.[2]

Agricultural chemicals had more to offer the developing nations than increased food production. Through increased efficiencies, agricultural chemicals also facilitated the economic growth necessary to raise the standard of living. Less land was needed to produce the same amount of food, and labor was freed up for other productive purposes. The sale of cash crops provided a valuable source of foreign exchange necessary to purchase advanced technologies. Without the use of pesticides in the United States, the price of farm products might increase by 50 percent. Pesticides had proven effective in making food more affordable in developing countries as well. Finally, pesticide use had been tremendously effective in reducing the incidence of a variety of pest-borne diseases like malaria, and yellow fever.[3]

The Risks of Chemical Use

There were indisputable benefits for developing countries that adopted modern technologies like agricultural chemicals. Unfortunately, as the Bhopal disaster had shown, there were also risks. India was very different from the United States, which had developed most of the industrial technology for producing pesticides. The Indian infrastructure was not developed along Western lines and the culture had completely different standards about the purpose and value of human life. A complex technology like pesticide production was at best an awkward fit.

The dangers of pesticide manufacture and use were not understood in Third World countries. Annual pesticide poisonings ranged from one-quarter to three-quarters of a million people, with more than 10,000 dying. While LDCs used only 15 percent of the world's pesticides, they reported more than half of the accidental poisonings and more than three-fourths of the deaths. Over half the fatalities were children.[4]

These fatalities occurred because people did not use the pesticides appropriately. For example, fishermen living along the shore of Lake Volta in Ghana used them to kill fish. Local people who ate the fish and drank the water developed the blurred vision, dizziness, and vomiting that were symptoms of pesticide poisoning.

The boomerang effect meant that people in developed countries also were affected. They ingested excess amounts of pesticides on the fruits and vegetables imported from LDCs. Pesticides banned in the United States were sold by U.S. firms abroad and came back to the United States in foreign produce. This impact on people in developed nations was very hard to control.

In addition, many insects developed resistance to the pesticides, eventually becoming immune to them. Consequently, more powerful pesticides, with greater toxicity to humans, animals, and the environment, were developed, marketed, and applied. This pesticide use phenomenon, called the treadmill, greatly disturbed scientists, who pointed to the increasing concentrations of very deadly pesticides throughout the biosphere.

The regulatory apparatus in Third World countries was completely inadequate to deal with these problems. Not only was the importation of products banned in developed countries permitted, but also no labeling or handling requirements were imposed on these dangerous substances. The few pesticide regulations on the books were poorly enforced. Moreover, LDC regimes had little awareness of the alternatives to available pesticides.

As a legacy of their recent colonial pasts, the developing countries tended to put restrictions on foreign firms operating within their countries. The Indian government, for instance, passed laws limiting the degree of control that a foreign corporation could exercise over an Indian subsidiary.

The Bhopal Accident

A multinational corporation had much to gain and to give by expanding markets for its products and doing business in developing countries, but Bhopal made it clear that there were costs to consider as well. At the conference next week, John and representatives of other chemical firms would attempt to work out a set of guidelines to determine whether investment in a developing country was worthwhile and, if so, under what conditions. John reviewed the history of the accident at Bhopal to better consider the specific lessons to be learned.

The Setting. Located in central India, Bhopal is the capital of one of the country's least industrialized states. Although the area around Bhopal had a fairly good base of natural resources such as water and timber, which would have helped in its economic development, the feudal history of the region had kept it a mainly agricultural region. Beginning in the 1950s, the Indian government actively encouraged industrial development in the region, but without a particularly comprehensive planning effort, the infrastructure of roads, utilities, and communications services remained poor.

By the 1980s, stagnation in agricultural production had driven thousands of people to the cities to look for work. Bhopal's 1981 population of 672,000 had grown sixfold since 1961, almost three times the national average. The severe housing shortage forced the migrants to build shantytowns in any available open space; areas near industrial plants where work might be found were favorite choices. The land around the walls of Union Carbide's Bhopal plant was crowded with squatters' dwellings. When the plant was built in the 1960s, it stood in open fields within two miles of the local commercial and transportation center.

At the time of its start-up, the plant processed chemical components that had been manufactured overseas and shipped to Bhopal where they were mixed into the final pesticide formulations ready for sale. The plant did not pose much threat to neighboring residential areas. Union Carbide had built and begun operating a plant to manufacture much more dangerous pesticide components. The plant was a greater health hazard than before. Some local authorities objected to the plant at its present location, but state and national government officials overruled them. The plant was too important a part of the local economy to risk losing.[5]

Among the pesticide components manufactured at the Bhopal plant was a highly toxic and highly unstable compound called methyl isocynate (MIC), which is used to make the active ingredient in the pesticide Sevin. MIC was manufactured in batches and stored in three refrigerated tanks set in concrete. Each tank was equipped with pressure and temperature gauges, a high-temperature alarm, a level indicator, and high- and low-level alarms. Several safety systems were designed to handle accidental leaks: a vent-gas scrubber that neutralized toxic gases with a caustic soda solution, a flare tower that could burn off the gases, the refrigeration system to keep the chemical at low, stable temperatures, and a set of water-spray pipes that could control escaping gases or extinguish fires.[6]

The Evening of December 2, 1984. When Suman Dey, a control room operator at the Bhopal plant, came on duty at 11:00 P.M. on December 2, 1984, everything seemed normal. He performed a routine check of the gauges in the control room and noticed that the pressure in the MIC storage tanks was within the normal range of 2 to 25 pounds per square inch (psi). At about 11:30 P.M., however, a worker noticed an MIC leak near the vent-gas scrubber and notified Dey. A tea break was scheduled at 12:15 A.M., so the workers planned to fix the leak afterward. By the time the break was over at 12:40 A.M., it was too late. The pressure in one of the tanks shot up to 30 psi shortly after the break began and minutes later exceeded the gauge's upper limit, 55 psi.

Dey ran outside to the storage area to investigate. He heard a tremendous rumbling sound beneath the concrete. As he watched, 60 feet of concrete six inches thick cracked open, unleashing heat so intense that Dey couldn't get close. A white cloud of MIC began to shoot out of the vent gas tower attached to the tank and settle over the plant.[7]

Within a few minutes, the fire brigade arrived and began to spray a curtain of water in the air to knock down the cloud of gas. The tower from which the gas was escaping was 120 feet high, however, and the water reached only about 100 feet in the air. The system of water spray pipes was also too low to help.

Dey ran inside the control room and turned on the vent-gas scrubber. It did not work. The scrubber had been under maintenance and had not been charged with a caustic soda solution. Even if the scrubber had been operational, it would have been ineffective since the temperature of the escaping gas was at least 100 degrees Fahrenheit hotter than the system was designed to handle.

By this time, the plant superintendent had raced to the plant on his bicycle. He conferred with Dey on what to do next. They were afraid to turn on the flare tower for fear of igniting the large cloud of gas that had enveloped the plant. The superintendent then remembered that the flare tower was also being repaired and was missing a four-foot section. Likewise, the coolant in the refrigeration system had been drained weeks before so it could be used in another part of the plant. The two considered routing the escaping gas into an empty MIC storage tank, but contrary to established safety procedures, no empty tanks were available. There seemed to be nothing they could do.

As the gas began to escape, a warning alarm was sounded, but it was shut off shortly afterwards. Four buses parked near the entrance and intended for emergency use were left sitting as workers fled by foot in panic. By 1:30 A.M. the gas had permeated the control room and Dey dashed for his gas mask and oxygen tank. The few remaining control room workers fled, one of them breaking his leg as he scrambled over the fence surrounding the plant. Dey left the control room and waited upwind for the cloud of gas to disperse, periodically putting on his mask to enter the control room and check the pressure gauge. By 2:30 A.M. the gas had stopped shooting out of the vent stack. By 3:30 A.M. the gas had dispersed from the plant.

Meanwhile, in the shantytowns and neighborhoods outside the plant, chaos reigned. The gas seeped into the rooms of the sleeping population, suffocating hundreds in their sleep and driving others out into a panicked run through the narrow streets where they inhaled even more of the gas. Blinded by the gas and with their lungs on fire, thousands of people fled the city. According to one source, 45 tons of MIC spread over 25 square miles of the city, killing more than 2,000 residents and seriously injuring 40,000 more.[8]

The Costs of the Accident. Long after the accident, victims continued to suffer from breathlessness, coughing, lung diseases, eye disorders, abdominal pain and vomiting, and menstrual disorders, as well as psychological trauma. The psychological problems were most severe for women of childbearing age, many of whom suffered from reproductive illnesses. These women were afraid to tell their families or spouses about their problems because of the cultural prejudices against infertile women.[9]

The economic consequences of the accident were as devastating as the physical consequences. Many victims were unable to work and their families suffered as a result. Estimates of business losses ranged up to $65 million. The Union Carbide plant was closed and 650 high-paying jobs were lost. So were 1,500 government jobs peripherally related to the presence of the plant. In addition, the business reputation of the city and the whole developing world suffered as a consequence of the accident.[10]

Union Carbide was hard hit by the accident. The Indian government filed a $3 billion lawsuit against the company on behalf of the victims. The company's reputation came under attack from the worldwide news media. Activist groups undertook a variety of campaigns against the company, and communities where Union Carbide had proposed building plants canceled the plans. The company's stock dropped from $48 per share to a low of $32 3/4 within a few weeks. The company's debt rating was reduced by Standard & Poor. Union Carbide stockholders sued the company for not informing them of the risks of doing business abroad. Further damaging the company's and the industry's reputation was the revelation in early 1985 that 28 major MIC leaks had occurred at the Union Carbide plant in Institute, West Virginia, during the five years preceding Bhopal.[11]

The Investigation. After the accident, a horde of reporters, Indian government officials, and Union Carbide technical experts descended on the plant at Bhopal to find out what had gone wrong. It gradually became apparent that the accident resulted not only from technical malfunctions in the plant's equipment but also from human errors and organizational shortcomings. The unpreparedness of the emergency infrastructure of the local government further exacerbated the problem.[12]

Union Carbide scientists who analyzed the residue that remained in the tank after the accident determined that the chemical reaction that led to the leak was caused by the introduction of approximately 1,100 pounds of water into the tank. Water reacts exothermically with MIC to produce a hot, highly pressurized mixture of liquid, foam, and gas. The pressure in the tank had reached 180 psi, more than enough to blow open the safety valve and allow the deadly gas to escape. The question that remained was how had the water gotten into the tank.

There were two main theories. Most experts believe the water leaked into the tank on the evening of December 2 when an employee washed out some of the pipes leading to the tank. Investigations revealed that the employee had failed to use a device called a slip blind to ensure that water could not leak past a series of valves leading to the tank. Union Carbide, on the other hand, argued that the accident was the result of sabotage by an unhappy employee who deliberately unscrewed a gauge and stuck a water hose into the tank. As support for its theory, Union Carbide cited the statements of some employees who remembered seeing a running water hose near the tank after the accident. The company also argued that it wouldn't have been possible to introduce such a large quantity of water into the tank during the washing of the pipes.

Whatever the cause of the accident, it was clear that the magnitude of deaths and injuries was the result of more than a few leaking valves or an act of sabotage. The safety policies and procedures intended to prevent such an accident were not followed; the reasons why were rooted partly in the deteriorating financial condition of the Bhopal plant.

Simply put, the Bhopal plant was an unprofitable unit in an unimportant division of the company. Competitors in the country's pesticide market had introduced new, inexpensive products and the Indian economy had been in a downturn for several years. The Bhopal plant had lost money for three years in a row. As profits fell and the plant's budgets were cut, maintenance was deferred, employees were laid off, and training programs were scaled back. Half the operators in the MIC unit were laid off between 1980 and 1984, leaving only six. Because of the layoffs and rumors that the plant was a candidate for divestment, morale was low and many of the best employees quit. Labor-management conflicts were common. A 1982 company safety inspection determined that many basic safety rules were ignored; for example, maintenance workers were signing permits that they were unable to read and others were working in prohibited areas without permission. Safety training was inadequate—there had been many small accidents and one death in the past—and workers had no training in dealing with emergencies. In fact, the plant had no emergency plans at all, so when the MIC leak occurred, employees reacted in a disorganized manner, shutting off the warning siren, for example. The plant management and workers knew little about the toxic effects of MIC and could not supply the local authorities with any information on how to deal with the accident.[13]

The plant relied on manual operating systems to a much greater degree than its counterparts in the United States. The construction and final technical engineering of the plant had been done by Indian workers and engineers, and the Indian engineers had designed the plant to use more manual labor than comparable plants overseas, partly to generate more jobs. The communications system of the plant relied heavily on runners to bring messages between parts of the plant or outside the plant. The local police were not notified of the accident until 3 A.M., more than two hours after the gas release began, partly because the phones weren't working and partly because the plant management had an informal policy of not involving the local authorities with gas leaks.[14]

The Indian Government's Role. While the Indian government laid responsibility for the accident completely at the door of Union Carbide, it played a significant role in contributing to the conditions that created the disaster. Like many developing countries, India had strict rules regarding the degree to which foreign companies were allowed to own and operate businesses within its borders. Intent on developing the self-sufficiency of Indian industry, the government placed restrictions on the equipment that could be imported, the source of the raw materials used in manufacturing processes, and the makeup of the labor force.

Because of these regulations, the company turned over almost complete control of the Bhopal plant to its Indian subsidiary, Union Carbide India Limited in 1982, and the plant was operated solely by Indians. However, Union Carbide's top management in Connecticut received monthly reports concerning the plant and continued to make major decisions concerning financial, maintenance, and personnel decisions. The Indian personnel were responsible for making safety inspections and operating the plant according to the processing manuals supplied by headquarters.

Many aspects of the local and national infrastructure also contributed to the severity of the accident. The Department of Labor of the state of Madhya Pradesh, in which Bhopal is located, was responsible for safety inspections of industrial facilities located there. Grossly understaffed, the department had only 15 inspectors to cover more than 8,000 industrial plants, and some of the inspectors lacked even typewriters and telephones to assist them in their duties. The two inspectors responsible for the Bhopal plant were trained as mechanical engineers and had little understanding of the hazards of a chemical plant. The government, fearful of discouraging job-producing industries, was reluctant to place a heavy burden of safety and environmental regulations on business.[15]

When an Indian journalist wrote a series of articles in 1982 detailing the death of an employee that was caused by a chemical leak at the plant and warned of the possibility of a catastrophe, neither the plant management nor the government took action, even after the journalist wrote a letter to the chief minister of Madhya Pradesh to warn him of the danger. A high-level government bureaucrat was transferred to another post after he requested that the plant be moved to another location because of the threat it posed to neighboring slum residents. When migrants began building dwellings adjacent to the plant, government officials even issued deeds allowing the squatters the right to stay for 30 years.[16]

Besides an indifferent bureaucracy, the local social services infrastructure contributed to the severity of the accident. There was only one telephone per 1,000 residents and dead lines were common. Running water was available for only a few hours each day and was of poor quality. The streets in the older parts of the city were only 12 feet wide and were crammed with animals, carriages, scooters, cars, buses, bicycles, and people, making evacuation difficult. The hospitals and dispensaries were unequipped to handle the flood of victims.

Inappropriate Technology?

Some critics argue that a highly complex technology like pesticide production is inappropriate for a country like India whose people are unfamiliar with the hazards of such technologies. The squatters who lived around the plant thought that it produced some kind of beneficial plant medicine and had no idea that there was any threat to their safety.[17] The employees of the plant were unfamiliar with the nature of the health threat posed by MIC and were unable to advise the doctors treating the injured. Further, preventive maintenance is a somewhat foreign concept in a subsistence economy where the idea of spending money now in order to save money later is unfamiliar.

Others argue that modern technologies like pesticides are the developing world's best hope of achieving a better standard of living and that without such technologies to increase the food supply, millions would die. An accident like that at Bhopal, they contend, is part of the price developing societies pay for modernization.

When Is It Worth the Risk? John closed the folder and began to collect his thoughts. Under what circumstances was it worthwhile to invest in a developing nation like India? The Bhopal disaster demonstrated that the actions of one small plant in a distant subsidiary could threaten the survival of an entire multinational corporation. There was a definite need for a list of guidelines for corporations investing in the developing countries, which would help ensure that mistakes such as those contributing to the Bhopal disaster would not be repeated.

Discussion Questions

1. What did U.S. chemical companies have to offer developing countries?
2. What were the risks of chemical use in developing countries?
3. Why did the Bhopal accident take place?
4. What lessons can be learned from the Bhopal accident?
5. What should John Brown say to the management of W. R. Grace about investing in developing countries?

Endnotes

1. Written by Mark Jankus with the editorial guidance of Alfred Marcus.
2. From David E. Whiteside, "Note on the Export of Pesticides from the United States to Developing Countries," case 384–097, Harvard Business School, 1983, p. 127.

3. Ibid., p. 129.
4. Ibid., p. 129.
5. Paul Shrivastava, *Bhopal: Anatomy of a Crisis* (Cambridge, Mass.: Ballinger, 1987), p. 41.
6. Ibid., pp. 41, 45.
7. Stuart Diamond, "Workers Recall Horror," *New York Times*, January 30, 1985, p. I1.
8. Shrivastava, *Bhopal*; "The Union Carbide Corporation and Bhopal: A Case Study of Management Responsibility," *Business Ideologies and Social Responsibilities*, p. 303.
9. Ibid., p. 74.
10. Ibid., p. 72.
11. Shrivastava, *Bhopal*, pp. 76–78; see also Alfred Marcus and Robert Goodman, "Corporate Adjustments to Catastrophe: A Study of Investor Reaction to Bhopal," *Industrial Crisis Quarterly* 3 (1989), pp. 213–34.
12. Shrivastava, *Bhopal*, p. 48.
13. Ibid., pp. 49–51.
14. Diamond, "Workers Recall Horror."
15. Ibid.
16. S. Hazarika, "Indian Journalist Offered Warning," *New York Times*, December 11, 1984, p. I9.
17. "Slumdwellers Unaware of Dangers," *New York Times*, January 31, 1985, p. I8.

CHAPTER

18

Product Liability

A Firm's Obligations

The Reasonable Man invariably looks where he is going and is careful to examine the immediate foreground before he executes a leap or bound; who neither stargazes nor is lost in meditation when approaching trap doors or the margin of a dock; . . . who never mounts a moving omnibus, and does not alight from any car while the train is in motion.

A. P. Herbert, "The Reasonable Man"[1]

Introduction and Chapter Objectives

Businesses invariably cause harm to innocent bystanders. How careful must they be? According to classic legal doctrine, businesses have to act as a "reasonable person" would under the circumstance. If they do not conform to this standard, they are at fault and have to compensate the victims. In modern legal theory, fault does not have to be proved in product liability cases. Businesses are held strictly liable. Strict liability, however, does not mean that businesses are without a defense. They have to show that the product has no design or manufacturing defect, that they have provided adequate warnings, and that users have voluntarily assumed some of the risk. This chapter begins with a real-world example describing what a group of U.S. litigation attorneys has done to protect victims' rights in the Dalkon Shield case, which resulted in the bankruptcy of A. H. Robins Company, a large pharmaceutical company. It then compares litigation in Japan and the United States, summarizes the classic U.S. legal doctrine of harm, and shows how this doctrine has evolved from a fault-based system to one based on the doctrine of strict liability.

Litigation in Different Countries

There are vast differences in the number of judges, lawyers, and civil litigation in different countries. In the United States more than 2,000 lawyers exist for every million persons.

Real-World Example

The Law Firm of Robins, Kaplan, Miller, and Ciresi

A 200-member Twin Cities law firm, Robins, Kaplan, Miller, and Ciresi, achieved distinction when Solly Robins, one of its partners, won a case that established the principle of strict liability in Minnesota.[2] The case involved a girl who had been scalded by hot water from a vaporizer. The court decided that it was unnecessary to prove negligence in the manufacture of the product. Product defect was enough to establish liability.

Michael Ciresi, another attorney for the firm, successfully challenged A. H. Robins Company, the manufacturer of the Dalkon Shield. His case was the first to win a major award against A. H. Robins. Eventually Ciresi won more than $37 million in settlements of 198 Dalkon Shield lawsuits; A. H. Robins paid over $375 million before it filed for bankruptcy. Ciresi won an $8.75 million award from Searle Company in the Esther Kociemba Copper-7 intrauterine device case.[3]

The A. H. Robins Company was a successful multinational enterprise with more than $700 million in sales and 6,100 employees in 1985. Its strong product lines—Chapstick, Robitussin, and Sergeant's flea and tick collars—were well known. The company had bought the rights to sell the intrauterine device (IUD) called the Dalkon Shield, which was invented by Dr. Hugh Davis, a professor at Johns Hopkins University. Davis performed the first clinical trials of the Dalkon Shield, during which he followed 640 users of the shield for five and a half months. This time frame was not long enough to discover whether the low pregnancy rate, 1.1 percent, was accurate or whether the women in the study developed pelvic infections. At the time, the Food and Drug Administration did not require A. H. Robins to do any premarket testing. Ultimately, the company sold 2.9 million Dalkon Shields in the United States and controlled 40 percent of the market for IUDs. A. H. Robins sold the Dalkon Shield for $4.35; it cost $.25 to manufacture.[4]

As more Dalkon Shields were sold, more customers reported that it was ineffective in preventing pregnancy. Worse still, it caused serious infections of the reproductive system and abdominal area, resulting in miscarriages and sterility among many women. The cause of the infections often was traced to a string on the shield. The string served as a safety device so that doctors could see if the shield had been properly placed. If not properly placed, the Dalkon Shield could perforate the uterus and enter the abdomen. Unlike the string on competitors' IUDs, the string on the Dalkon Shield was made of interwoven fibers that acted like a wick, drawing bacteria into a woman's body.[5]

Roughly 4 percent of the women who used the Dalkon Shield suffered some type of injury. In the trials, it was shown that top company officials knew about the dangers of the shield and had ordered the destruction of documents on the product's wicking tendencies. Before it filed for bankruptcy, A. H. Robins estimated that payouts to Dalkon Shield victims would exceed $1 billion by the year 2002.

Attorney Michael Ciresi next filed suit against G. D. Searle and Company for its Copper-7 IUD.[6] Ten million women had used the Copper-7 and Ciresi claimed that it had problems similar to those discovered in the Dalkon Shield. In preparing for the *Kociemba* case, Robins, Kaplan, Miller, and Ciresi attorneys reviewed more than 600,000 pages of Searle documents. They found evidence that Searle officials knew of potential problems but decided not to warn the women who used the Copper-7. Deleted from the label on the IUD package were warnings about the potential high risks of infection, the increased risks to women who had never had children, and recommendations that young women, women who had never been pregnant, and women who had multiple sex partners seek another birth control device.

Opponents of Ciresi accused him of histrionics, combativeness in the courtroom, and overaggressiveness. They also argued that his campaign against the drug companies was making the companies too cautious: Fear of litigation kept important innovations from coming on the market in a timely fashion. For women who wanted more birth control options, this was a real problem.[7]

Victims, however, knew that they would find a forceful advocate in Robins, Kaplan, Miller, and Ciresi. The Indian government, for instance, chose the firm to represent it in its lawsuit against the Union Carbide Company for the Bhopal disaster.

EXHIBIT 18–1 Number of Lawyers, Civil Cases, and Judges: Selected Countries

	Lawyers (per million population)	*Civil Cases (per thousand population)*	*Judges (per million population)*
United States	2,348.7 (1980)	44 (1975)	94.9 (1980)
Australia	911.6 (1975)	62.1 (1975)	41.6 (1977)
Canada	890.1 (1972)	46.6 (1970)	59.3 (1981–2)
West Germany	417.2 (1973)	23.4 (1977)	213.4 (1973)
France	206.4 (1973)	30.7 (1975)	84 (1973)
Japan	91.2 (1973)	11.7 (1978)	22.7 (1974)

SOURCE: Adapted from M. Galanter, "Reading the Landscape of Disputes: What We Know and Don't Know. . ." *UCLA Law Review* 4 (1983).

No country in the world is close to this figure. Japan has fewer than 100 attorneys for every million persons (see Exhibit 18–1).[8]

Some attribute differences in economic vitality to these differences. U.S. competitiveness, according to this view, is diminished when lawyers engage in expensive and time-consuming litigation that results in the redistribution of existing resources instead of the creation of new ones.

Although the United States has more attorneys per capita, the number of civil cases brought in the United States is similar to the number brought in other countries whose legal systems are based on English common law. These countries as a whole are more likely to engage in lawsuits than countries whose law is based on other systems. The U.S. estimate is about 44 civil cases per 1,000 persons. In Australia, more than 62 civil cases are brought for every 1,000 persons, whereas in Canada the number is about the same as in the United States. Other international competitors of the United States, however, have far fewer suits: in Japan about 12 cases per 1,000 persons and in Germany about 23 cases.[9]

Litigation in Japan

What accounts for these differences? In Japan, the opportunity for conflict certainly exists. It is a small island nation with a large and homogeneous population. Its industrial output has grown rapidly since the end of World War II. The amount of industrial activity per square kilometer of inhabitable space is the greatest in the world.[10]

Real conflict among the Japanese may not be reflected in the official statistics. When

Japanese are involved in traffic accidents, police give them a minor violation. They are expected to apologize and visit the victim every week for up to a year. The obligation is enforced by local custom and by members of the community. No suit is brought and the courts are not involved.

When a Japanese Airlines plane crashed, killing over 200 people, the CEO personally approached all the families saying he was sorry for what had happened. Notables in the Japanese community, particularly the police and bankers, are available for conflict resolution. Insurance companies offer conflict-resolution services that promise fast and cheap settlements. The full burden of dispute resolution does not fall on the judicial system because so many conflicts are dealt with through informal mechanisms.

Japanese traditions stress the group's obligations to society instead of the rights of the individual. The constitutional reforms adopted by Japan after the end of World War II, however, gave individuals legal rights comparable to those possessed by people in the United States. Nonetheless, conflicts rarely advance to the stage of formal legal proceedings because of Japan's long-standing tradition of informal dispute resolution.[11]

Informal Dispute Resolution

Japan has institutionalized many of these informal dispute resolution techniques and applied them to pollution damages when it passed a law for the Resolution of Pollution Disputes in 1970. The intent of the law was to anticipate controversy and defuse grievances at the outset. A Citizen's Complaint Referral Service gives authority to some 3,000 complaint counselors who operate under local ordinances in more than 400 prefectural and local governments.[12] The law also created Local Pollution Review Boards and a Central Dispute Coordination Committee. All of these groups operate outside the formal legal process to encourage mediation (where the parties reach agreement by themselves), conciliation (where committees formulate nonbinding draft agreements for the parties), and arbitration (where arbitrators bind the parties to an agreement). A similar movement to have environmental disputes resolved outside the court system has arisen in the United States, but it has not made as much progress as the movement in Japan.[13]

A Reluctance to Sue

The Japanese reluctance to sue is based on a number of factors. When asked, most Japanese respond that they think suing is un-Japanese and that lawyers are despicable. The reputation of a person who sues suffers. Other people shun doing business with the person.

Because the costs of litigation in Japan are great, suing ordinarily does not pay in Japan. If the court costs are 1,200 yen, it makes no sense to sue to recover 1,000 yen. Suing also is unprofitable because of a shortage of judges and attorneys; this makes suing expensive because it leads to court delays, expensive bond-posting requirements, and a lack of appropriate remedies.

Thus, the Japanese reluctance to sue is based on a mixed set of motives best summed up by the idea that "suing is both wrong and unprofitable." The result is fewer lawsuits.[14]

Legal Predictability

The predictability of Japanese law is another reason that may explain why the Japanese are less prone to sue than Americans. Japanese courts do not have juries; judges determine outcomes. The parties to a conflict appear in front of the judge in intervals over a long period of time during which the judge can suggest what the likely outcome is going to be. When the parties have a good indication of how the judge is going to decide, they have strong reason to settle informally without pressing their case any further.[15]

Another difference between the United States and Japan is that Japanese judges have been more willing to codify portions of the law. (The Japanese system of law tends to be code-based, similar to continental European nations such as France and Germany.) They have established well-accepted formulas for resolving difficult cases that involve damage awards. Again, the parties know in advance what the likely outcome will be so there is less reason to sue.

Litigation in the United States

Unlike Japan, the United States has seen a growing amount of litigation. Most observers have pointed to an increase in the number of product liability cases filed and to the average and median awards that have been made.[16] The question is whether these increases are disproportionate to the growth in population and concentrated only in the product liability area. Legal scholar Marc Gallanter holds that in proportion to population growth, the increase in the number of suits is not out of line; moreover, most of the increase in federal court filings has been in areas other than product liability law. Still, there have been numerous well-publicized liability cases involving very large settlements.[17]

Business Executive Opinion. Forty-seven percent of business executives surveyed reported that increased litigation had resulted in improved product usage and warnings, 35 percent claimed that it had improved the safety of their products, and 33 percent reported that their companies had redesigned product lines (see Exhibit 18–2).

However, the same business executives also reported that increased litigation had adverse impacts, including discontinued product lines, the decision not to introduce new

EXHIBIT 18–2 Executive Opinion of Increased Litigation

Positive Impact		*Negative Impact*	
Improved product usage warnings	47%	Discontinued product lines	47%
Improved safety	35%	Decision not to introduce new products	39%
Redesigned products	33%	Decline in product research	25%
		Lost market share	22%

SOURCE: Adapted from *The Polling Report* 21 (1987).

products, a decline in product research, and lost market share. The decision not to introduce new products, they argued, had hurt the global competitiveness of U.S. business.[18]

The general public views the increasing number of suits with mixed feelings. Of the people surveyed in 1987, 51 percent believed that awards had been excessive, and 63 percent blamed attorneys who were looking for big fees. However, most people felt that no limit should be placed on the size of damage awards, and that juries, not judges, should continue to set the amount of the damages.[19]

Reforming U.S. Liability Laws

Executives most favored a reform that would replace the strict liability system with a fault-based one. However, most executives believed that the type of reform most likely to occur was the imposition of caps on punitive damages.[20]

Indeed, many states, including Alaska, Colorado, Minnesota, and Utah, have introduced some type of cap on damages (see Exhibit 18–3). However, there was little agreement in the business community and in the general public about what type of reform would be best. Among the many reform proposals that were made were the following:[21]

1. A cap, or upper limit, on the amount that victims can recover. A cap can come in many forms—on pain and suffering damages, on punitive damages, on lawyer's contingency fees, and so on.
2. Allowing judges, not juries, to award punitive damages.
3. Limiting the principle of joint and several liability principle (in which each contributor to the damage—no matter how small its role—can be held fully liable for all the costs).

The Contract with America and Liability Reform

As part of its Contract with America, the Republicans who controlled the House of Representative in 1995 passed new standards limiting awards in civil suits. The purpose was to reduce the number of lawsuits. The legislation put caps on the damage awards that litigants could win in cases involving devices such as lawnmowers, toaster-ovens, and artificial hearts. It also limited the damages a person could win for pain and suffering in a medical malpractice suit.[22]

Under existing federal law, a plaintiff could win punitive damages to punish willfully malicious conduct where the court believed that the manufacturer had shown flagrant indifference to consumer safety. Punitive damages were money payments that went beyond the compensation for economic losses (e.g., medical costs and lost wages) and intangibles (e.g., mental distress, pain, and suffering). Under the House bill, punitive damages could be awarded only when a plaintiff showed with clear and convincing evidence that the defendant meant to cause harm or showed conscious, flagrant, and indifferent regard to the rights of others. The limit on punitive damages was three times the amount of economic damages or $250,000, whichever was greater. Awards for pain and suffering could be no more than $250,000. A person who used drugs or alcohol could be barred from winning an award if the court determined that he or she was more than 50 percent

EXHIBIT 18–3 States with Caps on Damages

State	Cap on Noneconomic Damages
Alaska	$500,000
Colorado	$500,000
Florida	$450,000
Maryland	$350,000
Minnesota	$400,000
New Hampshire	$875,000
Virginia	$350,000
Washington	$493,000
Wisconsin	$1 million

SOURCE: Adapted from National Conference of State Legislatures, *Liability Insurance,* May 1987.

responsible for the harm. The law established a 15-year statute of limitations on any liability award for a defective manufactured product. It also made drug companies immune from damage awards if the Food and Drug Administration had approved their product.

The House Republicans passed the Attorneys Accountability Act. Under this act, the loser in a civil suit is required to pay the legal costs of his or her opponent, which puts great pressure on both parties to settle before going to court.

The Evolution of U.S. Liability Laws

tort law
Branch of law dealing with private harm or injury and the compensation for these wrongs.

Before discussing reform in more detail, it is necessary to understand how the law of damages evolved in the United States. In legal terminology, this branch of the law is called torts. Derived from French and Latin roots and meaning "to twist," **tort law** deals with private harm or injury. When a person is harmed by another person, the plaintiff (i.e., the person claiming to have been harmed) may bring an action against the defendant (i.e., the person alleged to have caused the harm). The purpose is to restore the situation to the condition before the harm was caused, and inasmuch as possible, to compensate the plaintiff for the damage that was done.

Tort law also has a deterrent effect. If a person knows that a victim must be compensated, then the person will be less likely to commit an act that causes harm. Insofar as tort law aims to restore a situation to its prior condition, its purpose is to promote a sense of justice in society.[23]

The Classic Theory

According to the classic theory, the plaintiff has to prove three things.

1. *Breach of duty.* Even if harm is unintentional, the defendant owes the plaintiff the *duty of care* that a reasonable person would show under the circumstances; that is, the

defendant has a legal duty to prevent harmful acts from happening. The defendant is held liable—that is, negligent and at fault—for the breach of this standard.

There is, however, no precise statutory definition of the standard of *reasonable care*. Instead, the courts rely on custom, practice, and tradition to decide if it is exercised in a particular case. Because of the admirable flexibility of the standard, it has been subject to parody and ridicule. For example, a reasonable person is always supposed to be thinking of others. Prudence is supposed to be the person's guide, and "safety-first" the rule to which the reasonable person steadfastly clings (see the opening quotation of this chapter). Difficulties in defining the reasonable person's behavior have resulted in much legal disputation.[24]

"negligence in the air"
Carelessness or breach of duty without harm.

2. *Actual damages*. An additional element in the classic theory is that the plaintiff must show real damages. Carelessness or breach of duty without harm is called **"negligence in the air."** In this respect, the requirements of the law and ethics diverge. Although ethically the defendant is worthy of blame for carrying out actions that might result in harm, if no actual harm results, the defendant is not legally responsible and does not have to compensate the plaintiff.

The harms for which a plaintiff can be compensated are broad. They include relatively concrete matters such as medical bills and lost wages, and less tangible harms such as emotional distress and loss of companionship. For wrongful death, the victim's heirs are entitled to the present value of future wages that the victim would have earned less the amount that would have been spent on personal consumption. How to value a human life has been strenuously debated (see Chapter 17). The use of the present value of future wages as a standard does not take into account the emotional loss of the heirs.

The intent of tort law is compensation, not punishment, but there are exceptions to this rule. When the defendant means to inflict harm or acts in reckless disregard of the safety of others, punitive damages may be awarded. Punitive awards have been large, and companies like Johns Manville have been threatened with bankruptcy (see the special feature, "The Threat of Bankruptcy" at the end of this chapter). The trials that end in the award of punitive damages are long and complex, and attorneys' fees usually consume more than half of the awards.[25]

3. *Causation*. The third element that the plaintiff must demonstrate is causation. If there is damage, and the defendant has acted carelessly but is not directly responsible for the damage, then the defendant has no legal obligation to compensate the plaintiff. The actions of the defendant must be the immediate and proximate cause of the harms suffered by the plaintiff.[26]

For example, a theologian's arguments that the damage was caused by an act of God or a psychologist's arguments that the damage was caused by childhood experiences would have no legal bearing. The courts seek clear evidence of a direct cause-and-effect relationship, for example, a car that strikes another car or a bullet that is fired within view of reliable witnesses.

A case familiar to most law students is the 1928 Supreme Court decision in *Palsgraf* v. *Long Island Railway Co.* The plaintiff, Mrs. Palsgraf, was standing on a railroad platform. The guard for Long Island Railway helped a man board a train after it had started to move and jarred loose a package that the man had been carrying. Covered in newspapers and filled with fireworks, the package fell on the track and exploded. The explosion upset a set of scales at the other end of the platform where Mrs. Palsgraf was standing, causing injuries for which she sued. The Court decided against Mrs. Palsgraf. In the majority decision Justice Cardozo held that the railroad guard's actions were too far removed in the chain of causes to result in Mrs. Palsgraf's injuries.[27]

Long Latencies

The courts have difficulty assigning responsibility in cases of long latencies—the time between a person's first exposure and the onset of a disease. The California Supreme Court fashioned a unique response to long latency in the case of *Sindell* v. *Abbott Laboratories* in 1980. Several drug companies manufactured and sold diethylstilbestrol (DES), which was used to prevent miscarriages. The FDA banned DES in 1971 when it was found to cause vaginal and cervical cancer in women whose mothers had taken the drug. The drug companies were sued. Over 200 companies had manufactured DES, making it impossible to determine which one sold the drug that harmed a particular woman. The California Supreme Court allowed the plaintiffs to recover by apportioning responsibility based on each company's market share at the time the plaintiff's mother took the drug.[28]

The Case against Smoking

Problems in determining causation affect many tort cases. One reason that smokers have not recovered from cigarette manufacturers is that the evidence showing a link between smoking and lung cancer—no matter how conclusive it may be to scientists—does not stand up in the courts. The scientific argument is statistical: It shows a greater tendency among smokers to contact cancer. However, scientists cannot say with complete assurance that a particular cancer is a result of a person's smoking. Unlike asbestos, which is associated with one type of cancer, smoking is associated with many types. Other factors, including genetic and environmental circumstances, also can intervene.

Assume that the person smoked two packs of cigarettes a day for 20 years and contacted a form of lung cancer. What if the same type of cancer was found among nonsmokers in the person's family? What if the person lived in an area of high concentration of sulfur dioxide and other air pollutants? It would be hard for the victim's lawyers to prove that cigarette smoking was the immediate and proximate cause of the person's illness. The "but-for" test is the criterion the courts apply—but for A, the courts ask, would B have occurred?[29] Even without smoking, such a person might have contacted cancer. In the courts, probabilistic evidence usually is insufficient; there has to be a preponderance of evidence on the side of the plaintiff.

Landmark Case: *Cipolione* v. *Liggett Group*. The landmark 1988 case of Antonio Cipolione was the first to be won by a plaintiff against a cigarette company. A federal jury in Newark, New Jersey, awarded $400,000 in damages to Cipolione whose wife died of cancer in 1964. The jury granted this large award because it found that the Liggett Group implied wrongly that cigarettes were safe in its advertising prior to 1966. The jury found that Liggett should have warned customers about the dangers of cigarette smoking prior to 1966, the year in which Congress required that warning labels be put on cigarette packages.[30]

Lawyers for the plaintiff spent about $3 million and five years gathering evidence. Their aim was to bring to light thousands of pages of internal documents showing that prior to the congressional action the manufacturers knew of the dangers of cigarette smoking, but even with this knowledge they sold cigarettes to the public without a warning. The plaintiff's lawyers hoped that exposing these documents would make it easier to win awards in future cases.

The lawyers showed that cigarette manufacturers made many implied promises in their advertising about the safety of their products. In the 1940s, R. J. Reynolds claimed that "more doctors smoke Camels," and in the 1950s Lorillard said that the micronite filter on its Kent cigarettes was "so safe, so effective, it has been selected to help filter the air in hospital operating rooms." The lawyers alleged that with these claims, the cigarette manufacturers had established an explicit warranty about the safety of the product.

Landmark Cases: A Flood of Lawsuits. It takes landmark cases, such as the *Cipolione* case with its large award, to start a flood of lawsuits against products (e.g., asbestos and intrauterine devices) in which juries award huge sums for damages. Of course, asbestos and intrauterine devices have a number of characteristics that distinguish them from cigarettes, so it is easier to argue that victims have been unwittingly exposed to hazards. In contrast, many juries believe that smokers voluntarily engage in the practice and know its dangers.

Lawyers for the cigarette manufacturers have adhered to traditional defenses:

1. Smokers have a sense that tobacco involves risks and that they must take some responsibility for their conduct.
2. The evidence linking smoking to any particular type of cancer is ambiguous at best. Significantly, the jury in the *Cipolione* case found that smoking was at least partially responsible for Mrs. Cipolione's death, but it did not find that the defendants conspired against Mrs. Cipolione to suppress evidence that smoking was unsafe. Future cases are likely to press forward with the conspiracy argument.

Arguments for the Defense

The classic theory of torts provides defendants with a number of arguments for refuting the claims against them (see Exhibit 18–4). They may argue, for example, that their actions were responsible under the circumstances, that the plaintiff suffered no actual harm, or that their actions were not the direct causes of the plaintiff's injuries. Defendants also can claim contributory negligence and assumption of risk, which will be addressed in the next two sections.[31]

Contributory Negligence

contributory negligence
If a consumer blatantly misuses a product, the manufacturer cannot be held liable

Contributory negligence is based on the principle that both defendant and plaintiff must act according to the standard of reasonable care. For example, suppose the plaintiff is suing the defendant for failure to properly remove snow from a sidewalk, causing the plaintiff to fall and break an arm and a leg. Suppose also that the plaintiff approached the sidewalk

Exhibit 18–4 Classic Tort Law

Plaintiff has to prove:	Defendant can argue:
1. Breach of duty.	1. Contributory negligence.
2. Actual damages.	2. Assumption of risk.
3. Causation.	

in a stupor after having imbibed a few too many strong alcoholic drinks. In this case, the defendant can claim that the plaintiff did not exercise reasonable care.

However, when the courts find fault with the actions of both parties they are not faced with an either/or situation. The courts have the right to apportion blame on a percentage basis (this is true in most states). This reduces the plaintiff's burden to prove that the defendant is at fault. By applying a standard of comparative negligence, the states can reduce the award the defendant owes the plaintiff by the percentage the plaintiff is responsible. Some states will grant an award only if the defendant is 50 percent or more responsible; any percentage above 50 percent is paid by the defendant. Other states will allow awards to the plaintiff at percentages below 50 percent responsibility.[32]

The exact apportioning of responsibility between defendant and plaintiff is one of the most controversial aspects of tort law. Deciding who is responsible for an automobile accident is particularly difficult. Therefore, many states have adopted some form of no-fault insurance, which simplifies the process by eliminating costly and lengthy court procedures. It also guarantees that regardless of who is at fault, the victim will receive some form of compensation.

Assumption of Risk

assumption of risk A plaintiff who is aware of the risk of damage, loss, or injury cannot press claims against the defendant who caused the damage.

Defendants can also claim that the plaintiff was aware of the risks but decided to pursue the activity anyway. This is called **assumption of risk**. The protection offered by this claim has grown in importance as U.S. society becomes more litigious. The plaintiff's awareness of risk need not be conscious and explicit, but the defendant's argument is strengthened if a consciousness of the risks involved is specific. Therefore, patients in hospitals are commonly required to sign papers acknowledging their awareness of risks before surgery is performed. It is also common for ski lodges, baseball franchises, and transportation companies to put disclaimers on the back of tickets saying that in the event of harm the ticketholder was aware of the dangers. Because of the customers' implied assumption of risk, cigarette manufacturers and diet pop makers are not as unhappy as they might be about the warning labels that they are required to place on packages and bottles.

When the plaintiff has been warned, the courts are unlikely to take punitive action against the defendant. A plaintiff can still recover even after admitting awareness of risk, but the awards will be limited to compensation for tangible medical costs and lost earnings rather than intangible emotional distress or pain and suffering, which means that awards will be substantially lower.

Strict Liability

strict liability
Part of tort theory which states that the plaintiff does not have to prove fault.

The classic theory of torts puts the burden of proof on the plaintiff to prove that the defendant is at fault. However, modern tort theory has moved toward a theory of **strict liability** where the plaintiff no longer has to prove fault. The strict liability theory derives from the treatment the courts give to inherently dangerous activities. For example, if a person owns wild animals such as snakes or leopards, and those animals injure someone, the owner is responsible regardless of the care exercised. Likewise, a company that uses explosives is responsible for harm even if it observes safety rules. According to strict liability, responsibility exists without the sense of moral opprobrium that applies under the classic theory (see Exhibit 18–5).

What is the justification for strict liability? Why should a defendant have to pay when the harm inflicted is unintentional and the defendant's actions are reasonable and appropriate under the circumstances? First, it is necessary to recognize that someone will have to bear the costs of damages, either the victim, the injurer, or society at large through its governmental institutions. Modern tort law has decided to make the defendant or the defendant's insurance company mainly responsible.

Strict liability is developed most fully in the area of consumer injuries. The manufacturer of a defective product is held strictly liable whether or not the manufacturer is at fault. Strict liability is justified in part by the buyer's expectations. The buyer does not expect to be injured by the product.

Evolution of the Doctrine of Strict Liability

It is worth tracing the evolution of the doctrine of strict liability. The issues have claimed national attention because of the large awards, the increases in liability insurance, and the withdrawal of companies from making products such as infant vaccines.[33]

The evolution of product liability doctrine consists of roughly three periods:

- Recovery was mainly governed under contract law in the first period, which lasted until the beginning of World War I.
- The classic theory of torts developed during the second period, which lasted from World War I to the mid-1960s.
- A strict liability standard emerged during the third period, which has been in effect since the mid-1960s.[34]

EXHIBIT 18–5 Strict Liability

Plaintiff does not have to prove:
- Breach of duty.

Why?
- Someone has to pay.
- Buyer doesn't expect to be injured.
- Manufacturer knows more about the product than the buyer.

Contract Law

privity of contract A plaintiff can sue only when a legally binding contract exists with the defendant.

Under contract law, if the manufacturer causes the product defect, the consumer has no right to recovery because the consumer's transaction is with the retailer, not the manufacturer. **Privity of contract** means that a plaintiff can sue only when he or she has a legally binding contract with the defendant. The *Winterbottom* v. *Wright* case decided in England in 1842 held that a person thrown from an imperfectly constructed wagon had no right to recovery against the wagon manufacturer because the wagon had been purchased from the retailer, not the manufacturer. The privity of contract exists between the consumer and the retailer, not between the consumer and a third party, which in the *Winterbottom* decision was the manufacturer.[35]

Legal analysts, however, subsequently viewed the privity of contract requirement as prejudicial to customers, who lacked the knowledge, expertise, and power of the manufacturers. Today, the courts do not allow human risk to be allocated contractually. In product defect cases, contract-based warranties apply only to the repair of the product and to property damage, not to human injury. Warranties remain in effect to cover characteristics such as product durability, responsibility for labor and parts repairs, and the uses to which a product may and may not be put.

implicit warranties Warranties read into the contract by court cases and statute.

Warranties. Two types of warranties exist—express and implicit. Express warranties are a written part of the contract and the bargain for sale. **Implicit warranties** are read into the contract by court cases and statute. For example, the Uniform Commercial Code covers an implied warranty of merchantability, which requires that goods be fit for their intended use.

Express warranties serve two purposes. First, they enable the seller to support its contention that the product has superior qualities by showing that the seller is willing to back them up with a warranty. Second, express warranties divide the risks efficiently between the manufacturer and the purchaser. A manufacturer, for example, may be better able to fix refrigerator compressors and therefore takes on this responsibility; the purchaser is in a better position to take precautions against damage to the refrigerator door and therefore takes on that responsibility.

Standard warranties usually contain disclaimers against implicit warranties, stipulate that the warranted good is free from defects in material and workmanship, and limit the time within which claims can be made and the seller is obliged to repair or replace defective parts. Time limitations are established to assure that claims are due to the seller's defective workmanship or materials, not to the buyer's reckless or irresponsible use of the good in question.

Express warranties usually exempt the seller from liability for consequential (large scale or significant) damage because buyers are supposed to be in a better position than sellers to cease activities that will cause this type of damage. The insurance cost to the seller, therefore, would be greater than the insurance cost to the buyer. By placing the responsibility on the buyer, overall costs to society should be reduced.

Critics of express warranties maintain that the seller has greater bargaining power than the buyer and that the seller will impose its terms. Defenders hold that if the product market is competitive, the seller will not have the power to impose its terms. Even so, critics respond, buyers are incapable of reading or understanding the "fine print" in warranties and are still at a disadvantage. Moreover, buyers will not draft warranties that are advantageous to them because they are unaware of low-probability events and are unwilling to take precautions to protect themselves against them.[36]

Magnuson-Moss Warranty Act
Restricts a seller's ability to disclaim implied warranties and imposes labeling and disclosure requirements.

Magnuson-Moss Act. In 1966, Congress passed the **Magnuson-Moss Warranty Act** to protect buyers from unscrupulous warranty terms in contracts and bills of sale. This act restricts a seller's ability to disclaim implied warranties and imposes labeling and disclosure requirements on the seller. A seller must say if a warranty is "full" or "limited." If full, the warranty cannot exclude consequential damages and the manufacturer has to repair defects promptly without charge. If repair is impossible, the manufacturer must replace the item or give a refund within a specific time period.

Classic Tort Law

Contract law, as discussed under the topic of warranties, is designed to assist individuals in ordering their private relations. Classic tort law applies when it is too costly for individuals to foresee all contingencies and to devise detailed rules to cover cases of potential damage. For example, it is impractical for drivers to enter into contractual relations with all other drivers and with all pedestrians concerning potential accidents. Tort law supplements contract law by devising rules for apportioning losses in these instances.

The *MacPherson v. Buick Motor Co.* decision of 1916 ended the privity of contract requirement in product liability cases. A buyer typically purchases a car from a dealer, not a manufacturer. The buyer has no direct contractual relations with the manufacturer, nor do the passengers in the buyer's car. Regardless of any contractual obligations, the court held the manufacturer responsible for injuries caused by its products. After this decision, product liability became a subset of tort law rather than contract law. This meant, that a buyer then had to prove *fault*, which typically was defined to mean that reasonable safety features or adequate warnings had not been provided.[37]

Hand's Rule. *Reasonable precaution* was defined in economic terms in a famous decision handed down in 1947 by Judge Learned Hand (see discussion of the Hand rule in Chapter 13). In *United States* v. *Carroll Towing Co.*, Judge Hand ruled that if the expected injury exceeded the costs of precaution and the defendant failed to take the precaution, the defendant was negligent:

> Since there are occasions when every vessel will break away from her moorings, and since, if she does, she becomes a menace to those about her; the owner's duty, as in other similar situations, to provide against resulting injuries is a function of three variables: (1) the probability that she will break away; (2) the gravity of the resulting injury, if she does; and (3) the burden of adequate precautions.[38]

If the probability of breaking away times the gravity of injuries is greater than the cost of precaution, then the defendant was at fault.

Final Blow to Warranties. The final blow to the use of warranties in product safety cases came in *Henningsen* v. *Bloomfield Motors*. Decided by the New Jersey Supreme Court in

1960, this case held that warranty terms for exclusion of liability for consequential damages did not have bearing. Mrs. Henningsen was driving the family automobile, but the warranty contained an express limitation of liability to the original purchaser, Mr. Henningsen. In addition, the manufacturer only accepted liability for defective parts for 90 days and 4,000 miles, but the accident occurred after this time and mileage had elapsed. The manufacturer waived any liability for consequential damage, but when the steering mechanism failed and Mrs. Henningsen was injured, the court decided to allow her to sue the manufacturer for her injuries. Its decision signified that tort law was dominant and that warranty provisions in contracts had no bearing when human injury occurred.[39]

Judge Traynor's Decision. The movement away from a fault-based system took place gradually. The first major breakthrough was a case against Coca Cola Bottling Co., decided by Justice Traynor of the California Supreme Court in 1944, in which a Coca-Cola bottle had exploded in the hands of a waitress. Justice Traynor decided against Coca-Cola Bottling, ruling that "a manufacturer incurs an absolute liability when an article that he has placed on the market, knowing that it is to be used without inspection, proves to have a defect that causes injury to human beings . . ."[40]

Three points were implicit in Justice Traynor's decision, which has become part of the standard rationale for strict liability:

1. It is cheaper for society to have a strict liability standard. A plaintiff has to prove only damage and causation, not fault; the burden of proof—and the time and expense of legal proceedings—is reduced. While there may be more trials, the ease of their execution should reduce the total costs to society.

2. It is less expensive for the manufacturer to bear the cost of the damage than it is for the victim. The cost of a single accident can be devastating for the victim, who is often uninsured and unprepared. On the other hand, the costs of an accident may be trivial to the manufacturer, which should have the foresight to acquire insurance. Also, accident costs can be passed on to consumers in the form of higher prices—probably only a few pennies for each product sold. The option of spreading the risk, available to the manufacturer, is unavailable to the customer.

3. The final rationale implicit in Justice Traynor's decision is that the manufacturer's intimate knowledge of the product dwarfs the consumer's knowledge or capability to change the situation. The consumer buys mass-produced, technically sophisticated goods that pass through a long and complex chain from factory to retailer. The consumer is unlikely to know where in the chain of design, production, and distribution a defect is likely to occur. Therefore, if the consumer is seriously injured, the manufacturer is responsible.

The Second Restatement of Torts: Strict Liability

The three points from Justice Traynor's decision were incorporated into the 1965 Second Restatement of Torts by the American Law Institute. Thus, strict liability became the norm and, in effect, replaced the slogan, Let the Buyer Beware (caveat emptor). Seller beware! A seller is held strictly liable even if it exercises "all possible care in the preparation and sale."[41]

EXHIBIT 18–6 Absolute Liability?

Movement away from absolute liability:
- Need to show product defect.
- Contributory negligence defense allowed.
- Assumption of risk defense alowed.

Movement toward absolute liability:
- Manufacturer needs to find out about unknown dangers.
- State-of-the-art defense unacceptable.
- Curtailments of product misuse and assumption-of-risk defense put in place.

A Movement toward Absolute Liability?

The Second Restatement of Torts has since undergone a number of refinements that have made it more like the classic law of torts. Nonetheless, a countertrend has pushed legal doctrine in the direction of absolute liability. These two forces, which have moved strict liability both away from and toward absolute liability, are briefly examined (see Exhibit 18–6).

First, pushing strict liability toward classic tort law is the need to show product defect so that a manufacturer can be held liable. A defect can occur in the design or manufacture of the product or by virtue of a failure to warn. Determining whether a defect has occurred, especially in product design, is similar to determining whether fault has taken place under the classic theory. The concept of reasonable behavior under the circumstances, often formulated as a state-of-the-art defense, plays an important role.

A second element pushing strict liability toward classic tort law is the continued consideration of contributory negligence. Most courts would hold that a manufacturer cannot be held liable if the consumer blatantly misuses the product. If a consumer uses a lawnmower to trim hedges, for example, no liability would attach to the manufacturer because the product is not being used in its intended fashion. The consumer assumes the risk.

A third way in which strict liability is similar to the classic doctrine is that it retains the concept of assumption of risk. Thus, warning labels and disclaimers are common, for the reasons discussed earlier.

Beshada v. *Johns-Manville*

These refinements of the doctrine of strict liability have been challenged in some cases. For example, *Beshada* v. *Johns-Manville Products Corp.*, which was decided by the New Jersey Supreme Court in 1982, pushed the law toward absolute liability. The defendant claimed that the dangers of asbestos were unknown to science at the time. The court said that even if this claim were true, the manufacturer would still be responsible, implying that the manufacturer has a responsibility to find out about unknown dangers and that a state-of-the-art defense is unacceptable. The manufacturer may have to conduct product tests and warn workers if a problem exists even if scientists are not yet aware of the problem. Failure to do so may be grounds for paying damages.[42]

In addition, some states have curtailed the application of product-misuse and assumption-of-risk defenses. Courts may expect manufacturers to foresee product misuse (e.g., driving under the influence of alcohol) and to design products so that damage cannot result even under these extreme conditions.

Greater Manufacturer Liability

A controversy has arisen in the academic community over the reasons why the movement toward greater manufacturer liability has taken place. On the one hand, G. L. Priest of Yale University maintains that manufacturer liability has gained acceptance not because it is the right doctrine but because its proponents have been skillful in propagating it. Their arguments—that manufacturers have unfair bargaining power over consumers, that they can absorb the losses better, and that they are in a better position to invest in precaution and in research in superior technology—are powerful, but Priest believes they are mistaken because they remove the consumers' incentives for precaution and provide a sense of entitlement without a concomitant sense of responsibility.

A contrary view, proposed by W. M. Landes and R. A. Posner of the University of Chicago, is that the movement toward manufacturer liability promotes general economic efficiency. Their argument is that the expense to consumers of learning about product defects is greater than the expense to manufacturers when mechanization and the complexity of goods bought and sold are great. Mass markets, which separate manufacturers from consumers, make the bargaining costs of allocating risks through contractual mechanisms prohibitively high. Thus, social welfare is served in most cases by a strict liability standard. Landes and Posner have found that the movement away from a contractual standard toward strict liability correlates with measures of urbanization and economic development.[43]

Assessing Existing Reform Proposals

As indicated, efforts have been made to reform product liability law. Many states have decided to put a cap, or upper limit, on the amount that victims can recover. For example, in medical malpractice suits in Missouri, victims can recover up to $350,000. In New Mexico, there is a recovery limit of $50,000 from tavern owners in cases of drunken driving. The federal government also has passed the Risk Retention Act in 1981, which allowed firms in the same industry to form insurance pools as an alternative to the high cost of commercial products liability insurance.

Additional reform proposals have been made:

1. *Returning to the classic negligence theory.* The system of strict liability would be replaced with a fault-based system. Strict liability would be restricted to cases of inherently dangerous activities (e.g., keeping wild animals or using explosives) and not extended to all products.

2. *Maintaining the strict liability principle, but clarifying that the system has not evolved toward absolute liability.* This can be accomplished by strengthening the state-of-the-art defense. Defendants would be able to mount a defense against a design defect if they did not know in advance about the product's dangers, or if there was no practical or feasible alternative way of designing or manufacturing the product.

3. *Establishing a reasonable-prudence standard.* A product would be held to be

unreasonably dangerous if the manufacturer knew, or through the exercise of reasonable prudence should have known, about the dangers, and if a reasonably prudent person in the same or similar circumstances would not have manufactured the product or used the design or formulation that the manufacturer used.

4. *Strengthening assumption-of-risk and contributory-negligence defenses*. This implies a return to contractlike principles wherein warnings are seen as implicit contracts agreed to by consumers, who are presumed to understand that the products they use have certain risks. The consumers then would have to take more responsibility for their actions.

Although there have been many proposals for such tort reform, Congress has failed to pass any of them. Instead, it has put a cap on recovery (see earlier discussions). Robert Cooter from the University of California, Berkeley, and Thomas Ulen from the University of Illinois argue that putting a ceiling on recovery awards is similar to a ceiling on any price, and like rent control or other rate regulations, these limits are economically inefficient: if potential defendants are aware of the cap, they will not take sufficient precaution. However, Cooter and Ulen admit that the intellectual underpinnings of the product liability system have gone awry:

> The most efficient liability standard for this area is strict liability with the defenses of product misuse and assumption of risk . . . [which] would duplicate the sort of standard that would have been achieved by the consent of the manufacturer and consumer through voluntary exchange if the costs of bargaining were low. The current system has evolved beyond this standard and toward absolute manufacturer liability. It is this extension beyond strict liability with the usual defenses that is at the root of the current crisis.[44]

These attorneys support a uniform federal liability statute that would require:[45]

- Corroborating objective evidence (not only the testimony of experts) to prove defects in construction, design, or manufacture.
- A rejection of market share liability.
- The awarding by judges, not juries, of punitive damages.
- The awarding of punitive damages only in cases of proven reckless disregard of consumer safety.
- The deduction of workers' compensation and other insurance benefits from damage awards.

Companies support a number of different types of laws, but none has passed.

A type of reform adopted in Japan for compensating the victims of pollution and other hazardous substances has two main features:[46]

1. *Granting injured persons the right to receive administrative relief*. Instead of relying on the court system and litigation, a person can make a claim before an administrative body. Based on proof of exposure, existence of the disease or injury, and compensable damages, the person can collect without having to show fault. The injured person would receive medical costs plus a portion of lost earnings but would not have the right to receive punitive damages.

2. *Assessing damages according to the principle of proportional liability*. If the person chooses to sue, the courts can establish liability and distribute compensation based on the

Real-World Example

The Threat of Bankruptcy

In recent years, filings of Chapter 11 bankruptcy petitions have become a common practice for large American corporations.[47] Economic theory assumes that if a firm goes bankrupt, its assets will be liquidated and the firm no longer will exist. The process of exiting from the market is an integral part of the discipline imposed upon firms by the capitalist system. Investors have to accept risk; if the companies in which they invest do not succeed, they will lose large portions of their investment. Then new investors will have the chance to purchase the liquidated assets at favorable terms; they can form new firms and enter the market. Because of some combination of lower costs, better management, and greater productivity, the new firm should be able to succeed, whereas the old one could not. In this way, capitalism is a dynamic system that perpetually revitalizes itself. It increases the growth and productivity of society at large by weeding out losing ownership teams and rewarding winning ones.

The discipline of the market, however, has been eroded by changes in the bankruptcy laws that make it harder for firms to fail. Until 1893, the United States did not have a permanent bankruptcy law. Under common law, debtors were sent to prison. Efforts to create a permanent bankruptcy law (in 1800, 1841, and 1867) came to naught because of disputes between Jeffersonians, Jacksonians, and Southern and Western Democrats who favored liberal bankruptcy laws, and Tories, Federalists, Whigs, and Republicans who opposed them. The first enduring national bankruptcy act called for strict liquidation of failing firms. It was not until 1938 that an alternative to strict liquidation was made part of law. The 1938 Bankruptcy Act is the predecessor to current laws. Passed during the Great Depression when many people were debtors and comparatively few were solvent, it allows for corporate reorganization rather than liquidation.

The 1938 act was amended in 1977 when a new bankruptcy code took effect. Under the new code, liquidation takes place under Chapter 7 proceedings. However, an alternative to liquidation—reorganization under Chapter 11—remains. The 1977 amendments eliminate the need to be insolvent when filing for Chapter 11 status. As soon as a petition for Chapter 11 bankruptcy is filed, the stay of creditors claims is automatic. Creditors do not have to be paid. Troubled firms then start a process of negotiations with creditors' committees. They can negotiate with employees about collective bargaining agreements and with executives about their compensation contracts.

These negotiations are designed to establish the conditions under which the distressed companies can remain going concerns. The bankruptcy judge acts as a mediator or arbitrator in this process. Legal fees must be paid first. Employees, customers, and the government (taxes) next have claim to the company's assets. Following in line are bondholders and preferred stockholders; common shareholders are the last to be paid back. They are referred to as the "residual claimants" and have claim to all remaining profit when the firm is doing well, and take the risk of losing everything when the firm does poorly.

Under 1984 amendments to the Bankruptcy Act, standards were established for judging the reasonableness of an employer's use of Chapter 11 to reject collective bargaining agreements.[48] These amendments were passed after Bildisco and Bildisco, Inc., used a Chapter 11 filing to unilaterally abrogate its collective bargaining agreements. Continental Airlines in 1983 and Frontier Airlines in 1986 also used Chapter 11 filings to modify collective bargaining agreements.

The most significant uses of the Chapter 11 filing to modify claims, however, have been in product liability. The cases involving Johns-Manville in 1982 and A. H. Robins in 1986 attracted substantial attention[49] (see the Real-World Example: "The Law Firm of Robins, Kaplan, Miller, and Ciresi" at the beginning of this chapter). Johns-Manville faced an unpredictable number of claims relating to the damage caused by asbestos. At the time of its filing for bankruptcy, it had 16,500 existing asbestos claims against it, which were being settled at an average of $40,000 per suit.

Five large punitive damage awards, however, had averaged over $600,000 since 1982. With 500 new claims being made every month, the estimates of the total number of claims against Johns-Manville were more than 50,000 and the total liability was at least $2 billion. The lawyers were receiving $1.71 for every dollar that went to the victims and Johns-Manville's long-term legal costs could have been very large. Its insurers refused to pay, arguing that the damage had been inflicted upon the victims years ago. Long latencies with respect to the onset of the disease meant that different insurers had been around when the victims first suffered exposure. Present-day insurers argued that they were not accountable. Johns-Manville's out-of-court settlement with the insurers netted the company only $730 million.

The company's filing for Chapter 11 reorganization came as a surprise. It was the first time a company had used the bankruptcy laws to stay the claims of a group of creditors who were the victims of the company's past actions. Under the bankruptcy filing, Johns-Manville created a separate fund under which all present and future asbestos claims would be reimbursed. Meanwhile, the company could continue normal business operations. The fund for the reimbursement of victims was to receive $2.5 billion over 25 years and it had the right to at least 50 percent of the common voting shares of the corporation. The company had to pay up to 20 percent of its operating profits into the fund over 20 years. It was required to divest itself of its asbestos divisions, which were its most profitable. But Johns-Manville no longer could be sued by victims. With the stay of suits came an end to punitive damage awards.

Many felt that this use of the bankruptcy laws to evade punitive damage awards was unjustified—Johns-Manville deserved to be punished. The company defended itself by claiming that asbestos brought many advantages to society (e.g., fireproofing and insulation and better brake linings, which added to automotive safety). The company intended to do no wrong. Its position was that it did not know definitely until 1964, after a major study showed illness among asbestos workers, that exposure was dangerous. It relied on a state-of-the-art defense, which is typical in tort cases of this kind: at the time of production, the company was conforming to what it believed to be the best practice in the industry.

However, attorneys for the plaintiffs held that the company had to have known that asbestos caused health-related problems.[50] One of its founders, Henry W. Johns, had died of chronic lung disease that was suspected to have come from his exposure to the substance. Medical studies going back 50 years showed that people who had been exposed to asbestos were likely to have severe pulmonary problems; their lungs would be damaged and breathing would be difficult. As early as 1918, insurers understood the health problems and refused to sell health insurance to asbestos workers.

Moreover, in 1933 top officials of asbestos manufacturers, including Johns-Manville, met together to discuss the health risks to asbestos workers. These risks had been revealed in a report by the Metropolitan Life Insurance Company commissioned by the industry. Extensive notes taken during this meeting were locked away in a safe in one of the companies. Lawyers for the victims referred to these notes whenever attorneys for the asbestos companies maintained that the companies had no early knowledge of asbestos dangers. The notes were used to show that the asbestos companies acted in reckless disregard of the health of their workers and deserved to be assessed punitive damages. Also, it was alleged that punitive damages were necessary in this case as a deterrent to other companies.

The plaintiffs' attorneys had additional evidence that showed the asbestos manufacturers knew of the health risk (e.g., a former doctor for Johns-Manville said that he had informed top company officials in the 1940s that only 4 of the 708 asbestos workers that he had X-rayed had healthy lungs). The lawyers had won large awards by showing that company officials knew of the risks but failed to do anything about them. With the Chapter 11 filing, however,
thing about them. With the Chapter 11 filing, how-

ever, the victims would no longer be able to collect punitive damages.

Many questioned, therefore, whether the Johns-Manville filing was done in good faith. The company in all other ways was financially sound, but representatives for Johns-Manville justified the use of Chapter 11 as a procedure that was set up for companies that were not currently insolvent but might become so. Still, Johns-Manville was probably the healthiest company ever to declare itself bankrupt.

principle of probable causation. The courts can rely on epidemiological evidence, which they have refrained from using in the United States.

Chapter 11 bankruptcy Reorganization under the U.S. bankruptcy code that eliminates the need for a company to show complete insolvency and allows it to obtain an automatic stay of creditors.

Because of large liability awards in cases such as asbestos, pollution, and intrauterine devices, some companies have used the bankruptcy laws to avoid paying plaintiffs, even though they are technically solvent. The use of the bankruptcy laws, such as **Chapter 11 bankruptcy**, to avoid paying the victims is an unprecedented legal development brought on by the liability crisis in the United States (see the real-world example).

Conclusions

The litigation rate in the United States is high especially compared with Japan. In Japan, suing is considered to be both wrong and unprofitable. In addition, the Japanese legal system is more predictable, which takes away the incentive to sue. The U.S. litigation rate has been rising, and scholars disagree about whether this growth is inconsistent with population growth and with changing rates of death and injury. Business executives admit that their products are safer, but complain about discontinued product lines, decisions not to introduce new products, and lost market share. This chapter has reviewed the evolution of legal doctrine with respect to the harm caused by corporations. It has examined the many proposals made to reform product liability laws.

Tort law in the United States has evolved from an emphasis on contracts and warranties, to the classic tort doctrine, and now to strict liability. Under the classic doctrine, a plaintiff must show breach of duty, actual damages, and causation. Strict liability eliminates the need to show fault, but even under strict liability companies can use the defense of contributory negligence and assumption of risk. Plaintiffs, moreover, have to prove product defect for manufacturers to be held liable. The *Beshada* case questioned whether companies can use a state-of-the-art defense and suggests a movement toward absolute liability. Without a state-of-the-art defense, companies are forced to try to discover unknown dangers and to analyze the future effects of their products.

Large liability awards have caused some companies to use the bankruptcy laws to avoid paying creditors and victims. This is an unprecedented legal development in which the company's main obligation switches from shareholders to victims.

Discussion Questions

1. Explain why there is less litigation in Japan than in the United States.
2. Why has the litigation rate in the United States been growing?
3. How do business executives feel about the growth of litigation? How does the public feel about it?
4. What are some of the proposals to reform product liability laws? Is reform needed? What did Congress do in 1995? Which proposals do you think are the best?
5. Explain what tort law means. What is the intent of tort law?
6. Under the classic doctrine, what must the plaintiff prove?
7. What is the relevance of the *Palsgraf* case?
8. What is the relevance of the *Sindell* case?
9. Why haven't plaintiffs been able to win large awards in cigarette cases? To what extent was the *Cipolione* case a breakthrough?
10. What defenses does a company have if it is sued under classic tort law? What defenses does it have if it is sued under strict liability?
11. What is the difference between strict liability and the classic doctrine?
12. Why did tort law move from contract law to the classic doctrine? What were some of the significant cases that brought about this movement? What was decided in these cases?
13. Why was Judge Traynor's decision important? What was his argument? Do you agree with it? Why or why not?
14. What does the Second Restatement of Torts say?
15. What court cases suggest a movement toward absolute liability? Why might this movement be taking place?
16. What is the difference between Chapter 11 and Chapter 7 bankruptcy? In what sense does Chapter 11 erode the foundations of a capitalist society? Do you agree with the argument that it does? Why or why not?
17. Do you think it was right for Johns-Manville to seek protection under Chapter 11? Why or why not?

Endnotes

1. A. P. Herbert, *The Reasonable Man,* cited in R. Cooter and T. Ulen, *Law and Economics* (Glenview, Ill.: Scott, Foresman, 1988), p. 329.
2. F. Schwadel, "Robins and Plaintiffs Face Uncertain Future," *The Wall Street Journal,* Aug. 23, 1985.
3. P. M. Barrett, "Hearings Set in Robins Chapter 11 Case to Fix Amount of Dalkon Shield Fund," *The Wall Street Journal,* Nov. 3, 1987, p. A4; G. Warchol, "Hit 'Em and Hit 'Em Hard," *Twin City Reader,* Aug. 24–30, 1988, pp. 10–12.
4. B. J. Feder, "What A. H. Robins Has Wrought," *The Wall Street Journal,* Dec. 13, 1987, p. F2; R. Koenig and S. Wermeil, "Supreme Court Refuses to Hear Challenges in A. H. Robins Case,"

The Wall Street Journal, Nov. 7, 1989, p. A3; G. A. Steiner and J. F. Steiner, *Business, Government, and Society: A Managerial Perspective* (New York: McGraw-Hill, 1991).

5. Feder, "What A. H. Robins Has Wrought," p. F2.
6. Warchol, "Hit 'Em and Hit 'Em Hard."
7. Ibid.
8. M. Galanter, "Reading the Landscape of Disputes: What We Know and Don't Know (and Think We Know) about Our Allegedly Contentious and Litigious Society," *UCLA Law Review* 4 (1983); M. Galanter, "Beyond the Litigation Panic, " *Proceedings of the Academy of Political Science*, 1988, pp. 18–30.
9. N. Glazer, "Towards an Imperial Judiciary," *Public Interest* 104 (1975); Silberman, "Will Lawyering Strangle Democratic Capitalism?" *Regulation* 15 (1978), pp. 15–22; D. Oberdorfer, "The Tangled Saga of the Dalkon Shield," *Minneapolis Star and Tribune*, September 15, 1985, p. 1A; Galanter, "Reading the Landscape of Disputes."
10. S. Reed, "*Environmental Pollution Policies in Japan*," paper presented at the annual meeting of the American Political Science Association, Washington, D.C., 1979; M. R. Reich, "Environmental Policy and Japanese Society," *International Journal of Environmental Studies* 20 (1983) Part I, pp. 191–98, and Part II, pp. 199–207.
11. J. Gresser, K. Fujikura, and Morishma, *Environmental Law in Japan* (Cambridge, Mass.: MIT Press, 1981); A. A. Marcus, "Japan," in *International Public Policy Sourcebook: Education and Environment*, vol. 2, ed. F. N. Bolotin (Westport, Conn.: Greenwood Press, 1989), pp. 275–92.
12. Ibid.
13. Douglas Amy, "Environmental Mediation: An Alternative Approach to Policy Stalemates," *Policy Sciences* 15 (1983), pp. 345–52; Douglas Amy, "The Politics of Environmental Meditation," *Ecology Law Quarterly*, 1983; A. Sarat, "Alternative Dispute Resolution: Wrong Solution, Wrong Problem," *Proceedings of the Academy of Political Science*, 1988, pp. 162–73; Reich, "Environmental Policy and Japanese Society"; A. Marcus, M. V. Nadel, and K. Merrikin, "The Applicability of Regulatory Negotiation to Disputes Involving the Nuclear Regulatory Commission," *Administrative Law Review* 36 (1984), pp. 213–38.
14. J. M. Ramseyer, "Reluctant Litigant Revisited: Rationality and Disputes in Japan," *Journal of Japanese Studies*, 1987, pp. 111–23; J. Trauberman, "Statutory Reform of 'Toxic Torts': Relieving Legal, Scientific, and Economic Burdens on the Chemical Victim," *Harvard Environmental Law Review* 7 (1979), pp. 177–296.
15. Ramseyer, "Reluctant Litigant Revisited," p. 112.
16. P. W. Huber, *Liability: The Legal Revolution and Its Consequences* (New York: Basic Books, 1988); R. E. Litan, P. Swire, and C. Winston. "The U.S. Liability System: Background and Trends" in *Liability: Perspectives and Policy*, ed. R. E. Litan (Washington, D.C.: Brookings Institution, 1988), pp. 1–15; W. Olson, "The Liability Revolution," *Proceedings of the Academy of Political Science*, 1988, pp. 1–3; W. K. Viscusi, "The Dimensions of the Product Liability Crisis," *The Journal of Legal Studies* 1 (1991), pp. 147–78.
17. Galanter, "Beyond the Litigation Panic"; Litan, Swire, and Winston, "The U.S. Liability System."
18. "Lawsuits and Liability," *The Polling Report* 21 (1987), p. 1; E. P. McGuire, *The Impact of Product Liability*, research report no. 908, The Conference Board, 1988; W. K. Viscusi, "Structuring an Effective Occupational Disease Policy: Victim Compensation and Risk Regulation," *Yale Journal on Regulation* 2 (1984), pp. 53–81.
19. Media General/Associated Press Poll, August 7–17, 1987, of 1,223 adults nationwide.
20. McGuire, *The Impact of Product Liability*.
21. C. L. Allen, "The Angry Retort against Tort Law," *Insight on the News*, October 31, 1988, pp. 8–14; C. L. Allen, "Reformers Gather Steam," *Insight on the News*, October 31, 1988, pp. 17–19;

P. M. Barrett, "Tort Reform Fight Shifts to State Courts," *The Wall Street Journal*, September 19, 1988, p. 27; P. M. Barrett, "Courts May Have to Lead Product Liability Reform," *The Wall Street Journal*, October 7, 1988, p. B1; P. Huber, "The Legal Revolution in Product Liability," *Contemporary Issues Series* 33, Center for the Study of American Business, Washington University, July 1989; M. E. Kriz, "Liability Lobbying," *National Journal*, January 23, 1988, pp. 191–93; R. L. Miller, "Drawing Limits on Liability," *The Wall Street Journal*, April 4, 1984; R. Neely, *The Product Liability Mess: How Business Can Be Rescued from the Politics of State Courts* (New York: Free Press, 1988); J. O'Connell, "Neo-No-Fault: A Fair-Exchange Proposal for Tort Reform," *Proceedings of the Academy of Political Science*, 1988, pp. 186–95; D. Rosenberg, "The Causal Connection in Mass Exposure Cases: A 'Public Law' Vision of the Tort System," *Harvard Law Review* 97 (1984), pp. 851–929; W. K. Viscusi, "Toward a Diminished Role for Tort Liability: Social Insurance, Government Regulation, and Contemporary Risks to Health and Safety," *Yale Journal on Regulation* 1 (1989), pp. 65–108; S. Wermeil, "High Court Urged to Rule on Punitive-Damages Issue," *The Wall Street Journal*, October 21, 1988; S. Wermeil, "High Court Will Get Chance to Put Limits on Punitive Damages," *The Wall Street Journal*, September 28, 1990, p. A1.

22. Neil Lewis, "House Passes New Standards Limiting Awards in Civil Suits," *New York Times*, March 11, 1995, pp. 1, 7.
23. Cooter and Ulen, *Law and Economics*,
24. Ibid.
25. S. Shavell, "Uncertainty over Causation and the Determination of Civil Liability," *Journal of Law and Economics* 28 (1985), pp. 587–611; L. Tribe, "Trial by Mathematics: Precision and Ritual in the Legal Process," *Harvard Law Review* 84 (1971), pp. 1329–93.
26. Shavell, "Uncertainty over Causation," pp. 587–611; Tribe, "Trial by Mathematics," pp. 1329–93; M. Rizzo and F. Arnold, "Causal Apportionment in the Law of Torts: An Economic Theory," *Columbia Law Review* 80 (1980), pp. 1399–429; Rosenberg, "The Causal Connection in Mass Exposure Cases."
27. Cooter and Ulen, *Law and Economics*.
28. G. Robinson, "Multiple Causation in Tort Law: Reflections on the DES Cases," *Virginia Law Review* 68 (1982), pp. 713–69; Shavell, "Uncertainty over Causation."
29. Cooter and Ulen, *Law and Economics*.
30. D. Marcus and W. Lambert, "Tobacco Liability Case Nears High Court," *The Wall Street Journal*, March 4, 1991, p. B8.
31. Cooter and Ulen, *Law and Economics*.
32. Ibid.
33. E. Kitch, "Vaccines and Product Liability: A Case of Contagious Litigation," *Regulation*, May/June 1985, pp. 11–18.
34. Cooter and Ulen, *Law and Economics*.
35. Ibid.
36. Ibid.
37. Ibid.
38. Ibid., p. 361.
39. Ibid.
40. Ibid., p. 431.
41. Ibid.
42. Ibid.
43. G. L. Priest, "Understanding the Liability Crisis," *Proceedings of the Academy of Political Science*, 1988, pp. 196–211; G. Priest, "Products Liability Law and the Accident Rate," in *Liability: Perspectives and Policy*, ed. R. E. Litan (Washington, D.C.: Brookings Institution, 1988), pp. 184–

222; W. M. Landes and R. A. Posner, *The Economic Structure of Tort Law* (Cambridge, Mass.: Harvard University Press, 1987), pp. 438–39; F. K. Upham, "After Minamata: Current Prospects and Problems in Japanese Environmental Legislation," *Ecology Law Quarterly* 2, pp. 213–69.

44. Cooter and Ulen, *Law and Economics*, p. 462.
45. Cooter and Ulen, *Law and Economics; Asbestos in the Courts: The Challenge of Mass Toxic Torts* (Santa Monica, Calif.: Rand Corporation Institute for Civil Justice, 1985).
46. S. Reed, "Environmental Pollution Policies in Japan," paper presented at the Annual Meeting of the American Political Science Association, Washington, D.C., 1979.
47. "Chronology of Chapter 11 Events," *Manville News Background Information*, Oct. 1987; P. Brodeur, "The Asbestos Industry on Trial," *New Yorker*, June 10, 1985, pp. 49–101; June 17, 1985, pp. 45–111; June 24, 1985, pp. 37–77; Aug. 1, 1985, pp. 36–80; A. Cifeli, "Asbestos Defendants Try a New Approach," *Fortune*, Nov. 12, 1984, pp. 110, 165; W. Glaberson, "Of Manville, Morals and Mortality," *New York Times*, Oct. 9, 1989, p. F1; "Manville Chapter 11 Plan of Reorganization," *Manville News Background Information*, Oct. 1987; "Note. The Manville Bankruptcy: Treating Mass Tort Claims in Chapter 11 Proceedings," *Harvard Law Review* 96 (1984), pp. 1121–42; W. F. Todd, "Aggressive Uses of Chapter 11 of the Federal Bankruptcy Code," *Economic Review* 3 (1986), pp. 20–26; Trauberman, "Statutory Reform of 'Toxic Torts,'" pp. 177–296; "When Firms Go Bust," *Economist*, Aug. 1, 1992, pp. 62–64.
48. Todd, "Aggressive Uses of Chapter 11."
49. S. Labaton, "Manville Trust for Asbestos Victims Is Running Short of Funds," *New York Times*, Oct. 24, 1989, p. A18; W. Lambert and P. M. Barrett, "Nationwide Plan Set for Asbestos Cases," *The Wall Street Journal*, Aug. 13, 1990, p. B3; Rogene Buchholz, William Evans, and Robert Wayley, *Management Response to Public Issues* (Englewood Cliffs, N.J.: Prentice Hall, 1985), pp. 322–37.
50. P. Brodeur, *Outrageous Misconduct: The Asbestos Industry on Trial* (New York: Pantheon, 1985).

Case 18–A
Auto Safety Policy at Ford

Revisiting the Pinto[1]

Karen Carlson, the newest staff member of Ford's automotive safety department and a recent M.B.A. graduate, had a lot on her mind. She had been assigned to review the facts of the Pinto controversy and to develop some ideas about what the company could learn from it in order to avoid similar situations in the future. Her presentation was scheduled for the next week.

Auto Safety Today

The issue of auto safety did not go away at Ford. On April 5, 1990, the company again was hit with a huge settlement in a personal injury lawsuit. It had to pay $6 million in a case involving the safety of lap-only rear seat belts.[2] This problem had been emerging for many years as an important product liability issue for the automobile manufacturers. A number of companies had reached multimillion-dollar settlements with litigants, but the Ford settlement was one of the largest ever.

The case presented Ford with many of the same dilemmas it had confronted nearly 15 years earlier with its Pinto model. The company believed that it was adhering in good faith to state-of-the-art technology concerning safety, only to be challenged in the courts. Attorneys for victims of injuries occurring while driving or riding in a Pinto claimed that the company knew that certain features of the automobile could not adequately protect occupants, but that it did not want to spend the extra money to do something about it. This claim had been made in the Pinto case and was brought up again with Ford's Escort model; attorneys for the plaintiffs argued that "three-point" lap and shoulder belts should have been installed in that model because the company knew they would save lives.

Ironically, the Escort was the successor to the Pinto, and its reputation also was being threatened by this new controversy over safety. In both instances, Ford's subcompact challenge to Japan's dominance in this segment of the market was being put to a test on the safety issue.

The similarity between the cases did not end there. When both vehicles were first marketed, no government regulations required Ford do anything other than what it was doing, either with the placement of the gas tank on the Pinto or the installation of three-point lap belts on the Escort. Not until December 1989 did the government mandate such a safety feature in the rear seats of vehicles. In the meantime, more than 140 million vehicles had been sold in the United States with lap-only rear belts.

The failure of the government to mandate three-point belts in the rear seat, however, did not prevent attorneys from bringing many successful suits. The Institute for Injury Reduction, a Maryland-based organization founded by trial lawyers to put together information on product safety cases, predicted that the rear belt issue would be one of the biggest sources of auto litigation in history.

Ford was very concerned. The company understood that the issue was serious not only for itself but for the auto industry as a whole, which faced increased competition from the Japanese and continued loss of market share. In March 1990, Toyota's share of the U.S. auto market was 9.2 percent, up from 6.2 percent a year earlier, while Ford's share of the U.S. market had declined from 22.6 percent a year earlier to 21.1 percent. To maintain sales, Ford had to offer $500 rebates on many of its 1990 models.

Most American automobile executives had concluded that safety did sell. Since the publication in 1963 of Ralph Nader's book *Unsafe At Any Speed*, consumers had obtained a great deal of information about the relative safety of various cars from consumer groups, government regulatory agencies, and insurers. Foreign automakers had introduced high-tech safety features while U.S. automakers had been slower to do so.

Consumers consistently shunned automobiles that had poor safety records. For instance, when critics charged that the Audi 5000 luxury sedan tended to self-accelerate, sales plummeted. Similarly, Suzuki's Samurai sport utility vehicle lost 70 percent of its sales after drivers claimed that it easily rolled over during sharp turns.

Today, no one disputes the contention that safety sells, but auto executives still were asking how much safety and at what cost. What types of safety policies did they have to implement in new auto design to reassure consumers?

The Pinto History

Shortly after Lee Iacocca took over as Ford's president in 1967, Ford started the accelerated development program to bring the Pinto to market by 1971. Ford had a fairly strong position in the small-car market with its Falcon and Mustang models. Iacocca knew something about small cars and their appeal, having master-minded the introduction of the highly popular Mustang in 1964, and he wanted a new, competitive small car brought to the market quickly.

By 1967 it appeared that foreign imports like the Volkswagen were posing a threat to Ford's small-car niche. The company needed an inexpensive, fuel-efficient subcompact to be fully competitive. Ford executives believed that to compete in the small-car market was the socially responsible thing for the company to do. It saved American jobs, conserved energy, and reduced pollution. It gave people who might otherwise not be able to afford a car the chance to obtain inexpensive transportation. In suburban America, where a car was a necessity, providing an inexpensive option to the standard-size American vehicle was important. Single people and families needing a second car would find the Pinto attractive. Of course, other managers thought Ford should stick to producing the large models where the profit margins were much higher.

Iacocca developed the "rule of 2,000" to help define what he wanted. The car could weigh no more than 2,000 pounds or cost no more than $2,000. Even at that price the car would be more expensive than the subcompacts offered by foreign producers, who didn't have Ford's high labor costs.[3]

Pinto's product objectives were as follows:

1. True subcompact:
   a. Size.
   b. Weight.
2. Low cost of ownership:
   a. Initial price.
   b. Fuel consumption.
   c. Reliability.
   d. Serviceability.
3. Clear product superiority:
   a. Appearance.
   b. Comfort.
   c. Features.
   d. Ride and handling.
   e. Performance.

Critics later pointed out that passenger safety was not on this list.

The Successful Introduction of the Pinto

Pinto made it into production in time for the 1971 model year as Iacocca had demanded. Instead of the usual 43-month development period, it arrived in dealer showrooms in 38 months. In the six years following its introduction in August 1970, the Pinto fulfilled many of the company's expectations and became one of Ford's all-time best-selling models. The 2 million Pintos sold between 1970 and 1977 helped retain Ford's market position during a period of rapidly escalating gas prices. The Arab oil embargo had caught the other major American auto manufacturers without an adequate line of small, fuel-efficient cars, and the Pinto sold well among cars in its size range.[4]

The first public criticism of the Pinto came not from consumers but from Byron Bloch, an independent auto safety expert. He warned on national television in 1973 that the fuel system was extremely vulnerable to even minor damage and called for the recall of Pintos to repair this hazard. The Nader-funded group, the Center for Auto Safety, claimed that attorneys engaged in liability lawsuits and its own research provided grounds for a defect investigation. It demanded that the newly formed National Highway Traffic Safety Administration (NHTSA) investigate the Pinto. NHTSA reviewed the complaints and decided that statistical studies showed no greater problem with Pintos than with other vehicles. Therefore, no investigation was necessary.

The Insurance Institute for Highway Safety, however, released a study in 1975 showing a growth in the number of fire-related incidents of which Ford had a disproportionate share. Twenty percent of vehicles on the road were manufactured by Ford, while the company's cars had 35 percent of the fire-related incidents.

"Pinto Madness"

In August 1977, precisely seven years after production of the Pinto began, the popular muckraking journal, *Mother Jones*, called a news conference in Washington to announce the publication of a piece called "Pinto Madness." Although not the first published article to suggest that Ford executives had known about the Pinto's explosive defects before the car was produced—columnist Jack Anderson had written on the subject in late 1976—it generated additional attention to the issue.[5] "Pinto Madness" contained a number of serious allegations that can be summarized as follows:

1. The Pinto's accelerated development schedule meant that crash tests were conducted after assembly tooling had already begun, making changes in design prohibitively expensive.

2. The safety of the car was not a serious consideration in its design because top executives like Iacocca believed "safety doesn't sell."

3. Pinto's designers knew of the car's defects but chose not to remedy them (even though the modifications might have cost as little as $1 per car for materials) based on a cost-benefit analysis that crassly assigned a dollar value to human life.

4. Ford mounted a concerted campaign to delay implementation of the relevant safety standards, succeeding in postponing their final adoption until the 1977 model year.

Stories in the press quoted top Ford officials as saying that the *Mother Jones* article was "unfair and distorted."[6] The article made no pretense of objectivity, concluding, for example, with this question: "One wonders how long the Ford Motor Company would continue to market lethal cars were Henry Ford II and Lee Iacocca serving 20-year terms in Leavenworth for consumer homicide."[7] Nevertheless, the article raised some troubling questions about the company's behavior.

A Public Relations Disaster

Ford management considered the allegations misrepresentations and the controversy a public relations disaster. Yet the public believed the charges. Opponents of the Pinto's design suggested that it might be more likely than the average car to explode into flames when rear-ended by another vehicle. They asserted that many Ford customers had died fiery deaths. But how many people actually had died?

In *Mother Jones*, Mark Dowie claimed 500 deaths, but the National Highway Traffic Safety Administration counted only 38 cases of rear-end collisions of Pintos that resulted in fuel tank damage, leakage, and ensuing fires. In these 38 cases, NHTSA reported 27 fatalities and 24 instances of nonfatal burns.

Ford argued that its placement of the car's gas tank between the rear bumper and the differential housing on the rear axle was *state of the art* for the period in which the car was introduced. Legally, that was all that was required of Ford—to meet a state-of-the-art standard.

The company was well into the design process when an internal engineering study suggested an alternative: The "safest place" for the fuel tank might be directly above the rear axle. This option, which was diligently considered by Ford, was rejected for very sound *safety* reasons.

1. Moving the fuel tank closer to passengers actually increased the threat that they would be consumed by fire.
2. Doing so required the use of a circuitous filler pipe that could be easily dislodged in an accident.

3. If the fuel tank was placed closer to the front, it would shift the car's center of gravity, making it more difficult to control. This was precisely the problem with the Corvair that Ralph Nader protested so vigorously in *Unsafe At Any Speed.*
4. If the fuel tank placement was different, then the car could not be serviced as easily, which presented another safety hazard.

In addition, moving the fuel tank would reduce trunk size and make it harder to offer a station wagon or hatchback option in the future.

Ford and the Government Regulations

Ford was not violating any existing government regulations when it placed the fuel tank where it did. In January 1969, under NHTSA's proposed rear-end safety standard, the vehicle was tested striking a 4,000-lb. *moving* barrier at 20 miles per hour (mph). The vehicle was supposed to leak less than an ounce of fuel per minute. In the four tests Ford conducted, the vehicles slightly exceeded this limit in three cases, and in the fourth massive leakage occurred because of improper welding (the fuel tank split at the seams). Before production began, however, Ford made modifications so that its car would conform to the 4,000-lb. moving-barrier test.

The government, though, did not go with this standard. Instead, it contemplated pushing the limit upward to a 4,000-lb. *fixed*-barrier test, which Ford considered to be the equivalent of a 4,000-lb. moving-barrier test at 40 mph. Auto engineers believed that this standard was highly unrealistic because more than 85 percent of rear-end collisions took place at speeds less than 20 mph. The cars did not strike stationary objects, but hit other moving vehicles. In any case, only 0.45 percent of all auto injuries were the result of fires. At speeds of 40 mph or more, the occupants would die or be hurt because of the impact, not because of the fire.

At that time (1971), Pinto was already on the market and many Pintos were being driven. Ford did not want to unduly alarm people about a contentious issue that still was in the very early stages of consideration. Still, it retested the Pinto using the 20 mph and 30 mph fixed-barrier tests proposed by the government. When Ford found excessive leakage and concluded that it would have to completely modify the design, it decided to stay with the 20 mph moving-barrier standard for current models. In the meantime, it could do the necessary engineering that would enable it to meet a future 30 mph moving-barrier test, which it believed NHTSA ultimately would adopt.

In early 1971, a junior engineer conducted a study that explored various ways to meet the 30-mph moving-barrier standard. Almost all the options (e.g., an over-the-axle gas tank, a repositioned spare tire, installation of body rails, and a redesigned filler pipe) involved extensive redesign of the vehicle. Only a rubber bladder could be installed without extensive redesign, but it would not work well in either cold weather or hot weather.

Wide Media Coverage

Though few in number, the accidents where Pintos were struck from behind at closing speeds between 30 and 35 mph received wide media coverage. In these occurrences, the gas tank was smashed between the bumper and differential housing, and fuel sprayed over the pavement and inside the vehicle. It ignited from a spark, perhaps from sheet metal scraping the pavement, and it caused enormous fires, killing or maiming the vehicle's occupants in a hideous way.

Two such incidents were reported very widely:

- In an accident on a California freeway in 1972, a Pinto was struck from behind while going 30 to 50 mph. The woman driving the car, Lily Gray, died from the subsequent fire. Her 13-year-old passenger, Richard Grimshaw, suffered burns over 80 percent of his body, losing his nose, an ear, and much of a hand. The boy underwent scores of reconstructive skin graft operations but nonetheless remained scarred for life. A California jury awarded Grimshaw $2.8 million in February 1978 for wrongful injuries and set punitive damages at $125 million, at the time the largest punitive damage award ever. The court later reduced the punitive damages to $3.5 million.[8] The jury was strongly influenced by the films of the Pinto crash tests performed before the car went on the market in 1970. The tests showed a Pinto backing into a wall at 20 mph after which the nonflammable liquid in the car's gas tank sprayed into the passenger compartment. A juror told a reporter that "it looked like a fireman had stuck a hose inside the car and turned it on. In my mind, that film beat the Ford Motor Company."[9]

- In a 1978 accident in Indiana, three teenaged girls were burned to death in a Pinto when they were struck from behind by a van. A prosecutor for the county where the accident occurred brought charges of reckless homicide against the company (the first time a corporation had been charged with murder), and the subsequent trial drew national attention. A jury found Ford Motor Company not guilty of the charges, but the publicity did significant harm to its reputation.[10]

NHTSA's Investigation

Under pressure from consumer advocate Ralph Nader and others who expressed outrage over the Pinto's explosive potential, NHTSA finally opened an investigation into the Pinto in the fall of 1977. Mark Dowie, author of "Pinto Madness," claimed that NHTSA would "never force the company to test or recall the more than two million pre-1977 Pintos still on the highway. Seventy or more people will burn to death in those cars every year for many years to come. If the past is any indication, Ford will continue to accept the deaths."[11] In late 1977, Ford issued a press release responding to the Dowie article and the issues it raised. In part, it said:

> The truth is that in every model year the Pinto has been tested and met or surpassed the federal fuel system integrity standards applicable to it . . . It is simply unreasonable and unfair to contend that a car is somehow unsafe if it does not meet standards proposed for future years or embody the technological improvements that are introduced in later model years.[12]

NHTSA informed Ford that a public hearing on safety defects in the fuel system would be held in June 1978. Shortly before the hearing was to begin, Ford announced a recall of all 1971–1976 model Pintos to remedy the defect. NHTSA canceled the planned hearing after the recall announcement, since Ford's repairs would eliminate the fire danger to the degree required by law. The recall cost Ford an estimated $20 million; the previous year the company had earned $1.5 billion after taxes.[13]

60 Minutes

Shortly after the recall announcement, the CBS news program *60 Minutes* aired a segment on the Pinto controversy. Correspondent Mike Wallace discussed the Grimshaw accident and interviewed a former Ford engineer who said Ford had known of the safety defect but the cost had kept the company from remedying the problem. Wallace's interview with Herbert Misch, Ford's executive in charge of environmental and safety engineering, made Misch appear unable to answer pointed questions about the controversy. A public image of Ford as a company that willfully sacrificed the safety of its customers in return for larger profits began to take hold.[14]

Production of the Pinto ceased in 1980. By then, both of the company's top executives during the controversy, CEO Lee Iacocca and chairman Henry Ford II, had left, and the company began to develop an emphasis on quality—its advertising theme was "At Ford, Quality Is Job One." It tried to reduce damageability and increase the safety of its vehicles.[15]

Charges and Countercharges

To help clarify the policy questions involved, Karen Carlson, Ford's new automotive safety staff member, reviewed the charges that had been brought against Ford.

Charge 1: The accelerated development program was responsible for the design flaws. While Mark Dowie claimed that the Pinto was rushed into production in 25 months instead of the usual 43, Ford records indicated that it actually took 38 months and that the early introduction of the vehicle provided competitive advantage—five months of market dominance when the car's leadership was uncontested by any rival. The faster development of the car meant that assembly tooling (i.e., where the machine tools are made) had to start before crash tests occurred. Tooling usually took place after crash tests were completed, but Ford was able to make adjustments in the gas tank design before production. This allowed the Pinto to meet the existing federal safety standard designed to protect passengers from rear-end fires.[16]

According to Dowie, secret company documents showed that the company had also crash-tested 11 Pinto prototypes before production at an average of 31 mph, and that only 3 had escaped with gas tanks intact. Dowie argued that Ford refused to adopt modifications because assembly tooling had already begun, and modifications to the machine tools would cut into profits.

The preproduction test-crash films introduced as evidence in the Grimshaw trial suggested that engineers within the company were aware that the tanks were vulnerable. Still, at that time the applicable proposed federal standard (there was no actual standard) was for a moving 20 mph test, not a fixed 25 mph test.

Ford pointed out that the Pinto was involved in fewer fire-related collisions than would be expected given the number of Pintos on the road.[17] Dowie, however, claimed that the studies commissioned by NHTSA showed that more than 3,000 people were burning to death in 400,000 auto fires per year and that the rate was increasing five times faster than building fires.[18]

Charge 2: Ford placed little importance on safety considerations in its design process. According to Dowie, design engineers who learned of the Pinto's explosive faults were loathe to inform Lee Iacocca of their findings. He quoted several former company officials on the subject, one of whom told him: "Safety wasn't a popular subject around Ford in those days. With Lee it was taboo. Whenever a problem was raised that meant a delay on the Pinto, Lee would chomp on his cigar, look out the window and say, 'Read the product objectives and get back to work.'" The emphasis was on styling and price considerations, not safety. The company's design departments seemed to take to heart a maxim attributed to Iacocca: "Safety doesn't sell."[19]

Charge 3: The Pinto's designers chose not to incorporate inexpensive design modifications that could have saved the lives of many of the burn victims, and made this decision on the basis of a cost-benefit analysis that assigned a value to human life. Dowie's article claimed that four design changes the company tested in preproduction could have reduced the chances of fatal fires occurring.

- A $1 plastic device placed between the tank and the differential housing could shield the tank from the sharp bolts on the housing that tended to pierce the tank in crashes.
- A piece of metal could be placed between the tank and the rear bumper to absorb some of the impact of a crash.
- A $5.08 rubber liner could be placed inside the gas tank to keep gas from spilling out if the tank was pierced.
- The gas tank could be placed above the drive shaft, away from the rear axle and bumper. Ford had a patent on this tank design and used it on its Experimental Safety Vehicle, which had withstood rear-end impacts of 60 mph.

Ford denied that these were the options it considered in the preproduction stage. Still, a former Ford engineer testified at the Grimshaw liability trial that 95 percent of the people who had died as a result of the Pinto fires would have survived if an alternative tank placement had been used. He estimated the additional cost at $9.95 per car.[20]

Ford never explicitly used cost-benefit analysis in evaluating different methods for containing damage from rear-end collisions. Yet Dowie attacked Ford for using a cost-benefit analysis as part of its case against the 1973 NHTSA proposed standard for fuel leakage in *rollover accidents*. Ford argued that if it put an $11 valve on each of the 12.5 million cars it made to prevent leakage in a rollover, the cost would greatly exceed the social benefit. Assuming that 180 people would die in auto fires if the valve were not installed and another 180 would be seriously burned, that damages per death were $200,000—a NHTSA-supplied figure that included $10,000 for the victim's pain and suffering—and that lost dollar damages for a surviving burn victim were $67,000, Ford calculated that installation of the valves would mean a net loss to society of $87.5 million.[21]

The rollover cost-benefit calculations were widely publicized in the press and made Ford appear to be valuing profit over human suffering and death. Little attention was given to NHTSA approval of this method of calculating the social costs of a proposed regulation or to the fact that this cost-benefit analysis had nothing to do with exploding rear fuel tanks.

Charge 4: Ford mounted a campaign against the rear-end safety standards that delayed their adoption for eight years. When a federal agency like NHTSA proposes a new regulation, it requests public comment on the effects and feasibility of the regulation. Ford submitted evidence supporting its contentions that various aspects of the standard were unnecessary, unrealistic, or otherwise excessive. Critics characterized Ford's actions about the standards as cynical.[22]

There was no doubt that Ford's top management was hostile toward some aspects of federal safety regulation. NHTSA was a new, inexperienced agency. Its leadership during the Carter administration came from the ranks of ex-Naderites, and it lacked not only the capacity to be objective but the technical competence to do a good job. Combined with the effects of inflation, foreign price competition, and the cost burden of complying with other regulations concerning fuel efficiency and pollution controls, the costs of safety regulations added significantly to the automakers' competitive worries.

Conclusion

Having finished her review of the Pinto controversy, Karen Carlson had a number of questions she still was considering and some ideas on how company automobile safety policy could be better handled in the future:

- Was the company negligent for not voluntarily improving its gas tanks to a higher standard than that proposed by the NHTSA?
- Should Ford allow a compressed development schedule that requires assembly tooling to begin before crash tests occur?
- If potential customers were more concerned with a car's style, fuel efficiency, and price than with safety features that could make the car more expensive, was Ford at fault for not incorporating state-of-the-art safety design anyway, regardless of the cost?
- Was Ford behaving wrongly by trying to fight the adoption of standards that would cost the company and the car buyer money? Added costs might hurt the company's competitive position, with an eventual loss of jobs for employees and communities.
- How should society determine whether the good arising from a proposed regulation outweighs the costs to society?
- If statistics showed that even one person's life could be saved by requiring a design change, would it be worth any cost, no matter how high?

- If cost-benefit analyses are necessary, what is the appropriate way to value human life and suffering?

Carlson was considering the possibility of some type of internal standard of reasonableness whereby Ford would proceed with the development of a new vehicle if the income generated was likely to exceed the probability of a safety recall times the cost. However, she was aware that some people might consider this reasonableness standard as a form of cost-benefit analysis, which would be repugnant to them on ethical grounds. She also wondered about the legality of the standard and whether it would stand up well in the courts.

Discussion Questions

1. Why did the Pinto controversy take place?
2. What lessons should Ford learn from Pinto?
3. What should Karen Carlson say in her presentation?

Endnotes

1. This case was prepared by Mark Jankus and Alfred Marcus.
2. Neal Templin, "Ford Settles Big Lap Belt Injury Suit," *The Wall Street Journal*, April 5, 1990, p. B1.
3. Dekkers L. Davidson, "Managing Product Safety: The Ford Pinto," case no. 383–129, Harvard Business School, 1984, p. 114.
4. Ibid., p. 14.
5. Mark Dowie, "Pinto Madness," *Mother Jones*, September/October 1977, pp. 18–32; Jack Anderson and Les Whitten, "Auto Maker Shuns Safer Gas Tank," *Washington Post*, December 30, 1976, p. B7.
6. "Ford is Recalling Some 1.5 Million Pintos, Bobcats," *The Wall Street Journal*, June 12, 1978, p. 2.
7. Dowie, "Pinto Madness," p. 32.
8. Russell Mokhiber, *Corporate Crime and Violence: Big Business and the Abuse of the Public Trust* (San Francisco: Sierra Club Books, 1988), p. 378.
9. Roy J. Harris, Jr., "Why the Pinto Jury Felt Ford Deserved $125 Million Penalty," *The Wall Street Journal*, February 14, 1978, p. A1.
10. See Francis T. Cullen, William J. Maakestad, and Gray Cavender, *Corporate Crime under Attack: The Ford Pinto Case and Beyond* (Cincinnati: Anderson Publishing, 1987), pp. 245–308.
11. Dowie, "Pinto Madness," p. 32.
12. Cited in Davidson, "Managing Product Safety," p. 117.
13. Ibid., p. 118–19.
14. Cullen et al., *Corporate Crime under Attack*, p. 167.
15. Ford 1982 annual report, cited in G. Starling and O. W. Baskin, "Ford Pinto," in *Issues in Business and Society: Capitalism and Public Purpose* (Boston: Kent, 1985), p. 439.
16. Davidson, "Managing Product Safety," p. 114–15.
17. Ibid., pp. 115, 117.
18. Dowie, "Pinto Madness," p. 28.
19. Ibid., p. 21.
20. Mokhiber, *Corporate Crime and Violence*, p. 377.
21. Dowie, "Pinto Madness," pp. 24, 26.
22. Ibid., p. 27.

Name Index

Subject Index